HANDBOOK OF PRACTICAL PROGRAM EVALUATION

HANDBOOK OF PRACTICAL PROGRAM EVALUATION

FOURTH EDITION

Kathryn E. Newcomer
Harry P. Hatry
Joseph S. Wholey

JOSSEY-BASS
A Wiley Imprint
www.josseybass.com

Published by John Wiley & Sons, Inc., Hoboken, New Jersey
Published simultaneously in Canada

For general information about our other products and services, please contact our Customer Care Department within the United States at (800) 762-2974, outside the United States at (317) 572-3993 or fax (317) 572-4002.

Wiley publishes in a variety of print and electronic formats and by print-on-demand. Some material included with standard print versions of this book may not be included in e-books or in print-on-demand. If this book refers to media such as a CD or DVD that is not included in the version you purchased, you may download this material at http://booksupport.wiley.com. For more information about Wiley products, visit www.wiley.com.

Library of Congress Cataloging-in-Publication Data:
Handbook of practical program evaluation / Kathryn E. Newcomer, Harry P. Hatry, Joseph S. Wholey, editors. — Fourth edition.
    pages cm. — (Essential texts for nonprofit and public leadership and management) Includes index.
ISBN 978-1-118-89360-9 (hardback : alk. paper) ;
ISBN 978-1-118-89361-6 (pdf); ISBN 978-1-118-89369-2 (epub)
    1. Policy sciences. 2. Political planning—Evaluation. I. Newcomer, Kathryn E., editor. II. Hatry, Harry P., editor. III. Wholey, Joseph S., editor.
H97.H358 2015
658.4—dc23

                                2015009201

Printed in the United States of America

V10013855_091119

CONTENTS

FIGURES, TABLES, AND EXHIBITS

Figures

Tables

Exhibits

PREFACE

Our main objective in this handbook has been and continues to be to make the practice of program evaluation as accessible and practical as possible. This fourth edition introduces many changes aimed at considerably improving the contents so as to better meet this objective.

We are pleased to note that we have added a number of chapters on new subjects, further improving this handbook's practicality and usefulness. These new subjects address:

- Culturally Responsive Evaluation (Chapter Twelve),
- Adopting designs and tools to evaluate multi-service community change programs (Chapter Eleven), and
- Using role playing to collect data (Chapter Fifteen).

In addition, we have added new materials about important topics to existing chapters on:

- Using cognitive interviewing to pre-test surveys (Chapter Fourteen),
- Coding qualitative data (Chapter Twenty-Two), and
- Employing data visualization techniques to present quantitative data (Chapter Twenty-Three).

Intended Audience

The intended audience for this handbook includes (1) managers, management analysts, policy analysts, and evaluators in federal, state, and local governments and school districts; (2) managers and analysts in foundations and non-profit organizations; (3) independent evaluators, auditors, and management consultants; and (4) faculty members and students in professional schools, such as schools of public policy, public administration, business administration, education, public health, and social work.

The information presented here is intended to help those involved in program evaluation, those who fund programs and evaluation studies, those who operate programs, those who are staff members in the legislative and executive branches of government, those in universities, and those in the consulting world—both individuals new to evaluation and experienced evaluators (who may find new ideas to add to their current toolkit). Even though the language is U.S. English and the authors are primarily people who live and work in the United States, the material presented here should be applicable in any country.

Scope

Considerable diversity exists in the training and skills possessed both by those charged with evaluating public and nonprofit programs and by program managers and staff members seeking to collect useful data on their programs.

Evaluators and program managers may have a variety of evaluation objectives in mind. They may have specific questions, or they may be unsure of how to frame useful questions about their programs. Careful analysis of the program to be evaluated and the context in which it operates is a significant precursor to the planning and design of any evaluation endeavor. Identification of the theory underlying the program and the contextual factors that affect its operations and success is critical.

This handbook covers a variety of approaches to analyzing the operations and results of past and current programs. Guidance for designing ongoing program performance monitoring systems is provided, along with advice on designing and implementing studies of program processes and program outcomes. A variety of evaluation approaches are discussed, including both qualitative and quantitative approaches for evaluating program operations and impact. (Note that, except in discussions about ways for evaluators to develop options and recommendations for program improvement, the term *program evaluation* as used in this handbook does not include assessing the effectiveness of *future* programs.)

The program evaluation approaches and tools covered here may provide feedback on program expenditures, program operations, or program results. They can be useful in developing new legislative proposals and in reauthorizing existing programs; in developing, debating, and deciding among budget alternatives; in implementing, operating, and improving public programs and programs operated by for-profit or nonprofit organizations; and in managing, auditing, and reporting on the uses of public funds.

Need for Program Evaluation

The demand for program evaluation, and "evidence-based" information on results, has become extraordinary. National and state legislatures, local legislative bodies, public agencies, foundations, and other funding agencies are increasingly demanding information on how program funds have been used and what funded programs have produced. Both program advocates and fiscal conservatives need information on program results. Performance management (or managing for results) initiatives are involving increasing numbers of program managers and staff in developing performance goals, monitoring performance, and then reporting on performance to inform decision making. The public is also becoming more demanding about how their tax dollars and fees are being used.

National governments, such as those in the United States, Australia, Canada, Chile, France, Mexico, Peru, the Scandinavian countries, and the United Kingdom, have developed experience with and expertise in program evaluations, including *performance audits*, also known as *value-for-money* audits. In the United States, the Government Performance and Results Act (GPRA) of 1993, along with the GPRA Modernization Act of 2010, require federal agencies to develop and update strategic plans, to establish annual performance targets, and to report annually on program performance. The Chief Financial Officers Act of 1990 requires federal agencies to provide a list of their program evaluations as well as to provide "systematic measurement of performance" and information on the "results of operations." The World Bank and other multilateral and regional banks have been pressing for evaluations of the work for which they provide support.

Handbook Organization

This handbook is divided into four parts. These address evaluation planning and design, data collection, data analysis, and evaluation use. In Part One,

the authors of Chapters One through Twelve explore a variety of approaches
to planning and designing evaluation studies and performance monitoring
systems. Evaluation planning and design should ensure that the benefits of
evaluation outweigh its costs. The chapters in Part One provide an overview
of program evaluation; suggest strategies for involving intended users and
other key stakeholders in evaluation planning and design; and discuss the
use of logic models, evaluability assessment and other exploratory evaluation approaches, performance measurement systems, case studies, and various experimental and quasi-experimental designs. The evaluation designs presented provide information on how to analyze program theories—including
program activities, outputs, program outcomes, and contextual factors affecting the extent to which program activities have produced desired program
results. Chapter authors discuss the purpose of each evaluation design, the
types of questions that can be answered, and requirements that must be
met to use each design properly. In addition, Part One contains chapters
on recruitment and retention of evaluation study participants, multisite evaluations, complex community change programs, and culturally responsive
evaluation.

In Part Two, the authors of Chapters Thirteen through Twenty-One
describe practical data collection procedures, that is, methods for collecting
data on program performance within tight time and resource constraints. They
describe both well-established and newer procedures for collecting information on program performance, including the use of agency records, surveys,
role playing, ratings by trained observers, the Internet, focus groups, and semi-
structured interviewing and the collection of data in the field and of "stories"
for evaluation studies. They discuss uses of these data collection procedures in
program evaluations and indicate the types of quality control needed to ensure
that the resulting data are valid and reliable.

In Part Three, the authors of Chapters Twenty-Two to Twenty-Five
provide advice on important methods for data analysis, looking at methods for analyzing qualitative data, use of appropriate statistics and statistical tests, cost-effectiveness and cost-benefit analysis, and meta-analyses and
evaluation syntheses. They discuss the requirements that must be met to
use these data analysis techniques and present examples illustrating their
application.

In Part Four, the authors of Chapters Twenty-Six to Thirty describe methods for getting evaluation results used. They offer advice on avoiding evaluation pitfalls, developing options and recommendations for policy and program
change, reporting findings persuasively, contracting for evaluations, and overcoming political and bureaucratic challenges to the use of evaluation findings.

The final chapter discusses challenges and issues in evaluation, including quality control of the evaluation process, selection and training of evaluators, and evaluation standards and ethics, and it also examines the relationships between performance measurement systems and evaluation studies. This chapter—and the handbook—closes with a discussion of current and future trends in program evaluation.

Acknowledgments

The editors and authors acknowledge the significant impact Joseph Wholey has had on all of our thinking about evaluation. While Joe has retired, and did not participate as actively in this edition, his influence remains significant. We are most grateful to the chapter authors. They gracefully and patiently handled the often numerous modification requests made by the editors. We are truly indebted to them. We thank our excellent copyeditors from this and previous editions and the entire Jossey-Bass/Wiley team, especially Dawn Kilgore, who encouraged and assisted us throughout this project and produced a high-quality publication from our manuscript.

We especially thank our energetic and capable research assistants, Rachel Breslin and Joselynn Hawkins Fountain, doctoral students in the Trachtenberg School at George Washington University, who kept the project on track throughout the entire process. In addition, we thank Adam Bethke, Master of Public Administration student, and Estelle Raimondo, Nick Hart, and Ryan Baker, doctoral students in the Trachtenberg School at George Washington University for their valuable contributions to the success of this endeavor.

THE EDITORS

KATHRYN E. NEWCOMER is the director of the Trachtenberg School of Public Policy and Public Administration at The George Washington University. She teaches public and nonprofit program evaluation and research design. She routinely conducts research and training for federal and local government agencies and nonprofit organizations on performance measurement and program evaluation, and has designed and conducted evaluations for several U.S. federal agencies and dozens of nonprofit organizations.

Newcomer has co-edited three books in addition to previous editions of this handbook: *Improving Government Performance* (1989), *Meeting the Challenges of Performance-Oriented Government* (2002), *Getting Results: A Guide for Federal Leaders and Managers* (2005), and co-authored (with James Kee) *Transformational Leadership: Leading Change in Public and Nonprofit Agencies* (June 2008). She is also the editor of a volume of *New Directions for Public Program Evaluation, Using Performance Measurement to Improve Public and Nonprofit Programs* (1997), and of numerous articles in journals, including the *Public Administration Review* and the *American Journal of Evaluation*. She is a Fellow of the National Academy of Public Administration and currently serves on the Comptroller General's Educators' Advisory Panel. She served as president of the Network of Schools of Public Affairs and Administration (NASPAA) in 2006–2007, and on the board of the American Evaluation Association in 2012–2014. She has received two Fulbright awards, one for Taiwan (1993) and one for Egypt

(2001–2004). In 2008, she received the Elmer Staats Award for Achievements in Government Accountability, awarded by the National Capital Area Chapter of the American Society for Public Administration. She has lectured on program evaluation and performance measurement in Ukraine, Brazil, Israel, the United Arab Emirates, Egypt, Taiwan, Colombia, Italy, Nicaragua, and the U.K.

Newcomer earned a bachelor of science degree in education and an MA degree in political science from the University of Kansas and her Ph.D. degree in political science from the University of Iowa.

HARRY P. HATRY is a Distinguished Fellow and director of the Public Management Program at the Urban Institute in Washington, D.C. He received his BS degree in engineering from Yale University and his MS degree from Columbia University's Graduate School of Business. He is a principal author of *Performance Measurement: Getting Results* (2nd ed., 2006), *How Effective Are Your Community Services? Procedures for Measuring Their Quality* (3rd ed., 2006), the Legislating for Results series of municipal action guides (2008), *Making Results-Based State Government Work* (2001), *Practical Program Evaluation for State and Local Government* (second edition, 1981), and an editor and author of the six-volume series Outcome Management for Nonprofit Organizations (2004).

He has been a national leader in developing performance measurement and evaluation procedures for public agencies at all three levels of government since the 1970s. He has led a number of efforts by public and nonprofit organizations to develop outcome measurement procedures for a number of public services.

Hatry is a Fellow of the National Academy of Public Administration. He was a member of the U.S. Department of Education's Evaluation Review Panel and a member of the White House Office of Management and Budget's Performance Measurement Advisory Council, 2002–2003. He received the 1985 Elmer B. Staats Award for Excellence in Program Evaluation and a 1984 American Society for Public Administration award naming him Outstanding Contributor to the Literature of Management Science and Policy Science. In 1993, he received a National Public Service Award from the American Society for Public Administration and National Academy of Public Administration. In 1996, he received the Evaluator of the Year award from the Washington Evaluators Association. In 1999, the Center for Accountability and Performance of the American Society of Public Administration presented him with a lifetime achievement award for his work in performance measurement and established the Harry Hatry Award for Distinguished Practice in Performance Measurement. In 2000, he received a 50th Anniversary Einhorn-Gary award from the Association of Government Accountants for "sustained commitment to advancing government accountability."

JOSEPH S. WHOLEY is professor emeritus, University of Southern California, Price School of Public Policy. His work focuses on the use of strategic planning, performance management, and program evaluation to improve the performance and accountability of public and nonprofit organizations. Wholey is the author or coauthor of numerous journal articles and five books, including *Zero-Base Budgeting and Program Evaluation* (1978), *Evaluation: Promise and Performance* (1979), *Evaluation and Effective Public Management* (1983), and *Improving Government Performance* (with Kathryn Newcomer, 1989) and is coeditor of three books, including *Handbook of Practical Program Evaluation* (1994, 2004, 2010) and *Performance and Credibility* (with Mark Abramson and Christopher Bellavita, 1986). He has consulted with and provided training for the World Bank and a wide variety of government agencies, nonprofit organizations, and foundations in this country and abroad. He has served as president of the Evaluation Research Society and is a cofounder of the American Evaluation Association.

Wholey has served as special assistant to the deputy assistant secretary for program analysis and director of evaluation in the U.S. Department of Health, Education, and Welfare; director of evaluation studies at the Urban Institute; deputy assistant secretary for planning and evaluation in the U.S. Department of Health and Human Services; senior advisor to the deputy director for management in the White House Office of Management and Budget; and senior advisor for evaluation methodology and senior advisor for performance and accountability in the U.S. Government Accountability Office.

Wholey is a Fellow of the National Academy of Public Administration. In 1979 he received the Gunnar and Alva Myrdal Prize from the Evaluation Research Society, and in 1983 he received the Elmer B. Staats Award from the National Capital Area chapter of the American Society for Public Administration. In 1999 the Center for Accountability and Performance of the American Society for Public Administration presented him with a lifetime achievement award for a lifetime of outstanding scholarship in performance measurement and performance management and established the Joseph S. Wholey Distinguished Scholarship Award.

Wholey held elective office for eight years as a member of the County Board of Arlington, Virginia, serving three times as chairman. He chaired Arlington's Long-Range County Improvement Program, which stimulated high-density development that locates high-rise office buildings, shops, apartments, condominiums, and hotels close to subway stops. He also chaired the Washington Metropolitan Area Transit Authority, the Virginia Board of Social Services, and the International Hospice Institute. He was president of Hospice of Northern Virginia and president of the Arlington Partnership for Affordable Housing. He is a cofounder and board member of the Alliance for Housing Solutions.

Wholey holds an MA degree in mathematics and a Ph.D. degree in philosophy from Harvard University and a BA degree in mathematics from The Catholic University of America.

THE CONTRIBUTORS

WILLIAM C. ADAMS is a professor at the Trachtenberg School of Public Policy and Public Administration at The George Washington University. After receiving his BA and MA in political science from Baylor University, he earned his Ph.D. in political science from The George Washington University, while working at the Rand Corporation, where he coauthored *An Assessment of Telephone Survey Methods*. His most recent book is *Election Night News and Voter Turnout*. Other books that he has authored or edited are *Television Coverage of the 1980 Presidential Campaign*, *Television Coverage of International Affairs*, *Television Coverage of the Middle East*, and *Television Network News: Issues in Content Research*. His scholarly studies have been published in journals such as *Policy Studies Journal*, *Public Opinion Quarterly*, *Journal of Politics*, *Journal of Communications*, and *Public Administration Review*. Adams has traveled extensively in more than 160 countries, lectured at many universities abroad, and was a Fulbright Fellow in 2010 at the University of Malaya, Kuala Lumpur.

CLAUDIA L. ARANDA is a Senior Research Associate at the Metropolitan Housing and Communities Policy Center at the Urban Institute, where the focus of her work is housing discrimination, fair housing, and housing market research. Her most recent projects include the Housing Discrimination Studies funded by the Department of Housing and Urban Development, all of which utilized the role playing methodology to measure the differential treatment experienced by persons with disabilities, families with children, and black, Hispanic, and Asian homeseekers. Aranda and her team have managed data collection efforts in the rental and sales markets of more than forty metropolitan areas nationwide. She works closely with fair housing and other advocacy and community organizations, helping implement best practices in testing methodologies, field staff recruitment, and management. She is an alumna of Stanford University and Columbia Law School.

JAMES B. BELL is the president of James Bell Associates, a firm that specializes in national evaluations of innovations in health and human services programs, such as the first Medicaid managed care demonstrations in the early 1980s. In recent years he has focused on evaluating the clinical outcomes and costs of integrated services for persons living with HIV/AIDS and co-occurring mental health and substance use disorders. Bell also oversees an evaluation of innovations in the management of patient safety and medical liability risk, as well as an evaluation of a promising child maltreatment prevention program. From 1974 to 1979, Bell worked with Joseph Wholey and other members of the Urban Institute's Program Evaluation Studies Group to develop evaluability assessment and other approaches to planning useful evaluations of federal programs. He received a BA degree in political science from the University of California, Los Angeles and an MA degree in political science from California State University at Northridge.

BARBARA J. COHN BERMAN, president of the Institute for Publicly Engaged Governing, works with nonprofits and governments to bring their organizations in closer alignment with the public they serve. Two of her books, *Listening to the Public* (2005) and *When Governments Listen* (2012), emerged from her research and work with seventy cities and counties in the United States and Canada. Her work in improving organizational performance, executive development, introducing technology, and research has resulted in numerous publications, presentations, invitations and recognition in the United States and abroad. She was founding director of the Center on Government Performance at the National Center for Civic Innovation and its affiliated Fund for the City of New York (vice president). In New York City government she was assistant housing commissioner for rent control and deputy city personnel director. Her undergraduate degree is from New York University, and she attended graduate schools at the City University of New York and The New School for Social Research, where she also taught graduate courses in addition to the Harriman School at SUNY Stony Brook. She was appointed a post-graduate Loeb Fellow at Harvard University.

ROBERT F. BORUCH is University Trustee Chair Professor in the Graduate School of Education and the Statistics Department of the Wharton School at the University of Pennsylvania. He is a Fellow of the American Statistical Association, the American Educational Research Association, the American Academy of Arts and Sciences, and the Academy for Experimental Criminology. Boruch is a founder of the international Campbell Collaboration, which instituted an award in his name for scholars who have made distinctive contributions to enhancing the use of dependable evidence. He serves on the board of directors of the American Institutes for Research and on the Advisory Boards for the Coalition for Evidence Based Policy and the Center for Evidence Based Crime Policy. Boruch's current research focuses on randomized controlled trials, research ethics and policy, big data, including administrative records and MOOCs, and failure analysis.

KEESHAWNA S. BROOKS is currently a school psychology doctoral student at Loyola University Chicago and a Diversifying Faculty in Illinois (DFI) fellow. Prior to enrolling in her doctoral program, Brooks worked as a survey director on several large-scale federal health surveys, including the National Children's Study and the Racial and Ethnic Approaches to Community Health in the U.S and co-founded a small research services business. She received her BA in psychology and MA in the social sciences at the University of Chicago and most recently received her MEd in educational psychology at Loyola University Chicago. Her research interests include survey research, bullying and violence prevention, individual and collective self-esteem and their impact on academic performance, social emotional learning, and educational issues related to ethnic/racial minorities. After completing her doctoral program, Brooks plans to work as a licensed psychologist and school psychology faculty member.

JOHN M. BRYSON is McKnight Presidential Professor of Planning and Public Affairs at the Hubert H. Humphrey School of Public Affairs at the University of Minnesota. He works in the areas of leadership, strategic management, collaboration, and the design of engagement processes. He wrote *Strategic Planning for Public and Nonprofit Organizations* (4th ed.) (Jossey-Bass, 2011), and co-wrote with Barbara C. Crosby *Leadership for the Common Good,* (2nd ed.) (Jossey-Bass, 2005). Dr. Bryson is a Fellow of the National Academy of Public Administration and received the 2011 Dwight Waldo Award from the American Society for Public Administration for "outstanding contributions to the professional literature of public administration over an extended scholarly career."

MARY ANNE CASEY is an independent consultant and has taught at the University of Minnesota, the University of Michigan, and the University of South

Florida. She works with organizations, helping them gather information to improve their programs and services. She has been a consultant and evaluator at the international, national, state, and local levels on topics relating to health, wellness, community development, education, agricultural policy, and environmental issues. Previously, she worked for the W. K. Kellogg Foundation and the State of Minnesota. Casey is the coauthor of several books on focus group interviewing. She received her Ph.D. degree from the University of Minnesota. She lives in Saint Paul, Minnesota.

STEPHANIE RIEGG CELLINI is an associate professor of public policy and public administration and of economics, at George Washington University. She is also a faculty research fellow at the National Bureau of Economic Research and an associate editor of *Education Finance and Policy*. Her research interests include education policy, labor economics, and public finance. Recent papers focus on the labor market returns to a for-profit college education and the responses of for-profit postsecondary institutions to changes in federal and state financial aid programs. Her work has been published in the *Quarterly Journal of Economics,* the *Journal of Policy Analysis and Management,* and the *American Economic Journal: Policy,* among others. Dr. Cellini teaches cost-benefit analysis and economics for public decision making in the Trachtenberg School of Public Policy and Public Administration at George Washington University. She received an M.A. and Ph.D. in economics from the University of California, Los Angeles, and a B.A. in public policy from Stanford University.

DYLAN CONGER is an associate professor and director of the masters in public policy program at New York University. She is also a research affiliate at the George Washington Institute of Public Policy and New York University's Institute for Education and Social Policy. Dylan's research concerns disadvantaged, immigrant, and minority youth with a focus on education policies and urban areas. Current projects include examining the effects of public policies and programs on the educational outcomes of undocumented immigrant and English language learners from early schooling through post-secondary; estimating the effect of Advanced Placement and other advanced high school courses on educational outcomes; and identifying the sources of gender disparities in secondary and post-secondary educational outcomes. Dylan is currently serving on the editorial boards of *Educational Evaluation and Policy Analysis* and *Educational Researcher.* She is also a technical panel member for the National Center for Education Statistics' National Assessment of Educational Progress High School Transcript Study and a member of the scientific review panel of the U.S. Department of Education's Institute of Education Sciences. Dylan received her BA in ethnic studies from the University of California at

Berkeley, her MPP from the University of Michigan, and her Ph.D. in public policy from New York University.

SCOTT C COOK is a clinical psychologist with extensive experience serving diverse inner-city populations with multiple medical, social, and economic challenges. He is currently at the University of Chicago and has more than twenty years of experience in behavioral health intervention as well as designing, implementing, and evaluating health promotion and disease prevention programming in health care and community settings. His career has focused on health care disparities research, intervention, program evaluation, and technical assistance provision for multiple disadvantaged populations, including LGBTQ patients and communities. He joined the team at the University of Chicago after eight years in leadership roles in research, community services, and clinical coordination at Howard Brown Health Center, a clinic that serves diverse communities of varied racial, ethnic, sexual, and gender identities in Chicago. Cook received his master's and doctoral degrees from the University of Missouri at Columbia. He completed his internship at Cook County Hospital (now John H. Stroger, Jr., Hospital), the major public hospital in Chicago that serves an indigent, multiethnic population.

JOSEPH FIRSCHEIN is deputy associate director and community affairs officer at the Board of Governors of the Federal Reserve System. In this capacity, he leads the board's community development and policy analysis teams that are responsible for analyzing emerging consumer and community development policies and practices in order to understand their implications for the economic and supervisory policies that are core to the central bank's functions. Prior to joining the Federal Reserve Board, Firschein served as a director in Fannie Mae's Housing and Community Development Division and also had senior policy roles at the U.S. Treasury Department Community Development Financial Institutions Fund and the U.S. Office of Management and Budget. Firschein is an adjunct professor at George Washington University, where he teaches courses on community development finance and policy.

SHARA GODIWALLA is a board member of The Alliance for Early Childhood. With more than eighteen years of experience in the field of survey research and project management with academia and with nonprofit, government, and international organizations, she last served as senior survey director. Her expertise lies in survey management, public health, children's health, health disparities, and international health. She served as associate project director with the NORC at the University of Chicago for the National Children's Study, a survey that follows children from before birth to twenty-one years of age. Prior to this, she was based at the Centers for Disease Control and Prevention and worked with twenty-two federal agencies as the director of the Federal Interagency Forum on Child and Family Statistics, which publishes national reports on children and families. She received her BA degree in bio-chemistry from the University of Texas at Austin and her MPH degree from The Johns Hopkins University.

DELWYN GOODRICK is a consultant in evaluation and organization development and works with both government and nongovernment clients. She delivers professional development in qualitative and mixed-method evaluation and research methods in Australia, New Zealand, Singapore, and the United Kingdom and is on the faculty of The Evaluators' Institute at George Washington University. She previously held academic appointments at Victoria University and the Royal Melbourne Institute of Technology and led the development of an evaluation support unit within the Victoria Department of Human Services while working in a policy role. She has undertaken evaluations of a range of public-sector initiatives in health and education, including initiatives in communities of practice, leadership, and adult learning. She earned her BA (honors) and master's degrees in psychology and education from the University of Waikato, New Zealand, and her Ph.D. degree, with a specialization in evaluation, from the University of Melbourne. She is coeditor of the *Evaluation Journal of Australasia.*

GEORGE F. GROB is a career program evaluator with extensive experience in working with policymakers. He served as director of Planning and Policy Development at the U.S. Department of Health, Education, and Welfare, responsible for coordinating the development of its annual legislative program. Subsequently, he was deputy inspector general for evaluation and inspections, overseeing the preparation of some nine hundred evaluations that were sent to senior departmental officials and to the Congress. He testified before Congress two dozen times. Based on this experience, he developed his ideas on how to effectively use evaluations to influence policy makers. He concluded that, in addition to the substance of reports, their writing style is also important. After forty years of federal service and he started the Center for Public Program Evaluation to extend his work as an evaluator of government and private sector programs.

GARY T. HENRY holds the Patricia and H. Rodes Hart Chair and serves as a professor of public policy and education in the Department of Leadership, Policy, and Organization, Peabody College, Vanderbilt University. Henry teaches the doctoral course in causal inference and a graduate evaluation course at Vanderbilt. He formerly held the Duncan MacRae '09 and Rebecca

Kyle MacRae Distinguished Professorship of Public Policy in the Department of Public Policy and directed the Carolina Institute for Public Policy at the University of North Carolina at Chapel Hill. Henry specializes in education policy, educational evaluation, teacher quality research, and quantitative research methods. He has published extensively in top journals, such as *Science, Educational Researcher, Journal of Policy Analysis and Management, Educational Evaluation and Policy Analysis, Journal of Teacher Education, Education Finance and Policy,* and *Evaluation Review.* Henry has received over $20 million dollars of sponsored research funding, and his research has been funded by the Institute of Education Sciences, U.S. Department of Education, Spencer Foundation, Lumina Foundation, National Institute for Early Childhood Research, Walton Family Foundation, and numerous state legislatures, governors' offices, and agencies. Henry currently serves as panel chair for the Continuous Improvement in Education Research panel and previously served as a principal member of the Standing Committee for Systemic Reform, Institute of Education Sciences, U.S. Department of Education.

STAFFORD HOOD is the Sheila M. Miller Professor and Founding Director of the Center for Culturally Responsive Evaluation and Assessment (CREA) in the College of Education at the University of Illinois at Urbana-Champaign, where he is also a professor of curriculum and instruction and educational psychology. For twenty-five years, his research and scholarly activities have focused primarily on the role of culture/cultural context in program evaluation and educational assessment. This work has included major collaborations with prominent evaluators (in the United States and internationally), educational researchers in culturally responsive pedagogy and computer scientists addressing issues of culture and cultural context. Additionally, he has served as a program evaluation and testing consultant to the federal government, state departments of education, school districts, universities, social service agencies, and private foundations in the United States, as well as continuing scholarly and practitioner based collaborations on evaluation in New Zealand and Ireland.

RODNEY K. HOPSON is a professor of education policy and evaluation in the College of Education and Human Development and a senior research fellow in the Center of Education Policy and Evaluation at George Mason University. He serves as an affiliated faculty member of the Center for Culturally Responsive Assessment and Evaluation (CREA) at the University of Illinois, Urbana-Champaign. His work focuses on comparative and international education policy and politics, especially on official, indigenous, and medium of instruction language issues; critical, cultural issues in education and social policy and evaluation; neighborhoods and education policy; and interpretive, qualitative, and ethnographic methods. In addition to his academic work, Hopson applies evaluation in school districts, philanthropic agencies, universities, and in government settings. Hopson received his Ph.D. from the Curry School of Education, University of Virginia, and has done post-doctoral/sabbatical studies in the Faculty of Education, University of Namibia, the Johns Hopkins Bloomberg School of Public Health and the Centre of African Studies, Cambridge University.

PRIYA JOHN is a research project professional for the University of Chicago Diabetes Research and Training Center. Her work includes overseeing projects that use decision analysis and epidemiological methods to characterize elderly patients with diabetes. Additionally, she works on a trial that looks at the integration of health information technology and decision analysis and its ability to help physicians and patients with treatment goals. She also assists with the Robert Wood Johnson Foundation's National Program Office for Finding Answers: Disparities Research for Change, a project that aims to reduce racial and ethnic disparities in health care. Prior to working at the University of Chicago, she worked on a trial using personal digital assistants as a weight management tracking device for veterans. She has also done extensive work in the area of health policy and its effects on obesity. She received her BS degree in health sciences from Purdue University and her MPH degree from Indiana University, Bloomington.

GRETCHEN B. JORDAN is an independent consultant specializing in evaluation for the full range of publicly funded research, development, and market adoption initiatives, using a systems view of innovation to develop logical frameworks. She has planned and managed program evaluations and performance monitoring for more than twenty years, primarily for the U.S. Department of Energy. Until December 2011 she was a Principal Member of Technical Staff with Sandia National Laboratories. Jordan has written articles and book chapters on logic modeling and co-authored guides on evaluation. She is co-editor of the journal *Research Evaluation*. Jordan is co-founder and co-chair of the American Evaluation Association Research Technology and Development Evaluation Topical Interest Group. She has a Ph.D. in economics and a B.A. in mathematics.

JAMES EDWIN (JED) KEE is a Professor Emeritus of the Trachtenberg School of Public Policy and Public Administration at George Washington University. He joined GW after a career in government in the states of New York and Utah. In New York, Kee served as a legal assistant to Senator Robert F. Kennedy and legislative counsel to the New York State Assembly. In Utah, he held a series of cabinet positions, including budget director and executive director of the Department of Administration. At GW, Kee was senior associate dean of the School of Business and Public Management and from 1997 to 2003 was the Giant Food Inc. Professor of Public/Private Management. Kee's teaching and research interests are in the areas of leadership, cross-sector collaborations, contracting out and public financial management. He has authored or coauthored three books and more than forty book chapters and journal articles.

KAREN E. KIRKHART is a professor of social work in the David B. Falk College of Sport and Human Dynamics at Syracuse University and an affiliated faculty member of the Center for Culturally Responsive Assessment and Evaluation (CREA) at the University of Illinois, Urbana-Champaign. She has been active in the evaluation profession for more than thirty-five years, receiving the Robert Ingle Award for Outstanding Services to the American Evaluation Association in 2007. She has been recognized with the Paul F. Lazarsfeld Award for Outstanding Contribution to Evaluation Theory for her work in culture, validity, and evaluation influence. Her most recent publication, coauthored with Joan LaFrance and Richard Nichols, is "Cultural Views of Validity: A Conversation," in S. Hood, R. K. Hopson, & H. Frierson (eds.) (2015), *Continuing the Journey to Reposition Culture and Cultural Context in Evaluation Theory and Practice.* Kirkhart earned an MSW and a Ph.D. degree in social work and social science from the University of Michigan.

RICHARD A. KRUEGER is professor emeritus at the University of Minnesota. He is an internationally recognized authority on the use of focus group interviewing within the public environment. He has written seven books, authored many journal articles, and lectured throughout the world. In addition, he is a former president of the American Evaluation Association. He holds a Ph.D. in research methods and holds academic appointments in education, epidemiology, and public health. Although trained as a quantitative researcher, he was drawn to qualitative research and has spent the past thirty years learning about, practicing, and teaching qualitative research.

DIANE K. LEVY is a Senior Research Associate in the Metropolitan Housing and Communities Policy Center at the Urban Institute. She has examined housing discrimination in mortgage lending, rental, and sales markets through a number of HUD-sponsored paired-testing studies. Recent studies have focused on differential treatment based on race, ethnicity, and physical disabilities. Her work broadly has focused on low- and moderate-income housing and neighborhoods—including studies of housing conditions, effects of federal and local programs on residents and neighborhoods, and implementation and viability of housing provision models such as mixed-income housing and affordable housing development via inclusionary zoning. Levy earned master's degrees in anthropology and city and regional planning from the University of North Carolina at Chapel Hill.

KARIN MARTINSON is a principal associate with Abt Associates in Bethesda, Maryland. With more than twenty years of experience as both a researcher and policy analyst, she has conducted evaluations of a wide range of programs and policies for low-income families, particularly employment and training and income support programs. She has directed and participated in numerous large-scale demonstration projects using experimental designs and field-based implementation studies using multiple data collection and analysis strategies. Much of her research has focused on examining policies and service delivery systems for families facing barriers to employment and identifying promising models and practices to improve service delivery and employment outcomes. She has provided technical advice and methodological consultation to numerous projects and has authored a wide range of publications, including evaluation reports, policy briefs, and book chapters. She also served as a senior researcher at the Urban Institute and MDRC. Martinson received her MPP degree from the University of California, Berkeley, and her BA degree in economics from Oberlin College.

JOHN A. McLAUGHLIN is an independent consultant in strategic planning, performance measurement, and program evaluation. For the past forty years, he has assisted in the design, delivery, and evaluation of programs at major university-based research and training centers and federal/state/local government levels and has designed and implemented training and technical assistance for federal/state/local managers as they moved their organizations to becoming performance-based. The centerpiece to McLaughlin's work has been the creation of a performance management framework with three interdependent functions: logic modeling, developing performance measures grounded in the logic models, and subsequently program evaluation strategies aimed at increasing understanding of performance as measured through performance indices referenced to the logic models. McLaughlin has been a faculty member and administrator at four universities in the United States and has authored texts and articles on performance measurement and program evaluation.

CLAIRE MORGAN is a senior research associate at WestEd, where she promotes evidence-based policy and practice and provides education research, evaluation, and technical assistance for departments of education and other governmental and non-governmental entities. Morgan provides research support and technical assistance for the Puerto Rico Research Alliance for Dropout Prevention and the U.S. Virgin Islands College and Career Readiness Research Alliance through the federally funded Regional Educational Laboratory (REL) Northeast & Islands. In addition to her work for REL-NEI, Morgan conducts other research projects, including systematic reviews of education development issues in developing nations and needs assessment for non-governmental organizations providing technical assistance in developing countries. This work informs policymakers and practitioners about the effectiveness of certain education interventions in low-income countries. Morgan's evaluation work includes evaluating alternative teacher preparation programs, university-school STEM partnerships, community schools initiatives, and various other federally funded programs. She earned an MA in international education administration and policy analysis from Stanford University.

DEMETRA SMITH NIGHTINGALE is the chief evaluation officer at the U.S. Department of Labor. She is also a professorial lecturer at the Trachtenberg School of Public Policy and Public Administration at the George Washington University, a Fellow of the National Academy of Public Administration, and a senior research affiliate with the Poverty Center at the University of Michigan. Her research focuses on employment policy, workforce development, labor markets, and social policy, and she has evaluated federal, state, and local programs aimed at increasing employment, skills, and income for workers and families. She is the author or coauthor of several books, including *Repairing the U.S. Social Safety Net* (with Martha Burt) and *Reshaping the American Workforce in a Changing Economy* (with Harry Holzer). She previously was a Senior Fellow at the Urban Institute for many years, on the faculty at Johns Hopkins University's graduate program in public policy, and a senior consultant to the World Bank. She was also an expert advisor to the White House Welfare Reform Working Group in 1992–1993. She received her B.A. in political science and Ph.D. in public policy, both from the George Washington University.

CAROLYN O'BRIEN is a senior research associate with Capital Research Corporation in Arlington, Virginia. She has more than thirty years of experience in the evaluation of policies and programs, particularly in the areas of employment and training, income support and services for low-income families. Her extensive experience in designing and conducting process and implementation studies includes multiple data collection methods—case studies, focus groups, staff surveys, and semi-structured telephone and in-person interviews with program administrators and staff at the federal, state and local levels. She has directed and participated in dozens of studies for a variety of federal and state agencies as well as foundations. Prior to joining Capital Research Corporation, O'Brien was a senior research associate at the Urban Institute. She received her BA degree in sociology from Duke University and her MA degree in sociology from The George Washington University.

MICHAEL QUINN PATTON is an independent organization development and program evaluation consultant. He is former president of the American Evaluation Association. He is author of the fourth editions of *Qualitative Research and Evaluation Methods* (2015) and *Utilization-Focused Evaluation* (2008). He also authored *Developmental Evaluation: Applying Complexity Concepts to Enhance Innovation and Use* (2011). He has received the Myrdal Award for Outstanding Contributions to Useful and Practical Evaluation Practice and the Lazarsfeld Award for Lifelong Contributions to Evaluation Theory from the American Evaluation Association. He is coauthor of *Getting to Maybe: How the World Is Changed* (Random House Canada, 2006) with Frances Westley and Brenda Zimmerman. He regularly teaches in The Evaluators' Institute and the International Program for Development Evaluation Training.

ANTHONY PETROSINO, is a senior research associate at WestEd and Senior Research Fellow at the Center for Evidence-Based Crime Policy, George Mason University. He has twenty-five years of experience working on evaluation projects. Current projects include co-directing five research projects funded by the U.S. Department of Justice and a multi-site randomized trial of a teen pregnancy prevention program (funded by the U.S. DHHS). Petrosino was one of the founding members of the Campbell Collaboration (C2), an international organization that prepares, updates, and disseminates systematic reviews of research. Specifically, he helped develop the C2's first register of experimental studies, its first review (on the "Scared Straight" juvenile delinquency prevention program), and one of its first substantive groups (Crime & Justice Group). He received a Distinguished Service Award from the Campbell Crime and Justice Group for his service. Petrosino, who holds a Ph.D., is also an Honorary Fellow for the Academy Experimental Criminology.

THEODORE H. POISTER is professor of public management at the Andrew Young School of Policy Studies at Georgia State University, where he specializes in public management systems and applied research methods. His research focuses on strategic planning, performance measurement and management, and stakeholder feedback, and he has published widely on these and other subjects in the major public administration journals and elsewhere. In addition to earlier books on public program analysis, program evaluation, and performance monitoring, he was lead author of the second edition of *Managing and*

Measuring Performance in Public and Nonprofit Organizations, published by Jossey-Bass in 2014. In addition to the field of transportation, Poister has worked with numerous federal, state, and local agencies in a wide variety of other areas, including criminal justice, housing, mental disabilities, public health, child support enforcement, and nursing regulation. He has also conducted professional development programs for a number of public agencies, and he regularly teaches course on applied statistics and performance measurement for the Evaluators' Institute at George Washington University. He earned an MPA degree and a Ph.D. in social science from the Maxwell School at Syracuse University, and he taught at Southern University and Penn State University prior to moving to Georgia State.

CHRISTOPHER V. POWERS is a licensed marriage and family therapist and was coordinator of recruitment and retention for both the Research Unit of the UCSF AIDS Health Project and the Research Department of Howard Brown Health Center in Chicago. Working for more than ten years in behavioral health research, he has collaborated with city health departments, community-based organizations, universities, the National Institutes of Health, and the Centers for Disease Control and Prevention. His focus has been on addressing health disparities that affect individuals in the lesbian, gay, bisexual, transgender, queer, and HIV-positive communities. He has presented at the National HIV-Prevention Conference and the Conference of the American Public Health Association. Powers holds a BA in psychology from the University of Michigan and an MA in counseling psychology from the California Institute of Integral Studies.

DEBRA J. ROG is a Westat associate director and president of the Rockville Institute, with more than thirty years of experience in research and evaluation. In her current roles, Rog is directing several evaluations in the areas of homeless systems and services, housing, public health, among others. She also serves in evaluation advising roles within the organization. Throughout her career, Rog has directed numerous evaluation studies involving programs and policies for vulnerable populations. Before joining Westat in January 2007, Rog was director of the Washington office of Vanderbilt University's Center for Evaluation and Program Improvement (CEPI) for seventeen years, and was a senior research associate in CEPI. Rog has served as the co-editor of the *Applied Social Research Methods Series* (more than fifty textbooks to date) and the *Handbook of Applied Social Research Methods*, and is on faculty of The Evaluators' Institute. She has to her credit numerous publications on evaluation methodology, housing, homelessness, poverty, mental health, and program and policy development and has contributed and served on the editorial boards of the *Encyclopedia of*

Homelessness and *the Encyclopedia of Evaluation*. She was the 2009 president of the American Evaluation Association (AEA) and a member of AEA since its inception.

PATRICIA J. ROGERS is professor of public sector evaluation at the Centre for Applied Social Research in at the Royal Melbourne Institute of Technology (RMIT University), Australia. She is also on the faculty of The Evaluators' Institute at George Washington University, where she teaches courses in qualitative data analysis and theories of change. She earned her BA degree in political science and Ph.D. degree (with a specialization in evaluation) from the University of Melbourne and completed a postdoctoral fellowship in evaluation with Carol Weiss at Harvard University. She is a recipient of the American Evaluation Association's Myrdal Prize for evaluation practice and the Australasian Evaluation Society's Evaluation Training and Services Award and Best Evaluation Study Award. Her current research focuses on decision support to choose appropriate evaluation methods to suit a particular situation and practical evaluation methods for complicated and complex interventions, including the book *Purposeful Program Theory: Effective Use of Logic Models and Theories of Change* (with Sue Funnell, 2010).

SHELLI B. ROSSMAN was a Senior Fellow in the Justice Policy Center of Urban Institute, with more than thirty years of research and management experience on projects for federal/national, state, and local governments, as well as private-sector clients in the areas of (1) criminal justice, including reentry, problem-solving courts, community-based and correctional supervision, case management and comprehensive service delivery for offender populations, delinquency prevention and intervention, and victimization; (2) public health, focused on substance abuse, HIV/AIDS, and reproductive health; and (3) community safety. In both national and international settings, her projects have addressed improving the standards and monitoring of service delivery for at-risk and high-risk populations, as well as cultural competency and gender equity issues. She recently completed the largest problem-solving court research study ever conducted: *NIJ's Multi-Site Evaluation of Adult Drug Courts (MADCE)*–a study of twenty-three courts and six comparison jurisdictions in eight states, during which researchers completed nearly five thousand in-person surveys, conducted multiple site visits documenting core activities, and performed more than one thousand research-conducted drug screens.

SIERRA STONEY is a graduate student at the Harris School of Public Policy at the University of Chicago, where she specializes in community development, public finance, and quantitative research methods. Her independent research focuses on identifying significant differences in economic outcomes between groups of people and evaluating the extent to which differential access to economic opportunity influences these observed outcomes. She is pursuing her MPP at Harris to complement her MA in applied economics from Georgetown University. Prior to working with the Urban Institute's Metropolitan Housing and Community Policies Center, she was a quantitative research intern with the Migration Policy Institute and an analyst with a small consulting firm.

CELIA A. TAYLOR is an associate professor of quantitative research in the Division of Health Sciences at the University of Warwick. Her research includes evaluation of interventions to enhance patient safety and health services delivery, using a variety of research designs and including economic evaluation. She also has an interest in the selection and assessment of health care students and professionals. Taylor teaches medical statistics and evidence-based medicine.

BRETT THEODOS is a senior research associate with the Metropolitan Housing and Communities Policy Center at the Urban Institute. His expertise is in performance measurement and program evaluation of interventions supporting vulnerable communities and families, focusing on affordable housing and economic/community development. Efforts he has evaluated include the New Markets Tax Credit program, four Small Business Administration loan and investment programs, HUD's Section 108 program, and HUD's Strong Cities, Strong Communities National Resource Network. Theodos has also conducted several research studies of neighborhood change, including examining the importance of residential mobility. He is also working to grow nonprofit capacity in the areas of evaluation and performance measurement: he directs Measure4Change, an initiative sponsored by the World Bank, which provides technical assistance to nonprofits.

CAROLE J. TORGERSON is a professor of education in the School of Education at Durham University and a Fellow of the Academy of Social Sciences. Her research interests include randomized trials in educational research and systematic reviews of educational experiments. She has published widely in the field of education and experimental methods. She is co-author of *Designing Randomised Trials in Health, Education, and the Social Sciences* (with David Torgerson, 2008).

DAVID J. TORGERSON is director of the York Trials Unit and a professor in the Department of Health Sciences, University of York. He has published widely on the methods and methodology of randomized trials in health and the social sciences. He is the coauthor of *Designing Randomised Trials in Health, Education and the Social Sciences* (with Carole Torgerson, 2008).

TIMOTHY TRIPLETT is a senior survey methodologist and part of the Urban Institute's Statistical Methods Group. At the Urban Institute, his primary work involves working on studies that include survey data collection, complex sample designs and random experimental designs. He conducts methodological research addressing such issues as estimating non-response bias, weighting strategies, and imputation procedures. He also works extensively with the decennial Census, American Community Survey, and the Annual Social and Economic Supplement (ASEC) to the Current Population Survey in order to create survey weights, impute for missing data, or to analyze non-response for the numerous surveys collected for or by the Urban Institute. He has more than thirty years of survey research experience, including responsibility for national, statewide, and regional projects, sample design, developing questionnaires, and managing statistical and computer programming. He has written and presented more than twenty-five survey methodology papers and served as the program chair for the 1998 International Field Directors and Technology Conference.

VERNA VASQUEZ is a vice president of the Institute of Publicly Engaged Governing, working with nonprofits and governments to bring their organizations in closer alignment with the public they serve. For the last three years, she has also managed the after-school enrichment program at an independent school. Previously, she served as associate director of the Center on Government Performance of the Fund for the City of New York and its affiliate organization, the National Center for Civic Innovation. During her fifteen-year tenure at the Center, she helped develop a computerized neighborhood environment tracking program from inception, managed a street smoothness survey project, and facilitated the launch and continuous operation of a program that encouraged governments to listen to the public, learn how they assess government performance, and incorporate the public's views into their government reports and management strategies. Before that, she worked as an analyst in California's State Department of Conservation. She has a B.A. in government from Claremont McKenna College and an MPA from Columbia University's School of International and Public Affairs.

PART ONE

EVALUATION PLANNING AND DESIGN

The chapters in Part One discuss a variety of techniques and strategies for planning and designing credible, useful evaluation work. Chapter authors provide guidance relevant to engaging stakeholders, designing evaluation studies including impact evaluations, and designing ongoing monitoring systems.

The chapters cover the following topics:

- Evaluation planning and design
- Engaging stakeholders
- Logic modeling
- Evaluability assessment and other exploratory evaluation approaches
- Performance monitoring
- Comparison group designs
- Randomized controlled trials
- Case studies
- Recruitment and retention of evaluation study participants
- Multisite evaluations
- Evaluating community change programs
- Culturally responsive evaluation

Evaluation design involves balancing evaluation costs with the likely usefulness of the evaluation results. In general, the higher the level of precision, reliability, and generalizability of an evaluation, the higher the evaluation costs in terms of time (calendar time and the time of managers, staff, clients, and others affected by the evaluation process); financial costs; and political and bureaucratic costs, such as perceived disruptions and loss of goodwill among those affected. The value of an evaluation is measured: in the strength of the evidence produced; in the credibility of the evaluation to policymakers, managers, and other intended users; and especially in the use of the evaluation information to improve policies and programs. Matching design decisions to available time and resources is an art, supported by the social sciences.

An evaluation design identifies what questions will be answered by the evaluation, what data will be collected, how the data will be analyzed to answer the questions, and how the resulting information will be used. Each design illuminates an important aspect of reality. Logic modeling is a useful strategy for identifying program components and outcomes, as well as important contextual factors affecting program operations and outcomes. Evaluability assessment explores the information needs of policymakers, managers, and other key stakeholders; the feasibility and costs of answering alternative evaluation questions; and the likely use of evaluation findings—for example, to improve program performance or to communicate the value of program activities to policymakers or other key stakeholders. Performance monitoring systems and descriptive case studies answer questions that ask for description: What's happening? Comparison group designs, randomized experiments, and explanatory case studies answer questions that ask for explanation: Why have these outcomes occurred? What difference does the program make? Many evaluations use a combination of these approaches to answer questions about program performance.

The Chapters

The editors, in Chapter One, describe how to match evaluation approaches to information needs, identify key contextual elements shaping the use of evaluation, produce the methodological rigor needed to support credible findings, and design responsive and useful evaluations.

John Bryson and Michael Patton, in Chapter Two, describe how to identify and engage intended users and other key evaluation stakeholders and how to work with stakeholders to help determine the mission and goals of an evaluation. They highlight the need for flexibility and adaptability in responding to rapidly changing evaluation situations.

John McLaughlin and Gretchen Jordan, in Chapter Three, discuss the *logic model*, which provides a useful tool for: planning, program design, and program management; communicating the place of a program in a larger organization or context; designing performance monitoring systems and evaluation studies; and framing evaluation reports so that the evaluation findings tell the program's *performance story*. They describe how to construct and verify logic models for new or existing programs. They also present examples of both basic and complex logic models and identify resources and tools that evaluators can use to learn about and construct logic models.

Joseph Wholey, in Chapter Four, describes evaluability assessment, rapid feedback evaluation, evaluation synthesis, and small-sample studies, each of which produces evaluation findings and helps focus future evaluation work. *Evaluability assessment* assesses the extent to which programs are ready for useful evaluation and helps key stakeholders come to agreement on evaluation criteria and intended uses of evaluation information. *Rapid feedback evaluation* is an extension of evaluability assessment that produces estimates of program effectiveness, indications of the range of uncertainty in those estimates, tested designs for more definitive evaluation, and further clarification of intended uses of evaluation information. *Evaluation synthesis* summarizes what is known about program effectiveness on the basis of all relevant research and evaluation studies. *Small-sample studies* can be used to test performance measures that are to be used in evaluation work. Wholey describes each of these four exploratory evaluation approaches and indicates when one or another of these approaches might be appropriate.

Theodore Poister, in Chapter Five, discusses *performance measurement systems*: systems for ongoing monitoring of program outcomes. He describes how to design and implement performance measurement systems that will provide information that can be used to improve program performance—without creating disruptions and other negative consequences. Poister focuses particular attention on development of good performance measures and effective presentation of performance information to decision makers.

Gary Henry, in Chapter Six, describes a variety of *comparison group designs* that evaluators frequently use to make quantitative estimates of program impacts (the causal effects of programs) by comparing the outcomes for those served by a program with the outcomes for those in a comparison group who represent what would have occurred in the absence of the program. He notes that comparison group designs represent alternatives to randomized controlled trials, in which members of the target population are randomly assigned to program participation (treatment) or to an untreated control group, and notes that comparison group designs are often the only practical means available for evaluators to provide evidence about program impact. Henry's chapter will help evaluators to improve their evaluation designs as much as circumstances permit—and will help evaluators to state the limitations on the findings of evaluations based on comparison group designs.

Carole Torgerson, David Torgerson, and Celia Taylor, in Chapter Seven, discuss *randomized controlled trials* (RCTs), in which participants are randomly assigned to alternative treatments. These authors discuss the barriers to wider use of RCTs but argue that carefully planned RCTs are not necessarily expensive and that the value of the information they provide on program impact often outweighs their cost.

Karin Martinson and Carolyn O'Brien, in Chapter Eight, discuss case studies, which integrate qualitative and quantitative data from multiple sources and present an in-depth picture of the implementation and results of a policy or program within its context. They distinguish three types of case studies: *exploratory case studies*, which aim at defining the questions and hypotheses for a subsequent study; *descriptive case studies*, which document what is happening and why to show what a situation is like; and *explanatory case studies*, which focus on establishing cause-and-effect relationships. Martinson and O'Brien present guidelines that show how to design and conduct single-site and multiple-site case studies, how to analyze the large amounts of data that case studies can produce, and how to report case studies in ways that meet the needs of their audiences.

Scott Cook, Shara Godiwalla, Keeshawna Brooks, Christopher Powers, and Priya John, in Chapter Nine, discuss a range of issues concerning recruitment and retention of study participants in an evaluation study. They share best practices in *recruitment* (obtaining the right number of study participants with the right characteristics) and *retention* (maximizing the number of participants who continue to provide needed information throughout the evaluation period). Cook and his colleagues describe how to avoid a number of pitfalls in recruitment and retention, noting, for example, that evaluators typically overestimate their ability to recruit and retain study participants and typically underestimate the time required to obtain study clearance from an institutional review board or from the White House Office of Management and Budget.

Debra Rog, in Chapter Ten, provides principles and frameworks for designing, managing, conducting, and reporting on *multisite evaluations*: evaluations that examine a policy or program in two or more sites. She presents practical tools for designing multisite evaluations, monitoring evaluation implementation, collecting common and single-site data, quality control, data management, data analysis, and communicating evaluation findings.

Brett Theodos and Joseph Firschein, in Chapter Eleven, describe how to design evaluation of multi-service community change programs. They identify the characteristics of these programs that require special consideration in evaluation. They also describe the challenges evaluators face when designing and implementing evaluations of these programs, and offer guidance on how to address the challenges.

Stafford Hood, Rodney Hopson, and Karen Kirkhart, in Chapter Twelve, provide a historical overview of the development of culturally responsive evaluation (CRE), describe the theory that guides CRE practice, and discuss how practical applications of CRE have informed and contributed to CRE in the field. They provide a useful framework to clarify how CRE informs all stages of evaluation practice. They also discuss how CRE practice can bolster the validity, rigor, and responsibility of evaluation work.

All of the authors in Part One discuss challenges in the evaluation designs that they describe. They offer practical advice on implementing evaluation designs and illustrate the use of their designs in a number of policy areas. Although many of the authors discuss data collection and data analysis methods, those topics are addressed more thoroughly later in this handbook.

CHAPTER ONE

PLANNING AND DESIGNING USEFUL EVALUATIONS

Kathryn E. Newcomer, Harry P. Hatry, Joseph S. Wholey

The demand for systematic data on the performance of public and non-profit programs continues to rise across the world. The supply of such data rarely matches the level of demand of the requestors. Diversity in the types of providers of pertinent data also continues to rise.

Increasingly, elected officials, foundations and other nonprofit funders, oversight agencies, and citizens want to know what value is provided to the public by the programs they fund. Members of program staff want to know how their programs are performing so that they can improve them and learn from the information they gather. Increasingly, executives want to lead *learning organizations*, where staff systematically collect data, learn what works and does not work in their programs, and use this information to improve their organizational capacity and services provided. Leaders and managers also want to make evidence-based policy and management decisions, informed by data evaluating past program performance.

As we use the term in this handbook, a *program is a set of resources and activities directed toward one or more common goals, typically under the direction of a single manager or management team.* A program may consist of a limited set of activities in one agency or a complex set of activities implemented at many sites by two or more levels of government and by a set of public, nonprofit, and even private providers.

Program evaluation is *the application of systematic methods to address questions about program operations and results. It may include ongoing monitoring of a program as well as one-shot studies of program processes or program impact. The approaches used are based on social science research methodologies and professional standards.* The field of program evaluation provides processes and tools that agencies of all kinds can apply to obtain valid, reliable, and credible data to address a variety of questions about the performance of public and nonprofit programs.

Program evaluation is presented here as a valuable learning strategy for enhancing knowledge about the underlying logic of programs and the program activities under way as well as about the results of programs. We use the term *practical program evaluation* because most of the procedures presented here are intended for application at reasonable cost and without extensive involvement of outside experts. We believe that resource constraints should not rule out evaluation. Ingenuity and leveraging of expertise can and should be used to produce useful, but not overly expensive, evaluation information. Knowledge of how trade-offs in methodological choices affect what we learn is critical.

A major theme throughout this handbook is that evaluation, to be useful and worth its cost, should not only assess program implementation and results but also identify ways to improve the program evaluated. Although accountability continues to be an important goal of program evaluation, the major goal should be to improve program performance, thereby giving the public and funders better value for money. When program evaluation is used only for external accountability purposes and does not help managers learn and improve their programs, the results are often not worth the cost of the evaluation.

The objective of this handbook is to strengthen program managers' and staff members' abilities to meet the increasing demand for evaluation information, in particular information to improve the program evaluated. This introductory chapter identifies fundamental elements that evaluators and organizations sponsoring evaluations should consider before undertaking any evaluation work, including how to match the evaluation approach to information needs, identify key contextual elements shaping the conduct and use of evaluation, produce methodological rigor needed to support credible findings, and design responsive and useful evaluations. A glossary of some key evaluation terms is provided at the end of this chapter.

Matching the Evaluation Approach to Information Needs

Selecting among evaluation options is a challenge to program personnel and evaluators interested in allocating resources efficiently and effectively. The value of program evaluation endeavors will be enhanced when clients for the information know what they are looking for. Clients, program managers, and evaluators all face many choices.

Since the turn of the twenty-first century, the demand for evidence to inform policymaking both inside the United States and internationally has grown, as has the sophistication of the public dialogue about what qualifies as strong evidence. Relatedly, the program evaluation profession has grown in terms of both numbers and professional guidance. There are many influential organizations that provide useful standards for evaluation practice and identify competencies needed in the conduct of evaluation work. Three key sources of guidance that organizations and evaluators should consult before entering into evaluation work include:

- *Joint Committee on Standards for Educational Evaluation* (2010). This organization
  has provided four key watch words for evaluators for many years: *utility, feasibility, propriety,* and *accuracy* (see the committee's website, www.jcsee.org/program-evaluation-standards, for more information on the standards).
- *American Evaluation Association* (2004). The AEA's *Guiding Principles for Evaluators* is a detailed list of guidelines that has been vetted regularly by evaluators to ensure its usefulness (see www.eval.org/p/cm/ld/fid=51)
- *Essential Competencies for Program Evaluators Self-Assessment* at www.cehd.umn.edu/OLPD/MESI/resources/ECPESelfAssessmentInstrument709.pdf

Select Programs to Evaluate

Resources for evaluation and monitoring are typically constrained. Prioritization among evaluation approaches should therefore reflect the most urgent information needs of decision makers. There may be many demands for information on program performance. Not all of these can likely be met at reasonable cost. What criteria can guide choices?

Five basic questions should be asked when any program is being considered for evaluation or monitoring:

- Can the results of the evaluation influence decisions about the program?
- Can the evaluation be done in time to be useful?
- Is the program significant enough to merit evaluation?
- Is program performance viewed as problematic?
- Where is the program in its development?

One watchword of the evaluation profession has been *utilization-focused evaluation* (see Patton, 2008). An evaluation that is *utilization-focused* is designed to answer specific questions raised by those in charge of a program so that the information provided by these answers can affect decisions about the program's future. This test is the first criterion for an evaluation. Programs for which decisions must be made about continuation, modification, or termination are good candidates for evaluation, at least in terms of this first criterion. Programs for which there is considerable political support are less likely candidates under this criterion.

Timing is important in evaluation. If an evaluation cannot be completed in time to affect decisions to be made about the program (the second criterion), evaluation will not be useful. Some questions about a program may be unanswerable at the time needed because the data are not currently available and cannot be collected in time.

Significance can be defined in many ways. Programs that consume a large amount of resources or are perceived to be marginal in performance are likely candidates for evaluation using this third test, assuming that evaluation results can be useful and evaluation can be done in a reasonable amount of time.

The fourth criterion, perceptions of problems by at least some program stakeholders, matters as well. When citizens or interest groups publicly make accusations about program performance or management, evaluation can play a pivotal role. Evaluation findings and performance data may be used to justify decisions to cut, maintain, or expand programs in order to respond to the complaints.

Placement of a program in its life cycle, the fifth criterion, makes a big difference in determining need for evaluation. New programs, and in particular pilot programs for which costs and benefits are unknown, are good candidates for evaluation.

Select the Type of Evaluation

Once a decision has been made to design an evaluation study or a monitoring system for a program, there are many choices to be made about the type of approach that will be most appropriate and useful. Figure 1.1 displays six important continua on which evaluation approaches differ.

FIGURE 1.1. SELECT AN EVALUATION APPROACH THAT IS APPROPRIATE GIVEN THE INTENDED USE.

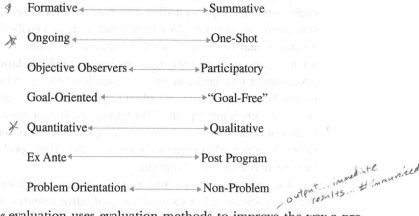

Formative ←————————————→ Summative

Ongoing ←————————————→ One-Shot

Objective Observers ←————————————→ Participatory

Goal-Oriented ←————————————→ "Goal-Free"

Quantitative ←————————————→ Qualitative

Ex Ante ←————————————→ Post Program

Problem Orientation ←————————————→ Non-Problem

output... immediate results... # immunized

overall results... w/# contract disease

is goal = longer life expectan

Formative evaluation uses evaluation methods to improve the way a program is delivered. At the other end of this continuum is *summative* evaluation, which measures program <u>outcomes</u> and impacts during ongoing operations or after program completion. Most evaluation work will examine program implementation to some extent, if only to ensure that the assessment of outcomes or impacts can be logically linked to program activities. There are a variety of designs for formative evaluation, including *implementation evaluation, process studies,* and *evaluability assessment,* and they are covered later in this handbook. And there are a variety of specific designs intended to capture outcomes and impacts, and they are covered later in this text as well.

The timing of the evaluation can range across a continuum from a one-shot study of a specific aspect of implementation or one set of outcomes to an ongoing assessment system. The routine measurement of program inputs, outputs, or intermediate outcomes may be extremely useful for assessment of trends and should provide data that will be useful for more focused one-shot studies.

Traditional social science research methods have called for objective, neutral, and detached observers to measure the results of experiments and studies. However, as professional evaluation standards prescribe, program stakeholders should also be involved to ensure that the results of evaluation work of any kind will be used. The issue really is the level of participation of these stakeholders, who can include program staff, clients, beneficiaries, funders, and volunteers, to name a few. For example, various stakeholders could be consulted or given some degree of decision-making authority in evaluation design, data collection, interpretation of findings, and framing of recommendations.

Evaluators make judgments about the value, or worth, of programs (Scriven, 1980). When making determinations about the appropriateness, adequacy, quality, efficiency, or effectiveness of program operations and results, evaluators may rely on existing criteria provided in laws, regulations, mission statements, or grant applications. Goals may be clarified, and targets for performance may be given in such documentation. But in some cases evaluators are not given such criteria, and may have to seek guidance from stakeholders, professional standards, or other evaluation studies to help them make judgments. When there are no explicit expectations for program outcomes given, or unclear goals are espoused for a program (i.e., it appears to be "goal-free"), evaluators find themselves constructing the evaluation criteria. In any case, if the evaluators find unexpected outcomes (whether good or bad), these should be considered in the evaluation.

The terms *qualitative* and *quantitative* have a variety of connotations in the social sciences. For example, a qualitative research approach or mind-set means taking an inductive and open-ended approach in research and broadening questions as the research evolves. Qualitative data are typically words or visual images whereas quantitative data are typically numbers. The most common qualitative data collection methods are interviews (other than highly structured interviews), focus groups, and participant observation. Open-ended responses to survey questions can provide qualitative data as well. The most common sources of quantitative data are administrative records and structured surveys conducted via Internet and mail. Mixed-method approaches in evaluation are very common, and that means that both quantitative and qualitative data are used, and quantitative and qualitative data collection methods are used in combination (see Greene, 2007, for more on use of mixed methods). The extent to which an evaluation uses more quantitative or more qualitative methods and the relative reliance on quantitative or qualitative data should be driven by the questions the evaluation needs to answer and the audiences for the work.

And finally, the relative importance of the primary reason for the evaluation matters. That is, are assumptions that problems exist driving the demand for the application of evaluation methods the driver? When evaluators are asked to investigate problems, especially if they work for government bodies such as the U.S. Government Accountability Office, state audit agencies, or inspector general offices, the approaches and strategies they use for engaging stakeholders, and collecting data may be different from those used by evaluators in situations in which they are not perceived as collecting data due to preconceptions of fault.

Identify Contextual Elements That May Affect Evaluation Conduct and Use

The context for employing evaluation matters. The *context* includes both the broader environment surrounding evaluation and the immediate situation in which an evaluation study is planned. Since the beginning of the twenty-first century, daunting standards for evaluation of social programs have been espoused by proponents of *evidence-based* policy, management, and practice. Nonprofit organizations have promoted the use of evaluation to inform policy deliberations at all level of governments (For example, see Pew-MacArthur, 2014). The Cochrane and Campbell Collaborations and similar organizations have given guidance that randomized controlled trials (RCTs) are the "gold standard" for evaluation. Yet, ethical prohibitions, logistical impossibilities, and constrained resources frequently do not allow random assignment of subjects in evaluation of some social services, and some government programs with broad public mandates, such as environmental protection and national security. In such situations, less sophisticated approaches can provide useful estimates of program impact.

The key question facing evaluators is what type and how much evidence will be sufficient? Will the evidence be convincing to the intended audiences—be they nonprofit boards, legislators, or the public? The stakes have risen for what constitutes adequate evidence, and for many social service providers the term *evidence-based practice* is intimidating. There is not full agreement in virtually any field about when evidence is sufficient. And funders are likely to be aware of the rising standards for hard evidence and some may be unrealistic about what can be achieved by evaluators operating with finite resources.

It is usually difficult to establish causal links between program interventions and behavioral change. Numerous factors affect outcomes. Human as well as natural systems are complex and adaptive; they evolve in ways that evaluators may not be able to predict. Increasingly, attention has been drawn to using systems theory to inform evaluations of interventions designed to change behaviors in such complex systems.

Programs are typically located in multicultural environments. *Cultural competence* (also discussed as cultural humility) is a skill that has become more crucial for evaluators to develop than ever before. There are many important differences across program stakeholders, and expectation for evaluators to understand and address these differences in their work are high. Adequate knowledge of the social, religious, ethnic, and cultural norms and values of program stakeholders, especially beneficiaries who may present a large number of different backgrounds, presents another very important challenge to evaluators trying to understand the complex context in which a program operates. Evaluators need to understand the human environment of programs so that data collection and interpretation are appropriate and realistic. Chapter Twelve describes culturally responsive evaluation and provides guidance on incorporating cultural competency into evaluation work.

Characteristics of the particular program to be evaluated can also affect the evaluation approach to be used. Evaluators may find themselves working with program staff who lack any experience with evaluation or, worse, have had bad experiences with evaluation or evaluators. Many organizations are simply not evaluation-friendly. A compliance culture has grown up in many quarters in which funders' requirements for data have risen, and so managers and administrators may feel that providing data to meet reporting demands is simply part of business as usual but has nothing to do with organizational learning to improve programs (for example, see Dahler-Larsen, 2012).

Finally, the operational issues facing evaluators vary across context. Challenging institutional processes may need to be navigated. Institutional review board processes and other clearances, such as the U.S. federal requirements for clearance of survey instruments when more than nine persons will be surveyed, take time and institutional knowledge. Site-specific obstacles to obtaining records and addressing confidentiality concerns can arise. Obtaining useful and sufficient data is not easy, yet it is necessary for producing quality evaluation work.

Produce the Methodological Rigor Needed to Support Credible Findings

The strength of findings, conclusions, and recommendations about program implementation and results depends on well-founded decisions regarding evaluation design and measurement. Figure 1.2 presents a graphical depiction of the way that credibility is supported by the methodological rigor ensured by wise decisions about measurement and design. This section focuses first on getting the most appropriate and reliable measures for a given evaluation and then on designing the evaluation to assess, to the extent possible, the extent to which the program being evaluated affected the measured outcomes.

Choose Appropriate Measures

Credible evaluation work requires clear, valid measures that are collected in a reliable, consistent fashion. Strong, well-founded measurement provides the foundation for methodological rigor in evaluation as well as in research and is the first requirement for useful evaluation findings. Evaluators must begin with credible measures and strong procedures in place to ensure that both quantitative and qualitative measurement is rigorous. The criteria used to assess

FIGURE 1.2. DESIGN EVALUATION STUDIES TO PROVIDE CREDIBLE FINDINGS: THE PYRAMID OF STRENGTH.

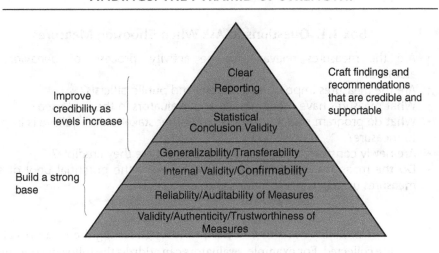

the rigor of quantitative and qualitative data collection, and inferences based on the two types of data, vary in terminology, but the fundamental similarities across the criteria are emphasized here.

The *validity or authenticity of measurement* is concerned with the accuracy of measurement, so that the measure accurately assesses what the evaluator intends to evaluate. Are the data collection procedures appropriate, and are they likely to provide reasonably accurate information? (See Part Two for discussions of various data collection procedures.) In practical evaluation endeavors, evaluators will likely use both quantitative and qualitative measures, and for both the relevance, legitimacy, and clarity of measures to program stakeholders and to citizens will matter. Often the items or concepts to measure will not be simple, nor will measurement processes be easy. Programs are composed of complex sets of activities to be measured. Outcomes to be measured may include both individual and group behaviors and may be viewed as falling on a short-term to long-term continuum, depending on their proximity to program implementation.

Measures may be *validated,* that is, tested for their accuracy, through several different processes. For example, experts may be asked to comment on the *face validity* of the measures. In evaluation work the term *experts* means the persons with the most pertinent knowledge about and experience with the behaviors to be measured. They may be case workers involved in service delivery, they may be principals and teachers, or they may be the program's customers, who provide information on what is important to them. Box 1.1 provides tips for probing the validity and authenticity of measures.

Box 1.1. Questions to Ask When Choosing Measures

- Are the measures relevant to the activity, process, or behavior being assessed?
- Are the measures important to citizens and public officials?
- What measures have other experts and evaluators in the field used?
- What do program staff, customers, and other stakeholders believe is important to measure?
- Are newly constructed measures needed, and are they credible?
- Do the measures selected adequately represent the potential pool of similar measures used in other locations and jurisdictions?

Credibility can also be bolstered through testing the measures after data are collected. For example, evaluators can address the following questions with the data:

- Do the measures correlate to a specific agreed-upon standard or criterion measure that is credible in the field?
- Do the measures correlate with other measures in ways consistent with existing theory and knowledge?
- Do the measures predict subsequent behaviors in ways consistent with existing theory and knowledge?

Choose Reliable Ways to Obtain the Chosen Measures

The measures should be reliable. For quantitative data, r*eliability* refers to the extent to which a measure can be expected to produce similar results on repeated observations of the same condition or event. Having reliable measures means that operations consistently measure the same phenomena and consistently record data with the same decision criteria. For example, when questions are translated into multiple languages for respondents of different cultural backgrounds, evaluators should consider whether the questions will still elicit comparable responses from all. Data entry can also be a major source of error. Evaluators need to take steps to minimize the likelihood of errors in data entry.

For qualitative data, the relevant criterion is the *auditability* of measurement procedures. Auditability entails clearly documenting the procedures used to collect and record qualitative data, such as documenting the circumstances in which data were obtained and the coding procedures employed. See Chapter Twenty-Two for more on coding qualitative data in a clear and credible manner.

In order to strengthen reliability or auditability of measures and measurement procedures, evaluators should adequately pretest data collection instruments and procedures and then plan for quality control procedures when in the field and when processing the information back home. (Also see Box 1.2.)

Box 1.2. Tips on Enhancing Reliability

- Pretest data collection instruments with representative samples of intended respondents before going into the field.
- Implement adequate quality control procedures to identify inconsistencies in interpretation of words by respondents in surveys and interviews.
- When problems with the clarity of questions are uncovered, the questions should be revised, and evaluators should go back to resurvey or re-interview if the responses are vital.
- Adequately train observers and interviewers so that they consistently apply comparable criteria and enter data correctly.
- Implement adequate and frequent quality control procedures to identify obstacles to consistent measurement in the field.
- Test levels of consistency among coders by asking all of them to code the same sample of the materials.

There are statistical tests that can be used to test for intercoder and interobserver reliability of quantitative data, such as Cronbach's alpha. When statistical tests are desired, research texts or Web sites should be consulted (for example, see the Sage Research Methods website at http://srmo.sagepub.com/view/encyclopedia-of-survey-research-methods/n228.xml).

Supporting Causal Inferences

In order to test the effectiveness of programs, researchers must ensure their ability to make well-founded inferences about (1) relationships between a program and the observed effects (internal validity) and (2) generalizability or transferability of the findings. With quantitative data this may include testing for the statistical conclusion validity of findings.

Internal Validity

Internal validity is concerned with the ability to determine whether a program or intervention has produced an outcome and to determine the magnitude of that effect. When considering the internal validity of an evaluation, the evaluator should assess whether a causal connection can be established between the program and an intended effect and what the extent is of this relationship. Internal validity is also an issue when identifying the unintended effects (good or bad) of the program. When employing case studies and other qualitative research approaches in an evaluation, the challenge is typically to identify and characterize causal mechanisms needed to produce desired outcomes, and the term *confirmability* is more often applied to this process.

When making causal inferences, evaluators must measure several elements:

- The timing of the outcomes, to ensure that observed outcomes occurred after the program was implemented;
- The extent to which the changes in outcomes occurred after the program was implemented; and
- The presence of confounding factors: that is, factors that could also have produced desired outcomes.

In addition, observed relationships should be in accordance with expectations from previous research or evaluation work. It can be very difficult to draw causal inferences. There are several challenges in capturing the *net impacts* of a program, because other events and processes are occurring that affect achievement of desired outcomes. The time needed for the intervention to change attitudes or behavior may be longer than the time given to measure outcomes. And there may be flaws in the program design or implementation that reduce the ability of the program to produce desired outcomes. For such reasons, it may be difficult to establish causation credibly. It may be desirable to use terms such as *plausible attribution* when drawing conclusions about the effects of programs on intended behaviors. Box 1.3 offers tips about strengthening causal inferences about program results.

Some evaluations may be intended to be relevant to and used by only the site where the evaluation was conducted. However, in other situations the evaluation is expected to be relevant to other sites as well. This situation is discussed in the next section, on generalizing findings.

Box 1.3. Tips on Strengthening Inferences About Program Effects

- Measure the extent to which the program was actually implemented as intended.
- Ask key stakeholders about other events or experiences they may have had that also affected decisions relevant to the program—before and during the evaluation time frame.
- Given existing knowledge about the likely time period needed to see effects, explore whether enough time has elapsed between implementation of the program and measurement of intended effects.
- Review previous evaluation findings for similar programs to identify external factors and unintended effects, and build in capacity to measure them.

Generalizability

Evaluation findings possess *generalizability* when they can be applied beyond the groups or context being studied. With quantitative data collection the ability to generalize findings from a statistical sample to a larger population (or other program sites or future clients) refers to statistical conclusion validity (discussed below). For qualitative data, the *transferability* of findings from one site to another (or the future) may present different, or additional, challenges. Concluding that findings from work involving qualitative data are fit to be transferred elsewhere likely require more extensive contextual understanding of both the evaluation setting and the intended site for replication (see Cartwright, 2013 and Patton, 2011, for guidance on replicating and scaling up interventions). All the conditions discussed previously for internal validity also need to be met for generalizing evaluation findings. In addition, it is desirable that the evaluation be conducted in multiple sites, but at the least, evaluators should select the site and individuals so they are representative of the populations to which the evaluators hope to generalize their results.

Special care should be taken when trying to generalize results to other sites in evaluations of programs that may have differential effects on particular subpopulations such as youths, rural groups, or racial or ethnic groups. In order to enhance generalizability, evaluators should make sampling choices to identify subpopulations of interest and should ensure that subsamples of the groups are large enough to analyze. However, evaluators should still examine each sample to ensure that it is truly representative of the larger population to which they hope to generalize on demographic variables of interest (for example, age or ethnic grouping). Box 1.4 offers tips about strengthening the generalizability of findings.

Statistical Conclusion Validity

Statistical generalizability requires testing the statistical significance of findings from probability samples, and is greatly dependent on the size of the samples used in an evaluation. Chapter Twenty-Three provides more background on the use of statistics in evaluation. But it bears noting that the criterion of statistical significance and the tests related to it have been borrowed from the physical sciences, where the concern is to have the highest levels of confidence possible. In program evaluation practice, where obstacles may exist to obtaining large samples, it is reasonable to consider confidence levels lower than the 95 or 99 percent often used in social science research. For instance, it may be reasonable to accept a 90 percent level of confidence. It is entirely appropriate to report deliberations on this issue, reasons why a certain level was chosen, and the exact level of significance the findings were able to obtain. This is more realistic and productive than assuming that evaluation results will not be discussed unless a, perhaps unrealistically, high level of confidence is reached.

Box 1.4. Questions to Ask to Strengthen the Generalizability of Findings

- To what groups or sites will generalization be desired?
- What are the key demographic (or other) groups to be represented in the sample?
- What sample size, with adequate sampling of important subgroups, is needed to make generalizations about the outcomes of the intervention?
- What aspects of the intervention and context in which it was implemented merit careful measurement to enable generalizability or transferability of findings?

In order to report properly on an evaluation, evaluators should report both on the statistical significance of the findings (or whether the sample size allows conclusions to be drawn about the evaluation's findings), and on the importance and relevance of the size of the measured effects. Because statistical significance is strongly affected by sheer sample size, other pertinent criteria should be identified to characterize the policy relevance of the measured effects.

Reporting

In the end, even careful planning and reasoned decision making about both measurement and design will not ensure that all evaluations will produce perfectly credible results. There are a variety of pitfalls that frequently constrain evaluation findings, as described in Chapter Twenty-Six. Clarity in reporting findings and open discussion about methodological decisions and any obstacles encountered during data collection will bolster confidence in findings.

Planning a Responsive and Useful Evaluation

Even with the explosion of quantitative and qualitative evaluation methodologies since the 1970s, designing evaluation work requires both social science knowledge and skills and cultivated professional judgment. The planning of each evaluation effort requires difficult trade-off decisions as the evaluator attempts to balance the feasibility and cost of alternative evaluation designs against the likely benefits of the resulting evaluation work. Methodological rigor must be balanced with resources, and the evaluator's professional judgment will arbitrate the trade-offs.

Wherever possible, evaluation planning should begin before the program does. The most desirable window of opportunity for evaluation planning opens when new programs are being designed. Desired data can be more readily obtained if provision is made for data collection from the start of the program, particularly for such information as clients' pre-program attitudes and experiences. These sorts of data might be very difficult, if not impossible, to obtain later.

Planning an evaluation project requires selecting the measures that should be used, an evaluation design, and the methods of data collection and data analysis that will best meet information needs. To best inform choices, evaluators learn how the evaluation results might be used and how decision making might be shaped by the availability of the performance data collected. However, it is important to recognize that evaluation plans are organic and likely to evolve. Figure 1.3 displays the key steps in planning and conducting an evaluation. It highlights many feedback loops in order to stress how important it is for evaluators to be responsive to changes in context, data availability, and their own evolving understanding of context.

Planning Evaluation Processes

Identification of the key evaluation questions is the first, and frequently quite challenging, task faced during the design phase. Anticipating what clients need

FIGURE 1.3. REVISE QUESTIONS AND APPROACHES AS YOU LEARN MORE DURING THE EVALUATION PROCESS.

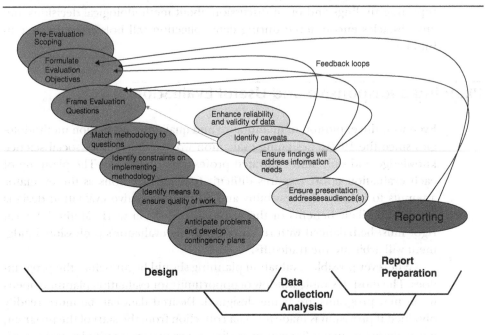

to know is essential to effective evaluation planning. For example, the U.S. Government Accountability Office (GAO) conducts many program evaluations in response to legislative requests. These requests, however, are frequently fairly broad in their identification of the issues to be addressed. The first task of GAO evaluators is to more specifically identify what the committees or members of Congress want to know, and then to explore what questions should be asked to acquire this information. (See Box 1.5 for more information on the GAO's evaluation design process.)

Box 1.5. GAO's Evaluation Design Process

Stephanie Shipman

U.S. Government Accountability Office

Each year, GAO receives hundreds of requests to conduct a wide variety of studies, from brief descriptions of program activities to in-depth evaluative assessments of program or policy effectiveness. Over time, GAO has drawn lessons from its experience to develop a systematic, risk-based process for selecting the most appropriate approach for each study. Policies and procedures have been created to ensure that GAO provides timely, quality information to meet congressional needs at reasonable cost; they are summarized in the following four steps: (1) clarify the study objectives; (2) obtain background information on the issue and design options; (3) develop and test the proposed approach; and (4) reach agreement on the proposed approach.

Clarify the Study Objectives

The evaluator's first step is to meet with the congressional requester's staff to gain a better understanding of the requester's need for information and the nature of the research questions and to discuss GAO's ability to respond within the desired time frame. Discussions clarify whether the questions are primarily descriptive—such as how often something occurs—or evaluative—involving assessment against a criterion. It is important to learn how the information is intended to be used and when that information will be needed. Is it expected to inform a particular decision or simply to explore whether a topic warrants a more comprehensive examination? Once the project team has a clearer understanding of the requester's needs, the team can begin to assess whether additional information will be needed to formulate the study approach or whether the team has enough information to commit to an evaluation plan and schedule.

In a limited number of cases, GAO initiates work on its own to address significant emerging issues or issues of broad interest to the Congress. In these studies, GAO addresses the same considerations in internal deliberations and informs majority and minority staff of the relevant congressional committees of the planned approach.

Obtain Background Information

GAO staff review the literature and other work to understand the nature and background of the program or agency under review. The project team will consult prior GAO and inspector general work to identify previous approaches and recommendations, agency contacts, and legislative histories for areas in which GAO has done recent work. The team reviews the literature and consults with external experts and program stakeholders to gather information about the program and related issues, approaches used in prior studies, and existing data sources. Evaluators discuss the request with agency officials to explore their perspectives on these issues.

GAO evaluators explore the relevance of existing data sources to the research questions and learn how data are obtained or developed in order to assess their completeness and reliability. Evaluators search for potential evaluative criteria in legislation, program design materials, agency performance plans, professional standards, and elsewhere, and assess their appropriateness to the research

(Continued)

question, objectivity, suitability for measurement, and credibility to key program stakeholders.

Develop and Test the Proposed Approach

The strengths and limitations of potential data sources and design approaches are considered in terms of which ones will best answer the research questions within available resource and time constraints. Existing data sources are tested to assess their reliability and validity. Proposed data collection approaches are designed, reviewed, and pretested for feasibility given conditions in the field. Evaluators outline work schedules and staff assignments in project plans to assess what resources will be required to meet the desired reporting timelines. Alternative options are compared to identify the trade-offs involved in feasibility, data validity, and the completeness of the answer likely to be obtained.

Evaluation plans are outlined in a design matrix to articulate the proposed approach in table format for discussion with senior management (see Figure 1.4 later in this chapter). The project team outlines, for each research question, the information desired, data sources, how the data will be collected and analyzed, the data's limitations, and what this information will and will not allow the evaluators to say. Discussions of alternative design options focus on the implications that any limitations identified will have on the analysis and the evaluator's ability to answer the research questions. What steps might be taken to address (reduce or counterbalance) such limitations? For example, if the primary data source relies on subjective self-reports, can the findings be verified through more objective and reliable documentary evidence?

Discussion of "what the analysis will allow GAO to say" concerns not what the likely answer will be but what sort of conclusion one can draw with confidence. How complete or definitive will the answer be to the research question? Alternatively, one might characterize the types of statements one will not be able to make: for example, statements that generalize the findings from observed cases to the larger population or to time periods preceding or following the period examined.

Reach Agreement on the Proposed Approach

Finally, the proposed approach is discussed both with GAO senior management in terms of the conclusiveness of the answers provided for the resources expended and with the congressional requester's staff in terms of whether the proposed information and timelines will meet the requester's needs. GAO managers review the design matrix and accompanying materials to determine whether the proposed approach adequately addresses the requester's objectives, the study's risks have been adequately identified and addressed, and the proposed resources are appropriate given the importance of the issues involved and other work requests. The GAO team then meets with the requester's staff to discuss the engagement methodology and approach, including details on the scope of work to be performed and the product delivery date. The agreed-upon terms of work are then formalized in a commitment letter.

Matching evaluation questions to a client's information needs can be a tricky task. When there is more than one client, as is frequently the case, there may be multiple information needs, and one evaluation may not be able to answer all the questions raised. This is frequently a problem for nonprofit service providers, who may need to address multiple evaluation questions for multiple funders.

Setting goals for information gathering can be like aiming at a moving target, for information needs change as programs and environmental conditions change. Negotiating evaluable questions with clients can be fraught with difficulties for evaluators as well as for managers who may be affected by the findings.

The selection of questions should drive decisions on appropriate data collection and analysis. As seen in Figure 1.4, the GAO employs a design tool it calls the *design matrix* that arrays the decisions on data collection and analysis by each question. This brief, typically one-page blueprint for the evaluation is used to secure agreement from various stakeholders within the GAO, such as technical experts and substantive experts, and to ensure that answers to the questions will address the information needs of the client, in this case the congressional requestor. Although there is no one ideal format for a design matrix, or evaluation blueprint, the use of some sort of design tool to facilitate communication about evaluation design among stakeholders is very desirable. An abbreviated design matrix can be used to clarify how evaluation questions will be addressed through surveying (this is illustrated in Chapter Fourteen).

A great deal of evaluation work performed for public and nonprofit programs is contracted out, and given current pressures toward outsourcing along with internal evaluation resource constraints, this trend is likely to continue. Contracting out evaluation places even more importance on identifying sufficiently targeted evaluation questions. Statements of work are typically prepared by internal program staff working with contract professionals, and these documents may set in stone the questions the contractors will address, along with data collection and analysis specifications. Unfortunately, the contract process may not leave evaluators (or program staff) much leeway in reframing the questions in order to make desired adjustments when the project gets under way and confronts new issues or when political priorities shift. Efforts should be made to allow the contractual process to permit

FIGURE 1.4. SAMPLE DESIGN MATRIX.

Issue problem statement:
Guidance:

1.   Put the issue into context.
2.   Identify the potential users.

Researchable Question(s)	Criteria and Information Required and Source(s)	Scope and Methodology, Including Data Reliability	Limitations	What This Analysis Will Likely Allow GAO to Say
What question(s) is the team trying to answer?	What information does the team need to address the question? Where will they get it?	How will the team answer each question?	What are the engagement's design limitations and how will they affect the product?	What are the expected results of the work?
Question 1				
Question 2				
Question 3				
Question 4				

Source: U.S. Government Accountability Office.

contextually-driven revisions. See Chapter Twenty-Nine for more guidance on effectively contracting out evaluation work.

Balancing clients' information needs with resources affects selection of an evaluation design as well as specific strategies for data collection and analysis. Selecting a design requires the evaluator to anticipate the amount of rigor that will be required to produce convincing answers to the client's questions. Evaluators must specify the comparisons that will be needed to demonstrate whether a program has had the intended effects and the additional comparisons needed to clarify differential effects on different groups.

The actual nature of an evaluation design should reflect the objectives and the specific questions to be addressed. This text offers guidance on the wide variety of evaluation designs that are appropriate given certain objectives and questions to address. Table 1.1 arrays evaluation objectives with designs and also identifies the chapters in this text to consult for guidance on design. The wide range of questions that be framed about programs is matched by the variety of approaches and designs that are employed by professional evaluators.

Resource issues will almost always constrain design choices; staff costs, travel costs, data collection burdens on program staff, and political and bureaucratic costs may limit design options. Evaluation design decisions, in turn, affect where and how data will be collected. To help evaluators and program

TABLE 1.1. MATCHING DESIGNS AND DATA COLLECTION TO THE EVALUATION QUESTIONS.

Evaluation Objective	Illustrative Questions	Possible Design	Corresponding Handbook Chapter(s)
1. Describe program activities	Who does the program affect–both targeted organizations and affected populations? What activities are needed to implement the program (or policy)? By whom? How extensive and costly are the program components? How do implementation efforts vary across delivery sites, subgroups of beneficiaries, and/or across geographical regions? Has the program (policy) been implemented sufficiently to be evaluated?	Performance Measurement Exploratory Evaluations Evaluability Assessments Multiple Case Studies	Chapter 4 Chapter 5 Chapter 8 Chapter 11 Chapter 12
2. Probe implementation and targeting	To what extent has the program been implemented? When evidence-based interventions are implemented, how closely are the protocols implemented with fidelity to the original design? What key contextual factors tare likely to affect the ability of the program implementers to have the intended outcomes? What feasibility or management challenges hinder successful implementation of the program?	Multiple Case Studies Implementation or Process evaluations Performance Audits Compliance Audits	Chapter 4 Chapter 8 Chapter 10 Chapter 11 Chapter 12

(Continued)

TABLE 1.1. MATCHING DESIGNS AND DATA COLLECTION TO THE EVALUATION QUESTIONS. *(Continued)*

Evaluation Objective	Illustrative Questions	Possible Design	Corresponding Handbook Chapter(s)
	To what extent have activities undertaken affected the populations or organizations targeted by the regulation?		
	To what extent are implementation efforts in compliance with the law and other pertinent regulations?		
	To what extent does current program (or policy) targeting leave significant needs (problems) not addressed?		
3. Measure program impact	Has implementation of the program produced results consistent with its design (espoused purpose)?	Experimental Designs, that is Random Control Trials (RCTs)	Chapter 6 Chapter 7 Chapter 25
	How have measured effects varied across implementation approaches, organizations, and/or jurisdictions?	Difference-in-Difference Designs Propensity Score Matching (PSM) Statistical Adjustments with Regression Estimates of Effects	
	For which targeted populations has the program (or policy) consistently failed to show intended impact?	Multiple Time Series Designs Regression Discontinuity Designs	
	Is the implementation strategy more (or less) effective in relation to its costs?	Cost-Effectiveness Studies Benefit-Cost Analysis	
	Is the implementation strategy more cost effective than other implementation strategies also addressing the same problem?	Systematic Reviews Meta-Analyses	

(Continued)

TABLE 1.1. MATCHING DESIGNS AND DATA COLLECTION TO THE EVALUATION QUESTIONS. *(Continued)*

Evaluation Objective	Illustrative Questions	Possible Design	Corresponding Handbook Chapter(s)
	What are the average effects across different implementations of the program (or policy)?		
4. Explain how and why programs produce intended and unintended effects	How and why did the program have the intended effects? Under what circumstances did the program produce the desired effects? To what extent have program activities had important unanticipated negative spillover effects? What are unanticipated positive effects of the program that emerge over time, given the complex web of interactions between the program and other programs, and who benefits? For whom (which targeted organizations and/or populations) is the program more likely to produce the desired effects? What is the likely impact trajectory of the program (over time)? How likely is it that the program will have similar effects in other contexts (beyond the context studied)? How likely is it that the program will have similar effects in the future?	Multiple Case Studies Meta-Analyses Impact Pathways and Process Tracing Contribution Analysis Non-Linear Modeling, System Dynamics Configurational Analysis, e.g., Qualitative Case Analysis (QCA) Realist-Based Synthesis	Chapter 8 Chapter 25

personnel make the best design decisions, a pilot test of proposed data collection procedures should be considered. Pilot tests may be valuable in refining evaluation designs; they can clarify the feasibility and costs of data collection as well as the likely utility of different data analysis strategies.

Data Collection

Data collection choices may be politically as well as bureaucratically tricky. Exploring the use of existing data involves identifying potential political barriers as well as more mundane constraints, such as incompatibility of computer systems. Planning for data collection in the field should be extensive in order to help evaluators obtain the most relevant data in the most efficient manner. Chapters Thirteen through Twenty-One present much detail on both selecting and implementing a variety of data collection strategies.

Data Analysis

Deciding how the data will be analyzed affects data collection, for it forces evaluators to clarify how each data element will be used. Collecting too much data is an error that evaluators frequently commit. Developing a detailed *data analysis plan* as part of the evaluation design can help evaluators decide which data elements are necessary and sufficient, thus avoiding the expense of gathering unneeded information.

An analysis plan helps evaluators structure the layout of a report, for it identifies the graphs and tables through which the findings will be presented. Anticipating how the findings might be used forces evaluators to think carefully about presentations that will address the original evaluation questions in a clear and logical manner.

Identifying relevant questions and answering them with data that have been analyzed and presented in a user-oriented format should help to ensure that evaluation results will be used. However, communicating evaluation results entails more than simply drafting attractive reports. If the findings are indeed to be used to improve program performance, as well as respond to funders' requests, the evaluators must understand the bureaucratic and political contexts of the program and craft their findings and recommendations in such a way as to facilitate their use in these contexts.

Using Evaluation Information

The goal of conducting any evaluation work is certainly to make positive change. When one undertakes any evaluation work, understanding from the outset how the work may contribute to achieving important policy and program goals is important. Program improvement is the ultimate goal for most evaluators. Consequently, they should use their skills to produce useful, convincing evidence to support their recommendations for program and policy change.

Box 1.6. Anticipate These Challenges to the Use of Evaluation and Performance Data

1. Lack of visible appreciation and support for evaluation among leaders
2. Unrealistically high expectations of what can be measured and "proven"
3. A compliance mentality among staff regarding collection and reporting of program data and a corresponding disinterest in data use
4. Resistance to adding the burden of data collection to staff workloads
5. Lack of positive incentives for learning about and using evaluation and data
6. Lack of compelling examples of how evaluation findings or data have been used to make significant improvements in programs
7. Poor presentation of evaluation findings

Understanding how program managers and other stakeholders view evaluation is also important for evaluators who want to produce useful information. Box 1.6 lists some fairly typical reactions to evaluation in public and nonprofit organizations that may make it difficult for evaluators to develop their approaches and to promote the use of findings (for example, see Hatry, 2006; Mayne, 2010; Newcomer, 2008; Pawson, 2013; and Preskill and Torres, 1999). Clear and visible commitment by leadership is always critical, as are incentives within the organization that reward use. The anticipation that evaluation will place more burdens on program staff and clients is a perception that evaluators need to confront in any context.

The most effective evaluators are those who plan, design, and implement evaluations that are sufficiently relevant, responsive, and credible to stimulate program or policy improvement. Evaluation effectiveness may be enhanced by efficiency and the use of practical, low-cost evaluation approaches that encourage the evaluation clients (the management and staff of the program) to accept the findings and use them to improve their services.

Efforts to enhance the likelihood that evaluation results will be used should start during the planning and design phase. From the beginning, evaluators must focus on mediating obstacles and creating opportunities to promote use. Box 1.7 provides tips for increasing the likelihood that the findings will

be used. Six of these tips refer to actions that need to be taken during evaluation design. Evaluators must understand and typically shape their audiences'
expectations, and then work consistently to ensure that the expectations are
met. Producing methodologically sound findings and explaining why they are
sound both matter.

Box 1.7. Tips on Using Evaluation Findings and Data

1. Understand and appreciate the relevant perspectives and preferences of the audience (or audiences!) to shape communication of evaluation findings and performance data.
2. Address the questions most relevant to the information needs of the audience.
3. Early in the design phase, envision what the final evaluation products should contain.
4. Design sampling procedures carefully to ensure that the findings can be generalized to whomever or wherever the key stakeholders wish.
5. Work to ensure the validity and authenticity of measures, and report on the efforts to do so.
6. Address plausible alternative explanations for the measured program outcomes.
7. Clearly communicate the competence of the evaluators and the methodology employed to enhance the credibility of findings.
8. When quantitative analytical techniques are used, clarify why these techniques were appropriate and that adequate sample sizes were used.
9. In recommendations, to the extent politically feasible, state who should take what actions, where, and when.
10. Tailor reporting vehicles to address the communication preferences of different target audiences.
11. Provide an executive summary and a report written clearly and without jargon.
12. Work consistently from the beginning to develop strong working relationships with program staff and other pertinent stakeholders so that they will be willing to implement recommendations.

Clear presentation of both findings and feasible recommendations is also
necessary, and these skills are discussed in depth in Chapters Twenty-Seven and
Twenty-Eight.

Credibility of evaluation work in the eyes of the audiences, especially those
people who need to implement recommended changes, is the goal for all evaluators. In the end, production of credible performance data and evaluation
study findings that are communicated to funders and the broader public can
contribute to the public good through informing policy and program management decisions.

Glossary

Case study. A rich description and analysis of a program in its context, typically using multiple modes of qualitative data collection.

Comparison group design. An assessment design that compares outcomes for program participants with outcomes for people in a comparison group.

Cost-benefit study. An analysis that compares the dollar value of program costs with the dollar value of program impacts.

Evaluation design. A plan for conducting an evaluation that specifies (1) a set of evaluation questions, (2) the targeted groups from whom data will be collected, and the timing of collection, (3) the data that will be collected, (4) the analyses that will be undertaken to answer the evaluation questions, (5) the estimated costs and time schedule for the evaluation work, and (6) how the evaluation information may be used.

Evaluation stakeholders. The individuals, groups, or organizations that can affect or are affected by an evaluation process or its findings, or both.

Experimental design. An assessment design that tests the existence of causal relationships by comparing outcomes for those randomly assigned to program services with outcomes for those randomly assigned to alternative services or no services. Also called a randomized experiment or random control trial (RCT).

Implementation evaluation. An assessment that describes actual program activities, typically to find out what actually happened or is happening in the program.

Interrupted time-series design. An assessment design that tests the existence of causal relationships by comparing trends in outcomes before and after the program.

Logic model (or program logic model). A flowchart that summarizes key elements of a program: resources and other inputs, activities, outputs (products and services delivered), and intermediate outcomes and end outcomes (short-term and longer-term results) that the program hopes to achieve. Logic models should also identify key factors that are outside the control of program staff but are likely to affect the achievement of desired outcomes. A logic model shows assumed cause-and-effect linkages among model elements, showing which activities are expected to lead to which outcomes, and it may also show assumed cause-and-effect linkages between external factors and program outcomes.

Outcomes. Changes in clients or communities associated with program activities and outputs.

Outputs. Products and services delivered to a program's clients.

Pre-post design. An assessment design that compares outcomes before and after the program.

Process evaluation. An assessment that compares actual with intended inputs, activities, and outputs.

Program. A set of resources and activities directed toward one or more common goals, typically under the direction of a single manager or management team.

Program logic model. See *logic model.*

Quasi-experimental design. An assessment design that tests the existence of a causal relationship where random assignment is not possible. Typical quasi-experimental designs include pre-post designs, comparison group designs, and interrupted time-series designs.

Randomized experiment or Random Control Trial (RCT). See *Experimental design.*

Regression discontinuity design. An experiment that assigns units to a condition on the basis of a score cutoff on a particular variable.

Stakeholder. See *evaluation stakeholders.*

Theory-based evaluation (TBE). A family of approaches that seek to explicate and test policy-makers', managers', and other stakeholders' assumptions (or 'theories') about how a program intends to bring about a desired change. Core elements of these theories are mechanisms (the 'nuts and bolts' of an intervention) and how they relate to context and outcomes.

References

American Evaluation Association. "The AEA's Guiding Principles for Evaluators." www.eval.org/p/cm/ld/fid=51. 2004.

Cartwright, Nancy. "Knowing What We Are Talking About: Why Evidence Doesn't Always Travel." *Evidence & Policy,* 2013, *9*(1), 97–112.

Dahler-Larsen, Peter. *The Evaluation Society.* Stanford, CA: Stanford University Press, 2012.

Greene, Jennifer. *Mixed Methods in Social Inquiry.* San Francisco, CA: Jossey-Bass, 2007.

Hatry, Harry. *Performance Measurement: Getting Results* (2nd ed.). Washington, DC: Urban Institute Press, 2006.

Joint Committee on Standards for Educational Evaluation. "Program Evaluation Standards." www.jcsee.org/program-evaluation-standards. 2010.

Mayne, J. "Building an Evaluative Culture: The Key to Effective Evaluation and Results Management." *Canadian Journal of Program Evaluation*, 2009, 24, 1–30.

Newcomer, Kathryn. "Assessing Program Performance in Nonprofit Agencies." In Patria de Lancer Julnes, Frances Stokes Berry, Maria P. Aristigueta, and Kaifeng Yang (Eds.), *International Handbook of Practice-Based Performance and Management Review*. Thousand Oaks, CA: Sage, 2008.

Patton, Michael Quinn. *Utilization-Focused Evaluation* (4th ed.). Thousand Oaks, CA: Sage, 2008.

Patton, Michael Quinn. *Developmental Evaluation: Applying Complexity Concepts to Enhance Innovation and Use*. New York: The Guilford Press, 2011.

Pawson, Ray. *The Science of Evaluation: A Realist Manifesto*. Thousand Oaks, CA: Sage, 2013.

The Pew Charitable Trusts. "Evidence-Based Policymaking: A Guide for Effective Government Pew Charitable Trusts." www.pewtrusts.org/en/research-and-analysis/reports/2014/11/evidence-based-policymaking-a-guide-for-effective-government. November 13, 2014.

Preskill, Hallie S., and Torres, Rosalie. *Evaluative Inquiry for Learning in Organizations*. Thousand Oaks, CA: Sage, 1999.

Sage Research Methods. http://srmo.sagepub.com/view/encyclopedia-of-survey-research-methods/n228.xml.

Scriven, Michael. *The Logic of Evaluation*. Inverness, CA.: Edgepress, 1980.

Shadish, William., Cook, Thomas D., and Campbell, Donald Thomas. *Experimental and Quasi-Experimental Designs for Generalized Causal Inference*. Boston, MA: Houghton Mifflin, 2002.

Williams, Bob, and Hummelbrunner, Richard. *Systems Concepts in Action: A Practitioner's Toolkit*. Stanford, CA: Stanford University Press, 2011.

CHAPTER TWO

ANALYZING AND ENGAGING STAKEHOLDERS

John M. Bryson, Michael Quinn Patton

Evaluators overwhelmingly acknowledge the importance of working with stakeholders in evaluation and of focusing evaluations on optimizing intended use by intended users, which is the guiding principle of utilization-focused evaluation (Patton, 2008). In this chapter we focus on the processes of analyzing and engaging stakeholders in order to (1) identify who the key stakeholders are and in particular who the intended users of evaluation information are; (2) clarify the purposes and goals of the evaluation; and (3) specify which stakeholders should be worked with, in what ways, and at which stages of the evaluation process, in order to increase the chances that the evaluation will serve its intended purpose for its intended users. We start from the premise that careful analysis should precede stakeholder engagement, although some engagement may be necessary in order to do good analysis. Seven particularly useful stakeholder identification and analysis techniques will be described.

The chapter has seven sections in addition to this brief introduction. The first discusses what is meant by the term *stakeholder*. Stakeholders' interests and goals may be compatible or may be in direct conflict initially, but it is generally possible to find considerable common ground and agreement on what an evaluation's purposes are and how best to proceed. The second section summarizes what the evaluation literature says about identifying and engaging with primary intended evaluation users. In the third section, we present stakeholder identification and analysis techniques. The fourth section offers

additional suggestions on how to use stakeholder analysis to help determine
more precisely the evaluation's purpose and goals. The fifth section presents a
final stakeholder analysis technique, a matrix helpful for figuring out ways to
engage stakeholders and reasons for engaging them during the various steps
in an evaluation process. The sixth section discusses the need for flexibility,
adaptability, and situational responsiveness in rapidly changing evaluation situations; our suggestions involve continuing analysis and probably changing
engagement tactics. The chapter's final section offers a summary and several
conclusions.

Understanding Who Is a Stakeholder—Especially a Key Stakeholder

Paying attention to stakeholders in evaluation practice is a strategy that has
gained prominence for both practical and ethical reasons. The accumulated
evidence demonstrates that attention to and involvement of key stakeholders
enhances the design and implementation of evaluations and the use of
evaluation results in decision making (Patton, 2008). Beyond that, the Joint
Committee on Standards for Educational Evaluation (1994) argues that several principles should guide any evaluation: utility, feasibility, propriety, and
accuracy. Following this advice would appear to be quite difficult without careful attention to stakeholders. Similarly, it would be hard to follow the Guiding
Principles for Evaluators of the American Evaluation Association (1995) without attending to stakeholders. These principles include systematic inquiry, the
provision of competent performance to stakeholders, integrity and honesty,
respect for people, and responsibility for the general and public welfare.

The definition of *stakeholder* is consequential as it affects *who* and *what*
count (Mitchell, Agle, and Wood, 1997). We define *stakeholders* as *individuals,
groups, or organizations that can affect or are affected by an evaluation process or its
findings.* The definition is purposefully broad so that the full range of possible stakeholders is considered. *Key stakeholders* are a subset of this group, but
who is key will always be a judgment call and a matter for negotiation. Beyond
that, Patton (2008) defines *primary intended users* as a subset of key stakeholders. They are those "*specific* stakeholders selected to work with the evaluator throughout the evaluation to focus the evaluation, participate in making
design and methods decisions, and interpret the results to assure that the evaluation is useful, meaningful, relevant, and credible. Primary intended users
represent key and diverse stakeholder constituencies and have responsibility
for transmitting evaluation findings to those constituencies for use" (p. 72).

Beginning by defining stakeholders broadly leads inevitably to the finding that the stakeholders of any particular evaluation will have diverse and often competing interests. No evaluation can answer all potential questions equally well. This means that some process is necessary for narrowing the range of possible questions to focus the evaluation, which in turn necessitates focusing not just on the subset of key stakeholders but on the further subset of key stakeholders who are the primary intended users of the evaluation.

Identifying and Working with Primary Intended Users

As context for the specific stakeholder identification and analysis techniques presented in subsequent sections, we present here what research on evaluation use has revealed about identifying and working with primary intended users (Patton, 2008). Our summary is presented in the form of a set of guidelines for evaluators.

1. Develop Facilitation Skills

Evaluators need skills in building relationships, facilitating groups, managing conflict, walking political tightropes, and engaging in effective interpersonal communications in order to work with evaluation stakeholders. Technical skills and social science knowledge aren't sufficient to get evaluation results used. People skills are critical. Ideals of rational decision making in modern organizations notwithstanding, personal and political dynamics affect what really happens. Evaluators without the savvy and skills to deal with people and politics will find their work largely ignored or, worse yet, used inappropriately.

How do you improve these skills? Practice and feedback. Look for opportunities to observe and engage in facilitation with experienced evaluators. When you do facilitate, evaluate how it went; get formal feedback from those involved. That's how you get better.

2. Find and Train Evaluation Information Users

In order to work with primary intended users to achieve intended uses, the evaluation process must surface those people who want to know something and are therefore willing to use information that an evaluation might provide. The number of people found may vary from one prime user to a fairly large group representing several constituencies—for example, a task force of program staff, clients, funders, administrators, board members, community representatives, and officials or policymakers. One survey of evaluators indicates that six is the median number of primary intended users typically involved directly in an evaluation project (Cousins, Donohue, and Bloom, 1996). Although stakeholders' points of view may vary on any number of issues, what they should share is a genuine interest in using evaluation, an interest manifest in a willingness to take the time and effort to work through their information needs and interests. They should also be willing to take the time to be trained in evaluation options and to learn enough about methods to make informed choices (Patton, 2015). Even people initially inclined to value evaluation often will still need training and support to become effective information users. If users are not willing to be trained, perhaps people whose opinions they value can be found and persuaded to convince them. If they still are not willing, the chances increase that the evaluation will not serve its primary intended users well and, indeed, will be misused. (It may be more diplomatic to talk about building or increasing the capacity to use evaluation or about supporting professional development for use rather than "training." Whatever the language, the point is to develop the mind-set and skills needed to support and enhance use.)

How do you find and train evaluation information users? Inquire into the skills, interests, and interpersonal approaches of those being considered as primary intended users. Make training primary intended users an explicit part of the evaluation design so that adequate time and resources are included in the evaluation plan.

3. Find Tipping Point Connectors

Formal position and authority are only partial guides in identifying primary users. Evaluators must find strategically located people who are committed, competent, and connected—in short, who are *tipping point* connectors, people who are looked to by others for information (Gladwell, 2000). Research on evaluation use suggests that more may sometimes be accomplished by working with a lower-level person displaying these characteristics than by working with a passive, disinterested person in a higher position. However, the lower-level person needs to be able to connect with, have credibility with, and be able to influence higher-level people. Evaluation use is clearly facilitated by having genuine support from the program and organizational leadership. These leaders are not always the best choice for detailed, hands-on engagement along the way, but reaching them with findings remains essential.

How do you find tipping point connectors? Create a stakeholder influence diagram (described later in this chapter) of those being considered as primary intended users. Ask about who is viewed as connected to whom and who has influence with key decision makers.

4. Facilitate High-Quality Interactions

Quality, quantity, and timing of interactions with intended users are all important—but *quality* is most important. A large volume of interaction with little substance between evaluators and users may backfire and actually reduce stakeholder interest. Evaluators must be strategic and sensitive in asking for time and involvement from busy people and be sure they're interacting with the right people around relevant issues. Increased contact by itself is likely to accomplish little; nor will interaction with people not oriented toward use be productive. It is the nature and quality of interactions between evaluators and decision makers that is at issue. Our own experience suggests that where the right people are involved, the amount of direct contact can sometimes be reduced, because the interactions that do occur are of such high quality.

How do you facilitate high-quality interactions? Given the specific evaluation situation and people involved, develop explicit criteria with those people for what constitutes high quality, then evaluate with them how well the process is unfolding in terms of those criteria.

5. Nurture Interest in Evaluation

Evaluators will typically have to work to build and sustain interest in evaluation use. Identifying and working with intended users is part selection and part nurturance. Potential users with low opinions of or little interest in evaluation may have had bad prior experiences or just not have given much thought to the benefits of evaluation.

How do you nurture interest in evaluation? Find out what issues are relevant to those involved in terms of the evaluation process and the intended use of evaluation findings and work with these individuals and groups to make those issues the focus of the evaluation.

6. Demonstrate Cultural Sensitivity and Competence

Involvement of stakeholders and primary intended users has to be adapted to cultural and contextual factors (SenGupta, Hopson, and Thompson-Robinson, 2004; Symonette, 2004). Respecting and honoring culture is a significant dimension of making evaluation credible to people from different backgrounds. Culture is personal. Everyone who comes to the evaluation table brings culture with him or her. To ignore it is to disrespect those present and imperil use.

How do you demonstrate cultural sensitivity and competence? Check in with those involved about their priority cultural sensitivities and issues. Don't just guess. Don't just operate out of your own stereotypes or biases. Inquire about these issues with knowledgeable people and those involved. Get feedback and use it.

7. Anticipate Turnover of Intended Users

When personal connections are important to evaluation use, turnover may become a problem. Indeed, turnover in primary intended users can be the Achilles' heel of utilization-focused evaluation unless evaluators watch for, anticipate, and plan for it. The longer the time frame for the evaluation, the more important it is to engage with multiple intended users, build in some overlap, and when turnover happens, bring new people up to speed quickly. This will sometimes involve making some later-stage design changes, if that is possible, to get the buy-in of the new people and increase their sense of ownership of the evaluation.

How do you anticipate turnover? In the initial selection of primary intended users, also identify backups and potential substitutes. As the evaluation unfolds, check in regularly with those involved about whether their circumstances are changing.

With these guidelines as context, we now turn to specific stakeholder identification and analysis techniques.

Using Stakeholder Identification and Analysis Techniques

Practical program evaluators will find three stakeholder identification and analysis techniques particularly useful. These techniques are basic and will be relevant in any evaluation:

- Conducting basic stakeholder identification and analysis
- Choosing evaluation stakeholder analysis participants
- Drafting a purpose network diagram (or purpose hierarchy)

In this section we discuss these techniques in enough detail for readers to get a good idea of what is involved in using them. Also, as you will see, there may be overlapping activities involved when a technique builds on previous work the evaluator has done. Further guidance on these and additional techniques can be found in Bryson (2004, 2011), Patton (2008), and Bryson, Patton, and Bowman (2011).

All of the techniques are fairly simple in concept and easy to carry out. The first and third can be completed in one to two hours, although considerable additional time may be spent discussing and modifying the results. The technique for choosing evaluation stakeholder analysis participants will take longer, but even it should not take more than one or one and one-half workdays to complete. The key resources needed to undertake these analyses are some time, some effort, and reasonably informed participants. For example, an individual or a small analysis group must initiate the process. (Note that this analysis group will likely not be the same as the evaluation's primary intended users, a group that will be finalized as a result of the analyses.) *Evaluation sponsors* (persons with enough authority or power, or both, to commission an evaluation) or *process champions* (persons who will focus on managing the day-to-day effort and keeping everyone on track) may be part of the group or may be identified during the group's process. The actual evaluator(s) also may be among this group or may be selected later. Additionally, applying the techniques relies on standard facilitation materials such as flip charts, marking pens, tape, colored stick-on dots, and so on. The bottom line is that the typical necessary resource expenditures are miniscule when compared with the opportunity costs of a less-than-adequate evaluation.

After completing the techniques discussed in the following sections, it should be possible to articulate

- Who the evaluation sponsor(s) is.
- Who the day-to-day process champion(s) is, meaning the day-to-day evaluation process manager; this person may be the evaluator, but maybe not.
- Who the stakeholders, key stakeholders, and primary intended users are.
- What the purpose(s) or intended use(s) of the evaluation is.
- Who the members of the evaluation coordinating committee or task force are, if such a group is to be formed.
- How the different stakeholders will be involved at different stages in the evaluation process.
- Who the evaluator(s) is, or at least what his or her qualifications should be, and who the members of any required evaluation team might be. Note that, depending on the circumstances, this team may or may not be the

same as either the initial analysis group mentioned previously or the primary intended users.

Conducting Basic Stakeholder Identification and Analysis

The basic stakeholder identification and analysis technique is a good place to start. It is an adaptation of a technique described by Bryson (2004, 2011). It offers a quick and useful way of identifying stakeholders and their interests in the program or the evaluation. It can also surface or highlight some key evaluation issues and begin the process of identifying coalitions of either support for or opposition to use of the evaluation's results. Bryson (2011) describes how this technique was used in one state to begin evaluating the performance of the state's department of natural resources and how it showed participants how existing strategies ignored important stakeholders—who refused to be ignored—as well as what might be done to satisfy the stakeholders. The evaluation results were used to successfully bring about major changes in the organization. Once a small analysis group of reasonably well-informed participants who think doing a user-focused evaluation might be a good thing has been assembled and a skilled group facilitator identified, the technique employs the following steps:

- The analysis group brainstorms the list of potential stakeholders (individuals or groups).
- The facilitator prepares a separate flip chart sheet for each stakeholder.
- She places a stakeholder's name at the top of each sheet.
- She creates two columns.
- She labels the left-hand column "Stake or Interest in the Program," meaning: What does this stakeholder want to get out of the program or want the program to produce?
- She labels the right-hand column "Stake or Interest in the Evaluation," that is, What does this stakeholder want to get out of the evaluation or want the evaluation to produce?
- For each stakeholder, group members enter as many possibilities in each column as they can think of.
- If appropriate, the facilitator has the group members examine the left-hand column and make an initial assessment of how well they think the stakeholder thinks the program is doing *from the stakeholder's point of view,* not the evaluator's or someone else's point of view. Use colored dots to indicate a stakeholder judgment of *good* (green), *fair* (yellow), or *poor* (red).

- The group members identify and record what can be done quickly to satisfy each stakeholder.
- The group members identify and record longer term issues with individual stakeholders and with stakeholders as a group regarding both the program and the evaluation.
- Additional steps might be included, such as:
  - Discussing how each stakeholder influences the program or the evaluation or both.
  - Deciding what the evaluator needs from each stakeholder.
  - Ranking the stakeholders according to their importance to the evaluation. When doing so, the group should consider the stakeholder's power, legitimacy, and attention-getting capacity (Mitchell, Agle, and Wood, 1997).

Choosing Evaluation Stakeholder Analysis Participants

It may be necessary to engage a larger group to do the stakeholder analyses, rather than the small group mentioned with the previous technique. Deciding who should be involved, how, and when in doing stakeholder analyses is a key strategic choice. In general, people should be involved if they have information that cannot be gained otherwise, or if their participation is necessary to assure a successful evaluation process built on the analyses. There can be too much or too little participation, but determining the appropriate amount depends on the situation, and there is little hard-and-fast guidance to be offered. There are likely to be important trade-offs between early or later participation in the analyses and one or more of the following: broad representation of stakeholders, analysis quality, analysis credibility, analysis legitimacy, the ability to act based on the analyses, or other factors, and these will need to be thought through. Fortunately, these choices can be approached as a sequence of choices, in which an individual, who may be the evaluator, or a small stakeholder analysis group begins the effort by doing a preliminary version of the basic analysis technique or a purpose network diagram; then other participants are added later as the advisability of doing so becomes apparent.

One way to approach the task is to use a four-step process in which a decision can be made to stop any time after the first step. You might stop, for example, because you have enough information and support to proceed, timelines are short, the analyses are too sensitive, or for some other good reason. The steps are as follows:

1. The evaluator or a small stakeholder analysis group initiates the process by brainstorming and listing all potential stakeholders. (If the group has already carried out the first step in the basic analysis technique and has created a stakeholder list there, it can use that existing list here.) This step is useful in helping sponsors and champions of the evaluation effort think strategically about how to proceed. This step is typically backroom work. Necessary additional information inputs may be garnered through the use of interviews, questionnaires, focus groups, or other targeted information-gathering techniques in this and subsequent steps, or in conjunction with the other techniques outlined in this chapter. The step is important not only to help make sure all stakeholders are identified but also to do so at the right level of aggregation, meaning at a level that makes sense from a strategic perspective (Eden and Ackermann, 1998). For example, usually "the government" is not a stakeholder, but some parts of it, or individuals in it, might be.

2. After the evaluator or analysis group reviews the results of the first step, a larger group of stakeholders can be assembled. This meeting can be viewed as the more public beginning of the evaluation effort. The assembled group should be asked to brainstorm the list of stakeholders who might need to be involved in the evaluation effort (or review and revise as necessary a previously developed list). After this work has been completed, the group should be encouraged to think carefully about who is not at the meeting who should be at subsequent meetings. The group should consider actual or potential stakeholders' power, legitimacy, and attention-getting capacity. The group should carefully think through the positive and negative consequences of involving (or not) other stakeholders or their representatives, and in what ways to do so.

3. After these conversations have been completed, the full group should be assembled—that is, everyone who should be involved in the stakeholder analyses. The previous analyses may need to be repeated, at least in part, with the full group present, in order to get everyone "on the same page" and "bought in" and to make any needed corrections or modifications to prior analyses.

4. Last of all, after the full group has met, it should be possible to finalize who the primary intended users of the evaluation are and who will have some role to play in the evaluation effort—for example, sponsors and champions; the primary intended users themselves; the evaluation team, if there will be one; the coordinating group or task force, if there will be one; and various advisory or support groups (Bryson, 2004; Bryson, Patton, and Bowman, 2011; Patton, 2008).

Note that this staged process embodies a kind of technical, political, and ethical rationality. The process is designed to gain needed information, build political acceptance, and address some important questions about legitimacy, representation, and credibility. Stakeholders are included when there are good and prudent reasons to do so, but not when their involvement is impractical, unnecessary, or imprudent. Clearly, the choices of whom to include and how, when, and why to include them can be quite challenging to make. There is no way of escaping the need for wise, politically savvy, and ethical judgments if a credible evaluation is to be produced that will be used as intended by its intended users.

Creating a Purpose Network Diagram

Stakeholder analysis and involvement as part of an evaluation process should be undertaken for a clear purpose and that purpose (or purposes) should be articulated as clearly and as early as possible in the process—while also understanding that purposes may change over time. Creating a purpose network diagram can be very helpful in this regard. This technique is adapted from Bryson, Ackermann, and Eden (2007).

A purpose network (or hierarchy) diagram indicates the various interrelated purposes that the evaluation might serve. These ideally will include the overarching purpose; the major subordinate purposes, or goals; and the purposes subordinate to and supportive of goals, which typically are referred to as objectives. Note that the evaluation's overarching purpose and major subordinate purposes must mesh at least in part—and certainly not directly conflict with—the interests of key stakeholders; otherwise the evaluation process is unlikely to get off the ground, and even if it does the process and its findings will be misused or ignored. To ensure buy-in by key stakeholders, the evaluation should align with and address their interests and concerns. The other techniques discussed in this chapter can help ensure this alignment of key stakeholder interests and evaluation purposes. Of particular use in this regard is the bases of power–directions of interest diagram discussed later.

Once the network of purposes is created, it is typically possible to identify the primary intended purpose(s) or use(s) of the evaluation, at least in draft form, and to think strategically about subsequent stakeholder identification, analysis, and involvement. A final version of the diagram may have to wait until some of the techniques presented later are put to use and their results assessed. In other words, the initial analysis group should consider constructing an initial purpose network diagram very early in the process to help clarify evaluation purposes and to guide subsequent stake-holder identification, analysis, and engagement efforts. But the stakeholder analysis group clearly should recognize that this early diagram is tentative. It should be revisited and, typically, revised as additional information becomes available.

Follow these steps to create a purpose network diagram. Note that prior to using this technique, analysis group participants should familiarize them-selves with the generic intended uses, or purposes, of evaluation discussed in this chapter's next major section. These purposes relate to (1) the type of eval-uation being undertaken, (2) the stage of the program's development, and (3) the desired outcomes of the evaluation process itself, in contrast to the findings.

- The facilitator tapes four flip chart sheets to a wall to form a single surface two sheets high and two sheets wide, with one-inch overlaps where the sheets join.
- The analysis group then brainstorms a list of possible purposes (that is, the potential set of goals, aims, outcome indicators, aspirations, mandated requirements, and critical success factors) for the evaluation, and the per-sons suggesting the ideas place their statements of each purpose on a 3 × 5 inch sticky note (such as a Post-it label). Purpose statements should begin with a verb (*obtain, produce, create, show, demonstrate,* and so forth), and each statement should describe only a single purpose (this means that the group will not use *and, or,* or *in order to* in the statement).
- The facilitator places the labels on the flip chart sheets.
- The group members then rearrange the labels as needed to construct a causal network (or hierarchy), indicating how purposes are linked by inserting arrows to indicate the direction of causation (or of influence or support). Arrows indicate how fulfilling one purposes helps to fulfill one or more subsequent purposes; in other words, the arrows go from a means to an end, or an action to an outcome, in the form of links in a chain. Arrows should be made with a soft-lead pencil so that the group can move labels around, erase arrows, or otherwise change its mind.
- Through this process of creating the network (or hierarchy), the group members decide which purpose is the actual primary intended purpose and which purposes are subsidiary purposes of the evaluation. Note that the primary intended purpose may end up being different from what group

members or other stakeholders originally thought it was. It is also possible—perhaps even likely—that purposes may change somewhat based on further stakeholder analyses.

Dealing with Power Differentials

We turn now from basic and universal issues involved in identifying and engaging with stakeholders to the challenge of dealing with power differentials. Sometimes an evaluation involves only one primary intended user or a small number of intended users who know each other and have a history of working together. For larger, more complex evaluations, however, where there are a number of different stakeholder constituencies with competing or even conflicting interests, power and status differences come into play.

These differences should not be ignored, which requires sensitive facilitation and thoughtful preparation. Preparation means helping participants in the process get ready to take on these issues. Both stakeholder and evaluator readiness require careful situation analysis to understand what approach will be most appropriate for a particular group within a particular context. Readiness exercises include introducing and discussing evaluation standards and principles, conducting a retrospective use study on how evaluations have been used in the past, and articulating ways evaluations could be useful in the future. (See Patton, 2012, for details about these and other readiness exercises.) These basic readiness exercises pave the way for taking on more sensitive power differential issues.

The three techniques that follow are analytical frameworks that are especially relevant in those situations where significant power and status differences exist among stakeholders. These techniques are

- Using a power versus interest grid
- Using a stakeholder influence diagram
- Using a bases of power–directions of interest diagram

Power Versus Interest Grid

Power versus interest grids are described in detail by Eden and Ackermann (1998; see also Bryson, 2004; Bryson, Patton, and Bowman, 2011; Patton, 2008). These grids array stakeholders on a two-by-two matrix where the dimensions are the level of a stakeholder's interest (in a political sense as opposed to simple inquisitiveness) in the evaluation or issue at hand and the level of the stakeholder's power to affect the evaluation process or use of evaluation findings. Four categories of stakeholders result:

- *Players—people with both an interest and significant power.* Players have high potential as primary intended users. They are often key stakeholders who are in a prime position to affect evaluation use, including using it themselves as well as drawing the attention of others.
- *Subjects—people with an interest but little power.* It may be important to support and enhance subjects' capacity to be involved, especially when they may be affected by findings, as program participants may be, for example.
- *Context setters—people with power but little direct interest.* It may be important to increase the interest of context setters in the evaluation if they are likely to pose barriers to use through their disinterest.
- *The crowd—people with little interest or power.* On the one hand the crowd may need to be informed about the evaluation and its findings. On the other hand, if communication is badly done, controversy may quickly turn this amorphous crowd into a very interested mob.

Power versus interest grids typically help evaluators to determine which players' interests and power *must* be taken into account in order to produce a useful evaluation. Players, in other words, are almost by definition key stakeholders. These grids also highlight coalitions to be encouraged or discouraged and people whose buy in should be sought or who should be co-opted. Finally, they may provide some information on how to convince stakeholders to change their views. Interestingly, the knowledge gained from deploying this grid can be used to advance the interests of the relatively powerless subjects (Bryson, Cunningham, and Lokkesmoe, 2002).

A power versus interest grid is constructed as follows:

- The facilitator tapes four flip chart sheets to a wall to form a single surface two sheets high and two sheets wide.
- He then draws the grid's two axes on this surface, using a marking pen. He labels the vertical axis *interest* and makes it a continuum, running from *low* (bottom of the grid) to *high* (top of the grid), and he labels the horizontal axis *power* and makes it a continuum running from *low* (on the left) to *high* (on the right).
- Analysis group participants individually brainstorm the names of stakeholders, with each participant writing the names he or she thinks of on 1.5 × 2 inch sticky notes or labels, one stakeholder name per label. Alternatively,

if the choosing stakeholder analysis participants or basic analysis technique has been performed, the names can be taken from those lists.

- The facilitator then places each label in the appropriate spot on the grid according to the group's judgment. He collects the labels in round-robin fashion, one label per group member, until all labels (other than duplicates) have been placed on the grid or eliminated for some reason.
- He moves the labels around until all group members are satisfied with the *relative* location of each stakeholder on the grid.
- The group members then discuss the implications of the resulting stakeholder placements.

Stakeholder Influence Diagram

Stakeholder influence diagrams begin with a completed power versus interest grid and indicate how the stakeholders on that grid influence one another. This technique is taken from Eden and Ackermann (1998, pp. 349–350; see also Bryson, Cunningham, and Lokkesmoe, 2002). Understanding influence relationships adds depth to a power versus interest grid analysis in three ways: (1) it reveals which actors are central to moving the evaluation process or use of findings forward and which are more peripheral, (2) it indicates where existing channels of influence are and where they might need to be created, and (3) it clarifies where coalitions in support of the evaluation process and use of findings exist or might be formed. The steps in developing a stakeholder influence diagram are as follows:

- The analysis group starts with a completed power versus interest grid (on flip chart sheets) and then, for each stakeholder on the grid, suggests lines of influence from one stakeholder to another. Two-way influences are possible, but participants should attempt to identify the primary direction in which each line of influence flows. Specific types of influence might be noted as well, for example, money, authority, access to decision-makers, and so forth, by using different kinds of arrows or writing on the arrows themselves.
- The facilitator draws in the lines and directional indicators with a soft-lead pencil.
- Group members engage in an ongoing dialogue about which influence relationships exist, which are most important, and what the primary direction of influence is.
- Once final agreement is reached, the pencil lines are made permanent with a marking pen.

- The results and implications of the resulting stakeholder influence diagram are discussed, including identifying who the most influential or central stakeholders are and what the implications are for coalition formation.

Bases of Power–Directions of Interest Diagram

The bases of power–directions of interest diagram builds on the completed power versus interest grid and stakeholder influence diagram and involves looking at selected stakeholders in more detail, including the most influential or central stakeholders. A bases of power–directions of interest diagram can be created for each stakeholder or for a subset of stakeholders. The technique is an adaptation of Eden and Ackermann's "star diagrams" (1998, pp. 126–128, 346–349; see also Bryson, Cunningham, and Lokkesmoe, 2002).

A diagram of this kind indicates both the sources of power available to the stakeholder and the goals or interests the stakeholder seeks to achieve or serve (see Figure 2.1). Power can come from access to or control over various resources, such as expertise, money, votes, network centrality, or formal authority, or from access to or control over various sanctions, such as regulatory authority or votes of no confidence (Eden and Ackermann, 1998, pp. 126–127). Directions of interest indicate the aspirations or concerns of the stakeholder. When used in the context of evaluation, this diagram typically focuses on the stakeholder's bases of power and directions of interest *in relation to* the program (or other object of evaluation) or the evaluation; that is, it seeks to identify the power that might affect achievements of the program or the evaluation.

There are two reasons for constructing bases of power–directions of interest diagrams. First, they help the stakeholder analysis group find the common ground—especially in terms of interest—among the stakeholders. After exploring the power bases and interests of each stakeholder, the team will be in a position to identify commonalities across the stakeholders as a whole or across particular subgroups. Second, the diagrams are intended to provide background information on each stakeholder so that the evaluator will know how to tap into stakeholder interests or power to advance the evaluation's purpose, credibility, and use.

A bases of power–directions of interest diagram is constructed as follows:

- The facilitator attaches a flip chart sheet to a wall and writes the name of a stakeholder of interest in the middle of the sheet.

FIGURE 2.1. BASES OF POWER–DIRECTIONS OF INTEREST DIAGRAM.

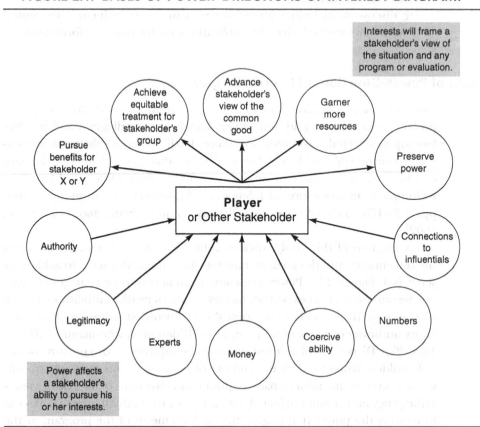

Source: Adapted from Eden and Ackermann, 1998, p. 127; Bryson, Cunningham, and Lokkesmoe, 2002, pp. 575–576.

- The group decides or the evaluator specifies whether the focus is on the stakeholder's power and interests in general or as they relate to the program or the evaluation.
- The analysis group then brainstorms possible bases of power for the stakeholder, and the facilitator writes these bases on the bottom half of the sheet and draws arrows connecting from them to the stakeholder. In other words, the arrows indicate the sources of power the stakeholder has, or on which he or she can draw.
- The group members discuss how one power base may be linked to another, and the facilitator draws additional arrows on the diagram to indicate the group's determinations about these linkages.

- The group members then brainstorm goals or interests they believe the stakeholder has, either in general or in relation to the program or the evaluation. The facilitator writes these goals and interests on the top half of the sheet and draws arrows connecting from the stakeholder to them. In other words, the arrows indicate the interests toward which the stakeholder's efforts are directed.
- As in a previous step, members discuss how goals and interests may be linked to one another, and the facilitator draws appropriate additional arrows.
- The group members engage in an open discussion of the evaluation design implications that might be inferred from the goals and interests that they have now identified.

Determining the Evaluation's Purpose and Goals

When clarifying the evaluation's purpose and goals, it is useful to keep in mind a number of generic purposes or intended uses of evaluation that depend on (1) the type of evaluation being undertaken, (2) the stage of a program's development, and (3) the desired outcomes of the evaluation process itself, in contrast to the evaluation findings. Patton (2008, 2012) identifies six of these generic uses. The findings may be intended to facilitate (1) overall summative judgment; (2) formative program improvement and learning; (3) accountability; (4) monitoring; (5) development of the program to adapt to complex, emergent, and dynamic conditions; and (6) knowledge generation to enhance general understandings and identify generic principles of effectiveness. Each purpose implies the selection of pertinent evaluation questions, evaluation approaches, and strategies to promote use among the primary intended users. Most evaluation efforts are likely to embody some blend of purposes, and early consultation with key stakeholders, and especially with primary intended users, can settle what the precise blend should be in order to help ensure an appropriate evaluation design and effective use of findings.

Finally, a number of purposes are associated with the evaluation process itself, in contrast to its findings. *Process use* refers to the impacts on those involved in the evaluation process, for example, what primary intended users learn about evaluation by being involved in the evaluation design process. Patton (2008) identifies six process uses that are distinct from findings uses:

- Infusing evaluative thinking into an organization's culture
- Enhancing shared understandings related to the program and evaluation

- Supporting and reinforcing program interventions or treatments to increase program impact and the value of the evaluation
- Using evaluation instrumentation to focus on program priorities and increase participant learning
- Increasing participant engagement, self-determination, and commitment to the evaluation
- Improving program and organizational development in terms of capacity building, contributions beyond the specific evaluation findings, and enhancement of ongoing adaptability.

Some of these purposes complicate attribution as the effects of the program become intertwined with the evaluation, in effect making the evaluation part of the intervention. In practice any actual evaluation process, either intentionally or unintentionally, serves a number of process purposes. Gaining clarity about the process purposes or uses to be served, in addition to the finding uses, can lead to a greatly improved evaluation design and to more effective engagements with stakeholders.

Any particular evaluation must be guided by a more specific statement of purposes than the three analytical frameworks we have been discussing initially provide, and here is where stakeholder analyses can help. Previously, we recommended that one of these frameworks, the purpose network diagram, be developed very early on in the process of organizing an evaluation study. As additional stakeholder analysis techniques are used or as additional people are using them, additional information on purposes is likely to surface. Evaluators and those they work with should consider how best to consider and possibly add new information to this purpose network diagram to gain further clarity about their evaluation's purposes, goals, and objectives.

Two techniques are likely to be particularly helpful in refining the purpose diagram: using basic stakeholder analysis and creating bases of power–directions of interest diagrams. As noted, the former technique involves gaining clarity about stakeholders' expectations of the program or evaluation. The latter often involves trying to gain greater understanding of stakeholders' interests more broadly. The enumerated expectations and interests may imply important purposes, goals, or objectives for the evaluation. Once again, the way in which this information will be incorporated into the statement of the evaluation's purpose(s) is a judgment call. Here are three examples of general purpose statements for different kinds of evaluations undertaken in three different kinds of organizations:

Overall purpose of a federal government evaluation initiative. Improve effectiveness of programs at every level in the department and demonstrate efficient use of taxpayer dollars in accordance with congressional mandates and executive priorities.

Overall purpose of evaluation in a philanthropic foundation: Support the foundation's mission attainment, build knowledge about what works and what doesn't work, and learn collaboratively with our grantees.

Overall purpose of a nonprofit organization's program evaluations: Improve services to those in need so as to help them improve their quality of life.

Engaging Stakeholders

All of the techniques considered so far are relevant to planning for stakeholder participation. The final stakeholder technique we want to offer is the *evaluation stakeholder engagement planning matrix* (Figure 2.2), which pulls stakeholder analysis information together to help evaluators and those they are working with closely develop a carefully articulated plan for engaging or responding to different stakeholders throughout the evaluation. The matrix adapts material from the International Association for Public Participation (2007), specifically that group's notion of a spectrum of levels of public participation, and also uses the generic steps in an evaluation process. The levels of participation range from not engaging at all to empowerment, in which the stakeholders or some subset of them are given final decision-making authority over the evaluation. Each level implies a different kind of promise from the evaluator to the stakeholder—implicitly if not explicitly (see Figure 2.2). Evaluators can enter the names of the stakeholders in the appropriate cells in the matrix to indicate the extent to which each stakeholder will be involved in each step as the evaluation progresses.

Note that even though the majority of evaluators endorse the idea of engaging stakeholders, there are likely to be sharp differences about the advisability of involving stakeholders—other than the evaluator(s)—in the second step, where choices are made on evaluation design, measurement and data collection methods (Patton, 2015); the third step, where the data are collected and organized; and the fourth step, where the data are analyzed and interpreted, judgments about findings are made, and recommendations are developed. Many would argue that only evaluation professionals may legitimately make these choices; if others make them, the merits of the evaluation may be severely compromised. In addition, many evaluators believe that any decisions about adoption and implementation of recommendations in the last step (what many would consider the post-evaluation phase) are beyond an

FIGURE 2.2. EVALUATION STAKEHOLDER ENGAGEMENT PLANNING MATRIX.

Type of involvement	Do Not Engage	Engage as Data Source	Inform	Consult	Involve	Collaborate	Empower
Promise evaluator makes	No promise.	We will honor human subject protocols and treat you and the data with respect.	We will keep you informed of the evaluation's progress and findings.	We will keep you informed, listen to you, and provide feedback on how your input influenced the evaluation.	We will work with you to ensure your concerns are considered and reflected in options considered, make sure you get to review and comment on options, and provide feedback on how your input is used in the evaluation.	We will incorporate your advice and suggestions to the greatest extent possible, and give you meaningful opportunities to be part of the evaluation decision-making process.	This is your evaluation. We will offer options to inform your decisions. You will decide and we will support and facilitate implementing what you decide.
Those engaged are especially important and useful for . . .	. . . not being involved!	. . . providing needed data.	. . . dissem-inating findings and creating interest in the results.	. . . anticipating issues, identifying landmines, suggesting priorities, and enhancing the credibility of the evaluation.	. . . affirming the importance, appropriateness and utility of the evaluation, attracting attention to findings, and establish credibility.	. . . serving as primary intended users because of their high interest, interpersonal style, availability, influential positions or connections, and sense of ownership of the evaluation.	. . . capacity development, using the evaluation to build their capacity to engage in evaluative thinking and practice.

(Continued)

FIGURE 2.2. EVALUATION STAKEHOLDER ENGAGEMENT PLANNING MATRIX. *(Continued)*

Type of involvement	Do Not Engage	Engage as Data Source	Inform	Consult	Involve	Collaborate	Empower
Step 1: evaluation planning							
Step 2: evaluation design							
Step 3: data collection and organization							
Step 4: data analysis and interpretation, judgments about findings, and recommendations							
Step 5: decision making and implementation of evaluation recommendations							

Source: Adapted from Bryson, 2004, p. 33; Patton, 2008, p. 81; International Association for Public Participation, 2007.

evaluator's purview. The matrix simply poses the questions of who might or should be engaged and when, how, and why at each step, and implies that the choices should not be left to chance, and indeed, that the possible choices to be made in the last step might actually inform those made in the earlier steps.

In other words, the participation planning matrix prompts evaluators and those they are working with closely to think about engaging or responding to different stakeholders in different ways over the course of an evaluation process and its aftermath. The same stakeholder might be engaged differently in different steps. As a result, the benefits of taking stakeholders seriously may be gained while avoiding the perils of inappropriately responding to or engaging stakeholders. The evaluator's process for filling out the matrix is as follows:

Begin using this matrix relatively early in any evaluation effort.

Fill out the matrix with stakeholders' names in the appropriate boxes, and then develop action plans for how to follow through with each stakeholder.

Cycle back and revise the matrix as the evaluation design and methods unfold.

Meeting the Challenges of Turbulent and Uncertain Environments

As noted earlier, the guiding principle of utilization-focused evaluation is to design evaluations to achieve intended use by intended users. This emphasis on intentionality assumes that we can identify key stakeholders and work with them to determine evaluation purposes. However, in very turbulent situations, evaluators may experience uncertain and changing political and other stakes for different stakeholders. Unanticipated factors can suddenly change the stakeholder landscape, as the global financial meltdown did in 2007 to 2009, because it severely affected many nonprofit programs, government agencies, and private sector initiatives. Everything was in flux. Changes in political administrations also bring huge uncertainties about what new stakeholder alignments will emerge and how those alliances, and conflicts, will affect evaluation priorities.

Evaluators in complex adaptive systems—systems characterized by high uncertainty and emergent self-organizing groups and organizations—will need flexibility, adaptability, and situational responsiveness to track and map any changes in stakeholders, relationships among stakeholders, and the purposes an evaluation is meant to serve. Attention to such changes provides a framework for understanding such common evaluation issues as unintended consequences, irreproducible effects, lack of program fidelity in implementation, multiple paths to the same outcomes, unexpected changes in program requirements, and difficulty in specifying treatment interventions— all of which are made more challenging in a dynamic stakeholder environment (Patton, 2011). In other words, while striving for intended use by intended users is the utilization-focused evaluation ideal, the realities of complex adaptive systems alert us to be attuned as well to dynamic and emergent stakeholder relationships and evaluation issues that may have been unknown and unintended at the outset of an evaluation but that become critically important as the evaluation unfolds. Various network analysis techniques can be used to identify stakeholders and their interrelationships (the stakeholder influence diagram presented earlier is one) and to map any changes. (See Bryson, Ackermann, and Eden, 2014; Bryson, Ackermann, Eden, and Finn, 2004; and Durland and Fredericks, 2005, for more information on several other useful techniques.) In a related vein, evaluation efforts focused on examining initiatives aimed at changing all or major parts of a system should probably include the mapping of changed relationships among key stakeholder groups, especially changed relationships among those stakeholders directly involved in the evaluation.

Conclusion

The vast majority of evaluators agree that it is important to identify and work with evaluation stakeholders in order to design and manage evaluation processes in such a way that evaluations serve their intended purposes for their intended users. What is generally missing from the literature, however, is practical advice on how to do this stakeholder work. This chapter is intended to at least partially fill that gap.

A starting premise is that, even though some stakeholder engagement may be necessary to do the analysis effectively, stakeholder analysis should precede the main efforts toward stakeholder engagement. In other words, at least some stakeholders may have to be engaged right from the start to give the evaluator and the analysis group access to the information needed to fully understand stakeholders—their interests and expectations, their powers, their interrelationships, and the various roles they might need to play in order for a well-designed and utilization-focused evaluation to be assembled and to serve its intended purpose for its intended users.

The techniques we offer are easy to use and generally take no more than an hour or two for a group to complete, although the results may prompt considerable additional important discussion. This represents a time commitment that is a small fraction of the time and opportunities evaluators can lose if they have to address ill effects from *not* doing stakeholder analyses. That said, some evaluators will wonder what to do when they have little time, say a week or a month, to prepare an evaluation and potential stakeholders have little time, say at most thirty to ninety minutes, to speak with evaluators during the evaluation planning and design steps. Our response is threefold. First, take all the time you can and use at least the basic stakeholder analysis technique. Second, let the intended evaluation users know that the research evidence indicates they are running a serious risk of evaluation misuse or inappropriate nonuse by shortcutting stakeholder analyses. (As Yogi Berra supposedly said, "If you don't know where you're going, you'll end up somewhere else.") And third, given the principles for evaluators espoused by the American Evaluation Association and the Joint Committee on Standards for Educational Evaluation, one has to wonder about the professional ethics of proceeding without doing some serious stakeholder analysis work.

Evaluators are likely to differ most on the advisability of engaging stakeholders in the following evaluation steps: evaluation design, data collection and organization, data analysis and interpretation, judgments regarding findings, and evaluation recommendations. The strong evidence that engaging stakeholders is effective and important for improving use should certainly give pause to the naysayers who are against all stakeholder involvement in these steps. We believe that evaluators and intended users should at least seriously consider the pros, cons, and mechanics of engaging stakeholders in these steps and not simply rule out such involvements right from the start.

We hope this chapter has provided enough information for evaluators to achieve a good grasp of the stakeholder analysis and engagement techniques we believe are fundamental to good utilization-focused evaluation practice. The promise of effective stakeholder analysis and engagement is that evaluation users will end up with more useful evaluations—leading to a world made better, one evaluation at a time.

References

American Evaluation Association, Task Force on Guiding Principles for Evaluators. "Guiding Principles for Evaluators." In W. R. Shadish, D. L. Newman, M. A. Scheirer, and C. Wye (eds.), *Guiding Principles for Evaluators.* New Directions for Program Evaluation, no. 66. San Francisco: Jossey-Bass, 1995.

Bryson, J. "What to Do When Stakeholders Matter: A Guide to Stakeholder Identification and Analysis Techniques." *Public Management Review*, 2004, *6*(1), 21–53.

Bryson, J. *Strategic Planning for Public and Nonprofit Organizations* (4th ed.). San Francisco: Jossey-Bass, 2011.

Bryson, J., Ackermann, F., and Eden, C. "Putting the Resource-Based View of Management to Work in Public Organizations." *Public Administration Review*, 2007, *67*(4), 702–717.

Bryson, J., Ackermann, F., Eden, C., and Finn, C. B. *Visible Thinking: Unlocking Causal Mapping for Practical Business Results.* Hoboken, NJ: Wiley, 2004.

Bryson, J., Ackermann, F., and Eden, C. *Visual Strategy: Strategy Mapping for Public and Nonprofit Organizations.* San Francisco: Jossey-Bass, 2014.

Bryson, J., Cunningham, G., and Lokkesmoe, K. "What to Do When Stakeholders Matter: The Case of Problem Formulation for the African American Men Project of Hennepin County, Minnesota." *Public Administration Review*, 2002, *62*(5), 568–584.

Bryson, J., Patton, M. Q., and Bowman, R. A. "Working with Evaluation Stakeholders: A Rationale, Step-Wise Approach, and Toolkit." *Evaluation and Program Planning*, 2011, *34*, 1–12.

Cousins, J. B., Donohue, J. J., and Bloom, G. A. "Collaborative Evaluation in North America: Evaluators' Self-Reported Opinions, Practices and Consequences." *Evaluation Practice*, 1996, *17*(3), 207–225.

Durland, M., and Fredericks, K. (eds.). *Social Network Analysis in Program Evaluation.* New Directions for Evaluation, no. 107. San Francisco: Jossey-Bass, 2005.

Eden, C., and Ackermann, F. *Making Strategy.* Thousand Oaks, CA: Sage, 1998.

Gladwell, M. *The Tipping Point: How Little Things Can Make a Big Difference.* Boston: Little Brown, 2000.

International Association for Public Participation. *IAP2 Spectrum of Public Participation.* www.iap2.org/associations/4748/files/IAP2%20Spectrum_vertical.pdf. 2007.

Joint Committee on Standards for Educational Evaluation. *The Program Evaluation Standards.* Thousand Oaks, CA: Sage, 1994.

Mitchell, R. K., Agle, B. R., and Wood, D. J. "Toward a Theory of Stakeholder Identification and Salience: Defining the Principle of Who and What Really Counts." *Academy of Management Review*, 1997, *22*(4), 853–886.

Patton, M. Q. *Utilization-Focused Evaluation* (4th ed.). Thousand Oaks, CA: Sage, 2008.

Patton, M. Q. *Developmental Evaluation: Enhancing Innovation and Use in Complex Adaptive Systems.* New York: Guilford Press, 2011.

Patton, M. Q. *Essentials of Utilization-Focused Evaluation.* Thousand Oaks, CA: Sage, 2012.

Patton, M. Q. *Qualitative Research and Evaluation Methods* (4th ed.). Thousand Oaks, CA: Sage, 2015.

SenGupta, S., Hopson, R., and Thompson-Robinson, M. "Cultural Competence in Evaluation: An Overview." In M. Thompson-Robinson, R. Hopson, and S. SenGupta (eds.), *In Search of Cultural Competence in Evaluation: Toward Principles and Practices.* New Directions for Evaluation, no. 102. San Francisco: Jossey-Bass, 2004.

Symonette, H. "Walking Pathways Toward Becoming a Culturally Competent Evaluator: Boundaries, Borderlands, and Border Crossings." In M. Thompson-Robinson, R. Hopson, and S. SenGupta (eds.), *In Search of Cultural Competence in Evaluation: Toward Principles and Practices.* New Directions for Evaluation, no. 102. San Francisco: Jossey-Bass, 2004.

CHAPTER THREE

USING LOGIC MODELS

John A. McLaughlin, Gretchen B. Jordan

Those who are responsible for designing, conducting, reporting, and using program evaluations are the primary audience for this chapter. We believe that program managers and staff will also find the logic model tool useful for conceptualizing, planning, and communicating with others about their program. The logic model serves as a useful advance organizer when evaluators and others are designing evaluation studies and performance measurement systems. It helps them to focus on the important elements of the program and to identify what evaluation questions should be asked and why and what measures of performance are key. The logic model in various forms has been around since the late 1960s, but it has come into increasing use in the past two decades because of the emphasis on managing for results and measuring performance. The logic model also helps evaluators frame evaluation reports so that findings from the evaluation and measurement can tell a performance "story" and results can be linked to program elements and assumptions about them. Evaluators can use this tool when asked to evaluate a program during its design phase, after it has ended, or at any other point in its life cycle. Managers may use this tool in program planning and design and when communicating the place of the program in a larger organization or context. The process of developing a logic model helps build shared understanding and expectations among program staff and other participants. We believe that while it is important for the evaluation to address the question of program results, it is equally important to focus the evaluation efforts on program implementation and early outcomes so the managers and staff know what's working and not working and where necessary make informed mid-course corrections to enhance the probability of longer-term success.

We use the term *program* loosely throughout this chapter. We have used logic models to describe internal management functions, websites, and the performance-based management process itself. A program can be described as an intentional transformation of specific resources (inputs) into certain activities (processes) to produce desired outcomes (results) within a specific context. We present a tool that evaluators and program managers can use to describe the unique program elements and show how they go together. This completed model can then be used for the purposes of communicating and testing the assumptions that program staff members have made about how the program is supposed to work.

A program can also be thought of as a hypothesis or theory of change: if a program is implemented as planned, then certain results are expected to follow, given the context within which it is implemented. Logic modeling is a tool that can be used to unpack this hypothesis in order to understand the underlying assumptions and create strategies to test the hypothesis.

The material in this chapter supports subsequent chapters in several ways. One of the assumptions that evaluators make is that a useful evaluation approach is based on an understanding of the objectives of the program and of the ways in which the program intends to achieve these objectives. Conducting an evaluation of a program without this understanding can be both costly and potentially harmful. Logic modeling can be a useful tool for performing an evaluability assessment. It can serve as an advance organizer for designing and conducting an implementation evaluation. The model presents a description of how the program staff members or other stakeholders believe the program works. If the evaluation finds that the program is successful in achieving its aims but works differently in practice, the logic model may be revised. If the evaluation determines that the program is not successful, it may be possible for the evaluator to recommend that the staff exert more pressure on the actual delivery of the program to bring it in line with their logic. Collecting and interpreting evaluation information is also aided by the logic model, as it establishes a framework for understanding the elements of the program, the assumed causal relationships, and the potential role of context. Finally, using the logic model in preparing and presenting the evaluation findings and recommendations can increase the probability that the evaluation results will be used.

What Is a Logic Model?

A *logic model* is a plausible and sensible model of how a program will work under certain environmental conditions to solve identified problems (Bickman, 1987). It can be the basis for a convincing story of the program's expected performance, telling stakeholders and others the problem the program focuses on and how the program is qualified to address it. The elements of the logic model are resources, activities, outputs, short-term outcomes, intermediate outcomes, and long-term outcomes (Wholey, 1987). Some have added the customers reached to the logic model, as well as the relevant external contextual (antecedent and mediating) influences (McLaughlin and Jordan, 1999). (A historical review of logic modeling as a tool for planning and conducting evaluations can be found in McLaughlin and Jordan, 2004.) The interest in logic modeling has spawned a number of books and guides with instructions and examples. These include Centers for Disease Control (2010), Frechtling (2007), Funnell and Rogers (2011), Knowlton and Phillips (2008 and 2013), Taylor-Powell (2008), and W.K. Kellogg Foundation (2005).

Logic models can take many different forms, including diagram, narrative, and tabular forms. Evaluators can prepare a logic model at any time in the life cycle of a program, and they often revise this model as more program information is collected. A basic logic model is shown in Figure 3.1. It has three basic parts: program structure, outcomes structure, and context. These are consistent with the desirable dimensions of performance measurement and evaluation. That is, the goal of evaluation is to observe and explain change. The necessary information for explanation comes from performance measurement in the program and outcomes structure and context. Here are descriptions of the elements of the logic model:

- *Resources*: human and financial resources as well as other inputs required to support the program, such as partnerships. Information on the type and level of the problem addressed by the program is an essential resource for the program.
- *Activities*: the essential action steps necessary to produce program outputs.
- *Outputs*: the products, goods, and services provided to the program's direct customers or program participants. For example, the reports generated for other researchers or the number of clients completing a workshop could be outputs of an activity. Customers or "reach" is sometimes put explicitly in the middle of the chain of logic. Many evaluators do not separate out activities and outputs in their models. However, activities typically represent what the

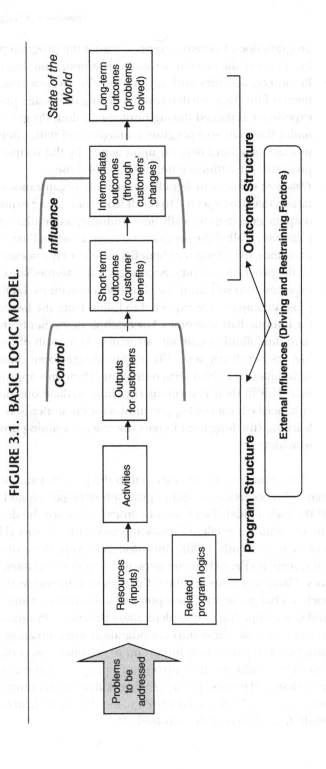

FIGURE 3.1. BASIC LOGIC MODEL.

State of the World

Long-term outcomes (problems solved)

Intermediate outcomes (through customers' changes)

Short-term outcomes (customer benefits)

Influence

Outputs for customers

Control

Activities

Resources (inputs)

Related program logics

Problems to be addressed

Outcome Structure

Program Structure

External Influences (Driving and Restraining Factors)

program does, whereas outputs are what the program produces, and so we like to break the two out because this supports implementation evaluation.

- Resources, activities and outputs are the *program structure*, and these elements of the logic are determined during the design phase and modified as experience is gained during implementation. Program structure is mostly under the control of program managers and staff, whereas short and intermediate outcomes depend upon action by the recipients of outputs, and programs can influence but not control those.

- *Outcomes*: changes or benefits to people, organizations, or other program targets that are expected to result from their being exposed to activities and outputs. Programs typically have multiple, sequential outcomes, sometimes collectively called the program's *outcome structure*. First, there are short-term outcomes, the changes or benefits most closely associated with, or "caused" by, the program's outputs. Second are the intermediate outcomes, which are expected to result from the short-term outcomes. Long-term outcomes or program impacts are expected to follow from the benefits accrued though the intermediate outcomes. For example, a teacher training program might have the following outcome structure. As a result of participating in training, teachers learn new skills and knowledge about classroom management techniques (the short-term outcome). Then they appropriately apply these new skills in their classrooms (the intermediate outcome), which leads to enhanced educational opportunities for the students, resulting in improved learning (the long-term impact the teacher training program was designed to achieve).

Key contextual factors external to the program and not under its control may influence its success either positively or negatively and are critical features of the logic model. Two types of context influence the design and delivery of the program: antecedent factors and mediating factors (Harrell, Burt, Hatry, Rossman, and Roth, 1996). *Antecedent* factors are those the program starts out with, such as client characteristics, geographical variables, and economic factors. *Mediating* factors are the influences that emerge as the program unfolds, such as changes in staff, new policies, a downturn or uptick in the economy, and new competing or complementary programs. Program planners and evaluators must take these into consideration when creating and evaluating the program. It is particularly important to consider how certain client characteristics might influence the outcome of a program. For example, if the program were designed to increase the reading skills of adult immigrants, the developer would consult the related research to identify useful instructional methods for adults from the countries involved.

The Utility of Logic Models

The utility of logic models has increased as managers are being challenged by oversight agencies at all levels of government and in the nonprofit sector. At the federal level, Congress and the White House Office of Management and Budget are asking managers to tell their programs' stories in a way that both communicates the program's outcome goals and shows that these outcomes have been achieved. For many public programs, there is also this implicit question: Are the results proposed by the program the correct ones? That is, do the results address problems that are appropriate for the program and that stakeholders deem to be important to the organizational mission and national needs?

The emphasis on accountability and managing for results that is now found in state and local governments and in nonprofit organizations such as the United Way of America and the American Red Cross represents a change in the way managers have to describe their programs and document program successes. In the past, program managers were not as familiar with describing and measuring outcomes as they were with documenting inputs and outputs. Program managers and evaluators have not been in the habit of using clear, logically consistent methods to make explicit their understandings about programs and how those programs work to achieve their outcomes given their specific operating contexts.

There is an increasing interest among program managers in continuous improvement and managing for quality. Yet, choosing what to measure and then collecting and analyzing the data necessary for improvement are new to many managers. Although tools such as flowcharts, risk analysis, and systems analysis can be used to plan and describe programs, logic models more comprehensively address the increasing requirements for both outcomes measurement and measurement of how the program is being implemented to allow for improvement. (Box 3.1 summarizes the benefits of using a logic model.) The logic modeling process can also be used by managers of existing programs to enable program staff members to step back and reexamine their existing program, asking, for example: Are the challenges the program is responsible for still relevant? Have they changed in any way? Are the strategies we have been using consistent with prevailing professional practice? Should we consider other approaches? Have new partners or technologies emerged that we can take advantage of? For planning, the logic model is worked from desired outcomes to chosen activities, whereas for evaluation and measurement, the important viewing is from the activities to the emerging outcomes.

Box 3.1. Benefits of Using the Logic Model Tool

- It points to evaluation issues and a balanced set of key performance measurement points, thus improving data collection and usefulness and helping managers and staff to meet performance reporting requirements.
- It helps with program design or improvement by identifying program activities that are critical to goal attainment, are redundant, or have inconsistent or implausible linkages to program goals.
- It communicates the place of a program in the organization or problem hierarchy, particularly if there are shared logic charts at various management levels.
- It builds a common understanding of the program and expectations for resources, customers reached, and results, and thus is good for sharing ideas, identifying assumptions, team building, and communication.

One of the uses of the logic model that should not be overlooked is communication. The process of developing a logic model brings people together to build a shared understanding of the program and program performance standards. The model also helps to communicate the program to those outside it in a concise and compelling way and helps program staff to gain a common understanding of how the program works and their responsibilities to make it work.

Logic models are increasingly used for program design and management. This usually requires development of a theory of change and means that more resources and time are needed to complete and update the logic model. The traditional linear, cause-and-effect logic models emphasize activities or sequence of outcomes and are often used for evaluability assessment, evaluation planning, or outcomes assessment. Logic models such as the ones put forth by Funnell (2000) and Funnell and Rogers (2011) are more dynamic, and they include behavioral change, risk, context, and mediating variables. These models take more time to develop but have added utility as integrating frameworks for evaluation and performance measurement.

Theory-Driven Evaluation

Assumptions about resources and activities and how these are expected to lead to intended outcomes are often referred to as *program theory*. A logic model is a useful tool for describing program theory and is often referred to as describing the program's *theory of change*. The program's theory of change evolves through persistent dialogue between the evaluator and program representatives. The logic model is then used to provide a graphic description of the theory of change. The hypothesis, often implicit, is that if the right resources are transformed into the right activities for the right people, then these are expected to lead to the results the program was designed to achieve. Some evaluators believe that making explicit the underlying assumptions about how a program is supposed to work increases the potential for evaluation utility. Although developing the program theory prior to the evaluation is considered most beneficial for predicting relationships, developing program theory at any point in the evaluation helps explain observed causal relationships.

The aim of evaluation is to explain observed performance. According to Mayne and Stern (2013), "explanation is impossible without theory." Logic modeling is a process through which evaluators can tease out theory through deep discussions with mangers and staff regarding their assumptions and beliefs about how their program will work or is working to achieve intended outcomes and results. The discussion between evaluators and staff centers on relationships between various elements in the program's performance spectrum. After these causal associations are sufficiently described the role of the evaluators is the design and conduct of a study that tests the degree to which the hypothesized relationships hold up. The "tests" might occur at multiple points in the life cycle of a program: during the design stage, at implementation, emergent outcomes, and end outcomes or results.

Leeuw (2003) provides an excellent review of three approaches to restructuring program theories after the program has been implemented:

- The *policy-scientific approach* is more empirical than the other approaches and consists of generating a series of propositions, or assumptions, about how the program is supposed to work. The evaluator then tests these propositions through a review of relevant scientific research, interviews with key staff, and document reviews.
- The *strategic assessment approach* is driven through conversations or dialogues with program staff and participants. The focus is to draw out the underlying assumptions about how the program works and then subject these to open debate among stakeholders and staff.
- The *elicitation approach* aims at recovering the mental models or cognitive maps that program staff hold about their program. The various maps are then compared, contrasted, and assessed for their validity through open dialogue and reviews of existing related research.

The central theme in all three approaches is discovering the underlying *theory* and assumptions held about how the program is believed to be working to achieve its outcomes and then testing these assumptions once they have been made public. All three approaches make the program transparent, allowing the evaluator and others to see how it is supposed to work or thought to be working from multiple perspectives. Logic modeling is a tool that can effectively be used to display the assumption pathways. Most evaluators do not actually enter statements about the underlying theory in the model. The model is a *graphic* representation of the elements and how they go together. The arrows connecting the elements (see Figures 3.1 and 3.3) represent the theory or assumptions. (Box 3.2 offers some tips to consider before starting to construct a logic model.)

Building the Logic Model

A logic model is constructed in five stages:

Stage 1: collecting the relevant information

Stage 2: clearly defining the problem the program will solve and its context

Stage 3: defining the elements of the program in a table: early sense making

Stage 4: drawing the model to reveal the program's theory of change

Stage 5: verifying the program logic with stakeholders

Box 3.2. Tips to Consider Before Starting

- Think of developing a logic model as a process. In general, it is important that program managers and staff be involved in developing their logic model. They should be able to "do it themselves" after having had training in the logic modeling technique.
- Do not try to do the job alone. It is important to involve a workgroup with a full range of key stakeholders who are associated in some way with the implementation of the model and its results.
- Be careful with jargon. Because logic modeling is often a new way of thinking about the program, using familiar language helps others understand it. The format and terminology used in creating the logic model should be adapted to the program.

- View logic modeling as part of long-term cultural change. Do not shortcut the process. Make the model an iterative process, updating it as program and program context change.
- *Avoid* letting the logic modeling process become a time sink. Leave some elements unknown. Plan costs and a schedule that can include downstream activities such as choosing performance measures or planning next steps.

Stage 1: Collecting the Relevant Information

Building the logic model for a program should be a team effort in most cases. If the evaluation function is external to the program, the evaluator, in collaboration with the program manager and staff, should carry out the process of creating the model. If the program manager does the work alone, there is a risk that she may leave out or incorrectly represent essential parts because she has limited knowledge of the program or its context. There are times when a manager may push back on the use of the logic model. The evaluator should be prepared to talk about the potential benefits of logic modeling such as those described in this chapter. In particular, we advise taking a step back to review the rationale of existing programs. It is often valuable to revisit the underlying assumptions of prevailing practice to explain why a program might be working well or might need improvements. In the end, deep engagement in the process is the best way to demonstrate utility.

In the following stages of building the logic model, we refer to the manager as the key player. However, we also recommend that persons knowledgeable about the program's planned performance, including partners and customers, be involved in a workgroup to develop the model. As the building process begins, it will become evident that there are multiple realities or views of program performance. Developing a shared vision of how the program is supposed to work will be a product of persistent discovery and negotiation between and among stakeholders.

When a program is complex or poorly defined or communication and consensus are lacking, we recommend that a small subgroup or perhaps an independent facilitator perform the initial analysis and synthesis through document reviews and individual and focus group interviews. The product of this effort can then be presented to the larger workgroup as a catalyst for the logic model process.

Whether designing a new program or describing an existing program, it is essential that the evaluator or workgroup collect information relevant to the program from multiple sources (see Box 3.3 for some tips). The information will come in the form of program documentation and from interviews with key stakeholders internal and external to the program. Although strategic plans, annual performance plans, previous program evaluations, pertinent legislation and regulations, and the results of targeted interviews should be available before the logic model is constructed, this will be an iterative process requiring the ongoing collection of information. Conducting a literature review to gain insights on what others have done to solve similar problems and on key contextual factors to consider in designing and implementing the program can reveal important evidence as to whether or not a program approach is correct. All those involved in the process, and particularly the evaluators, should adopt the role of skeptic, repeatedly asking why they should believe that a particular relationship is true, or conversely, why a step in the logic may not happen.

Box 3.3. Tips on Collecting Relevant Information to Build a Logic Model

- Interview people associated with the program, starting with those closely associated with its design and implementation and then moving to others either affected by the program or having a stake in its results. (Evaluators might find the interview guide developed by Gugiu and Rodriguez-Campos, 2007, helpful when facilitating this interviewing.)
- Analyze documents with a small group, perhaps assisted by an independent facilitator, especially for complex, poorly defined programs or where communication and consensus are lacking.
- Stay alert to changes in the context that could influence performance, such as staff turnover, new policies, or changes in the economy.

Stage 2: Clearly Defining the Problem and Its Context

Clearly defining the need for the program is the basis for all that follows in the development of the logic model. The program should be grounded in an understanding of the problem that drives the need for the program. This understanding should be expressed in clear descriptions of the overall problem and any ancillary problems, of who is involved, and of the factors that "cause" the problem. The program will address some or all of these factors to achieve the longer-term goal of solving the problem. (Box 3.4 offers some tips on problem definition.)

For example, there are economic and environmental challenges related to the production, distribution, and end use of energy. U.S. taxpayers face problems such as dependence on foreign oil, air pollution, and the threat of global warming from the burning of fossil fuels. The causal factors that might be addressed to increase the efficiency of the end use of energy include limited knowledge, risk aversion, consumers' budget constraints, lack of competitively priced clean and efficient energy technologies, externalities associated with public goods, and the structure of U.S. electricity markets. To help solve the problem of economic and environmental challenges related to the use of energy, a program would choose to focus on one or more factors related to developing clean and efficient energy technologies and changing customer values and knowledge.

One of the greatest challenges that workgroups developing logic models face is describing where their program ends and others start. For the process of building a specific program's logic model, the program's performance ends with addressing the problem it is designed to solve with the resources it has acquired, with recognition of the external forces that could influence its success in solving that problem. Generally, the manager's concern is determining the reasonable point of accountability for the program. At the point where the actions of customers, partners, or other programs are as influential on the outcomes as the actions of the program are, there is a shared responsibility for the outcomes and the program's accountability for the outcomes should be reduced. For example, the adoption of energy-efficient technologies is also influenced by financiers and by manufacturers of those technologies. Not recognizing these other factors reduces the probability for long-term success.

Box 3.4. Tips on Defining the Problem Addressed by the Program

- Look for what drives the need for the program. Some evaluators put client and customer needs as the first point in the model.
- Define all the major factors that "cause" the problem.
- Define the factors that the program addresses. Factors that "cause" the problem but that aren't addressed by the program are part of the context within which the program operates.
- Determine whether the program can be modified to address or take advantage of the contextual factors identified.
- Identify possible performance partnerships with other programs or organizations whose results affect those of the program.
- If necessary, reflect legislative language, perhaps by adding an additional layer of outcomes.

When defining the problem, it is important to examine the external conditions under which a program is implemented and how those conditions affect outcomes. Such an examination clarifies the program's niche and the assumptions on which performance expectations are set. Understanding program context provides an important contribution to program improvement (Weiss, 1997). Explaining the relationship of the problem addressed through the program, the factors that cause the problem, and external factors should enable the manager to argue that the program is addressing an important problem in a sensible way. Those developing the logic model must not only elicit the key external, or contextual, factors but also develop measures for the most critical of these factors so that these data can be factored into discussions about the program results.

One reason why it is important to recognize contextual factors before the program starts is that the program may be able to do something about them. For example, we once were asked to participate in the evaluation of a preservice teacher training program before it started. When we met with program staff, we began the logic modeling process to get a grasp on how they thought the program might work. One outcome identified was that student teachers would practice technology integration in their practicum sites. We asked if there were any factors that could influence reaching this outcome. Staff members said that participating classroom teachers would have to be skillful in the use of technology. As a result of this interchange, the staff decided to amend their initial logic to include training for classroom teachers who would be working with the preservice teachers.

Many of the problems that programs or organizations address are highly complex, resulting from a number of causal factors. Most programs are uniquely qualified to address a few of these factors, but if the problem is to be solved, then many of these factors must be addressed. We recommend that program staff identify all the factors that need to be addressed and then develop performance partnerships with other programs whose mission is to solve the same problem. Until the performance partnerships are established, all factors that are not under the control of the program fall into the context and may have a negative impact on the program's long-term success. For example, many federal programs depend on state and local programs to carry out policies established at the federal level. One of the performance goals of the U.S. Environmental Protection Agency is to ensure the availability of clean and safe water. This will not happen if states and localities do not develop and enforce guidelines for protecting sources of water.

Stage 3: Defining the Elements of the Program in a Table: Early Sense Making

The purpose of this stage is to uncover all the salient elements of the program. We find it helpful to introduce this stage by comparing it to the first step in completing a puzzle. The first action after opening the box is to dump all the pieces on the table that will make up the puzzle. Then you begin by sorting them into piles of like colors and shapes. The aim is putting the puzzle together but you first have to get an idea of what the pieces look like. This step in building a logic model requires the workgroup to categorize the information collected into "bins," rows, and columns in a table. The manager and other workgroup members review the information and tag each "piece" as a resource, activity, output, short-term outcome, intermediate outcome, long-term outcome, or external factor. Because they are building a model of how the program is intended to work, not every program detail has to be identified and catalogued, just those that are key to enhancing program staff and stakeholder understanding of how the program works.

Just like in puzzle building the modeling team begins to look for relationships between and among the pieces. The group organizes the elements in the table into chains of activities, outputs, and outcomes. (Box 3.5 offers some tips for this process.) An example of a logic model table for a middle school science technology engineering and math (STEM) program is shown in Figure 3.2. In this case the columns display the elements of the logic model and the rows show the program's description of significant program content associated with each element. This is, of course, a simplification of a nonlinear process.

Box 3.5. Tips on Defining the Elements of the Logic Model in a Table

- As you are categorizing elements of the logic model, define the target audiences and expected effects of the program for each.
- Put the outcomes into a sequence.
- Map both forward and backward to develop and check logic and assumptions. Ask questions such as, How do [did] we make this happen? Why do [did] we do this? If this, then that? If that, then what?
- Check for associations with other programs and partners for resources, delivery, or take up.
- Combine and summarize program elements, limiting the number of activity groups to no more than five to seven. These groupings are the program strategies that are expected to lead to results.
- *Avoid* giving the impression that program results occur in a linear process, even though they appear linear in the table format. Showing multiple rows feeding into one outcome and coloring rows to indicate the timing of events are possible ways to do this.

FIGURE 3.2. EXAMPLE OF A LOGIC MODEL TABLE FOR INCREASING THE NUMBER OF QUALIFIED GRADUATES ENTERING STEM CAREERS.

Resources	Activities	Outputs for Customers	Short-Term Outcomes	Intermediate Outcomes	Long-Term Outcomes
Need for increased STEM graduates Evidence-based STEM pedagogy Teachers, scientists, administrators, parents, middle school students Funding from federal and state agencies	Implement professional development for middle school teachers and scientists participating	Trained teachers and scientists	Middle school teachers and scientists have knowledge, skills and values to implement and support new STEM curriculum	Teachers and scientists accurately apply evidenced-based STEM in the classroom and prepare home activities for parents	
	Teachers, scientists conduct orientation sessions for school administrators and parents	School administrators, middle school students' parents complete orientation	Administrators and parents understand their roles in supporting STEM program	Administrators and parents carry out their responsibilities with fidelity	
Technologies	Install middle school STEM program with fidelity	Middle school students take advanced STEM courses, attend camps, clubs	Middle school students improve STEM learning and see value in pursuing a STEM career	Students elect to take advanced STEM courses and opt for STEM career paths in college	The number of STEM college graduates who choose STEM careers increases

External Context: Driving and restraining contextual factors such as state/federal policy, funding priority shifts, available technologies, competing/complementary school programs, need for scientists, changes in school leadership

As the elements of the logic model are being gathered, the manager, evaluator, and workgroup should continually check the accuracy and completeness of the information contained in the table. The checking process is best done by determining whether representatives of key stakeholder groups can understand the logical flow of the program implementation from resources to solving the longer-term problem. Thus, the checking process goes beyond determining if all the key elements have been identified to confirming that, reading from left to right (or top to bottom), there is an obvious sequence or bridge from one column to the next.

One way to conduct the check is to ask *how* and *why* questions. Start with an entry in any column in the table, and ask, in effect, "How did we get here?" For example, select a particular short-term outcome and ask, "Is there an output that leads to this outcome?" Or, ask "Why are we aiming for that outcome?" The answer should lie in a subsequent outcome in the intermediate or long-term outcome column. Ask such questions at any point in the logic model performance spectrum, from inputs or resources to outcomes or results. The process of asking how and why questions is sometimes called *forward and backward mapping.*

Another good way to elicit information from the workgroup is to ask why an outcome might *not* occur, a reverse logic. What are the non-program factors that will prevent success (where what success looks like has been carefully defined)? Sue Funnell (2000) suggests a *logic model matrix* to capture these aspects of the logic. For example, looking at the first row in Figure 3.2 suggests a number of non-program factors that could prevent accomplishing the desired outcomes, factors such as a lack of scientific and technical personnel in the area. If the program manager and workgroup think of a non-program factor that is particularly critical and know of no one else who is addressing that factor, the design of the program and its logic may have to change to address it.

Last, note that at the bottom of the table the workgroup has recorded factors from the implementation context that might have a positive or negative influence on the success of the project. These influences might be found in searching through previous evaluation studies or the professional experiences of the program designers. The contextual factors are identified throughout the modeling process by asking, "What else must happen to enable this event to occur?" If those factors are not included in the program then they become part of the context and the evaluation should examine the extent to which they actually influenced to program success. Finally, contextual factors can become an influence at any point along the program's performance spectrum.

Stage 4: Drawing the Logic Model to Reveal the Program's Theory of Change

The logic model captures the logical flow and linkages that exist in any performance story uncovering the hypothesized theory of change. Using the program elements in the table, the logic model further organizes that information, enabling an audience to better understand and evaluate the hypothesized linkages. Whereas resources, activities, and outcomes are listed in separate columns in the table, they are specifically linked in the model, so that an audience can see exactly which activities lead to what intermediate outcomes and which intermediate outcomes lead to what longer-term outcomes, or impacts. Remember that this graphic depiction is only a picture of how the program is supposed to work given its implementation context. The text associated with the model will describe the program theory and rationale for believing that certain elements go together in a certain way. The text should not only describe experiences but should relay relevant previous research and evaluation studies.

There are several ways to present a logic model, but usually it is set forth as a diagram with columns and rows of boxes containing abbreviated descriptions and causal linkages shown with connecting one-way arrows. We place program inputs or resources in the far left-hand column and the long-term outcomes and problem to be solved in the far right-hand column. The boxes in the second column show the major program activities. In the subsequent columns the intended outputs and outcomes from each activity are shown, and these boxes may also list the intended customer for each output or outcome. Another common format displays the logic top to bottom rather than left to right, usually with resources and activities at the top and the goals at the bottom of the model.

An example of a logic model for a middle school STEM program is depicted in Figure 3.3. Two levels of the same logic are shown in Figure 3.3: a very high level in the single line at the top, and below that a more detailed version showing the relationship of multiple program elements in a Z-shaped pattern, where one set of activities and outcomes leads to another. The rows are created according to activities or activity groupings. If there is a rough sequential order to the activities, as there is when the accomplishments of the program come in stages, the rows, reading from the top to bottom of the diagram, will reflect that order. When the outcomes from one activity serve as a resource for another activity chain, an arrow is drawn from those outcomes to that activity chain. The arrows represent the expected causal relationship between the program elements. The last in the sequence of activity chains identifies the efforts of participating students to gain STEM-related knowledge, skills, and values leading to developing an increased inclination to follow a STEM career path resulting in an increase in the probability of more STEM professionals available for the workforce.

Rather than using a sequence of activities, a program could take a multifaceted approach, using several concurrent strategies to tackle a problem. The arrangement of the boxes in the model would reflect that. For example, a program might prepare teachers scientists, administrators and parents concurrently and then implement the school/home-based program once the partnership has been established. Although the example in Figure 3.3 shows one-to-one relationships among program elements, this is not always the case. It may be that one program element leads to more than one outcome, all of which are of interest to stakeholders and are part of describing the value of the program. For example, the United Way might have identified infant mortality as a critical problem that needs to be addressed. One of its partners, a school system, discovers that several teenagers in a school are pregnant, and an after-school program is designed to address the needs of these students.

FIGURE 3.3. A Z LOGIC MODEL FOR INCREASING THE NUMBER OF QUALIFIED GRADUATES ENTERING STEM CAREERS, AT TWO LEVELS OF DETAIL.

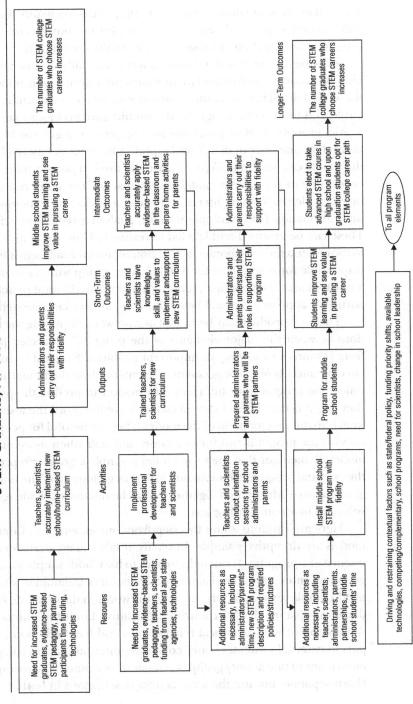

The outcomes of the program are increasing the participants' knowledge and skills related to prenatal health and caring for newborns. The impact of the program is a reduction in infant mortality in the community.

Activities can be described at many levels of detail. Because models are simplifications, activities that lead to the same outcome may be grouped to capture the level of detail necessary for a particular audience. As mentioned previously, a rule of thumb is that a logic model should have no more than five to seven activity groupings. Most programs are complex enough that logic models at more than one level of detail are helpful. A logic model more elaborate than the simple one shown in Figure 3.1 can be used to portray more detail for all or any one of the simple model's elements. For example, research activities may include performing literature reviews, conducting experiments, collecting information from multiple sources, analyzing data, and writing reports. These can be grouped and labeled as research. However, it may be necessary to formulate a more elaborate description of research sub activities for the staff responsible for research or for a stakeholder group with a specific interest in a research area. For example, funding agencies might want to understand the particular approach that will be employed to answer key research questions.

The final product may be viewed as a network displaying the interconnections between the major elements of the program's expected performance, from resources to solving an important problem. External factors that influence the success of the program may be entered into the model at the bottom, unless the program has sufficient information to predict the point at which they might occur. These external factors serve to record the assumptions that went into the development of the model. They are helpful for people not familiar with the program and for evaluators and staff when using or revising the model. Remember that the logic model is simply a graphic representation of the essential program elements and how they go together. The underlying program theory—why they go together—must be discussed, challenged, and then recorded in accompanying text.

Here are cautions about this step from our experience. Completed logic models are deceptively simple. In reality, it takes many drafts to describe the essence of a program. It can help to plan to have both simple forms of the diagram and more complex diagrams. Stakeholders unfamiliar with a program need a simple version. In this one, limit the words in the diagram. Provide more detail in separate charts or a written narrative. Limit the number of arrows, showing only the most critical relationships and feedback loops. Include outputs to external customers only, collapsing internal outputs such as management plans to one activity group or a separate document. Leave organizational charts separate, but use the same activity descriptions in both. In addition to this simple diagram, consider having more than one model with different levels of detail, different groups of activities, different levels at which performance could be measured, different stakeholder views, and different theories. Whatever the level of detail, avoid even the appearance that this logic model is set in stone by dating the model and including the *current external influences* on the same page.

The process of physically creating the logic model diagram, whatever tool is used, helps focus and organize. PowerPoint is frequently used, even though it is not as automatic as some of the newer tools. Every box and arrow in a model has to be copied from an earlier model or created by selecting a rectangular shape and creating a box of appropriate size. Ideally, the text within the rectangle, again entered with a text box, will display in at least a 10-point font. Other options are just to use a text box with black line selected or a rectangle filled with the allowed text, but these options make it harder to have boxes of a consistent size. Keep words to a minimum within boxes, and group activities into a small number so everything fits on one page. A draft may employ a smaller font and more numerous boxes until thinking is streamlined. Detail can also be moved to separate logic models that look in more depth at one or more aspects of the higher-level logic. Other than with symbols or words, there is no easy way to link models together in a nested fashion in PowerPoint. (Box 3.6 provides tips on tools for developing a logic model diagram.)

Box 3.6. Tools for Drawing Logic Models

- PowerPoint is simple to use and it has the advantage that workgroup members can take ownership of the diagrams.
- Inspiration is inexpensive, easy-to-learn, mind-mapping software that automatically generates arrows and new boxes and also has a feature through which each box can be linked to a nested, expanded logic.
- Flow Charting 6 is similar to Inspiration. These more sophisticated diagrams are easily exported into word processing software such as Microsoft Word. The downside is that to modify the diagram a person would have to have access to or purchase the modeling software.
- More sophisticated drawing tools such as SmartDraw are also available and have features beyond those already discussed here, including the ability to draw very large models that can hang on a wall, but there is a steep learning curve.
- *Easy Outcomes*, available from OutcomesModels.org [www.outcomesmodels.org] is a user-friendly and free version of a more formal approach (systematic outcomes analysis). It can be implemented with DoView software which can be used to build linked models that project well for group work.

Stage 5: Verifying the Program Logic Model with Stakeholders

As the logic model process unfolds, the workgroup responsible for producing the model should continuously evaluate it with respect to the overall goal of representing the program logic—how the program works under what conditions to achieve its short-term, intermediate, and long-term aims. The verification process should engage the appropriate stakeholders in the review process. The workgroup will use the logic model diagram and the supporting table and text. During this time, the workgroup also can address the information needed about performance, setting the stage for performance measurement and evaluation plans.

In addition to why and how questions, we recommend that three measurement and evaluation design questions be addressed in the final verification process:

- Is the program logic theoretically sound? Do all the elements fit together logically? Are there other plausible pathways to achieving the program outcomes?
- Have all the key external contextual factors been identified and their potential influences described?
- Does the program logic suggest the performance measures and major evaluation questions that must be covered?

In our experience, the exercise of defining performance measures makes a draft logic model more concrete to staff and stakeholders and often uncovers elements or relationships that have been missed. Having a logic model in place at the beginning of performance measurement and evaluation is important because it serves as an advance organizer or focusing mechanism for the measurement of key variables and for the evaluation of assumed causal relationships. As noted elsewhere in this volume, performance measurement describes *levels of performance* in relation to some standard and is typically a univariate measure, whereas program evaluation enables the explanation of why certain levels of performance were observed and is thus multivariate, using a number of performance measures to support the explanation. Logic modeling enables the identification of useful performance measures and sets up a pattern for putting them together to test underlying assumptions.

Evaluation should examine or test the underlying assumptions about how the program works to achieve intended outcomes. Weiss (1997), citing her earlier work, noted the importance of not only capturing the program process but also collecting information on the hypothesized linkages. According to Weiss, measurement should "track the steps of the program." Cooksy, Gill, and Kelly (2001) show how logic modeling can be used to focus data collection, organize data for analysis, and guide the interpretation of findings. In the logical model, boxes are the steps that can simply be counted or monitored, and the lines connecting the boxes are the hypothesized linkages or causal relationships that require in-depth study to determine and explain what happened. It is the testing of the linkages, the arrows in the logic chart, that allows the evaluator to determine whether the program is working. Monitoring the degree to which elements are in place, even the intended and unintended outcomes, will not explain the measurements or tell the evaluator if the program is working. It is essential to test the program hypotheses through impact evaluation. Even if the evaluator observes that intended outcomes were achieved, the following question must be asked: What features, if any, of the program contributed to the achievement of intended and unintended outcomes?

Special note should be made here about the relationship of the Z model to performance measurement. As noted previously and presented in Figure 3.3, the Z model describes the elements of the program's system and their interdependence. If one link in the system fails, then the end goal will not be achieved. Therefore, when the evaluator encounters a program in which there are interlocking parts, we recommend that linkage measures be developed to assess the degree to which the dependencies are operating effectively, that is, the degree to which the parts of the Z fit together functionally. In this way the Z model serves as a focusing mechanism for performance measurement and evaluation.

An example of linking performance measurement and evaluation to program logic is set forth in Figure 3.4. The linkage is developed after stage 5 in the logic model development process. The program described in Figure 3.4 is designed to increase middle school students' interest in selecting a career in science, technology, engineering, or mathematics (STEM). The underlying assumptions for the program were that if scientists and teachers collaborated in the delivery of eighth-grade science materials using problem-based challenges in cooperative learning groups and if they talked to students about how such exercises mirrored what scientists do in real life, then students would develop a more positive attitude toward school and a science career, resulting in their taking advanced math classes in high school and pursuing a science career.

Note that in this model, questions are directed at the program structure as well as the outcome structure. Further, questions are aimed at specific elements of the logic model in the program and outcome structures. The diagram also reveals that the evaluation should address potential contextual factors that might influence either the program implementation fidelity or the expected

FIGURE 3.4. SAMPLE LOGIC MODEL WITH PERFORMANCE MEASUREMENT AND EVALUATION FOCUS: MIDDLE SCHOOL STEM PROGRAM.

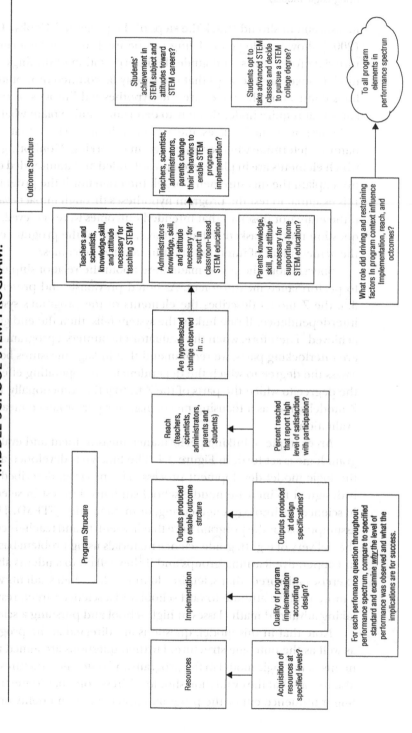

outcomes. This logic model was used to gain agreement among project staff and other key stakeholders about what would be studied throughout the program implementation, and then used this information for analyses. Remember, the first question seeks to assess levels of performance with respect to a particular program or outcome element. Next, the evaluator asks *why* a particular level of program performance was observed. The answer to the why question comes from a multivariate examination using program performance *and* context measures. Without answers to the why questions the program staff cannot make accurate decisions regarding necessary mid-course corrections in the program to enhance success. Further, the why question results enable staff and managers to communicate more confidently with external audiences regarding program performance. Having the logic model helps focus performance measurement and evaluation strategies and the use of findings.

A logic model is dynamic, so even after the evaluator, manager, and staff agree on the logic and the evaluation questions and data collection strategies are developed the process of verification continues. The logic model is a draft document that captures the program staff's or other stakeholders' concept of how the program works at a point in time. In fact, the program may not work that way at all. Thus the evaluator needs to test the logic model, developing what Patton (2008) has called the *theory in practice*. If discrepancies are found, the evaluator, manager, and program staff should discuss the ramifications of the discrepancies and either redesign the program or increase implementation fidelity to enhance the chance for success.

Stufflebeam (2001) noted that for many programs it will be very difficult to establish a defensible theory of change either because existing social science research has not produced sufficient evidence to support theory development or there is insufficient time to develop the theory. He argues, as we do, that logic modeling is appropriate as long as not too much time is taken for it and as long as the evaluator understands that the model is a draft that needs to be assessed in reality.

Yin (1989) discusses the importance of pattern matching as a tool to study the delivery and impact of a program. The use of the logic model process results in a pattern that can be used in this way. It thus becomes a tool to assess program implementation and program impacts. An iterative procedure may be applied that, first, determines the theory in practice and then moves on to either revision of the espoused theory or tightening of the implementation of the espoused theory. Next, the revised pattern can be used to address the extent to which the program yields desired outcomes and impacts and also the influence of context.

Conclusion

Program managers across the public and nonprofit sectors are being asked to describe and evaluate their programs in new ways. People want managers to present a logical argument for how and why a particular program is addressing a specific problem and how measurement and evaluation will assess and improve program effectiveness. Managers do not typically have clear and logically consistent methods to help them with this task, but evaluators do, and they can bring this tool to managers and help them meet the new challenges.

This chapter has presented the logic modeling process in enough detail that both evaluators and program managers and staff can use it to develop and tell the performance story for their program. The logic model describes the logical linkages among program resources, activities, outputs for customers reached, and short-term, intermediate, and long-term outcomes. Once this model of expected performance is produced, critical monitoring and evaluation areas can be identified. Because the logic model and the measurement plan have been developed with the program stakeholders, the story these tools tell should be a shared vision with a clear and shared expectation of success. Last, we must reiterate that we believe that while it is important for the evaluation to address the question of program results, it is equally important to focus the evaluation efforts on program implementation and early outcomes so the managers and staff know what's working and not working and where necessary make informed mid-course corrections to enhance the probability of longer-term success. The logic modeling process makes this possible.

References

Bickman, L. "The Functions of Program Theory." In L. Bickman (ed.), *Using Program Theory in Evaluation*. New Directions for Evaluation, no. 33. San Francisco: Jossey-Bass, 1987.

Centers for Disease Control and Prevention. *Logic Model*. www.cdc.gov/nccdphp/dnpao/hwi/programdesign/logic_model.htm, 2010.

Cooksy, L. J., Gill, O., and Kelly, P. A. "The Program Logic Model as an Integrative Framework for a Multimethod Evaluation." *Evaluation and Program Planning*, 2001, *24*, 119–128.

Gugiu, P. C., and Rodriguez-Campos, L. "Semi-Structured Interview Protocol for Constructing Logic Models." *Evaluation and Program Planning*, 2007, *30*(4), 339–350.

Frechtling, J. *Logic Modeling Methods in Program Evaluation*. San Francisco: Jossey-Bass, 2007.

Funnell, S. "Developing and Using a Program Theory Matrix for Program Evaluation and Performance Monitoring." In P. Rogers, T. Hacsi, A. Petrosino, and. T. Huebner (eds.),

Program Theory in Evaluation: Challenges and Opportunities. New Directions for Evaluation, no. 87. San Francisco: Jossey-Bass, 2000.

Funnell, Sue C., and Patricia J. Rogers. *Purposeful Program Theory: Effective Use of Theories of Change and Logic Models.* Vol. 31. Hoboken, NJ: John Wiley & Sons, 2011.

Harrell, A., Burt, M. R., Hatry, H. P., Rossman, S. B., and Roth, J. A. *Evaluation Strategies for Human Services Programs: A Guide for Policymakers and Providers.* Washington, DC: Urban Institute, 1996.

Knowlton, L. W., and Phillips, C. C. *The Logic Model Guidebook: Better Strategies for Great Results.* Thousand Oaks, CA: Sage, 2008, and Second Edition 2013.

Leeuw, F. L. "Restructuring Program Theories: Methods Available and Problems to Be Solved." *American Journal of Evaluation,* 2003, *24*(1), 5–20.

Mayne, J., and Stern, E. *Impact Evaluation of Natural Resource Management Research Programs: A Broader View.* ACIAR Impact Assessment Series Report. 2013, aciar.gov.au/files/ias84.pdf.

McLaughlin, J. A., and Jordan, G. B. "Logic Models: A Tool for Telling Your Performance Story." *Evaluation and Program Planning,* 1999, *22*(1), 65–72.

McLaughlin, J. A., and Jordan, G. B. "Logic Models." In J. S. Wholey, H. P. Hatry, and K. E. Newcomer (eds.), *Handbook of Practical Program Evaluation* (2nd ed.). San Francisco: Jossey-Bass, 2004.

Patton, M. Q. *Utilization-Focused Evaluation* (4th ed.). Thousand Oaks, CA: Sage, 2008.

Stufflebeam, D. L. "Evaluation Models." In D. L. Stufflebeam (ed.), *Evaluation Models.* New Directions for Evaluation, no. 89. San Francisco: Jossey-Bass, 2001.

Taylor-Powell, E., and Henert, E. *Developing a Logic Model: Teaching and Training Guide.* www.uwex.edu/ces/pdande/evaluation/pdf/lmguidecomplete.pdf. 2008.

W. K. Kellogg Foundation. *Logic Model Development Guide.* www.wkkf.org/resource-directory/resource/2006/02/wk-kellogg-foundation-logic-model-development-guide, 2005.

Weiss, C. "Theory-Based Evaluation: Past, Present, and Future." In D. Rog and D. Founier (eds.), *Progress and Future Directions in Evaluation: Perspectives on Theory, Practice, and Methods.* New Directions for Evaluation, no. 76. San Francisco: Jossey-Bass, 1997.

Wholey, J. S. "Evaluability Assessment: Developing Program Theory." In L. Bickman (ed.), *Using Program Theory in Evaluation.* New Directions for Evaluation, no. 33. San Francisco: Jossey-Bass, 1987.

Yin, R. K. *Case Study Research: Design and Methods.* Thousand Oaks, CA: Sage, 1989.

CHAPTER FOUR

EXPLORATORY EVALUATION

Joseph S. Wholey

Policy and management environments are typically complex, and program goals and strategies are often poorly defined both in government and in the nonprofit sector. In many cases, there is disagreement over which resources and activities are part of the program to be evaluated and which are part of the context in which the program operates. Given these realities, evaluators often find it difficult to determine the appropriate focus for their work, evaluations often fall short of their designs, and completed evaluations often sit on the shelf. Therefore, rather than proceed directly to the design of an evaluation, it is often helpful first to conduct a rapid, low-cost *exploratory evaluation* that will produce evaluation findings and help evaluators and others to identify priorities for further evaluation work and ensure the feasibility and usefulness of further evaluation.

This chapter describes evaluability assessment, rapid feedback evaluation, and two other exploratory evaluation approaches. Each of these approaches produces evaluation findings while helping to focus future evaluations. All of these approaches can be accomplished relatively quickly, and each approach enhances the likelihood that further evaluation will prove to be feasible, accurate, and useful.

Evaluability assessment (EA), which is given the most extensive treatment here, assesses the extent to which programs are ready for future evaluation and helps key stakeholders come to agreement on realistic program goals, evaluation criteria, and intended uses of evaluation information.

Rapid feedback evaluation (RFE) is an extension of EA that begins only after there is agreement on the goals (including goals for assessing, controlling, or enhancing important side effects) in terms of which a program is to be evaluated. RFE then uses evaluation synthesis, small-sample studies, program data, site visits, and discussions with knowledgeable observers to (1) estimate program effectiveness and indicate the range of uncertainty in the estimates, (2) produce tested designs for more definitive evaluation, and (3) further clarify intended uses of evaluation. EA and RFE are the first two steps in a *sequential purchase of information* process in which resources are invested in further evaluation only when the likely usefulness of the new information outweighs the costs of acquiring it. Though EA is well documented in the literature, RFE is not, and readers should note that RFE is different from other common forms of rapid assessment. Program evaluation takes time but policymakers, executives, managers, and other stakeholders often cannot—or will not—wait. Most budget projections are done on the basis of quick but unsystematic assessments. Auditors perform rapid assessments that typically focus on whether program activities are in accordance with legislation or regulations. Though these and other rapid assessments may have some of the characteristics of rapid feedback evaluation as the term is defined here, their goal is *not* to set the stage for further evaluation. Rapid feedback evaluation goes beyond such assessments by producing additional products; in particular, designs for further evaluation work.

Evaluation synthesis summarizes what is known about program effectiveness on the basis of all relevant research and evaluation studies.

Small-sample studies, as this chapter defines them, begin only after there is agreement on the goals in terms of which a program is to be evaluated. Before proceeding to evaluation of a program, evaluators are advised to verify that proposed performance measures will work by testing them. Small-sample studies use samples larger than those typically used in testing data collection instruments to (1) test the performance measures that are to be used in either a performance measurement system or an evaluation study and (2) produce initial evaluation findings in terms of those measures.

Table 4.1 identifies the purposes of these four exploratory evaluation approaches and provides rough estimates of the cost of each approach in terms of calendar time and staff time. Each approach can be used to increase transparency and accountability, to improve program management and program performance, and to support resource allocation and other policy decision making; each approach helps evaluators to focus further evaluation work. In times when evaluation resources are limited, it is important for evaluators to understand these rapid, low-cost evaluation methods.

TABLE 4.1. PURPOSE AND COST OF FOUR EXPLORATORY EVALUATION APPROACHES.

Approach	Purpose	Cost in Time
Evaluability assessment	Assess whether programs are ready for useful evaluation; get agreement on program goals and evaluation criteria; clarify the focus and intended use of further evaluation.	1 to 6 months; 2 staff-weeks to 3 staff-months
Rapid feedback evaluation	Estimate program effectiveness in terms of agreed-on program goals; indicate the range of uncertainty in the estimates; produce tested designs for more definitive evaluation; clarify the focus and intended use of further evaluation.	3 to 6 months; 3 to 12 staff-months
Evaluation synthesis	Synthesize findings of prior research and evaluation studies.	1 to 4 months; 1 to 3 staff-months
Small-sample studies	Estimate program effectiveness in terms of agreed-on program goals; produce tested measures of program performance.	1 week to 6 months; 1 staff-week to 12 staff-months

Evaluability Assessment Assesses a Program's Readiness for Evaluation

Evaluability assessment answers the question of whether a program is ready for useful evaluation, not whether the program can be evaluated (any program can be evaluated). Research has shown that evaluation is likely to be useful only if four standards (also listed in Box 4.1) are met: (1) *program goals are agreed on and realistic*: there is a reasonable level of agreement on the goals in terms of which the program is to be evaluated, and important side effects have been addressed through goals for assessing, controlling, or enhancing those side effects. Program goals are realistic given the resources committed to the program and the program activities under way: there is some likelihood that the program goals will be achieved; (2) *information needs are well defined*: there is agreement on the input, process, output, and outcome goals that should be the focus of evaluation, and there is agreement on the intended use of the resulting information; (3) *evaluation data are obtainable*: there are feasible quantitative or qualitative measures of key program inputs, activities, outputs (products or services delivered to intended recipients), and outcomes (results); and (4) *intended users are willing and able to use evaluation information*: for example, to enhance transparency and accountability, to improve program quality, or to communicate the value of the program to policymaking levels. Evaluability assessment clarifies program designs and if necessary helps managers and policymakers to redesign programs so that they meet these four evaluability standards. A program is "evaluable" to the extent that these four standards are met (see Horst, Nay, Scanlon, and Wholey, 1974; Wholey, 1979, 1983, 2004).

Box 4.1. Evaluability Standards: Readiness for Useful Evaluation

- Program goals are agreed on and realistic.
- Information needs are well defined.
- Evaluation data are obtainable.
- Intended users are willing and able to use evaluation information.

Evaluability assessment compares and contrasts the expectations of key stakeholders with the reality of the program activities under way and the outputs and outcomes that are occurring. It assesses the demand for evaluation information and the feasibility of meeting that demand at reasonable cost. EA may be either a separate process or the initial step in a larger evaluation.

Evaluability assessment is most useful in large, decentralized programs in which policymaking and management responsibilities are dispersed, program results are not readily apparent, and evaluation criteria are unclear (see Strosberg and Wholey, 1983). If there already is agreement on the goals and criteria in terms of which a program is to be evaluated, EA may not be appropriate.

The Evaluability Assessment Process

Evaluability assessment is a six-step process: (1) *involve intended users and other key stakeholders;* (2) *clarify the program design* (program inputs; intended program activities and outputs; intended short-term, intermediate, and long-term outcomes; and assumed causal linkages among inputs, activities, outputs, and outcomes); (3) *explore program reality;* (4) *assess the plausibility of the program* (the likelihood that program activities will lead to intended outputs and outcomes); (5) *reach agreement on any needed changes in program design or in program implementation;* and (6) *reach agreement on the focus and intended use of any further evaluation.* Although the steps need not be completed in this order and some have advocated placing step 3 before step 2, each of the six steps helps ensure that any further evaluation work will be relevant, feasible, and useful. It is often helpful to perform all six of these steps early in the evaluation assessment and then redo portions of the assessment as often as necessary to achieve well-informed decisions on evaluation priorities and, when appropriate, decisions on any needed changes in program design or implementation. Each iteration allows the evaluator to provide new information and to get a better sense of which options for further evaluation will be most useful. Evaluability assessment should not be prolonged, however.

Step 1: Involve Intended Users and Other Key Stakeholders. The evaluators first review relevant program documentation: authorizing legislation, regulations and guidelines, grant applications, budget justifications, research and evaluation studies, monitoring and audit reports, and reports of program accomplishments. The evaluators then meet with a small number of policymakers, managers, and other stakeholders to identify those likely to be most closely involved in the evaluability assessment. Key policymakers, managers, and stakeholders are briefed or otherwise kept informed as the evaluability assessment proceeds.

Step 2: Clarify the Program Design. Both at headquarters and in the field, the evaluators interview small numbers of policymakers, managers, those involved in service delivery, and other key stakeholders in order to clarify their expectations, concerns, and information priorities (see Boxes 4.2 and 4.3). In their review of program documentation and in the interviews, the evaluators explore various perspectives on program design, performance, results to date, results expected in the next year or two, problems that inhibit effective performance, and uses and intended uses of information that is available or desired. The evaluators thus identify key program inputs (including important contextual factors); intended program activities and outputs (products and services to be delivered to intended recipients); intended short-term, intermediate, and long-term outcomes (including important potential side-effects to be minimized, controlled, or enhanced); and assumed causal linkages among inputs, activities, outputs, and outcomes—thus clarifying the program design (the intended program) from the perspectives of policymakers, managers, and other key stakeholders. (Agreement with intended users on key intermediate outcomes is important in the design of evaluations both for policy use and for management use.)

Using the program documentation and information from these interviews and meetings, evaluators typically develop program *logic models*: flowcharts that identify key program inputs, intended program activities and outputs, intended outcomes, and assumed causal linkages among inputs, activities, outputs, and outcomes, as seen by policymakers, managers, those involved in service delivery, and other program stakeholders (see Figures 3.1 and 3.3 in Chapter Three). The evaluators may develop more than one logic model if there are important differences in key stakeholders' perspectives or in the levels of detail appropriate for various stakeholders. The evaluators may also develop *tables of performance indicators* that list program inputs, intended program activities and outputs, and intended outcomes; identify the types of data that would indicate the occurrence of those activities, outputs, and outcomes; indicate potential data sources; and thus help clarify and get agreement on the meanings of terms that appear in the logic models. Evaluators now brief key policymakers, managers, and other key stakeholders on the extent to which there is agreement on the program design and help to get agreement with intended users on the program design; in particular, evaluators seek agreement on intermediate outcomes, which connect program activities to end results and often are the focus of useful evaluation.

Box 4.2. Guide for Review of Documentation and Interviews with Policymakers, Managers, and Other Key Stakeholders

- From your perspective, what is the program trying to accomplish, and what resources does it have?
- What results have been produced to date?
- What results are likely in the next year or two?
- Why would the program produce those results?
- What are the program's main problems? How long will it take to solve those problems?
- What kinds of information do you get on the program's performance and results?
- What kinds of information do you need?
- How do you (how would you) use this information?
- What kinds of program performance information are requested by key stakeholders?

Step 3: Explore Program Reality. Although program reality is complex, the portion of a program that can usefully be evaluated may be relatively simple, especially when evaluation resources are limited.

In this step evaluators compare the program design (the intended program) with actual program inputs, activities, outputs, and outcomes; identify feasible performance measures; and identify problems inhibiting effective program performance. Evaluators typically use three information sources: existing documentation (from program data systems, project reports, monitoring and audit reports, research reports, and evaluation studies); a small number of site visits or telephone interviews; and discussions with knowledgeable observers, including those involved in service delivery. Here the evaluators explore the issues identified in Box 4.3. Using information from all three sources, the evaluators now identify a list of problems that inhibit effective program performance: for example, insufficient resources devoted to key program activities, unrealistic schedules, intended program activities not yet under way, program activities not producing intended outputs, or contextual factors that minimize the likelihood that program activities will lead to intended outcomes.

Box 4.3. Guide for Review of Documentation and Interviews with Operating-Level Managers and Staff

- What are your goals for the project or program?
- What are the major project activities?
- Why will those activities achieve those goals?
- What resources are available to the project? Number of staff? Total budget? Sources of funds?
- What outputs are being delivered by the project? To whom?
- What evidence is necessary to determine whether goals are met?
- What happens if goals are met? What happens if they are not met?
- How is the project related to local priorities?
- What data or records are maintained? Costs? Services delivered? Service quality? Outcomes? Something else?
- How often are these data collected?
- How is this information used? Does anything change based on these data or records?
- What major problems are you experiencing? How long will it take to solve those problems?
- What results have been produced to date?
- What results are likely in the next two to three years?

Step 4: Assess the Plausibility of the Program. With what has been learned in steps 1 to 3, the evaluator now may be able to make rough estimates of the likelihood that intended outputs (products or services) will be delivered to intended recipients and the likelihood that intended outcomes will occur—thus producing a preliminary evaluation of program effectiveness. Examination of program reality may show that the actual program is far from the inputs, activities, outputs, and outcomes envisioned by program managers or those at policymaking levels.

Step 5: Reach Agreement on Any Needed Changes in Program Design or in Program Implementation. With the information from the work in steps 1 to 4 in hand, the evaluators now work with intended users of evaluation information to explore what has been learned to date and what steps should be taken. At a minimum, evaluators should now be able to achieve more informed agreement—between themselves and primary intended users of evaluation— on what constitutes the design of the program to be evaluated: key program inputs (including important contextual factors), intended program activities and outputs, intended short-term, intermediate, and long-term outcomes (including any important side effects to be minimized or controlled), and assumed causal linkages among inputs, activities, outputs, and outcomes.

The evaluators may already have learned, moreover, that insufficient resources have been allocated for effective program performance, that the intended program has been poorly implemented, or that current program activities will not achieve intended outcomes. If the evaluability assessment has shown that key intended outcomes are unlikely to occur given the level of resources allocated to the program, the way the program is currently being operated, or the contextual factors at work, the evaluators may now be able to help managers and policymakers to agree on changes in program activities designed to achieve improved outcomes—or to agree to drop intended outcomes that appear unrealistic at current or likely resource levels.

Step 6: Reach Agreement on Evaluation Focus and Intended Use. The evaluators now determine a set of *evaluation options*. Each of these options identifies (1) the data that would be collected on specific program inputs, activities, outputs, and outcomes; (2) the data analyses that would be undertaken; (3) the estimated costs of data collection, data analysis, and dissemination of evaluation information (dollar costs; calendar time; political and bureaucratic costs; and the time of evaluation staff, program managers and staff, people involved in service delivery, and people served by the program); and (4) the ways in which the resulting evaluation information would be used: for example, in making changes in program activities in order to improve performance or in communicating the value of the program to policymaking levels in efforts to maintain or increase program resources. By including and explaining the implications of a "status quo" option (no further evaluation) and the costs and potential uses of other evaluation options, the evaluator encourages policymakers, managers, or other stakeholders to commit themselves to using the evaluation information at the time that they commit themselves to any further evaluation. When policymakers, managers, or other stakeholders select one or more of these evaluation options, they are at least tentatively agreeing

EXHIBIT 4.1. EVALUABILITY ASSESSMENT OF THE TRUST FOR AMERICA'S HEALTH.

The Trust for America's Health (TFAH) is a nonprofit organization that aims to raise awareness on public health issues, help secure better funding for public health agencies and activities, and strengthen the accountability of public health agencies for their uses of public funds.

In approximately thirty staff-days over a five-month period in 2008, three Urban Institute (UI) staff members used evaluability assessment in designing an evaluation of TFAH (under a $35,000 contract with the Robert Wood Johnson Foundation [RWJ], the principal TFAH sponsor and funder). UI evaluators reviewed four TFAH strategic policy reports, ten issue reports and briefs, four annual reports, and nine other TFAH documents; and interviewed five RWJ staff members, five TFAH managers, and nine other key informants. The evaluators then developed a TFAH logic model and a list of illustrative intermediate outcomes sought by TFAH.

The evaluators examined actual TFAH resources, program activities, and outputs; analyzed the plausibility of the program; reached agreement with RWJ on what constitutes the TFAH program design; reached agreement with RWJ on the focus and intended use of evaluation; and presented recommendations to RWJ for in-depth evaluation that would, in particular, examine progress toward three of the intended outcomes of the TFAH efforts: the extent to which the organization has succeeded in having key recommendations implemented; the extent to which TFAH has become a "go-to" organization for information and policy input; and the extent to which the media trust and use TFAH reports and other materials. The recommended in-depth evaluation also included conducting a case study of TFAH's overall advocacy approach, monitoring elements of specific activities, assessing the quality of specific reports, and documenting the extent to which TFAH provides estimates of the cost of implementing its recommendations. The evaluators estimated that the full evaluation would cost approximately $500,000.

RWJ accepted the evaluability assessment recommendations, decided to proceed with in-depth evaluation as recommended, and awarded a follow-on contract to UI for the in-depth evaluation.

on intended use of the evaluation information that would be produced. Exhibit 4.1 describes an evaluability assessment of the Trust for America's Health, a nonprofit organization funded by the Robert Wood Johnson Foundation (see Hatry, Bovbjerg, and Morley, 2008).

Issues, Problems, and Potential Solutions

This section identifies issues and problems that may arise in performing an evaluability assessment and suggests solutions based on experience with EA.

Holding the support of key stakeholders. To hold the support of key stakeholders and get needed feedback, evaluators should use briefings to present preliminary evaluability assessment products such as the perspectives of policymakers, managers, people involved in service delivery, and other key stakeholders; findings from site visits; options for changes in program activities to improve performance; and options for further evaluation.

Gaining agreement on evaluation focus and intended use. The most important step in evaluability assessment is getting at least implicit agreement on the input, process, output, and outcome goals that will be the focus of future evaluation, and agreement on how the resulting information will be used. To secure the necessary agreements, evaluators should provide preliminary EA products as suggested above; brief managers, policymakers, and other key stakeholders on EA findings and options for future evaluation; get intended users' views on the evaluation options; and provide the additional information needed to clarify the EA findings and prepare for implementation of the highest-priority evaluation options.

Documenting policy and management decisions. Evaluators should conclude each phase of an evaluability assessment with a brief memorandum documenting significant decisions made in meetings with managers, policymakers, and other key stakeholders; decisions on any changes to be made in program design or program implementation; decisions on the input, process, output, and outcome goals on which further evaluation will focus; and decisions on intended use of the resulting evaluation information.

Controlling evaluability assessment costs. In the most effective evaluability assessments, evaluators keep moving through all six steps in the EA, emphasize the spirit of EA, and—to the extent possible—communicate the information required for decision making through briefings rather than written reports. Focusing on the essentials makes the assessment more efficient and thus controls its costs.

Significance

In typical programs, there is no "right" set of performance measures. Managers cannot manage their programs for results, however, unless they can get agreement on realistic, measurable goals. Useful evaluation is seldom feasible unless the intended users of the evaluation are willing and able to clarify program goals and high-priority information needs. Evaluability assessment provides a way of screening programs to determine whether there is sufficient clarity and definition to make it likely that evaluation will be useful. EA helps managers, policymakers, and other key stakeholders to agree on realistic, measurable program goals by (1) bringing together information on the expectations, priorities, and information needs of policymakers, managers, and other key stakeholders; (2) suggesting potential performance indicators; and (3) providing informed estimates of the likelihood that various program goals will be achieved. Evaluators can then (4) help intended evaluation users to come to agreement on the program goals (in particular, the intermediate outcome goals) in terms of which the program is to be evaluated; identify priority information needs; and identify intended uses of evaluation information. In what can be thought of as a *program repair shop*, evaluators assess program designs in terms of the evaluability standards (Box 4.1) and then help managers, staff, and other stakeholders to redesign programs to meet those standards.

Rapid Feedback Evaluation Produces Tested Evaluation Designs

By definition, rapid feedback evaluation begins only after there is agreement on the goals (including goals for assessing, controlling, or enhancing important side effects) in terms of which a program is to be evaluated. Given intended users' agreement on those goals, either from evaluability assessment or some other process, rapid feedback evaluation synthesizes existing and new information on program performance in terms of those goals, produces an evaluation of program effectiveness that includes pilot-testing of data collection and analysis schemes that could be used in future evaluation work, indicates the extent of uncertainty in the estimates, and produces one or more tested options for more definitive evaluation—either through performance measurement systems or evaluation studies.

RFE provides policymakers, managers, and other stakeholders with two products: (1) an evaluation of program performance in terms of the goals to be used in future evaluation work, together with an indication of the extent of uncertainty in the estimates, and (2) a set of *evaluation options* specifying the data that would be collected; the sources of those data; the data collection instruments that would be used; sample sizes; techniques that would be used to analyze the data; quality control procedures; work plans and schedules for data collection, data analysis, and dissemination of the evaluation information; and specific intended uses of the evaluation information. In RFE the evaluation options are specified in greater detail than in EA; both EA and RFE estimate the costs and consequences of a status quo option (no further evaluation).

By quickly providing a preliminary evaluation that presents new information but speaks frankly of its limitations, evaluators can be responsive to immediate information needs, avoid "quick and dirty" evaluations that may mislead, and lay the groundwork for more definitive evaluation. Given intended users' agreement on the goals in terms of which a program is to be evaluated, rapid feedback evaluation strengthens or amends that agreement by providing information on program performance in terms of those goals. The rapid feedback evaluation may fully or partially meet users' information needs and may facilitate informed decisions on the scope and intended use of any additional data collection and analysis. In some cases policymakers or managers may conclude that the RFE has provided sufficient information for policy or management decisions, or the RFE may show that additional data collection and analysis are unlikely to be sufficiently conclusive or useful to justify their costs. In such cases evaluation may stop with the RFE, thus averting the cost of a full-scale evaluation. The primary purpose of RFE, however, is to provide a good foundation for further evaluation work by getting agreement on feasible designs for further evaluation and agreement on specific intended uses of the evaluation information.

There is no sharp dividing line between EA and RFE, though evaluability assessment is a qualitative process and rapid feedback evaluation is more quantitative. Rapid feedback evaluation builds on evaluability assessment and produces more fully developed evaluation options than those identified in EA. In RFE, evaluators estimate the effectiveness of a program by using three data sources: (1) prior research and evaluation studies, monitoring and audit reports, agency records, and other existing data on program performance; (2) discussions with knowledgeable observers such as experts in the program area, program staff, local service providers, and clients; and (3) pilot-testing performance measures that may be used in future evaluation, using samples that are smaller than those used in typical evaluations but still large enough to allow preliminary estimates of program accomplishments (see Wholey, 1979, 1983).

The Rapid Feedback Evaluation Process

Rapid feedback evaluation is a five-step process: (1) collect existing data on program performance in terms of which a program is to be evaluated; (2) collect limited amounts of new data on program performance in terms of those goals; (3) estimate program effectiveness and state the range of uncertainty in the estimates ("quick and clean" evaluation); (4) develop and analyze options for more definitive evaluation in terms of each option's likely feasibility, cost, and usefulness; and (5) reach agreement on the design and intended use of any further evaluation.

Step 1: Collect Existing Data on Program Performance. First, the evaluators review and synthesize existing quantitative and qualitative data on performance in terms of the agreed-on program goals. Data sources may include agency records, program data systems, monitoring and audit reports, and research and evaluation studies. The focus on agreed-on program goals limits the calendar time and staff time required for this review.

Step 2: Collect New Data on Program Performance. Again using the agreed-on program goals as guides, the evaluators next collect new data on program performance in terms of those goals. Data sources may include information from knowledgeable observers such as experts in the program area, program staff, local service providers, and clients (using data collection instruments that might be used in future, larger-scale evaluations); and site visits to a small number of local projects. Telephone surveys may be used to collect information from project sites or from knowledgeable observers. Site visits are typically used to determine how the program is actually being implemented, to determine whether specific measures and analyses are feasible, to collect data on program performance, and to corroborate or correct information from other sources.

Step 3: Estimate Program Effectiveness and State the Range of Uncertainty in the Estimates. Using both the existing data and the new data on program performance, the evaluators now estimate program effectiveness *and* state the range of uncertainty in the estimates (uncertainty due to conflicting evidence or small sample sizes, for example). In some cases existing and new quantitative data may be sufficient to allow quantitative estimates of program effectiveness; in most cases evaluators also use qualitative data, including information from knowledgeable observers, in estimating program effectiveness. In contrast to quick and dirty evaluations in which evaluators present their best estimates of program effectiveness but keep their uncertainties to themselves, in RFE evaluators also state the range of uncertainty in the estimates of program effectiveness and—in the next step—indicate how additional evaluation work could reduce that uncertainty.

Step 4: Develop and Analyze Designs for More Definitive Evaluation. At this point the evaluators explore options for more definitive evaluation in terms of their feasibility, cost, likely conclusiveness, and likely use. (Here, as noted earlier, the options include a status quo option (no further evaluation) and costs include the burden on program staff and recipients of services as well as the costs of disseminating evaluation information.) Each option specifies the data that would be collected, the data analyses that would be completed, uses that would be made of the resulting evaluation information, and the costs and schedule for that option. The analysis examines the strengths and weaknesses of alternative performance measures, the costs of alternative sample sizes, and the strengths and weaknesses of various nonexperimental, quasi-experimental, or experimental designs that might be used to test causal assumptions.

Step 5: Reach Agreement on the Design and Intended Use of Any Further Evaluation. The evaluators now present the findings of the RFE to intended users of evaluation information; discuss remaining uncertainties regarding program effectiveness; provide options for policy or management use of the findings to date; discuss options for further evaluation work, including the likely costs and conclusiveness of the new information and possible uses for that information; and help intended users to agree on one or more options for further evaluation and thus to agree—explicitly or implicitly—on intended use of the evaluation information that would be produced. Additional staff time and calendar time may be required to get the intended users' response to the RFE findings.

Exhibit 4.2 describes the first test of the rapid feedback evaluation approach, an exploratory evaluation for the U.S. Department of Housing and Urban Development (see Wholey, 1979).

Issues, Problems, and Potential Solutions

This section identifies issues and problems that may arise in rapid feedback evaluation and suggests solutions based on experience with RFE.

Estimating program effectiveness. To avoid the pitfalls of quick and dirty studies, in RFE evaluators present both estimates of program performance and results *and* the range of uncertainty in those estimates. Comparing and contrasting information from three sources facilitates development of both products: the evaluators draw on existing data on program performance, information from knowledgeable observers, and limited amounts of new data collected in the process of testing data collection instruments that may be used in further evaluation work. In some cases the preliminary evaluation may provide sufficient information to meet the needs of policymakers or managers.

Correcting users' misperceptions. To help avert the danger that a rapid feedback evaluation will be taken as providing fully conclusive information on program effectiveness, evaluators should identify the sources of their findings and

EXHIBIT 4.2. RAPID FEEDBACK EVALUATION OF A HOUSING PRODUCTION PROGRAM.

The first test of rapid feedback evaluation was in response to a request from the U.S. Department of Housing and Urban Development (HUD) for development of a design for evaluation of a demonstration program designed to stimulate industrialized housing production. Though HUD had originally requested only the development of an evaluation design, it agreed to allow a test of the RFE approach as part of the evaluation design process.

In the rapid feedback evaluation, the evaluators collected information from HUD documents and files, from other sources of existing data, and through telephone surveys and site visits. The evaluators interviewed seventy-three people and visited four of the nine industrialized housing production sites. The evaluators then developed models of program inputs, activities, and outcomes; developed rough estimates of the parameters in the model; assessed the extent of progress toward program objectives; analyzed the costs and value of options for further evaluation; and developed a recommended evaluation design and work statement. The RFE was completed in six months, with approximately ten staff-months of effort. The RFE concluded that (1) many of the intended program accomplishments were occurring, including industrialized production and marketing of new housing and adoption of statewide building codes; (2) some of the intended accomplishments apparently were not occurring, such as effective housing market aggregation by state and local authorities, changes in the involvement of savings and loan institutions in financing industrialized housing production, and significant innovation in housing production technology; and (3) because of the program's design and scale, it would be impossible to determine the program's effects on the nation's housing production or on constraints on industrialized housing production.

The preliminary evaluation facilitated decisions about the full-scale evaluation that HUD had promised to Congress. The rapid feedback evaluation report was presented to Congress, and a full-scale evaluation was undertaken along the lines proposed in the RFE report.

The two-stage evaluation provided information more quickly and at lower cost than the single large-scale evaluation originally planned by the department. Many who examined the RFE report concluded that it provided essentially all that could be learned from a larger, more expensive evaluation and that the full-scale evaluation was not really necessary.

the range of uncertainty in their estimates and should present their evaluation as part of a report that describes future evaluations that could provide more conclusive information on program effectiveness.

Meeting users' needs for rapid response. In some cases an evaluation organization may be mistakenly perceived as an organization that can turn out rapid feedback evaluations in days or weeks rather than months, and the organization may be pressured to produce quick and dirty evaluations. To meet such demands for instant information, an evaluation office or its parent organization should maintain a staff with the ability to synthesize or package existing information to respond to short-term information requests.

Significance

The significance of rapid feedback evaluation rests on the following line of argument: (1) focusing on a specific set of program goals will limit required data collection and analysis. (2) in developing evaluation designs, evaluators should assess the likely feasibility, cost, and utility of evaluation alternatives, the evaluation resources available, and the information needs of the primary intended users of evaluation information. (3) evaluators should not develop an evaluation design without first synthesizing what is already known about program effectiveness and having contact with the reality of program activities under way and program outcomes occurring; (4) prior research, evaluation, program monitoring, and audit work may allow preliminary estimates of program effectiveness and help shape the design for further evaluation work; (5) estimates of program effectiveness may also be obtained from the opinions of knowledgeable observers; (6) evaluation designs should not be implemented without first testing any data collection instruments to be used; (7) samples larger than those typically used in testing data collection instruments may both allow the testing of data collection instruments and yield data that can be used to make rough estimates of program effectiveness; (8) An evaluation of program effectiveness can often be obtained almost as a by-product of the document review and the quantitative and qualitative data collection needed to ensure that designs for evaluation work will lead to feasible, useful evaluations. In a few months RFE evaluators may be able to provide as much relevant information on program effectiveness as other evaluators would have produced in a more costly, less-focused evaluation; (9) an RFE provides occasion for interactions between evaluators and intended users that may further clarify information priorities and intended uses of evaluation information; and (10) in some cases policymakers, managers, and other stakeholders can learn as much from the RFE as could be learned from any further evaluation.

Two of the processes used in rapid feedback evaluation are themselves exploratory evaluation methods: evaluation synthesis and small-sample studies.

Evaluation Synthesis Summarizes What Is Known About Program Performance

Evaluation synthesis summarizes what has been learned about program effectiveness through a systematic review of all relevant prior research and evaluation studies. In evaluation synthesis, evaluators collect prior research and evaluation studies from a variety of sources, such as both published and unpublished reports and a variety of designs including experimental, quasi-experimental, and qualitative studies; extract and code data on the studies; and perform both quantitative and qualitative analyses of study findings (see Chapter Twenty-Five in this volume and also Labin, 2008; Light and Pillemer, 1984; U.S. General Accounting Office, 1992). Evaluation synthesis examines more studies than meta-analysis does; most meta-analyses perform quantitative analyses of prior studies that were randomized controlled trials and only the most rigorous quasi-experimental studies.

To the extent that there is agreement on the goals in terms of which a program is to be evaluated (including any goals for assessing, controlling, or enhancing important side-effects), evaluation synthesis takes less time and less staff time than when no such agreement exists. When intended users need evaluation information quickly, the scope and duration of evaluation synthesis can be limited accordingly.

Small-Sample Studies May Be Useful in Vetting Performance Measures

Before proceeding to evaluation of a program, evaluators are well advised to verify that performance measures will work by testing them. Measures for behaviors or other outcomes that are new, or proposed revisions to measures in place that have been questioned due to problems with validity and/or reliability, are most appropriate for this testing. This section explains how modest expansion of such testing can allow evaluators to test data collection schemes to be used in future evaluation work, produce rough estimates of program effectiveness in terms of specific program goals, and help to ensure the feasibility and usefulness of future evaluation work (see Wholey, 1979, 1983). Surprisingly small samples can yield useful evaluation information on the way to developing useful performance measures.

As is noted in Chapter Twenty-Three, random sampling reduces the amount of data that must be collected to obtain reliable estimates of program effectiveness and also makes it possible to generalize with known confidence to the universe from which the data were collected. Targeting random selection for the testing prescribed here will be more useful if over-sampling is undertaken with sub-populations or at program delivery sites that are expected to present challenges to measurement.

In approaching the problem of efficient sampling, it is helpful to be aware of the *square-root law* at a given confidence level, the precision of an estimate based on a simple random sample varies with the square root of the number of respondents contacted or records sampled (Riecken and Boruch, 1974, p. 71). Assume that evaluators planned, for example, to use random sampling in estimating the *proportion of patients who received satisfactory care in a prenatal program.* At the 95 percent confidence level, a random sample of approximately one hundred of the patients would yield an estimate within 10 percentage points of the *actual proportion of patients who received satisfactory care in the program's entire patient population*; and an even smaller random sample of approximately twenty-five of the patients would yield an estimate within 20 percentage points of the actual proportion. Random samples of one hundred, fifty, or even twenty-five can therefore be used in making rough estimates of program effectiveness.

Selecting an Exploratory Evaluation Approach

Evaluators often find it difficult to produce useful work and, in particular, to determine where future evaluations should focus. In this typical situation it is often helpful to conduct an exploratory evaluation that will provide preliminary findings and help to ensure the feasibility and usefulness of further evaluation. In this chapter I have described four exploratory evaluation approaches, each of which could have a place in an evaluator's toolkit. But how can an evaluator choose among them? Table 4.1 presented the purposes and costs of the four approaches; Table 4.2 suggests when one or another of these approaches might be appropriate.

Conclusion

Exploratory evaluations clarify program goals and evaluation criteria, provide evaluation findings that may be useful in the short term, and help in designing more definitive evaluations to further inform managers, policymakers, and other evaluation stakeholders. Each of these exploratory evaluation approaches provides information that may improve program quality or

TABLE 4.2. SELECTING AN EXPLORATORY EVALUATION APPROACH.

Approach	When Appropriate
Evaluability assessment	Large, decentralized program; unclear evaluation criteria.
Rapid feedback evaluation	Agreement exists on the goals in terms of which a program is to be evaluated; need for evaluation information "right quick"; potential need for more definitive evaluation.
Evaluation synthesis	Need for evaluation information "right quick"; potential need for more definitive evaluation.
Small-sample studies	Agreement exists on the goals in terms of which a program is to be evaluated; collection of evaluation data will require sampling.

help communicate the value of the program to policymaking levels; all four approaches help evaluators and users to decide among designs for further evaluation work. Each of the exploratory evaluation approaches discussed in this chapter has its own value.

Either evaluation synthesis or evaluability assessment may provide a good starting point for evaluation work: evaluation synthesis summarizes what is known from the relevant research and evaluation studies; evaluability assessment helps evaluators and staff to get agreement on program goals and on the focus and intended use of further evaluation work. Either approach can be undertaken before there is agreement on program goals.

Once there is agreement on program goals, small-sample studies produce tested measures of program performance in terms of the agreed-on goals, and rapid feedback evaluations produce tested designs for evaluating the program in terms of the agreed-on program goals. Both of these exploratory evaluation approaches deserve wider application.

References

Hatry, H. P., Bovbjerg, R. R., and Morley, E. *Evaluability Assessment of the Trust for America's Health.* Report prepared for the Robert Wood Johnson Foundation. Washington, DC: Urban Institute, 2008.

Horst, P., Nay, J., Scanlon, J. W., and Wholey, J. S. "Program Management and the Federal Evaluator." *Public Administration Review,* 1974, *34*(4), 300–308.

Labin, S. "Research Synthesis." In N. L. Smith and P. R. Brandon (eds.), *Fundamental Issues in Evaluation.* New York: Guilford Press, 2008.

Light, R. J., and Pillemer, D. B. *Summing Up: The Science of Reviewing Research.* Cambridge, MA: Harvard University Press, 1984.

Riecken, H. W., and Boruch, R. F. (eds.). *Social Experimentation.* New York: Academic Press, 1974.

Strosberg, M. A., and Wholey, J. S. "Evaluability Assessment: From Theory to Practice." *Public Administration Review*, 1983, *43*(1), 66–71.

U.S. General Accounting Office. *The Evaluation Synthesis.* Washington, DC: U.S. General Accounting Office, 1992.

Wholey, J. S. *Evaluation: Promise and Performance.* Washington, DC: Urban Institute, 1979.

Wholey, J. S. *Evaluation and Effective Public Management.* Boston: Little Brown, 1983.

Wholey, J. S. "Evaluability Assessment." In J. S. Wholey, H. P. Hatry, and K. E. Newcomer (eds.), *Handbook of Practical Program Evaluation* (2nd ed.). San Francisco: Jossey-Bass, 2004.

CHAPTER FIVE

PERFORMANCE MEASUREMENT

Monitoring Program Outcomes

Theodore H. Poister

Performance measurement systems can be thought of as both evaluation tools and management systems that are designed to provide useful feedback on performance in order to strengthen decision making and improve program and organizational performance.

Performance measurement has become orthodox practice in the public sector and increasingly in the nonprofit sector as well. In the age of outcomes the challenge of convincing agencies, managers, policymakers, funding agencies, governing bodies, and the like of the importance of focusing on results and monitoring performance on an ongoing, systematic basis has largely been met. Over the past thirty years, performance measurement has become widely accepted, outcome focused, more sophisticated, and institutionalized in both government and the nonprofit world.

The main question faced by public and nonprofit managers in this regard is not whether to monitor performance but how to design and implement measurement systems that provide meaningful information that can be used to improve program performance without creating disruptions and counterproductive results in the process—in short, systems that add value. This chapter provides a brief overview of performance measurement in terms of types of measures and the connection between performance measurement and program evaluation studies; discusses the development of measures, and particularly the criteria for good performance measures; and examines how to convert performance data into information and present it effectively to decision makers. The chapter then turns to two particular challenges in performance measurement, using the data to improve performance and developing measurement systems in networked governance structures, and concludes with brief comments on the outlook for performance measurement at this point in its evolution.

Performance Measurement and Program Evaluation

Performance measurement systems track sets of key measures of program or agency performance over time on a highly systematic basis. Some critics have argued that performance measurement is a fundamentally different enterprise from program evaluation on the grounds that they serve different purposes, and that while program evaluation encompasses a set of tools used by evaluators, performance measurement is used principally by managers (Feller, 2002; Perrin, 1998). Some observers view the two as complementary processes that employ essentially the same generic kinds of tools to assess program processes and effectiveness (McDavid, Huse, and Hawthorn, 2013). And others have dismissed the separation of the two and highlighted the need to apply evaluation thinking and tools to enhance performance measurement practice (Bernstein, 1999; Newcomer and Brass, 2015). The view here reflects Bernstein who noted, "Involving evaluators and evaluation methods in performance measurement helps refine program models and identify appropriate measures for appropriate uses" (Bernstein, 1999, p. 90).

The data generated by performance measurement systems are basically descriptive, and performance monitoring systems by themselves do not provide a rigorous methodology for isolating cause-and-effect relationships and identifying observed results as the impacts of a particular program. Although ongoing monitoring systems track what is in fact occurring with respect to program outputs and outcomes, on their own they cannot address the "how" and "why" questions about how programs produce desired outcomes. Program evaluation studies can examine program operations and results, provide, or at least are expected to provide, considerably stronger evidence on program implementation, and even program impact.

Nevertheless, when program and agency managers are confident about the underlying program logic connecting activities, products, and services to intended results—that is, when the validity of the program design and its fit to the operating context have been validated by science or evaluation research—they can track output and outcome data generated by monitoring systems and interpret them in terms of real results of their programs. In addition, performance monitoring systems build up databases that often lend themselves to more rigorous program evaluations, especially evaluations employing time-series designs. Conversely, the results coming from an in-depth program evaluation might well suggest additional measures that should be incorporated in an ongoing performance measurement system and provide data-based evidence to explain and explore program results, or the lack thereof.

The performance data can also raise red flags regarding chronically poor or deteriorating performance and signal when comprehensive program evaluation studies are needed. Many state and federal programs develop an agenda of evaluation activities each year, and they often target particular programs for evaluation based on issues that emerge from performance monitoring systems. In addition, measurement instruments such as customer surveys or trained observer ratings used in established monitoring systems can often be readily adapted to obtain data for in-depth evaluations.

Measurement Systems

Performance measurement systems are designed to track selected measures of program, agency, or system performance at regular time intervals and report these measures to managers or other specified audiences on an ongoing basis. Their purpose is to provide objective information to managers and policymakers in an effort to improve decision making and thereby strengthen performance and also to provide accountability to a range of stakeholders, such as higher-level management, central executive agencies, governing bodies, funding agencies, accrediting organizations, clients and customers, advocacy groups, and the public at large. A number of useful sources are available to program evaluators who are interested in learning more about methodological approaches to developing performance measurement systems (Ammons, 2001; Hatry, 2006; Poister, 2003).

Outcomes and Other Types of Performance Measures

One of the initial issues in developing a performance monitoring system is determining the types of measures to be emphasized. The principal classes of performance measures focus on outcomes, cost effectiveness, outputs, efficiency, service quality, and customer satisfaction.

Outcomes.   Measures of outcomes tend to be strongly emphasized in monitoring systems developed today because they represent the kinds of results that

a program is intended to produce. Thus the outcomes of a state's highway traffic safety program would be measured by the numbers of accidents, injuries,
and fatalities per 100,000 vehicle miles each year, and the overall effectiveness of a sexually transmitted diseases prevention system would be monitored
by examining trends in the incidence and prevalence of syphilis, gonorrhea,
chlamydia, and AIDS.

Outcome measures can be challenging and costly to operationalize
because they often require follow-up with clients after they have completed
programs: for example, staff and stakeholders are likely to want to know the
percentage of crisis stabilization consumers who are in crisis status again within
thirty days of discharge, the percentage of youths discharged from juvenile
detention centers who are attending school or engaged in gainful employment one year later, or the percentage of job training program participants
who have been placed in jobs—and perhaps the wages they are earning—six
months after completing the program.

Cost-Effectiveness. Cost-effectiveness measures relate costs to outcomes.
Thus, for a crisis stabilization unit, cost-effectiveness would be measured as
the cost per successfully discharged consumer. For a vocational rehabilitation
program, the most relevant indicators of cost-effectiveness would be the cost
per client placed in suitable employment and the cost per client successfully
employed for six months or more, and for a local police department's criminal investigation activity, cost-effectiveness would be measured as the cost per
crime solved.

Outputs. Although outcome measures are usually considered the most
important measures in a performance monitoring system, outputs are also critical because they represent the immediate products or services produced by
public and nonprofit organizations. Thus, output measures typically indicate
the amount of work performed or units of service produced, such as the number of seminars presented by an AIDS prevention program, the number of
detoxification procedures completed by a crisis stabilization unit, the number
of criminal investigations conducted by a local police department, or the miles
of guardrail replaced by highway maintenance crews. Sometimes, output measures focus on the number of cases dealt with: for example, the number of
crimes investigated by the police or the number of clients served, such as the
number of individuals who have received counseling in a drug abuse prevention program.

Efficiency. Paralleling cost-effectiveness measures, efficiency measures relate outputs to the resources used in producing them, most often focusing on the ratio of outputs to the dollar cost of the collective resources consumed. Thus, the cost per crime investigated, the cost per AIDS seminar conducted, the cost per ton of residential refuse collected, and the cost per client completing a job training program are all standard efficiency measures. Although the most useful efficiency measures focus on the cost of producing specific outputs, such as the cost per psychiatric assessment completed or the cost per group therapy session conducted in a crisis stabilization unit, performance monitoring systems sometimes incorporate efficiency measures relating cost to more general outputs, such as the cost per highway lane-mile maintained or the cost per client per day in group homes for mentally disabled persons.

Another type of efficiency measure, the productivity indicator, relates output produced to some specific resource over some particular unit of time. Productivity indicators usually focus on labor productivity, such as the miles of highway resurfaced per maintenance crew per day, the number of clients counseled per vocational rehabilitation counselor per month, or the number of claims processed per disability adjudicator per week.

Service Quality. The most common dimensions of the quality of public services are timeliness, turnaround time, accuracy, thoroughness, accessibility, convenience, courtesy, and safety. Whereas output measures typically represent the quantity or volume of outputs produced, indicators of service quality measure the quality of those outputs. Thus, the percentage of customers who wait in line more than fifteen minutes before renewing their driver's licenses, the number of calls to a local child support enforcement office that are returned within twenty-four hours, and the percentage of claims for disability benefits that are adjudicated within seventy working days are typical service quality measures. Quality indicators often measure compliance with established standards, such as the percentage of highway maintenance jobs that are performed according to prescribed operating procedures, but some others focus on the quality of the outputs themselves or the need for rework, such as the number of completed highway crack-sealing projects that have to be done again within six months. In addition, service quality measures sometimes overlap with outcome measures. For example, the goal of many public health programs and health policy initiatives is to improve the quality of health care services made available to vulnerable populations, and thus, indicators of service quality also constitute central outcome measures.

Customer Satisfaction.   Measures of customer satisfaction are usually closely related to service quality and to program outcomes, but it may be more helpful to consider them as constituting a separate category of performance measures. Determining the level of satisfaction might involve surveying citizen satisfaction with the timeliness and quality of a government-provided service such as tax-assistance from the Internal Revenue Service. Such customer satisfaction ratings may or may not square with more tangible measures of service quality and program effectiveness, but they do provide a complementary perspective.

Identifying, Operationalizing, and Assessing Performance Measures

Evaluators can identify the kinds of outcomes a program are intended to produce through interviews or focus group sessions with key internal and external stakeholder groups and by examining formal statements of the program's goals and objectives. In addition, program logic models can be extremely helpful in identifying both the outcomes and outputs to be monitored by performance measurement systems (Funnell and Rogers, 2011; Knowlton and Phillips, 2012). Although logic models often do not elaborate the process side of program performance, pertaining to how a program operates, they are often very useful in clarifying the logic of how program outputs are supposed to be linked with immediate, intermediate, and long-term outcomes. Figure 5.1 shows a logic model depicting the logic underlying state nursing regulation programs. As illustrated by this example, logic models often outline parallel and interrelated strands of logic that lead from a program's resources and activities to immediate, intermediate, and long-term outcomes. The four principal components of nursing regulation—establishing and revising the scope of nursing practice, reviewing and approving nursing education programs, licensing nurses to practice, and investigating and taking action on disciplinary cases—all have their own processes, outputs, and immediate and intermediate outcomes through which they all contribute to the longer term outcome of consumers receiving safe and competent care from nurses.

In addition to, or instead of, program logic models, public agencies may use goal structures as performance frameworks for developing measurement systems. For example, one of numerous goals established by the U.S. Department of Health and Human Services is to "Promote the safety, well-being, resilience, and healthy development of children and

FIGURE 5.1. STATE BOARD OF NURSING PROGRAM LOGIC.

Components and Inputs	Program Components and Resources	Processes and Activities	Outputs	Immediate Outcomes	Intermediate Outcomes	Longer Term Outcomes

Components and Inputs

Practice
Questions, inquiries and practice issues

Education
Initial and continuing nursing education program applications

Licensure
Applications for RN, LPN, licenses

Discipline
Complaints and reports of misconduct or incompetent practice

Program Components and Resources

Practice
- Staff
- Dollars

Education
- Staff
- Dollars

Licensure
- Staff
- Dollars

Discipline
- Staff
- Dollars

Processes and Activities

- Drafting legislative changes
- Markig rules
- Responding to inquiries
- Communicating with nurses and other stakeholders
- Establish philosophy, policy, standards, etc
- Reviewing applicatons
- Reviewing faculty credentials and qualifications
- Conductind sitevisits
- Providing consultation
- Establish philosophy, policy standards, etc
- Reviewing initial and renewal applications
- Following up on incomplete applications
- Establish philosphy, policy, standards, etc
- Triaging cases to detemine riske and course of action
- Conducting investigations
- Reviewing complaints with subjects and complainants

Outputs

- Lesgislation proposed
- Rules promulgated
- Advice and clarification provided; information disseminated, e.g., website, newsletters, etc
- Decisions regarding approvals of programs
- Initial and renewal licenses and certificates issued or denied
- Borad actions taken:
  - Cases dismissed
  - Nurses disciplined
  - Nursesr remediated without discipline

Immediate Outcomes

- Lesgislation passed
- Nurses and other stakeholders know ledgable about regulations and the role of the borad
- Students are adequately supervised
- Programs are high quality
- Only qualified nurses are practicing
- Unsafe or incompetent parctioners are removed from practice
- Nurses are remediated

Intermediate Outcomes

- Nursing regulations are current and reflectstate of the aet practice
- Consumers receive safe and competentcare from student nurses
- Nursing programs graduate competent, knowledgeable and safe practitioners
- Nurses are deterred from violating regulations
- Nurses adher to regulations and strndards of practice

Longer Term Outcomes

- Consumers receive safe and competent care from nurses

Source: National Council of State Board of Nursing.

114

youth" (www.performance.gov/content/promote-safety-well-being-resilience-and-healthy-development-children-and-youth?view=public#overview). A few of the measures that the Department monitors include the following:

- The percentage of all children who exit foster care after twenty-four or more months who exit into permanency through reunification with family, living with a relative, guardianship, or adoption
- The percentage of youth living in safe and appropriate settings after exiting ACF-funded transitional living programs
- The percentage of middle and high school students who report current substance abuse
- The percentage of children receiving trauma informed services showing clinically significant improvement

Over the past two decades, many public and nonprofit agencies have used the *balanced scorecard* model as a framework for creating a balanced approach to monitoring performance, using a variety of measures, not just performance-based measures.

In contrast to focusing on the flow of activities to outputs and outcomes, the balanced scorecard prompts managers to identify goals and associated performance measures for each of four perspectives: customers, financial performance, internal business processes, and innovation and learning. This model has become popular because it encourages managers to take a comprehensive view of performance, tie performance measures directly to goals, and develop *strategy maps* showing linkages among goals established for the various perspectives (Niven, 2003). Some government and nonprofit agencies have modified this model by adding considerable flexibility in terms of the performance perspectives incorporated, adding, for instance, outreach to external stakeholders as a key results area. Logic models and balanced scorecards can be complementary rather than mutually exclusive, with balanced scorecards focusing more on organizational performance which logic models focus more on program performance.

Data Sources

As is the case with program evaluation studies, performance monitoring systems use data from a wide variety of sources. First, a lot of measures—particularly those for internal processes, service delivery, and outputs—are based on transactional data maintained by agencies on an ongoing basis and regarding such things as requests for service, clients admitted and discharged, production records, inventories, permits issued or revoked, activity logs, incident reports, claims processed, treatments administered, follow-up visits made, and complaints from clients or others. Such data are usually maintained in management information systems and therefore often have the advantage of being readily available.

Performance measures, particularly outcome measures, however, often require additional sources and data collection procedures developed specifically to measure performance. These procedures include direct observation, such as trained-observer surveys of street cleanliness or mechanized counts of traffic volumes, medical or psychiatric examinations of clients, and tests typically used in measuring the effectiveness of education and training programs. Outcomes measures are often operationalized most directly through follow-up contacts or interviews with clients at specified lengths of time after they have completed programs.

Finally, surveys of clients, employees, or other stakeholders administered on a regular basis are often important sources of data used in performance monitoring systems, as are customer response cards. Obviously, monitoring performance through trained-observer surveys, clinical examinations, special testing procedures, follow-up contacts, and surveys entails significantly greater effort and cost than does relying on existing agency records, but such tools are often the best or only means of obtaining suitable measures of performance, particularly in terms of effectiveness and client satisfaction.

Criteria for Good Performance Measures

From a methodological perspective the sine qua non of good measurement is a high degree of *validity*, the degree to which an indicator accurately represents what is intended to be measured, and *reliability*, which concerns consistency in data collection. Validity is a matter of avoiding systematic bias or distortion in the data. Thus, in developing measurement systems, program evaluators must try to anticipate and guard against such problems as observer bias or subject bias, systematic overreporting or underreporting, poor instrument design, and nonresponse bias due to missing cases. The latter problem can be particularly likely when performance measures must be operationalized by follow-up contacts with clients and those contacts are not initiated until the clients have completed a program or left an agency because that is when the intended results are expected to materialize.

With respect to reliability, it is important to maintain consistency in data collection procedures in order to generate valid trend data over time. Thus, it is critical to develop a clear definition of each performance measure and the procedures for making observations and collecting data to operationalize it. In addition, data input in many monitoring systems is decentralized, with data fed in by numerous local offices around a state, for instance, and in such cases the need to guard against sloppy reporting in the field and to ensure uniform measurement and data collection procedures among reporting units is of paramount importance. Moreover, because performance monitoring systems are designed to track performance measures at regular intervals and to assess change over time, ensuring that measurement instruments and data collection procedures are applied the same way in each successive reporting period is particularly important.

Meaningful and Understandable.   In order for performance data to be useful, they must have a high degree of stakeholder credibility. This means that the measures must be meaningful to decision makers, focusing on goals and objectives, priorities, and dimensions of performance that are important to them. In addition the measures should be readily understandable by their intended audiences. Thus, measures should have obvious face validity to the users, and where they come from and what they mean should be clear. More complicated or less obvious indicators should be accompanied by clear definitions of what they represent.

Balanced and Comprehensive.   Collectively, the set of measures tracked by a monitoring system should provide a balanced and comprehensive picture of the performance of the program or agency in question, in terms of both the components covered and the classes of measures employed. Using program logic models or a framework such as the balanced scorecard can be immensely helpful in this regard.

Timely and Actionable.   One common problem with performance monitoring systems is that they sometimes fail to provide timely results to decision makers. When data are no longer fresh when they are made available or are not provided to decision makers when most needed, monitoring systems are not particularly useful. In addition, performance measures are really useful to decision makers only when they are actionable, when they focus on results over which decision makers can exert some leverage, such as dimensions of performance that can be affected by program elements or organizational strategies. Otherwise, the performance data may be interesting, but they will not serve to improve decisions and strengthen performance.

Goal Displacement. Performance measurement systems are intended to stimulate improved performance. In addition to providing information to higher-level decision makers, the very fact of measuring performance on a regular, ongoing basis provides a powerful incentive for managers and employees to perform well on the measures that are being tracked. However, with inappropriate or unbalanced measures this can lead to goal displacement, in which people will perform toward the measures but sacrifice the real program or organizational goals in the process. For example, newspapers around the United States have published hundreds of stories containing allegations of "collateral damage" from the standardized testing in the nation's public schools required by the federal No Child Left Behind legislation. These reported harmful effects include administrator and teacher cheating, student cheating, exclusion of low-performing students from testing, counseling low-performing students out of school systems, teaching to the test, narrowing of the curriculum, and declining teacher morale (Nichols and Berliner, 2007).

Thus, in designing monitoring systems, it is critical to ensure that indicators are directly aligned with goals and objectives, to anticipate problems such as the selective treatment of cases, or *creaming*, that can result from overly simplified measures, to avoid focusing on some parts of program logic or goal structures to the exclusion of others, and to focus directly on real outcomes as well as outputs wherever possible. In addition, evaluators who are developing sets of performance measures should try to anticipate whether an agency's emphasis on improving performance on one particular measure, schedule adherence in a local public transit system, for example, might be likely to result in behavior that runs counter to other important program goals, such as reckless driving in the local transit system. If so, evaluators need to incorporate additional performance measures, such as measures relating to safe driving and customer injuries, that will foster a more balanced incentive structure.

Practical Considerations and Cost. The need to incorporate well-balanced and meaningful sets of measures that are highly reliable and resistant to goal displacement is often offset by more practical considerations and cost factors. Although for some measures the data will likely be readily available, others will require the development of new instruments or data collection procedures. Some measures may simply be too difficult or time-consuming to collect in the field in a systematic and consistent manner, and others might impose undue burdens on the employees at the operating level who would have to keep track of the data sources and be responsible for reporting the data.

In comparing candidate measures, performance measurement system designers must often weigh trade-offs between the usefulness of a measure and the quality of the data on the one hand and issues of feasibility, time, effort, and costs on the other. Ultimately, such decisions should be made on the basis of ensuring accurate and reliable data whose usefulness exceeds the cost of maintaining the system. Thus, evaluators should engage in a systematic assessment of proposed measures and select or revise the measures to be incorporated in the system accordingly. Table 5.1 presents an example that can be used as a template for organizing and summarizing the results of this kind of review of the strengths and weaknesses of various indicators.

Quality Assurance

Because the quality of the data is crucial for maintaining the credibility and usefulness of a performance monitoring system, it is important to have procedures in place for ensuring data integrity. Thus, it is imperative to define indicators clearly in terms of their constituent data elements and to develop uniform procedures for the collection of performance data. If performance measures are revised over time, changes in data definition and collection procedures should be carefully documented. Particularly when data input will be decentralized, it is critically important to provide training on these procedures to the individuals who will be responsible for collecting data and entering data into the system. In addition, identifying *data owners* for individual performance measures or measure sets and making them responsible for overseeing data collection and ensuring the overall quality of the data can help to eliminate errors in the data.

Procedures for collecting and processing the data should provide clear data trails so that someone could, if necessary, track the data back to records of initial transactions or observations in order to reproduce the results. Although it is usually neither necessary nor practical to independently check all the data along these lines, conducting selective data audits on a small random sample can go a long way toward ensuring high-quality data. Such an audit process provides an overall reading on the accuracy of reported data, identifies problems in data collection that can then be resolved, and serves as an incentive for people to guard against sloppy reporting. Moreover, conducting data audits, even on a small-sample basis, can be a safeguard against deliberate false reporting or other manipulation of the system, particularly if appropriate sanctions or penalties against such forms of cheating are in place.

TABLE 5.1. REVIEW OF PERFORMANCE INDICATORS FOR DISABILITY ADJUDICATORS' CLAIMS PROCESSING.

Performance Indicators	Type of Indicator	Preferred Direction of Movement	Validity	Reliability	Actionable	Target	Resistant to Goal Displacement
Number of initial applications adjudicated	Output	N/A	Very strong	Very strong	Yes	N/A	N/A
Cases cleared per FTE work month	Labor productivity	Up	Strong	Questionable	Yes	≥ 20	No. Regions can pick and choose which files to do to meet target.
Workweeks pending	Workload	Down	Strong (denominator based on previous month's work, which can vary)	Strong	Yes	≤ 10	Yes
Cumulative expense per case	Efficiency	Down	Strong	Questionable	Yes	N/A	Yes
Percentage of cases adjudicated within 70 days	Service quality	Up	Strong	Strong	Yes	≥ 95%	No. Regions can pick and choose which files to do to meet target.
Initial accuracy rate	Service quality	Up	Fairly strong (based on small sample)	Fairly strong	Yes	≥ 98%	Yes
Percentage of claimants satisfied with process	Customer satisfaction	Up	Fairly strong (based on sample)	Fairly strong	Yes	≥ 80%	No

Converting Performance Data to Information

Although selecting appropriate measures and maintaining the integrity of the data are of critical importance, performance monitoring systems are effective only when they provide information that is useful for management, program staff, and decision makers. Thus the performance data need to be examined in some kind of comparative framework: namely, comparisons over time, actual performance against targets, comparisons among operating units, other kinds of breakouts, or comparisons against external benchmarks. Ammons (2008) points out that, while more advanced statistical models can sometimes be helpful In this regard, it is often the case that simple descriptive statistics such as means, ranges, standard deviations, and percentages are all that are required to summarize the data and provide a portrait of what performance looks like in the aggregate at a particular point in time. Furthermore, he shows how breaking the data down for simple comparisons and relating one performance measure to others can help analyze staffing patterns, the demand for services, workload and production capacity, and the costs of operating programs and capital projects. Hatry (2006), on the other hand, focuses more on outcomes and analyzing change in outcomes over time, examining clusters of outcomes, and relating outcome data back to output data and other performance measures.

Trends Over Time

Because monitoring systems make repeated observations of a set of indicators at regular time intervals, they automatically accumulate time-series databases that facilitate tracking trends over time. For example, as is the case for virtually all public transit systems in the United States, the most critical outcomes produced by the Metropolitan Atlanta Rapid Transit Authority (MARTA) focus on ridership, since the extent to which they produce public value depends on the extent to which they are actually utilized. As shown in Figure 5.2, the number of passenger trips taken on MARTA's bus and rail systems tracked each other closely over the first several years of the decade, dropping precipitously from 2002 to 2004 and then leveling off for the next two years. While ridership on the bus system remained at the lower level for the following two years, however, it increased to new decade-high levels on the rail system over the same period. Reversing again, then, ridership on both systems declined significantly from 2009 to 2011, most likely in response to the economic recession that was taking hold at that point.

FIGURE 5.2. MARTA REVENUE PASSENGERS 2002–2011.

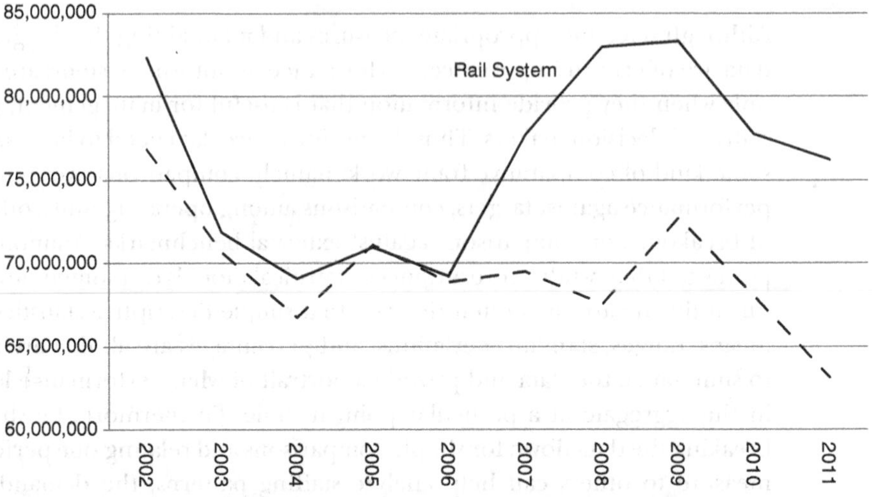

Source: National Transportation Database. www.ntdprogram.gov/ntdprogram/

Actual Performance Versus Targets

In the context of results-oriented approaches to managing public and non-profit organizations, monitoring systems often track actual performance against previously determined goals, objectives, standards, or targets. Tracking actual performance can help when setting growth-oriented but realistic targets. Using actuals to set realistic targets is often overlooked, leaving management (and politicians) to set unrealistic but widely popular targets that then cannot be achieved, or setting unrealistically low targets so that the agency looks good achieving and surpassing the targets (a form of creaming).

For example, the Atlanta Police Department sets differential targets for the percentage of specific types of reported crimes that will be solved each month: for instance, a 67 percent clearance rate for homicides and a 15 percent clearance rate for burglaries. As shown in Table 5.2, in October 2009 the department exceeded its target clearance rates for homicides, rapes, aggravated assaults, and larcenies but fell short of the targets for robberies, burglaries, and auto theft.

Comparisons Among Units

Although governing bodies, funding organizations, and chief executive officers tend to be interested principally in tracking performance data for a

TABLE 5.2. CITY OF ATLANTA POLICE DEPARTMENT SCORECARD, OCTOBER 2009.

Improve Clearance Rate of Crimes (10%)

Name	Actual	Target	Variance	Variance %	Time Period
Crime Clearance Rates—Homicide	81.7%	67.0%	14.7	21.9%	Jul FY 10
Crime Clearance Rates—Rape	64.7%	49.0%	15.7	32.0%	Jul FY 10
Crime Clearance Rates—Robbery	21.9%	31.0%	(9.1)	(29.4%)	Jul FY 10
Crime Clearance Rates—Aggravated Assault	61.2%	56.0%	5.2	9.3%	Jul FY 10
Crime Clearance Rates—Burglary	9.9%	15.0%	(5.1)	(34.0%)	Jul FY 10
Crime Clearance Rates—Larceny	20.3%	19.0%	1.3	6.8%	Jul FY 10
Crime Clearance Rates—Auto Theft	10.3%	14.0%	(3.7)	(26.4%)	Jul FY 10

Source: Atlanta Police Department, 2009.

program or agency as a whole, senior and middle managers often find it useful to compare these measures across operating units or project sites. For example, the Division of Sexually Transmitted Diseases Prevention of the Centers for Disease Control and Prevention (CDC) provides grants to each of the fifty states as well as fifteen large city governments for the prevention and treatment of syphilis, gonorrhea, and chlamydia. A key performance measure of control over syphilis outbreaks is the proportion of newly identified cases of primary or secondary syphilis who are interviewed within seven, fourteen, or at most thirty days from the date of the initial report in order to identify current or recent sexual partners so that these people may be contacted, counseled against spreading the disease, and advised to avail themselves of treatment. As shown in Figure 5.3, the CDC monitors this measure for the nation as a whole but also breaks the performance data down by the ten federal regions in order to identify regions whose performance along these lines is lagging.

Other Breakouts

Performance data are often much more meaningful when they are broken out by different types of cases. For example, in support of an effort to improve

FIGURE 5.3. PROPORTIONS OF PRIMARY AND SECONDARY SYPHILIS CASES INTERVIEWED WITHIN 7, 14, AND 30 DAYS: MEDIANS FOR UNITED STATES AND U.S. DEPARTMENT OF HEALTH AND HUMAN SERVICES REGIONS.

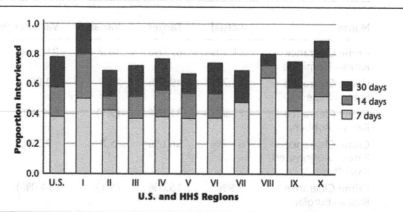

Source: Centers for Disease Control and Prevention, Division of Sexually Transmitted Diseases Prevention, 2004.

safety in city parks and recreation areas, a medium-size suburban municipality might track the number of reported personal injuries at these facilities on a monthly basis. Even though reducing the total number of injuries is officials' principal concern here, breaking these incidents down by type of venue will help pinpoint the problem venues. Thus, the monitoring system might break out the number of reported injuries occurring on sports fields, tennis courts, jogging trails, picnic areas, and parking lots, in swimming pools, and on other venues on a monthly basis. For many education, human service, job training, and other programs focusing on outcomes for individual clients, it is often useful to break results data down by client groups defined by, for example, relevant characteristics such as race, socioeconomic status, or risk levels.

External Benchmarking

Increasingly, public and nonprofit agencies are experimenting with external benchmarking, comparing their own performance data against the same measures for other similar agencies or programs. Such a comparative framework can help an agency assess its own performance and perhaps set future target levels, within the context of its larger public service industry. For instance, Figure 5.4 shows the number of regulated child-care spaces per thousand

FIGURE 5.4. REGULATED CHILD-CARE SPACES IN ONTARIO MUNICIPALITIES PER 1,000 LOW-INCOME CHILDREN.

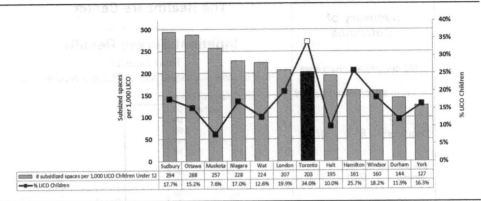

	Sudbury	Ottawa	Muskota	Niagara	Wat	London	Toronto	Halt	Hamilton	Windsor	Durham	York
# subsidized spaces per 1,000 LICO Children Under 12	294	288	257	228	224	207	203	195	161	160	144	127
% LICO Children		17.7%	15.2%	7.6%	17.0%	12.6%	19.9%	34.0%	10.0%	25.7%	18.2%	11.9%	16.3%

Source: 2011 Performance Measurement and Benchmarking Report C I T Y M A N AG E R' S O FFI C E MARCH 2013, page 49. www.toronto.ca/legdocs/mmis/2013/ex/bgrd/backgroundfile-57525.pdf.

low-income children in Toronto, Canada, as compared with other municipalities in the Province of Ontario. The data show that Toronto falls in the middle of the pack on this indicator, lagging behind such cities as Sudbury, Ottawa, and London, but ahead of others such as Hamilton, Windsor, and York. In addition, Figure 5.4 also shows the percentage of all children in each of these jurisdictions who are considered to be low-income children; in Toronto that figure exceeds 30 percent, while in most of the other jurisdictions the percentage of low-income children hovers around 15 percent. Thus, thus comparative performance data indicate that, while Toronto has the highest percentage of low-income children, it does not have a commensurately high number of regulated child care spaces per thousand low-income children.

Figure 5.5 shows another benchmarking example, a variety of performance data for one particular public hospital in Georgia, drawn from an intensive survey of patients discharged during a particular three-month period. The survey was conducted for the hospital by an independent firm that conducted the same survey for twenty other hospitals in the city on a quarterly basis. Thus the data reported back to each hospital included not only that hospital's scores on a number of indicators, but also some comparisons against the other hospitals being surveyed. In addition to having its overall performance benchmarked against twenty other hospitals, each hospital is further compared against a leading-edge institution that represents the hospital's aspirations on indicators of several specific dimensions of performance.

FIGURE 5.5. SATISQUEST PATIENT SURVEY RESULTS SUMMARY.

Summary of Outcomes

400 completed interviews

Benchmark Hospital

	Benchmark	Hospital
Quality of Care Score	91.1	87.7
Overall Nursing	95.1	91.8
Overall Physician	95.9	95.9
Willingness to Return	96.9	93.5
Willingness to Recommend	96.7	93.2
Helpfulness of Visit	95.7	94.8

The Healthcare Center

Inpatient Survey Results

Third Quarter
From patients discharged August 21st thru September 30th

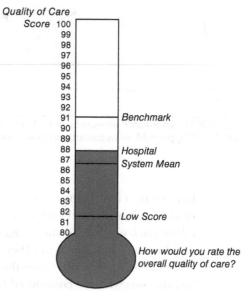

Quality of Care Score

Benchmark
Hospital System Mean
Low Score

How would you rate the overall quality of care?

Overall Assessment

The overall quality of care score for the hospital is

87.7

This puts the hospital 8th among 20 hospitals measured.

The aggregate score (computed by taking the average score for all attributes and functional area items) is

92.0

Reasons for Visits

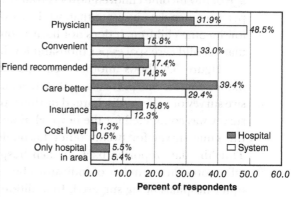

Reason	Hospital	System
Physician	31.9%	48.5%
Convenient	15.8%	33.0%
Friend recommended	17.4%	14.8%
Care better	39.4%	29.4%
Insurance	15.8%	12.3%
Cost lower	1.3%	0.5%
Only hospital in area	5.5%	5.4%

Percent of respondents

Q1. Why was this hospital chosen for this visit?

Source: SatisQuest^{sm}. Reprinted with permission.

Presenting and Analyzing Performance Data

Presenting data in useful formats can also facilitate understanding what they mean. Thus evaluators and others who are involved in developing measurement systems are encouraged to use a variety of display formats (dashboards, spreadsheets, graphs, pictures, and maps) to present performance data clearly. They are also urged to keep presentations simple and straightforward and to focus on conveying meaningful information effectively rather than presenting glitzy visuals.

Incorporating *roll up–drill down* features facilitates examination of data aggregated for an entire program or disaggregated down to organizational subunits, contractors delivering services, or individual program sites. For example, the Ohio Department of Transportation (DOT) has developed a set of indices, with values ranging from 0 to 100, to track its performance in a number of areas, such as construction management, contract administration, equipment and facilities, and finance, as well as its overall performance, as shown in Table 5.3. Managers can track the department's overall performance over time but can also drill down into each of its twelve districts and within any district drill down further to check performance in any one of the activity areas and drill down even further (not shown here) to view performance on a particular indicator that constitutes a part of an index for that activity area.

Evaluators should also employ a systematic process to analyze the data and gain a holistic picture of what a program's performance looks like first, by examining changes over time in individual key outcome indicators; comparing actual performance against targets; comparing the data against data for other similar programs; breaking the data down by organizational units, geographical areas, or grantees if service delivery is decentralized; and breaking the data down by other relevant factors such as client characteristics. Then they can examine trends in multiple outcome indicators collectively to see whether a composite portrait of a program's performance emerges. In addition they can assess the meaning of the outcome data in conjunction with other types of performance indicators, such as indicators for outputs, service quality, efficiency, or client satisfaction, to get a fuller picture of program operations and performance.

Furthermore evaluators can track explanatory variables that may be facilitating or impeding improved outcomes, in order to gain insight on the level of program effectiveness, and they may consider reporting adjusted performance measures for comparative data in order to control for key external influences. For example, data used in comparisons of crime rates across a number of cities

TABLE 5.3. OHIO DOT ORGANIZATIONAL PERFORMANCE INDEX: EXECUTIVE SUMMARY.

District	Total Index Value	Construction Management	Contract Administration	Equipment and Facilities	Finance	Information Technology	Plan Delivery	Quality and Human Resources	System Conditions
1	95.8333	83.3333	100.0	72.0238	100.0	88.8889	100.0	75.0	100.0
2	91.6667	79.1667	100.0	82.7381	100.0	100.0	50.0	87.5	95.0
3	97.9167	91.6667	100.0	85.119	100.0	100.0	80.0	93.75	91.6667
4	97.9167	91.6667	100.0	83.9286	100.0	100.0	95.0	68.75	100.0
5	100.0	91.6667	100.0	91.6667	100.0	100.0	95.0	93.75	100.0
6	83.3333	83.3333	100.0	86.3095	100.0	88.8889	83.333	93.75	93.3333
7	95.8333	91.6667	100.0	88.6905	100.0	100.0	65.0	87.5	100.0
8	100.0	91.6667	100.0	87.5	100.0	100.0	95.0	87.5	98.3333
9	89.5833	87.5	100.0	66.6667	100.0	100.0	50.0	75.0	100.0
10	95.8333	100.0	100.0	90.4762	100.0	100.0	90.0	56.25	93.3333
11	93.75	79.1667	100.0	95.8333	100.0	100.0	65.0	87.5	100.0
12	91.667	79.1667	100.0	82.7381	100.0	100.0	70.0	81.25	93.3333
ODOT INDEX	93.2192	91.6667	100.0	90.4762	100.0	94.4444	83.333	87.5	98.3333

Source: Ohio Department of Transportation, 2004.

are often adjusted for the percentage of each city's population living below the poverty level, and data for comparisons of hospitals in terms of health outcome measures might be adjusted by hospital for the severity of patients' illnesses at intake, using simple regression models. In addition, providing explanatory comments and other relevant information in narrative comment fields along with the quantitative data in performance reports provides decision makers with a context within which to assess the meaning of the performance data.

Analyses of performance might be used to determine when a more thorough evaluation study might be appropriate. Studies might be undertaken to: explain inconsistent results; explore high priority programs that consistently do not achieve targets; identify causal factors affecting program performance; and /or as part of a comprehensive system of accountability.

Current Challenges to Performance Measurement

Does performance measurement contribute to improved decision making and improved program performance? This should be the bottom line for judging whether monitoring systems really add value, but we lack systematic evidence to answer this question on an objective basis. On the one hand we have some celebrated performance management systems such as the New York Police Department's CompStat and Baltimore's CitiStat, but on the other hand we have cases where measurement systems have allegedly had damaging effects (see Radin, 2006).

There has been only some research to date on the effectiveness of performance measurement, and "hard evidence documenting performance measurement's impact on management decisions and service improvements is rare" (Ammons and Rivenbark, 2008). In a report published in 2003, researchers did state that a variety of federal agencies were using outcome data to trigger corrective action, identify and encourage best practices, motivate staff, and plan and budget more effectively in order to help improve programs, but they also found that many obstacles to the use of outcome data still existed (Hatry, Morley, Rossman, and Wholey, 2003).

However, institutional constraints such as the lack of flexibility regarding personnel actions, budget execution, and procurement often tie managers' hands in trying to respond to performance information in order to improve performance (Moynihan, 2008). While some public managers do make productive use of performance data, others are more inclined to make very passive use, more political use, and even perverse use of the performance information they receive (Moynihan, 2009). On the other hand, recent research is also beginning to show that, by some means or other, more extensive use of performance management practices is associated with higher levels of performance in the U.S. public transit industry (Poister, Pasha, and Edwards, 2013) and in the New York City School System (Sun and van Ryzin, 2014).

Using Performance Data to Improve Performance

Government and nonprofit organizations vary widely in their interest in implementing performance monitoring systems, depending on a variety of factors including the nature of their programs, the existence or lack of political consensus on policy goals, the degree of control they have over their outputs and outcomes, and the extent to which decision making relies on professional norms (Jennings and Haist, 2004). Even given good data on appropriate and potentially useful performance measures, there is no guarantee that performance data will actually be employed as a basis for strengthening decision making and management and eventually improving program performance. Top decision makers, heavily caught up in responding to short-term crises and routine day-to-day management issues, may not be invested in the system, and the performance data may receive passing interest at best or simply be ignored.

In addition, monitoring systems may not be linked systematically to other management and decision-making processes in a meaningful way, and so the data may generate passing attention but not be seen as real-time information to be used in addressing either short-term operational problems or long-term strategic issues. In the face of this sometime bureaucratic tendency to fail to connect performance measurement with ongoing decision-making processes or to capitalize on performance measures as actionable data, managers, evaluation staff, consultants, and others trying to develop monitoring systems that really add value should:

- Clarify the purpose of the measurement system, its intended audience(s), what audience information needs are, and how the performance data will be used at the outset.
- Build ownership by involving managers and decision makers in identifying measures, targets, and data collection procedures and in developing a plan for using the data effectively.
- Generate leadership to encourage others to buy into the measures and to demonstrate or encourage executive commitment to using them.

- Identify *results owners*, individuals who have lead responsibility for maintaining or improving performance on particular measures.
- Delegate increased authority and flexibility to agencies, divisions, programs, and managers, where possible, in exchange for holding them accountable for results.
- Establish a regular process for reviewing the performance data, and use it to ask hard questions and to identify problems, causes, and if possible, potential corrective actions.
- Initiate follow-up investigations when persistent problems emerge from the performance data, through task forces, process improvement teams, or in-depth program evaluations.
- Informally monitor the usefulness and cost-effectiveness of the measurement system itself, and make adjustments accordingly.

It is important to bear in mind the limitations of performance measurement systems and not to expect performance data to drive decisions or solve problems single-handedly. Rather, evaluators and managers should encourage the meaningful consideration of performance data within the usual, ongoing management and decision-making processes. Performance measurement provides just part of the information public and nonprofit leaders need to make decisions. It does not replace the need for expenditure data, budget analysis, more thorough and comprehensive evaluations, or political judgments, nor is it a substitute for common sense, good management, leadership, and creativity. As one of the leading advocates of performance measurement observes: "A major purpose of performance measurement is to raise questions. It seldom, if ever, provides answers by itself about what should be done" (Hatry, 2006, p. 6).

Implementing Performance Measures in Networked Environments

An emerging challenge facing evaluators and others interested in performance measurement—and one that will loom larger in the future—concerns the development of systems for monitoring the performance of programs that are managed through networked environments rather than by single organizations. In addition to the traditional federal, state, and local government units in the intergovernmental system, these networks also involve nonprofit organizations and for-profit firms as well as other public entities that are grantees and contractors or that collaborate as partners.

Moreover, in many program areas a variety of such stakeholders are involved in making or influencing policy in addition to delivering services.

Implementing and maintaining effective measurement systems is much more challenging in networked environments for a variety of reasons: partners in a network may have substantive goal conflicts; program implementation and service delivery are likely to be decentralized; program implementation may vary substantially throughout the network; and the degree of commitment to a program may vary considerably among program stakeholders (Frederickson and Frederickson, 2007).

In addition, network members may have different levels of interest and expertise, including lack of interest, in monitoring performance; some members may lack the data, staff, analytical capabilities, or other resources to support measurement; and some may not display the voluntary cooperation among stakeholders that enables performance measurement to work at all. To increase the likelihood of value-adding performance measurement in the context of these challenges, evaluators and others in the position of developing performance measurement systems in heavily networked environments should try the following:

- Communicate the purpose and intended use of the performance measures to all members of the network.
- Work in the spirit of *negotiated accountability* to develop consensus among key stakeholders regarding goals and objectives, measures, targets, and data collection systems.
- Develop multiple or perhaps overlapping (but non-duplicative) sets of measures, if necessary, for different stakeholder groups and different uses.
- Use logic models to clarify how one agency's immediate outcomes often constitute changes in processes or outputs produced by others. (See Figure 5.6 for an example regarding the National Breast and Cervical Cancer Early Detection Program managed by the U.S. Centers for Disease Control and Prevention.)
- Develop hybrid monitoring systems that combine some mandated performance measures with more localized measures reflecting specific interests or concerns of individual stakeholders.
- Challenge entities in the network who do not subscribe to common measures to identify their own measures and to share the results.
- Provide technical assistance, and additional funding if possible, to help agencies with data collection, data analyses, and use of results.
- Integrate performance data from different stakeholders in the same reports to provide a more meaningful picture of overall system performance.

FIGURE 5.6. NATIONAL BREAST AND CERVICAL CANCER EARLY DETECTION PROGRAM.

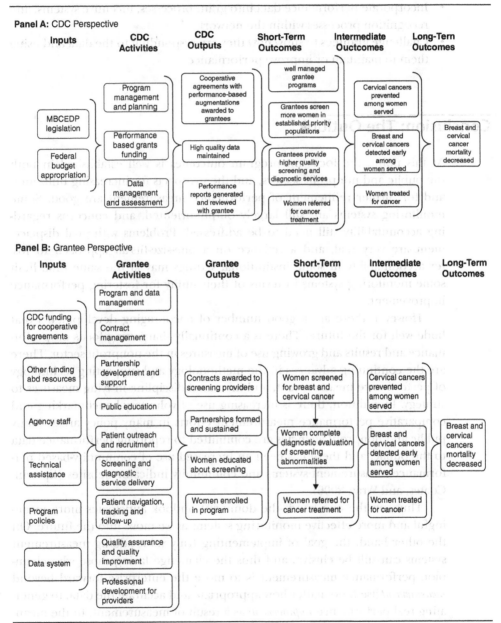

Source: Centers for Disease Control and Prevention. Used with permission.

- Delegate increased program management authority and flexibility to grantees in exchange for holding them accountable for results.
- Incorporate performance data into grant processes, incentive systems, and recognition processes within the network.
- Challenge grantees to show how they are responding to the data and using them to maintain or improve performance.

Conclusion: The Outlook

At this point, the focus on program outcomes is well established in both the public and nonprofit sectors, and the prospects for increasing utilization and for further refinement of performance measurement are good. Some monitoring systems are still largely output-oriented, and concerns regarding accountability still need to be addressed. Problems with goal displacement are very real, and a reliance on a one-size-fits-all approach to foster accountability in some institutional settings may at the same time limit some monitoring systems in terms of their utility for fostering performance improvement.

However, there are a good number of encouraging developments that bode well for the future. There is a continually sharpening focus on performance and results and growing use of measures in the nonprofit sector. There are the continuing advances in the methodology and supporting technology of performance measurement, and increased discipline in tying measures to strategy. In addition, there is increasing use of voluntary benchmarking and comparative performance measurement efforts in many policy areas. Many public and nonprofit agencies are committed to reporting performance data to the public, and there has been an increased use of community-based performance measurement systems and community indicator websites (Epstein, Coates, and Wray, 2006).

Thus, on the one hand, the dominant outlook anticipates more meaningful and more effective monitoring systems as we move into the future. On the other hand, the goal of implementing truly value-adding measurement systems can still be elusive, and thus the challenge facing those who champion performance measurement is to move the enterprise forward beyond *measurement* itself, no matter how appropriate and accurate the data, to generating real performance *improvement* as a result of measurement. In the meantime the tips in Box 5.1 can help make performance measurement more useful.

> ## Box 5.1. Final Tips for Practice
>
> - Take a results-driven rather than a data-driven approach in identifying relevant outcomes and other performance measures.
> - Involve internal and external stakeholders in developing performance measurement systems, in order to build commitment to using the data to strengthen performance.
> - Design integrated measurement systems to serve their intended purposes—strategic management, budgeting, program management, and so on—in order to improve decision making and strengthen performance.
> - Be wary of misinterpretation or misuse of performance data.
> - Use program evaluation and performance measurement as complementary tools to design and manage programs more effectively.
> - Periodically review the measures, performance reports, and procedures for follow-up, and revise the system as appropriate.

References

Ammons, D. N. *Municipal Benchmarks: Assessing Local Performance and Establishing Community Standards.* Thousand Oaks, CA: Sage, 2001.

Ammons, David N. "Analyzing Performance Data." In Patria De Lancer Julnes, Francis Stokes Berry, Maria P. Aristigueta, and Kaifeng Yang (eds.), *International Handbook of Practice-Based Performance Management.* Thousand Oaks, CA: Sage, 2008.

Ammons, D. N., and Rivenbark, W. C. "Factors Influencing the Use of Performance Data to Improve Municipal Services: Evidence from the North Carolina Benchmarking Project." *Public Administration Review,* 2008, *68*(2), 304–318.

Atlanta Police Department. "ATLStat Performance Management: Police." http://web.atlantaga.gov/atlstat/scorecards/apd/Atlanta_Police_Department-2009–10.pdf. 2009.

Bernstein, D. "Comments on Perrin's 'Effective Use and Misuse of Performance Measurement.'" *American Journal of Evaluation,* 1999, *20*(1), 85–93.

Centers for Disease Control and Prevention, Division of Sexually Transmitted Diseases Prevention. Unpublished slideshow presentation by Dayne Collins. Atlanta, GA: Centers for Disease Control and Prevention, Division of Sexually Transmitted Diseases Prevention, 2004.

City Manager's Office [Toronto], Executive Management Division. 2007 Performance Measurement and Benchmarking Report. Toronto: City Manager's Office, Executive Management Division, 2009.

Epstein, P. D., Coates, P. M., and Wray, L. D. *Results That Matter: Improving Communities by Engaging Citizens, Measuring Performance, and Getting Things Done.* San Francisco: Jossey-Bass, 2006.

Feller, I. Performance Measurement Redux. *American Journal of Evaluation,* 2002, *23*(4), 435–452.

Frederickson, D. G., and Frederickson, H. G. *Measuring the Performance of the Hollow State.* Washington, DC: Georgetown University Press, 2007.

Funnell, S. C., & Rogers, P. J. *Purposeful Program Theory: Effective Use of Theories of Change and Logic Models.* San Francisco: Jossey-Bass, 2011.

Hatry, H. P. *Performance Measurement: Getting Results* (2nd ed.). Washington, DC: Urban Institute Press, 2006.

Hatry, H. P., Morley, E., Rossman, S. B., and Wholey, J. S. *How Federal Programs Use Outcome Information: Opportunities for Federal Managers.* Washington, DC: IBM Endowment for The Business of Government, 2003.

Jennings, E. T., and Haist, M. P. "Putting Performance Measurement in Context: The Art of Governance: Analyzing Management and Administration." In P. W. Ingraham and L. E. Lynn (eds.), *The Art of Governance: Analyzing Management and Administration.* Washington, DC: Georgetown University Press, 2004.

Knowlton, L. W., & Phillips, C. C. *The Logic Model Guidebook: Better Strategies for Great Results.* Thousand Oaks, CA: Sage, 2012.

McDavid, J.C., Huse, I., and Hawthorn, L.R.L. *Program Evaluation and Performance Measurement: An Introduction to Practice.* (2nd ed.). Thousand Oaks, CA: Sage, 2013.

Moynihan, Donald P. *The Dynamics of Performance Management: Constructing Information and Reform.* Washington, DC: Georgetown University Press, 2008.

Moynihan, Donald P. "Through a Glass, Darkly: Understanding the Effects of Performance Regimes." *Public Performance & Management Review,* 2009, *32*(4), 592–603.

Newcomer, K. E., and Brass, C. "Forging a Strategic and Comprehensive Approach to Evaluation Within Public and Nonprofit Organizations: Integrating Measurement and Analytics Within Evaluation." *American Journal of Evaluation,* Forthcoming, 2015.

Nichols, S. L., and Berliner, D. C. *Collateral Damage: How High-Stakes Testing Corrupts America's Schools.* Cambridge, MA: Harvard Education Press, 2007.

Niven, P. R. *Balanced Scorecard Step-By-Step for Government and Nonprofit Agencies.* Hoboken, NJ: Wiley, 2003.

Ohio Department of Transportation. Unpublished slide show presentation by Leonard Evans. 2004.

Perrin, Bert. "Effective Use and Misuse of Performance Measurement." *American Journal of Evaluation,* 1998, *19*(3), 367–379.

Poister, T. H. *Measuring Performance in Public and Nonprofit Organizations.* San Francisco: Jossey-Bass, 2003.

Poister, T.H., Pasha, Obed Q., and Edwards, Lauren Hamilton. "Does Performance Management Lead to Better Outcomes? Evidence from the U.S. Public Transit System." *Public Administration Review,* 2013, *73*(4), 625–636.

Radin, B. A. *Challenging the Performance Movement: Accountability, Complexity, and Democratic Values.* Washington, DC: Georgetown University Press, 2006.

Sun, R., and Van Ryzin, G. G. "Are Performance Management Practices Associated with Better Public Outcomes? Empirical Evidence from New York City Schools." *The American Review of Public* 2014.

CHAPTER SIX

COMPARISON GROUP DESIGNS

Gary T. Henry

Evaluators frequently employ comparison group designs to assess the impact of programs or policies on their intended outcomes. Comparison group designs represent alternatives to randomized experiments when the goal of the evaluation is to provide a quantitative estimate of the causal effects of a program. (Throughout, I use the term *randomized experiment* to mean a study in which target population members are randomly assigned to program participation [treatment] or a control condition [no treatment]. Such studies are also known as *randomized controlled trials* or *random assignment studies*; see Chapter Seven for more information.) The purpose of most impact evaluations is to isolate the effects of a program to help officials and citizens decide whether the program should be continued, improved, or expanded to other areas. To conduct an impact evaluation, evaluators must provide an answer to the question: What would have happened in the absence of the program? In comparison group designs, the outcomes of the target population served by the program are compared to those of another group who represent what would have occurred in the absence of the program. By contrasting the outcomes of these two groups, evaluators can estimate the impact of the program on its intended outcomes.

The need for a comparison group may be best explained by an example. Many policymakers, parents, and taxpayers want to know if publicly subsidized prekindergarten (pre-K) programs boost children's cognitive, social, and communication skills. These skills can be measured directly after children have participated in the pre-K program, but it is impossible to know from these measures of the prekindergarteners' outcomes alone how much they were affected by the program. Even with an accurate measure of the children's problem-solving skills, it is impossible to isolate the effect of pre-K from the effects of other influences, including children's skills prior to entering pre-K, their interactions with family and others during the year, and other resources in the communities where they live. To obtain an estimate of the pre-K program's contribution to the children's outcomes, the skills of the children who participated in the program must be compared to those of another group. This is the essential logic behind comparison group designs. Although the logic of these designs is relatively straightforward, planning and implementing an evaluation that *accurately* isolates the effects of a program on the target population is one of the most difficult challenges that evaluators undertake.

Some readers may already be wondering about the definition of *comparison group design*. Fundamentally, comparison group designs are approaches to assessing causal effects that measure an important program outcome and estimate impact by comparing the difference between treated and untreated groups when random assignment to the groups has *not* been used. Thus the term *comparison group* distinguishes an untreated but not randomly assigned group from a randomly assigned *control group* used in randomized experiments. Both control and comparison groups are used to estimate what would have happened in the absence of a program, but group members are selected differently.

This chapter describes a variety of comparison group designs that evaluators have frequently used to assess program impacts. The tasks involved in developing and carrying out a comparison group design that accurately and convincingly estimates the effects of a program are arduous. Fortunately, in the past few years a stronger base of theory and empirical studies that examine the accuracy of alternative comparison group designs has begun to emerge. However, it is important to understand at the outset that (1) none of the comparison group designs is without its limitations; (2) some are better than others; and (3) in a world in which the most convincing estimate of program impacts is *not the top priority* for most policymakers and the public, evaluators will need to be knowledgeable and resourceful in exploring alternative comparison group designs when planning impact evaluations. Also, evaluators need to be able to explain the strengths and limitations of each design to sponsors and stakeholders so that informed choices can be made and evidence concerning program impacts can be accurately interpreted.

Comparison group designs have previously been grouped together under labels such as quasi-experimental, pre-experimental, non-experimental, or observational studies. They also include some designs that are possible when evaluators have longitudinal data, such as administrative data that tracks program participants over time or studies that collect data on multiple cohorts that participate in a program. This chapter strips away the distinctions among these labels by referring to all designs for impact evaluations that do not involve random assignment to treatment and control as *comparison group designs*. The unifying concept is that all comparison group designs involve using the difference between treated and untreated comparison groups in order to estimate the effects of a program. The idea behind comparison group designs is simple, but the program impact estimates can be quite misleading if the conditions for implementing them are not present or they are carried out incorrectly. Only in a limited number of situations, when circumstances are favorable and the comparison group designs are implemented in specific ways, have studies shown that the program impact estimates are sufficiently accurate for potential issues with the design to be ignored (Bifulco, 2012; Cook, Shadish, and Wong, 2008; Glazerman, Levy, and Myer, 2003; Shadish, Clark, and Steiner 2008). However, in an imperfect world, evaluators must sometimes choose between better and worse designs rather than the best design or no evaluation. The goal of this chapter is to help practicing evaluators improve their designs as much as circumstances and resources permit and be able to carefully state the limitations on the findings for any comparison group study that they carry out.

In the next section of the chapter, I describe the ideal situation for assessing program impacts. Surprisingly to some, this ideal is not a randomized experiment. In the view of many evaluators, statisticians, and social scientists, randomized experiments are the closest approximation to the ideal that is possible. However, randomized experiments are not the ideal, as we shall see, and they require that certain assumptions be made to consider their estimates truly accurate or unbiased. Randomized experiments are usually the best potential design because they require the fewest assumptions to be made in order to consider the estimates that they produce accurate and convincing. Under certain circumstances, however, comparison group designs can produce accurate estimates of program impact; indeed, at least one of the designs is considered by many to be as compelling as randomized experiments. Having acknowledged that comparison group designs can produce accurate effect estimates, it is important to also say that these designs impose significant technical conditions and data requirements that must be met in order to produce accurate and convincing estimates of program impact.

Introduction to Causal Theory for Impact Evaluation

Impact evaluations seek to provide quantitative estimates of the causal effects of programs or policies. The potential outcomes framework provides a new way to think about this task. The ideal way to calculate the causal impact of a program is to compute the difference between the outcome for every member of the target population after participating in a program *and* the outcome for the same subjects after not participating in the program. Applying this idea to the earlier example, an impact evaluator would like to be able to observe the outcomes for a specific four-year-old after attending prekindergarten *and* after not attending prekindergarten. Of course, each child either attends or does not attend a pre-K program when he or she is four years old. So in reality we can never directly observe or measure the treatment effect, a situation that Paul Holland (1986) refers to as the "fundamental problem of causal inference." Because we need to be able to acquire actual evidence about the impacts of policies and programs, evaluation designs that approximate the ideal have been developed and tested.

The most ideal alternative to this impossible situation for generating an unbiased effect estimate is a study that would involve random sampling and random assignment (Imai, King, and Stuart, 2009; Murnane and Willett, 2012). In such a study, a random sample of the target population for a program would be selected, then each of the randomly selected sample members would be randomly assigned to treatment or control. Why would this be considered an ideal? Random sampling ensures that the sample is an accurate statistical model of the population or has external validity (Henry, 1990). Random assignment of individuals to the treated groups or untreated control groups ensures that all the other factors that influence the outcomes are unrelated to whether the individual is treated or untreated. In other words, random assignment to one or the other group can be expected to balance all of the influences on the observed outcomes after program participation *other than the program*. When individuals are randomly assigned to treatment, differences between the treatment group and control group means on outcomes can be reasonably attributed to the effects of the program, when chance variation can be dismissed as an explanation, and the sample has been selected at random from the target population, the effects can be inferred to the target population. Comparison group designs are usually implemented in situations when random assignment is not possible, and therefore we will focus on those situations.

In the world of practical program evaluations, random assignment is always difficult and frequently impossible. A principal advantage of random assignment in impact evaluations is that the means by which individuals enter the treated or untreated groups is free of selection bias or, in other words, assignment to treatment is not related to the outcomes of the program participants. For example, if a fair lottery is used to assign eligible children to Pre-K when the demand for slots exceeds availability, then comparing outcomes of the children who received a slot and those who did not is free of selection bias. If, however, the spaces are allocated on a first-come first-served basis, parents who are more motivated for their children to succeed in school may be more successful in enrolling their children. After the program, any differences in outcomes measured for the four-year-olds who participated and the four-year-olds who did not participate (who were untreated) could be due in part to parental motivation as well as in part to the program. It is wise for evaluators to assume that selection bias does operate when designing impact evaluations, even if some argue that it is nonexistent or of minimal consequence. Comparison group designs differ in the extent to which they can minimize this type of bias.

Randomized experiments stand out as the preferred method for eliminating selection bias from impact evaluations. However, other sources of bias can and often do occur with randomized experiments, such as non-random selection from the target population when those who volunteer for participation are different from the target population that is of interest to evaluation stakeholders, when participants leave the study, or when samples are too small to rule out chance as an explanation for observed differences in outcomes. For these reasons and for a number of practical concerns—such as the length of time it takes to design, implement, and obtain findings from a randomized experiment, the costs of randomized experiments, and ethical issues—comparison group designs are useful and powerful approaches for evaluators to consider when designing impact evaluations. Often, comparison group designs are the only practical means available for evaluators to provide evidence about program impact within time and resource constraints imposed by evaluation sponsors.

Comparison Group Designs

Numerous comparison group designs are available for impact evaluations. These designs differ in their data requirements, the circumstances in which they can be applied, and the extent to which they are likely to reduce bias. Although theory (Holland, 1986; Rosenbaum and Rubin, 1983) and careful application of logic (Shadish, Cook, and Campbell, 2002) provide guidance about the relative strengths of alternative comparison group designs, neither theory nor logic can predict the extent of bias that any particular impact evaluation design will produce. Our understanding about the extent of selection bias in any specific evaluation is largely based on judgments about the plausibility of alternative explanations for the results and on empirical studies that compare program impact estimates of randomized experiments and comparison group designs.

The next eight sections of this chapter review alternative comparison group designs, beginning with the most basic design, which is labeled the *naïve* design. Even though this design is the least likely to produce estimates that are accurate and convincing, it illustrates the most elementary approach to comparison group design. These eight sections end with a review of a very rigorous and sophisticated design—*regression discontinuity*—that has strong theory supporting the accuracy of its causal inferences and mounting empirical evidence about its accuracy. In between these two extremes are additional comparison group designs that are described roughly in order of their likelihood of producing more and more accurate impact estimates, but also in order of increasing complexity and greater requirements for data and technical proficiency. I say roughly in order of each design's ability to yield accurate estimates of program impact because this accuracy depends on the circumstances in which the design is used, the data that are used for the evaluation, and how well the design is implemented. A poorly implemented randomized experiment can produce flawed findings, and a poorly implemented comparison group design can as well. None of the designs are in any sense guaranteed to produce accurate impact estimates, but in moving us in the direction of providing evidence about program effects, they represent efforts to provide the best available evidence about program effects when randomized experiments are infeasible, unethical, or not available in the time frame in which decisions need be made. Finally, it is important to note that elements of these designs can be combined to enhance the accuracy of program impact estimates, although describing the possible combinations is beyond the scope of this chapter.

1. Naïve Design

The most basic means of estimating program impacts is the comparison of the statistical means for *naturally occurring* treated and untreated groups. Usually, this design involves comparing one or more outcome measures for a group that participated in or had access to treatment with those for another group that did not have such treatment or access to it. The outcome measures may be available from administrative data, such as student test scores or patient lengths of stay in the hospital, or from surveys that include both treated and untreated individuals. To continue with the pre-K example, we could compare children who participated in pre-K and those who did not on teachers' ratings of their school readiness when they begin kindergarten. An estimate of impact is the difference between the group means:

$$\delta = \overline{Y}_t - \overline{Y}_u$$

In this case, δ is the treatment effect or program impact (for example, the pre-K program impact estimate),

$$\overline{Y}_t$$

is the mean score on the readiness assessment for the treated (for example, prekindergarteners), and

$$\overline{Y}_u$$

is the mean score for the untreated (for example, children who did not attend pre-K). Naïve comparisons can also be expressed in a simple regression format (this chapter also uses this format for depicting other designs, and therefore it is shown here for clarity):

$$Y_i = \alpha + \delta Z_i + \varepsilon_i$$

where Y_i is the outcome (for example, the readiness score for each kindergartener), α is the average score for the untreated (for example, kindergarteners who did not participate in pre-K), δ is a regression coefficient that represents the difference between the treated and untreated group means and is identical to the δ in the previous equation,

$$Z_i$$

is an indicator variable that is coded 1 for treated and 0 for untreated individuals, and

$$\varepsilon_i$$

is each individual's deviation from the group mean, also described as the *error term*.

This design for producing program impact estimates when the treated and untreated groups have occurred naturally is considered naïve because these two groups could differ for reasons other than participation in the program. The treated group could have been in greater need of the program and started out far behind the untreated group in skills, family resources, or motivation. In some situations the reverse might be expected. For example, families or individuals who perceive greater benefits from program participation, like pre-K, after-school, or job training programs, may have been the most likely to enroll.

Frequently, in addition to individuals making a choice to participate (self-selection), program operators choose individuals to participate based on such loose criteria as the operator's perceptions about need or the extent to which an individual will benefit from the program. In situations where participants or program operators exercise judgments in selecting program participants, selection bias is likely to render the simple comparisons highly inaccurate. In any case, after program participation has occurred, it is impossible to discern conclusively that selection bias did not occur. Selection bias is the most pernicious form of bias that plagues evaluators' attempts to accurately estimate program impacts. Also, it is often difficult to explain to evaluation sponsors and stakeholders why this simple design is unlikely to be accurate.

We can gain a better understanding of the reasons why bias is likely to be a problem by recourse to the *potential outcomes framework*: for selection bias to be reduced to the point at which it can be ignored, *the potential outcomes if neither group was exposed to the program* must be similar for the two groups. Evaluators must ask the following question and be able to answer it in the affirmative for the naïve design to be a reasonable approach for an impact evaluation: Do we expect that if the program had not been offered, the outcomes of the treated and untreated comparison groups would have been roughly the same? In other words, evaluators must be able to assume that if no treatment had been offered to anyone in either group, the mean outcomes of the treated and untreated groups would have been the same *and* that assumption must be both valid and plausible to the consumers of the evaluation.

In most cases, good and valid reasons exist to doubt that the outcomes would have been roughly the same. Moreover, evaluators and evaluation sponsors and stakeholders cannot be sure that the outcomes would be roughly the same for both groups had the program not been provided. Thus, in the great majority of cases, the assumption of equivalent outcomes for the treated and untreated groups in the absence of the program is likely to be implausible and naïve. Therefore, the naïve design is a very questionable choice for impact evaluations in most cases.

2. Basic Value-Added Design: Regression Adjusted for a Preprogram Measure

As mentioned previously, one of the difficulties of the naïve design is that evaluators cannot rule out the possibility that differences between the treated and untreated groups prior to participating in the program could cause differences in their outcomes after the program has been offered to the treated group. When the same measure that is used for the outcome has been observed for both the treated and untreated group *prior to program participation*, the preprogram measure can be used to adjust the impact estimates for this preexisting difference. Adding this preprogram measure to the regression equation adjusts the program impact estimates for preexisting differences between treated and untreated on an outcome of interest for the evaluation. Here is a regression approach to estimating program impact (δ) using a preprogram measure of the outcome:

$$Y_{it} = \alpha + \delta Z_i + \beta_1 Y_{it-1} + \varepsilon_i$$

As in the previous equations, δ represents the program impact estimate, Z_i is coded 1 for the treated group members and 0 for the untreated, Y_{it} is the measure of the outcome at time t, which occurs after treatment, Y_{it-1} is the measure of the outcome at time $t-1$, which occurs before the program, and α is the constant or intercept term. The preprogram measure is the best measure of the individuals' differences prior to the program and therefore adjusts the program impact for the initial difference in the outcome variable between the treated and untreated groups within limitations of measurement error and assuming that the values of the preprogram measures for the two groups substantially overlap.

This comparison group design of program impact adjusting for a preprogram measure of the outcome variable is commonly referred to as a *value-added design*, because the program impact estimate represents the amount of gain since program participation began or, more precisely, since the preprogram measure was observed. Fortunately, this type of longitudinal design is now possible more frequently due to administrative data sets that record the status of individuals eligible for a program at regular intervals, such as the test scores measures that are now available for most students in all states. In addition, much has been done to assess the accuracy of value-added approaches and the threats to the accuracy of the estimates that are generated. Common problems with value-added designs include regression to the mean (high and low scores at preprogram move toward the mean after the program), differences in program effects for those with either high or low preprogram scores, and omission of other covariates that are related to both program participation and the outcome. The latter problem, which is sometimes called *omitted variable bias*, is a persistent problem with comparison group designs. Omitted variable bias, which refers to the bias of program impact estimates due to omitting other variables that are related to the outcome and program participation, will be confronted but not entirely removed in the next design, the regression-adjusted covariate design.

3. Regression-Adjusted Covariate Design

A frequent first impulse to improve program impact estimates over the naive estimates is to use multiple regression to adjust the impact estimates by adding covariates (control variables) that account for some of the other variables that influence outcomes. To the extent that the treated and the untreated groups differ on covariates systematically associated with the outcome, the estimates of program impact can be adjusted for the imbalances between the groups. This chapter calls this design *regression adjusted for covariates*, and it can be represented as follows:

$$Y_i = \alpha + \delta Z_i + \beta_1 X_{1i} + \cdots + \beta_c X_{ci} + \varepsilon_i$$

where β_1 is the regression coefficient for the first of c covariates, X_{1i} is the value of the first of c covariates for individual i, X_{ci} is the value for the last of the c covariates, and δ is the adjusted coefficient that is used to estimate the program impact. When samples are large enough, many covariates can be added to the multiple regression equation. The choice of covariates should be guided by theory that delineates the various factors that influence the outcomes of interest. Where possible, it is advantageous to use empirically validated theory that prior research has shown to be systematically associated with the outcomes in the target population for the program being evaluated. Where the covariates are better at explaining the variation in the outcome and differ between treated and untreated groups, the bias reduction is likely to be significant.

Studies (Glazerman, Levy, and Myer, 2003; Shadish, Clark, and Steiner, 2008) find that this type of design does substantially reduce bias; however, their findings also indicate that substantial bias can still remain, depending on the quality of the covariates. For example, in an evaluation of a state pre-K program, Henry and Rickman (2009) report that 51 percent of the mothers of Head Start participants received food stamps, but only 18 percent of the mothers of children enrolled in Pre-K received food stamps. An adjustment for the difference could be attempted by adding food stamp receipt as a covariate in an equation that includes the indicator for participation in Pre-K. In addition to food stamp participation, additional covariates, variables on which the two groups could be expected to differ and which are expected to affect the outcome, could be added to adjust the estimates further. Larger reductions in bias may be achieved when the covariates include all variables that have affected selection into treatment and the outcomes that are being assessed. However, the extent of bias remaining cannot be directly tested in most evaluations, and for that reason, covariate-adjusted estimates of program impact are frequently viewed with skepticism. A large number of covariates based on a well-conceived theory about the factors influencing the outcome variables will improve this design.

4. Value-Added Design Adjusted for Additional Covariates

When a preprogram measure of the variable used as a post-program outcome is combined with additional covariates, the design can be referred to as a *value-added design adjusted for additional covariates*. For example, in the evaluation of a state Pre-K program, Henry, Gordon, Henderson, and Ponder (2003) measured children's cognitive and communication skills on four different assessments in fall 2001, when the children began Pre-K, Head Start, or some other preschool program. Because these same measures were used as the outcome variables after the Pre-K program, they could be added along with other baseline covariates expected to explain a great deal of the variation in children's developmental outcomes into the regression analysis, which can be represented as follows:

$$Y_{it} = \alpha + \delta Z_i + \beta_1 Y_{it-1} + \beta_2 X_{1i} + \cdots + \beta_{c+2} X_{c+1i} + \varepsilon_i$$

where the covariates include Y_{it-1} to represent the preprogram measure of the outcome, as it did in the value-added design above. The preprogram outcome measure is also known as the *lagged value* of the outcome variable. The preprogram score on the same measure as the outcome provides an adjustment for differences in the children in the treated and untreated comparison groups on that measure before the participation in the program began for the treated group. In addition, it can improve the precision of the estimates of treatment effects. Including the preprogram score in the equation changes the interpretation of the coefficients, $\beta_2 - \beta_{c+2}$, to the effect of the covariate since the time the preprogram score was measured. Some recent research has indicated that estimates are likely to be improved if all the preprogram measures, such as measures of skills for four-year-olds, are included in the regression. Doing this appears to mitigate a part of the measurement error that can occur in any single measure of the children's skills and abilities. To continue with this example, preprogram measures can also be used to adjust for other outcome measures, such as teachers' ratings of school readiness, but the coefficients are not interpreted as value added.

When a preprogram measure of the outcome variable is available, it is possible to develop a special type of covariate-adjusted, value-added program impact estimate that substantially reduces bias (Glazerman, Levy, and Myer, 2003). The process for this special adjustment begins by assembling a rich set of covariates and using the preprogram score on the outcome variable as a temporary substitute for the post-treatment outcome variable in a regression analysis. First, the preprogram score is substituted as the dependent variable, as shown here:

$$Y_{it-1} = \alpha + \delta Z_i + \beta_1 X_{1i} + \cdots + \beta_c X_{ci} + \varepsilon_i$$

The object of the analysis is to find a set of covariates that render the coefficient on the indicator for treatment (δ) statistically insignificant (that is, not statistically different from 0). This indicates that the covariates included in the equation make the two groups statistically similar prior to program participation. Then the program impact is estimated using the equation for the value-added design adjusted for covariates presented earlier in this section, with the complete complement of covariates included in the specification in which the treated and untreated groups were found to be statistically more similar.

5. Interrupted Time-Series Designs

Interrupted time-series designs are longitudinal designs applicable in situations when new programs are started or major reforms occur and data are available for before and after the change. These situations are often referred to as *natural experiments,* but they compare groups that cannot be assumed to be equivalent, as groups in randomized experiments can be. Interrupted time-series designs include several observations of an outcome that is expected to be affected by the reform or new program *prior to the change* and several observations of the same measure *after the change.* In the most basic form of interrupted time-series designs, the treated group before the reform is compared to itself after the reform. However, this design is considered relatively weak because other changes occurring at the same time as the reform might produce a different pattern in the outcome variable after the interruption.

A much stronger interrupted time-series design involves comparing post-program change from the pattern of preprogram observations in the treated group to the change for an untreated group over the same time. This design is frequently assessed for an average increase in the outcome during the post-program period in comparison to the change in the untreated group's outcome, which can be done using the following formula:

$$Y_{it} = \alpha + \beta_1 Z_i + \beta_2 T + \delta Z_i T + \beta_3 X_{ci} + \cdots + \beta_{c+3} X_{c+1i} + \varepsilon_i$$

where the estimate of the effect is the coefficient δ on an interaction term that designates observations of the treated group after the reform or change, Z_i is coded 1 for the treated group and 0 for the untreated group, and T_t is coded 1 for the period after the interruption and 0 for the pre-interruption period. The program impact coefficient is interpreted as the average increase (or decrease, if negative) in the outcome for the treated group in the post-interruption period less the average difference in the outcome for the untreated group in the post-interruption period.

This interrupted time-series design is considered relatively strong. The principal issue with the design is that the treated group could have been selected based on criteria that make them react to the reform or program change differently from the untreated group. For example, this design has been used to assess the impact of various types of state policy reforms on the intended outcomes of the policy. But if a state adopts a reform of a particular policy in a period when pre-interruption outcomes are particularly low, then factors other than the policy may be contributing to any increase that is found.

Impact evaluations are currently making use of this design more frequently. For example, Henry and Gordon (2003) assessed the effects of a public information campaign that announced action days during which members of the Atlanta public were asked to reduce car travel due to predictions that ozone levels would exceed U.S. Environmental Protection Agency regulations. Upcoming action days were communicated to the public on the day prior to the predicted violation through electronic highway signs and in weather forecasts in the newspapers and in radio and television broadcasts. Thirty-five action days occurred intermittently during the 153-day study period, and so driving behavior on the action days was contrasted with driving behavior on the other days. Rather than a single switch or interruption, this design used multiple switches or interruptions to estimate the program effects. Henry and

Gordon found that overall, individuals reduced their average miles driven on action days by 5.5 miles, and individuals whose employers had joined in the local clean air campaign reduced their driving even more.

6. Fixed-Effect Designs for Longitudinal Evaluations

With longitudinal data sets becoming more commonly available for studies such as education and labor market studies and for panel studies such as the Panel Study of Income Dynamics and the Early Childhood Longitudinal Studies, a study design known as a *fixed-effect design* has gained popularity. In these designs each individual effectively serves as his or her own comparison. The treatment effects are estimated based on comparing outcomes for an individual during periods when he or she received a particular treatment with outcomes during periods when he or she received an alternative treatment or no treatment.

$$Y_{it} - \overline{Y}_i = \alpha + \delta \left(Z_{it} - \overline{Z}_i \right) + \beta_c \left(X_{cit} - \overline{X}_{ci} \right) + \left(\varepsilon_{it} - \overline{\varepsilon}_i \right)$$

The individual fixed effects remove all of the non-time varying characteristics of the individual, which essentially allows for each individual to serve as his or her own control. An evaluation of the Teach For America (TFA) program, by Xu, Hannaway, and Taylor (2008) illustrates individual fixed effects. The objective of the evaluation was to obtain the effects of TFA by estimating the differences in student achievement when students were taught by a TFA teacher and when they were taught by a traditionally prepared teacher. The evaluation used data from the twenty-three school districts in North Carolina where TFA teachers were employed between the 2000–2001 and 2006–2007 school years. Treatment effects were the aggregated differences between end-of-course achievement test scores for courses taught by TFA teachers and end-of-course test scores for courses taught by traditionally prepared teachers for each student who had experienced both types of teachers. The student fixed effects essentially eliminated the influence of any student characteristic that did not change during the study period. Xu, Hannaway, and Taylor (2008) found that students in courses taught by TFA teachers averaged scores about one point higher on their tests (0.10 standard deviation units) than they did when these students were taught by other teachers. Although fixed effects can eliminate an important source of bias, only study subjects who have experienced treatment on some occasions and not experienced it on others can be included in impact estimates. In the example, students who did not experience both types of teachers were excluded from the effect estimate, which may limit the generalizability of the effect estimate.

7. Matching Designs

Designs in which members of an untreated group are matched to each member of a treated group are referred to as *matching designs*. Matching members of the comparison group to members of the treatment group using preprogram covariates is intended to make the two groups as similar as possible prior to the treatment. These designs have a venerable but checkered tradition in evaluation. There are instances in which matching did not produce results that most careful observers would regard as unbiased. One such case was the now infamous Westinghouse study of Head Start (Cicarelli, 1971). In this evaluation, children who had participated in Head Start were matched with members of their kindergarten classes who had not participated, and differences in outcomes between these two groups were used to estimate the effects of Head Start. However, when the data were reanalyzed using several different techniques, the evaluators concluded that substantial bias was likely (Datta, 1982). The issue for matching designs is that the groups can be made very similar on the covariates that have been measured and used in the matching, but unobserved differences in the treated and untreated groups may remain, and these differences may bias the impact estimates.

One strategy for reducing the differences between a treated group and an untreated comparison group is to increase the number of covariates that are used to match them. However, as more covariates are added it becomes difficult to find exact matches for every member of the treated group in the pool of untreated group members. The result is inexact matches or incomplete matches, either of which could affect the accuracy of the impact estimates. Recent developments in matching designs indicate that an approach referred to as *propensity score matching* may substantially reduce bias in effect estimates (Cook, Shadish, and Wong, 2008; Diaz and Handa, 2005; Glazerman, Levy, and Myer, 2003; Stuart 2010). Paul Rosenbaum and Donald Rubin developed the propensity score matching approach, and they have established some very desirable properties for the procedure (see Rosenbaum and Rubin, 1983; Rosenbaum, 2002; Rubin, 2001).

Several different types of matching designs have become available since compelling theoretical properties for propensity score matching (PSM) were developed by Rosenbaum and Rubin (1983). PSM replaces matching on several covariates with matching on a single propensity score that is an estimate of the likelihood that each member of the study sample could be in the treated group. PSM makes assignment to the treated and comparison groups independent of the covariates that are used to estimate the propensity of an individual to be in the treatment group. PSM has both intuitive and technical advantages over using regression-based approaches by themselves. These advantages include creating a comparison group that is more similar to the treatment group and accounting for nonlinearities between covariates and the outcome (Stuart and Green, 2008). However, the theory supporting PSM does not address the extent of the bias that could be caused by imbalances between treatment and comparison groups that result from variables not included in estimating the propensity score. Therefore, the amount of bias that remains after the matching is uncertain. If assignment to the two groups is not independent across the unobserved covariates, the treatment effect estimates using PSM could be biased, due to these differences between the treated and comparison groups that are uncontrolled by the matching.

Propensity score matching has been frequently used in recent years to obtain more accurate estimates of program impact. In a recent study, Henry, Gordon, and Rickman (2006) matched a group of children who participated in a state Pre-K program with a group of Head Start recipients to investigate the differences in developmental outcomes attributable to participating in Head Start when compared with an alternative Pre-K program. They found that the children who attended the state Pre-K program scored higher on direct assessments of language and cognitive skills at the beginning of kindergarten than the children who participated in Head Start.

When PSM procedures are followed, within-study comparisons indicate significant bias reduction (Cook, Shadish, and Wong, 2008; Diaz and Handa, 2005; Glazerman, Levy, and Myer, 2003; Stuart 2010). However, some researchers find the amount of bias that remains is too large to ignore (Glazerman, Levy, and Myer, 2003; Wilde and Hollister, 2007). There are a variety of ways to obtain estimates of the treatment effect using the matched sample. A common approach, which Glazerman, Levy, and Myer (2003) find to reduce bias, simply adds the propensity score (P_i) to the regression equation used for the estimation of the treatment effect, as illustrated in this equation, which assumes that a lagged outcome measure is available:

$$Y_i = \alpha + \delta Z_i + \beta_1 Y_{it-1} + \beta_2 P_i + \beta_3 X_{1i} + \cdots + \beta_{c+3} X_{c+1i} + \varepsilon_i$$

The accuracy of program impact estimates using propensity score matching remains an empirical question because the influence of unobserved variables depends on the quality of the covariates used in the estimation of the propensity score and in the previous equation. Having a large group of covariates that are related to the outcome and selection into the treated group has been shown by empirical research to be important for the accuracy of the program impact estimates.

8. Regression Discontinuity Designs

Regression discontinuity (RD) designs lay the strongest claim of all of the comparison group designs to producing unbiased estimates of program impacts. These designs rely on a quantitative index to assign subjects to treatment or to an alternative condition, such as business as usual or no treatment. Including the quantitative index in the equation used to estimate the difference between the treated and comparison groups can effectively eliminate selection bias in the program impact estimates (Imbens and Lemieux, 2007; also see Chapter Seven in this volume). Frequently, the quantitative variable that assigns subjects to treatment measures an individual's need for the program or the subject's risk of adverse social consequences. The variable does not have to perfectly measure the need, but it must be strictly used to assign all cases on one side of a cutoff value to the treated group, and the treatment must be withheld from all cases on the other side of the cutoff.

Cook, Shadish, and Wong (2008) provide evidence that the differences in estimates from RD designs and randomized experiments are negligible. RD design produces impact estimates that are unbiased by selection into treatment by including the variable that indicates whether a subject was assigned to the treated group or comparison group and the quantitative index used to assign subjects to the two groups along with higher-order terms of this variable in a multiple regression (Imbens and Lemieux, 2007, p. 10). Including variables in the estimation equation that perfectly model the relationship between the assignment index and the outcome variable breaks up any possible correlation between the treatment indicator variable and the individual error term. Including this term along with exponential functions of this term as needed removes selection bias from the estimate of the treatment effect.

Here is a typical equation for estimating the treatment effect (δ):

$$Y_i = \alpha + \delta Z_i + f(I_i - I_c) + \beta_1 Z_i * f(I_i - I_c)_i + \beta_2 X_{1i} + \cdots + \beta_{c+2} X_{c+1i} + \varepsilon_i$$

where the novel term, $f(I_i - I_c)$, can be broken down as follows: I_c is the value of the assignment index at the cutoff, I_i is the value of the index for each individual, which makes the term $I_i - I_c$ the distance of each individual from the cutoff. The entire term refers to a polynomial function of the distance, which is operationalized by including exponential functions such as the squared and cubed terms of the distance from the cutoff on the assignment variable as additional variables until the higher order terms are no longer significant. Basically, the terms associated with the assignment index I will "soak up" the selection bias that may be attributable to omitted variables, so that even though the *other* coefficients may be biased, the program impact estimate will be correspondingly purged of selection bias. The covariates are included to eliminate small sample biases and increase precision without altering the benefits of the RD design (Imbens and Lemieux, 2007, p. 11).

In an evaluation of the impact of Oklahoma's state pre-K program, Gormley, Gayer, Phillips, and Dawson (2005) used a novel RD design to estimate the effects of the program in Tulsa. The evaluation team used the children's ages as the assignment variable and the eligibility dates as the cutoff on the assignment variable. The children's outcomes on direct assessments were measured in the fall after the older children had attended pre-K and before pre-K began for the younger children. The evaluators compared the test scores of children with ages slightly above the cutoff to the test scores of children slightly too young to have been eligible for pre-K the prior year. Significant differences in children's knowledge of letters and words, spelling skills, and problem-solving skills were found, indicating that the Tulsa pre-K program was effective in increasing these outcomes. For a more complete discussion of this design see Lipsey, Weiland, Yoshikawa, Wilson, and Hofer (2014).

RD designs have also been implemented when a few cases close to the cutoff have ended up in a group other than the one to which they should have been assigned. This type of RD design is referred to as a *fuzzy* discontinuity design, as opposed to a *sharp* discontinuity design. In addition, RD designs have been implemented in situations in which settings or clusters of individuals, such as school districts, are assigned to treatment using a quantitative index of need. Currently, the interest in RD designs is high and their use is enjoying a renaissance. A well-designed RD study effectively eliminates selection bias, but researchers must take care to assess other sources of bias. A primary validity concern for RD designs is the generalizability of the intervention effect estimate. RD designs estimate the effect of the intervention at the cutoff, and this estimate can be different from the average treatment effect estimate obtained in random assignment studies. Other sources of bias are "hidden" treatments for either group that occur precisely at the cutoff for assignment. Even with these potential biases, RD designs are generally considered second only to randomized experiments in terms of producing accurate estimates of program effects.

Conclusion

A common use of comparison group designs in evaluation is to estimate the impact of programs by calculating the difference between the outcomes for those exposed to a treatment and the outcomes for those in an untreated comparison group. When random assignment is impossible or impractical, a comparison group design can be used to contrast the outcomes of a group that participated in a program with the outcomes of an untreated comparison group in an attempt to quantify the program's causal effects from the comparison of the two group means. This chapter showed how stronger comparison group designs can be used to improve on naïve comparisons by making adjustments that reduce bias in the estimates of program impacts.

Value-added designs, interrupted time-series designs, fixed-effect designs, matching designs, and regression discontinuity (RD) designs appear to have the capacity to significantly reduce the bias likely to occur in naïve program impact estimates. Regression discontinuity designs have the most compelling underlying theory for causal inference. As the developments in propensity score matching and RD designs indicate, this is a dynamic area for research and development. As richer data sources continue to become more available, evaluators will have increasing opportunities to implement stronger comparison group designs. In addition, these designs are frequently being combined – such as in the use of matching and interrupted time series (Henry, Smith, Kershaw, and Zulli, 2013) or longitudinal data and regression discontinuity (Wing and Cook, 2013) to further reduce bias in causal effect estimates.

References

Bifulco, Robert. "Can Nonexperimental Estimates Replicate Estimates Based on Random Assignment in Evaluations of School Choice? A Within-Study Comparison." *Journal of Policy Analysis and Management,* 2012, *31*(3), 729–751.

Cicarelli, V. "The Impact of Head Start: Executive Summary." In F. Caro (ed.), *Readings in Evaluation Research.* New York: Russell Sage Foundation, 1971.

Cook, T. D., Shadish, W. R., and Wong, V. C. "Three Conditions Under Which Experiments and Observational Studies Produce Comparable Causal Estimates: New Findings from Within-Study Comparisons." *Journal of Policy Analysis and Management,* 2008, *27*(4), 724–750.

Datta, L.-E. "A Tale of Two Studies: The Westinghouse-Ohio Evaluation of Project Head Start and the Consortium for Longitudinal Studies Report." *Studies in Educational Evaluation,* 1982, *8*, 271–280.

Diaz, J. J., and Handa, S. "An Assessment of Propensity Score Matching as a Nonexperimental Impact Estimator: Evidence from Mexico's PROGRESA Program." *Journal of Human Resources*, 2005, *41*(2), 319–345.

Glazerman, S., Levy, D. M., and Myer, D. "Nonexperimental Versus Experimental Estimates of Earnings Impacts." *Annals of the American Academy of Political and Social Science*, 2003, *589*, 63–93.

Gormley, W. T. Jr., Gayer, T., Phillips, D., and Dawson, B. "The Effects of Universal Pre-K on Cognitive Development." *Developmental Psychology*, 2005, *41*(6), 872–884.

Henry, G. T. *Practical Sampling.* Thousand Oaks, CA: Sage, 1990.

Henry, G. T., and Gordon, C. S. "Driving Less for Better Air: Impacts of a Public Information Campaign." *Journal of Policy Analysis and Management*, 2003, *22*(1), 45–63.

Henry, G. T., Gordon, C. S., Henderson, L. W., and Ponder, B. D. "Georgia Pre-K Longitudinal Study: Final Report 1996–2001." Atlanta, GA: Georgia State University, Andrew Young School of Policy Studies, 2003.

Henry, G. T., Gordon, C. S., and Rickman, D. K. "Early Education Policy Alternatives: Comparing the Quality and Outcomes of Head Start and State Pre-Kindergarten." *Educational Evaluation and Policy Analysis*, 2006, *28*, 77–99.

Henry, G. T., and Rickman, D. K. "The Evaluation of the Georgia Pre-K Program: An Example of a Scientific Evaluation of an Early Education Program." In K. Ryan and J. B. Cousins (eds.), *The Sage International Handbook of Educational Evaluation.* Thousand Oaks, CA: Sage, 2009.

Henry, Gary T., Smith, Adrienne A., Kershaw, David C., and Zulli, Rebecca A. "Formative Evaluation: Estimating Preliminary Outcomes and Testing Rival Explanations." *American Journal of Evaluation*, 2013, *34*, 465–485.

Henry, G. T., and Yi, P. "Design Matters: A Within-Study Assessment of Propensity Score Matching Designs." Paper presented at the meeting of the Association for Public Policy Analysis and Management, Washington, D.C., Nov. 7, 2009.

Holland, P. W. "Statistics and Causal Inference." *Journal of the American Statistical Association*, 1986, *81*, 945–960.

Imai, Kosuke, King, Gary, and Stuart, Elizabeth A. "Misunderstandings Between Experimentalists and Observationalists About Causal Inference." *Journal of the Royal Statistical Society*, 2008, *171*, 481–502.

Imbens, G. W., and Lemieux, T. "Regression Discontinuity Designs: A Guide to Practice." *Journal of Econometrics*, 2007.

Lipsey, M. W., Weiland, C., Yoshikawa, H., Wilson, S. J., and Hofer, K. G. "The Prekindergarten Age-Cutoff Regression-Discontinuity Design: Methodological Issues and Implications for Application." *Educational Evaluation and Policy Analysis*, 2014.

Murnane, Richard J., and Willett, John B. *Methods Matter: Improving Causal Inference in Educational and Social Science Research.* New York: Oxford University Press, 2012.

Rosenbaum, P. R. "Covariance Adjustment in Randomized Experiments and Observational Studies (with Discussion)." *Statistical Science*, 2002, *17*, 286–327.

Rosenbaum, P. R., and Rubin, D. B. "The Central Role of the Propensity Score in Observational Studies for Causal Effects." *Biometrika*, 1983, *70*(1), 41–55.

Rubin, D. B. "Using Propensity Scores to Help Design Observational Studies: Application to the Tobacco Litigation." *Health Services & Outcomes Research Methodology*, 2001, *2*(1), 169–188.

Shadish, William R., Clark, M. H., and Steiner, Peter M. "Can Nonrandomized Experiments Yield Accurate Answers? A Randomized Experiment Comparing Random and Nonrandom Assignments. *Journal of the American Statistics Association*, 2008, *103*(484), 1334–1356.

Shadish, William R., Cook, T. D., and Campbell, D. T. *Experimental and Quasi-Experimental Designs*. Boston, MA: Houghton Mifflin, 2002.

Stuart, E. A. "Matching Methods for Causal Inference: A Review and a Look Forward." *Statistical Science*, 2010, *25*(1), 1–21.

Stuart, E. A., and Green, K. M. "Using Full Matching to Estimate Causal Effects in Non-Experimental Studies: Examining the Relationship Between Adolescent Marijuana Use and Adult Outcomes." *Developmental Psychology*, 2008, *44*(2), 395–406.

Wilde, E. T., and Hollister, R. "How Close Is Close Enough? Evaluating Propensity Score Matching Using Data from a Class Size Reduction Experiment." *Journal of Policy Analysis and Management*, 2007, *26*(3), 455–477.

Wing, C., and Cook, T. D. "Strengthening the Regression Discontinuity Design Using Additional Design Elements: A Within-Study Comparison." *Journal of Policy Analysis and Management*, 2013, *32*, 853–877.

Xu, Z., Hannaway, J., and Taylor, C. *Making a Difference? The Effects of Teach For America in High School*. Washington, DC: Urban Institute and CALDER, 2008.

Further Reading

Angrist, Joshua D., and Pischke, J-S. *Mostly Harmless Econometrics: An Empiricist's Companion*. Princeton, NJ: Princeton University Press, 2008.

Morgan, S. L., and Winship, C. *Counterfactuals and Causal Inference: Methods and Principles for Social Research*. New York: Cambridge University Press, 2007.

Rubin, D. B. "Causal Inference Using Potential Outcomes: Design, Modeling, Decisions." *Journal of the American Statistical Association*, 2005, *100*, 322–331.

CHAPTER SEVEN

RANDOMIZED CONTROLLED TRIALS

Carole J. Torgerson, David J. Torgerson, Celia A. Taylor

When policymakers require evidence of "what works?" in public policy-making, this often involves the use of quasi-experimental evaluations, which have been described in detail by Gary Henry in Chapter Six of this book. As Henry notes, randomized controlled trials (RCTs) are generally acknowledged by methodologists to be the gold-standard method in evaluation research. This is so because RCTs enable causal inferences to be derived through the observation of unbiased estimates of effect (Shadish, Cook, and Campbell, 2002), provided they are rigorous in their design and execution. The randomized trial is one of the key methodological breakthroughs for program evaluation that has occurred in the last one hundred years. Therefore, when an RCT is possible, this design should generally be used in preference to alternative evaluative approaches.

The RCT is a simple concept. If participants are allocated to one or more groups *at random* then we can be sure that all *known* and *unknown* factors or variables that might affect outcome are equally present across the groups, except by chance. Because any factor that is associated with outcome is the same in each group, the effects are balanced or cancelled out. Therefore, if we offer one of the groups an intervention condition that is different from the control or comparison condition the other group receives and we see a difference at outcome, we can be confident (if the sample size is large enough) that the difference is due to the intervention and alternative explanations can be ruled out. Although the basic concept of a RCT is straightforward, its implementation is often rather more complex and requires careful thought in order to maintain the rigor of initial random allocation.

For the purposes of this chapter, we define *efficacy evaluation* as research that seeks to observe whether an intervention *can be effective* under optimum implementation conditions, and we define *effectiveness evaluation* as research that seeks to observe whether an intervention *is effective* when it is tested in authentic settings, where fidelity of implementation might be less than optimal. RCTs are not a panacea when researchers are addressing all such questions, but they are amenable to research questions that seek to investigate the relative efficacy or effectiveness of different policies or programs, such as different approaches for reducing criminal activity, different educational programs, different methods of improving voter turnout, and varying ecological or agricultural practices.

This chapter focuses on the use of RCTs in evaluating social policy interventions. In the field of social policy, public officials often intervene by introducing new policies, programs, and practices without their effectiveness having first been demonstrated using a rigorous design (such as an RCT). Biases and limitations that compromise the integrity of RCTs can be introduced at any stage in their design and conduct. However, all such biases and limitations also affect other research designs (quasi-experiments); and alternative methods usually have additional problems and sources of bias (Berk, 2005). The only exception to this is the regression discontinuity design. In this chapter, we highlight the key characteristics of well-designed RCTs and demonstrate how biases and limitations in the method can be avoided.

History of RCTs

The modern randomized controlled trial has its origins in the writings of Fisher in an agricultural context (Fisher, 1971). This research method was adopted for use with humans by education researchers in the 1930s (Lindquist, 1940; Walters, 1931), with medical researchers first using the technique about a decade later (Medical Research Council, 1944, 1948). Since those times, the use of RCTs in medical research has exploded, and now no new pharmaceutical product will be licensed until it has been tested in several large RCTs with human participants. This might be partly due to the many disasters that have occurred in the field of health care research when interventions, usually pharmaceutical interventions, were licensed in the absence of RCT evidence of their effectiveness in human participants (Silverman, 2004). Although occasionally using the RCT as their evaluative method, researchers in other areas (such as education and criminal justice) have used RCTs much less frequently than health care researchers have. Mistakes in health care can often be counted in terms of morbidity levels; mistakes in other policy areas are less noticeable, but often as important. Society imposes regulations to ensure that a new cream for wart treatment must be tested in a large RCT, yet the same level of evidence is not required before new programs and practices are imposed on school or justice systems, even though an incorrect decision about education pedagogy or a criminal justice innovation may have a greater detrimental impact on society than the use of an ineffective wart treatment.

In recent times in the United States and the U.K., there has been a renewed interest in the use of experimental methods in education research—an interest driven by policymakers who are realizing that the RCT is the most robust method for providing firm answers to pressing questions of how to educate children and young people. Government policy initiatives are especially ripe for RCT evaluations. Changes to national or local policies incur huge costs and affect many thousands, if not millions, of citizens. Where possible, policy initiatives should be evaluated using the RCT design, as this could lead to more effective policies and large resource savings by avoiding the implementation of ineffective, but costly, policies.

Why Randomize?

It is possible for researchers to know that one intervention is more or less effective than an alternative intervention only when they can compare groups that are equal *in all known and unknown variables that relate to outcome* before each of these groups receives the experimental or the control intervention. Any differences observed thereafter can be safely assumed to be results of the intervention.

Randomization is simple. Researchers form groups of participants using a method akin to tossing a coin (although it is best to use a secure computer system to do the coin tossing). Random allocation is virtually the only method in which two or more groups that are similar in all known and unknown characteristics can be formed. If researchers form groups by virtually any other method, they are at risk of introducing selection bias. *Selection bias* occurs when the determination of group membership means that membership correlates with final outcome. For example, in a comparison of the performances of children attending private schools and children attending public schools, selection (particularly if it related to income) could bias or confound any results.

Trial Design

In its simplest form, the randomized controlled trial is used to assemble two groups through random allocation. One of the groups is then exposed to the treatment intervention, and the other (control or comparison) group is exposed to an alternative intervention or to no intervention. Both groups are then followed for a specified period of time and the outcomes of interest are observed. The nature of the control or comparison condition depends on the research question. For example, if the question is which of two methods for teaching reading is more effective, the comparison condition is one of the two experimental conditions. If the research question is whether a supplementary program for improving reading is effective, then the control condition will be a no-treatment condition.

Although, in theory, random allocation ensures comparable groups at baseline, bias can be introduced at any stage, including initial randomization. Even when two groups have been carefully formed through a rigorous randomization procedure, the groups might not remain comparable unless due diligence is observed in avoiding the introduction of all possible post-randomization biases. In the following sections, we highlight the main potential sources of bias (pre- and post-randomization) and illustrate how these can be minimized or avoided.

Biased Allocation and Secure Allocation

A crucial issue in the design of an RCT is ensuring that the initial allocation is truly random. There is a wealth of evidence, mostly from health care research, that some "randomized" trials are not RCTs at all (Berger, 2005). Anecdotal and statistical evidence has shown that some trials have suffered from subversion of the random allocation process (Berger, 2005; Hewitt and others, 2005; Schulz, Chalmers, Hayes, and Altman, 1995). In these cases, rather than using a random method of assigning participants to groups, the researchers used a systematic or selective approach to group allocation. This might have occurred through ignorance or might have been due to deliberate research misconduct. For instance, a survey of the extent of this problem in the health care field found examples where researchers had deliberately placed patients who were likely to fare better than others (because they were younger and fitter, for example) into the experimental group in order to "prove" that an experimental treatment was superior (Hewitt, Torgerson, and Berger, 2009). In addition, through ignorance, some researchers have overridden an initially random allocation because, by chance, it had led to groups of different sizes, and they thought, in error, that they should correct this.

In the last ten to fifteen years, health care researchers have become aware that research misconduct does exist in the conduct of some randomized trials and that, consequently, rigorously designed trials should always use third-party randomization services to avoid this potential problem. Health care research is not likely to be the only field experiencing this problem; consequently, it should be accepted good practice to separate the randomization procedure from the researcher who is enrolling participants in the trial.

Contamination and Cluster Randomization

For many policy interventions, there is a huge potential for *contamination* of the control participants with the treatment condition. For example, in an experiment investigating the effectiveness of teacher praise in motivation, schoolchildren in the same classes were randomized as individuals to either receive or not receive praise from their teachers. However, the teachers could not prevent themselves from praising the children in the control group as well as the children in the treatment group (Craven, Marsh, Debus, and Jayasinghe, 2001). And one can readily envisage other examples where contamination might be a problem. For example, in one study, investigators wished to know whether an intervention to improve recycling household waste was effective (Cotterill, John, Liu, and Nomura, 2009). The intervention consisted of volunteers knocking on doors to urge householders to sort their waste for recycling. To evaluate this initiative, an RCT was undertaken. The outcome was the amount of sorted waste by household; however, randomizing by house might have introduced contamination, as neighboring households might (on seeing their neighbors recycling waste) have modified their own behavior. Consequently, street-level randomization, rather than house-level allocation, was undertaken.

When confronted with the likelihood of contamination, it is best to randomize at a level *higher* than the level of the individual. Classically, this has occurred in education research, where the class or school is usually the most appropriate unit of allocation (Lindquist, 1940). Such trials are called *cluster randomized* trials or experiments. Even when it is theoretically possible to randomize individuals, sometimes it is not feasible for practical or administrative reasons. For instance, in a trial evaluating the use of financial incentives to encourage attendance at adult literacy classes, cluster or class-based randomization was used (Brooks and others, 2008). This prevented control students from finding out about the incentives and the fact that they were not going to receive them, as this knowledge might have altered their behavior: for example, they might have reduced their attendance if they felt resentful demoralization.

Ascertainment and Blinded Follow-Up

A major potential source of bias in RCTs is the way in which the assessment is conducted at follow-up. If the observer undertaking the posttest or follow-up measure is aware of individuals' group allocation, then he or she might consciously or unconsciously bias the outcome. It is important, therefore, that whenever possible, data collection be undertaken by an observer who is masked or blinded to the intervention status of the participants. Tests should be selected, administered, and assessed by personnel who are not aware of participants' group allocations. Failure to take this precaution can certainly introduce either conscious or unconscious bias on the part of those doing the data collection at follow-up.

Crossover and Intention to Treat

In many, if not most, randomized trials, some participants will receive a treatment different from the one to which they were assigned. In such cases it is tempting but scientifically incorrect to analyze participants by the condition that they *received* rather than that to which they were originally assigned. Randomization ensures that baseline confounders or covariates are equally distributed. If after randomization some participants in the control group gain access to the intervention, then these participants will invariably be different from those who do not gain access to the treatment condition. If the data from these participants are excluded from the analysis or, worse, included in the intervention group's data, this inclusion will result in bias. Therefore, their data should be included in the analysis *as if they had remained in their original randomized group.* This is known as *intention to treat* (ITT) analysis. Doing this will, of course, dilute any treatment effects toward the null. However, the worst that can happen in such an analysis is that it will be concluded that there is no difference when, in fact, there is a difference. If the data from the crossover participants were to be included with the intervention group's data, then it might be concluded that an intervention is beneficial when in truth it is harmful. Furthermore, if the crossover can be measured accurately, it will be possible to adjust the analysis using a statistical technique known as *complier average causal effect* (CACE) analysis (Hewitt, Torgerson, and Miles, 2006), which will under many circumstances provide an unbiased estimate of effect (as discussed later).

Attrition

Another potential threat to the reliability of an RCT is the problem of attrition. In many RCTs, some participants drop out of the study. If this dropping out is nonrandom, which it often is, then bias can be introduced. For example, if boys with low pretest scores are at increased risk of dropping out of an experimental group, then at analysis researchers might mistakenly conclude that the intervention either has no effect or makes things worse, as boys with low test scores are present in the control group, but their counterparts are no longer available in the experimental group. Consequently, it is important to ensure that attrition is kept to a minimum. Often participants confuse failure to comply with the intervention with dropping out of the study. Noncompliance is a problem, as noted previously; however, it is better to retain participants in the study for the posttests, even when they no longer comply with the intervention. When noncompliant participants are retained, bias due to attrition is avoided. Once it is explained to participants that failure to comply does not equate with dropping out and that their posttest data will be included in the analysis, they are usually happy to provide these data. When students change schools, it is worthwhile putting procedures into place to obtain their posttest outcomes by having research staff administer the posttest in their new schools. One quality assurance check for a good trial is that it has both low dropout rates overall and equivalent dropout rates between groups. If the dropout rates are different (for example, 20 percent in the control group and 10 percent in the intervention group), then there is a real worry that this might introduce attrition bias.

Resentful Demoralization: Preference Designs

Participants might have a preference for one of the options under evaluation, or policymakers might insist that their preferred intervention is rolled out to all. These issues pose problems for researchers evaluating a novel intervention using trial methodology. However, these problems are not insurmountable and, with a little thought, can often be addressed through careful trial design (Torgerson and Torgerson, 2008). Researchers do need to deal with the issue of treatment preference to avoid the potential for bias posed by this problem. They can do this through several different approaches. One approach is the *participant preference design*—also known as the Brewin-Bradley approach (Brewin and Bradley, 1989). In this design, participants are asked about their preferences before randomization, and only those who are indifferent to the conditions are randomized; the remainder receive their preferred intervention and are then followed up in a nonrandomized study. (Note that in the field of education, issues of treatment preference may relate more to teachers or parents than to students.) In the Brewin-Bradley approach, those who are randomized provide an unbiased comparison, whereas the outcomes of the nonrandomized participants are likely to be biased.

Another alternative is the *randomized cohort design*. In this design, participants are initially recruited to a cohort study—that is, they consent to undertake pretests and to be followed up with posttests at regular intervals (Relton, Torgerson, O'Cathain, and Nichol, 2010). At recruitment they are also informed about potential interventions and asked whether they would consider using these at some point in the future. Participants who indicate an interest in one or more of the potential interventions are randomly assigned to produce a randomized experiment.

In some instances, it might be possible to randomize participants without their knowledge. For instance, an evaluation of a policy of reducing benefits to parents who do not have their children vaccinated before attending school randomized people, without their consent, to be either informed or not informed about this policy. An alternative to this is Zelen's method (Zelen, 1979), where participants are randomized and then *only those allocated to the novel intervention* are asked for their consent to receive the intervention. A major problem with these approaches is one of ethics: some ethics committees will refuse permission for a design where full informed consent is not part of the design. There are scientific problems with these methods as well. In the latter approach, if significant numbers of participants refuse the intervention and cross over to the control treatment, then study power is lost and, correspondingly, more participants are required. This occurs because the effects of the intervention will be diluted, and to maintain the randomized allocation, researchers will need to use ITT analysis (as noted earlier).

Waiting List and Stepped Wedge Designs

Alternative approaches to dealing with some of these issues include the *waiting list design* (where participants are informed that they will receive the intervention at a later date), and the *stepped wedge design*. Generally, researchers need a prima facie case for testing a new intervention in public policy, such as prior but not highly rigorous evidence of its effectiveness. A potential problem then faced by researchers undertaking an RCT is that the participants in the control group might be unhappy at being denied the promising intervention. In evaluating an intervention where the evidence is uncertain, there is no ethical problem; indeed, it is ethically correct to offer the participants a chance (random possibility) to be enrolled in the most effective intervention, which might very well be the control condition. However, potential participants might not be convinced that the control intervention is as likely as the new intervention to be beneficial. When they anticipate a benefit from the experimental intervention, those allocated to the control group might suffer resentful demoralization and either refuse to continue with the experiment or deliberately or subconsciously do worse merely because they have been refused the new intervention. Thus, it might also be desirable to evaluate the "real-world" implementation (pragmatic trial) of an intervention that had previously been shown to be effective in a laboratory-type RCT (explanatory or efficacy trial).

In a waiting list study, participants are told explicitly that they will receive the intervention; however, some will receive it straightaway, and others will receive it later. It is then possible to evaluate the effectiveness of the intervention by measuring both groups at pretest, implementing the intervention in one group, and giving a posttest measurement, and after this giving the intervention to the participants in the control group. Consider an RCT undertaken by Brooks, Miles, Torgerson, and Torgerson (2006), for example. This study evaluated the use of a computer software package in a secondary school. Such packages were usually implemented arbitrarily, as there were insufficient laptop computers for all pupils to receive the software at the same time. For the evaluation, the researchers changed the arbitrary assignment to random allocation and adopted a waiting list design, which permitted a rigorous evaluation of this software package. Moreover, the use of the waiting list in this instance allowed all the children to receive the package eventually and might have reduced any demoralization, either among the children or among their teachers.

A special form of the waiting list design is known as the stepped wedge, or multiple baseline, method. Policymakers, particularly politicians, are often anxious to implement an intervention as soon as possible, which in some cases does lead to problems in evaluation. However, sometimes policymakers can be persuaded to adopt a staged approach in rolling out a program. It is then possible to randomize the order in which areas or units receive the intervention. More information on the stepped wedge design can be found in a recent systematic review of the method (Brown and Lilford, 2006).

The stepped wedge design differs from the waiting list design in that it operates as a series of waiting lists (Hayes and Moulton, 2009). Indeed, staged implementation might result in a more efficient method of rollout than the so-called big bang approach. For example, consider the implementation of a novel method of offender supervision by probation officers in the North of England (Pearson, Torgerson, McDougall, and Bowles, 2010; Pearson, McDougall, Kanaan, Torgerson, and Bowles, 2014). Two areas wanted to implement the program, which required training probation officers in the new system. Researchers managed to persuade one area to implement the program office by office. Hence, the probation offices were randomly assigned to a waiting list so that implementation commenced in the first office, followed by a three-month gap, and then implementation began in the second office, and so on until all the offices had received the new training. In each three-month gap, the reoffence rates were monitored for all offenders attending all probation offices, thus enabling an unbiased estimate of the impact of the new service. In the second area, this approach was not taken and a big bang method was adopted. However, it was found that implementation was suboptimal because there were insufficient resources to deliver the training to all the sites in a short period of time. Process measures (such as measures of referrals to other services) indicated that the area that had adopted the stepped wedge approach was using services, such as alcohol counseling, more effectively than the big bang area was. Thus, in this case, adopting a rigorous method of evaluation ensured rigorous research *and* better training.

One potential weakness of the stepped wedge design is that it is necessary to measure outcomes at each step, that is, whenever an individual or cluster moves from the control to the intervention section of the wedge. This can be costly or intrusive to participants. Therefore, the stepped wedge design might work best when the outcomes are based on routinely collected data, such as national education assessments. Furthermore, it is important to monitor the implementation of the intervention in different sites in order to assess whether the nature of the intervention evolves with each step. This is important when interpreting the results, as the intervention in the last cluster could be substantially different from the intervention in the first cluster, as it inevitably changes with the increased experience of those implementing it.

Of course, a huge problem with any form of waiting list design is that, even if the evaluation shows that the intervention is ineffective, it might prove politically difficult to withdraw the intervention. Furthermore, considerable amounts of resources might have already been expended by giving the control group an ineffective intervention, which could have been avoided had a non-waiting-list design been used.

Design Issues in Cluster Randomized Trials

Most trials evaluating policy interventions use *cluster randomization*. As noted above, cluster randomization (for example, allocation of classes or schools

TABLE 7.1. EXAMPLE OF MINIMIZATION ON TWO IMPORTANT VARIABLES.

Variable	Intervention	Control
Large	3	2
Small	2	3
Rural	3	2
Urban	2	3

rather than individual students) will minimize contamination bias. However, there are some potential issues that need to be considered in the design of a cluster trial. First, multiple clusters are required in each group. A cluster trial consisting of two units (for example, two schools, two hospitals, two prisons) will not produce any valid results, as this is effectively the same as a two-person trial. Confounding at the level of the cluster (for example, special teacher characteristics or differences in offender populations) will not allow researchers to make any judgment about the effectiveness or otherwise of the intervention. Furthermore, statistical tests cannot be undertaken on a sample of two. Consequently, assignment of several clusters to each group is required. Some methodologists recommend at least seven clusters per group, whereas others state that five per group will suffice (Donner and Klar, 2000; Murray, 1998). However, greater numbers of clusters than these are usually required if researchers are to have the power to observe an important difference. Nevertheless, cluster trials tend to have fairly small numbers of units, usually fewer than fifty. In this instance, some form of restricted allocation method might improve the precision of the trial. One method of allocating small numbers of groups is *minimization* (Torgerson and Torgerson, 2007). In this method, a simple arithmetic algorithm is used to ensure that the clusters are allocated so that cluster-level covariates (for example, size or past performance) are balanced. Table 7.1 illustrates the key step in minimizing on two key variables. In the table, ten clusters have been randomized. The researchers' goal here is to ensure balance between the intervention and control groups on two key variables: unit size and whether the unit is in a rural or urban area. An eleventh cluster has the characteristics of being *large* and *rural*. To assess the group into which Cluster 11 should be allocated, researchers would add up the number of existing units across those two variables. As the table shows, this sums to six units for the intervention group and four units for the control group. To ensure that this imbalance is minimized, the eleventh cluster would be assigned to the control group. If the sums for the groups were exactly the same, then the allocation would be done randomly. Minimization is particularly attractive when researchers wish to ensure balance across several variables. The use of minimization will ensure that statistical power is maximized and that the groups are comparable at baseline.

A more important issue that is frequently overlooked in the design of cluster trials is ensuring that the individual participants in each cluster are either a random sample or a census. Randomization of the clusters will ensure that selection bias is avoided if all, or a random sample, of the cluster members are included in the analysis. One way of introducing bias into a cluster trial is to randomize the clusters and then ask each cluster member to consent to taking part in the study. Inevitably there will be some individuals who do not consent, and if their choice is influenced by knowledge of the likely intervention, bias is likely to be introduced (Torgerson and Torgerson, 2008). To avoid this possibility, cluster members need to provide consent *before* randomization of the clusters occurs. In education research, this should be straightforward, as researchers could obtain parental and student consent prior to random allocation of the clusters.

Sample Size Issues

Many trials (particularly in the field of education) are relatively small (Torgerson, Torgerson, Birks, and Porthouse, 2005). Small trials are likely to have the consequence that researchers are able to observe a difference between the groups that might be of policy significance but is not of statistical significance. As a general rule, few education interventions, when compared against an *active* control (such as usual teaching or other business as usual), will yield an effect size bigger than half a standard deviation or half an effect size (that is, the difference in group posttest means divided by the standard deviation of the control group). Indeed, many effective education interventions might generate an effect size difference on the order of only a quarter or a fifth of a standard deviation. However, small effect sizes matter. Consider an effect size of 0.10 (a tenth of a standard deviation difference), which is considered small; however, if this effect occurred in a population taking an examination, it would lead to an additional 4 percent of that population achieving a passing grade. This could matter a great deal in a high-stakes testing situation.

The arithmetical calculation of a sample size is relatively straightforward, and most statistical packages have a sample size function. Indeed, several computer packages that can be downloaded for free work quite satisfactorily (for example, PS Power from the Biostatistics Department at Vanderbilt University: http://biostat.mc.vanderbilt.edu/twiki/bin/view/Main/PowerSampleSize).

Determining what difference is worthwhile to policymakers and consumers requires a complex judgment. Such a difference would be influenced by the cost of the intervention, its ease of implementation, and various political and social factors. For instance, the aforementioned recycling program was relatively costly compared with simply sending leaflets to all households and would, all other things being equal, have needed to produce a relatively large effect size in order to justify its additional cost.

If a cluster design is being proposed, then the relationship between members of the cluster needs to be taken into account in the sample size calculation. This will generally lead to an increase in the number of individuals in the trial on the order of at least 50 percent, if not more. To adjust for the effects of clustering, the standard sample size needs to be multiplied by $[(m - 1) 3 ICC] 1 1$, where m is the size of each cluster and ICC is the intracluster correlation coefficient, which can be obtained from previously published studies. As a rule of thumb, ICC values are generally between 0.01 and 0.02 for human studies (Killip, Mahfoud, and Pearce, 2004). A final point concerning cluster studies is that there is a diminishing marginal return from increasing cluster size beyond twenty to thirty individuals per cluster (see the graph in Brown and others, 2008; also see Campbell and others, 2004).

Increased Power for Very Little Cost

It is almost automatic when randomizing participants or clusters to different treatments in a trial to attempt to have the same number of cases in each treatment group—a 1:1 allocation ratio of intervention group to control group. This tradition has grown up because a 1:1 ratio, for any given sample size, usually ensures maximum statistical power—where *power* is the likelihood of correctly finding a difference between the groups for a predetermined effect size. However, where resource shortages limit the number of people who can be offered the intervention treatment, power can be increased by randomly allocating more participants to the control group, thereby increasing the total sample size. For example, there might be sufficient resources to offer an intervention to only sixty-three participants. If equal allocation were used, then the sample size would be constrained to 126 participants. This would give 80 percent power to detect a difference of half a standard deviation between the two groups. However, if the allocation ratio is set to 2:1, then 189 participants can be randomized, with 126 in the control group and sixty-three in the intervention group, which will increase power to 90 percent. If this is done, statistical power is increased at little or no additional cost when the control group participants simply receive normal treatment anyway. The allocation ratio can be set as high as is desirable, although once it exceeds 3:1 the extra increase in power tends to be slight and it might not be worth the effort of following up a much larger sample.

In summary, increasing the size of the control group in this way can give increased power for very little cost. Of course, if the *total* sample size is constrained, then using unequal allocation will reduce power—although not by much unless the ratio exceeds 2:1. For example, in a trial with 100 participants, if thirty-two were allocated to one group and sixty-eight allocated to the other group, the decline in power would be only 5 percent, compared with the power in a situation where fifty were allocated to each group. This loss of power might be worthwhile if considerable resource savings can be achieved.

Analytical Issues

The statistical analysis of most randomized controlled trials is relatively simple. Because selection bias has been minimized through the initial randomization, there is, in principle, no reason to use complex multivariate methods. However, in some trials, particularly in education, the pretest has a very strong relationship with the posttest. Similarly, in the aforementioned recycling trial, previous recycling behavior correlated strongly with future behavior. Therefore, it is desirable to control for pretest values in such trials. This is particularly important in order to improve statistical power. This relationship can be used either to increase power for a given sample size or in order to use smaller sample sizes. For example, a pretest-posttest correlation of 0.7 (that is, an R^2 value of 0.49) leads to an approximate halving of the required sample size (for any given power, significance value, and effect size). Often correlations are in excess of 0.7 in education trials, and this will further drive down the required sample size.

If cluster trials are undertaken—if randomization is, for example, at the class, school, hospital, prison, or district level—then the clustering needs to be taken into account in any analysis. The simplest way of doing this is to calculate the group means from the cluster means and perform an unpaired t test comparing the group means. To take covariates into account, such as pretest scores, one could extend this analytical framework to use a regression approach, taking into account cluster-level pretest scores. Note that a t test or simple regression analysis of individuals who have been randomized in clusters is always incorrect, no matter how few or how many clusters have been randomized. There are alternative approaches, including multilevel modeling, that also adjust for clustering and have some advantages, particularly when there is a complex design with many different levels (for example, children within classrooms, within schools, or within areas).

Generalizability or External Validity

In this chapter, we have focused on the internal validity of the RCT. That is, we have looked at whether researchers and stakeholders can rely on the results of a trial within an experimental sample. This is the correct focus, because without this internal reliability the results cannot be applied outside the study sample. Yet, it is important that the results of a trial should be transferable. The main point of an RCT is to influence policy beyond any particular evaluation. In this section, we look at some of the issues that need to be considered in order to make trials externally valid.

One of the criticisms of RCTs is that they are often not conducted in real-world, authentic settings. Many RCTs of education interventions, for example, are conducted in the laboratory setting of a university psychology department. However, trials are needed that have, first, been conducted with student participants in educational settings that are representative of normal educational practice and, second, replicated in diverse educational settings, as this will increase their generalizability. Consequently, pragmatic trials are needed where whole classes or schools are allocated to either receive a new program or to continue with business as usual. These schools need to be chosen to ensure that they represent the general population of schools. Indeed, this is where social science trials are different from medical experiments. Health care trials—specifically pharmaceutical trials—are more likely to transfer beyond their experimental population than education trials are. For example, an educational program developed in the United States might not apply to U.K. students and, even if we ignore language differences, is unlikely to apply further afield. The reason for this is that educational achievement can be profoundly affected by cultural and socioeconomic factors. This also applies to other fields. Criminal activity and types of offending behavior vary significantly between countries: for example, violent crimes involving the use of firearms are more prevalent in the United States, whereas those involving knives are more prevalent in the United Kingdom. Thus, interventions to prevent violent crime might require a focus in the United States that is different from the focus chosen in the United Kingdom.

Quality of Randomized Trials

Earlier we discussed some of the potential problems with undertaking RCTs. Many RCTs do not describe their methods in sufficient detail for outsiders to be sure that, for example, randomization was undertaken in a robust manner. Similarly, significant numbers of RCTs do not use an independent, blinded follow-up or ITT analysis (Torgerson, Torgerson, Birks, and Porthouse, 2005). We have proposed elsewhere that when reporting their RCTs, researchers should adopt a modified version of the CONSORT statement used in health care research (Torgerson and Torgerson, 2008). The CONSORT statement is a checklist of twenty-two items that correspond to quality issues in the design, conduct, and reporting of RCTs and that need to be addressed in the trial manuscript if the reader is to be assured of the RCT's internal and external validity. Items include justification of the sample size, method of randomization, description of the population and intervention, and use of confidence intervals. Various papers about the CONSORT statement can be accessed online (www.consort-statement.org). Health care research methodologists developed the statement in response to the substantial number of poorly reported RCTs in health care research. Subsequently, it has been adopted by all the major health care journals, the major psychology journals, and more recently, some education journals, with other researchers such as political scientists also starting to use it (Cotterill, John, Liu, and Nomura, 2009).

Barriers to the Wider Use of RCTs

Many arguments are made against the wider use of RCTs and experimental methods when evaluating education interventions, some of which do not withstand sustained scrutiny. Policy implementation without evaluation using randomized designs is often justified on the ethical grounds that it is unethical to withhold promising interventions. Policies introduced by one set of politicians can easily be undone by a future group, particularly if there is no rigorous evidence to support their continuance. However, it is unethical to widely implement a policy that increases costs and might not result in benefit. For example, an enhanced sex education program in Scotland was implemented in state schools before the results of the trial on unwanted pregnancies became known. The trial showed that the program led to an *increase* in unwanted pregnancies and cost fifty times more than the existing program (Henderson and others, 2007).

Cost is often cited as a reason for not undertaking RCTs. Yet the cost of not doing them is in the long run likely to be greater. Furthermore, a carefully planned RCT is not necessarily expensive, and the value of an RCT can be estimated using value of information methods (Claxton and others, 2004).Involvement with stakeholders at an early stage is crucial. One of the reasons that quasi-experiments are so widely used is that the policy has already been implemented and then researchers have been asked to evaluate the decision after rollout. When early engagement with stakeholders occurs, then sometimes randomization can be implemented. For example, the involvement of researchers early on *before* a novel policy in the probation service (described earlier; Pearson, Torgerson, McDougall, and Bowles, 2013; Pearson, McDougall, Kanaan, Torgerson, and Bowles, 2014) was implemented allowed them to persuade one of the probation services to use random allocation in its implementation strategy. Consequently, the early engagement of research and the appropriate stakeholders allowed a rigorous implementation and evaluation in one of the two districts. Note, however, despite early engagement between researchers and stakeholders, one of the districts refused to implement random allocation. Nevertheless, a 50 percent success was better than nothing!

Conclusion

The widespread use of random allocation is one of the most important methodological contributions to health and social science research of the last century. In education and additional fields other than health care, there is increasing interest in using the approach more widely. Although this renewed interest is welcome, it is necessary to ensure that trials are conducted to the highest standard; otherwise, there is a risk that their integrity will be compromised. Health care trials can contribute to informing our methodological deliberations. Although the traditional, placebo-controlled drug trial is unlike most educational program evaluations, there are many nonpharmaceutical health care research interventions that are similar to educational programs in key ways: for instance, health promotion or health education programs. For example, health care researchers have undertaken large, cluster randomized trials involving schools to assess new health promotion programs. Evaluations of literacy or numeracy programs can use the same method. If researchers in the field of health promotion can design and conduct rigorous trials of new programs in their field, there should be no methodological barrier preventing researchers from doing the same in the field of education. Many of the methodological advances in health care trial methods can be applied to educational program trials, and there is now published guidance for the evaluation of complex interventions in health care (Medical Research Council, 2009). One example is the need to monitor the fidelity with which an intervention is implemented.

It is important that trials that are undertaken be rigorous; otherwise funders of randomized controlled trials might turn away from them in the future.

Consequently, at the same time that we urge evaluators to use the RCT, we note that it is equally important that they use the most rigorous methods available.

References

Berger, V. W. *Selection Bias and Covariate Imbalances in Randomized Clinical Trials.* Hoboken, NJ: Wiley, 2005.

Berk, R. A. "Randomized Experiments as the Bronze Standard." *Journal of Experimental Criminology,* 2005, *1,* 417–433.

Brewin, C. R., and Bradley, C. "Patient Preferences and Randomised Clinical Trials." *British Medical Journal,* 1989, *299,* 313–315.

Brooks, G., Burton, M., Coles, P., Miles, J., Torgerson, C., and Torgerson, D. "Randomized Controlled Trial of Incentives to Improve Attendance at Adult Literacy Classes." *Oxford Review of Education,* 2008, *34,* 493–504.

Brooks, G., Miles, J.N.V., Torgerson, C. J., and Torgerson, D. J. "Is an Intervention Using Computer Software Effective in Literacy Learning? A Randomised Controlled Trial." *Educational Studies,* 2006, *32,* 133–143.

Brown, C. A., and Lilford, R. J. "The Stepped Wedge Trial Design: A Systematic Review." *BMC Medical Research Methodology,* 2006, *6,* 54.

Brown, C. A., and others. "An Epistemology of Patient Safety Research: A Framework for Study Design and Interpretation. Part 2: Study Design." *Quality & Safety in Health Care,* 2008, *17,* 163–169.

Campbell, M. K., and others. "Sample Size Calculator for Cluster Randomised Trials." *Computers in Biology and Medicine,* 2004, *34,* 113–125.

Claxton, K., and others. "A Pilot Study on the Use of Decision Theory and Value of Information Analysis as Part of the NHS Health Technology Assessment Programme." *Health Technology Assessment,* 2004, *8*(31), 1–103.

Cotterill, S., John, P., Liu, H., and Nomura, H. "Mobilizing Citizen Effort to Enhance Environmental Outcomes: A Randomized Controlled Trial of a Door-to-Door Recycling Campaign." *Journal of Environmental Management,* 2009, *91,* 403–410.

Craven, R. G., Marsh, H. W., Debus, R. L., and Jayasinghe, U. "Diffusion Effects: Control Group Contamination Threats to the Validity of Teacher-Administered Interventions." *Journal of Educational Psychology,* 2001, *93,* 639–645.

Donner, A., and Klar, N. *Design and Analysis of Cluster Randomization Trials in Health Research.* London: Hodder Arnold, 2000.

Fisher, R. A. *The Design of Experiments.* New York: Hafner, 1971.

Hayes, R. J., and Moulton, L. H. *Cluster Randomised Trials.* London: Chapman & Hall, 2009.

Henderson, M., and others. "Impact of a Theoretically Based Sex Education Program (SHARE) Delivered by Teachers on NHS Registered Conceptions and Terminations: Final Results of Cluster Randomised Trial." *British Medical Journal,* 2007, *334,* 133.

Hewitt, C. E., Torgerson, D. J., and Berger, V. "Potential for Technical Errors and Subverted Allocation Can Be Reduced If Certain Guidelines Are Followed: Examples from a Web-Based Survey." *Journal of Clinical Epidemiology,* 2009, *62,* 261–269.

Hewitt, C. J., Torgerson, D. J., and Miles, J.N.V. "Taking Account of Non-Compliance in Randomised Trials." *Canadian Medical Association Journal,* 2006, *175,* 347–348.

Hewitt, C., and others. "Adequacy and Reporting of Allocation Concealment: Review of Recent Trials Published in Four General Medical Journals." *British Medical Journal*, 2005, *330*, 1057–1058.

Jacob, B. A., and Lefgren, L. "Remedial Education and Student Achievement: A Regression-Discontinuity Analysis." *Review of Economics and Statistics*, 2004, *86*(1), 226–244.

Killip, S., Mahfoud, Z., and Pearce, K. "What Is an Intracluster Correlation Coefficient? Crucial Concepts for Primary Care Researchers." *Annals of Family Medicine*, 2004, *2*(3), 204–208.

Lindquist, E. F. *Statistical Analysis in Educational Research.* Boston, MA: Houghton Mifflin, 1940.

Medical Research Council. "Clinical Trial of Patulin in the Common Cold." *Lancet*, 1944, *2*, 370–372.

Medical Research Council. "Streptomycin Treatment of Pulmonary Tuberculosis: A Medical Research Council Investigation." *British Medical Journal*, 1948, *2*, 769–782.

Medical Research Council. *Developing and Evaluating Complex Interventions: New Guidance.* London: Medical Research Council, 2009.

Murray, D. M. *Design and Analysis of Group-Randomized Trials.* New York: Oxford University Press, 1998.

Pearson, D.A.S., Torgerson, D. J., McDougall, C., and Bowles, R. "Parable of Two Agencies, One Which Randomizes." *Annals of the American Academy of Political and Social Sciences*, 2010, *628*, 11–29.

Pearson, D.A.S., McDougall, C., Kanaan, M., Torgerson, D. J., and Bowles, R. "Evaluation of the Citizenship Evidence-Based Probation Supervision Program Using a Stepped Wedge Cluster Randomized Controlled Trial." *Crime and Delinquency*, 2014,

Relton, C., Torgerson, D. J., O'Cathain, A., and Nichol, J. "Rethinking Pragmatic Randomized Controlled Trials: Introducing the 'Cohort Multiple Randomized Controlled Trial' Design." *British Medical Journal*, 2010, *340*, c1066.

Schulz, K. F., Chalmers, I., Hayes, R. J., and Altman, D. G. "Empirical Evidence of Bias: Dimensions of Methodological Quality Associated with Estimates of Treatment Effects in Controlled Trials." *JAMA*, 1995, *273*, 408–412.

Shadish, W. R., Cook, T. D., and Campbell, T. D. *Experimental and Quasi-Experimental Designs for Generalized Causal Inference.* Boston, MA: Houghton Mifflin, 2002.

Silverman, W. "Personal Reflections on Lessons Learned from Randomized Trials Involving Newborn Infants from 1951 to 1967." *Clinical Trials*, 2004, *1*, 179–184.

Torgerson, C. J., and Torgerson, D. J. "The Use of Minimization to Form Comparison Groups in Educational Research." *Educational Studies*, 2007, *33*, 333–337.

Torgerson, C. J., Torgerson, D. J., Birks, Y. F., and Porthouse, J. "A Comparison of Randomised Controlled Trials in Health and Education." *British Educational Research Journal*, 2005, *31*, 761–785.

Torgerson, D. J., and Torgerson, C. J. *Designing Randomised Trials in Health, Education and the Social Sciences.* Basingstoke, UK: Palgrave Macmillan, 2008.

Walters, J. E. "Seniors as Counselors." *Journal of Higher Education*, 1931, *2*, 446–448.

Zelen, M. "A New Design for Randomized Clinical Trials." *New England Journal of Medicine*, 1979, *300*, 1242–1245.

CHAPTER EIGHT

CONDUCTING CASE STUDIES

Karin Martinson, Carolyn O'Brien

Unlike quantitative methods of research that focus on the questions of who, what, where, how much, and how many, case studies are the preferred strategy when *how* or *why* questions are asked. Case studies can be used for several purposes, including defining the questions and hypotheses of a subsequent study, presenting a complete description of an event within its context, or establishing cause-and-effect relationships. Case studies are used in many disciplines, including public policy, education, psychology, medicine, and law. In the field of program evaluation, case studies are frequently used to examine program implementation. Because programs must adapt to organizational context and local conditions, case studies are often the method used to examine variations across program sites. This includes understanding the unexpected consequences of implementation and why implementation looks the way it does.

Case studies integrate quantitative and qualitative information from a variety of sources to give an in-depth picture of the issue being studied and the broader environment. The strength of case studies is their flexibility and ability to assemble a comprehensive array of quantitative and qualitative data to provide rich analysis and valuable insight.

What Are Case Studies?

A case study is a method for developing a complete understanding of a process, program, event, or activity. The goal of this type of study is to develop a comprehensive understanding of a case, or complex *bounded system,* including the context and circumstances in which it occurs, through extensive description and analysis (Smith, 1978). A core feature of the case study approach is a reliance on systematic and detailed data collection from multiple sources, particularly firsthand observations.

The case study approach has both benefits and challenges. Case studies provide a detailed picture of program operations, often at a number of locations, and can result in a deeper understanding of how and why program operations relate to outcomes. However, case studies are unlikely to be statistically representative, and thus generalizing the findings is often problematic. In addition, because of the multiple sources of data, the depth of the analysis, and the common desire to include multiple sites, case studies can be time consuming and costly (Love, 2004).

Case studies generally fall into one of three categories: exploratory, descriptive, or explanatory. An *exploratory* case study is aimed at defining the questions and hypotheses of a subsequent and broader study. It informs the development of the evaluation questions, measures, designs, and analytical strategy for this larger study, which may or may not be a case study (U.S. General Accounting Office, 1991). A *descriptive* case study (sometimes called an *illustrative* study) presents a detailed and nuanced description, and aims to capture relevant details of an event within its context. Studies in this category primarily describe what is happening and why, in a limited number of instances, in order to show what a situation is like. Finally, an *explanatory* case study focuses on establishing local cause-and-effect relationships, explaining which causes produced which effects in a specific context. This type of case study typically describes an event in one or a limited number of sites, with little focus on statistical generalizability (Yin, 1993). Box 8.1 provides examples of each of these categories.

Box 8.1. Examples of Three Case Study Categories

Exploratory case study. In a national study of state and local efforts to modernize the food stamp program, exploratory case studies were conducted in four states identified as being more advanced in the implementation of innovative strategies to increase access to benefits and to improve operational efficiency. Findings from the four case studies were used to identify and define types of modernization activities and to guide future evaluation efforts to study modernization across all states (O'Brien and others, 2007).

Descriptive case study. The Assessing the New Federalism project described changes to a wide range of programs and policies affecting low-income families in the aftermath of the enactment of the Personal Responsibility and Work Opportunity Reconciliation Act of 1996, which provided states with significantly more authority and discretion in the design and operation of these programs. A major component of this study was a set of in-depth case studies of a range of income, work support, and health programs. Conducted in thirteen states that accounted for over half of the low-income population receiving these services, these case studies formed the basis for numerous publications describing both individual state circumstances and cross-site findings on the evolution of federalism in the late 1990s (see, for example, Martinson and Holcomb, 2002).

Explanatory case study. Murray Levine's book *From State Hospital to Psychiatric Center: The Implementation of Planned Organizational Change,* describes the transformation of what is now the Harlem Valley Psychiatric Center, in New York State, from an inpatient state mental hospital providing custodial care to a community-based treatment facility following deinstitutionalization in the mid-1970s. Based primarily on data gathered through semi-structured interviews, the study examines the strategies employed in making this transition, addressing the political, fiscal, and social factors that had an effect on the process and contributed to the successes, challenges, and outcomes (Levine, 1980).

Researchers go through four primary steps in any case study project: designing the study, conducting the study, analyzing the data, and preparing the report. The following sections discuss each of these steps. Box 8.2 lists the steps and substeps.

Box 8.2. Key Steps in Case Studies

Designing the Case Study
- Define the research questions.
- Develop a framework to identify study dimensions.
- Determine the unit of analysis.
- Establish a single-case or multiple-case design.

Conducting the Case Study
- Develop protocols.
- Select qualified staff and provide training.
- Implement strategies for collecting data, typically from multiple sources.

(Continued)

Analyzing the Data
- Create a database.
- Use specific techniques to analyze the data.

Preparing the Report
- Determine the audience and the organizational structure for the report.
- Include context and data collection strategies in addition to findings.
- Outline limitations or cautions.

Case studies are not always conducted as discrete, stand-alone research efforts. They are often one component of larger, mixed method studies that contain multiple quantitative and qualitative research techniques and methods. For example, the national study of state and local efforts to modernize the food stamp program (see Box 8.1), included three separate but related data collection activities: exploratory case studies conducted in four states; a nationwide web-based survey of state, local, and partner agency program administrators; and in-depth case studies in fourteen states. Results from each sequential phase of the study, conducted over a three-year period, informed the next component and led to some modifications and additions to the research questions as well as the instrumentation and data collected. Researchers undertaking such mixed-method studies must take steps to integrate the methods so that measures and procedures overlap or complement each other. Otherwise, a single study using mixed methods runs the risk of becoming multiple separate studies (Yin, 2006).

Designing Case Studies

The design of a case study is critical to its success, and evaluators must carefully consider a number of issues. These include defining the research questions, determining the unit of analysis, deciding between single- and multiple-case designs, and site selection.

Defining Research Questions

As in designing any other research study, the first step in developing a case study is the definition of the questions that will be addressed by the study. In case study research, understanding the context in which the case exists is particularly important in identifying the research questions. This requires reviewing the available literature on the issue to be studied and accumulating evidence related to the goals and design of the program being evaluated, often through interviews with program officials and other stakeholders, to fully inform the development of the issues that the study will be addressing.

For example, for a formative evaluation of job search services (often called job clubs) provided by faith-based and community-based organizations, Trutko, Barnow, O'Brien, and Wandner (2014) conducted case studies in six locations across the country to learn more about the characteristics of these job clubs and how they differ from or are similar to those offered by publicly funded workforce agencies. A second goal of the study was to identify potential approaches that might be used for a more rigorous evaluation. Prior to conducting the case studies, the researchers conducted telephone interviews with several key stakeholders knowledgeable about these types of job clubs. The information collected during these interviews helped to inform and refine the focus of the topics addressed during the on-site semi-structured interviews (See Trutko, Barnow, O'Brien, and Wandner, 2014).

After developing the initial set of research questions, it is critical to develop a framework to structure the specific research questions that will be addressed and specific hypotheses about the program or case being studied. Logic models (described in Chapter Three) can function as diagrammatic or graphic models to specify the key elements of the issues addressed. Figure 8.1 presents a conceptual framework for case studies of efforts to improve a food assistance program, describing the motivations for the changes, the types of changes, and the outcomes of interest.

Evaluators can use a framework like this to identify and establish the dimensions of what they will study and report. From these dimensions, research questions can be developed and clarified and the types of data required to address each question identified. A common pitfall in case study research is *collecting too much information*, that is, collecting both pertinent information and information that is irrelevant to understanding the program or event being studied. A *clearly structured research framework* is critical to focusing and defining the data collection efforts and avoiding this issue.

An example of the study dimensions and research questions for a case study is presented in Table 8.1. This study examined a state program designed to provide integrated services to long-term welfare recipients. However, much of this discussion is likely to be applicable to many other case study topics.

This program sought to improve on the performance of other, similar welfare-to-work efforts by coordinating services provided by multiple systems in a defined service area. The research questions focused on examining how

FIGURE 8.1. CONCEPTUAL FRAMEWORK FOR CASE STUDIES OF FOOD ASSISTANCE PROGRAM MODERNIZATION INITIATIVE.

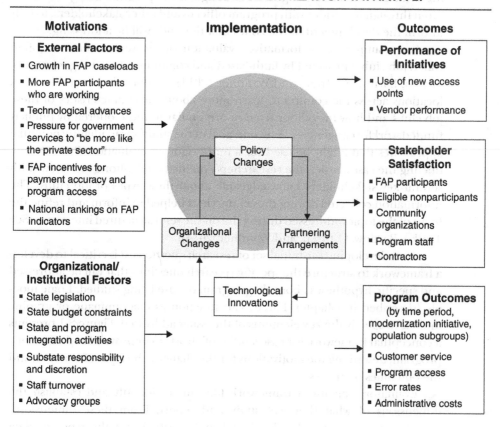

localities offer integrated services across delivery systems, identifying factors that contributed to localities' success or created challenges, and understanding how efforts differed across localities. To address these questions, researchers identified a range of factors that would affect implementation of the program, and from these, specific research questions were derived. Data sources (for example, program staff interviews and program data) for each research question were also identified.

GAO's sample design matrix, presented in Chapter One (see Figure 1.4), is also a useful tool for systematically making decisions about appropriate data collection and analysis methods for each research question.

TABLE 8.1. RESEARCH QUESTIONS ADDRESSED AND DATA SOURCES FOR A STUDY OF INTEGRATED SERVICES.

Dimension	Research Questions Addressed	Data Sources
Program goals	What are the key goals of the program? To what extent does the program focus on employment, reducing welfare dependency, or improving outcomes for children?	Interviews with program staff; documents
Program scale and target group	What is the definition of the target group? What are the demographic characteristics of the target group? How do the demographics of target group "match" the program services? How are members of the target group actually identified and informed about available services? Does the program target both parents and children for services? How large is the program? Did the program meet its goals in terms of program scale?	Interviews with program managers and line staff; baseline demographic data
Service strategies	What organization(s) is (are) involved in planning and providing services? What are the program's linkages with other service providers? What are the barriers to effective coordination and how are they resolved? What informal and formal guidelines are put into place to guide service delivery? How are management responsibilities divided up and coordinated? How is the program staffed? How are line staff recruited and trained, and how is their performance assessed?	Interviews with program managers and line staff; focus groups
Service delivery structure	What programmatic features were implemented to achieve the program goals? What services (e.g., assessment, case management, training, support services, supported employment, counseling, mentoring) are provided? What are the timing and triggers for key services? What specialized services are provided, including mental health, substance abuse, health, criminal justice, and child welfare? To what extent do the services address the needs of children of the participants? What methods of assessment are used? Where are the services provided (e.g., office, home visits, other locations)?	Interviews with program managers and line staff

(Continued)

TABLE 8.1. RESEARCH QUESTIONS ADDRESSED AND DATA SOURCES FOR
A STUDY OF INTEGRATED SERVICES. *(Continued)*

Dimension	Research Questions Addressed	Data Sources
Service receipt and intensity	What services did participants receive? What is the length and intensity of services? How many hours per week did participants engage in work and work-related activities? To what extent did they receive employment-related services and other specialized services such as substance abuse and mental health services, etc.? To what extent did they participate in sanction-resolution activities?	Program data; focus groups
Implementation of accomplishments and challenges	What factors—including resources, staff, and service availability—affect program implementation? What issues were encountered in setting up and running the program? How did the program overcome or resolve these issues?	Interviews with program managers and line staff
Participant experiences	What were participants' experiences in the program? Did they find the services beneficial?' How did the program compare to services they had previously received?	Focus groups

Determining the Unit of Analysis

A key decision in designing case studies is selecting the unit of analysis. Case studies may focus on a range of issues, including policies, specific programs, key decisions, the implementation process, program effects, and organizational change. The unit of analysis is closely related to the initial research questions. In some cases, defining the unit of analysis can be relatively straightforward. For example, if the primary study objective is to document how localities implemented the delivery of a back-to-school supplemental payment for public assistance recipients, the primary unit of analysis will be the public offices that administer this benefit. If the research objective involves understanding how families spent the benefit, the unit of analysis would be the families who received the payment.

In other cases, the choice of the unit of analysis is more complicated. For example, if the goal is to understand the implementation of innovative approaches for providing employment and parenting services to noncustodial fathers, the unit of analysis could be an individual project, an organization operating several projects, or a nationally sponsored program consisting of many funded projects (Yin, 1993). In some studies, such as those examining how states and localities implemented the landmark welfare reform legislation in the late 1990s, the unit of analysis can be more than one organization or program. In this welfare reform situation, the case studies focused on the network of local service delivery systems, including welfare offices, workforce development organizations, and nonprofit service providers.

Choosing Single-Case or Multiple-Case Designs

Another key decision in designing case studies is choosing between single- and multiple-case designs. Yin (2003) notes that single-case designs are appropriate when the case represents a "critical" test of existing theory, a rare and unique circumstance, or when the case serves a revelatory purpose. Classic examples of the single-case study include Graham Allison's study (1971) of the Cuban missile crisis and Pressman and Wildavsky's study (1973) of the implementation of an economic development program intended to benefit unemployed African Americans in Oakland in 1966. Single-case designs can also be appropriate and valuable when a typical or representative case can be identified, although this can be difficult to achieve, particularly for program implementation studies.

Multiple-case designs are used to provide descriptions and make comparisons across cases to provide insight into an issue. Multiple-case designs are generally preferred to single-case designs because of the possibility of missing an important occurrence if only one case or one program site is studied. Evidence from multiple-case designs is often considered more compelling and the findings more robust (Yin, 2003). A common example of a multiple-case study is an evaluation of a school innovation (such as the introduction of a new curriculum or a modification of a class schedule) in which individual schools implement some type of change. Each school is the subject of an individual case study, but the study as a whole covers several schools. Although multiple-case study designs are typically preferred, they are often more expensive to conduct.

Selecting Cases or Sites

Selecting specific cases to examine is a critical piece in the case study design. This process is generally more straightforward in single-case designs, where the focus of study is likely to be a unique occurrence or critical instance. For example, an examination of a federal, state, or local emergency agency's response to the Hurricane Katrina disaster of 2005 would be a single-case design.

Case selection is typically more difficult in multiple-case study designs. Although it is possible to randomly select cases under some circumstances, in general this approach is not used in program evaluation studies because the relatively small number of cases selected (often due to budget constraints) will not ensure a representative sample.

Purposive sampling is common because this case selection method ensures that the cases selected represent an adequate range of conditions. Various criteria can be used to select cases, depending on the study questions examined. Purposive sampling strategies include (1) bracketing, or looking at what is happening at the extremes; (2) examining best cases, or what accounts for an effective program, and worst cases, or why the program is not working; and (3) being representative, or selecting those cases that represent important variations across a group of programs as a whole (U.S. General Accounting Office, 1991). In the field of program evaluation, generalizability is typically an important goal, so diversity among best and worst cases or representation of important variations across all models is typically desired.

Again, the strategy used to select cases or sites is tied to the specific research questions the study will address. For example, studies focused on identifying best practices might concentrate on programs that have made more progress in implementing the policy or that are believed to have had successful outcomes. A case study with the goal of identifying strategies for making food stamp benefits more accessible to working families would select sites that have made innovations in this area.

In contrast, case studies focused on representing the breadth and range of implementation experiences with a particular intervention would select cases or program sites that provide variation in key areas of interest. For example, in an evaluation of a federal grant program of over 160 industry-focused job training projects, nine case study sites were chosen, based on a number of key program dimensions (Nightingale and others, 2008). These dimensions included type of industry (such as production and trade, technology, or services), geographical region, substantive focus of grant activities, and types of partner organizations. The study sites were then selected to represent the range of grant projects that were developed.

It is also important to consider the number of sites selected, and again, there is no hard-and-fast rule. Evaluators using multiple-case designs generally aim for at least three sites to provide adequate variation and representation, but more often strive for six to nine cases. Studies using more than fifteen cases can be difficult to conduct, given the amount of data that must be collected, processed, and synthesized. Unlike quantitative analyses, which can easily handle additional cases, case studies may be overwhelmed by data from too many cases and may also find these additional data of limited value in discerning patterns and trends. Case studies are less about the number of cases selected and more about making the right match between the purposes of the study and the selection process, taking into account the diversity of the programs.

Conducting Case Studies

Contrary to popular opinion, conducting in-depth case studies is rarely inexpensive, easy, or quick. It can require lengthy and in-depth data collection and sensitivity to the setting that can take time to develop. Case study research also demands a significant investment of time for data analysis, interpretation, and reporting. This section discusses the key steps in conducting major case studies. Note, however, that smaller case studies often are appropriate. These smaller studies can be inexpensive, relatively easy, and quick to do. Regardless of study scope, the key steps involved in conducting case studies stay the same.

Preparation

Conducting a successful case study requires careful preparation, including establishing clear protocols and procedures in advance of the fieldwork, developing data collection instruments, training the staff conducting the study, and, if possible, conducting a pilot study prior to going into the field, in order to identify and avoid barriers and problems.

Development of Protocols and Data Collection Instruments. Protocols provide a road map for how the data will be collected in the field and then be used to guide investigators through the study. Particularly in multiple-case studies, protocols increase the reliability of results by providing uniformity and consistency in the data collection effort. Because other chapters in this volume present more detail on specific interviewing and data collection strategies, here we note only the general areas that a protocol should cover.

Protocols lay out the general procedures for collecting data needed for the case study, focusing on the data that will be collected in the field. They address:

- The sites in the study
- The sources of data to be collected in each site
- The key respondents to be interviewed

- The plans to complete other types of data collection activities, such as focus groups and observations of key program activities, information on the study, and confidentiality for respondents
- A schedule for completing the data collection procedures in each site

At the heart of the protocol are the data collection instructions for the semi-structured interviews that provide the substantive questions that will be asked. These should be tailored as necessary for each respondent. The main purpose of these questions is to keep the interviewer on track as the data collection proceeds and to ensure that the interview covers all key topics.

Staff Qualification and Training.   A well-trained researcher is highly desirable for case study research. Because data collection is nonroutinized, interviewers should be able to discern what is important from what is not. The judgment and interpretive skills of the researcher determine the findings and conclusions of the study. This is another nonroutine process, particularly when compared to analyses of quantitative data. Yin (2003) identifies several skills common to effective case study evaluators, including the ability to

- Ask good questions.
- Be a good listener (including being able to read between the lines and pursue a line of inquiry as needed).
- Be adaptive and flexible in real-life situations (such as an unexpected change—like lack of office space in which to conduct interviews).
- Have a firm grasp of the issues being studied.
- Be unbiased.

It is important to provide training for staff conducting site visits. Training should cover:

- A review of the research questions
- A review of the instruments used for data collection
- Strategies for gaining and maintaining respondent cooperation and handling unforeseen situations
- Formats for narrative reporting and for taking field notes

Training and ongoing oversight are especially needed to enhance quality control and consistency of data collection.

Pilot-Testing. If possible, a pilot test using each data-gathering method should be conducted so that problematic areas can be uncovered and corrected. Pilot-testing assists researchers in anticipating key problems and events, identifying key people, revisiting rules for confidentiality, and indicating where data collection strategies should be modified in order to more fully address or add to the original set of research questions. Pilot-testing is also useful for identifying which and what types of questions are confusing or need rewording and what additional questions to include.

Data Collection Strategies

The hallmark of a case study is an in-depth portrait of the case. Case study plans thus generally call for collecting data from multiple sources. *The richness and complexity of the data collected in case studies distinguishes them from many other forms of qualitative research.* Consequently, determining which data sources to use and how to collect data is critical in designing any case study. Here we review the range of data sources typically used in case studies, including interviews, document review, direct observation, and program data.

Interviews. Interviews are among the most important sources of case study information. Most interviews in case studies use open-ended questions, in which key respondents are asked to comment on certain events, with the opportunity to propose solutions or provide insight into those events. Even in open-ended interviews, some type of semi-structured interview guide is generally used to guide the researchers through the key topics that need to be covered (see Chapter Nineteen). Interviews are generally conducted one on one, although in some cases it can be appropriate to conduct interviews with groups of individuals with similar experiences: for example, a group discussion with several staff who process child support cases or a focus group with new mothers receiving home visits (see Chapter Twenty).

A critical component of the interviewing process for case studies is taking the time to obtain multiple perspectives on key areas of interests. For example, a focus group with individuals receiving Temporary Assistance for Needy Families (TANF) benefits can provide a viewpoint of the relative success of the process that is different from the viewpoint provided by one-on-one interviews with the staff who deliver the services. Evaluators need to take careful, detailed notes. These are critical for conveying the complexity and essence of what has happened in an interview.

Document Reviews.   Documents play an important role in corroborating and augmenting data from interviews and other sources and are critical for every type of case study. They may be organizational charts, letters, memoranda, grant applications, policies and procedures manuals, staff training materials, agendas and minutes from planning meetings, recruitment materials, project descriptions and timelines, curricula, aggregate statistical reports, press articles, customer satisfaction survey findings, or other documents. This kind of documentation can inform the research process at several stages of the study. It can provide important details that fill in the blanks for outstanding questions remaining after site visits. In addition these materials may offer rich contextual information and a better overall understanding of the implementation and operational processes at a site.

Direct Observation.   Observations of key program activities can be a valuable component of the data collection activities conducted during site visits. They provide researchers with the opportunity to see, in a real-time setting, how staff implement policies and procedures and how they interact with participants. Observations, for example, might focus on staff-client interactions, program workshops, or classroom sessions. These can provide a more accurate view of program operations than can be gained solely from interviews with staff. Direct observation can range from a relatively casual viewing of program activities to using formal protocols. Formal protocols might involve, for example, a checklist of observation topics and questions—with space to record activities and procedures, including unanticipated or noteworthy practices.

Program Data.   In some program evaluations a useful component of a case study is an understanding of the levels and types of services received by program participants. Interviews can get at this to some extent. However, program data on enrollment, services received, completion, and program outcomes (information often collected for monitoring and management purposes) can provide highly useful information for a case study.

Analyzing the Data

Case studies can generate large amounts of data that must be analyzed sufficiently and with appropriate techniques in order to be useful. The first step is to create a database of the range of quantitative and qualitative data collected. This includes interview notes and any quantitative program data collected.

A number of tools can be helpful for organizing and analyzing the information range of data collected. These can be particularly useful in multiple-case evaluations, where analysis of qualitative data across sites is a critical component. In a multiple-case study, it can be particularly challenging to compare programs that exist in very different contexts and adopt different approaches. Strategies to organize and analyze these data include the following:

- Describe each case in detail, and provide an analysis of the issues or themes that each case presents and that the cases as a group present.
- Focus on the specific dimensions identified as part of the study design, including analytical tables that systematically organize the key preliminary findings for each site under each main study topic.
- Detail site timelines or chronologies of the key stages of program development and implementation.
- Prepare diagrams of the key elements of program design and operation.
- Map participant flow through the program elements.
- Conduct meetings with field staff to discuss the findings, the team's preliminary interpretations, the strengths and weaknesses of different types of evidence, and possible alternative interpretations.

The analysis phase should include sorting the data in many different ways to expose or create new insights and looking for conflicting data to disconfirm the analysis. Several analytical techniques can be used to identify findings and work toward conclusions. These strategies help researchers to move beyond initial impressions to develop accurate and reliable findings. They include:

- Comparing multiple sources of evidence before deciding there is a finding. This is sometimes known as *triangulation* (U.S. General Accounting Office, 1991)
- Analyzing information within each case for themes and then across all cases for themes that are either the same or different (Miller and Salkind, 2002)
- Examining how data collection and analysis findings compare to original expectations and hypotheses (Yin, 2003)
- Analyzing all the information collected to develop a picture of what is happening and why, using the information to structure hypotheses (Elmore, 1982)
- Ensuring that the analysis addresses all major rival interpretations, so that these can be ruled out or targeted for additional study (Yin, 2003)

Using these strategies enables the researcher to synthesize, analyze, and highlight preliminary findings, themes, and lessons. Throughout the evaluation and analysis process, it is critical that the researcher remain open to new interpretations and insights. In all cases, in order to avoid premature or inaccurate conclusions, researchers must assess all available data to identify any evidence that may not support initial findings. The data analysis ends when the best possible fit has been reached between the observations and interpretations (U.S. General Accounting Office, 1991; also see Chapter Twenty-Two in this volume).

Preparing the Report

Case studies should report the data in a way that transforms a complex issue into one that can be easily understood, allowing the reader to question and examine the study and reach an understanding independent of the researcher. Case study reports may vary significantly in length and detail, and the preferences of the potential audience should play a key role in developing the structure of the case study report (Yin, 2003). It is critical to identify the audience for the report and their specific needs and goals when designing and writing the final report.

Among the common techniques for structuring a report are (1) addressing each case in a separate chapter, with a final chapter summarizing cross-site conclusions; (2) treating the case study as a series of chronological events and describing these events in sequence; or (3) identifying specific themes or topic areas and discussing each case within these areas. Again, the choice of appropriate report structure is driven in large part by needs and interests of the probable audience and the study funders as well as by the specific research questions addressed and the number of sites in the study. For example, some funders want detailed information on each case, requiring a chapter, or at the minimum a report appendix, to provide in-depth, case-specific information.

Regardless of the organizational approach, the following elements are critical to an exemplary report:

- Situating each case within its context or setting
- Specifying site selection and data collection activities
- Providing explicit explanations of the key evidence used to draw conclusions
- Offering an interpretation of the meaning of the analysis by providing *lessons learned*

- Outlining any limitations or cautions regarding the study's conclusions

It can also be important to have the case study report reviewed in order to gain validation of the key information it presents (Yin, 2003). In addition to research peers, it is important that key study respondents and stakeholders review the report. This review procedure has been identified as a way of verifying facts and evidence presented in the case. Although respondents may disagree with specific conclusions and interpretations, it is critical that the basic information presented about each case be correct.

Avoiding Common Pitfalls

In the course of describing how to conduct case studies, we have mentioned several pitfalls that await researchers conducting case studies and also the strategies for avoiding them. This information is summarized in Box 8.3 and described in more detail in the rest of this section.

The first common pitfall is that case studies are unlikely to be representative, and thus generalizing the findings is often problematic. There are strategies to improve generalizability, even if a representative sample of cases cannot be studied. For example, multiple-case designs are usually preferable to single-case designs because the evidence collected from multiple observations is considered more compelling and the findings more robust. In addition, in program implementation studies, purposively selecting cases to represent diversity among the best and worst cases or selecting cases that represent important variations across all programs can help to address generalizability issues.

Because case studies focus on collecting in-depth information from multiple sources, another problem frequently encountered is that the wealth of information gathered cannot be adequately analyzed and synthesized. It is critical for the researcher to develop a well-defined framework that describes the specific hypotheses that will be addressed by the study and the dimensions of what will be studied and reported. Well-designed protocols and data collection instruments can be then be developed to keep the project on track.

Difficulties can also arise if the case study evaluator is not impartial and develops conclusions before the research has been completed. These premature conclusions can be identified and, if necessary, removed through multiple strategies, including adequate supervision and training of researchers and use of multiple data collection strategies to verify or refute findings. It can also be useful to have respondents review a summary or transcript of their interviews to ensure their views are appropriately represented. A related pitfall is drawing conclusions before the data have been completely analyzed or developing inappropriate conclusions from data. Here the solution is to analyze all available data using multiple techniques and addressing rival hypotheses. In all cases, researchers must consider and assess all available data to identify any evidence that may not support initial findings and thus avoid inaccurate conclusions.

Box 8.3. Tips for Avoiding Common Case Study Pitfalls

- Problem: Limited generalizability
- Solutions:
  Select the sites through a careful process.
  Acknowledge limitations of conclusions.
- Problem: Too much data
- Solutions:
  Use a well-defined research framework.
  Use well-developed protocols.
- Problem: Need for impartiality on the part of the evaluator
- Solutions:
  Ask individuals who were interviewed to review a summary of their interview.
  Use multiple data collection methods.
  Provide adequate supervision and training.
- Problem: Premature or inappropriate conclusions
- Solutions:
  Analyze all available data using multiple techniques.
  Address rival hypotheses.
- Problem: Unintegrated report narrative
- Solutions:
  Understand what the audience needs from the case study report.
  Provide an explicit interpretation of the analysis by describing the lessons learned.

Source: Adapted from U.S. General Accounting Office, 1991.

Finally, some case studies suffer from a report narrative that does not integrate findings across all data sources or sites. This makes it difficult for readers to digest the large amount of information collected. When designing a summary report, it is critical to identify the audience for the report and to take into consideration their specific needs and goals so that information is provided with the appropriate level of detail. In addition, the final report should offer an interpretation of the data and analysis by drawing out lessons learned or other conclusions that integrate data sources and cross-site findings.

Conclusion

The case study is a powerful tool in the program evaluator's toolkit. Case studies can be used to inform the development of future studies (exploratory evaluations); document what is happening and why to show what a situation is like (descriptive case studies); or focus on establishing cause-and-effect relationships, explaining which causes produced which effects (explanatory case studies). Box 8.2 gave step-by step guidelines for conducting a case study. Tips for avoiding some of the common challenges faced by case studies are provided in Box 8.3. Nightingale and Rossman, in Chapter Seventeen, provide an in-depth discussion of field procedures.

The case study offers the evaluator a proven yet flexible method for providing detailed information and valuable insight into the "hows" and "whys" of program implementation. It gives evaluators the ability to integrate qualitative and quantitative data from multiple sources and to present an in-depth picture of the implementation and results of a program or policy within its context. Although there are limitations to the case study method, when systematically conducted by skilled evaluators, it can provide useful evaluative information not otherwise available.

References

Allison, G. *Essence of Decision: Explaining the Cuban Missile Crisis.* New York: Little, Brown, 1971.

Elmore, R. "Backward Mapping: Implementation Research and Policy Decisions." In W. Williams and others (eds.), *Studying Implementation: Methodological and Administrative Issues.* Chatham, NJ: Chatham House, 1982.

Levine, M. *From State Hospital to Psychiatric Center: The Implementation of Planned Organizational Change.* San Francisco: New Lexington Press, 1980.

Love, A. "Implementation Evaluation." In J. S. Wholey, H. P. Hatry, and K. E. Newcomer (eds.), *Handbook of Practical Program Evaluation* (2nd ed.). San Francisco: Jossey-Bass, 2004.

Martinson, K., and Holcomb, P. *Reforming Welfare: Institutional Change and Challenges.* Assessing the New Federalism Occasional Paper no. 60. Washington, DC: Urban Institute, 2002.

Miller, D. C., and Salkind, N. J. (eds.). *Handbook of Research Design and Social Measurement* (6th ed.). Thousand Oaks, CA: Sage, 2002.

Nightingale, D. S., and others. *Implementation Analysis of High Growth Job Training Initiative (HGJTI) Programs.* Washington, DC: Urban Institute, 2008.

O'Brien, C., and others. Enhancing Food Stamp Certification: Food Stamp Modernization Efforts: Report on Phase 1 Initial Site Visits. Unpublished report prepared for the U.S. Department of Agriculture, Food and Nutrition Service, by the Urban Institute, 2007.

Pressman, J. L., and Wildavsky, A. *Implementation: How Great Expectations in Washington Are Dashed in Oakland: or, Why It's Amazing That Federal Programs Work at All, This Being a Saga of the Economic Development Administration as Told by Two Sympathetic Observers Who Seek to Build Morals on a Foundation of Ruined Hopes.* Berkeley, CA: University of California Press, 1973.

Smith, L. M. "An Evolving Logic of Participant Observation, Educational Ethnography, and Other Case Studies." In L. Shulman (ed.), *Review of Research in Education.* Itasca, IL: Peacock, 1978.

Trutko, J., Barnow, B., O'Brien, C., and Wandner, S. *Formative Evaluation of Job Clubs Operated by Faith- and Community-Based Organizations: Findings from Site Visits and Options for Future Evaluation.* Final Report prepared for the U.S. Department of Labor, Chief Evaluation Office by Capital Research Corporation and George Washington University, March 2014.

U.S. General Accounting Office. *Case Study Evaluations.* Washington, DC: U.S. General Accounting Office, 1991.

Yin, R. K. *Applications of Case Study Research.* Thousand Oaks, CA: Sage, 1993.

Yin, R. K. *Case Study Research: Design and Methods* (3rd ed.). Thousand Oaks, CA: Sage, 2003.

Yin, R. K. "Mixed Methods Research: Are the Methods Genuinely Integrated or Merely Parallel?" *Research in the Schools,* 2006, *13*(1), 41–47.

CHAPTER NINE

RECRUITMENT AND RETENTION OF STUDY PARTICIPANTS

Scott C. Cook, Shara Godiwalla, Keeshawna S. Brooks, Christopher V. Powers, Priya John

This chapter introduces readers to a range of issues concerning recruitment and retention of participants in evaluation studies. First, we discuss how recruitment and retention are considered in planning and designing evaluations and how applications to institutional review boards are handled. Next, details around hiring, training, and supervising staff are covered. Best practices for general implementation of recruitment and retention are then shared, followed by a discussion of the need to closely monitor recruitment and retention. We then discuss the specific attention, resources, and sensitivity required when the evaluation involves members of minority populations or underprivileged groups. The chapter ends with a summary of the recruitment and retention challenges and potential solutions.

Recruitment for evaluation purposes means obtaining the right number of program participants with the appropriate eligibility characteristics to take part as members of the needed comparison groups. Evaluators need to ensure that appropriate participants are included because failing to do so may lead to rejecting the null hypothesis when it is true or failing to reject the null hypothesis when it is false in the evaluation outcome. For randomized controlled trials, this means recruiting and retaining participants for both the treatment and control groups. At the very least, inappropriate eligibility characteristics may alter or reduce the generalizability of the findings and the potential validity of the conclusions that could be drawn from the evaluation.

Retention, for evaluation purposes, means maximizing the number of participants who continue the intervention throughout the evaluation period and who are willing to provide follow-up information to the evaluators, often at a time after services for these participants have ended. Some evaluations will need outcome data at only one point in time, while other evaluations may have multiple data collection points.

There are evaluations that take a prospective, or ex ante, approach where baseline and post-implementation data are collected from treatment and referent groups and other ex-post evaluations that retrospectively use existing program data that may or may not include baseline data collection points. This chapter addresses primarily ex-ante evaluations, for which the evaluation planning and participant consent process includes the evaluation data collection. However, this chapter also applies to the many ex-post evaluations that require recruitment and retention of participants to specifically obtain follow-up evaluation information after they have already started participating in the program.

Whether a team is evaluating a biomedical intervention, a new counseling approach, or the effects of a program on the people to which it was delivered, successful recruitment and retention of participants is foundational for conducting a high-quality evaluation. For example, the way program participants are treated can directly affect the ability to obtain their consent to provide information for the evaluation. Recruitment and retention is important in evaluations, such as randomized controlled trials, in which study participants are receiving the program's services and in after-the-fact evaluations where all participants whose outcomes are being evaluated have completed the program. For some evaluations, recruitment may be needed only at the beginning of the evaluation. For other evaluations, recruitment may need to be done over a period of time based on participation goals. It is a multifaceted effort composed of technological, cultural, and other dynamic factors.

Planning for Recruitment and Retention

Planning for recruitment and retention is best done early. Evaluators need to define the target population, consider how data collection design will influence participant motivation, and prepare for pretesting.

The Importance of Early Planning

Planning the general evaluation methodology and the methods for recruitment and retention of participants are mutually influential processes. They should occur simultaneously from the earliest planning stages. Projects that retain participants for services whose outcomes are to be later evaluated also require detailed retention goals and protocols planned prior to implementation. Moreover, recruitment and retention planning needs to apply to the participants in comparison groups as well as to those in intervention groups. Unfortunately, most evaluators typically overestimate their ability to recruit and retain participants and spend too little time on this aspect of their evaluation in the design phase. This critical error can lead project staff to significantly underestimate the time and resources necessary to achieve the recruitment and retention targets, can send the project over budget, and can ultimately jeopardize the ability to meet the evaluation goals.

One example of the importance of early planning for recruitment and retention would be a project that relies on young participant populations living in unstable housing. Members of this type of target population could have higher levels of study withdrawal or loss to follow up over the course of the evaluation period, compared to members of populations who are older and more likely to live in stable housing. To ensure an adequate number of retained participants, such projects could predict an atypically large dropout rate and require recruitment of more participants than necessary for data analyses. They could also plan for additional activities designed to maximize participant retention. By making such predictions in early-stage planning, the evaluation team may also realize that the pool of potential participants is not large enough to accommodate this need and may revise the evaluation methodology so as to require fewer participants.

Evaluation teams should take the approach of hoping for the best but planning for the worst. They can achieve this by deliberately overestimating the challenges of recruiting and retaining participants and then incorporating methodological flexibility. Examples of this flexibility include extending the time allotted to recruitment, minimizing the length of follow-up periods, and maximizing flexibility in data collection methods (for example, allowing phone instead of face-to-face interviews for hard-to-retain participants). If the project team fortunately experiences fewer challenges than anticipated, then excess recruitment and retention resources such as time, personnel, and monetary funds can be redirected to other needs or activities.

Defining the Target Population

To ensure enrollment of the desired target population, evaluators have to carefully consider the screening and eligibility criteria. Common eligibility criteria include age, race, ethnicity, gender, location of residence, health behaviors, physical and mental health status indicators (such as blood pressure readings or a diagnosis of depression), and income. However, due to the vast array of potential evaluation goals, eligibility criteria may consist of almost any combination of factors and demographic variables. The estimated availability of possible participants who meet eligibility criteria, the anticipated rate of agreement to participate, and the estimated retention rate at each data collection point will help evaluators determine the resources necessary to meet recruitment and retention goals.

In some cases, an evaluation protocol may require a significant investment of staff and participant resources (such as time or financial resources) to determine eligibility for enrollment. To control costs, it becomes important to minimize resources spent on participants who are ultimately ineligible. For example, evaluation of health-related interventions may require screening potential participants for a particular disease state or lack of disease state to determine eligibility. These candidates often need at least two encounters or appointments prior to possible enrollment (for example, first, to collect lab specimens and, second, to deliver screening test results and enroll the participant if she is eligible and willing). Prescreening potential participants may prove beneficial by ensuring that those who meet most or all other eligibility criteria are the only ones asked to provide their time and energy for time-consuming or costly aspects of the recruitment protocol (such as collecting and processing lab specimens to determine final eligibility).

Some evaluation protocols may be unduly influenced by participants who have already been exposed to a condition or situation that renders them atypical in relation to the population being targeted or that is significantly related to the evaluation variables of interest. For example, the team designing an evaluation to determine the success of an after-school substance use prevention program for youths may preclude data collection from program participants who had used specific substances prior to program participation. This would be reasonable if the evaluation is attempting to measure success at preventing first-time substance use. However, if the intervention being evaluated focuses on relapse prevention, then inclusion of youths with substance use or abuse prior to intervention exposure will be appropriate. Similarly, specific prior life experiences may influence the dependent variables of the evaluation and thus should be part of any set of exclusion criteria. For example, it is possible that individuals who received outpatient behavioral health therapy for depression over the last year may best be screened as ineligible for evaluation of a depression intervention.

When considering exclusion criteria, it is important to determine whether potential participants have participated in prior evaluation projects that may render them atypical compared to the target population. For example, some organizations conducting regular evaluation or research studies recruit for multiple projects over time from the same general population. This increases the chance that participants recruited for the current evaluation project may have previously participated in a similar evaluation or research project. The evaluation team may determine that certain prior participation could unduly influence individuals' responses for the current evaluation.

Participant Motivation and Data Collection Design

Evaluators are often eager to collect as much data as possible from participants. However, this desire *must be balanced with the impact of study burden on participant motivation* to enroll and remain available for follow-up contacts. To maximize recruitment and retention over the life of the evaluation project it is essential to minimize the complexity and number of steps or actions required of participants. Each step of the recruitment and enrollment process introduces the risk of losing a percentage of the overall pool of potential participants. Similarly, participant attrition can occur at each step of the retention process. Participant motivation is also influenced by the mode and location of data collection.

Participant motivation. Participant motivation significantly affects the level of effort ultimately required for recruitment and retention and is directly influenced by data collection protocols. The questions of what data to collect and how much data to collect are primarily answered by factors unrelated to recruitment and retention (such as statistical power analyses and sample size estimations). However, during the planning stage, evaluation teams often overestimate the motivation of their anticipated participants and, once recruitment begins, discover that potential participants perceive the data collection burden as excessive and decline participation. Or participants may enroll in the evaluation but drop out after experiencing the data collection burden. In other situations, participants may continue their participation but provide lower quality or unreliable data due to decreased attention span, decreased energy, or rising frustrations as the protocol progresses. Therefore, participants' motivation to provide the data requested should directly inform the creation of data collection protocols, including which measures to use. Assessing participant motivation should include the influence of participant literacy and comprehension, how data collection tools are presented and explained by staff members, and the methods of data collection and recording.

Modes of Data Collection. Different modes of data collection have their own pros and cons, and these may also differ by target population or subpopulation.

The most common modes of data collection are paper-and-pencil question-naires, computerized interfaces, face-to-face interviews, telephone interviews, and focus groups. Web-based methods are increasingly being used. If data collection is likely to require substantial information from participants, their perceptions of convenience, comfort, or confidentiality can affect their willing-ness to enroll or to remain as participants. This, in turn, affects the resources required to reach recruitment and retention goals.

Location of Data Collection. The geographical location and the physical characteristics of the study site will also have an impact on recruitment and retention as well as on the quality of the data. Data collection may occur on the street, in the home, at an office, or elsewhere, but decisions about the location must consider the factors that will affect adherence to the evaluation protocol. Individuals' perceptions about whether the location is convenient, comfortable, and culturally welcoming will affect recruitment and retention.

Pretesting

Once screening, enrollment, and data collection protocols are created, imple-mentation staff should pretest them to assess their viability in the field, includ-ing ease of use for staff and potential participants. Role playing best- and worst-case scenarios can be immensely informative. Best-case scenarios help staff develop a baseline understanding for ideal implementation. Worst-case sce-narios help to identify potential challenges and allow consultation with the rest of the evaluation team to alter protocols as necessary prior to implemen-tation. Worst-case scenarios might include encountering resistance from the implementing staff; dealing with potential participants with limited time and motivation, participants who are uncooperative, participants with limited read-ing ability, or participants wary of research; explaining ineligibility to individ-uals highly motivated to participate; and working with participants previously deemed ineligible who attempt to reenter at a later date.

Recruitment and retention are time-, location-, and culture-bound. Particular recruitment and retention methodologies that were successful in the recent past may not work today, even for the same organization with the same target population and study parameters. This is often due to overlooked changes in the population targeted for intervention. In cities where neighborhoods are racially and ethnically segregated, target population centers may shift geographically over time. In other cities, target populations may experience overall changes in socioeconomic status (as, for example, large employers expand or decrease job opportunities). Also, socioeconomic status, health status, or other demographic variables may shift as immigrant populations become more acculturated.

Recruiting for the same evaluation project in different sites at the same time will often reveal differences in culture, resources and participant populations across sites that significantly impact recruitment and retention. Finding Answers: Disparities Research for Change conducted thirty-three different program evaluations with most recruiting and retaining participants across multiple sites (Finding Answers: Disparities Research for Change, n.d.). Most of the thirty-three evaluation projects reported significant variance across sites in their ability to recruit and retain participants. Important site variables that impacted recruitment and retention included participant subpopulations that varied by race and ethnicity, income, preferred language, staff buy-in and motivation, as well as space and staff time for recruitment and retention activities. Focus groups, pilot interviews and other pretest efforts can illuminate changes in the target population and help to identify unforeseen obstacles and challenges early; allowing program staff to alter recruitment and retention protocols and goals accordingly.

Institutional Review Boards and the Office of Management and Budget

Institutional review boards (IRBs) oversee the rights and welfare of human subjects involved in research and evaluation projects. Another critical IRB function is maintaining ethical practices in research and evaluation. Evaluators need to consult their own institution's IRB for its standards and regulations. It is also helpful for evaluators to have a regular contact at their IRB to guide them through the application process and provide constructive feedback. The IRB may also have consent form templates, which can be a helpful time saver and facilitate the inclusion of all required consent form information. An IRB contact can also explain the proper language for the IRB application itself and for the participant consent form and other materials. Finally, in developing and distributing surveys supported with federal government funds, it is important that the lead organization obtains clearance from the White House Office of Management and Budget (OMB) to comply with the Paperwork Reduction Act (PRA). This clearance may take many months to obtain, so it is important to allow adequate time for this process (Martin and Thomas, 2006).

Evaluators should ensure that the original IRB application contains as many contingency plans as possible for additional recruitment and retention strategies that may need to be implemented if challenges arise. This will help to avoid the necessity of adding some procedure not included in the original IRB request and will ultimately save valuable time because such additions typically require a potentially time-consuming IRB review. For example, in the community setting it can be especially difficult to maintain phone contact and retain participants with unstable housing. If retention protocols rely on phone contacts, evaluation staff may want to plan for not being able to keep in contact with a participant via phone and needing to institute home visits. It is important that the initial IRB application contain language to this effect and provide for this specific contingency.

The IRB application should also include details related to participant incentives. Although incentives can motivate participants to continue their participation and express appreciation for participants' time and effort, they can also be perceived as coercive if excessive and, therefore, can raise IRB concerns. The possibility that the incentive might be coercive must be assessed by the likelihood that it could control or dominate someone's decision to participate (Nelson and Merz, 2002). It is important while planning recruitment and retention strategies to understand the IRB's policies on disbursing incentives. The review board may have particular requirements for incentive disbursement protocols. For tax purposes, many IRBs now encourage using prepaid gift cards instead of cash incentives. Another benefit of using prepaid gift cards is that they are traceable by serial number, which some institutions prefer for documentation purposes. Finally, using gift cards instead of cash decreases the likelihood that participants may use their stipend to purchase illegal or unhealthy items.

Recruitment and Retention Staffing

Successful recruitment and retention requires the right staff. Some evaluation projects will have resources to hire new permanent or temporary staff whose primary job responsibility is implementing recruitment and retention protocols. This approach is ideal and should be followed whenever possible. Other evaluation projects may not have adequate resources to specifically hire recruitment and retention staff. These projects must use current staff and train them to implement recruitment and retention protocols in addition to their primary job responsibilities. Using existing staff raises multiple complex challenges because these individuals were not hired to do the specialized work of recruitment and retention. Not surprisingly, they often do not have the requisite skill sets. They also may not have the interpersonal characteristics required for successful recruitment and retention, which are typically innate and thus difficult to train. Finally, because their primary job duties are not recruitment and retention, they typically have inadequate time to be appropriately trained or to fully implement recruitment and retention protocols.

Adding recruitment and retention duties to current staff members' responsibilities can easily give rise to conflicts related to time and resource management and can also result in decreased staff morale. This is often expressed via overt or covert staff resistance to the evaluation protocols. Recruitment and retention efforts typically lose out to preexisting duties when such conflicts arise. The potential for staff turnover then increases. Thus, it is critical that pragmatic and demonstrable buy-in and support of the evaluation project be obtained from all levels of organizational leadership as it is vital in addressing the challenges described here, should they arise. It is important to anticipate these potential challenges by proactively addressing them and maintaining active oversight throughout the evaluation project.

Staff Background

Once an adequate number of recruitment staff members are identified or hired, they must learn to adeptly recognize and react to cultural and social standards that factor into a potential participant's decision to take part in the evaluation and provide informed consent. Barriers to evaluation participation may include any stigma associated with participation and the ways in which the potential participant's peers may perceive participation. For example, recruitment of Alzheimer's disease patients and their caregivers from the Chinese American community could be hindered by a cultural belief that mental illness is the result of personal moral failure (Hinton, Guo, Hillygus, and Leykoff, 2000). To potentially lessen the sociocultural learning curve, consider recruiting staff who are culturally congruent with or familiar with the study population. This could mean recruiting staff from the same community, socioeconomic status, or health background as the target population. It is generally considered discriminatory to consider demographics such as race or ethnicity, health status, or socioeconomic status when assessing applicants. However, these may be acceptable criteria when judging applicants on their ability to establish and maintain culturally competent interactions with the population(s) targeted for recruitment and retention. Staff members should also be familiar and comfortable in interacting with potentially stigmatized populations such as those with non-heterosexual identities or sexual orientations, transgender identities, sex workers, intravenous drug users, and the homeless. These required abilities should be clearly indicated in the job description and posting. Evaluators should work closely with human resource personnel to address these issues while creating the job description and selecting candidates.

Interpersonal Qualities

Another critical factor in building a successful recruitment and retention team is attending to the interpersonal qualities that bolster successful recruitment. Staff personality traits and interpersonal skills can increase or decrease the likelihood that the targeted population will participate. Interpersonal qualities such as keeping up a conversation, being enthusiastic, and leaving a good impression will lead to a successful discourse between recruiters and potential participants. This will facilitate subsequent contacts. Instead of primarily feeling discouraged, staff should be able to learn from participants who refuse participation.

When participants are asked to take part in research or maintain their participation over time, staff must be able to respond suitably to their concerns. Staff members need to diagnose the reasons why a potential participant may refuse initial or ongoing participation, understand these barriers, and respond to the person's needs quickly, professionally, and confidently. Although the specific techniques for averting negative responses can be learned, how the initial message is delivered is extremely important. Therefore, interpersonal skills and each staff member's inherent interest and belief in the importance of the evaluation project play a critical role in recruitment and retention.

Communication Skills

Strong communication skills can increase the potential for successful recruiter-participant discourse. These skills include speaking confidently and clearly; a professional, modulated tone; and talking and pausing at an appropriate rate. These attributes can implicitly convey the importance of the evaluation and remove communication barriers that can sometimes inhibit a discussion. An attitude that exudes courtesy, respect, and sincerity can also make the difference between gaining cooperation and losing participant interest. Both interpersonal characteristics and communication skills develop a potential participant's first impression. The first thirty seconds of an interaction are considered key in gaining cooperation, so first impressions conveyed via a combination of interpersonal qualities and communication skills are vital to the work of recruitment.

Thus, to effectively screen, interview, and select recruitment and retention staff, consider these requirements and determine the elements of candidates' backgrounds that will help them empathize and connect with the population in which they will work. In addition, to properly assess candidates, supervisors should know the important interpersonal characteristics and communication skills required for a recruitment and retention position.

Training and Supervision

After screening and staff selection are complete, the next step in the recruitment and retention process involves preparing the staff for the upcoming evaluation work. One of the ultimate goals is to prevent staff turnover associated with burnout. Recruitment and retention work can be challenging due to a myriad of pressures associated with meeting recruitment and retention goals and project deadlines, handling participant rejection, or trepidation with contacting participants and establishing connections where none previously existed. To ease staff concerns, thoroughly train them on established processes and standardized administrative recruitment materials and evaluation instruments. This will lay a foundation for strong staff skills to successfully gain participant cooperation.

Training can address practicing basic communication skills, being persuasive, and learning the details of the specified evaluation needs. Using role-playing exercises for every part of the recruitment and enrollment process during training can teach all of these elements simultaneously. Potential participants will easily sense whether staff are unsure or uneasy. This anxiety can be detected during role-playing exercises and immediately discussed and counteracted before actual recruitment and retention activities begin. Role-playing exercises give staff the chance to gain additional information about participant perspectives.

Role playing also improves staff cohesion because recruiters can partner with one another and alternate between playing the staff role and potential participant role. This perspective-taking exercise becomes particularly useful when recruitment or retention work involves face-to-face or phone-based encounters or when enrollment or outcome-tracking processes are complex. In addition, role-playing exercises can prepare staff for difficult portions of the recruitment process, such as asking sensitive questions, performing sensitive procedures, or working with interpersonally challenging participants.

Solid staff preparation can also improve recruiters' ability to assess factors that preclude enrollment in the evaluation. For example, if a potential participant has a cognitive disability that inhibits his or her ability to understand study participant rights, role-playing exercises can provide staff with ways to successfully handle this type of interaction.

The training should also include a discussion of reasons for refusals and role-playing refusal scenarios that will help recruiters learn the best responses to frequently asked questions. Role plays should include practicing responses to refusals that are based on misunderstandings about the purpose of the study, what participation entails, and eligibility requirements. However, staff training must also include learning to accept refusals from individuals who are not at all motivated to participate. Persuading an unmotivated person to comply with enrollment may be a short-term recruitment success but a long-term retention challenge. Furthermore, learning to accept refusals without becoming discouraged is necessary if staff are to maintain the positive attitude required to sustain recruitment efforts.

Role playing difficult retention scenarios, such as reluctance to complete evaluation forms or return for future visits, will help staff to learn the balance between encouraging continued participation by addressing concerns held by the participant and acknowledging and accepting the participant's right to withdraw from further evaluation efforts at any time.

Supervisors should also consider implementing methods of preventing staff burnout. For example, sharing staff and using agencies that specialize in providing temporary staff are methods to bolster the workforce during particularly heavy recruitment and retention periods; both resources can provide staff who are attuned to the issues associated with recruitment and retention activities and staff who can approach the work with new perspectives. Because each evaluation project is unique, it is impossible to predict all staff training needs in advance. Therefore, regardless of the length of the evaluation project, supervisors should meet regularly with staff to assess and meet training needs as they arise. Although using the methods detailed here will likely decrease the likelihood of a large staff turnover, turnover will inevitably occur. To lessen the loss of momentum and morale due to staff turnover, supervisors should develop protocols for regularly sharing lessons learned and best practices. This information can also be used as a training resource for new staff.

Implementing Recruitment and Retention

This section addresses a number of specific considerations in recruiting and retaining evaluation participants such as methods of contact and gaining participants' cooperation. It is important to remember that every contact with a potential or current participant will have either a positive or negative impact on ultimately recruiting or retaining that individual. This includes written contact and phone or in-person contacts with staff members who are not part of the recruitment and retention team. Their interactions with each participant must be cordial, professional, in line with the protocol, and culturally competent. If the interactions lack these important characteristics, the participant will be more likely to resist or avoid follow-up visits and data collection efforts. Contacting participants is most commonly accomplished via written (such as mail, email, or web-based), phone, or face-to-face methods.

Modes of Contact for Recruitment and Retention

Written Contact. As staff interact with participants, it is important to keep the opportunity to contact the individual in the future intact. A prenotification or advance contact, by letter or email, is one method of initial contact for recruitment. Letters, emails, or texts can also be very useful for retention efforts. It is important that these communications avoid jargon, such as difficult legal or medical terminology, and consider the literacy level of the target population. Literacy in this context involves a measure of how adept participants are at interpreting terms and concepts associated with the evaluation topic. For example, if you are recruiting participants recently diagnosed with diabetes, it may be important to explain terms in common use among others with diabetes, such as *glucose meter*. At the same time, to bolster participant cooperation and to prevent misconceptions, evaluation staff should avoid the excessive use of terms associated with an issue or condition. Keep the discourse channels between the participant and the recruitment and retention team as open as possible. Assess the readability of all written materials using a Flesch-Kincaid assessment or a similar tool (Flesch, 1948; Microsoft Office Online, n.d.). A study conducted on the National Immunization Survey found that keeping the reading level of prenotification letters at an eighth-grade level or less facilitated participant cooperation (Barron, Brooks, Skalland, and Singelton, 2007).

Another way of collecting information from prenotification letters or email is to document contact failures (such as returned letters or failed email addresses) and lack of response. Returned letters can indicate respondent relocation. Most postal service providers, such as the United States Postal Service, indicate the reason that a letter was undeliverable and will also provide forwarding information if it is available. This information can inform staff about the most appropriate contact methods and provide invaluable information about a participant's current location. For potential participants who do not respond, evaluators can send a reminder letter. If there is still no response, evaluators can change the mode of contact. If all modes of contact are ineffective, evaluators should assess whether the lack of response affects which participants are being included or excluded in the evaluation.

Telephone Calls. Phone calls can serve the same purpose as the prenotification communication and can provide important information about participants, such as the best days and times of optimal contact and whether there are others in the household who may be involved in the decision to participate. For example, if a staff member calls a potential or ongoing participant and must typically leave messages with family members, the family then becomes a crucial part of the recruitment and retention activity. These family members could be considered *gatekeepers,* and recruiting staff should treat them as if they were the participants. Staff should provide clear information about the research, including how the participant can contact the recruitment staff. At the same time, staff should assess and implement all necessary confidentiality procedures that may be required by the IRB. Health-related evaluation projects may also be bound by local, state, and federal regulations regarding protected health information.

All methods of contact can deliver information about the participant to inform future contact attempts and to convey to supervisors the recruitment and retention strategies likely to be the most effective to implement. Every contact attempt and participant interaction with any staff member is an opportunity to build solid connections with the participant and can influence the level of comfort the participant has with the evaluation. Therefore, all staff, including those who are not directly a part of the recruitment and retention team, should be prepared for productive interactions with participants. Also, evaluators should identify any staff who have existing relationships with participants, as these staff may prove helpful in building long-term rapport.

Recruitment and Retention Efforts in a Health Care Setting

Recruitment and retention efforts are peripheral in a health care setting, such as a doctor's office or a hospital, where the primary activity is to provide medical care. Using medical records may be a good method to screen for participants with certain health conditions, as well as to obtain critical contact and basic demographic information. Later, this information about the starting pool of candidates can be compared to the participants who complete the program period covered by the evaluation to determine any major differences or patterns between the two groups.

Gaining access to hardcopy or electronic medical records will require careful planning and adherence to the laws associated with gathering this information, such as the privacy provisions of the Health Insurance Portability and Accountability Act (HIPAA) of 1996. In addition, if there is a need to access records across multiple systems, the ease of access may vary depending on the level of interdependence across the data sources. If the databases are housed in the same clinic or in different clinics that have existing data-sharing agreements, the task of accessing and connecting databases becomes less difficult.

The widespread use of electronic health records is relatively new and it is important to remember that obtaining data for the evaluation in this format may be difficult. Many health care organizations are relatively inexperienced with electronic health records and may have difficulty retrieving specific or accurate data. Additionally, information technology (IT) staff members are often overburdened with competing and high-priority programming and data extraction requests that can result in long wait times. IT staff will need specific guidance to extract the correct data. For example, when accessing data for recurring lab values, such as blood pressure, the evaluation team will need to clarify the subset of patients whose data are required and which blood pressure readings to extract (all readings or only one reading within a specific time period) and how to handle missing data. Even with all of the necessary information, the initial data extraction will often reveal unanticipated data challenges that will take time to resolve. For these reasons it is important to pretest data extraction protocols required for recruitment and retention (such as protocols to identify race, ethnicity, preferred language, or age of potential participants). Pretesting will allow recruitment and retention staff to proactively identify any challenges that may require altering or adding work flows (such as software reprogramming or implementing manual data extraction or manipulation).

Pretesting data extraction protocols will also allow recruitment and retention staff the time to assess data quality and develop alternative approaches if the data is not usable or reliable. For example, when extracting specific data points for the first time, many health care organizations will discover that different staff may have input the desired data into a variety of data fields; thus requiring an extended period of time to find all of the relevant data, verify accuracy, and retrain clinic staff on the proper data entry protocols.

When preparing to gather participant information, it is important to determine the most effective method of contacting participants. One way to ensure effective contact is to assess whether the participant has upcoming clinic appointments, which can provide a good opportunity for face-to-face interactions. In some studies, direct face-to-face contact can produce better recruitment and retention outcomes. However, it is also important to determine whether participants may be uncomfortable with being approached during medical appointments. Informing participants of recruitment and retention efforts through posters and signs or flyers in the clinic may better prepare them for interaction with recruitment and retention staff.

Evaluators should consider how recruitment and retention activities will affect routine clinic flow as they refine the methods of obtaining participant information for recruitment and retention and the most effective ways of contacting participants. Occasionally, HIPAA regulations and the IRB may specify that only clinic staff members contact patients, effectively prohibiting patient contact by non-clinic recruitment and retention staff members. It is important to have all clinic staff involved in the effort, even those who are not explicitly recruiting or retaining participants. Prepare clinic staff well in advance of upcoming recruitment or retention activities and ask that they remain flexible. This preparation can help in obtaining staff member buy-in, active involvement, and ongoing support of the recruitment and retention effort. Conversely, recruitment and retention staff should be flexible and willing to reasonably adjust protocols to accommodate unexpected changes in the clinic environment or when clinic staff members notify evaluation staff of challenges. Ideally, identify a clinic champion who is innately motivated by the evaluation project, can proactively monitor recruitment and retention activities, and will motivate other staff members.

Gaining Participant Cooperation

Several approaches are helpful in encouraging potential and ongoing participants to assist with an evaluation.

Diagnosing Objections.   In training exercises, recruitment and retention staff can learn to diagnose objections and develop and refine the skill of gaining participant cooperation. Understanding the reasons behind participant objections to enrolling or maintaining participation starts with understanding why people agree to participate in research or evaluations. People participate for an amalgam of reasons and according to several social norms, such as those listed in Table 9.1 (Cialdini, 2001; Groves, Cialdini, and Couper, 1992). People also

TABLE 9.1. SOCIAL NORMS FOR RESEARCH PARTICIPATION.

Social Norm	Example of Norm Application
Reciprocity	"You help me and I will help you."
Social validation	"If others do this, then so shall I."
Authority	"I will cooperate with legitimate authority."
Scarcity	"I will take advantage of a rare opportunity."
Liking	"I like you [that is, the provider, clinic, or university], therefore I will cooperate."
Consistency	"This is what I think or say and that means I have to act accordingly."
Altruism	"I want to contribute to the community, our society."

Source: Adapted from Groves, Cialdini, and Couper, 1992; Cialdini, 2001.

give different weight to different attributes of the project. For example, for some individuals, a monetary incentive to participate may be a highly salient attribute and their interest in contributing to important health knowledge may be lower. People weigh these factors for their level of personal saliency before making a decision to participate in research (Dillman, 1978; Gouldner, 1960).

Individuals may participate in evaluations to gather additional knowledge about a particular issue, engage in an important activity, fulfill civic duty, or satisfy curiosity. They may do it to combat loneliness or because they have difficulty in refusing. There are multiple motivations for participation, and these reasons may be dynamic. As recruiting and retention staff learn about participants' reasons, they should leverage them to gain cooperation for participation. It is critical that staff assess reasons for refusal and craft a response that creates an opportunity for subsequent and, hopefully, successful contact. Table 9.2 lists reasons for refusals and approaches to counteract them.

TABLE 9.2. REASONS FOR REFUSING TO PARTICIPATE AND POTENTIAL REBUTTAL APPROACHES.

Reasons	Rebuttal Approach
Busy	Give a reason why making the time to participate is important.
Private	Stress confidentiality and importance of the study.
Suspicious	Use a conversational and professional tone.
Fearful	Conduct your efforts on the participant's terms. Go at the participant's pace and focus on building trust.
Apathetic	Explain that they cannot be replaced.
Unpleasant	Leave the door open for another attempt.

Source: National Opinion Research Center, 2004.

Usually, people will not say that they do not understand something. Potential participants may say, "I am not interested" or "I'm busy." However, their "hidden" reason may be one of those listed in Table 9.2. Even though staff may never know the true reason for a refusal, it is important to pay attention to the spoken and unspoken cues from potential or current participants. If recruitment and retention staff determine that there is a hidden reason, they will have a greater chance at gaining cooperation if they can respond to it.

Questions from potential or current participants may give clues to their hidden reasons. They may ask, "What is this about again?" or "Why do I need to do this?" If their questions are answered thoroughly and professionally, staff could convince them that their participation is worthwhile. Another clue may be repeatedly rescheduling appointments or consistently failing to show up for appointments. This could indicate individuals' ineligibility or reluctance to participate. Respond to these clues by being prepared with various descriptions of the project and the reasons why the requested activity is important, and by having the motivational skills to guide participants' to consent. Diagnoses of objections and other efforts to gain participation must always be balanced with assessments of inherent motivation and interest. Someone who is especially difficult to enroll may or may not be especially difficult to retain. This requires staff to judge how challenging it will be to retain a difficult-to-enroll individual, based on staff members' prior experience, knowledge of the target population, and intuition.

Provide Answers to Frequently Asked Questions. One tool that can assist staff and participants with objections is a set of frequently asked questions (FAQs). FAQs accompanied by well-crafted, written responses give staff valuable information for their recruitment and retention efforts. Providing staff with multiple responses to FAQs allows them to tailor their responses to the conversation. Staff can take pieces from multiple FAQ responses to create a rebuttal that addresses a participant's specific reasons for a refusal.

In addition, staff can include a brief FAQs section in written materials for potential participants, such as advance written communication, consent forms, and brochures. These FAQs should provide succinct and clear information about the evaluation, including the overall purpose, the risks and benefits of participating, and methods to contact the evaluation staff. As an additional method of promoting recruitment and retention efforts, provide this same information to staff who meet the target population or staff whom a target individual knows and trusts. In a health care setting, these staff members could include receptionists and all clinical staff who have had previous contact with an individual and who can provide an accurate description of the evaluation requirements. In an educational setting, such staff might include teachers or other school personnel.

As staff consider the previous interactions and existing connections between a potential participant and the recruitment and retention staff, it is also important for them to understand the potential for a participant to feel coerced due to these existing relationships. It is important to emphasize to the participant that she can decline the request to participate at any time and that participating or not participating will not affect her current or future interactions with the service provider.

The Pros and Cons of Incentives. Incentives can be an important key to increasing participant cooperation rates. Some examples of incentives are monetary reimbursements, charitable donations, or logo-adorned items that carry the name of the evaluation project. Incentives have been shown to be a cost-effective method to boost response rates. For example, Berk, Mathiowetz, Ward, and White (1987) showed that response rates for one of their studies increased by 7 percentage points when a monetary incentive was provided with a mailed questionnaire (*prepaid incentive*) during study recruitment. Other studies have shown that incentives can improve data quality and lessen item nonresponse, including fewer *don't know* responses to questions (Singer, Van Hoewyk, and Maher, 2000; Willimack, Schuman, Pennell, and Lepkowski, 1995).

The type of incentive and the method of delivery can be the most critical elements in efforts to maximize the effectiveness of incentives. In several rounds of incentives research, Dillman (2000) found that unconditional, prepaid cash incentives work best to increase participation rates. The amount of an effective incentive can be equivalent to a reimbursement of travel expenses or a small token of appreciation. Although incentives can increase participation, they are costly and may not be the answer to specific recruitment and retention obstacles. Before instituting an incentive program or augmenting an existing protocol, evaluators should debrief with recruitment staff to explore other options to increase participation rates.

In addition, using incentives to increase participation may affect the representativeness of the sample. Groups that are less likely to be recruited into a sample and more likely to respond to an incentive offer include ethnic or racial minorities; less educated, younger participants; and participants from low-income households (Singer, Van Hoewyk, and Maher, 2000). Using a variety of recruitment strategies designed to reach different targeted subgroups can help evaluators reach a representative sample.

In addition to using flexible recruitment and retention incentive protocols, it is also important to watch for and avoid coercion. Staff members should
discuss any incentive as a token of appreciation for contributing to the overall
purpose of the evaluation, and not as a means to "buy" participants' recruitment or retention (Dillman, 2000; Erlen, Sauder, and Mellors, 1999). In addition, some participants' primary goal may be to obtain the incentive and not
legitimately participate in the study. These participants may attempt to be
rescreened and may then alter their responses to eligibility questions in an
attempt to be found eligible. Some participants may inform others about the
incentive and may encourage them to act eligible for the sake of receiving
the incentive. Therefore, staff should be prepared for the many ways in which
incentives can influence motivation. For these reasons, as well as others, it is
practical for recruitment and retention staff to minimize disclosure of specifics
to a potential participant who is found to be ineligible.

Retention-Specific Considerations

After recruitment is complete and those selected as participants have engaged
in the initial aspects of the research, it is important to retain these individuals as participants until completion. Successful retention relies on establishing
positive rapport throughout all phases of recruitment, enrollment, and active
participation. In addition, staff should collect more contact information than
they anticipate needing, including cell phone numbers, participant addresses,
e-mail addresses, and social networking sites. Then they can take advantage of
the multiple technological modes through which a participant may be accustomed to receiving information. In addition, gathering contact information
for individuals who do not live with participants but know them well gives
staff a means of contacting participants who relocate. Service providers such as
social workers, parole officers, and homeless shelter attendants can also facilitate contact, particularly for mobile populations or for those who may not have
a permanent residence.

Monitoring Recruitment and Retention Progress

To collect information about effective recruitment and retention strategies,
the team should keep detailed contact logs that describe each contact with
each potential participant and recruited participant. With these resources on
actual recruitment and retention protocol implementation, evaluators and
staff can make informed decisions on altering approaches. For example, staff

can document every attempted contact, the mode of attempted contact, and the days and times that work best for reaching participants by phone. The contact log should also contain information about specific messages left with alternate contacts or on voice mail. The best days and times may be related to unique characteristics of the target study population. For example, when recruiting migrant workers who move in and out of an area based on their employment, contact logs can reveal the days and times that will maximize the possibility of participant contact.

The team also needs to determine what venues work best with the target population and be willing to try different recruitment methods to learn more about a population. While assessing productivity and collecting information on effective recruitment and retention strategies, also track what modes and venues work best to effectively recruit participants. If participants tend to respond better to phone calls placed shortly after their visit to a primary health care provider, then document and implement this approach. If face-to-face recruitment and retention efforts or mailed correspondence improves participation, then consider incorporating these approaches into the existing protocol.

Supervisors can also develop standard recruitment and retention metrics to gauge overall progress and compare individual staff members' productivity levels. For example, reaching recruitment goals may require setting objectives of five participants recruited each day in a certain geographical area. Supervisors can use this as a metric when providing feedback to staff on how their performance compares to the standard and to others—and to shed light on unrealistic recruitment goals.

Monitoring Multiple Recruitment Strategies

Staff can learn from documentation of multiple recruitment methods. With a variety of strategies, staff can collect information from eligible and ineligible participants during the enrollment process about the ways in which they learned of the study before they made the decision to participate. By recognizing the recruitment methods that prove to be effective and those that do not work as well, low-yield strategies can be removed from the recruitment plan. This can save resources, which can then be invested in more fruitful recruitment strategies.

Evaluators may also find it helpful to compare the effectiveness of passive and active recruitment methods. For some evaluations, passive recruitment methods may be more effective than active methods. For example, in some HIV-prevention studies, HIV-negative participants respond better to direct outreach (for example, face-to-face contact) than to print ads and flyers, and need to be sold on study participation. HIV-positive participants, however, respond in higher percentages to print ads and flyers, and they are also more difficult to identify during direct outreach. The issues related to this example, such as stigma or perceptions and misconceptions about the possible benefits of participating, may apply to other populations and other types of research.

Monitoring Recruitment and Retention of Subpopulations

Another common challenge with recruitment and retention is differential recruitment of the various subcomponents of the target population. In the example of the after-school substance use prevention program for youths described earlier, the evaluation team may wish to recruit and enroll a representative sample of all program participants. However, while monitoring data during the enrollment period, staff may note that participants of a particular race are overrepresented in the evaluation, while others of another race are underrepresented. Depending on the target population, one or both of the racial groups may use substances at different rates than the target population overall does.

Similarly, for studies with multiple data collection points, differential retention can affect the outcome of the evaluation and how the results can be interpreted. Continuing the previous example, participants in the program and evaluation that live in a particular section of the city may be overrepresented in the group that is lost to follow-up. In addition to their home neighborhood, the members of this particular subgroup may be different in other important respects that would influence the outcome of the evaluation (for example, more or less access to substances in their neighborhood compared to other participants, or more or less household income). Thus, the evaluation team may wish to alter the study's retention protocols to address this challenge. For example, the recruitment and retention staff may learn that the problem with follow-up results from a reduction in available public transportation during the course of the evaluation. The evaluation team may institute home visits for subsequent data collection points or offer to pay for transportation costs as a potential solution.

There are innumerable potential reasons for differential recruitment and retention, and some of them are amenable to protocol changes and others are not. Because a non-representative sample of participants can affect the study's validity, the evaluation team may wish to engage in efforts to determine potential reasons, devise one or more potential solutions in the form of protocol changes, and then attempt one or more of these solutions to gain a more representative participant sample.

Cultural Considerations

Often, evaluations are directed at questions of disparities or other topics requiring data from very specific target populations. Efforts to recruit and retain specific target populations often take additional resources and care. It is important to consider the target population and its members' particular cultural considerations prior to implementation. Evaluation projects have a better chance of succeeding when cultural aspects of the population and intervention are addressed.

Inviting the collaboration of stakeholders from the communities in which the target populations reside is helpful for multiple aspects of the project. Stakeholders can inform pilot-testing and provide insight on all relevant project materials and protocols. Additionally, stakeholders can help to lead the project to the best recruitment and retention methods. They may help staff with understanding the population's perceptions relevant to research in general and the particular evaluation, the times to call, and the places to recruit, and with identifying community volunteers, specific language and educational materials, and, when necessary, translations of written materials. Stakeholder participation throughout the process is helpful in maintaining the trust of the population and making sure materials and protocols stay current and relevant. Pilot-testing any changes to protocols or materials that arise during the course of the project is recommended. Although pilot-testing and stakeholder participation consume additional time and money, they can help prevent frustration and bring greater understanding of the participants and study outcomes.

Also, having staff who are demographically concordant with the target population and staff who meet the population's language needs can lessen potential participants' concerns about becoming a part of the project and help to build participant trust. All staff should be culturally sensitive and program planning should include assessing cultural sensitivity and the need for demographically based staff-to-participant matching.

Respect for cultural beliefs related to the program or intervention being evaluated can be an integral part of successful recruitment and retention efforts. Recruiters can begin to understand participants' cultural beliefs by conducting structured interviews and focus groups while planning the recruitment and retention efforts. By conducting focus groups with specific subgroups of interest (for example, patients with severe diabetes or members of particular racial or ethnic groups), the team can gather participants' potential reactions to the study protocol before procedures are finalized. Note that different age cohorts also have specific cultures that typically require tailored recruitment protocols. Subsequently, staff can plan and tailor recruitment and retention efforts appropriately, based on focus group results. Focus group information can reveal how participants may react to recruitment and later follow-up efforts, how they may perceive the written materials, and what incentives, if any, may be appropriate.

It is also important to recognize how interactions between particular populations and health care organizations or government agencies can affect the decision to participate. For some populations, historical events have negatively affected their level of trust in health care providers and evaluators. They may feel they do not have access to adequate health care, for example. This type of barrier must be overcome to build the trust required for individuals to decide to participate in research. Another example of a cultural consideration in the health care setting is that some cultures heavily rely on holistic or other alternative approaches to health care. To forge a respectful and effective recruiter-participant interaction, these alternative approaches should be identified before approaching these communities. If the evaluation's approach to participants seems counter to the holistic health care approaches, gaining cooperation may prove difficult. Focus groups can help to inform staff about particular communities.

Finally, while determining how cultural beliefs can influence participants' perceptions and responses to evaluation efforts, it is imperative to avoid overgeneralizing to all members of the target population. Assuming that cultural beliefs apply the same way to every person within a group can be just as damaging to recruitment and retention efforts as not taking cultural beliefs into account at all. Although recruitment and retention efforts must appropriately apply knowledge about cultural beliefs and perspectives, this knowledge and its application must also incorporate the significant individual and subgroup variability that typically occurs in any cultural group. Even when a participant self-identifies as a member of a particular population, that does not automatically mean that he or she holds all of the same cultural beliefs. Thus, recruitment staff should be attentive not only to common cultural beliefs and customs in the target population but also to the significant variability in how these beliefs are experienced, held, and expressed within populations (Hawkins and others, 2008; Kreuter and others, 2005; Rofes, 1998).

TABLE 9.3. RECRUITMENT AND RETENTION CHALLENGES AND POTENTIAL SOLUTIONS.

Recruitment Pitfalls	Ways to Avoid Them
Recruitment staff turnover (for example, lack of job satisfaction). Insufficient number of participants to meet sample size requirements for research. Recruitment taking much longer than anticipated.	Hire more staff to account for underestimate of recruitment hours needed.
Implementing multiple recruitment strategies becomes resource intensive.	Early on, evaluate the effectiveness of recruitment strategies to eliminate those that are ineffective.
Those recruited are different from the original pool or sample. Certain subpopulations are under- or over-represented.	Implement multiple recruitment strategies to actively recruit from subgroups in the population. Compare the starting pool with those recruited for the research to identify differences. Review and amend recruitment strategies as appropriate to include those underrepresented, and reduce the number of those already well represented. Consider adding recruitment and retention staff from the target population. Collaborate with representatives from the target population from the earliest planning stages and request their feedback as the study proceeds.
IRB application required when additional recruitment strategy is implemented after evaluation starts.	Learn from recruitment experiences; include multiple recruitment strategies from the beginning.
Gatekeepers in a household are barriers, preventing staff from talking directly to a potential participant.	Treat gatekeepers as one would treat participants to gain their cooperation (also maintain and regularly review contact logs). Plan for and include gatekeepers, especially for elderly or disabled populations who may not live independently.
People are reluctant to participate.	Provide clear information about the research or intervention, using prenotification letters and frequently asked questions (FAQs). Make respondents aware of their rights as study participants up front. Use existing relationships that participants may have with study organization as a way to convey information about the research. Collaborate with representatives from the target population from the earliest planning stages and request their feedback as the study proceeds.

(Continued)

221

TABLE 9.3. RECRUITMENT AND RETENTION CHALLENGES AND POTENTIAL SOLUTIONS. *(Continued)*

Recruitment Pitfalls	Ways to Avoid Them
Lack of staff support and cooperation (also applies to retention).	When possible, hire permanent or temporary staff whose primary job responsibilities are implementing recruitment and retention protocols. Anticipate potential challenges and proactively address them. Maintain active oversight throughout the evaluation project. Obtain pragmatic and demonstrable buy-in and support of the evaluation project from all levels of organizational leadership.
Loss of participants over time.	Plan to collect information up front on reasons for loss; amend retention strategies to ameliorate loss. Keep all appointments and make several reminder contacts before visits (mail, phone, e-mail) and update contact information between visits, including alternate contacts. Collaborate with representatives from the target population from the earliest planning stages and request their feedback as the study proceeds.
Repeatedly attempting to contact particular potential participants with no success.	If the contact information is correct, ensure contact attempts are made during different days of the week and different times of the day and with alternate contacts (maintain and regularly review contact logs). Obtain information beyond phone and address. If population is highly mobile, ask for updated contact information at every visit, including alternate contacts, email and social networks. Provide adequate reminders before each visit or contact to prevent no-shows and losses to follow-up.

Conclusion

Table 9.3 summarizes the common recruitment and retention challenges and offers suggestions for avoiding them. Do not underestimate the difficulty of the tasks involved, the amount of staff time, or the number of staff needed to reach recruitment and retention goals. Obtain IRB approval for multiple strategies during the planning phase to save time later. Allow for time and attention to make sure the demographics of your sample match those of your intended target population. Revising strategies accordingly to address unintended oversampling or undersampling of specific subgroups is important to maintain the validity of the evaluation. Periodic review of the effectiveness of different recruitment strategies will also help the team decide what can be eliminated to save costs. However, be sure not to omit those strategies that are focused on underrepresented subgroups.

Losing participants over time is the biggest retention problem. Obtain and regularly update thorough contact information, including alternate contacts who would know how to reach participants, and maintain frequent contact with participants between visits. During recruitment and retention, gain support of family members and other gatekeepers by treating them with respect.

Recruitment and retention are dynamic processes that require routine and detailed monitoring of each individual being recruited and each successfully recruited participant to be retained, recruitment staff productivity, and overall recruitment and retention goals. In addition, flexibility is required to obtain an adequate number of participants who are representative of the entire target population and to meet sample size requirements to validly answer the questions of interest. Recruitment and retention challenges and successes throughout the life of the evaluation project can provide valuable information and insight when interpreting the evaluation outcomes and findings. For example, a sub-population that was only partially retained may help to explain differences between pre- and post-intervention data. Finally, a clear picture of the implementation of recruitment and retention processes can help to inform subsequent program decisions and execution.

References

Barron, M., Brooks, K., Skalland, B., and Singelton, A. "The Impact of Incentives on Representativeness in the National Immunization Survey." Methodological brief presented at the American Association of Public Opinion Research Annual Conference on Polls and Policy, Anaheim, California, 2007.

Bork, M. L., Mathiowetz, N. A., Ward, E. P., and White, A. A. "The Effect of Prepaid and Promised Incentives: Results of a Controlled Experiment." *Journal of Official Statistics,* 1987, *3*(4), 449–457.

Cialdini, R. B. *Influence: Science and Practice* (4th ed.). Boston, MA: Allyn & Bacon, 2001.

Dillman, D. A. *Mail and Telephone Surveys: The Total Design Method.* Hoboken, NJ: Wiley, 1978.

Dillman, D. A. *Mail and Internet Surveys: The Tailored Design Method* (2nd ed.). Hoboken, NJ: Wiley, 2000.

Erlen, J. A., Sauder, R. J., and Mellors, M. P. "Incentives in Research: Ethical Issues." *Orthopaedic Nursing*, 1999, *18*(2), 84–91.

Finding Answers: Disparities Research for Change. "Grants Portfolio," accessed April 6, 2015, www.solvingdisparities.org/sites/default/files/finding-answers-grants-portfolio-0.pdf. A national program of the Robert Wood Johnson Foundation with program direction and technical assistance provided by the University of Chicago. n.d.

Flesch, R. "A New Readability Yardstick." *Journal of Applied Psychology*, 1948, *32*, 221–233.

Gouldner, A. W. "The Norm of Reciprocity: A Preliminary Statement." *American Sociological Review*, 1960, *25*(2), 161–178.

Groves, R. M., Cialdini, R. B., and Couper, M. P. "Understanding the Decision to Participate in a Survey." *Public Opinion Quarterly*, 1992, *56*(4), 475–495.

Hawkins, R. P., and others. "Understanding Tailoring in Communicating About Health." *Health Education Research*, 2008, *23*(3), 454–466.

Hinton, L., Guo, Z., Hillygus, J., and Levkoff, S. "Working with Culture: A Qualitative Analysis of Barriers to the Recruitment of Chinese-American Family Caregivers for Dementia Research." *Journal of Cross-Cultural Gerontology*, 2000, *15*(2), 119–137.

Kreuter, M. W., and others. "Cultural Tailoring for Mammography and Fruit and Vegetable Intake Among Low-Income African-American Women in Urban Public Health Centers." *Preventive Medicine*, 2005, *41*(1), 53–62.

Martin, M., and Thomas, D. "Using the Office of Management and Budget (OMB) Clearance Process in Program Planning and Evaluation." *Preventing Chronic Disease*, 2006, *3*(1), A04–A07.

Microsoft Office Online. "Test your document's readability", accessed April 6, 2015, https://support.office.com/en-AU/article/Test-your-documents-readability-0adc0e9a-b3fb-4bde-85f4-c9e88926c6aa - bm2. n.d.

National Opinion Research Center. *General Training Module J: Approaching the Respondent and Gaining Cooperation.* Chicago, IL: National Opinion Research Center, 2004.

Nelson, R. M., and Merz, J. F. "Voluntariness of Consent for Research: An Empirical and Conceptual Review." *Medical Care*, 2002, *40*(9), V69–V80.

Rofes, E. *Dry Bones Breathe: Gay Men and Post-AIDS Identities and Cultures.* New York: Harrington Park Press, 1998.

Singer, E., Van Hoewyk, J., and Maher, M. P. "Experiments with Incentives in Telephone Surveys." *Public Opinion Quarterly*, 2000, *64*, 171–188.

Willimack, D., Schuman, H., Pennell, B., and Lepkowski, J. "Effects of a Prepaid Nonmonetary Incentive on Response Rates and Response Quality in a Face-to-Face Survey." *Public Opinion Quarterly*, 1995, *59*(1), 78–92.

CHAPTER TEN

DESIGNING, MANAGING, AND ANALYZING MULTISITE EVALUATIONS

Debra J. Rog

Little has been written about conducting multisite evaluations (Herrell and Straw, 2002; King and Lawrenz, 2011; Turpin and Sinacore, 1991), despite the fact that they are relatively common in evaluation practice. The uninitiated may assume that multisite evaluations (MSEs) are merely an extension of single-site evaluations, applying the same basic designs and methodologies across multiple sites. However, as this chapter describes, MSEs often require much more, such as cross-site collaboration, attention to diversity among the sites, and cross-site as well as individual-site analyses, among other activities that need to be considered in designing and implementing the effort.

This chapter, based on the author's own experiences, those of colleagues, and other examples in the literature, offers some general principles and frameworks for designing MSEs as well as practical tools and examples that can guide their conduct. The first section begins with an orientation to what is meant by multisite evaluation and the situations when a multisite approach to evaluation is appropriate, followed by a review of different types of multisite approaches and designs. The chapter then walks the reader through the stages of an MSE, including development of the study foundation and initial design, examination of implementation, data collection, quality control, data management, data synthesis and analysis, and communication of the results. The chapter concludes with tips for evaluators to follow regardless of the nature of the MSE.

Defining the Multisite Evaluation

Multisite evaluations involve examining a program or policy in two or more sites or geographical locations. In some instances the intervention is intended to be exactly the same across the different sites. For example, in a study of supportive housing programs for individuals with serious mental illness, each of the supportive housing programs was to follow the same basic model. In other situations the programs studied are of the same type but may vary from one another in various ways. For example, in an evaluation of community coalitions focused on violence prevention, the coalitions were expected to have activities that varied in response to the features and needs of each site's context.

Table 10.1 illustrates some of the variation possible in how MSEs are approached. As the top row illustrates, MSEs involve a continuum of approaches varying in the degree to which there is shared cross-site control, from studies that are led and driven by a cross-site evaluator to those that are highly collaborative to those that involve more of a compilation of individual studies or sites. Table 10.1 also illustrates some of the key distinguishing characteristics along which MSEs vary, including features of the evaluation and characteristics of the program being evaluated. Evaluation features include the purpose for the evaluation, its timing, (that is, whether the evaluation is examining each program's process and outcomes as the program is being conducted [prospectively[or whether the evaluation is looking "backward" in time and examining process and outcomes after the program has been in operation [retrospectively]), and whether the study sites will include only programs or also comparison/ control groups. Key program features include whether the interventions are existing programs or developed specifically for the research/evaluation, and whether the programs across the sites are the same model or differ.

Within the cross-site or central evaluator group on Table 10.1 are four examples of projects. The first, the Healthy Schools evaluation, is a current randomized study of two childhood obesity prevention models. The cross-site evaluation team is responsible for all aspects of the evaluation, including recruiting elementary schools into the study and randomizing them to receive either an on-site support model or an online model, both designed to create environments in which healthy eating and physical activity are encouraged. This randomized MSE anchors the continuum of examples in the chart, with a focus on examining the effects of the two standardized interventions on the selected schools and their students using a controlled study. The evaluation

TABLE 10.1. EXAMPLES OF MULTISITE EVALUATIONS.

	Cross-Site Evaluator				Coordinating Body with Collaboration		Facilitating Body with Some Collaboration	
	Healthy Schools[a] 130 sites	RWJ HFP[b] 9 sites	CSH[c] 9 sites	WFF HNF[d] 20 sites	HI[e] 6 sites	HF[f] 8 sites	Anthem Foundation[g] 4 sites	McKinney[h] 5 sites
Purpose Exploratory Process or Effectiveness	•	•	•		•	•		•
Timing Planned-Prospective or Retrospective	•	•		•	•	•	•	•
Source of intervention Program-Driven or Research -Driven	•	•	•	•	•	•	•	
Intervention Standardized or Varied	•	•		•	•	•	•	
Nature of Sites Program Only or with Comparison	•		•	•	•	•		•

[a] Healthy Schools Evaluation, Rockville Institute, ongoing.
[b] Robert Wood Johnson Foundation Homeless Families Program Evaluation; Rog and Gutman, 1997.
[c] Corporation for Supportive Housing Employment Initiative Evaluation; Rog, Hopper, Holupka, and Brito, 1996.
[d] Washington Families Fund High Need Family Program Evaluation, Rog, Henderson, Stevens, and Jain, 2014; Rog, Jain, and Reed, 2013).
[e] CMHS Housing Initiative, Rog and Randolph, 2002.
[f] Evaluation of the CMHS/CSAT Homeless Families Program; Rog, Rickards, Holupka, Barton-Villagran, and Hastings, 2005.
[g] Anthem Foundation Prevention of Family Violence Initiative Cross-Site Evaluation, Rog., Barton-Villagrana, and Rajapaksa, 2009.
[h] McKinney Demonstration Program for Homeless Adults with Serious Mental Illness; Center for Mental Health Services, 1994.

is assessing the comparative effectiveness of the two models, is collecting data prospectively, and is being conducted for research purposes (although both models have been in existence in other schools).

The second example in this group, The Robert Wood Johnson Foundation Homeless Families Program evaluation (Rog and Gutman, 1997), was conducted with nine demonstration efforts of the same model of services-enriched housing for families and was conducted as a descriptive outcome evaluation. Data were collected prospectively, both by the central evaluation team and the local site providers, with instruments developed by the central evaluators. There were no local evaluators or local evaluation designs (for example, comparison groups). The evaluation of the Corporation for Supportive Housing Employment Initiative (Rog, Hopper, Holupka, and Brito, 1996) also was conducted by a central evaluator with no local evaluators; the main differences with this evaluation were that data were collected retrospectively, using existing data, and on programs that varied across the nine sites. The final examples in this group approach, the Washington Families Fund High Needs Family evaluation (Rog, Henderson, Stevens, and Jain, 2014; Rog, Jain, and Reed, 2013), examined the implementation and outcomes of twenty supportive housing programs within Washington. The initial funding for the evaluation was limited, so data collection was modest. Data on program implementation were collected through telephone interviews with the providers, and data on families' history, experiences, and outcomes were collected by the providers' staff at baseline and every six months families stayed in the housing. Additional funding obtained midway through the effort allowed for more in-depth fidelity assessments at each site as well as the collection of state data on outcomes for the families involved in the program as well as two comparison groups constructed with the state data (a group of comparable families who entered shelter and a group of families who entered public housing only, without special supports).

In the middle of the continuum are a range of approaches that may offer more or less cross-site consistency and shared activity, including shared evaluation questions, protocols, and analyses. Each has a cross-site evaluation team, but is characterized as being highly collaborative with a coordinating body, such as a Steering Committee (see Straw and Herrell, 2002, for several examples). The Center for Mental Health Services Housing Initiative (Rog and Randolph, 2002), for example, involved examining the effectiveness of the same model of supportive housing for persons with mental illness through a collaborative model directed by a Steering Committee involving representatives from the local sites, the cross-site evaluation team, the federal government, and a consumer panel. All sites had a control group, but the nature of the control group differed across the sites. The Substance Abuse, Mental Health Services Administration Homeless Families Program had a similar cross-site collaborative design with a similarly structured steering committee (Rog, Rickards, Holupka, Barton-Villagrana, and Hastings, 2005). The key difference between these two MSE models is that the SAMHSA Homeless Families Program included a range of intervention models (that is, no one standardized model) across the local evaluation sites as well as a range of comparison and control groups.

The third group of MSEs on the continuum on the chart are multisite evaluations that have some level of collaboration, but are not as highly structured as the group just reviewed. In each MSE, there is a great deal of variation across the sites, but some area of shared activity, such as cross-site analysis. For example, the evaluation of the Anthem Foundation Family Violence Coalitions involved a cross-site evaluation of four community coalitions aimed at preventing family violence (Rog, Barton-Villagrana, and Rajapaksa, 2009). Each of the sites was located in a different county in one Midwestern state and funded through a local foundation. The sites received two-year planning grants, followed by five years of implementation funding. The initiative had a cross-site technical assistance provider as well as a cross-site evaluation team. The evaluation was modest in funding and scope and relied primarily on the collection of data through interviews, site visits, and documents. It was led by a cross-site evaluator, with local evaluators involved only in the planning stage. The design involved longitudinal case studies (Yin, 2014), with an emphasis on using the same lens in each site. The focus was initially on the implementation of the coalitions, followed by an assessment of their ability to achieve outcomes. Feedback was provided to the coalitions throughout the evaluation.

The cross-site evaluation of the McKinney Demonstration Program for Homeless Adults with Serious Mental Illness (Center for Mental Health Services, 1994) involved an effort of bringing together five randomized projects—all independently designed and implemented—during the analysis, interpretation, and writing stages.

The overall message from this chart is that there is no one MSE design, but rather a portfolio of possible designs varying on a number of dimensions. Although the full range of evaluations is covered in this chapter, the focus is on guiding those efforts in the middle and end sections of the continuum—studies that strive for consistency and shared activity across sites, but fall short of the standardization offered through RCTs.

Advantages and Disadvantages of Multisite Evaluations

Multisite evaluations offer opportunities to accelerate the development of knowledge in a program area. Whether an MSE examines a set of identical interventions or variations of a program, conducting an evaluation of multiple sites at one time with a coordinated approach is likely to offer the power of results that can rise above any single investigation. It not only provides for a larger sample size but a sample that is likely more diverse on the variables of interest. It has the unique advantage of providing for simultaneous replication (Mullen, 2003). In addition, by examining the implementation and outcomes of a program or policy across multiple sites that differ in geography, population composition, and other contextual features, we are likely to learn more about the generalizability of an intervention and its effects. Moreover, if the program follows some general guidelines but is implemented in different ways, there is also the opportunity to understand the trade-offs and relative advantages and disadvantages of the different types of program strategies. From a resource perspective, a multisite may offer more resources than a single site study and also may allow certain functions (for example, data entry) to be conducting more efficiently and uniformly by a central unit. Finally, if an MSE involves the active collaboration of investigators across the different sites, the multisite effort can create an "invisible college" (Reiss and Boruch, 1991), in which the evaluation benefits from the synergy, shared visions, and insights of the participants (Mullen, 2003). It can help to foster a "community of practice" (Goodyear, 2011) in which evaluation capacity-building occurs among the individual projects. Moreover, multisite evaluations provide multiple pathways through which process use and evaluation influence can occur (Mark, 2011) for local and central level decision makers and other stakeholders

Multisite evaluations also can have downsides. Highly collaborative MSEs are likely to take more funding than the individual sites would have needed if funded separately and are likely to take more time to design, implement, and analyze. Errors that occur in an MSE, because they are amplified by the number of sites, are likely to be more serious and long-lasting than errors in a single-site evaluation are (Kraemer, 2000). In addition, when an agency or foundation commits to funding an MSE, it is less likely to have funds for single evaluations or studies in the area that could provide a different perspective on a problem or program. Finally, multisite evaluations can be difficult to implement, analyze, and interpret. Idiosyncratic site effects can occur and challenge the statistical analysis (Mullen, 2003) So many differences can exist across the sites that pooling the data may not be advantageous as the MSE analysis may need too many variables to control the influence of the differences.

Multisite Approaches and Designs

The first stage of an MSE begins with developing the study's foundation, including establishing relationships, decision-making mechanisms, and communication protocols. Along with the foundation, another critical up-front decision in the MSE is determining the nature and scope of the design, including whether to sample sites to be used in the MSE.

Laying the Foundation for an MSE

Among the first decisions for an MSE is determining who the lead for the evaluation is and identifying the mechanisms by which cross-site decisions are made. Other key foundational elements are determining the nature of the relationships between the evaluation team and the evaluation sponsors, the level and nature of stakeholder involvement in the evaluation, and expectations and mechanisms for communication. In the family violence prevention coalitions MSE example, it was decided early on that there would be a cross-site evaluator who would be largely responsible for all key decisions. Local evaluators were initially involved, but the level at which they could be compensated was minimal, and it was ultimately determined that it would be best to have project directors provide any data that the MSE evaluator needed. In turn, we (the evaluators) tried to provide as much feedback as we could along the way. There also was an ongoing relationship with the foundation sponsor and the technical assistance (TA) provider.

Of the foundational elements noted, communication is the one that is most distinct for MSEs, compared to single-site evaluations. In MSEs there is a need to make certain that all study expectations, procedures, and developments are known by all key participants in the sites. For MSEs that are highly collaborative, it is important that participants in the local sites are clear on the role that they play, receive training, and are kept abreast of developments across the sites. For example, as noted later, it is likely that in the course of data collection (especially in the initial stages), there will be modifications to accommodate issues that were not anticipated. Although the way the modification gets made may depend on the overall MSE strategy, the decision still needs to be communicated to all involved in the data collection. The more decentralized the decision making is in the MSE, the more important it is that decisions and other information be communicated regularly and frequently. In addition, even when the decision making is more controlled, having frequent communication across the sites decreases the possibility that individuals in the sites will misunderstand the decisions, and that in turn decreases the possibility that these individuals will resent or actively attempt to thwart the decisions that were made.

Communication mechanisms should include a mix of in-person, telephone, and electronic communications. With improvements in technology, the range and variety of mechanisms for keeping in touch with individuals involved with or affected by the study in the various sites continues to grow and the costs tend to decrease. Therefore, in addition to routine meetings, other strategies for communicating procedures and updates to key parties include conference calls, webinars, and list servs. Mechanisms such as SharePoint provide access to a *virtual filing cabinet* that helps with version control on documents and provides a central place in cyberspace where team members can access up-to-date documents (such as data collection protocols).

If the MSE strategy is a collaborative one in which the design of the MSE is shared cooperatively (such as through a steering committee), there may be a need for interactive communication to ensure that all are on the same page in making decisions. This means making certain that all involved understand the specifics of the sites, the needs of the study, and other factors important to consider in designing the study. Sharing cross-site charts of the sites that illustrate how sites compare and contrast and having site representatives present information on their local study evaluations (if applicable) are two ways of ensuring that people in one site understand all the other sites that make up the MSE and why certain cross-site design decisions are warranted.

In the MSE of the family violence prevention coalitions, communication was largely conducted through e-mails and a list serv, as well as through the meetings where the MSE team presented findings to the project directors, TA providers, and the sponsoring foundation and engaged in a dialogue about their implications. In the WFF High Need Family MSE, the MSE evaluation team is working closely with the intermediary that is providing both TA support for the supportive housing providers and oversight of the evaluation for the foundation sponsor. We also had routine phone conversations with the provider directors and more frequent contact with the provider staff collecting the data. As noted later, because the evaluation team was not located in the same region as the providers, conference calls and webinars were used for contacts and training, with the intermediary as our local in-person contact and conduit to them.

A final element in the foundation phase of an MSE is determining the process for submitting materials for the Institutional Review Board (IRB) process. As with individual evaluations, MSE protocols must be approved by at least one IRB before the evaluation can begin. The IRB is charged with reviewing the design and methodological procedures of a study to ensure that it meets ethical guidelines. In most MSEs, multiple IRBs need to involved, typically one from each site but often more than that if multiple interventions or providers within a site are involved. The ethics review process has to be conducted separately with each IRB, making it often a time consuming and difficult process within an MSE (Gold and Dewa, 2005). Moreover, in addition to the time and effort involved, inconsistencies in the review process can result in unevenness in the human subjects protections provided (McWilliams, Hoover-Fong, Hamosh, Beck, Beaty, and Cutting, 2003). Ideally, MSEs should strive for more central IRB review, but these are uncommon. Therefore, sufficient time should be allotted in the beginning of the evaluation to allow for the IRB process and for the development and modification of key procedures and forms (for example, informed consent) to meet the ethical guidelines of the individual IRBs.

Determining the MSE Design

Much like individual evaluations, there is no one approach to MSE and, in turn, no single design. As noted earlier, the only distinction that MSEs share is that the evaluation examines an intervention in two or more sites. Building logic models in the initial stage of an evaluation—ideally together with the site evaluators—and reviewing them with all key stakeholders will help to foster agreement on the main purposes and goals of the intervention, and articulate a *theory of change* through the specification of short-term and longer-term outcomes.

How the intervention is evaluated, however, depends on a number of factors, much as in the design of a single-site evaluation. Among the factors that shape the MSE design are the nature of the evaluation questions(s), the readiness of the field in the intervention or program area, and the nature of the problem that the intervention is addressing; the reasons why an evaluation is being conducted; the nature, diversity, and number of sites; the framework for the program (some programs are developed and evaluated in phases, for example); and the resources (time, expertise, and funding) available for the interventions or programs in each site, for the local evaluations (if applicable), and for the cross-site evaluation. Therefore, as with single-site evaluations, a range of designs are often required to meet the variety of evaluation questions and purposes for the information. Designs include process and implementation studies, outcome and effectiveness studies, and even multisite evaluability assessments. The rigor and need for precision is driven by the decision-making needs of the study. However, the nature, number, and diversity of the sites have a strong bearing on the design that is desired and feasible. For example, if all study sites are expected to implement the same program, the evaluation will likely pay attention to measuring the fidelity of implementation of the program. If, however, the programs are diverse but still fit under a global program category, an examination of the sites may focus more on identifying the features that the sites share and those on which they differ. In addition, if the sites have evaluations of their own, the multisite evaluation may likely be designed to coordinate or build on these efforts; if the sites do not have their own evaluations, the MSE will likely use its own staff to collect data or will incorporate program staff into the data collection efforts of the evaluation. Finally, the number of sites will likely influence the study design, especially in determining the nature of data collection and management. The larger the number of sites, the more important are standards for data collection, quality control, and data submission. With a large number of sites, the multisite evaluator may be in the position of determining whether all or a sample of the sites should be included in the evaluation.

In the MSE of the Anthem Foundation family violence prevention coalitions, the coalitions were aimed at the same outcomes but used different approaches to developing their governance structures, developing their coalitions, selecting sectors (such as business or education) to target, and selecting the types of prevention strategies and activities to use in each of these sectors. The study design that lent itself best to this MSE was a multiple, comparative case study approach (Yin, 2014) in which each site was examined independently according to its own goals and design and was also examined by the MSE evaluator in terms of the extent to which it fit the overall intent of the initiative.

The design for the MSE of the WFF High Need Family supportive housing program reflects the readiness of the field and the resources available. Supportive housing for homeless families has been examined in other studies, and this has permitted the development of a model that is based on prior evidence and that can be assessed for fidelity and can support a screening process and a data collection process that are rigorous and standardized across the sites.

Sampling Sites

Although most MSEs encompass all the sites funded in a program or policy initiative, there are times when using a sample of sites is indicated, either to meet budget constraints or the design specifications of the MSE. For example, some MSE designs may examine representative sites from clusters of sites sharing similar characteristics. In other MSEs, sampling may be limited to sites that meet a threshold level of fidelity of implementation. One might even want to select only those sites that are ready for an evaluation, using evaluabilty assessment (Wholey, Chapter Four in this volume) as a tool to assess sites' readiness.

In addition, there may be sites within sites that have to be sampled. For example, in an MSE of mental health and substance abuse interventions for homeless families, each intervention was implemented in multiple shelters within a community. Data were collected from families across all shelters, but the fidelity study of interventions was restricted to the shelter sites that had the largest proportion of families participating in the evaluation.

Strategies for Multisite Data Collection

Data collection in MSEs involves a range of decisions. One of the first decisions to be made is whether the data collected from the sites should be the same across the sites or specific to each site. When common data will be collected across the sites, a common protocol is needed, whether the data are extracted from existing data sources or collected from primary sources. This section guides the evaluator through each of these decisions.

Collecting Common Versus Specific Site Data

One of the key decisions in MSE designs is whether the data collected from the sites will be the same across the sites or specific to each site. Among the factors that influence this decision are the resources and funding available to collect common data, the decision-making needs of the study, whether data exist in the sites that are relevant to the evaluation and can be readily accessed, and whether the sites have their own evaluation efforts and thus have their own ongoing data collection.

There are trade-offs to collecting common rather than site-specific data for an MSE. Overall, having common data across sites simplifies data collection and analysis, and it provides a one-voice dimension to reports and briefings that more clearly communicates the findings of the study. However, common data collection can be more expensive than assembling existing data, can impose an increased burden on the sites and potentially on program participants, and may not be feasible within the study time frame and funding constraints. In addition, the MSE may be able to tolerate the data differences among the sites. If, however, the findings are to inform policy and other decisions and there is a high need for rigor and precision, common data across the sites will likely be necessary.

In the current MSE of WFF's supportive housing for homeless families, we initially intended to use existing data from a management information system that is implemented across the country in communities to track service use and outcomes by homeless individuals and families. However, this data system was only in the design phase in the communities where the providers are located and thus not available for use. Other data sources were too disparate across the sites, and having data collected by outside interviewers was prohibitively expensive given the modest budget for the evaluation and the need for a longitudinal data system. In consultation with the providers and funder, it was decided that the best solution was to develop a data collection system that the providers could use both to assess the needs of families for clinical purposes and to fill the needs of the evaluation. The providers agreed to use standardized instruments as long as these tools lent themselves to clinical use, such as instruments that measured mental health status and outcomes, but could also be used to discern the need for services. When additional funding was obtained, we were able to augment the study with additional data on service receipt and other outcomes (for example, employment; criminal justice involvement; reunification with children in foster care) on the families in the housing as well as in two comparison groups constructed with the state dataset.

Developing a Common Protocol

When the decision is made to collect common data across the sites, a common protocol is required. If the MSE is a collaborative effort, with individual-site researchers working with the cross-site evaluation team, the first step will be to ensure that all sites agree with the research questions and overall framework. Ideally, the cross-site logic model or theory of change provides a basis delineating the measures needed to understand the implementation and outcomes of the program The next step involves determining the sources of the data. In some situations, existing data sources may be the most efficient sources for some domains; in other instances it may be more worthwhile to collect primary data.

Maximizing Existing Data

As noted for the MSE of the WFF High Need Family program, it is critical in the planning process for the MSE evaluator to critically evaluate whether the data will meet the study needs. The dimensions that need to be evaluated include the quality of the data (that is, their accuracy, validity, reliability, and completeness); how comparable the data are across the sites; whether the data systems can be modified to achieve greater consistency across the sites; and the steps, costs, and time needed to access the data. At times, especially for administrative data sources maintained by public entities, a number of review and approval hurdles need to be jumped in order to access the data. Even when the hurdles can be jumped, there may be delays in accessing the data that the evaluation time frame cannot accommodate.

Developing a Common Data Collection Tool

In many MSEs it is necessary to collect primary data and to develop a common data collection protocol across the sites. Especially when the programs and their contexts vary across the sites, it may be desirable to have a core set of data across the sites, with additional measures per site for program-specific elements or other site-specific interests.

A number of considerations and decisions are involved in designing a primary data collection effort across multiple sites. Evaluators need to determine:

- The population of interest and participant selection criteria
- The strategies for participant recruitment and tracking (if it is a longitudinal data collection effort)
- The data collection methods—whether to use in-person interviews, self-administered questionnaires, observational methods, or web questionnaires, and so forth
- The logistics for data collection—whether data collection will use paper and pencil only or computer programs (such as CAPI, CATI, or CASI), Optiscan, or web technology
- The instruments for data collection—whether standardized instruments will be used or new instruments will be developed
- Whom to hire as data collectors—whether outside interviewers will be needed; whether program personnel can collect any of the data; whether specific skills other than the ability to collect standardized data are needed (for example, whether interviewers need to be bilingual or multilingual or need clinical training)
- The training for the data collectors—whether any specialized training is needed
- The time frame for data collection—how often data will be collected; whether more than one wave of data collection is needed and the time intervals between the waves

Variation across the sites on any one of these decisions could increase the difficulties of combining data across the sites. The interest is in ensuring that the data collection strategies and the measures are the same across sites or similar enough that if differences in results do emerge across sites, they can be attributed to differences in the programs (if relevant) or in the populations served or in the contexts encompassing the programs, and not to differences in data collection methods.

Even if standardized data collection is desired, individual site customization may still be needed. For example, in drug studies, often the terms of art for specific illegal drugs differ across regions of the country and any items referring to specific drugs will collect more comparable data across sites if they employ terms typically used in each region.

Translating a data collection instrument into different languages also often requires tailoring to specific sites when multiple regions or countries are involved. For example, in an MSE involving projects serving homeless families in sites across the United States, we had the instrument translated into "generic" Spanish, and then customized to the specific dialect of Spanish used in each site (for example, Puerto Rican or Mexican).

In any data collection effort, it is important to pilot and pretest the instrument with several individuals before developing the final instrument. In MSEs, it is especially important to pilot the tool and accompanying procedures in all sites to identify what aspects of the instrument may not work the same across the sites.

Assessing Multisite Interventions

In most multisite evaluations, there is a need to assess the interventions. The nature of the assessment is based on the type of study being conducted and the extent to which the interventions are intended to be the same across the sites. At least four types of implementation assessment are possible: program fidelity, common ingredients, program implementation, and program participation.

Monitoring Fidelity

In some multisite efforts, a specific model is expected to be implemented in each of the sites and a fidelity assessment is used to assess the extent to which this expectation is met. A fidelity assessment typically involves developing a tool that measures the key elements and components of a program model. The assessment may look for specific types of staffing, the level of implementation of different types of program components, and even the existence of specific philosophical underpinnings. Elements may be measured according to whether they exist or not, or according to the extent to which they are present.

Measures of departures from fidelity can be included in cross-site analyses or can guide decisions as to whether sites have sufficient fidelity to be included in the data set. In MSEs with an ample number of sites, fidelity assessments can be used as a screening tool for determining whether a site provides an adequate test of a program and should be included in the MSE. In the MSE of WFF's supportive housing for families, fidelity assessments were used to provide feedback to the funder and the sites to help keep them on track and to determine why departures from the model occurred. When indicated, additional technical assistance was provided by the intermediary to those sites with less than desired fidelity. Similarly, Zvoch (2009) conducted an examination of different characteristics associated with fidelity outcomes and found that background characteristics of teachers and contextual factors in the school environment were related to protocol adherence. The findings highlighted the challenges of both achieving and maintaining fidelity of a complex intervention that is to be delivered by multiple teachers in multiple settings. As Zvoch (2009) noted, being able to measure and examine fidelity in an evaluation, especially a multisite evaluation, can separate design failure from implementation failure. Moreover, including a measure of fidelity in the MSE analyses can help to determine whether an intervention's effectiveness is related to the degree to which it is implemented according to the original design or program model (Zvoch, Letourneau, and Parker, 2007).

Assessing Common Ingredients

In some multisite programs, the programs across the sites may not be identical, but may share some common ingredients or features that qualify them to be under the same general program heading or concept. For example, in a study of behavioral interventions for homeless families, we examined how sites were delivering mental health or substance abuse services, or both, and the commonalities in how these services were being provided. Ultimately, we developed a measure that allowed us to discern whether each specific type of service was provided on-site or through referral, and if on-site, the array that was available.

Studying Implementation

Implementation assessment may be undertaken in lieu of an assessment of fidelity or common ingredients or in combination with one of those assessments. When the focus is on implementation, the question generally concerns how the programs are being put into place and whether the level of implementation is sufficient. Implementation assessment can therefore be conducted with or without a focus on fidelity or common ingredients.

Measuring Program Participation

All three of the assessments just discussed are typically focused at the program level and often involve data collected through program visits and a review of program documents. Examining program participation requires either collecting data directly from the participants or using administrative data on service use. When program participation is assessed, the desire is to gain a precise understanding of differences in service receipt or other types of program participation, especially when individual-level variation is expected, due to differences in attendance, tailoring of services, or other factors. Differences can be due to differences in program implementation, but also to the needs of participation as well as their motivation and ability to participate. There are likely differences within site as well as between sites that are important to examine. Participant-level implementation data provide an added benefit of enriching analyses by providing person-specific "dosage" information that can be related to relevant outcomes.

Assessing Comparison as Well as Treatment Sites

For MSEs that involve both treatment and comparison sites, it is useful to have an understanding of the nature and strength of the comparison sites equal to the understanding one has of the treatment sites. In a study of supported housing programs for individuals with mental illness, for example, we used the fidelity tool developed for the treatment housing programs to examine the comparison housing programs as well. We found that, in some instances, the level of fidelity was actually higher in the comparison programs than in the treatment programs, suggesting that many of the same service elements were in place in these programs in comparable strength. Examining the comparison conditions thus can reveal the extent to which they offer an adequate contrast to the treatment conditions. This knowledge may help to shape analyses, as well as assist in interpreting the final results.

Monitoring Multisite Implementation

In an MSE considerable attention needs to be placed on the extent to which the evaluation itself is being implemented as expected. Even when the procedures are dictated and implemented by a central, cross-site evaluation team, there may be site-specific issues that influence and affect the integrity of the study design and methods.

Design Features to Monitor

When individual study designs, such as randomized designs or quasi-experimental designs, are implemented in the study sites, it is important to understand the integrity of each design once it is in place. When the design is implemented from a central level, the focus is on ensuring the structures are in place and making adjustments when it is not feasible to maintain the integrity of the design. When the site-level investigators are in control of the design decisions, it is important to understand the decisions that are being made and the nature of the design that is being implemented. For example, sites may differ in how they construct and implement comparison groups, and this variation will affect the analysis and possibly the results.

In addition to monitoring the integrity of the study designs expected in each site, MSEs also need to monitor the implementation of agreed-on procedures related to participant selection, recruitment, and tracking as well as data collection and the logistics involved with data collection (described more completely later in discussing quality control). Monitoring MSE implementation assesses the extent to which the study design and procedures are being put into place as expected and what changes, if any, need to be made to ensure commonality across the sites. This monitoring is particularly important in those MSEs where certain aspects of the methodology are expected to be consistent across sites.

Procedures need to be in place to ensure that sites are using the same selection criteria, recruiting participants with the same methods, and placing the same emphasis on tracking to achieve high response rates. Although there may be agreed-on procedures, site contextual differences may influence the degree to which these procedures can be implemented and the extent to which modifications may be needed. For example, in some sites the agreed-on tracking procedures may not be sufficient to maintain contact with the study participants. Some populations are more mobile than others. In other sites, shifts in funding may create changes in the program and may also affect the participants. These types of changes cannot be controlled, but having monitoring systems in place can help to ensure that the responses to them are as uniform as possible across sites and that information is being collected that can at a minimum explain their effects on the study results.

Monitoring Methods

It is generally prudent to have multiple monitoring strategies in place to ensure that all sites are implementing the study procedures as intended. If the study is being implemented in cooperation with local site personnel, frequent and routine contact should be made with designated individuals in each site, such as the principal investigators or project directors on design and program issues and the designated data coordinators on data collection issues. Other monitoring methods include regular site visits to review study procedures and reviews of status reports on various aspects of study implementation. Cross-site monitoring also can occur through group conference calls and in-person meetings that provide opportunities to foster cross-site exchange of information on implementation status and joint decision making on resolutions to any challenges confronted.

Quality Control in MSEs

Often in MSEs the sites vary in the populations served, the program models being evaluated, and local study designs. Rarely, however, is it also desirable for sites to vary in the data collected. Because data collection may be the only area that is within the control of the evaluator, the MSE evaluator is typically interested in developing methods for ensuring the collection of uniform data across the sites. The MSE therefore needs to have quality control procedures to ensure that all steps of the data collection process are being followed with integrity. In ensuring quality in MSEs, it is important to recognize the tensions between cross-site and local site data collection and to incorporate sensitivity to these tensions in the design of data collection procedures.

Maintaining integrity in cross-site data collection may be achieved through a multiplicity of strategies, including having common criteria for selecting and hiring data collectors; common training and booster sessions; common assessments of readiness of data collectors; and communication, supervision, and ongoing review of data collection (for example, reliability assessments).

Selecting and Hiring Data Collectors

For some MSEs, it is desirable to have interviewers with certain characteristics or backgrounds. In studies of homeless families, for example, when the mother is the respondent, it is desirable to have women as interviewers. In other studies, it is desirable to have interviewers who have some education or experience in common with participants. However, it may be important not to overprescribe the process in an MSE; at times it may not be feasible in all sites to find qualified interviewers with the same backgrounds. In addition, there may be site-specific interviewer conventions that are not common to all sites. For example, in a previous multisite study across the State of Tennessee, it was critical in the more rural areas of the state to have data collectors who were considered indigenous to the area.

Common Training and Booster Sessions

When the same protocol is being used across the sites, common initial training and booster sessions are recommended. When this results in a large number of interviewers to be trained, one strategy is to conduct a "train the trainers" session, in which each site designates one or more individuals to attend the cross-site training and then become the trainers of the interviewers in their site. Other strategies for maintaining cross-site integrity are to videotape the central training and use that video to supplement a live training in each site, or to hold webinar trainings in which all site trainers or all interviewers participate in the central training. Webinar trainings have been conducted with the individuals on the program provider's staff who are conducting baseline and follow-up interviews with families.

Training sessions generally cover the same topics that would be included in training for single site evaluations (that is, the basics of interviewing; the nature of the particular interview population; aspects of the program and phenomenon under study that are important for the interviewers to know; preparation for unusual interview situations; procedures for obtaining informed consent; the specifics of the data collection instrument, including the nature of the domains and measures, how to follow skip patterns, how to select individuals on whom to collect data [if relevant]; how to collect information for tracking the respondent for future interviews; and data coding instructions). The training should incorporate the use of whatever mode of data collection is to be used in the field, including computers, web technology, Optiscan forms, or hard-copy interviews. In addition to providing training on technical skills, we have at times included training on the nature of the problem, such as homelessness, to provide the interviewers with a greater understanding of and comfort with the people they will be interviewing. The session on improving understanding of homelessness has been most powerful when conducted by formerly homeless individuals. In the MSE of supportive housing for homeless families, an additional topic for the training was how the data for individuals could be used for clinical assessment as well as for the evaluation.

In longitudinal studies, booster training sessions for interviewers are generally needed to reinforce aspects of the original training. Often, even the best of interviewers can get into interview ruts where they are not following all procedures exactly as initially intended. Having boosters at various points in the study often helps interviewers either avoid the ruts or get out of them.

Readiness of Interviewers

In some data collection efforts, there are sections of the interview or process that are less standardized than others but still need to follow certain procedures. For example, in many studies of homeless individuals and families, their housing history is measured through the use of a residential follow-back calendar (New Hampshire-Dartmouth Psychiatric Research Center, 1995) that involves asking a series of questions about an individual's or family's previous housing and homeless episodes. Respondents often have difficulty in recalling each episode. The interviewer is thus trained to ask a number of probes and to administer the calendar in flexible ways to obtain the key information. In an MSE, there is greater likelihood that the interviewers could adopt different strategies for administering the calendar without more focused attention on standardization.

A readiness assessment can be conducted to determine whether an interviewer is prepared to use this process in as standard a manners as possible. A gold-standard interviewer, typically the trainer in a site, is an individual who has mastered the data collection process in an MSE training. All other interviewers are assessed according to this gold standard. In the case of the homeless family interviews, a person's history would be assessed by a trainee interviewer on one day and then, within a couple of days, reassessed by the gold-standard interviewer (or vice versa). If the gold-standard and trainee interviewers collect 90 percent of the same data, the trainee interviewer is considered ready to go into the field. Typically, both interviews are audiotaped so evaluators can assess whether any lack of agreement is due to differences between the interviewers in applying the process or to the unreliability of the interviewee. At times the data collected may not be the same, despite the two interviewers' using highly similar processes; in these cases, allowances can be made to permit the trainee interviewer to begin data collection. In addition, we found that in this particular data collection process, gaining agreement on number of days spent in each housing or homeless situation was nearly impossible, and we therefore created "windows" of agreement. That is, the interviewers' results were considered in agreement as long as the length of stay for each episode did not differ by more than seven days between the two interviews.

Communication, Supervision, and Ongoing Review

Key to quality control in MSEs is communication between the cross-site evaluation team and the interviewers and others in the site. With a large number of sites, it may be useful to have site data coordinators who work as the local supervisors of the interviewers and also serve as the key contacts with the cross-site team. The data coordinators are responsible for monitoring the data collection effort and fielding concerns raised by the interviewers. Particularly in the early stages of a data collection effort, situations arise that are not covered by the training or specifications. For example, despite years of experience in conducting studies involving homeless families, I continue to have definitional issues arise that I did not anticipate and thus did not delineate in the study procedures (for example, configurations of families that do not quite fit within a study definition or certain residential arrangements that are difficult to code). When these situations arise, it is important to have a procedure in place that brings them to the attention of the cross-site team, a process for arriving at a decision, and then a process for communicating that decision to all sites so that similar situations can be handled in the same way.

Decision rules can be added to the existing training materials so that these materials are kept current. SharePoint and other electronic tools that create a *virtual filing cabinet* offer extremely useful ways of communicating these decision rules and other study developments to all involved and also of storing all this information.

Depending on the size of the study, interviewer supervision may be required both at the site and cross-site levels. At the site level, supervision may be provided by the data coordinator or the gold-standard interviewer or some other senior interviewer. This person in turn should be in regular communication with the cross-site team. Site supervisors need to be up to date on all procedures and, in turn, provide updates to the team on any issues being confronted in the data collection, the rate at which participants are being recruited and tracked, and the rate at which data are being collected.

Ongoing review of data, both tracking data and data from the primary collection efforts, is also part of the supervision and ongoing communication.

A data collection management system, tracking the numbers of respondents identified, contacted, recruited, and completing each data collection point, is often necessary to keep the sites on track and the cross-site team informed of the progress within and across the sites. Information from this system is typically one of the key areas of discussion in routine calls between the data coordinator and the cross-site team.

Once data are collected and submitted to the cross-site team, the team should review them quickly to confirm that they are being collected and coded as expected. Early reviews can identify areas in which directions are not being followed or coding decisions were not fully explicated.

Once the study is up and running, routinely scheduled reliability assessments are recommended for primary data collection efforts involving interviews. These assessments involve audiotaping the interviews so that a member of the cross-site team can review the completed interview information while listening to the audiotape to determine whether the data collection and coding procedures were followed. A good rule of thumb is for the cross-site team to conduct at least two reviews for each interviewer in every quarter of the data collection effort, although the exact numbers will depend on the overall number of interviews conducted. The results of the review should then be communicated to the interviewer and the supervisor, ideally in writing, highlighting both the areas that the interviewer followed as expected and areas where reminders or retraining is indicated. Consistent problems may warrant further training or dismissal.

Data Management

This section outlines key tips for managing both quantitative and qualitative data, including various options for data submission and storage, and strategies for safeguarding confidentiality.

Computerizing and Managing Qualitative Data

For qualitative data, software packages such as NVivo and ATLAS.ti, among others, are often useful for organizing the data collected across the sites. Although these packages offer powerful analytic capabilities, for MSEs they are a convenient and efficient way to store and organize qualitative data by source and domain. Program-level data obtained through site visits and document reviews can be stored in these databases by site to allow within-site and cross-site analyses.

Computerizing and Managing Quantitative Data

Like individual evaluations, MSEs have a number of options for computerizing and managing quantitative data. The options range from direct electronic submission from computer-assisted data collection modes to submission of hard-copy scannable forms (either through the mail or by scanning the data to a central computer program that can read and enter the data into the system) to submission of hard-copy forms that are manually keyed. These methods have trade-offs, depending on the number and nature of the sites, the number and nature of the study participants, and the size, complexity, and sensitivity of the data collection.

Computer-assisted technology can improve data quality, especially when the data collection tool is complex or when the data to be collected are highly sensitive. However, not all participant populations are comfortable with computerized data collection, and in some instances, the up-front costs of programming the data collection instrument may be more expensive than can be borne by the budget, especially if the number of interviews across the sites is fewer than five thousand. If it is cost-effective, the programming may be a cost that is borne by the MSE central team, if applicable. Using Optiscan forms may be a cost-effective alternative and could offset computer entry costs for lengthy data collection instruments. The scanning or computer entry of hard-copy data may be best performed centrally or, at a minimum, with the same computer entry program across sites to ensure consistent strategies for building in skip patterns and data conventions. Other hybrid solutions may be possible, such as web survey tools that respondents can complete by themselves or that an interviewer can complete with a participant, especially if the tool is brief.

MSE evaluators must delineate a clear process for data submission from the sites (unless the cross-site team is collecting the data directly). The process has to delineate the data that need to be submitted, the schedule to be followed, and the expectations for on-site data cleaning and quality checking before submission.

IDs and Confidentiality

Assigning identification codes to individual respondents' data provides for both data control and confidentiality. ID codes are required in any study; in an MSE they are required to help maintain confidentiality and provide appropriate linkages to the site, to treatment or comparison condition (if relevant), and to specific organizational entities within the site. Therefore, the ID for any one family will likely have embedded within it the code for the site, the code for the organizational entity (such as a shelter), the code for whether it is a treatment or comparison program, and the code for the family. In some instances, codes also may be in place for individual respondents in the family.

Encryption for electronic submission of data, locked filing cabinets for hard copies, and password-protected files for computer access are all methods to ensure confidentiality that are equally relevant for MSEs and individual studies. These methods need to be in place in each site as well as at the cross-site location.

Quantitative Analysis Strategies

This section highlights the types of analytic challenges that often befall MSEs and strategies for controlling, limiting, or explaining the challenges. Steps to take in both preparing for analysis and developing an analysis plan are also outlined.

Challenges and Strategies

As with any quantitative data analysis effort in evaluation, MSE quantitative data analysis begins with attention to several data preparation steps: data cleaning and manual review when the data are collected on hard copy, and computerized data cleaning for all data submitted to assess validity and accuracy. In addition, early analyses of the baseline data should be conducted to assess site diversity. To what extent do the sites appear to be serving different populations? To what extent do the treatment and comparison conditions appear to be serving the same or different populations? To what extent do the programs across the sites look similar or different with respect to implementation data?

At this stage, graphical displays, such as box and whiskers graphs or other data visualization techniques that display the variation within and across the sites, can be very useful (Evergreen and Azzam, 2013; Henry, 1995; Tufte, 2001). Box and whiskers diagrams, for example, graph the summary data of a distribution—the minimum score, the lowest quartile, the median, the upper quartile, and the maximum score, as well as any outliers. Tables displaying the details of the data across the sites can also be useful for examining the similarities and differences among the sites and communicating the data to all sites.

For many MSEs, pooling data across the sites is generally preferred if the interventions are similar. In the MSE of supportive housing for homeless families, for example, the sample served by any one provider was too small to provide a sensitive assessment of outcomes; pooling provided greater statistical power overall and also allowed for analysis of the outcomes for key subgroups of families. Clusters of sites may also be pooled if there are greater similarities in subsets of the sites than across all sites. However, at times such pooling is difficult or impossible. The more diverse the sites are (in the populations served, the measurement and data collection processes, the programs evaluated, and the evaluation contexts) and the less cross-site control there is, the more challenges there are likely to be in the analysis. These analytic challenges fall into five major categories: those due to population differences, those due to program differences, those due to design differences, those due to methods differences, and those due to differences in the initial data results. Each of these categories is described in the following sections, along with strategies to control, limit, or explain the challenges.

Analytic Challenges Due to Population Differences. In an MSE where participant eligibility is not specified or is broadly defined, there may be significant differences among the site populations. Some of these differences may due to differences in whom the programs serve or in how the population is recruited or tracked. For example, in a past MSE of programs for homeless families with behavioral health conditions, despite screening for the existence of a condition across the sites, there were substantial differences among the sites in the nature and severity of the problems experienced by the populations served.

Even when the eligibility criteria are very specific and uniform across the sites in an MSE, significant differences in populations can be present due to contextual differences. Populations can differ in ethnicity or other characteristics that reflect the geographical area of the site. For example, homeless families in Baltimore, regardless of the selection criteria, will undoubtedly be majority African American, whereas homeless families in West Coast cities will be made up of a broader range of ethnicities. Heads of households in West Coast cities often have education levels higher than those of heads of households in East Coast cities.

Strategies for handling analytic challenges due to population differences can include one or more of the following:

- Using criteria in the analyses to rule each individual in or out
- Conducting attrition analyses (that is, analyses comparing those individuals who have dropped out of the study with those retained) to determine

whether there are differences among the sites in the nature of the population successfully retained, and including an attrition factor in the final
analyses if there are differences
- Examining the effects of the program on subgroups of like individuals
across the sites
- Using moderators to accommodate and explain site differences

The last two strategies require specific analytic expertise. Moderators
are variables that are hypothesized to interact with the program variable.
Individual-level moderators, such as gender, can also be considered subgroup
effects in that the intervention is expected to have different effects for men
and for women. Site-level moderators, such as community size, may be studied
quantitatively only when there are a large number of sites. However, patterns
within even a small set of sites may suggest the existence of contextual differences affecting the outcomes. For example, in a study of housing, it may be
reasonable to conclude that the data are affected by contextual effects if the
housing intervention is the same across the sites, but the outcomes in housing access and stability correlate with differences in the amount of housing
available in each site. The more consistent the pattern is across the sites, the
stronger the conclusion.

Analytic Challenges Due to Program Differences.   As noted earlier, the extent
to which the programs differ among the sites can present analytical challenges.
Even when programs start out the same, changes can occur in them over time
due to shifts in funding, staffing, and other variables.

Strategies for dealing with the variability among sites include using a priori criteria for determining when a site should be ruled in or ruled out of the
study; incorporating program fidelity data or implementation data in the analyses; and grouping subsets of sites by looking at their common ingredients.
In some MSEs it may be necessary to exclude one or more of the programs
from the analysis and to provide the descriptions needed to make appropriate
interpretations of the differences among the sites.

Analytic Challenges Due to Design Differences.   When each site in an MSE has
its own experiment, analytical challenges can be created by differences in how
these individual studies are designed. Challenges can include variability among
the comparison conditions or an overlap between treatment and comparison
conditions across the sites (when one site's comparison condition is similar to
another site's treatment condition).

Strategies for handling the design challenges include developing criteria for ruling in and ruling out comparison groups based on the level of contrast between a comparison group and a treatment group within a site and between that comparison group and treatment groups across all the sites; developing cross-site propensity scores for statistically matching treatment and comparison group participants on key covariates (Guo and Fraser, 2015; Rubin, 1997; also see Chapter Six in this volume); and, as discussed earlier, measuring the comparison conditions with the same tools used to measure the nature and implementation of the treatment conditions. A propensity score is a composite of variables that controls for known differences between the treatment and comparison group by creating matches, or subclassifications, in which cases are alike (see, for example, Rosenbaum, 2002; Rosenbaum and Rubin, 1984; Rubin, 1997). In nonrandomized studies, where outcome differences may be biased by differences in the participants in the treatment and comparison groups, propensity scores provide one method of controlling for these known differences by statistically matching participants.

Analytic Challenges Due to Method Differences. Analytic challenges can occur in an MSE when sites use different data collection procedures or instruments, resulting in different measures. Challenges can also occur if the sites are using data collected through different types of administrative records. Data may vary across the sites in what is measured, how it is measured, and when it is measured.

The strategies for handling these differences in the data depend on the nature of the differences. If the difference is in the data collection mode (for example, collecting data in person versus collecting data by telephone), it may be important to control on mode in the analysis or just account for the differences in the discussion and explanation.

Differences in measurement can at times be reconciled by rolling the measures up to the level that they share. For example, if sites measure ethnicity differently, it may be possible to collapse all differences to three categories: Caucasian, African American, and other. These three categories may lack sufficient sensitivity for individual sites, but may be all that is possible for the cross-site analyses. The concern for outcome variables is that the more the measures are rolled up to ordinal or categorical measures (for example, measuring yes versus no, rather than measuring various degrees of agreement), the less sensitive they are to assessing differences among conditions or assessing change over time.

Other analytic methods may be used to handle differences in the data created by differences in methods. If the same data are collected across sites but the time frame varies for example, hierarchical linear modeling (Gelman and Hill, 2007; Raudenbush and Bryk, 2002) may be used to smooth out the time-frame differences. If the individual studies vary to a great degree in the measures used, this may warrant keeping the sites separate and conducting a meta-analysis that computes and compares the effect sizes across the sites (Banks, McHugo, Williams, Drake, and Shinn, 2002).

Analytic Challenges Due to Differences in Initial Data Results.   Even with comparability in design, methods, and population, differences may arise that make it difficult, if not impossible, to pool the data across the sites in an MSE. For example, baseline data may reveal different patterns of missing data or different floor or ceiling effects across the sites. Modeling the missing data may reveal systematic differences that prevent pooling; ceiling or floor effects may suggest the need to exclude specific sites from certain analyses, or at least to consider their impact on the pooled analyses in the discussion of the data.

If initial data results suggest using a number of individual- and site-level moderators to control on differences, the addition of these variables to longitudinal models may tax those models and make them difficult to fit to the data. One strategy is to examine the outcomes in point-in-time linear and logistic regression models, which have a greater ability to accommodate multiple covariates and can test for the effect of the program on the outcome measures while controlling on other differences. Linear regression is appropriate for interval-level variables, whereas logistic regression (see Gelman and Hill, 2007) is used when the outcome measure is categorical, most typically a dichotomous variable (for example, housed or not housed).

Overall Analysis Plan

The MSE analysis plan, as with almost any evaluation plan, should be guided by the main research questions. A strategy, based on the study design, should be built into the plan, such as pooling the data across all sites or within a priori defined clusters of sites. However, it may also be useful to build contingencies into the plan, such as conducting individual-site analyses and meta-analyses (Banks, McHugo, Williams, Drake, and Shinn, 2002). In addition, especially in MSEs where there is less design control, it may be useful to build into the plan the set of analyses that will be conducted to review and diagnose the quality of the data and to assess and control for artifacts (such as attrition) and also to build in stepwise procedures for determining the analysis strategies that are most appropriate given the data that are collected. In some situations, I have employed a design sensitivity approach to the data analysis. Design sensitivity (Lipsey, 1990; Lipsey and Hurley, 2009) refers to maximizing the statistical power of a study—that is, a study's ability to detect a difference between treatment and control conditions on outcomes of interest if the effect is present. Lipsey's approach to study design is to focus on those factors that play a role in improving the statistical power of the study, such as having strong treatments with high dosage and integrity to the intended model; control conditions that provide a high contrast with the treatment condition and have integrity; large samples, with limited heterogeneity on baseline outcome measures or measurement controls on participant heterogeneity; measurement that is sensitive to change with the absence of floor or ceiling effects; and statistical analyses that optimize statistical power, such as the use of blocking variables.

At the analysis stage of an MSE, a sensitivity approach might include only those sites that have high fidelity to the treatment or participants who have received a threshold level of the program; only those sites in which there is a sufficient contrast in programs offered between the treatment and control conditions; moderators to control on the heterogeneity of the population; a focus on the most rigorous measures that have sufficient baseline variation as well as sensitivity to change over time; and analysis techniques that employ strategies, such as propensity scores (Rubin, 1997) and other covariates as needed. In the WFF High Need Family homeless families supportive housing MSE, our analysis plans involve descriptive outcome analyses that will include examining the role of program fidelity to determine whether it has an effect on outcomes, as well as other variables that may help account for differences in the outcomes, such as variables related to individual and family characteristics and needs and to context (for example, urban versus rural settings).

Finally, graphical analysis (Henry, 1995) and use of different data visualization techniques (Evergreen and Azzam, 2013) can be especially useful in MSEs, from examining early data problems and patterns in the data to elucidating differences and similarities across the sites.

Qualitative Analysis Strategies

Qualitative analysis strategies for MSEs are similar to those that would be used in any individual study. The difference in MSE studies is largely with respect to the scope of the effort. Typically, more structure is placed on qualitative data collection and analysis in an MSE than might be needed in a single-site evaluation, due to the potential volume of data to be collected and limitations on time and budget that prohibit a more exploratory or grounded approach.

Synthesis strategies for qualitative data generally involve a successive series of data reduction steps, beginning with data reduction within each site. For example, understanding the level of implementation in each site is likely to entail collecting a range of qualitative data through site visit interviews, document reviews, and observations according to a set of domains detailed in a data collection protocol. The first steps in analysis would involve summarizing the data on each implementation domain by the source (for example, project director interview), then across the sources (for example, all interviews, documents, and observations), and then possibly across all the domains that comprise the implementation-level inquiry, in order to arrive at an overall assessment of a site's implementation. The implementation level of all sites would then be compared and contrasted and possibly linked to other data to understand relationships and explain why varying levels of implementation occur.

Data reduction is greatly facilitated by the use of software packages, such as NVivo, that organize data in files representing each source and then perform runs by domain. Data displays that array data by various dimensions (such as chronological time) can also be useful for examining patterns within sites and across sites (Miles, Huberman, and Saldana, 2014).

In the Anthem Foundation family violence prevention coalition MSE, data collected through our site-visit interviews, focus groups, and document reviews were entered into NVivo and coded using an a priori coding system that aligned with our overall case study data collection protocol. The protocol was aligned with the main research questions.

Taking just the implementation question as an example, our data collection involved collecting data from a variety of sources within each coalition at regular points over time to determine the structure of each coalition (its membership and the role of members, its leadership and governance structure, and the role of its staff) and the nature of the coalition activities (the sectors being targeted in the community; the overall strategy for intervention, and each activity's goals and focus, evidence base, reach in the community, and so forth). Data on the structure of the coalition, for example, were collected through interviews with the project director of the coalition, selected members, and the TA providers and through routine surveys of members that collected information on their background, role in the coalition, attendance at meetings, and overall participation. The surveys of coalition members allowed us to have a sensitive assessment of the size, composition, and role of the membership over time, whereas the interview data provided us with an understanding of each aspect of the coalition's structure and how it operated. We continued to use steps to successively reduce the data within each structural domain, looking at themes that allowed us to summarize the data at their highest level and then to look for similarities and differences across the sites.

Telling the Story

MSE reports and briefings, like those of any other evaluation, need to be guided by the needs and interests of the funders and other stakeholders. Expectations for individual-site reports in addition to the cross-site reports need to be clarified in the early stages of a project. If the interest of the funder is truly in the cross-site story, developing individual-site reports may have limited value. The specifics of the individual-site stories are generally not as critical as the patterns of findings across the sites. Therefore, with a limited MSE budget, restricting formal reports to the cross-site findings may be prudent.

The nature of the MSE report is also likely to vary, depending on the intended audiences. Using graphs and tables to present the findings is often beneficial, especially when the findings are complex. Time is often needed to construct the presentation of the findings in a way that can visually communicate the patterns (or lack thereof) in the findings across the sites. Using *dot* charts, for example, that indicate the presence of a finding in a site can allow an audience to quickly scan a table and see where a particular outcome is prevalent among the sites (see Rog, Boback, Barton-Villagrana, Marrone-Bennett, Cardwell, Hawdon, Diaz, Jenkins, Kridler, and Reischl, 2004, for an example of a dot chart). We used dot charts in the family violence prevention coalition MSE to display the presence or absence of features of the coalitions as well as the extent to which there were changes in individuals, organizations, and communities where the coalitions intervened. The charts allowed the reader to quickly see the patterns of outcomes across the sites as well as in relation to features of the sites and their coalitions.

In highly collaborative MSEs it is important to clarify who is permitted to issue press releases, prepare publications, and otherwise report MSE findings. Developing publication policies in the early stages of the MSE is likely to clarify expectations, especially when individual-site investigators are involved.

Final Tips for the MSE Evaluator

MSEs often require a broad set of technical skills and expertise, including an understanding of mixed methods and a portfolio of complex analytic strategies. Moreover, MSEs require interpersonal acumen, especially in those projects that involve a high level of collaboration with individual-site evaluators. Controlling and accommodating egos, attending to equity, and being sensitive to individual-site concerns are among the challenges that an MSE evaluator is likely to face. Maintaining communication, keeping everyone up to date on the progress of the MSE as well as the status of each site, delivering on promises made, and taking care not to overpromise are strategies the evaluator can use to ensure that an MSE can be successful.

References

Banks, S., McHugo, G. J., Williams, V., Drake, R. E, and Shinn, M. "A Prospective Meta-Analytic Approach in a Multisite Study of Homelessness Prevention." In J. M. Herrell and R. B. Straw (eds.), *Conducting Multiple Site Evaluations in Real-World Settings.* New Directions for Evaluation, no. 94. San Francisco, CA: Jossey-Bass, 2002.

Center for Mental Health Services. *Making a Difference: Interim Status Report of the McKinney Demonstration Program for Homeless Adults with Serious Mental Illness.* DHHS no. (SMA) 94–3014. Rockville, MD: Substance Abuse and Mental Health Services Administration, 1994.

Evergreen, S., and Azam, T. "Data Visualization, Part 1." *New Directions for Evaluation,* 2013, *139,* 1–84.

Gelman, A., and Hill, J. *Data Analysis Using Regression and Multilevel/Hierarchical Models.* New York: Cambridge University Press, 2007.

Gold, J. L., and Dewa, C. S. "Institutional Review Boards and Multisite Studies in Health Services Research: Is There a Better Way?" *Health Services Research,* 2005, *40,* 291–307.

Goodyear, L. "Building a Community of Evaluation Practice Within a Multisite Program." In J. A. King and F. Lawrenz (eds.), *Multisite Evaluation Practice: Lessons and Reflections from Four Cases. New Directions for Evaluation,* 2011, *129,* 97–105.

Guo, S., and Fraser, M. W. *Propensity Score Analysis: Statistical Methods and Applications.* Thousand Oaks, CA: Sage, 2015.

Herrell, J. M., and Straw, R. B. (eds.). "Conducting Multiple Site Evaluations in Real-World Settings." *New Directions for Evaluation,* 94, 2002.

Henry, G. T. *Graphing Data: Techniques for Display and Analysis.* Thousand Oaks, CA: Sage, 1995.

King, J. A., and Lawrenz, F. (eds.). "Special Issue: Multisite Evaluation Practice: Lessons and Reflections From Four Cases." *New Directions for Evaluation,* 2011, *129.*

Kraemer, H. C. "Pitfalls of Multisite Randomized Clinical Trials of Efficacy and Effectiveness." *Schizophrenia Bulletin,* 2000, *26,* 533–541.

Lipsey, M. W. *Design Sensitivity: Statistical Power for Experimental Research.* Thousand Oaks, CA: Sage, 1990.

Lipsey, M. W., and Hurley, S. M. "Design Sensitivity: Statistical Power for Applied Experimental Research." In L. Bickmanand D. J. Rog (eds.), *The Sage Handbook of Applied Social Research Methods.* Thousand Oaks, CA: Sage, 2009.

Mark, M. "Toward Better Research on—and Thinking About—Evaluation Influence, Especially in Multisite Evaluations." *New Directors for Evaluation,* 2011, *129,* 107–119.

McWilliams, R., Hoover-Fong, J., Hamosh, A., Beck, S., Beaty, T., and Cutting, G. "Problematic Variation in Local Institutional Review of a Multicenter Genetic Epidemiology Study." *Journal of the American Medical Association,* 2003, *290,* 360–366.

Miles, M., Huberman, A. M., and Saldana, J. *Qualitative Data Analysis: A Methods Sourcebook.* Thousand Oaks, CA: Sage, 2014.

Mullen, E. " Multi-Site Evaluation and Research." *Socvet,* 2003, 175–193.

New Hampshire-Dartmouth Psychiatric Research Center. *Residential Follow-Back Calendar.* Lebanon, NH: Dartmouth Medical School, 1995.

Raudenbush, S. W., and Bryk, A. S. *Hierarchical Linear Models: Applications and Data Analysis Methods. Advanced Quantitative Techniques in the Social Sciences.* Thousand Oaks, CA: Sage, 2002.

Reiss, A. J., and Boruch, R. "The Program Review Team Approach and Multisite Experiments: The Spouse Assault Replication Program." In R. S. Turpin and J. M. Sinacore (eds.), *Multisite Evaluations.* New Directions for Program Evaluation, no. 50. San Francisco, CA: Jossey-Bass, 1991.

Rog., D. J., Barton-Villagrana, H., and Rajapaksa, S. "The Anthem Foundation of Ohio Prevention of Family Violence Initiative Cross-site Evaluation Findings." Prepared for the Anthem Foundation, Cincinnati, Ohio, 2009.

Rog, D. J., Boback, N., Barton-Villagrana, H., Marrone-Bennett, P., Cardwell, J., Hawdon, J., Diaz, J., Jenkins, P., Kridler; J., and Reischl, T. "Sustaining Collaboratives: A Cross-Site Analysis of the National Funding Collaborative on Violence Prevention." *Evaluation and Program Planning,* 2004, *27,* 249–261.

Rog, D. J., and Gutman, M. "The Homeless Families Program: A Summary of Key Findings." In S. Isaacs and J. Knickman (eds.), *To Improve Health and Health Care.* The Robert Wood Johnson Foundation Anthology, Vol. 1. San Francisco, CA: Jossey-Bass, 1997.

Rog, D. J., Hopper, K., Holupka, C. S., and Brito, M. C. *CSH Employment Initiative: Summary of First Year Evaluation Activities.* Prepared for the Corporation for Supportive Housing, New York, New York, 1996.

Rog, D. J., Jain, R., and Reed, M. *Washington Families Fund High Needs Family Program: Year Evaluation Report: Cross-Site Program Summary.* Rockville, MD: Westat, 2013.

Rog, D. J., and Randolph, F. L. "A Multisite-Evaluation of Supported Housing: Lessons Learned from Cross-Site Collaboration." In J. M. Herrell and R. B. Straw (eds.), *Conducting Multiple Site Evaluations in Real-World Settings.* New Directions for Evaluation, no. 94. San Francisco, CA: Jossey-Bass, 2002.

Rog, D. J., and the CMHS/CSAT Steering Committee. "Understanding and Responding to the Needs of the Homeless Families: Lessons Learned from the Evaluation of the Homeless Families Program." Presentation to SAMHSA, May 2005.

Rog, D. J., Rickards, L., Holupka, C. S., Barton-Villagrana, H., and Hastings, K. "Overview of the CMHS/CSAT Collaborative Program on Homeless Families: Women with Psychiatric, Substance Use, or Co-Occurring Disorders and Their Dependent Children." Unpublished manuscript, 2005.

Rog, D. J., Henderson, K. A., Stevens, K. C., and Jain, R. *Washington Families Fund High Needs Family Program: Year 5 Evaluation Report.* Rockville, MD: Westat, 2014.

Rosenbaum, P. R. *Observational Studies.* New York: Springer-Verlag, 2002.

Rosenbaum, P. R., and Rubin, D. B. "Reducing Bias in Observational Studies Using Subclassification on the Propensity Score." *Journal of the American Statistical Association,* 1984, *79,* 516–524.

Rubin, D. B. "Estimating Causal Effects from Large Data Sets Using Propensity Scores." *Annals of Internal Medicine*, 1997, *127*, 757–763.

Straw, R. B., and Herrell, J. M. "A Framework for Understanding and Improving Multisite Evaluations." In J. M. Herrell, and R. B. Straw (eds.), *Conducting Multiple Site Evaluations in Real-World Settings*. New Directions for Evaluation, no. 94. San Francisco, CA: Jossey-Bass, 2002.

Tufte, E. *The Visual Display of Quantitative Information*. Cheshire, CT: Graphics Press, 2001.

Turpin, R. S., and Sinacore, J. M. (eds.). *Multisite Evaluations*. New Directions for Program Evaluation, no. 50. San Francisco, CA: Jossey-Bass, 1991.

Yin, R. K. *Case Study Research: Design and Methods* (5th ed.). Thousand Oaks, CA: Sage, 2014.

Zvoch, K. "Treatment Fidelity in Multisite Evaluation: A Multilevel Longitudinal Examination of Provider Adherence Status and Change." *American Journal of Evaluation*, 2009, *30*, 44–61.

Zvoch, K., Letourneau, L. E., and Parker, R. P. (2007). "A Multilevel Multisite Outcomes-by-Implementation Evaluation of an Early Childhood Literacy Model." *American Journal of Evaluation*, *28*, 132–150.

CHAPTER ELEVEN

EVALUATING COMMUNITY CHANGE PROGRAMS

Brett Theodos, Joseph Firschein

There is growing interest in the use of community change (also referred to as "place-based") policies and programs to strengthen communities and improve outcomes for low-income families. Recent federal programs, such as the Department of Housing and Urban Development's (HUD) Choice Neighborhoods and the Department of Education's Promise Neighborhoods, and new foundation sponsored initiatives such as the Annie E. Casey Foundation's Family Centered Community Change, LISC's Sustainable Communities, and Living Cities' Integration Initiative are new and creative approaches to upgrade poor communities in an integrated way that cuts across traditional funding, organizational, and sectoral silos.

These efforts are shaped by the recognition that neighborhoods characterized by concentrated disadvantage, low performing institutions, inadequate housing, crime, and other indicators of distress have strong negative effects on the well-being of residents and on the vitality of towns and cities. Community change initiatives work to overcome these limitations by improving the built environment and quality of local services, creating opportunities for residents, and providing incentives and amenities that attract new residents and/or service providers. These types of programs also reflect an understanding that concentrated disadvantage has multiple causes and so improving affected communities requires a multifaceted approach (Theodos and Popkin, 2012). Distressed communities require more than decent housing; as important as that is; they require an array of amenities that support the social fabric of the community and build the capabilities of community residents (Bernanke, 2013).

The United States has a long history of using place-based development efforts to address the range of economic and social challenges associated with concentrated poverty. Early efforts date back to settlement houses in the 19th century. In the 1930s a number of federal community change programs emerged as part of the authorization of the Public Housing program in 1937. Under the Urban Renewal program—a widely criticized effort authorized by the Housing Act of 1949—the federal government attempted to redevelop entire communities. In the decades since, there have been multiple federal neighborhood development programs intended to address a range of problems: developing affordable housing, supporting small businesses, remediating environmental problems, repairing infrastructure, developing rural areas, and encouraging banks to invest in low-income communities. While many of these place-based development efforts have been funded or managed at the federal level, state and local governments also administer their own programs, including tax increment financing, industrial revenue bonds, state enterprise zones, tax abatements, and inclusionary zoning ordinances, to name just a handful of local tools.

In recent decades, private-sector investors and foundations have taken increasingly prominent roles in neighborhood redevelopment. Beginning in the 1990s, there was an effort to pursue "comprehensive community initiatives" (CCIs), often driven by national and community philanthropic foundations (Kubisch, Auspos, Brown, and Dewar, 2010). CCIs sought to go beyond the achievements of existing community-based organizations, including social service agencies and community development corporations, by concentrating resources in order to catalyze the transformation of distressed neighborhoods. Although CCIs have differed depending on the location, sponsor, and community capacity, many CCIs have similar design features. They have analyzed neighborhood problems and assets, created a plan to respond in a comprehensive way, engaged community actors, and developed a structure for implementing the plan (Kubisch, Auspos, Brown, and Dewar, 2010). Yet, relatively little evaluation of such complex efforts has been conducted until recently.

Defining Community Change Interventions

In discussing the evaluation of community change interventions, it is important to be able to define "what's in" and "what's out" of the universe of community change efforts. At a minimum, place-based interventions are defined as those targeting a geographically specified area, often a large housing development, neighborhood, small town, or Native American reservation, but sometimes a larger area such as the South Bronx or the Gulf Coast (Kubisch, Auspos, Brown, and Dewar, 2010). They adopt a "comprehensive lens," with goals that often include social, economic, physical, and civic upgrading and engagement (Kubisch, Auspos, Brown, and Dewar, 2010, p. 12). Many of these interventions are also characterized by efforts to ensure resident engagement in and ownership of the work.

Another dimension to defining place-based interventions is the extent to which the initiative seeks to change underlying social conditions within a community by changing institutional and structural factors, rather than simply funding new, improved, or expanded services. CCIs in particular often focus on the review and revision of programs and policies, strengthening of community institutions, and redirection of public and philanthropic dollars as the means to improve outcomes for families and children (Weitzman, Mijanovich, Silver, and Brecher, 2009). Some community change initiatives involve a "collective impact" framework with regard to assessing outcomes, although others do not (Kania and Kramer, 2011).

Despite these common elements of community change approaches, they are often pursued by multiple sponsor types—national, regional, statewide, city-based, or community-based organizations. Similarly, they can be segmented by primary focus of the work (Kubisch, Auspos, Brown, and Dewar, 2010). Importantly, community change approaches may primarily employ a human development/social services approach or a physical revitalization and economic development approach—or they can combine elements of both approaches.

Another way to differentiate alternative place-based intervention approaches is to segment by the delivery mechanism or "platform" used for delivering services to or engaging with the community. Five commonly used delivery platforms include: (1) working through private sector organizations to improve community economic conditions by fostering business development, developing real estate or community amenities, and increasing access to financing; (2) providing services through public housing authorities and/or properties; (3) delivering resources or services in schools; (4) providing services directly to residents; and (5) focusing on broader community engagement approaches including strengthening local leadership and building organizational capacity (Theodos and Popkin 2012).

With all of these approaches to segmenting and differentiating place-based approaches, it is still not always clear whether an individual program can be characterized as being part of a place-based strategy. For example, if a bank or nonprofit organization finances the revitalization of a manufacturing facility in a low-income community using an allocation of tax credits from Treasury's New Markets Tax Credit program, does that represent a place-based strategy? Similarly, if a city invests funds in affordable housing or infrastructure development using federal block grant funds, is that placed-based? While it's hard to argue that these two examples do not provide resources to defined low-income places, and therefore could be considered place-based strategies, the focus of this chapter is on evaluating more comprehensive and multi-year placed-based initiatives.

One additional note is helpful at this point. Many resources are available for how to evaluate programs—from how to design a survey instrument to how to field a random control trial—and many of those topics are represented in other chapters of this volume. This learning is highly relevant to evaluations of community change programs. In this chapter we have sought to avoid replicating that good work, and instead focus on challenges and potential solutions that are distinctive to measuring the effects of place-based work.

Challenges

Assessing whether programs accomplish their goals generally requires conducting formal evaluations. Evaluations of community change programs tend to be among the most challenging types of program evaluations to conduct. In several respects, evaluation of place-based programs involves an additional set of constraints than evaluation of "people-based" programs. Indeed, it is in many ways the same factors that make place-based work attractive—the ability to respond to people as they are actually situated in local contexts—that makes it difficult to evaluate such strategies.

1. *Community change initiatives often occur in contexts exemplified by variety, complexity, and dynamism.* Neighborhood complexity and change make it difficult to generalize findings from one initiative or place to another, and even for one place over time. An example of this dynamism is mobility: people and jobs move at rates much higher than is commonly understood. One initiative seeking to prepare children to be ready to succeed in kindergarten found that over half of all households moved over the course of three years during which the intervention was active, a surprise to those who designed and administered the program (Coulton, Theodos, and Turner, 2012; Fiester, 2011).

2. *Individual program investments are often small in size relative to the neighborhoods or areas in which they take place.* It is, therefore, difficult to assess an initiative's

impact relative to broader forces affecting the community. The implication of investments that are small, relative to their target areas, is that many residents are not reached by the intervention first-hand, especially if receipt of services or supports is unevenly distributed. Some properties, residents, or businesses may receive considerable support, with others receiving little or none. Alternatively, if spread evenly, the activities or services may be too limited; the "dosage" received by residents may be insufficient to accomplish program objectives.

3. *There are multiple programmatic elements in many initiatives' theories of change.* Community change interventions, and especially CCIs, often seek to saturate a neighborhood with several services or activities (Smith, 2011). The problems of distressed communities are multifaceted, so it stands to reason that the solutions would be as well. Yet, from an evaluation perspective, it is difficult to separate the contribution of each component in an effort to determine which, given scare resources, should be replicated.

4. The elements of the intervention's theory of change (for example, exposure, engagement, and social processes) are not always well defined and may shift as the intervention evolves. In contrast to programs with a more narrowly defined approach and set of objectives, community change interventions often contain a large set of varied objectives that evolve over time. In part, this is by design: place-based interventions are meant to be locally responsive, and it is rarely possible to fully identify the landscape of local opportunities and roadblocks in advance. The added complication is that multi-site community change interventions often do not administer a prescribed set approach, but rather evolve differently in their different contexts (Auspos and Kubisch, 2004).

5. *It can take considerable time for community change interventions to generate changes in the outcome(s) they seek to influence.* The issues place-based efforts are seeking to address are complex and deeply rooted. They relate not only to personal vulnerabilities and challenges, but also to local dynamics (for example, segregation, discrimination, transit access, and so forth), and even to national and global changes (for example, technology changes that adversely affect a locally dominant industry). Addressing these challenges takes a considerable amount of time, often more than a decade (Bernanke, 2013). Yet funders and policy makers rarely devote the long-term resources necessary to see a place-based reform to completion (Auspos and Kubisch, 2004). And some outcomes may develop too far into the future relative to when an evaluation is conducted.

6. *Only limited data about general populations in small geographies are available, and original data collection at the community-level is costly.* Original data collection is expensive in many contexts, but whereas national studies can describe

populations of interest for many research questions with a sample of only a few thousand Americans, place-based evaluations often require a sufficient sample for each study area. There are few sources of reliable, recurrent information about small-area geographies (Kubisch, Auspos, Brown, and Dewar, 2010). Additionally, some of the most important types of metrics related to community building—local civic capacity, engagement and participation, and networks—are very difficult to quantify.

7. *Interventions can suffer from a "small number" problem,* for example, when only a small set of communities are targeted, making it difficult to generate meaningful statistical inferences. Commonly used statistical tests rely on sufficient sample sizes to detect changes in outcomes of interest, for example, between pre- and post-intervention periods. Yet, in cases in which neighborhoods are the unit of analysis, it is often difficult to amass enough places to conduct quantitative analyses appropriate for large samples. If a place-based intervention invests in many communities, the odds are lessened, given constrained resources, that it will make a material difference to those places. However, concentrating investments in only a few communities can make statistical impact assessments more difficult.

8. *Finally, it is often quite difficult to identify or construct equivalent comparison communities.* Creating an appropriate counterfactual is especially difficult for place-based interventions. This is, in part, because, as described above, standardized, recurrent data are frequently not available—and also because devoting considerable effort and expense to measuring outcomes for untreated communities is often unpalatable. Statistical matching techniques have been used in several research contexts, although there is also skepticism in some circles about the validity of causal claims relying on these techniques, given the potential for factors associated with the selection of the location of an intervention also being associated with the outcomes of interest.

For all these reasons, evaluation of place-based programs may falter, or at a minimum, prove difficult. As a result, place-based evaluations have been inconsistent with respect to methods, evidence, and rigor, and also uneven with respect to coverage.

Guidance for Evaluators and Practitioners

Given these challenges, what can be done? We provide guidance in seven key areas that are likely to be encountered by program evaluators. While by necessity we list the seven issues in a certain order, it is not our experience that they can be grappled with in an isolated, linear fashion (see Box 11.1). Rather, each interacts with and informs the others, and as such, our recommendation is that evaluators consider all seven before deciding on a preferred evaluation strategy.

Box 11.1. Guidance Evaluating Community Change Programs

1. Define a comprehensive, parsimonious set of metrics through which to assess program performance.
2. Select the right unit of analysis.
3. Assess how "stable" or mobile is the unit of analysis.
4. Determine the right time period for evaluation.
5. Inventory what data are available and what original data collection is necessary.
6. Support the creation and management of a data system.
7. Choose the most appropriate evaluation method(s).

---

1. Define a Comprehensive, Parsimonious Set of Metrics Through Which to Assess Program Performance

Community change programs frequently have broad mandates with respect to project activity types. Furthermore, project location, initiation, and purpose decisions are frequently delegated to intermediaries, meaning that interventions can operate quite differently in different locations. Performance measurement must take into account this diversity so that initiatives can be evaluated against their intended purposes and desired outcomes.

The starting point for many evaluators is to examine what an intervention's theory of change or logic model indicates the program will accomplish and how it proposes to do so. Logic models or theories of change can be exceptionally helpful in designing an evaluation, but other times, in our experience, they can be simply "words on a page" reflecting a vague hope, more than a realistic sequence of events. In reviewing these documents, evaluators should incorporate other knowledge and previous findings about how plausible it is that the processes and effects will play out in the manner articulated.

As a next step, we strongly recommend evaluators not neglect the importance of designing—and subsequently tracking—input and output metrics. Understanding what activities place-based interventions actually undertake, for whom, and when, are especially important, given the complexity and non-linear fashion that residents, businesses, or properties receive supports. Tracking data related to service use and receipt will allow evaluators to gain insights into the dispersion and dosage concerns raised earlier. Aggregate and unit costs of services delivered will be important for any cost-benefit analysis.

Turning to outcomes, we first start with a caution. Too often evaluators have opted to assess place-based programs simply against change in neighborhood poverty levels, although, in recent years, employment levels and test scores have gained prominence. Other researchers assert that all community benefits will be capitalized in housing values, but such a metric is often too narrow to provide insights into a broad array of programmatic accomplishments.

What then are the appropriate outcome indicators of programmatic success? The options are almost limitless. They may include standard measures like employment, income, poverty, and test scores; however, depending on the intervention, a much broader set of metrics may be more fitting. This could include gauges of social capital, such as civic capacity, participation in local groups and events, political agency/control. Or it might include measures of physical capital, such as residential vacancy, foreclosure, or blight. Measures of infrastructure (such as street) conditions may also be pertinent. Crime rates or perceptions can be important in many contexts as well, as are measures of community members' physical and mental health.

An important consideration when thinking through appropriate outcome indicators is the different "levels" of effect. Most fundamentally, it is important to establish what the program accomplished for people, businesses, or properties receiving the services or activities. Next, did these activities result in any benefits or improvements that are detectable for the target neighborhood? Finally, did any of the direct services "spillover" or catalyze change for others. For example, did investment in a handful of properties induce other owners to upgrade their units as well? Many place-based interventions are explicitly designed to create spill-over benefits.

A final note is that evaluators should consider what external constraints are imposed in terms of indicator development. Evaluators will likely have to be responsive to client or program expectations with regard to outcome assessment. One recent example is that local groups implementing Promise Neighborhoods have been required by the Department of Education to collect a pre-determined set of indicators (Comey, Tatian, Freiman, Winkler, Hayes, and Franks, 2013).

2. Select the Right Unit of Analysis

Selecting the right unit of analysis is not altogether straightforward for many initiatives. Potential options include individuals (children and/or adults), households, housing units or properties, businesses or nonprofits, social networks or relations, neighborhoods, or cities. Often, evaluators would like the ability to describe outcomes for more than one unit of analysis—for example, employment gains for residents participating in a work-support intervention and increased employment rates for the broader neighborhood targeted by such a program. Given constrained resources, however, evaluators must consider the tradeoffs required when considering the collection and assessment of data on different units of analysis, and evaluators are unlikely to be able to track all of them equally well. As such, an evaluator may need to "satisfice" the most viable research design.

How does an evaluator weigh the benefits and costs of each type of unit of analysis? Again, a logic model or theory of change, together with program and client expectations, should inform the relative priority of each level or unit (see Box 11.2). Beyond that, evaluators should consider the relative priority of each type or level of outcome, together with the cost.

Box 11.2. An Example of Selecting the Appropriate Unit of Analysis

The designers of LIFT, a program that provided downpayment assistance to low and moderate income homebuyers, touted two main programmatic goals: directly helping interested buyers who received these forgivable loan funds and also stimulating local housing markets that had been hard hit by the foreclosure crisis (Pindus, Theodos, Stacy, Derian, and Hedman, 2015). Evaluators were weighing the importance of focusing on client versus neighborhood outcomes—that is, evaluating the program at the client or neighborhood level. Beginning with stakeholder interviews, evaluators heard skepticism from local sites about the extent to which the downpayment assistance was sufficiently concentrated within a narrow set of neighborhoods to stimulate housing market improvements. Administrative data confirmed that the forgivable loans were spread widely across the target cities. In addition, evidence from other evaluations indicates that housing-related investments only positively affect the immediately surrounding properties. These two facts convinced the researchers that, given the costs of the data, the evaluation should focus on client level rather than housing market outcomes.

Another complicating factor in place-based evaluation is the articulation of that place's boundaries. If selecting a "neighborhood" as the unit of analysis, evaluators should consider how neighborhoods are defined, as there is no consensus about what geography constitutes a neighborhood. A neighborhood is generally thought to be a spatially contained small area recognized by residents and outsiders in which people or physical structures cohere and provide opportunities for interaction (Coulton, Theodos, and Turner, 2012). Neighborhoods therefore are thought to embody both physical and social components (Schwirian, 1983).

Operationalizing this concept in the context of a particular intervention, however, can be difficult. A weakness of most research on place-based evaluations is the use of a census geography (for example, tract or block group) or a geometric formula (such as a quarter-mile radius of the area surrounding a point) as proxies for neighborhoods. These methods have advantages and are appropriate in some contexts, but may not be consistent with local perceptions and/or with the defined boundaries of a particular intervention. Previous research demonstrates that official boundaries can have little meaning for residents' views of their neighborhood (Coulton, Chan, and Mikelbank, 2011; Theodos, Coulton, and Pitingolo, 2015).

3. Assess How "Stable" or Mobile the Unit of Analysis Is

Most evaluations of community change efforts rely on stock data, often from the Census Bureau or a similar source. The use of these data is understandable given the costs associated with original data collection, and that census and other administrative cross-sectional data are regularly updated, publicly available at small areas of geography, and generally reliable.

An over-reliance on administrative and secondary data is not without consequences, however. These cross-sectional snapshots leave unanswered the fundamental question of whether interventions serve to shape a neighborhood's socioeconomic mix. Places can change either as a result of changes *within* people (for example, a place-based program providing in-home child development service and these children evidence improved development outcomes) or changes *of* people (for example, children who move into the neighborhood with their parents have higher developmental outcomes than those exiting the neighborhood).

The distinction is important and has been largely overlooked. One exception was the Annie E. Casey Foundation's sizable investment in fielding representative panel surveys that follow both the evolution of target neighborhoods and people (Fiester, 2011). These data allowed researchers to examine the components of neighborhood change—disaggregating changes (in poverty) that occurred for those residents living in target neighborhoods for successive years, or as a result of in and out movement (Coulton, Theodos, and Turner, 2012).

Our research on the Making Connections initiative, which should not be generalized to all communities or place-based initiatives, found, on balance, that mobility was a more important driver of neighborhood change than were changing circumstances for existing residents. Other research has found that some types of place-based work—especially those associated with large physical redevelopment efforts—can result in significant displacement. For example, while HOPE VI, a public housing revitalization program, resulted in substantial improvements to neighborhoods by many measures, many previous residents did not return to those communities, nor see their personal economic conditions improve (Popkin, Levy, Buron, Gallagher, and Price, 2010).

In sum, the inability to distinguish between the change in the "stocks" that are due to "flows," rather than due to changes in existing residents, limits the ability to guide planning and action for community change policy and programs. What steps should an evaluator take in light of this? First, evaluators should collect data longitudinally on residents and on places whenever possible. This is possible in more places than has been tried. Second, evaluators should examine residential mobility explicitly through qualitative and quantitative data. This can include asking residents and service providers about mobility, for example, how much churn they perceive or experience through caseloads or by asking how long people have been at their current address or in the neighborhood. Third, where longitudinal data collection is not feasible, evaluators should look for other metrics that can denote change of, rather than within, people (e.g., race/ethnicity). Fourth, evaluators should appropriately qualify any cross-sectional findings as to the program's impact on existing residents.

Finally, evaluators have a role to play in helping practitioners think clearly about the issue. It is important to communicate that residential mobility is higher than commonly perceived and that place-based interventions should grapple with the issue at the design stage. An initiative likely should not seek to stop or limit mobility as a course of events. Sometimes the best thing for people in distressed neighborhoods is to leave for a better school district (Theodos, Coulton, and Budde, 2014) or a better neighborhood, rather than wait for their local environment to turn around. But other times, moves are a result of instability, and place-based interventions need to do a better job of addressing housing instability by helping residents stay in place (Coulton, Theodos, and Turner, 2012). Further, place-based practitioners should decide whether and how people (or businesses) will continue to receive the service after they leave the neighborhood.

4. Determine the Right Time Period for Evaluation

Community change interventions often take considerable time to be implemented on the ground, and once they are, outcome development can also take a substantial amount of time. This is especially the case when evaluators are testing not just for immediate effects of an intervention, but for "spillover" effects, for example, where a new theater is expected not just to improve art-going opportunities, but also local foot traffic and receipts at nearby restaurants. Similarly, the theory of change of many place-based interventions assumes a certain duration of exposure in order for residents to make gains.

Standard evaluation practice and theory dictates that, for most research designs, a baseline survey is necessary, or at least helpful, in determining programmatic outcomes or impacts. Sending evaluators into an area to collect or access data before an intervention starts is often challenging, however. Site selection for place-based interventions is frequently iterative or incremental. For example, a local foundation might begin with a modest investment in a neighborhood and could take decades to deepen its work in that community. Even in the case of a new, externally driven community change initiative, external evaluators may need to rely on a local infrastructure to support data collection that is being built alongside, or even after, the intervention itself. In sum, evaluators should seek to design a data collection and evaluation approach before the intervention begins, or as early into its implementation as possible. (Although certainly, post-hoc evaluations are feasible for some place-based initiatives.)

If an evaluation should begin as soon as possible in the design of an intervention, how far out should evaluators look for outcomes or impacts? Frequently, after an initiative has been designed and begun to be implemented, there is a desire to know in the near term or even in "real time" whether it is working. Evaluators can provide early learning to program administrators. Dashboards can present evidence about how faithfully a program is being administered, for example, how many clients are seen weekly by case managers or whether foot patrols are occurring as frequently as intended. Qualitative data collection (for example, interviews with clients or staff) can also provide early feedback to program administrators about stakeholders' perceptions of its effectiveness.

It is important to remember that the need for near-term evidence about program implementation and effectiveness does not negate the need for rigorous evaluation. Rigorous evaluation can be time-consuming, but it must be to be responsive to initiatives that are designed to take years to achieve their desired objectives. In many cases, leading indicators can be identified, and evaluators should seek to develop an evaluation strategy that is able to present interim evidence about programmatic outcomes or impacts. However, our experience has been that program administrators and funders also need to invest in a sufficiently long-term evaluation that allows for the tracking of outcomes that may take a long time to develop. Spillover or catalytic processes occur over the course of several years, not one or two, and for a community change initiative to truly understand its ability to change a place requires observing changes in that community over a sustained period of time.

5. Inventory What Data Are Available and What Original Data Collection Is Necessary

Multiple forms and sources of data are available to assess community change interventions, with each providing a different set of strengths and limitations. Of course, many of these data sources can, and should, be used in combination. Qualitative data collection is frequently used in evaluating place-based efforts. The list of stakeholder evaluators can interview is long, including front-line staff, program managers, clients, family members of clients, businesses, lenders, community members not directly participating in the intervention, local policymakers, local funders, and others with insights into the target neighborhood(s), the intervention, or both. A recent example is in an evaluation of the New Markets Tax Credit program (Abravanel, Pindus, Theodos, Dumlao Bertumen, Brash, and McDade, 2013), where staff conducted over two hundred interviews with project participants (lenders, intermediaries, businesses) as well as local stakeholders. Qualitative data, together with other sources, often inform case studies. And case studies are widely used in assessing place-based initiatives because they allow a depth of focus on a particular location and efforts, and are appropriate for interventions operating in only one or a few locations (Burstein and Tolley, 2011).

Neighborhood surveys that are either cross-sectional or panel in design are also used to generate data to assess programmatic activities and outcomes. Original data collection, whether qualitative or quantitative, is frequently expensive and time-consuming. Yet, these approaches remain popular because existing data often do not allow evaluators to assess the particular population, metric, or time period most relevant to an intervention. One example is a recent evaluation of the Robert Wood Johnson Foundation's Urban Health Initiative which fielded two waves of telephone surveys of randomly generated samples of residents in the target areas (Weitzman, Mijanovich, Silver, and Brecher, 2009). In another example, the Annie E. Casey Foundation employed a data collection firm to field three waves of in-person and telephone survey of residents in areas targeted by the Making Connections initiative. The firm maintained representative cross sections of the areas over time by adding additional samples with each wave, but also created a panel of residents and followed them even if they moved outside the target area(Coulton, Theodos, and Turner, 2012; Fiester, 2011).

Increasingly, evaluators are making use of secondary data about communities, generated either at the local, state, or federal levels. Cities are increasingly making data available about their activities and residents, and while accessing these data is frequently a cumbersome process, existing groups in many communities see as their mandate the work of democratizing access to public information. (See, for example, the members of the National Neighborhood Indicator Partnership [http://neighborhoodindicators.org/) Cities frequently have, and make available, local data from or about business licenses, properties (such as sales prices, assessed values, building permits, tax delinquencies, code violations), vital statistics (births, deaths, and so forth), immunizations, Medicaid/SCHIP, TANF, SNAP, child welfare, child maltreatment, education records from public schools (proficiency scores, absenteeism, school mobility), health records, juvenile court statistics, and reported crimes.

These data may be available at the geography of a point or parcel, a block group, census tract, zip codes, or some other city-defined neighborhood boundary. Accessing individual-level data is more difficult, but not impossible. For example, the release of school records is possible after evaluators receive consent according to the Department of Education's Family Educational Rights and Privacy Act (FERPA). And accessing health records requires complying with the Health Insurance Portability and Accountability Act (HIPAA). It is worth noting, however, that obtaining such consent can be time-consuming and is sometimes sensitive.

Evaluators are increasingly designing and accessing individual-level data kept in Integrated Data Systems (IDSs), which keep merged data on people, with the data provided by each of the individual programs they receive services from. For example, a local IDS system may have geocoded child welfare data that is merged with individual school attendance records and foreclosure notices. Examples of well-established IDSs include the Childhood Integrated Longitudinal Data (CHILD) in Cuyahoga County, Ohio (Coulton and Fischer, 2012), and a jurisdiction-wide system operated by Allegheny County (Pittsburgh), Pennsylvania. Identities of the individuals need not necessarily be made know to the researchers; evaluators may be able to work with anonymized individual, household, or property-level records.

In addition to these locally generated data, a number of publicly available survey and secondary data describe local neighborhoods or activities. Researchers have used surveys such as the Decennial Census, American Community Survey, American Housing Survey, and Zip Business Patterns. The Federal Deposit Insurance Corporation makes available the locations of bank branches. The IRS releases rates of residential mobility and tax filing status at the Zip-code level. The National Center for Education Statistics Common Core makes several data fields available for every public school and school system in the country. Other nationally available data include the Bureau of Labor Statistics' Longitudinal Employer-Household Dynamics and Home Mortgage Disclosure Act data. Federal programmatic data are also available (such as locations of New Markets Tax Credit investments or the locations of public housing, Low-Income Housing Tax Credit developments, and other assisted housing).

Proprietary data is increasingly relied on in evaluating place-based initiatives. Credit bureaus have an array of data available at small geographies that they have provided to researchers for evaluation purposes. CoreLogic and other groups aggregate loan performance information, which is attached to individual property addresses, while DataQuick sells residential sales data, and CoStar sells commercial sales data. InfoUSA, Dun and Bradstreet, and other sources compile information about businesses, such as numbers of employees and revenues. Some of these data can be quite expensive, though others are not. For example, several studies have relied on relatively inexpensive college matriculation data from the National Student Clearinghouse.

Last, of course, place-based initiatives should seek to document their own activities, collecting data about service delivery. The use of program data is explored below.

6. Support the Creation and Management of a Data System

Creating a performance measurement and outcome tracking data system is increasingly de rigueur for community change initiatives, and with good reason. Program administrators are, more and more, seeing the value of such systems, not just to support formal outcome or impact evaluations, but also as a management tool to better understand programmatic efforts. Furthermore, costs of data collection and sharing are falling with technological developments. Standardized software platforms like Social Solution's Efforts to Outcomes, Salesforce, and Community Techknowledge (or CTK) allow program administrators to invest considerably less time than previously in creating data systems. Several efforts—for example PerformWell (www.performwell.org/)—have created "common indicators" for use in evaluating different service delivery efforts.

While data systems are increasingly in use, their quality is highly variable. Devoting scarce program resources to the design of these systems, as well as their upkeep, remains a challenge. Program staff often lack the training or skills to appropriately input, organize, clean, analyze, and report on administrative data (Winkler, Theodos, and Gross, 2009). And even when established, staff turnover in nonprofit organizations is common and is especially harmful in roles with specialized skills.

Then what should the role of an evaluator be vis-à-vis that of program staff? Evaluators should contribute to shaping the indicators that go into the data system, liaising with program staff early and often. Ideally, the same set of metrics would be useful for both performance measurement and evaluation purposes. Additionally, even if not a formal responsibility, evaluators should monitor closely the inputting of these data to ensure consistency, quality, and completeness. External review and accountability are often helpful, as it is hard to overemphasize the discrepancy between how many data systems appear on paper and how they operate in reality. In some instances, evaluators will assist program staff in cleaning, analyzing, and reporting on administrative data, but in other engagements, evaluators will not provide this kind of support.

In all cases, data safeguards are important to protect information collected about human subjects. This begins with gathering only information that is truly needed. Data systems also should be designed to use that information in secure ways (for example, not relying on Social Security numbers as unique identification numbers). Storing files securely (on encrypted drives) and making them accessible only to those who need to access them is important, as is storing identifying information separately from other sensitive information. In most cases, analysis and reporting should not reveal the identities of clients. Similarly, rules about data sharing must be created. Institutional Review Board approval of new data collection efforts may be required, but even where it is not, program staff should follow best practices in protecting human subjects. While these tasks may not initially seem like ones that an outside evaluator would need to explore, in reality, program staff will often need assistance in thinking through and designing solution for these issues.

7. Choose the Most Appropriate Evaluation Method(s)

Coming to causal conclusions about the effects of a place-based intervention is difficult. This stems in part from the reality that evaluators have frequently been unable to detect population level changes in target communities (Kubisch, Auspos, Brown, and Dewar, 2010). It also stems from the fact that community change interventions are mostly attempted in only one or a small number of locations. Quantitative techniques to measuring programmatic outcomes or impacts typically rely on a large number of observations, and in cases where neighborhoods, rather than people, are the unit of analysis, that poses challenges. Even when tried in multiple locations, place-based efforts, situated within local contexts, are often not administered identically in the different target areas.

What evaluation methods are available then? Random control trials are usually infeasible or inappropriate in evaluating entire community change programs. While there are thousands of communities in the United States, and place-based interventions could, in theory, be assigned at random to different communities, there is often opposition in practice or policy circles to deciding where to put interventions based on lottery. Furthermore, randomization is strengthened by large numbers of observations assigned to control and treatment groups, rarely a possibility for community change interventions studying neighborhoods.

There are, however, scenarios where randomization may be workable to determine an intervention's site. For example, HUD's Jobs Plus initiative was implemented in a handful of public housing developments that were assigned at random to receive the services, while others were assigned to be the control group. Randomization is also feasible in some scenarios to evaluate a part of a community change intervention where demand for a service outstrips the ability of the intervention to supply it to all, or to all at the same time.

If randomization continues to remain more the exception than the rule in place-based evaluation, what standards of evidence are appropriate or sufficient for understanding the effects of these efforts? This is the subject of a lively debate in evaluation circles. Some, like Lisbeth Schorr, have argued we need to expand our definition of what counts as credible evidence (Schorr and Farrow, 2011). This might include directly querying stakeholders to gauge their perceptions of impact.

Most will see the benefit in developing a robust performance measurement system and following the development of the intervention itself through a process study. Evaluators have frequently used case studies to examine place-based initiatives. Pre-post cross-sectional analysis has been used, but has also been open to criticism about its ability to attribute any changes to the intervention itself. Theory of change approaches have received attention in community change work, in part because they do not require the construction of a control or comparison group. This approach works by having those designing an initiative articulate the necessary steps of components of change the work will achieve. However, it is not always clear that the complicated world of community change initiatives play out according to a script that can be fully anticipated by those designing the effort. Meta-analysis has come under criticism as largely inappropriate for place-based efforts given the complexity and incomparability of these programs (Nichols, 2013).

Quasi-experimental evaluation approaches have been much more widely used in community change work than has experimental evaluation. Regression discontinuity techniques have taken advantage of programmatic rules to compare communities just above and below qualifying thresholds for a number of programs, for example, the Treasury Department's Low Income Housing Tax Credit, HUD's Community Development Block Grant, and the New Markets Tax Credit. Different forms of matching techniques have been used by many evaluators to compare treatment communities with untreated communities. Or evaluators have compared treatment communities to communities that would later receive treatment. A new approach is to create a "synthetic control," where evaluators assess the target community not against a real matched comparison, but an artificial comparison created by combining the most representative parts of non-treated areas (Abadie, Diamond, and Hainmueller, 2010).

Cost-benefit analysis and cost-effectiveness analysis are less commonly used in community change work than with other types of interventions. But as the field is better able to document impacts of place-based efforts and also track costs, there will be increasing calls to justify the benefits these programs produce relative to the funds invested in them.

Regardless of the analytic method used, evaluators should consider the local context that the intervention is situated in. An intervention operating in a single or a few locations will always raise questions of generalizability to other communities with different demographic, social, economic, transportation, institutional, and geographic features. Further, community change evaluations often intend to have spill-over effects on residents and communities in or near the treatment area. Evaluators should carefully consider the ability of the treatment's benefits to spill over into other people and communities before selecting an evaluation strategy (especially comparison sites).

Faced with this long list, how should an evaluator proceed? Certainly, researchers will want to invest in output and early outcome tracking (via a performance management system), and also likely a process study. Then, the tradeoffs of cost, time, local and funder priorities, and rigor will need to be balanced to implement the most appropriate evaluation design (Box 11.3). Where an evaluation's success is especially unclear or uncertain, an evaluability assessment may first prove helpful.

Box 11.3. Examples of Challenges and Opportunities in Evaluating Community Change Initiatives

An evaluation of the Robert Wood Johnson Foundation's (RWJF) Urban Health Initiative provides an example of a promising place-based evaluation design that integrates theory of change and quasi-experimental research approaches

(Weitzman, Mijanovich, Silver, and Brecher, 2009). This ten-year effort, launched in 1995, sought to improve city-wide health and safety outcomes in five distressed cities. The Urban Health Initiative focused on communities with deeply entrenched problems, with grant funding intended as "venture capital" to change public systems to produce better outcomes. As part of this ten-year commitment, participating cities collectively received over $80 million for systems engagement and services, technical assistance, and program evaluation, with a goal of measurable change in multiple domains relevant to the health and safety of children and youth.

The national evaluation team sought to address the challenges posed in evaluating a long-term, city-wide, comprehensive initiative by combining a quasi-experimental design, including a group of comparison cities. The theory of change was used to define the initial set of intended impacts that included short-term, medium-term, and long-term metrics. In the evaluation design, qualitative and quantitative data were used to test for program impacts. The evaluation included a difference-in-differences approach to examine whether the Urban Health Initiative cities experienced greater changes in intended outcomes than did the comparison cities. Differences between these changes were only attributed to the initiative if these outcomes were predicted by both program theory and implementation to be intended impacts.

It is instructive to compare and contrast the strength of the Urban Health Initiative evaluation and its approach to that used for the William and Flora Hewlett Foundation's investment of over $20 million in the Neighborhood Improvement Initiative between 1996 and 2006. This latter initiative was an ambitious effort to help three neighborhoods in the Bay Area reduce poverty and develop new leaders, better services, more capable organizations, and stronger connections to resources (Brown and Fiester, 2007). The Neighborhood Improvement Initiative's basic design elements included a one-year, resident-driven planning process; six years of implementation grants; technical assistance and training; designation or creation of a neighborhood-based organization to oversee implementation; local advisory committees with representatives from the public, private, and nonprofit sectors; partnership with community foundations to manage the work; site-level data collection and development of a tracking system; and a multi-site implementation evaluation.

As described in detail by Brown and Fiester, one of the limitations of the evaluation of the Neighborhood Improvement Initiative was that the Hewlett Foundation's staff did not develop a detailed theory of change that specified all the connections between each of the Initiative's goals, the strategies to achieve the goals, and the assumptions underlying the connections. In addition, there were challenges with the operational meaning of "resident-driven" as well as in the creation of a new neighborhood intermediary in each of the sites. Perhaps most challenging, in 2000 a leadership change at Hewlett brought a heightened focus on articulating

(*Continued*)

clear objectives and measuring progress toward them, rather than using the existing more narrative-focused, non-quantitative implementation evaluation. From the local sites' perspectives, the new framework represented a change in the rules of the game midstream and a challenge to the role of the residents in driving the work. Furthermore, at the start of the initiative, Hewlett gave its local foundation partners responsibility for establishing and tracking performance indicators at each site. By 2001, however, it was clear that none of the sites had a robust data tracking system. As a result, Hewlett staff hired a second evaluation firm to take responsibility for collecting performance data and conducting an impact evaluation. However, in the end it was difficult for the separate evaluation teams to integrate the two evaluations or otherwise garner any meaningful information about the program's impacts.

Conclusion

There is significant interest on the part of the public sector and the philanthropic community in the effectiveness of place-based policies and programs to strengthen communities and improve outcomes for low-income families. While such approaches have differed depending on the location, sponsor, and community capacity, many place-based approaches have analyzed neighborhood problems and assets holistically and created a plan to respond in a comprehensive way. In discussing the definition of "what's in" and "what's out" of the universe of community change efforts, there is only a fuzzy line separating what constitutes a place-based versus people-based approach given that most of the place-based approaches involve people-based solutions and vice versa.

Given the multiple challenges of evaluating community change initiatives, it is not surprising that some may approach the evaluation task with trepidation or see the task as insurmountable. However, as illustrated in the discussion, there are both qualitative and quantitative approaches that can be successfully utilized in evaluating place-based initiatives. While cost is an important consideration, investment in a well-designed evaluation can yield significant benefits for a range of stakeholders. By understanding the history of community change interventions and some of the challenges and potential benefits that come with their evaluation, our hope is that researchers and practitioners designing new evaluations will be able to avoid some of the pitfalls and increase their likelihood of success.

References

Abadie, Alberto, Diamond, Alexis, and Hainmueller, Jens. "Synthetic Control Methods for Comparative Case Studies: Estimating the Effect of California's Tobacco Control Program." *Journal of the American Statistical Association*, 2010, *105*(490), 495–505.

Abravanel, Martin, Pindus, Nancy M., Theodos, Brett, Dumlao Bertumen, Kassie, Brash, Rachel, and McDade, Zach. *New Markets Tax Credit (NMTC) Program Evaluation*. Washington, DC: Urban Institute, 2013.

Auspos, Patricia, and Kubisch, Anne. *Building Knowledge About Community Change: Moving Beyond Evaluations*. Washington, DC: Aspen Institute, 2004.

Bernanke, Ben. Creating Resilient Communities. Remarks at "Resilience and Rebuilding for Low-Income Communities: Research to Inform Policy and Practice." Federal Reserve System Community Development Research Conference. Washington, DC. April 12, 2013.

Brown, Prudence, and Fiester, Leila. *Hard Lessons about Philanthropy & Community Change from the Neighborhood Improvement Initiative*. Menlo Park, CA: William and Flora Hewlett Foundation, 2007.

Burstein, Meyer, and Tolley, Erin. *Exploring the Effectiveness of Place-Based Program Evaluations*. Toronto, Ontario, Canada: Policy Research Initiative, 2011.

Comey, Jennifer, Tatian, Peter, Freiman, Lesley, Winkler, Mary, Hayes, Christopher, and Franks, Kaitlin. *Measuring Performance: A Guidance Document for Promise Neighborhoods on Collecting Data and Reporting Results*. Washington, DC: Urban Institute, 2013.

Coulton, Claudia, and Fischer, Rob. *Cuyahoga County's Childhood Integrated Longitudinal Data System (CHILDS): Information for Program Improvement, Outcome Tracking, and Policy Analysis*. Cleveland, OH: Center on Urban Poverty and Community Development, Case Western Reserve University, 2012.

Coulton, Claudia, Theodos, Brett, and Turner, Margery. "Residential Mobility and Neighborhood Change: Real Neighborhoods Under the Microscope. "*Cityscape*, 2012, *14*(3), 55–90.

Coulton, Claudia, Chan, Tsui, and Mikelbank, Kristen. "Finding Place in Community Change Initiatives: Using GIS to Uncover Resident Perceptions of Their Neighborhoods." *Journal of Community Practice*, 2011, *19*, 10–28.

Fiester, Leila. *Measuring Change While Changing Measures: Learning In, and From, the Evaluation of Making Connections*. Baltimore, MD: Annie E. Casey Foundation, 2011.

Kania, John, and Kramer, Mark. "Collective Impact." *Stanford Social Innovation Review*, 2011.

Kubisch, Anne, Auspos, Patricia, Brown, Prudence, and Dewar, Tom. *Voices from the Field III: Lessons and Challenges from Two Decades of Community Change Efforts*. Washington, DC: Aspen Institute, 2010.

Nichols, Austin. *Evaluation of Community-Wide Interventions*. Washington, DC: Urban Institute, 2013.

Pindus, Nancy, Theodos, Brett, Stacy, Christina, Derian, Alexandra, and Carl Hedman. "Down Payment Assistance: An Assessment of the LIFT Program." Washington, DC: Urban Institute, forthcoming.

Popkin, Susan, Levy, Diane, Buron, Larry, Gallagher, Megan, and Price, David. *The CHA's Plan for Transformation: How Have Residents Fared?* Washington, DC: Urban Institute, 2010.

Schorr, Lisbeth, and Farrow, Frank. *Expanding the Evidence Universe: Doing Better by Knowing More*. Washington, DC: Center for the Study of Social Policy, 2011.

Schwirian, Kent. "Models of Neighborhood Change." *Annual Review of Sociology*, 1983, *9*, 83–102.

Smith, Robin. *How to Evaluate Choice and Promise Neighborhoods*. Washington, DC: Urban Institute, 2011.

Theodos, Brett, Coulton, Claudia, and Budde, Amos. 2014. "Getting to Better Performing Schools: The Role of Residential Mobility in School Attainment in Low-Income Neighborhoods." *Cityscape*, 2014, *16*(1), 61–84.

Theodos, Brett, Coulton, Claudia, and Pitingolo, Robert. "Housing Unit Turnover and the Socioeconomic Mix of Low Income Neighborhoods," 2015. Article accepted and will be published this summer in *The ANNALS of the American Academy of Political and Social Science*.

Theodos, Brett, and Popkin, Susan. *Platforms for Place-Based Development in the United States*. Washington, DC: Urban Institute, 2012.

Weitzman, Beth, Mijanovich, Tod, Silver, Diana, and Brecher, Charles. "Finding the Impact in a Messy Intervention: Using an Integrated Design to Evaluate a Comprehensive Citywide Health Initiative." *American Journal of Evaluation*, 2009, *30*(4), 495–514.

Winkler, Mary, Theodos, Brett, and Gross, Michel. *Evaluation Matters: Lessons from Youth-Serving Organizations*. Washington, DC: Urban Institute, 2009.

Further Reading

Coulton, Claudia. *The Catalog of Administrative Data Sources for Neighborhood Indicators: A National Neighborhood Indicators Partnership Guide*. Washington, DC: The Urban Institute. Available at www.urban.org/UploadedPDF/411605_administrative_data_sources.pdf, 2007.

Erikson, David. *The Housing Policy Revolution: Networks and Neighborhoods*. Washington, DC: Urban Institute Press, 2009.

National Neighborhood Indicators Partnership's Shared Indicators Systems. www.neighborhoodindicators.org/, forthcoming.

CHAPTER TWELVE

CULTURALLY RESPONSIVE EVALUATION

Theory, Practice, and Future Implications*,†
Stafford Hood, Rodney K. Hopson, Karen E. Kirkhart

In the last two decades, the evaluation literature reflects increasing attention to culture and cultural contexts in the field. A lion's share of this literature has focused on culturally responsive evaluation (CRE) concepts and frameworks.[1] Much less literature considers the practice, practical application, or ways in which those in the field maximize the use of such frameworks. As this chapter will reveal, most of the current CRE literature discusses either theory *or* practice; very few, if any, provide discussions of *both* theoretical *and* practical applications of CRE.

As the practice of evaluation by non-profits, consultants, academics, and the general public grows, the need to use CRE in evaluation practice has increased because evaluators work in diverse cultural, contextual, and complex communities in the United States and in many other parts of the world. In this fourth edition of the Handbook, this chapter provides a core resource on the history, theory, and application of CRE. This opportunity to bring CRE theory and practice to a wider audience is set within an increasing global demand for monitoring and evaluation of public programs and the requirements by

*Acknowledgements: The authors thank Kathy Newcomer and two anonymous reviewers. Additionally, authors credit Elizabeth Kahl and Kelly D. Lane for their assistance with the technical and graphic design support of Figure 12.2.
†This chapter reflects a long-term collaboration among these authors, each of whom made unique contributions to the conversation; therefore, the order of authorship is purposely alphabetical.

governments and international organizations to use evaluation, especially in settings and communities that have traditionally been underserved, underrepresented, or marginalized.

The purpose of the chapter is threefold: to provide a historical record of the development of CRE, to describe the theory that guides CRE practice, and to demonstrate how practice applications inform and contribute to CRE theory. The chapter begins with a summary and history of CRE, from its inception in the evaluation literature to its current moment and use in training, professional development workshops, publications, and practice.

The second part of the chapter presents a framework used to distinguish application of CRE in several dimensions of evaluation practice. Specifically, this section describes how core theoretical components of CRE provide a framework to guide practice from the outset of an evaluation to its conclusion. By integrating culturally responsive practices and applications throughout the evaluation cycle, practitioners gain better practical knowledge in ways to use CRE and how to provide more robust CRE learning in diverse cultural settings.

The third part of the chapter illustrates what CRE theory looks like in practice through the illustration of three practice applications published in the last decade. These practice applications describe an increasingly complex world of evaluation and show how the details of implementing CRE also build CRE theory on the ground. This third section depicts distinct ways to think about evaluation practice through a CRE theoretical framework and suggests that the practical application of CRE in national and international settings is increasingly timely and useful.

The fourth and final section of the paper highlights ways in which CRE challenges the evaluation profession to revisit basic premises such as validity, rigor and responsibility. As such, the final section provides implications and considerations for future culturally responsive evaluators who intend to extend practice even further.

Ultimately, the chapter lays out an affirmative statement on the boundaries of CRE in practical evaluation contexts and offers ways in which culturally responsive evaluators in multiple settings can apply CRE practically and usefully. As demonstrated in the history of CRE, this chapter intends to serve both as a reference point and a benchmark for further discussion and development of CRE for years to come.

What Is CRE?

CRE is a holistic framework for centering evaluation in culture (Frierson, Hood, Hughes, and Thomas, 2010). It rejects culture-free evaluation and recognizes that culturally defined values and beliefs lie at the heart of any evaluative effort. Evaluation must be designed and carried out in a way that is culturally responsive to these values and beliefs, many of which may be context-specific. CRE advocates for the inclusion of culture and cultural context in both evaluation theory and practice (Hood, 2014). Hopson (2009) expressed it as follows:

> CRE is a theoretical, conceptual and inherently political position that includes the centrality of and [attunement] to culture in the theory and practice of evaluation. That is, CRE recognizes that demographic, sociopolitical, and contextual dimensions, locations, perspectives, and characteristics of culture matter fundamentally in evaluation. (p. 431)

In examining the component parts of CRE, *culture* is understood as "a cumulative body of learned and shared behavior, values, customs and beliefs common to a particular group or society" (Frierson, Hood, and Hughes, 2002, p. 63). *Responsive* "fundamentally means to attend substantively and politically to issues of culture and race in evaluation practice" (Hood, 2001, p. 32). *Evaluation* refers to the determination of merit, worth or value of a program, project or other evaluand (Scriven, 1991). Thus, "an evaluation is culturally responsive if it fully takes into account the culture of the program that is being evaluated" (Frierson, Hood, and Hughes, 2002, p. 63) as well as "the needs and cultural parameters of those who are being served relative to the implementation of a program and its outcomes" (Hood and Hall, 2004, cited in Hood, 2014, p. 114).

CRE gives particular attention to groups that have been historically marginalized, seeking to bring balance and equity into the evaluation process. Relevant theoretical roots include indigenous epistemologies, social advocacy theories, and critical race theory (Hopson, 2009). CRE marries theories of culturally responsive assessment and responsive evaluation to bring program evaluation into alignment with the lived experiences of stakeholders of color. As the following section recounts, the historical foundations of CRE marry theories of culturally responsive assessment and pedagogy with responsive evaluation. As reflected later in the chapter, the historical foundation of CRE sets the record straight concerning the pioneers and legacy of CRE.

Pioneers in the Foundations of CRE

The historical foundation of CRE is largely framed in scholarship by Stafford Hood, as well as the significant contributions of others in the evaluation field

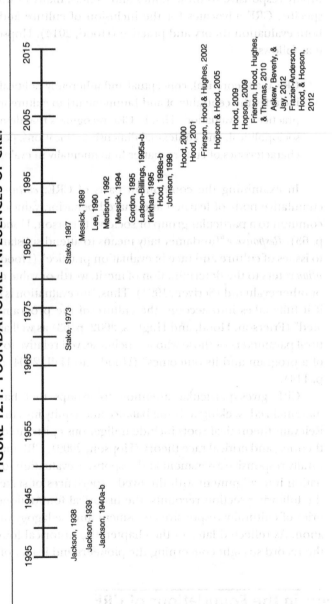

FIGURE 12.1. FOUNDATIONAL INFLUENCES OF CRE.

in the last ten to fifteen years. This section, as reflected in Figure 12.1, summarizes Hood's influences in culturally relevant pedagogy and culturally responsive assessment, responsive evaluation, validity, and social justice as one initial reference point.

The early roots of CRE began in education, specifically in the work of Carol Lee (1990) and Gloria Ladson-Billings (1995a-b) on culturally responsive pedagogy in conjunction with the work of Edmund Gordon (1995) and Sylvia Johnson (1998) in educational assessment. Hood (1998a) extended this thinking from culturally responsive pedagogy to culturally responsive assessment, and subsequently to culturally responsive evaluation. Interestingly, the bridge from culturally responsive assessment to culturally responsive evaluation was built within validity theory. Kirkhart's (1995) conceptualization and articulation of the construct multicultural validity in evaluation contributed significantly to Hood (1998a), extending his logic of cultural responsiveness from pedagogy and educational assessment to evaluation. Hood's initial thinking on culturally responsive assessment had been influenced by Messick's (1989) definition of validity and particularly Messick's articulation of a consequential basis of validity which emphasized "the salient role of both positive and negative consequences" in validation (Messick, 1994, p. 13). When Kirkhart (1995) introduced the concept of multicultural validity, also building upon Messick's attention to consequences, Hood resonated with Kirkhart's emphasis on social justice and saw in it a bridge from culturally responsive assessment to culturally responsive evaluation. Hood's (2000) commentary on "deliberative democratic evaluation" reflects this transition, which was also supported by the work of authors such as Madison (1992), who challenged evaluation to address race and culture.

Hood first used the term "culturally responsive evaluation" in his presentation at a May 1998 festschrift honoring Robert Stake and Stake's initial work in responsive evaluation (Stake, 1973/1987).[2] Hood's (1998b) description of "responsive evaluation Amistad style" attached responsiveness explicitly to culture and cultural differences, emphasizing the importance of shared lived experience between the evaluators/observers and persons intended to be served and observed. Examples included culturally specific use of language and non-verbal expression.[3]

Development of CRE continued through dialogue in a number of ways, both through Hood's work as co-founder of Arizona State University's national conference on Relevance of Assessment and Culture in Evaluation (RACE) in 2000 and his membership and leadership in two American Evaluation Association (AEA) committees: the Diversity Committee and the Advisory Oversight Committee of Building Diversity Initiative (BDI). As Hood (2014) reports:

The interface between the RACE conference and AEA Building Diversity Initiative provided an "expanded space" for the conversations among researchers, scholars, and practitioners about the role of culture and cultural context in evaluation and assessment as well as the need to increase the number of trained evaluators and assessment specialists of color. (p. 113)

In the 2001 *New Directions for Evaluation* volume on Responsive Evaluation (Greene and Abma, 2001), Hood explicitly infused Stake's model (1973/1987) with concerns for evaluation as a means of promoting equity and recognition of scholars of color as evaluation forefathers.[4] Equity and equality are focal issues in Hood (2001), bringing together concerns for racial equality with those of responsive evaluation. Hood demonstrates in his *Nobody Knows My Name* (2001) publication how four premises of responsive evaluation are visible in the work of early African American evaluators, whose contributions have not been duly recognized:

- Issues are the "advanced organizers" for evaluation study instead of objectives or hypotheses.
- Issues are the structure for continuing discussions and data gathering plan[s].
- Human observers are best instruments.
- Evaluators should get their information in sufficient amounts from numerous independent and credible sources so that it effectively represents the perceived status of the program, however, complex. (Stake, 1973/1987/1987, cited in Hood, 2001, p. 38)

The work of Reid E. Jackson (1935, 1936, 1939. 1940a-b) in the 1930's and 1940's would provide historical insight and clarity in the articulation of CRE. It is important to note that not only did Jackson receive his Ph.D. in 1938 but also that it was completed at Ohio State University, where Ralph Tyler marked the Eight Year Study as an historic marker in the evaluation history timeline. Hood (2001) had identified Reid E. Jackson as one of the earlier African American pioneers in educational evaluation. It was Hopson and Hood (2005) who connected the significance of Jackson's work as providing "one of the earliest glimpses of culturally responsive evaluative judgments" (p. 96). Jackson's evaluations of segregated schooling for African Americans in Kentucky (Jackson, 1935), Florida (Jackson, 1936), and particularly Alabama (Jackson, 1939, 1940a-b), provide concrete examples of an evaluator designing and implementing evaluations where culture was a central consideration.

Other significant publications further refined the theoretical and ideological roots of CRE. Table 12.1 summarizes the evolution of key points and principles of CRE as articulated by the authors of core publications. It is a cumulative list in the sense that characteristics introduced in earlier literature are not repeated. For example, the notion of shared lived experience is a foundational theme woven through all of the core literature on CRE; however, it appears in Table 12.1 only where it was first introduced in relation to CRE (Hood, 1998b).

From CRE Theory to CRE Practice

The theoretical parameters of CRE were translated into practice guidelines by Frierson, Hood, and Hughes (2002) and Frierson, Hood, Hughes, and Thomas (2010). These have been developed through workshop interactions (for example, Hopson, 2013; Hopson and Casillas, 2014; Hopson and Kirkhart, 2012; Kirkhart and Hopson, 2010) and practice applications (for example, Jay, Eatmon, and Frierson, 2005; King, Nielsen, and Colby, 2004; LaFrance and Nichols, 2010; Manswell Butty, Reid, and LaPoint, 2004; Thomas, 2004). While CRE does not consist of a unique series of steps set apart from other evaluation approaches, the details and distinction of CRE lie in how the stages of the evaluation are carried out. CRE is conducted in ways that create accurate, valid, and culturally-grounded understanding of the evaluand. The nine procedural stages outlined by Frierson, Hood, and Hughes (2002) and Frierson, Hood, Hughes, and Thomas (2010) illustrate the practice of CRE. See Figure 12.2, which depicts a guiding visual for incorporating the steps in the practice of CRE.[5]

Preparing for the Evaluation

Evaluators must work hard in preparing to enter a community, neighborhood, or organization; they have a responsibility to educate themselves. CRE requires particular attention to the context in which an evaluation will be conducted. This includes the history of the location, the program, and the people. What are the stories of this community and its people, and who is telling them? CRE evaluators are observant regarding communication and relational styles. How does one respectfully enter this community? What dimensions of diversity are most salient within this community and how is power distributed, both formally and informally? What relationships are valued or privileged and what relationships are discouraged or forbidden?

TABLE 12.1. KEY CHARACTERISTICS OF CULTURALLY RESPONSIVE EVALUATION (CRE) FROM CORE LITERATURE.

Citation	Core Characteristics of CRE
Hood, S. (1998)	Importance of shared lived experience between observers and observed Emphasis on understanding a program as it functions in the context of culturally diverse groups Need for a greater number of trained African American evaluators Both language and cultural nuance may require interpretation Importance of bridging understanding between cultures
Hood, S. (2001)	Recognizes the early work of African American scholars Explicit attention to culture and race, "substantively and politically" Increased participation of African Americans and other evaluators of color as a pragmatic necessity and moral obligation Broadens evidence to include qualitative as well as quantitative data Understanding as "vicarious experience" Inclusion of multiple stakeholder perspectives Social responsibility to address unequal opportunities and resources
Frierson, H. T., Hood, S., and Hughes, G. B. (2002)	Considers culture of the project or program as well as culture of participants Rejects "culture free" evaluation Proposes evaluation strategies consonant with cultural context Racial/ethnic congruence of evaluators with setting does *not* equate to cultural congruence or competence. Addresses the epistemology of what will be accepted as evidence Evaluators must recognize their own cultural preferences Represents all voices through a democratic process
Hood, S. (2009)	Attention to power differentials among people and systems Importance of historical and cultural antecedents Social justice agenda Evaluator understands own cultural values Requires long-term investment of time to acquire necessary skills and shared lived experiences Use of a cultural liaison/language translator Importance of how one enters relationships Explicitly links CRE to validity

(Continued)

TABLE 12.1. KEY CHARACTERISTICS OF CULTURALLY RESPONSIVE EVALUATION (CRE) FROM CORE LITERATURE.
(Continued)

Citation	Core Characteristics of CRE
Hopson, R. K. (2009)	Explicitly names white privilege Challenges knowledge claims that delegitimize the lives, values and abilities of people of color Positions CRE as multidimensional, recognizing demographic, sociopolitical and contextual characteristics of culture Warns against taking deficit perspectives that "evaluate down" Knowledge as situational and context-bound Important to think multiculturally rather than monoculturally Recognizes intergenerational and fictive kin relationships Theoretical support from Indigenous frameworks and critical race theory (CRT)
Frierson, H. T., Hood, S., Hughes, G. B., and Thomas, V. G. (2010)	Positions CRE as a holistic framework, guiding the manner in which an evaluation is planned and executed Legitimizes culturally -specific knowledge and ways of knowing Links validity of evaluation and service to the public good Expands context as totality of environment—geographic, social, political, historical, economic and chronological Recognizes both formal and informal positions of power or authority Understand and respects varying communication and relational styles Employ best practices of linguistic translation Importance of establishing trust and ownership of evaluation Mixed-method designs as more fully addressing complexities of cultural diversity Links procedural ethics and relational ethics to cultural responsiveness, including risks to both individuals and communities Evaluator self-reflection and reflective adaptation
Askew, K., Beverly, M. G., and Jay, M. (2012)	Careful attention to assembling the evaluation team. Draws theoretical support from collaborative evaluation Enumerates CRE techniques (in comparison with collaborative techniques) Intentionally creates space and obtains permission to bring up and respond to issues of race, power and privilege Bidirectional exchange of cultural content and knowledge between evaluator and stakeholder

(Continued)

TABLE 12.1. KEY CHARACTERISTICS OF CULTURALLY RESPONSIVE EVALUATION (CRE) FROM CORE LITERATURE.
(Continued)

Citation	Core Characteristics of CRE
Frazier-Anderson, P., Hood, S., and Hopson, R. K. (2012)	Provides a culturally specific example of CRE for work with and benefit of African American communities, taking an Afrocentric perspective Differentiates culture from race Comprehensive contextual analysis, including social capital and civic capacity Warns against perceiving one's own culture as the only one of value (cultural egoism) Underscores importance of history (of oppression and resilience) Need to establish competence and credibility of evaluation team in communities of color Protect or prevent the exploitation of cultural minority and economically disadvantaged stakeholders Uses sankofa bird to frame an Afrocentric logic model Inclusion of a CRE panel review of findings as a system of checks and balances

FIGURE 12.2. CULTURALLY RESPONSIVE EVALUATION FRAMEWORK.

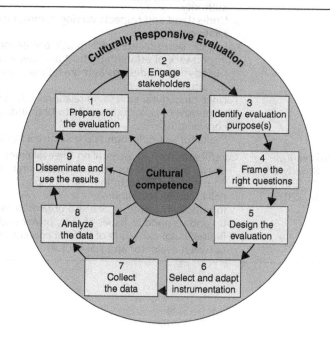

As they inventory resources available to support evaluation, CRE evaluators are mindful of ways in which culture offers rich opportunities in the evaluation process and challenges traditional evaluation that omits attention to culture. CRE evaluators are aware of their own cultural locations vis-à-vis the community, including prior experiences, assumptions, and biases. These understandings support the formation of an appropriate evaluation team. The collective life experiences of CRE team members should promote genuine connection with the local context. While this may include demographic similarities among evaluators and community members, team composition does not reduce to a simplistic "matching" exercise. Evaluation team members are required to have an array of skills, competencies, and sensibilities, consistent with the *Guiding Principles* of the evaluation profession (American Evaluation Association, 2004).

Engaging Stakeholders

Stakeholders are persons who are invested in a program or its evaluation by virtue of their roles, values, or perceived gains or losses. Not all stakeholders share the same investment; one person's benefit may come at another person's expense. CRE evaluators seek to develop a diverse stakeholder group, inclusive of persons both directly and indirectly impacted by a program, representative of the community and/or population of persons served by the program. To create opportunities for conversations about equity and fairness, CRE evaluators seek to include stakeholders of different status or with differing types of power and resources.

CRE evaluators must work to model and cultivate a climate of trust and respect among stakeholders. Toward this end, it is important that there be meaningful roles and activities for stakeholder engagement; token representation is insufficient and disingenuous (Mathie and Greene, 1997). CRE evaluators are guided in their interactions with stakeholders by the third edition of *The Program Evaluation Standards* (Yarbrough, Shulha, Hopson, and Caruthers, 2011). Standards U2 (Attention to Stakeholders) and P1 (Responsive and Inclusive Orientation) both speak to the importance of stakeholder relationships in evaluation.[6] Stakeholders can educate evaluators on important history and background, help define the parameters of what is to be evaluated (the evaluand), identify priority questions to be addressed by the evaluation, serve as sources of information, and offer advice on other sources of evidence as well as on strategies of information-gathering appropriate to context. Stakeholders can also aid in the interpretation of data and the skillful, clear communication of findings.

Identifying the Purpose and Intent of the Evaluation

Both the preparation of the evaluators and the engagement of stakeholders help refine the understanding of the evaluand, including the boundaries of what will and will not be examined. But appreciating the purpose(s) of CRE goes beyond specifying the evaluand. Is this evaluation required by funders to demonstrate accountability? Is it called for by a local citizens' group? Is it part of routine oversight or is it intended to clarify and troubleshoot an apparent problem? Is continuation, expansion, or reduction of program funding contingent upon conducting this evaluation or upon the content of the results? Is it intended to stimulate change and promote social justice? Because a given evaluation may have more than one purpose and not all purposes are overtly stated, evaluators must take time to understand different aspirations for the evaluation and how it could benefit the program and community. CRE evaluators in particular must be attuned to how the avowed purposes of the evaluation maintain or challenge current (im)balances of power and how social justice is served by the envisioned evaluation.

Framing the Right Questions

A pivotal point in the evaluation is coming to agreement on what questions are to be answered and how they should be prioritized. For contexts in which direct questions are culturally inappropriate, this stage identifies what it is that stakeholders seek to learn about the program or community (LaFrance and Nichols, 2009). Both the focus and the wording of questions or statements of intention are critical here in order to set the evaluation on the right path. Will the evaluation focus on community needs and strengths, on the daily operation of the program, on appropriate and equitable use of resources, on progress toward intended outcomes, or on overall effectiveness? CRE is particularly attentive to the perspectives of program recipients and community in framing the questions (for example, Is the program operating in ways that respect local culture? How well is the program connecting with the values, lifestyles, and worldviews of its intended consumers? How are the burdens and benefits of the program distributed?)

The process of revising and refining evaluation questions establishes critical dialogue among stakeholders in CRE. CRE evaluators work with stakeholders to reflect on nuances of meaning and how different expressions of intent may limit or expand what can be learned from an evaluation. Translation of ideas or terms may require the assistance of linguistic or language orthography experts (LaFrance, Kirkhart, and Nichols, 2015). This stage may appear tedious, but it is critical in establishing clear understandings and insuring that the evaluation will address the concerns of diverse stakeholders, authentically expressed. This includes reaching agreement on the most important questions to be answered with the available resources.

Closely related to the framing of questions or statements of desired learning is the matter of what will be accepted as trustworthy evidence in formulating answers. Conversations among stakeholders may reveal different perspectives on what "counts" as credible evidence. This is important information as CRE evaluators seek to maintain balance among stakeholder perspectives, moving into the design stage.

Designing the Evaluation

The design of a CRE evaluation is responsive to context; it is not dictated by the CRE approach itself. CRE designs are congruent with the questions to be answered/learnings desired, the evidence that is valued by stakeholders, and the cultural values represented in the setting. These often include an extended time frame in order to build the relationships necessary to establish trust.

An evaluation design typically maps out the sources of information that will be accessed to gather information (including people, documents or other archival sources, and databases), the time frames in which data will be collected, and the means by which data will be collected and analyzed. Frierson, Hood, and Hughes (2002) and Frierson, Hood, Hughes, and Thomas (2010) discuss instrumentation separately in the next stage, but the design stage explicitly frames the parameters of the evaluation. In CRE, mixed methods are now recommended (Frierson, Hood, Hughes and Thomas, 2010; LaFrance and Nichols, 2009); however, in early formulations of CRE, qualitative data were privileged over quantitative to restore balance to a historically quantitative enterprise (Hood, 2001). The descriptor, mixed methods refers not only to the nature of the information and its collection but also to the underlying epistemologies as well as the processes through which qualitative and quantitative data are combined (Greene, Benjamin, and Goodyear, 2001).

A final design consideration of particular relevance to CRE is the types of understandings sought. Are these holistic understandings? Are comparisons required among persons receiving services and those not yet connected to services? In order to answer the priority questions, will it be important to disaggregate the data by culturally relevant categories? These considerations have implications for both selection and assignment of participants in the evaluation.

Selecting and Adapting Instrumentation

A major concern in multicultural contexts is the validity of assessment tools and instruments. Working in the field of counseling psychology, Ridley, Tracy, Pruitt-Stephens, Wimsatt, and Beard (2008) argue that "much of the conduct of psychological assessment is culturally invalid and therefore an ethical problem" (p. 23). Similar concerns hold true for educational testing (Johnson, Kirkhart, Madison, Noley, and Solano-Flores, 2008). When selecting instruments for use in CRE, existing tools must be closely scrutinized for cultural bias in both language and content. Norms based on other populations and locations may be of little value in interpreting local scores. Instruments must be validated for use in culturally-specific contexts. When translation is used, it should follow best practices, addressing both semantic and content equivalence. For example, Frierson, Hood, Hughes, and Thomas (2010) suggest a combination of forward/backward translation (FBT), multiple forward translation (MFT) or translation by a committee (TBC). Single (forward) translation alone is never sufficient.

When appropriate existing instruments are not available or they cannot be satisfactorily adapted, original instruments must be developed specifically for CRE. Such instrument development will need to be reflected in both the timeline and the expertise of the CRE team.

Collecting the Data

Beyond the tools or instruments themselves, the procedures surrounding their use must also be responsive to cultural context. This applies equally to the collection of qualitative and quantitative data. Similar to when entering the community context as a whole, cultural protocols often dictate who the evaluator speaks to first and who has authority to grant access to other sources of information. Likewise, introducing oneself to individuals or groups holding valuable information must follow a respectful, culturally appropriate protocol. Time is required to establish trust and to ensure that participation is voluntary and information freely shared.

CRE evaluators appreciate how their own experiences and cultural locations affect what they can see or hear. Additionally, they recognize the importance of self as instrument (Hood, 2001; Manswell Butty, Reid, and LaPoint, 2004). Data collectors must be trained not only in correct use of observation tools, interview schedules, and questionnaire administration, but in cultural context and expression (written, oral, and nonverbal). Shared lived experience between the evaluator/observer and the persons providing information in CRE can anchor trustworthy communication and support valid understandings.

Analyzing the Data

Data do not speak for themselves; they are given voice by those who interpret them. Here again, understanding cultural context is necessary for accurate interpretation. To achieve this, CRE evaluators go beyond members of their own team. A cultural interpreter(s) may be needed to capture nuances of meaning. Stakeholders can be involved as reviewers to assist in interpretation, respond to drafts, and suggest alternate explanations.

CRE evaluators take an investigative approach to data analysis that goes beyond simple description or calculation of main effects. Diversity within groups can be examined by disaggregating data to explore, for example, how programs may affect some community members more or differently than others. Outliers can be studied to shed light on complexities or to challenge simple explanations with disconfirming information. Positive outliers—those who succeed without programmatic interference/assistance, for example— may be particularly helpful in appreciating resilience within a community. Data can be scrutinized for evidence of unintended outcomes—positive or negative. The existence of positive unintended outcomes can expand one's understanding of program benefits, while negative unintended outcomes suggest important caveats or cautions that must be considered to prevent harm.

Disseminating and Using the Results

This final stage closes the circle of the CRE evaluation framework illustrated in Figure 12.2 (Hopson and Kirkhart, 2014), often raising new questions that begin another evaluation cycle. For CRE evaluators, this stage holds potential for social betterment and positive change; therefore, it is extremely important. Cultural responsiveness increases both the credibility and utility of evaluation results. Benefit to community can be supported by inviting community review and comment on findings before wider dissemination. Community review also requires that the communication mechanisms themselves are culturally appropriate and respectful of cultural values and protocols. Knowledge gained from the evaluation must be effectively communicated to a wide range of diverse stakeholders; therefore, multiple, sometimes audience-specific, communication formats and procedures will be needed. This stage promotes use consistent with the purposes of CRE, emphasizing community benefit, positive change, and social justice.

Taken together, the steps or components form the guiding theoretical framework of CRE that centers evaluation in culture. Still, the core premise of the chapter suggests that CRE theory informs practice *and* CRE practice builds theory. The next section provides practice examples that illustrate how theory is elaborated in local application.

Case Applications of CRE Theory and Practice

Applications and practices of CRE are emerging from the seminal practice guidelines articulated by Frierson, Hood, and Hughes (2002) and Frierson, Hood, Hughes, and Thomas (2010). This section describes three recent applications of CRE in evaluation literature and illustrates how CRE practice contributes to and informs theoretical understandings of evaluation. The works cited below (Bowen and Tillman, 2014; Manswell Butty, Reid, and LaPoint, 2004; and Ryan, Chandler, and Samuels, 2007) are not the only references that define CRE in the last ten years (see, for example, Askew, Beverly, and Jay, 2012; Chouinard, 2013, 2014; Greene, 2006; Samuels and Ryan, 2011), but they are selected for their specific focus on CRE practice. In this section, we focus on how practice fleshes out the operational details of CRE theory, specific to the context of the evaluation.

Lessons Learned from Evaluating the Struggle of Brazil's Quilombos (Bowen and Tillman, 2014).

Bowen and Tillman (2014) explore an under-examined area of CRE practice by presenting lessons learned from the development, implementation, and analysis of surveys used to evaluate the struggle of Brazil's *quilombos* (former fugitive slave communities) for land rights and livelihood. With a purpose of producing "useful and culturally valid data on *quilombos*" (p. 4), the authors employ a mixed method CRE approach to inform land-based research projects in Brazil.

In the development of the surveys, the authors describe ways in which they lived and researched in *quilombo* communities previously, jointly participated in everyday activities at the local level in the land-based economy of the area, and conducted focus groups with locally elected associations in order to heighten their sensitivity and responsiveness to the culture and context of the *quilombo* communities. The authors also recount how *quilombo* feedback was sought through the entire planning stage of the survey development process, from electronic mail and telephone conversations to reframing questions and reducing the length of the survey to providing input on selection of communities for the study, remuneration for survey enumerators, and suggested ways of disseminating results.

In the implementation of the surveys, the authors describe the use of teams of enumerators to orally administer household and agriculture surveys, one team of a multi-racial and gendered group of university students who had research experience in rural communities but lived in cities and one team of *quilombola* students who were raised and resided in various communities in the study. Still, despite language issues that were addressed, authors and team members had challenges with survey implementation in regard to rephrasing or adding survey questions in the field to allow for greater understanding of the local household and cultural context and more comprehension among respondents as illustrated below:

> Some survey questions were rephrased in the field because neither the
> enumerators nor the respondents easily understood them. For example, one of
> the shortcomings of the household survey had to do with the definition and
> boundaries of the "household." According to the LSMS[7] household survey, which
> informed our work, a residential definition of the household includes members
> who have eaten and slept in the house at the time of interviewing for the last six
> to twelve months or "normally."' But the respondents did not easily comprehend
> this definition because there were household members who did not reside (or
> only sporadically) in the main residence but who contributed significantly to the
> expenses of the household and dependents from their income sources. (p. 9)

The authors illustrate where data analysis adjustments were made to attend to cultural nuances of the *quilombo* communities surveyed. They offer three examples from their study in the areas of analysis of land measurement, crop yields and marketed production, and wage labor versus self-employment, showing how they contextualized results sensitive to the local conditions of the community. Occupations considered as self-employment in the communities carry different meanings to international labor experts than they do to enumerators and respondents of the survey administered, illustrative of larger challenges in rural labor survey design.

Case Study of Culturally Responsive School-Based Evaluation in Southwestern U.S. (Ryan, Chandler, and Samuels, 2007)

Ryan, Chandler, and Samuels (2007) report on an instrumental, mixed-method case study evaluation of a culturally responsive school-based federally funded initiative involving three urban public schools and one Navajo reservation school in the southwestern United States that were not making "adequate yearly progress," the measurement defined by the No Child Left Behind Act (2002) to determine how public schools and school districts perform on standardized tests in the United States. By having teachers and principals participate in professional development workshops designed to assist them with skills needed to conduct and design culturally responsive and school-based evaluation for their respective schools, the funded project was designed to develop an empirically-based model for operationalizing culture in evaluation and to teach schools how to develop evaluation capacity.

The authors describe data collection methods designed to provide triangulation of interviews, focus groups with project team members, school and team leaders, and a national consultant. Additionally, the authors were informed by document analysis of evaluation plans and other relevant project information, including video of school team forums.

Several findings inform the case study. First, as reported by Ryan, Chandler, and Samuels (2007), the initial struggle with the meanings of culture by key school team leaders resulted in developing data-based decision-making influenced by nuanced notions of culture. Moving beyond initial recognition of ethnic and racial diversity (only), changes in understanding culture and contextual factors led to reconsidering their role in re-defining solutions to address their cultural realities. The authors write:

> Where schools may have initially balked at the concept of culture and evaluation, progress was made as one school later began to disaggregate school accountability data to target an underserved group of students and to provide additional support to that subgroup to address areas of shortfall. According to one participant, "teachers are starting to challenge the data. When teachers begin their grade level meetings, they start by reviewing the data . . . even individual student [data]." This level of understanding was not apparent across all participating schools, yet this kind of progress holds promise for schools doing culturally responsive evaluation by being more inclusive in their discussions about the meaning of data among key stakeholder groups. (p. 205)

As teachers began to think evaluatively, they began to have a better understanding of achievement and culture at their respective schools. Data collected and analyzed indicate they showed adequate understanding about explaining the context of the program, engaging stakeholders, determining the purpose of the evaluation and designing a culturally oriented evaluation, but challenges were evident in instrument design and dissemination and utilization of results.

The authors suggest that structural and theoretical issues play an important role in understanding the practical and logistical challenges with introducing the notion of culture in school-based evaluation. For instance, the authors indicate that values discussions and orientations are inevitable in applications and understandings of culture in school-based evaluation settings that tend to emphasize top-down, bureaucratic structures and processes. Being inclusive is one thing, but CRE evaluators must recognize the theoretical tensions in being inclusive and in shifting power dynamics in schools.

Additionally, the authors raise questions about what should be expected from novice, school-based evaluators who attempt to infuse culture in evaluation. Should standards and expectations for internal school evaluation teams be the same as standards and expectations for those who conduct external evaluations? The authors also note that open discussions about culture can raise tensions and that such conversations did not necessarily fit the bureaucratic, hierarchical structures and practices that existed among the four participating schools.

Successes and Challenges Evaluating an Urban School Talent Development Intervention Program in the U.S. (Manswell Butty, Reid, and LaPoint, 2004)

Manswell Butty, Reid, and LaPoint (2004) describe and analyze a Talent Development (TD) school program in partnership with Howard University's Center for Research on Education of Students Placed at Risk (CRESPAR). The authors describe a School-to-Career Transitions intervention that took place at a junior high school in an urban northeastern part of the United States. It was designed to improve the knowledge, attitudes, and practices of junior high school students related to school-to-career opportunities in their transition from elementary to middle school, middle to high school, and high school to post-secondary options through a variety of learning activities. Specifically, the intervention was a Breakfast Club (including interactive discussion groups and activities) that took place for one hour prior to the start of the formal school day. Participants were seventeen ninth-grade students who were expected to graduate during the academic year. Session evaluations, self-assessments, and pre- and post-tests were collected during the eight workshops that took place.

These authors provide a clear example of how the practice of CRE builds theory on the ground by operationalizing general principles of the CRE framework at each of the nine stages. Their work also illustrates how the stages overlap and repeat; they are not distinctly separate, linear activities as illustrated below:

Stage 1. Preparing for the Evaluation. The TD evaluation was interwoven with the TD intervention in the school, so evaluators met on multiple occasions with stakeholders to understand the sociocultural context of that particular school. Evaluators listened carefully to the perspectives of the principal, counselor, liaison, teachers, and students and also reviewed student profiles to determine program goals and aspirations. In a two-way exchange of information, evaluators brought relevant findings from prior research to inform program development. Student, family, and community factors were kept clearly in view as both the program and the evaluation were tailored to fit the specific context of application.

Stage 2. Engaging Stakeholders. Stage 1 preparation included stakeholder engagement, but in Stage 2, the authors gave particular attention to building solid relationships with the school principal, liaison, and counselor, who were identified as key stakeholders. The school liaison, was selected as the key point of contact for evaluators, and the authors were explicit in identifying the personal characteristics that made her ideal for this role. Her academic training, extensive experience of over thirty years in public education, and perhaps most significantly, her genuine commitment to the welfare of the students aligned her with the principles of CRE. This created an atmosphere in which ideas and suggestions could be freely exchanged and debated.

Stage 3. Identifying the Purpose and Intent of the Evaluation. This evaluation was intended to serve both formative and summative purposes, and the evaluation team laid these dual functions out clearly for the mutual understanding of all stakeholders. The formative purpose was to document and describe program operations, providing ongoing feedback to inform program staff so that they could continue to develop and improve the program. Feedback from the students participating in Breakfast Club "was used to fine-tune subsequent sessions to make them more valuable and enjoyable" (Manswell Butty, Reid, and LaPoint, 2004, p. 42). The summative purpose was to determine whether the Breakfast Club achieved its objectives, focusing on the direct effects on participants.

Stage 4. Framing the Right Questions. Following the CRE framework, the evaluation included questions of concern to key stakeholders—school principal, liaison, and counselor. Questions from the broader TD project level were adapted and tailored to local context. To confirm that the right questions were being posed, evaluators constructed a "data map" or visual matrix so that everyone was clear how the evaluation questions related both to the Breakfast Club intervention and to the evidence that was needed to answer each question.

Stage 5. Designing the Evaluation. This evaluation used mixed methods to promote both conceptual and methodological triangulation. Qualitative data included interviews and written assessments and quantitative data included surveys and self-assessments. Evaluators paid particular attention to both the preferred schedule and method of data collection, noting that "many students preferred discussions and other interactive activities rather than filling out surveys and self-assessments" Manswell Butty, Reid, and LaPoint, 2004, p. 43). The career self-assessment survey was administered to all ninth graders in the school, so the Breakfast Club participants were not singled out and comparisons could be made.

Stage 6. Selecting and Adapting Instrumentation. Many of the evaluation tools were developed or adapted specifically for use with the Breakfast Club audiences. Instruments were carefully selected with attention to their cultural sensitivity in form, language, and content. The authors report that one of the standardized tools was normed on majority populations, calling into question the validity of score interpretation for students of color. The authors countered this by augmenting that score with other outcome data that were more responsive to context.

Stage 7. Collecting Data. Overlapping instrumentation and data collection in CRE is the recognition of self-as-instrument. Those who are collecting the data must be attuned to the nuances of expression and communication specific to the contexts of this program, school, and community. TD evaluators shared a racial background with the stakeholders, entering the school with "an increased level of sensitivity and awareness to the plight and lived experiences of the various stakeholder groups" (Manswell Butty, Reid, and LaPoint, 2004, p. 44). The authors credited the (Stage 1) multiple meetings with stakeholders and participation in or observation of school-related functions with helping evaluators be responsive to context and culture.

Stage 8. Analyzing Data. The stakeholder conversations previously cited extended into data interpretation. Stakeholders advised on how best to analyze and interpret data to derive valid, contextualized meaning. Whole group data were disaggregated to examine differences by gender and age. The age disaggregation was especially relevant to this context, in which ninth-graders ranged in age from fourteen to sixteen and were therefore at considerably different developmental stages.

Stage 9. Disseminating and Using the Results. Evaluation findings were reported to stakeholders in formats tailored to communicating effectively with each audience. Feedback to participants was delivered "in a student-friendly manner" (p. 45). Results were explained to the principal, counselor, and liaison within the context of the Breakfast Club program, so that practice implications were clear. Successes as well as challenges were highlighted. Findings were also disseminated to funders and other project staff outside of the immediate context of application.

This study is unique in enumerating practice contributions to CRE theory at each stage of the framework. Overall, the authors also suggest that the culturally responsive evaluation approach is labor-intensive but effective. In ensuring a team, collaborative approach, responsive to aspects of culture and context at all stages of the evaluation, and flexible enough to combine evaluation approaches for different situations appropriate to the evaluand, the authors affirm that the approach "led to an intervention and evaluation that benefited stakeholders and participants, as evidenced by student and staff evaluations and positive student outcomes" (p. 45).

The three practice applications presented in this section illustrate the varied integration of the CRE theoretical framework and, even more importantly, how practice applications take a general framework and fill in context-specific details on the ground. Similarly, the three cases provide examples of practice in indigenous communities or communities of color and offer an opportunity to dig deeper into matters that pertain to cultural context in evaluation and ways in which culture is centered in evaluation practice.

The cases furthermore provide a clearer picture of the way theory informs practice and practice informs theory. Ultimately, the articles show over a decade how CRE practice happens in three distinct ways in international, indigenous, and minoritized school and community contexts and how CRE theory is deepened through practice in three different contexts.

Implications for the Profession

Whereas the previous sections examined how CRE theory is understood in its historical context, provided an overarching framework for evaluation practice, and described the ways in which CRE practice develops strategies that operationalize theory, this final section addresses how CRE presses the field itself to revisit basic premises. In short, this final section examines ways in which CRE challenges the evaluation profession to expand its thinking and examine the cultural location of core ideas such as validity, rigor, and the responsibilities of the evaluator role.

Validity, Rigor, and CRE

One of the benefits of centering evaluation in culture is that it pushes the profession to examine and reflect on respected standards of inquiry and to see these in a new light. Consider three points regarding validity and rigor congruent with CRE: (1) validity must be multicultural; (2) rigor should not be equated with precision; and (3) rigor (and in turn, validity) is supported by conceptual tools such as the Key Evaluation Checklist (Scriven, 2013) or A Culture Checklist (Kirkhart, 2013a-b).

Concerns for validity have accompanied the development of CRE from its earliest appearance as culturally responsive assessment (see, for example, Boodoo, 1998; Hood, 1998a; Qualls, 1998). In broad brush, validity marks the correctness or trustworthiness of evidence-based understandings and actions. But how should validity be understood in the context of CRE? Like other theories, validity theory needs to be congruent with evaluation context, so in the case of CRE, the concept of validity itself must be expanded and repositioned to address the core characteristics of CRE listed in Table 12.1. Validity must be understood as truly multicultural, open to perspectives previously marginalized (Kirkhart, 1995), and it must be repositioned to center it in culture (Kirkhart, 2013a) so that *all* definitions of validity are understood as culturally located.[8]

Kirkhart (1995; 2005) has argued for a vision of validity that reflects multiple cultural intersections. She uses the term multicultural validity *not* to specify a new type of validity but to suggest that validity is an expansive construct that can be understood from multiple perspectives, including those historically marginalized. In repositioning validity in culture, Kirkhart (2013a) has examined the perspectives from which validity is argued in feminist theory, CRT, Indigenous epistemology, queer theory, disability studies, and aging studies, as well as measurement theory and research design. Justifications have been identified in five categories at this writing; however, these understandings continue to evolve (LaFrance, Kirkhart, and Nichols, 2015). Each of the five justifications—methodological, relational, theoretical, experiential, and consequential—is congruent with CRE (see Table 12.2). These justifications may stand alone or be used in combination to argue the validity of CRE. Conversely, when a justificatory perspective is ignored or violated, it may weaken support for (threaten) validity (Kirkhart, 2011).

Rigor typically refers to compliance with strict standards of research methodology (Johnson, Kirkhart, Madison, Noley, and Solano-Flores, 2008). It is valued primarily because it supports methodological justifications of validity, but like validity, it requires an expanded conceptualization to make it useful to CRE. While scientific rigor can serve several purposes that "advance understanding and ultimately advantage communities of color and other underrepresented groups" (Johnson, Kirkhart, Madison, Noley, and Solano-Flores, 2008, p. 200), narrow definitions of scientific rigor undermine validity. What then does it mean to do rigorous evaluation that is culturally responsive? What are the hallmarks of rigor for CRE? Are these specific to CRE or are they, simply "good evaluation"?[9]

Nearly three decades after Lincoln and Guba (1986) cautioned that traditional criteria of rigor grounded in post-positivism were inadequate to the task of evaluating the quality of *all* evaluation, we have a better sense of alternate definitions of rigor and of criteria to achieve it. But whether one is working from a post-positivist or alternate paradigm such as CRE, rigorous inquiry has been historically rule-driven, with strict standards to be met or bars to be cleared. This understanding presents two challenges for rigor in CRE: equating rigor with precision and with fixed, preordinate criteria.

The first challenge emerges from implicitly associating rigor with precision. Precision values fixed, often narrowly defined, boundaries that reflect positivist yearning for singular truths. Sharp definitions and exact specifications are viewed as accurate and correct, while loose, holistic understandings

TABLE 12.2. JUSTIFICATIONS OF VALIDITY UNDER CULTURALLY RESPONSIVE EVALUATION (CRE)[a].

Justification[b]	Description	Applications in CRE
Methodological	Validity is supported by the cultural appropriateness of epistemology and method—measurement tools, design configurations, and procedures of information gathering, analysis and interpretation	Epistemology of persons indigenous to the community grounds the evaluation. Measurement tools have been developed for a particular ethnic group and/or validated for a context-specific use. The sampling frame insures inclusion of diverse cultural perspectives appropriate to the program being evaluated and its context. The study design employs a time frame appropriate to the cultural context. Evaluation questions represent a range of perspectives, values and interest.
Relational	Validity is supported by the quality of the relationships that surround and infuse the evaluation process	Evaluators respect local norms and authority in entering the community to undertake evaluation. Evaluators understand the historical and spiritual significance of the land and the geographic location of their work. Evaluators take time to build relationships and understandings as part of the early process of planning and design development. Evaluators reflect on their own cultural positions and positions of authority with respect to other participants in the evaluation process. Meaningful roles are established for stakeholder participation, and barriers to full participation are addressed.

(Continued)

TABLE 12.2. JUSTIFICATIONS OF VALIDITY UNDER CULTURALLY RESPONSIVE EVALUATION (CRE)[a]. (Continued)

Justification[b]	Description	Applications in CRE
Theoretical	Validity is supported by invoking culturally congruent theoretical perspectives.	Evaluators frame their work in CRE principles and practices, which in turn are drawn from culturally grounded social science theories. When social science research is used to develop program theory, it is first examined with respect to its multicultural validity and fit with context. Program theory is grounded in the cultural traditions and beliefs of program participants. Validity theory itself is examined for culturally-bound biases and limitations.
Experiential	Validity is supported by the life experience of participants.	Local citizens and program consumers contribute their wisdom to the evaluation process. Evaluators reflect on their own history and cultural positions, seeking assumptions and "blind spots." Evaluators employ a cultural guide to increase their understanding and appreciation of local culture. Evaluative data are understood and interpreted in terms of the realities of the people they represent.
Consequential	Validity is supported by the social consequences of understandings and determinations of value, and the actions taken based upon them.	History of evaluation in this community is acknowledged and addressed, especially if that history is oppressive, exploitive. Mechanisms are identified and negotiated by which evaluation and evaluators will give back to the community. Evaluation improves the ability of the community to advance its goals and meet the needs of its members. Evaluation promotes social justice.

[a]Table 2 is adapted from Hopson and Kirkhart (2012).
[b]Justifications of multicultural validity developed by Kirkhart (2005, 2013a-b).

are denigrated as imprecise or incorrect. Such a narrow perspective on rigor does not serve CRE well, however. To be responsive to culture and context, evaluation must include a broad vision, taking meaning not only from the minute and precise, but also from the holistic and expansive, for example, the history and worldview of the people who are stakeholders in the evaluation. Restricting the range of vision of evaluation methodology in the name of rigor undermines, rather than supports, valid understandings.

The second challenge is that preordinate criteria of rigor—those that are specified at the outset—often do not match the world of practice. CRE is often emergent in its design, grounded in its relationship with community, and fluid in its response to changing circumstances or resources. Rigor is not abandoned, but it may be more appropriately cast as criteria that guide evaluation practice rather than as fixed bars to be cleared.

The context-specific nature of CRE demands an understanding of rigor that is also fitted to context, providing guidance but not blocking the holistic vantage point or the emergence of new understandings. A CRE-compatible strategy is a non-linear, iterative, conceptual checklist such as Scriven's (1991; 2013) Key Evaluation Checklist (KEC), which can guide rigorous CRE and support the validity of resulting understandings. Drawing on multicultural validity theory, Kirkhart (2013a-b) proposed "A Culture Checklist" of nine conceptual elements that can serve as hallmarks of rigor in CRE and beyond: history, location, power, voice, relationship,[10] time, return, plasticity, and reflexivity (see Table 12.3). Each concept links back to and supports one or more justifications of multicultural validity; hence the elements are intertwined, not independent of one another. These represent concepts to be considered iteratively while planning and implementing CRE. Used reflexively, checklists such as these can be used to keep the CRE evaluation on course and flag considerations and activities that cannot be compromised. For any particular CRE application, it may also be necessary to create a contextually-specific list of core considerations that draws upon ideas and values central to that community (Kirkhart, 2013a).

Responsibility as a Core Principle of CRE

Central to the core principles of CRE (Table 12.1) as well as in the identity of the CRE evaluator are responsibility and responsiveness. CRE evaluators recognize the sense of "social responsibility" that requires the work to be responsive to the community that is served. Hood (2001) asserted that African American evaluators from the pre-Brown vs. Board of Education[11] era acted

TABLE 12.3. A CULTURE CHECKLIST (ADAPTED FROM KIRKHART, 2013b, PP. 151–152).

Element	Content Description	Questions Raised
History	History of place, people, program (or other evaluand), and evaluation's role. Knowledge of cultural heritages and traditions, including their evolution over time.	What is the story of this community? What is the story of how this program came to be in this place? How has what is here today been shaped by what came before it? What is the history of evaluation in this community or with this program?
Location	Cultural contexts and affiliations of evaluators and evaluand, including theories, values, meaning-making, and worldviews. Recognizes multiple cultural intersections at individual, organizational, and systems levels. Geographic anchors of culture in place.	What are the cultural identifications of persons in this community and how do these compare to those of the program staff and of the evaluators? What is valued here? How do people understand their lives? What is the geography of this place? How do people relate to the land?
Power	Understanding how privilege is attached to some cultural signifiers; prejudice to others. Attention to address equity and social justice, avoid perpetuating condescension, discrimination or disparity.	Who holds power in various ways, and what are the impacts of how power is exercised? What are the formal, legal, political, social and economic sources of power? What are the informal sources of power?
Connection	Connections among the evaluation, evaluand and community. Relating evaluation to place, time and Universe. Maintaining accountability to community with respect and responsibility. Establishing trust in interpersonal relationships.	How do members of the community relate to one another, to the program and its personnel, and to the evaluators? How do the evaluators relate to persons in the program and in the community? How does the evaluation relate to the core values of the cultures, community and context?

(Continued)

Element	Content Description	Questions Raised
Voice	Addresses whose perspectives are magnified and whose are silenced. Maps inclusion and exclusion or marginalization. Includes use of language, jargon, and communicative strategies.	Who participates in the planning, design, and implementation of the evaluation? Whose messages are heard and heeded? Whose methods of communication are reflected in the languages and expressions that are used to discuss the evaluation process, raise questions, interpret findings, and communicate results?
Time	Calls attention to rhythm, pace and scheduling and to the wide vision of past and future. Encourages evaluation to consider longer impacts and implications—positive or negative.	How does the rhythm of this evaluation fit the context? Is it moving too fast? Too slowly? Has it considered important outcomes at various points in time? Will it have the patience to watch carefully for small changes? For long-term consequences?
Return	Supports reciprocity by focusing attention on how the evaluation and/or the persons who conduct it return benefit to the evaluand and the surrounding community. Addresses returns both during and after the evaluation process. Positions the evaluation as non-exploitive.	How does evaluation advance the goals of this community or serve the needs of its people? Has the benefit returned to community compensated them fairly for their time and attention and for any disruption created by this evaluation? In what ways are persons better off? Have any been harmed or disadvantaged?
Plasticity	The ability to be molded, to receive new information, reorganize and change in response to new experiences, and evolve new ideas and forms. Applies both to the persons who do evaluation and to their designs, process and products. Because culture is fluid, not static, evaluation must be responsive.	How is this evaluation changing in response to local context? Are we evaluators staying open to new ideas or are we overly committed to following a fixed plan or timeline? What has surprised us here that changes how we think about evaluation? What have we learned here that is new and/or changes our understanding of good evaluation?

(Continued)

TABLE 12.3. A CULTURE CHECKLIST (ADAPTED FROM KIRKHART, 2013b, PP. 151–152). *(Continued)*

Element	Content Description	Questions Raised
Reflexivity	Applies the principles of evaluation to one's own person and work, from self-scrutiny to metaevaluation. Supports reflective practice. Underscores the importance of metaevaluation.	What do I think I know in this context and why? What do I know that I don't understand? What areas of new learning must I watch for and reflect upon? What do I need to let go of or relearn, and how can I work on that? What are the strengths and limitations of this evaluation and how it has addressed culture? How strong are the arguments supporting validity? What counterarguments challenge validity?

on their "social responsibility" to address the inequities of segregated schooling by using their research, evaluation, and scholarly skills in the evaluation of education systems in the South. The work of Reid E. Jackson was most notable in this regard (Hopson and Hood, 2005).

Hood and Hall (2004), in their implementation of their NSF funded Relevance of Culture in Evaluation Institute, along with the project's advisory board, devoted considerable thought to the characteristics of the "culturally responsible evaluator." First they made the distinction between being responsive and being responsible. Being "responsible" is viewed as an active behavior manifested in advocacy of social justice for those who had been traditionally disenfranchised. To act on this responsibility requires one to be responsive by being aware and recognizing the centrality of culture and cultural context in our evaluative work and identifying the appropriate methods and tools that will best serve the community. Culturally *responsible* evaluators are characterized as those who:

- Prioritize and are responsive to the needs and cultural parameters of those who are being served relative to the implementation of a program and its outcomes,
- Involve self in learning, engaging and appreciating the role of culture(s) within the context of the evaluation,
- Learn to recognize dissonance within the evaluation context, for example, between school and community groups being served, and
- Are committed to educating themselves, continuing to acquire training and experience in working in diverse settings.

The centrality of responsibility and responsiveness to our conceptualization of CRE is congruent with the work reported by the Māori and other indigenous members of our CRE family. It is particularly captured in the culturally specific evaluation of *Kaupapa Māori* (that is, a Māori way). Cram, Kennedy, Paipa, Pipi, and Wehipeihana (2015) inform us that *Kaupapa Māori* evaluation is grounded in the discovery of the true Māori *Kaupapa* to guide evaluators in their determination of not only the right methods but also the right people to undertake the evaluation. Ultimately, it is the responsibility of Māori to advance a Māori way of evaluation. This culturally specific/responsive approach is concretely illustrated by Paipa, Cram, Kennedy, and Pipi (2015) as these Māori evaluators utilize culturally responsive methods in a "family centered evaluation" approach. In this case the Māori evaluators act upon their responsibility and accountability "to identify culturally relevant ways of working that make sense to *whānau* [family] and align with *whānau* values with regard to kinship and relational connections" (p. 329).

The work of the pre-Brown African American evaluators in the 1930s to 1954 (Hood, 2001) and work that is currently being reported by indigenous evaluators such as the Māori (Paipa, Cram, Kennedy, and Pipi, 2015) may suggest a historical foundation connecting evaluators of color. This connection is possibly found in their mutual recognition and use of culturally responsive methods as they act upon their social responsibility to their communities (Hood, 2001). Just as pre-Brown African American evaluators took responsibility for being responsive in their own communities, there is a growing body of work in indigenous communities to address these same matters of responsiveness; that is, to find ways to use evaluations toward social and community responsibility.

Conclusion

Culturally responsive evaluation marks a significant advance in the ability of the evaluation profession to address culture. It not only provides a valuable framework for evaluation practice, but it challenges evaluators to reflect on power dynamics and sharpen their attention to social justice. This section summarizes key points elaborated in the chapter.

CRE has a defined theory base and conceptual framework to guide practice. The theory base incorporates existing evaluation approaches and is influenced by other culturally responsive notions in assessment and education. It builds on a framework developed by Frierson, Hood, and Hughes (2002) and

Frierson, Hood, Hughes, and Thomas (2010), where cultural context is integrated into evaluation practice and evaluation practice is centered in culture.

While there are many contributors to the development of CRE, its historical development was influenced by Stafford Hood's funded research, professional collaboration, and written work. From his Amistad paper to collaborative work, he has encouraged and hopefully inspired others to further refine the conceptualization of CRE as well as its applications.

CRE practice represents the fruits of this earlier conceptual work and it contributes to local CRE theory. To understand and appreciate CRE practice fully means understanding how it informs CRE and how CRE theory is ultimately fleshed out in the nuances and details of local context.

Future implications of CRE suggest that new approaches to core concepts such as validity deserve more exploration. Additionally, CRE requires understanding and recognizing the importance of our responsibility as evaluators and translating responsiveness in our practice. As illustrated in the chapter, the future of CRE will be advanced through well documented practice examples with rich detail (for example, Greene, 2015), combined with further reflection on and articulation of alignments between CRE and other evaluation approaches (for example, Askew, Beverly, and Jay, 2012). These advances coincide with the need to develop increasingly sophisticated ways to center evaluation in culture, both domestically and internationally. CRE stands poised to contribute and we as members of the CRE community are collectively compelled to use it as we act upon our responsibility to make a difference.

Notes

1. We carefully distinguish culturally responsive evaluation from other similar approaches such as culturally competent evaluation or cross-cultural evaluation (Chouinard, 2013; Chouinard, 2014; Chouinard and Cousins, 2009) which attend to matters of culture in local and international settings but have distinct histories and foci in evaluation.

2. Stake's more recent work also addresses cultural pluralism as part of responsive evaluation (Stake, 2004).

3. The title of this work references the historic Amistad trial, in which James Covey's role as "the portal between two conflicting cultures" (Hood, 1998b, p. 108) was the vehicle that made the defense of the Mende survivors culturally responsive. Hood describes how Covey had been born and raised Mende but was subsequently captured and held as a slave. After being freed from a slave ship by a British naval vessel, he learned to read and write in English and served as a sailor on a British brig of war. Covey's lived experience in both worlds made him essential to the understandings in the trial. Similarly, Hood argues, African American evaluators play a key role

in the evaluation of educational programs that serve African American students by deepening the understanding of a program, its value for participants, and potential improvements needed to increase benefits to culturally diverse groups.

4. The Nobody Knows My Name project takes its title from the 1961 collection of essays by James Baldwin, *Nobody Knows My Name; More Notes of a Native Son*. It initially focused on men of color who laid significant intellectual groundwork in evaluation. Scholarly contributions of women of color are a more recent addition. See, for example, Frazier-Anderson and Bertrand Jones (2015).

5. Note that Figure 12.2 is referenced in Bledsoe and Donaldson (2015), but was developed earlier in the presentation by Kirkhart and Hopson (2010).

6. *U2 Attention to Stakeholders.* Evaluations should devote attention to the full range of individuals and groups invested in the program and affected by its evaluation. *P1 Responsive and Inclusive Orientation.* Evaluations should be responsive to stakeholders and their communities.

7. This refers to the World Bank's Living Standards Measurement Survey (World Bank, 2011, cited in Bowen and Tillman, 2014).

8. While there may be no direct linguistic translation for the Western, English-language construct of validity, concerns for goodness, trustworthiness, and authenticity emerge in different cultural contexts (LaFrance, Kirkhart, and Nichols, 2015).

9. Interestingly, similar questions were raised when Ladson-Billings proposed culturally responsive pedagogy—isn't that just good teaching? (Ladson-Billings, 1995a).

10. Colleagues at the Aotearoa New Zealand Evaluation Association Conference in Wellington (July 2014) suggested that *relationship* be retitled *connection*. This change is reflected in Table 12.3.

11. *Brown v. Board of Education* was the landmark U.S. Supreme Court decision that found separate public schools for blacks and whites to be unconstitutional. Handed down in 1954, it was considered a major victory of the civil rights movement and led to the integration of American educational and public facilities in the South.

References

American Evaluation Association. *Guiding Principles for Evaluators.* www.eval.org/p/cm/ld/fid=51, 2004.

Askew, K., Beverly, M. G., and Jay, M. "Aligning Collaborative and Culturally Responsive Evaluation Approaches." *Evaluation and Program Planning*, 2012, *35*(4), 552–557.

Bledsoe, K., and Donaldson, S. "Culturally Responsive Theory-Driven Evaluations." In S. Hood, R. K. Hopson, and H. Frierson (eds.), *Continuing the Journey to Reposition Culture and Cultural Context in Evaluation Theory and Practice* (pp. 3–27). Greenwich, CT: Information Age Publishing, Inc., 2015.

Boodoo, G. M. "Addressing Cultural Context in the Development of Performance-Based Assessments and Computer Adaptive Testing: Preliminary Validity Considerations." *Journal of Negro Education*, 1998, *67*(3), 211–219.

Bowen, M. L., and Tillman, A. S. "Developing Culturally Responsive Surveys. Lessons in Development, Implementation, and Analysis from Brazil's African Descent Communities." *American Journal of Evaluation*, 2014, *35*(4), 507–524.

Chouinard, J. A. "The Case for Participatory Evaluation in an Era of Accountability." *American Journal of Evaluation*, 2013, *34*(2), 237–253.

Chouinard, J. A. "Understanding Relationships in Culturally Complex Evaluation Contexts." *Evaluation*, 2014, *20*(3), 332–347.

Chouinard, J. A., and Cousins, J. B. "A Review and Synthesis of Current Research on Cross-Cultural Evaluation." *American Journal of Evaluation*, 2009, *30*(4), 457–494.

Cram, F., Kennedy, V., Paipa, K., Pipi, K., and Wehipeihana, N. "Being Culturally Responsive Through Kaupapa Māori Evaluation." In S. Hood, R. K. Hopson, and H. Frierson (eds.), *Continuing the Journey to Reposition Culture and Cultural Context in Evaluation Theory and Practice* (pp. 289–231). Greenwich, CT: Information Age Publishing, Inc., 2015.

Frazier-Anderson, P. N., and Bertrand Jones, T. "Analysis of Love My Children: Rose Butler Browne's Contributions to Culturally Responsive Evaluation." In S. Hood, R. K. Hopson, and H. Frierson (eds.), *Continuing the Journey to Reposition Culture and Cultural Context in Evaluation Theory and Practice* (pp. 73–87). Greenwich, CT: Information Age Publishing, Inc., 2015.

Frazier-Anderson, P., Hood, S., and Hopson, R. K. "Preliminary Consideration of an African American Culturally Responsive Evaluation System." In S. Lapan, M. Quartaroli, and F. Riemer (eds.), *Qualitative Research: An Introduction to Methods and Designs* (pp. 347–372). San Francisco, CA: Jossey-Bass, 2012.

Frierson, H. T., Hood, S., and Hughes, G. B. "Strategies That Address Culturally Responsive Evaluation." In J. Frechtling (ed.), *The 2002 User-Friendly Handbook for Project Evaluation* (pp. 63–73). Arlington, VA: National Science Foundation, 2002.

Frierson, H. T., Hood, S., Hughes, G. B., and Thomas, V. G. "A Guide to Conducting Culturally Responsive Evaluations." In J. Frechtling (ed.), *The 2010 User-Friendly Handbook for Project Evaluation* (pp. 75–96). Arlington, VA: National Science Foundation, 2010.

Gordon, E. W. "Toward an Equitable System of Educational Assessment." *Journal of Negro Education*, 1995, *64*(3), 360–372.

Greene, J. C. "Evaluation, Democracy, and Social Change." In I. F. Shaw, J. C. Greene, and M. M. Mark (eds.), *The SAGE Handbook of Evaluation* (pp. 118–140). Thousand Oaks, CA: Sage, 2006.

Greene, J. C. "Culture and Evaluation from a Transcultural Belvedere." In S. Hood, R. K. Hopson, & H. Frierson (eds.), *Continuing the Journey to Reposition Culture and Cultural Context in Evaluation Theory and Practice* (pp. 91–107). Greenwich, CT: Information Age Publishing, Inc., 2015.

Greene, J. C., and Abma, T. A. (eds.) (2001). *Responsive Evaluation. New Directions for Evaluation*, 2001, *92*.

Greene, J. C., Benjamin, L., and Goodyear, L. (2001). "The Merits of Mixing Methods in Evaluation." *Evaluation*, 2001, *7*(1), 25–44.

Hood, S. "Culturally Responsive Performance-Based Assessment: Conceptual and Psychometric Considerations." *Journal of Negro Education*, 1998a, *67*(3), 187–196.

Hood, S. "Responsive Evaluation Amistad Style: Perspectives of One African American Evaluator." In R. Davis (ed.), *Proceedings of the Stake Symposium on Educational Evaluation* (pp. 101–112). Urbana-Champaign, IL: University of Illinois, 1998b.

Hood, S. "Commentary on Deliberative Democratic Evaluation." In K. Ryan and L. DeStefano (eds.), *Evaluation as a Democratic Process: Promoting Inclusion, Dialogue, and*

Deliberation. New Directions for Evaluation, No. 85, (pp. 77–84). San Francisco, CA: Jossey-Bass, 2000.

Hood, S. "Nobody Knows My Name: In Praise of African American Evaluators Who Were Responsive." In J. C. Greene and T. A. Abma (eds.), *Responsive Evaluation. New Directions for Evaluation,* 2001, *92,* 31–44.

Hood, S. "Evaluation for and by Navajos: A Narrative Case of the Irrelevance of Globalization." In K. E. Ryan and J. B. Cousins (eds.), *The SAGE International Handbook of Educational Evaluation* (pp. 447–463). Thousand Oaks, CA: Sage, 2009.

Hood, S. "How Will We Know It When We See It? A Critical Friend Perspective of the GEDI Program and Its Legacy in Evaluation." In P. Collins and R. K. Hopson (eds.), *Building a New Generation of Culturally Responsive Evaluators: Contributions of the American Evaluation Association's Graduate Education Diversity Internship Program, New Directions for Evaluation,* 2014, *143,* 109–121.

Hood, S., and Hall, M. *Relevance of Culture in Evaluation Institute: Implementing and Empirically Investigating Culturally Responsive Evaluation in Underperforming Schools.* National Science Foundation, Division of Research, Evaluation, and Communications, Directorate for Education and Human Resources (Award #0438482), 2004.

Hood, S., and Hopson, R. K. "Evaluation Roots Reconsidered: Asa Hilliard, a Fallen Hero in the 'Nobody Knows My Name' Project, and African Educational Excellence." *Review of Educational Research September,* 2008, *78*(3), 410–426.

Hopson, R. K. "Reclaiming Knowledge at the Margins: Culturally Responsive Evaluation in the Current Evaluation Moment." In K. Ryan and J. B. Cousins (eds.), *The SAGE International Handbook of Educational Evaluation* (pp. 429–446). Thousand Oaks, CA: Sage, 2009.

Hopson, R. K. "Culturally Responsive Evaluation 101." Workshop presented at the annual meeting of the Aotearoa/New Zealand Evaluation Association (ANZEA), Auckland, New Zealand, July 2013.

Hopson, R. K., and Casillas, W. D. "Culture Responsiveness in Applied Research and Evaluation." Workshop presented at the Claremont Graduate University, Claremont, California, August 2014.

Hopson, R. K., and Hood, S. "An Untold Story in Evaluation Roots: Reid Jackson and His Contributions Toward Culturally Responsive Evaluation at Three-Fourths Century." In S. Hood, R. K. Hopson, and H. T. Frierson (eds.), *The Role of Culture and Cultural Context: A Mandate for Inclusion, the Discovery of Truth, and Understanding in Evaluative Theory and Practice.* Greenwich, CT: Information Age Publishing, Inc., 2005.

Hopson, R. K., and Kirkhart, K. E. "Strengthening Evaluation Through Cultural Relevance and Cultural Competence." Workshop presented at the American Evaluation Association/Centers for Disease Control 2012 Summer Evaluation Institute, Atlanta, Georgia, June 2012.

Hopson, R. K., and Kirkhart, K. E. "Foundations of Culturally Responsive Evaluation (CRE)." Workshop presented at the annual conference of CREA (Center for Culturally Responsive Evaluation and Assessment), Oak Brook, Illinois, September 2014.

Jackson, R. E. "The Development and Present Status of Secondary Education for Negroes in Kentucky." *The Journal of Negro Education,* 1935, *4*(2), 185–191.

Jackson, R. E. "Status of Education of the Negro in Florida, 1929–1934." *Opportunity,* 1936, *14*(11), 336–339.

Jackson, R. E. "Alabama County Training Schools." *School Review,* 1939, *47,* 683–694.

Jackson, R. E. "An Evaluation of Educational Opportunities for the Negro Adolescent in Alabama, I." *Journal of Negro Education*, 1940a, *9*(1), 59–72.

Jackson, R. E. "A Evaluation of Educational Opportunities for the Negro Adolescent in Alabama, II." *Journal of Negro Education*, 1940b, *9*(2), 200–207.

Jay, M., Eatmon, D., and Frierson, H. "Cultural Reflections Stemming from the Evaluation of an Undergraduate Research Program." In S. Hood, R. K. Hopson, and H. T. Frierson (eds.), *The Role of Culture and Cultural Context: A Mandate for Inclusion, the Discovery of Truth, and Understanding in Evaluative Theory and Practice* (pp. 201–216). Greenwich, CT: Information Age Publishing, Inc., 2005.

Johnson, S. T. "The Importance of Culture for Improving Education and Pedagogy. *Journal of Negro Education*, 1998, *67*(3), 181–183.

Johnson, E. C., Kirkhart, K. E., Madison, A. M., Noley, G. B., and Solano-Flores, G. "The Impact of Narrow Views of Scientific Rigor on Evaluation Practices for Underrepresented Groups." In N. L. Smith and P. R. Brandon (eds.), *Fundamental Issues in Evaluation* (pp. 197–218). New York: Guilford, 2008.

King, J. A., Nielsen, J. E., and Colby, J. "Lessons for Culturally Competent Evaluation from the Study of a Multicultural Initiative." In M. Thompson-Robinson, R. Hopson, and S. SenGupta (eds.), *In Search of Cultural Competence in Evaluation: Toward Principles and Practices, New Directions for Evaluation*, 2004, *102*, 67–80.

Kirkhart, K. E. "Seeking Multicultural Validity: A Postcard from the Road." *Evaluation Practice*, 1995, *16*(1), 1–12.

Kirkhart, K. E. "Through a Cultural Lens: Reflections on Validity and Theory in Evaluation." In S. Hood, R. Hopson, and H. Frierson (eds.), *The Role of Culture and Cultural Context: A Mandate for Inclusion, the Discovery of Truth, and Understanding in Evaluative Theory and Practice* (pp. 21–39). Greenwich, CT: Information Age Publishing, Inc., 2005.

Kirkhart, K. E. "Missing the Mark: Rethinking Validity Threats in Evaluation Practice." Paper presented at the 34th Annual Conference of the Eastern Evaluation Research Society, Absecon, New Jersey, May 2011.

Kirkhart, K. E. "Repositioning Validity." Plenary panel presented at the Inaugural Conference of the Center for Culturally Responsive Evaluation and Assessment (CREA), Chicago, Illinois, April 2013a.

Kirkhart, K. E. "Advancing Considerations of Culture and Validity: Honoring the Key Evaluation Checklist." In S. I. Donaldson (ed.), *The Future of Evaluation in Society: A Tribute to Michael Scriven* (pp. 129–159). Greenwich, CT: Information Age Publishing, Inc., 2013b.

Kirkhart, K. E., and Hopson, R. K. "Strengthening Evaluation Through Cultural Relevance and Cultural Competence." Workshop presented at the American Evaluation Association/Centers for Disease Control 2010 Summer Evaluation Institute, Atlanta, Georgia, June 2010.

Ladson-Billings, G. "But That's Just Good Teaching: The Case for Culturally Relevant Pedagogy." *Theory into Practice*, 1995a, *34*(3), 159–165.

Ladson-Billings, G. "Toward a Theory of Culturally Relevant Pedagogy." *American Education al Research Journal*, 1995b, *32*(3), 465–491.

LaFrance, J., and Nichols, R. *Indigenous Evaluation Framework: Telling Our Story in Our Place and Time.* Alexandria, VA: American Indian Higher Education Consortium (AIHEC), 2009.

LaFrance, J., and Nichols, R. "Reframing Evaluation: Defining an Indigenous Evaluation Framework." *The Canadian Journal of Program Evaluation*, 2010, *23*(2), 13–31.

LaFrance, J., Kirkhart, K. E., and Nichols, R. (2015). "Cultural Views of Validity: A Conversation." In S. Hood, R. K. Hopson, and H. Frierson (eds.), *Continuing the Journey to Reposition Culture and Cultural Context in Evaluation Theory and Practice* (pp. 49–72). Greenwich, CT: Information Age Publishing, Inc., 2015.

Lee, C. "How Shall We Sing Our Sacred Song in a Strange Land? The Dilemma of Double-Consciousness and the Complexities of an African-Centered Pedagogy." *Journal of Education*, 1990, *172*(2), 45–61.

Lincoln, Y. S., and Guba, E. G. "But Is It Rigorous? Trustworthiness and Authenticity in Naturalistic Evaluation." *New Directions for Evaluation*, 1986, *30*, 73–84.

Madison, A. M. (ed.). *Minority Issues in Program Evaluation, New Directions for Program Evaluation*, Number 53. San Francisco, CA: Jossey-Bass, 1992.

Manswell Butty, J. L., Reid, M. D., and LaPoint, V. "A Culturally Responsive Evaluation Approach Applied to the Talent Development School-to-Career Intervention Program." In V. G. Thomas and F. I. Stevens (eds.), *Co-Constructing a Contextually Responsive Evaluation Framework: The Talent Development Model of School Reform, New Directions for Evaluation*, 2004, *101*, 37–47.

Mathie, A., and Greene, J. C. "Stakeholder Participation in Evaluation: How Important Is Diversity?" *Evaluation and Program Planning*, 1997, *20*(3), 279–285.

Messick, S. "Validity." In R. L. Linn (ed.), *Educational Measurement* (pp. 13–103). Washington, DC: American Council on Education and National Council on Measurement in Education, 1989.

Messick, S. "The Interplay of Evidence and Consequences in the Validation of Performance Assessments." *Educational Researcher*, 1994, *23*(2), 13–23.

No Child Left Behind Act of 2001, Pub. L. No. 107–110, § 115, Stat. 1425, 2002.

Paipa, K., Cram, F., Kennedy, V., and Pipi, K. "Culturally Responsive Methods for Family Centered Evaluation." In S. Hood, R. K. Hopson, and H. Frierson (eds.), *Continuing the Journey to Reposition Culture and Cultural Context in Evaluation Theory and Practice* (pp. 313–334). Greenwich, CT: Information Age Publishing, Inc., 2015.

Qualls, A. L. "Culturally Responsive Assessment: Development Strategies and Validity Issues." *Journal of Negro Education*, 1998, *67*(3), 296–301.

Ridley, C. R., Tracy, M. L., Pruitt-Stephens, L., Wimsatt, M. K., and Beard, J. "Multicultural Assessment Validity." In L. A. Suzuki and J. G. Ponterotto (eds.), *Handbook of Multicultural Assessment: Clinical, Psychological and Educational Applications* (3rd ed., pp. 22–33). Hoboken, NJ: Wiley, 2008.

Ryan, K. E., Chandler, M., and Samuels, M. "What Should School-Based Evaluation Look Like?" *Studies in Educational Evaluation*, 2007, *33*, 197–212.

Samuels, M., and Ryan, K. E. "Grounding Evaluations in Culture." *American Journal of Evaluation*, 2011, *32*, 83–98.

Scriven, M. *Evaluation Thesaurus* (4th ed.). Thousand Oaks, CA: Sage, 1991.

Scriven, M. Key Evaluation Checklist edition of July 25, 2013. Downloaded from http://michaelscriven.info/images/KEC_7.25.13.pdf, 2013.

Stake, R. E. "Program Evaluation, Particularly Responsive Evaluation." In G. F. Madaus, M. S. Scriven, and D. L. Stufflebeam (eds.), *Evaluation Models: Viewpoints on Education and Human Services Evaluation* (pp. 287–310). Boston, MA: Kluwer-Nijhoff, 1973/1987.

Stake, R. E. *Standards-Based and Responsive Evaluation*. Thousand Oaks, CA: Sage, 2004.

Thomas, V. G. "Building a Contextually Responsive Evaluation Framework: Lessons from Working with Urban School Interventions." In V. G. Thomas and F. I. Stevens (eds.), *Co-Constructing a Contextually Responsive Evaluation Framework: The Talent Development Model of School Reform, New Directions for Evaluation*, 2004, *101*, 3–23.

Yarbrough, D. B., Shulha, L. M., Hopson, R. K., and Caruthers, F. A. *The Program Evaluation Standards: A Guide for Evaluators and Evaluation Users* (3rd ed.). Thousand Oaks, CA: Sage, 2011.

PART TWO

PRACTICAL DATA COLLECTION PROCEDURES

Evaluation design is usually considered the glamorous part of program evaluation. Evaluators love to most appropriately analyze program activities and their measurable outcomes. Equally important, however, is collecting the data once the evaluation design has been selected. Even the best evaluation designs come to naught if accurate data cannot be obtained or if data are not collected in a reliable and valid way.

The Chapters

The next nine chapters discuss approaches to data collection. Some of these approaches are well known, such as use of agency record data and surveys. Others are not as common, such as using trained observer ratings, role playing, and using stories. The chapters in this part are presented in an order that roughly reflects the degrees to which quantitative data and qualitative data are sought, beginning with an emphasis on quantitative data and ending with an emphasis on qualitative data. The chapters cover using (1) agency records, (2) systematic surveys, (3) role playing, (4) trained observer approaches, (5) collection of data in the field, (6) the Internet, (7) semi-structured interviewing, (8) focus groups, and (9) stories. *Most evaluations will need to use more than one and possibly several of these approaches.*

Harry Hatry, in Chapter Thirteen, discusses the collection of data from agency, archive, or administrative records—probably the most common source of information for an evaluation. Most, and possibly all, public program evaluations require data from agency records, if only to obtain counts of the number of customers or cases the program has served. Agency records can pose a considerable challenge to evaluators, however. The field of evaluation is littered with examples of missing and incomplete records, differences in definitions and in data collection procedures for desired data elements, difficulties in gaining access to records, and other problems. The chapter author identifies and discusses such problems and provides a number of suggestions for alleviating them.

Kathryn Newcomer and Timothy Triplett, in Chapter Fourteen, discuss a well-known procedure, undertaking *systematic surveys*, whether surveys of a whole population or surveys of the clients of particular programs. No book on data collection for program evaluation would be complete without examining survey procedures. This chapter discusses many of the key elements needed for quality surveys. Surveys have been used by evaluators for decades. Often they are the key data collection procedure used to evaluate human services programs. Surveys are frequently the only way to obtain statistically reliable data from respondents on ratings of services they have received. Surveys can also be a major way to obtain factual information on changes in behavior and status of clients or customers, especially *after* these individuals have received a service. Surveys provide demographic information on clients or customers, as well as these respondents' perceptions of what needs to be improved in a service and how much the service contributed to any improvements they identified. The targets of surveys might be clients of particular services, households, businesses, or agencies or levels of government that are customers of a service.

Most of the procedures described in this chapter can be applied whether a sample of a population or the full population is surveyed. Surveys are especially attractive when costs can be kept relatively low, such as when mail or e-mail administration is feasible. As Newcomer and Triplett indicate, mail and electronic surveys are becoming more attractive and more competitive with telephone procedures, both because of growing problems in achieving high telephone response rates and the introduction of better mail survey procedures.

Claudia Aranda, Diane Levy, and Sierra Stoney, in Chapter Fifteen, describe how role playing can be used in evaluation, such as providing valid comparison groups. They describe role playing methodology, ways to implement role playing in the field, data analysis involved, and ethical considerations. They offer examples of role playing in evaluation practice and offer guidance on how to use the method effectively.

Barbara Cohn Berman and Verna Vasquez, in Chapter Sixteen, discuss the uses of *trained observer ratings* and procedures for undertaking them. Ratings by trained personnel using *anchored* rating scales can provide data on a variety of physical conditions. These ratings can be used to evaluate changes in such conditions as street cleanliness, street *ride-ability*, park and playground maintenance, housing conditions, the condition of schools and other buildings, and the maintenance quality of child-care and institutional facilities, among others. Ratings before and after specific program actions can be taken to help determine the effectiveness of those actions. Less widely, trained observer ratings have been applied to client functioning, such as in assessing the rehabilitation of persons with physical and mental disabilities.

Demetra Smith Nightingale and Shelli Rossman, in Chapter Seventeen, describe *field data collection* issues and procedures, such as steps and issues in conducting interviews with persons knowledgeable about program implementation, quality, or outcomes. Evaluators use such fieldwork to obtain qualitative and quantitative information on how programs are working. They often seek information on both successes and problems in implementing programs in order to provide feedback to agencies for improving their programs.

A major problem for evaluators is deciding what procedures and what staffing they should use to make information more systematic and therefore more valid and credible. The authors provide numerous suggestions for accomplishing this. They also address many of the difficulties in field studies and provide information on ways to alleviate them. Many federally funded and foundation-sponsored evaluations involve such examinations.

William Adams, in Chapter Eighteen, delves into a topic familiar to us all: the *Internet*. He identifies many uses for Internet-based functions in evaluation, many quite familiar to evaluators and some less likely to be familiar, including literature searches, online polls, and project Web sites. He provides numerous suggestions about particular access points and ways to better use the Internet.

William Adams, in Chapter Nineteen, addresses *semi-structured interviews*. Structured interviews are an important tool for evaluators. However, the details of how to best conduct them have been more in the arena of the survey profession and public opinion pollers than that of evaluators, who most likely contract out for any extensive survey work that primarily involves structured interviews. This chapter deals with person-to-person interviews that primarily involve open-ended questions. Such interviews are very important to field studies and case studies, such as those discussed in Chapters Eight and Seventeen.

Adams addresses the advantages and disadvantages of semi-structured interviews, discusses steps in arranging for them, provides recommendations for preparing the interview guides, and discusses various techniques in interviewing. He briefly addresses the analysis and reporting of the results for the interviews.

Richard Krueger and Mary Anne Casey, in Chapter Twenty, describe the use of *focus groups*, a popular information-gathering procedure. This approach is not intended to collect quantifiable data, because the number of persons involved in each group is intentionally kept quite small. Thus focus group information is not intended to be statistically representative of the full target population.

The authors emphasize that focus groups can be helpful in the design phase of evaluation (such as in designing an intervention or pilot-testing data collection instruments), and can also be a way to obtain richer information during an evaluation than, say, structured surveys can provide. In addition, after data are collected, such groups can assist evaluators in interpreting the data. Focus groups are frequently used in case studies and other fieldwork evaluations to assess how well a program is working. Participants in such instances may be program personnel rather than clients. The chapter provides detailed suggestions for setting up the groups, operating them, and then analyzing and reporting the findings.

In Chapter Twenty-One, the final chapter in Part Two, Richard Krueger addresses a controversial topic, the use of *stories* in evaluation. He stresses the power of reporting stories, but makes no claim that these stories should replace quantitative data. A growing area of thought is that including stories in an evaluation can considerably enhance the evaluation work and make the evaluation findings not only more readable for audiences, but also more likely to be used. While individual stories are typically criticized for being anecdotal, Krueger suggests adopting a systematic approach to storytelling to strengthen their credibility.

Other Data Collection Considerations

This set of chapters does not cover all data collection procedures that evaluators might use. For some public programs, mechanical or electronic recording devices are used to track program outcomes. Examples are the use of various recording instruments to assess air and water quality and noise levels. Some transportation agencies use ride meters to measure the bumpiness of roads.

When the readings from such equipment can be correlated with more end-oriented outcomes, they can be even more effective. For example, in some instances, ride meter readings of road roughness have been correlated with driving comfort and potential car damage, and air and water pollution levels have been correlated with levels of health hazards. Some measuring devices can be expensive, such as those that test water for toxic pollutants and the condition of fish tissue. In such instances the evaluators may need to use smaller samples and test less frequently.

Cost is an important consideration in all data collection procedures. Some of these chapters attempt to identify some of the less costly ways to acquire information. A common cost-reduction scheme in surveys and trained observer procedures is to use sampling and also to use smaller samples (yielding reduced precision levels). Evaluators in all cases should review their precision needs. Calling for more precision than necessary will add to the cost of the evaluation. For example, a 95 percent confidence level might be overkill for many evaluation applications. How often do the decision makers who will use the evaluation findings have such certainty in their decisions? Why not 90 percent, or an even lower level?

Another key issue for data collection is *quality control.* This element is addressed in most of these chapters. It needs to be given explicit attention when data collection is planned. Quality control should be built into the data collection process. This means taking such steps as

- Training thoroughly all data collection personnel
- Checking thoroughly the definitions and data obtained from other sources
- Attempting to triangulate field findings with confirmatory responses from more than one respondent and from multiple sources
- Pretesting data collection procedures before their full use
- Checking questionnaire wording for ambiguity and biases
- Checking sampling plans to ensure coverage of all relevant subgroups

One special way to ensure better data quality is for all members of the evaluation team to visit the program being evaluated, at least at one of its sites, possibly as part of a pretest. This on-site experience can give the evaluators a reality check and enable them to do a better job of planning data collection.

Finally, evaluators will need to make important decisions about the amount of data to be collected. Evaluators may be tempted to seek large amounts of information about a wide range of program and service quality characteristics. At some point, such over-collecting may overload the collection resources and cause significant difficulties in analysis of the data. In their initial planning, evaluators should make sure that each data element they include has a specific purpose and is likely to provide useful evaluative information. Advocates for particular data elements should be required to justify each element's inclusion. Otherwise the data collection efforts may be dissipated by being spread too widely and may produce more quantity than quality in data collection.

CHAPTER THIRTEEN

USING AGENCY RECORDS*

Harry P. Hatry

Traditional sources of data used by evaluators are records kept by either the agency delivering the service being evaluated or by other agencies that have records relevant to the work of the program being evaluated. The term *agency records* (also called *administrative records* or *archival records*), as used in this chapter, includes data formally entered into an agency's record system by a representative of the organization, such as a caseworker, nurse, or teacher. Such information is generally being regularly collected and recorded by an agency, whether or not an evaluation is being conducted. Some examples of the content of agency record data are

- Client characteristics
- Which services are used and how much of each
- Quantity of work done or amount of output
- Response times
- Disposition of work (such as number of clients successfully completing a service)
- Recidivism
- Number and type of complaints
- Number and categories of reported crimes
- Student grades and test scores
- School attendance and number of school dropouts

*Thomas Kingsley, a Senior Fellow at the Urban Institute and director of the National Neighborhood Indicators Partnership (NNIP), provided a number of useful ideas for this chapter.

- Number of reported cases of child abuse
- Number of violations of environmental regulations as reported by inspectors
- Number of water main breaks
- Number of businesses contacted that moved to the jurisdiction
- Clinical records on patients' conditions
- Program costs

Throughout this chapter, the word *client* is typically used as the general term for the subjects of an organization's work, programs, or evaluations. In actual agency records, the term for subjects will, of course, vary. Health programs often use the term *patients*. Many other programs use the term *customers* when referring to their clients. Some programs, such as criminal justice programs, work on what they refer to as *cases*. Other programs may have different terms for the subject of their work; for example, road maintenance programs focus on segments of roadways.

The potential substantial advantage of employing agency records for evaluations is that these data are already available. This eliminates the need for new (and perhaps expensive) data collection efforts. A primary limitation to the use of agency records as a source of evaluation information is that they may contain at best only a partial amount of the data needed to measure important outcomes, such as what happened to clients after a service ended for those clients. Thus, procedures described in the remaining chapters in Part Two will often be needed as well.

It is tempting to evaluators to accept agency records at face value and not look critically at the information they contain. But "programs differ widely in the quality and extensiveness of their records and in the sophistication involved in storing and maintaining them" (Rossi, Freeman, and Lipsey, 1998, p. 211). Thus, "[a]rchival data are never precisely what one wants or expects. Given this, the investigator is challenged to do what is possible given time and resources, in shaping the data according to needs" (Elder, Pavalko, and Clipp, 1993, p. 11). Such statements, while old, still hold water.

This chapter discusses issues and problems that can arise with use of agency records and suggests ways to alleviate these difficulties.

The published literature contains little direct discussion of the issues and problems in collecting data from agency records, except for the issue of imputing estimates for missing data (as discussed later). A very old source relevant to agency records, *Unobtrusive Measures*, by Webb, Campbell, Schwartz, and Sechrest (1966), is also one of the most useful on this subject. Some texts on research methods, such as Nachmias and Nachmias (2007), Rossi, Freeman, and Lipsey (1998), and Singleton and Straits (2010), at least briefly address this data source. Sometimes a government agency, as part of written descriptions of its procedures, briefly describes data collection problems and their alleviation, such as the Corporation for National and Community Service (2006) and the U.S. Department of Education (2007); occasionally, evaluation journal articles will be relevant as well. These latter materials primarily concern issues relating to the services of particular agency programs.

The use of administrative records in program evaluation has become considerably greater with the interest (stimulated by the United States Office of Management and Budget) in "rapid-response evaluation," such as noted in Coalition for Evidence-Based Policy (2012).

The considerable continuing improvement in information technology has meant that more and more data are being included in agency records. Evaluators will have increasingly large amounts of agency record information from which to draw when needed. In addition, recent trends have been to evaluate cross-cutting programs involving records from multiple programs and agencies.

Potential Problems and Their Alleviation

Table 13.1 lists a number of problems that evaluators are likely to face when using agency record information. Each problem is discussed in this section.

1. Missing or Incomplete Data

In many, if not most, evaluations, information on some clients or other work elements will be missing or incomplete. These gaps will affect the overall accuracy of the information. This applies whether the evaluators are attempting to obtain data on all clients (or all work elements) or are drawing samples from the available records. If the proportion of missing or incomplete cases is substantial for a category of cases, this will be a major evaluation concern.

Once a set of data is known to be missing, it is important to determine whether the missing data are random or whether they vary in a systematic fashion and also the extent to which the problem exists. For example, agencies may not have data files from a given time period or they may be missing complete client records from a subcontractor. Identifying the systematic nature of missing data is the first step in recapturing, or adjusting for, what was lost. In some rare cases, the missing data may be found to be random and can then be ignored.

TABLE 13.1. POTENTIAL PROBLEMS IN DATA OBTAINED FROM AGENCY RECORDS AND POSSIBLE WAYS TO ALLEVIATE THEM.

Problem	Possible Ways to Alleviate the Problem
1. Missing or incomplete data	Go back to the records and related data sources (interview program staff, for example) to fill in as many gaps as possible. Exclude missing data or provide a best estimate of the missing values. Determine whether part or all of the evaluation needs to be modified or terminated.
2. Concerns with data accuracy	Check reasonableness of the data. Have someone recheck all or a sample of the data. Have a second person enter the same data and then compare. Train or retrain the persons entering the data. Periodically audit at least a sample of the entered data against the data source.
3. Data available only in overly aggregated form	Where feasible, go back into the records to reconstruct the needed data. Undertake new, original data collection. Drop the unavailable disaggregations from the evaluation.
4. Unknown, different, or changing definitions of data elements	Make feasible adjustments to make data more comparable; define in detail each data element. Focus on percentage changes rather than absolute values. Drop analysis of such data elements when the problem is insurmountable.
5. Data need to be linked across programs and agencies	Be sure that the outcome data apply to the particular clients or other work elements covered by the evaluation. Track the clients or other work elements between agencies and offices. Look for variations in spellings, aliases, and so on.
6. Confidentiality and privacy considerations	Secure needed permissions from persons or organizations about whom individual data are needed. Avoid recording client names. Instead use unique code identifiers. Secure any lists that link unique codes to client names. Destroy these lists after the evaluation requirements are met. Obtain data without identifiers from agency employees (limiting subsequent analyses).

The evaluator should first determine whether it will be feasible to obtain the missing or incomplete information. This may not be possible, such as when data are sought for periods of time that are far in the past. In such cases, evaluators need to determine whether the number of missing cases will prevent them from answering questions important to the evaluation. Following this determination, the evaluators might even have to terminate the entire evaluation.

Missing data have caused substantial evaluation problems; for example, a number of state efforts to evaluate economic development programs have encountered this issue. In some programs, lists of businesses assisted by the programs were not carefully recorded. The evaluators needed the names of the businesses and their addresses in order to obtain business ratings of the services they had received. The evaluators had to ask program staff to put client lists together as well as they could, recognizing that these lists would be incomplete to an unknown extent.

The problem was even worse in a national evaluation of local programs that brought social services into schools to help reduce school dropouts. Many of the programs sampled did not have lists of clients served, data on the duration of their programs, or the extent of client participation in various program activities. The evaluators had to reconstruct this information from case files and staff memories.

Evaluators can handle missing information in a number of ways. Here are some key examples:

- Leave the data out of tabulations. To calculate percentages or averages, the evaluators would not count the missing data in the numerators or denominators. Suppose the evaluators are calculating the proportion of events completed on time. They know there were one hundred cases, but the records show that sixty were completed on time, twenty-five were not, and timeliness for the other fifteen cases could not be determined. The percentage of timely completion would be 60/85, or 71 percent.
- Include the number of missing data items in the denominator of the percentages so that the denominator represents the total number of cases, even though the case records on some may be missing or incomplete. Continuing the previous example, this would give a percentage of 60/100, or 60 percent. The second calculation is the more conservative figure for the on-time percentage.
- Impute values to the missing data elements. These values would be estimates that the evaluators believe represent the population of interest. For example, the evaluators might use the mean of the available observations. Thus, if data on earnings are missing for members of a particular ethnic group, the average earnings of those in the ethnic group for whom earning figures are available might be substituted for the missing data. The calculations of the overall average earnings for all ethnic groups would then include these estimates of earnings for the missing clients. In some instances, evaluators use more sophisticated procedures involving equations that attempt

to predict the values of the missing data based on a number of variables for which data are available. Each of these imputation methods, however, can result in biased estimates. (For technical discussions of these options, see, for example, Allison, 2001, and Little and Rubin, 2002.) Considerable detailed information can be obtained from the Internet, such as by searching on "data imputation methods."

• Delete the incomplete cases, but assign a weight to each complete case to compensate for the deleted cases. For example, say that other information on the population of interest indicates that males comprise 49 percent of the population, but the sample includes only 40 percent. Furthermore, suppose that this sample of male respondents gives a 25 percent favorable response to a question but that the sample of female respondents gives a 35 percent favorable response. To calculate the overall percentage of the population who have a favorable response, a simple approach is to weight the 25 percent by 0.49 and the 35 percent by 0.51. In this example, the modified weighting results in an estimate that 30 percent of the overall population think favorably, rather than the 31 percent estimated without the weighting. This is not much of a difference. Sometimes, sophisticated weighting techniques produce little change, as in this example.

Which of these options should be used will depend on the specific evaluation situation. Probably the best option is to analyze the data using all of these approaches to determine whether important findings are sensitive to the problem.

In any instances where data are missing, the evaluators need to identify those gaps for users of the evaluation findings, identify what statistical adjustments were made, and provide their best judgments as to the effects on the findings.

2. Concerns with Data Accuracy

A basic issue is the accuracy of the raw data used in subsequent calculations. Careless entry or mistakes by untrained staff are examples of the problems that can occur. Evaluations involving housing property data, for example, have found problems in incorrect classification of properties. Innumerable other such situations can arise. Errors can occur both:

• At the time of initial entry—whether intentional or unintentional
• At the time when the data are processed, such as when entered into the computer for processing—whether this is done manually or electronically

These two processes are increasingly being combined using various electronic means. For example, an inspector might enter a condition rating into a handheld calculator preprogrammed to automatically enter the rating into a data analysis program.

A major trend in evaluations is the effort to link data sets across agency programs and across agencies. This provides additional hurdles for evaluators, such as the need to reduce the possibility of attaching the record for one person to the wrong person.

Entry errors can be alleviated, where resources permit, by asking a second person to check the entries or at least check a random sample of entries. Entry errors can also be reduced by providing adequate training of the persons responsible for data entry and conducting periodic retraining, especially if error rates are increasing.

After the data have been entered into the computer, a variety of software has been emerging that automatically checks for unusual characteristics of the entered data. Such characteristics include:

- Data values outside an acceptable range for that data element
- Duplicate entries
- An unusual change in values from data for previous reporting periods
- Inconsistencies with other data in the record system

When data abnormalities appear, such as when data are kicked out by the data-checking software, someone has to sort out and correct, or at least alleviate, the problem. The options discussed earlier for missing or incomplete data apply here as well.

Finally, the evaluators should identify any significant effects on the findings from data accuracy problems that could not be corrected.

3. Data Available Only in Overly Aggregated Form

Sometimes the data are available only in aggregated form. This is a variation of the first problem. In most instances, evaluators are likely to want to obtain more detailed information. For example, they might want outcome data broken out by selected client demographic characteristics in order to calculate the outcomes for various disadvantaged populations. Or they might want to assess not only overall water quality but also water quality for various segments of a body of water using agency record data on various water quality characteristics (such as dissolved oxygen, clarity, and chemical content). The data available in the records might not provide sufficient past data on each segment of interest.

There may be little that evaluators can do in such instances. If time and resources permit, the evaluators can collect the new data. This will be possible if the evaluation is just beginning and the evaluator can build this data collection into the program's procedures. However, it is likely to be difficult or impossible to reconstruct past data in the detail desired.

This problem can be worse when evaluators are attempting to use comparison groups and these groups are served by another agency or even another government jurisdiction that did not collect or record the information in the detail needed. In such cases, the evaluators will likely have to forgo that break-out detail in their comparisons.

In some situations, the evaluators may be able to go back into the records to obtain the needed data. For example, public agencies often track complaints they receive but do not tabulate complaints or disaggregate them into categories, such as type of complaint, location of complaint, or other characteristics that may be important to the evaluators. In this case, the evaluators may be able to delve into individual case records and obtain the desired level of detail. If, however, the agency has changed its record-keeping procedures, such as switching from hard copy to digital records, or has used multiple generations of computer data management software, this may severely restrict an evaluator's ability to recapture the past data for comparisons over time.

Before the design phase of an evaluation is completed, the evaluators should check the availability of data needed for their proposed evaluation plan and make any needed adjustments. It will be a fortunate evaluation team that is able to obtain record data on all the disaggregations it would like to make.

The evaluators need to identify any significant adjustments to the data and any disaggregation gaps in the reported findings.

4. Unknown, Different, or Changing Definitions of Data Elements

Evaluators should ascertain not only the availability of data but also how the major data elements they are collecting are defined and collected. This information is essential if they are to assess the accuracy and comparability of the data used. It is particularly important when the evaluators obtain information from different sites or different agencies or collect data from several years during which data collection procedures might have changed.

Evaluators starting their work at the time that the data are just beginning to be collected (such as in randomized controlled trials) should, to the extent feasible, standardize new data collection, that is, try to maximize the likelihood that each type of data collected at all locations, by different people, and at different time periods, will be defined the same way across all these differences. Evaluators doing evaluations using already collected data need to assess the comparability of the data collected in different locations at different times and by different persons.

A common problem has been how to define *participant*, a unit often used as the denominator when calculating success rates. The question of whether such persons as those who sign up for a program but never show up or who just show up for one or two of a number of scheduled sessions are participants or not needs to be addressed.

Another classic example of the use of different definitions by different public agencies involves school dropout rates. Comparisons of school dropout data across school districts and states can be fraught with pitfalls. Dropout rates have been calculated in many different ways by school systems. For example, the rates may represent the ratio of the number of students graduating in a given year divided by the number of students entering at the beginning of that year. Or they may represent the number graduating in a given year divided by the number who entered as freshmen four years earlier. Agencies may or may not take into account the number of students who transferred into or out of the school system. Agencies may count GED (general educational development) students in different ways or handle differently the number of students who graduate earlier or later than the rest of their class. The U.S. Department of Education in its reporting of 2012 rates used a "status dropout rate," defined as the percentage of sixteen- through twenty-four-year-olds who are not enrolled in school and have not earned a high school credential (either a diploma or an equivalency credential such as a General Educational Development [GED] certificate).

Handling differences in definitions may be a matter of judgment as to how the rate should be defined or it may involve identifying logic errors. In any case, reasonable consistency and comparability across years and across school systems are needed when comparisons are being made. Do library usage counts include electronic accessing of library information sources from outside the library? Do data on program expenditure amounts include only direct expenditures? Or do they include overhead estimates as well? Do they or include funds obtained from other levels of government or not? Such questions will typically arise in evaluation work.

A problem sometimes found in human service programs is duplicated counts. Some records of clients may count a person each time he or she returns for service. In situations in which the evaluators need unduplicated counts, this may require the evaluators to reconstruct counts from the data files or to make estimates of the amount of duplication, perhaps based on sampling the records. Often, agencies keep track of the number of participations. However, it is harder, and has been much less done, to track how many *different* persons used a service during particular periods of time.

Another common problem is that of data that cover different periods of time. The evaluators might want to compare data across cities or states, but find that some report the data by calendar years and others by fiscal years, and those that report by fiscal years have different fiscal years.

Yet another typical situation arises with the definitions of cost elements. Currently, generally accepted standards of what to include in cost comparisons do not exist.

The following steps should help evaluators avoid, or at least alleviate, data definition problems:

- Identify the definitions and data collection procedures that have been used by the program and check for significant changes over the time period included in the evaluation. Evaluators should identify likely problems at the start of the evaluation.

- Where differences in definitions or data collection procedures are found over time or among comparison groups, make appropriate adjustments. For example, exclude data elements for which data are not available in compatible definitions across comparison groups, or examine the original information and make appropriate adjustments.

- Focus on *percentage changes* rather than absolute values. Compare the percentage changes from one year to the next for each comparison group (for example, in the reported crime rates of various cities), even though the data that are being compared are based on somewhat different definitions and data collection procedures. This adjustment may provide roughly accurate comparisons as long as the definitions and procedures for each individual agency or office remained stable over the time period covered by the evaluation.

- Keep a record of data definition problems that have not been fully solved, and estimate (and report) the collective impacts of these problems on the final evaluation findings.

A related problem sometimes arises, especially in human service programs. Evaluators may want to calculate the number and percentage of clients who achieved successful outcomes twelve months after the clients entered the program. Evaluators must be sure that the results data are for the clients they are tracking. The problem is perhaps best explained by an example. A state's department of human services calculates the number of successful case closures in each year and the number of cases served in the same year. It might divide one by the other to estimate the percentage of cases successfully closed. But the numerator and the denominator represent different cases. Instead, the system needs to track cohorts of incoming clients—clients entering in a given year—over a specific duration of time to identify the percentage of clients in a cohort who achieved specific outcomes by the end of the specified time period. (The outcome indicator might be, for example, the "percentage of children placed for adoption in the previous year who were adopted within twelve months after being placed.") If the evaluators find that an agency's reports provide such misleading information, they will likely have to examine individual records to obtain the more valid information.

A similar problem, particularly for human service programs such as social and mental health services, is the determination of when the follow-ups should be made to determine program outcomes. If samples of clients are drawn without consideration of how long a period has elapsed since service began or ended, and if outcomes are not all measured for the same time interval, the measurements will yield data on clients whose length of program participation will likely have varied widely. To avoid such inconsistencies, evaluators generally should use a standard time period for obtaining outcome indicators, such as "the percentage of clients starting service who twelve months later showed significantly improved functioning." (For such indicators, the evaluators will need precise definitions of "significantly improved functioning" and of the time envelope for "twelve months later" and apply these definitions to all clients being tracked.)

5. Data Need to Be Linked Across Programs and Agencies

Increasingly, evaluators are being asked to evaluate programs whose outcomes include important outcomes that are tracked in other programs or agencies. The evaluators then need record data from different agencies or different offices within the same agency. These activities require linking data from the program (such as demographic and activity data, for example, type and amount of the program's services provided to particular clients) to outcome information held by other programs or agencies.

These other offices and agencies may use different identifiers, or they may track clients (or other work elements, such as water quality or road condition) in different ways. Sometimes, they do not use the same name for the same element. They may use Social Security numbers or other special client identifiers rather than names. Different offices may use variations of clients' names. Some offices may identify clients by household and others by individual household member. All of these circumstances present problems to evaluation teams. (These other programs and agencies may also resist providing their data because of privacy or confidentiality issues. That problem is discussed later.)

The evaluators need to identify and address such problems. Some may require special data collection efforts, close examination of names to identify name variations (for example, considering multiple identifiers such as age, addresses, and Social Security numbers to verify identities), and perhaps special computer runs to identify and link together the relevant data on the units of analysis for the evaluation.

For example, for a variety of employment programs, evaluators are seeking employment and earnings information from state unemployment insurance (UI) offices. Usually, such information as Social Security numbers and names is used to identify the employment and earnings history of the employment program clients. Assuming the evaluators can obtain access to those files, a number of other problems typically arise:

- The data may not become available for many months, perhaps too late for the evaluation.
- Some individuals may not have been in employment covered by the UI database.
- Different names or Social Security numbers may exist for some clients, perhaps due to data entry errors.
- The clients may have worked in other states, making it much more difficult to access the data.

All of these difficulties can lead to a lower than desirable percentage of clients matched with the UI database. If these problems become too great, the evaluators may need to use surveys of clients (see Chapter Fourteen) to obtain the needed information.

6. Confidentiality and Privacy Considerations

Evaluators can face major obstacles in obtaining information from agency records because the data are confidential. This problem occurs often when human service, education, and criminal justice programs are being evaluated. It can also arise when evaluators seek any type of sensitive information, such as a person's income.

Evaluators must protect the privacy of anyone about whom they obtain data, whether from records, surveys, or interviews. Many evaluations will be subject to formal requirements to protect the rights and welfare of human subjects, such as those of the Health Insurance Portability and Accountability Act (HIPAA), the Family Educational Rights and Privacy Act (FERPA), and of institutional review boards (IRBs). (Current federal agency rules and regulations are to be found in the *Code of Federal Regulations*; see U.S. Department of Health and Human Services, 2009). Most research and evaluation organizations, such as universities doing research or evaluations involving human subjects, have an IRB. These boards review evaluation plans prior to implementation to ensure that, among other things, the evaluation will protect any private information obtained. This protection can be provided in a variety of ways:

- Do not record a person's name, Social Security number, or other identifiers obtained from the records. In some instances, it may be sufficient for the agency to provide the evaluators with a unique identifier rather than names or other identifiers. However, if the evaluators need to link this agency data with data from other sources, this procedure will not work.
- Assign a number to each client, and carefully secure the list that cross-references the numbers to clients' names. This procedure will also be useful should the evaluator need to return to the agency records to recapture or verify lost or anomalous data after a data check. Such lists should usually be destroyed after all the evaluation needs are met.
- Report only grouped data. Do not include in evaluation reports any information that might enable a reader to link a particular finding to an individual client. Sometimes, evaluators may want to cite a particular case. If so, no identifying information should be provided without obtaining permission, preferably in writing, from those able to give such permission. A classic example of this problem occurred in an evaluation of state export activities in the Northeast. Because the chemical export market in Delaware was dominated by the DuPont Corporation, the U.S. Census Bureau would not release information on the amount of chemical exports in the state. If this information were made public, business competitors could readily identify DuPont's level of activity. The evaluators therefore had to forgo using chemical export data on Delaware. Fortunately, such situations are rare.
- In advance of any data exchange, provide the agency with a detailed memo outlining the procedures that will be used to protect the privacy of individual clients. This demonstrates good faith on the part of the evaluator, and it reassures agency staff that the data are being handled in a responsible and professional manner.

Obtaining permission to access individual records can be a major problem for evaluators. This problem is even worse when the organization sponsoring the evaluation activity is different from the organization that has the needed data. For example, evaluators of a national school dropout prevention program needed permission from local program staff, administrators of the school systems that had implemented the program, and the parents of sampled students to review agency record information (such as grades, test scores, attendance records, and incidence of disciplinary action) on individual program participants. Examples of similar problems have occurred in evaluations seeking to access state unemployment insurance records or federal Social Security records. Securing such permissions can be quite time-consuming and expensive. This is especially so when consent agreements have to be obtained from each individual, as in cases in which evaluators need to obtain information on individual students or to access Social Security records (Olson, 1999).

When the evaluators are employees of the agency whose program is being evaluated and the needed data come from the agency's own records, obtaining permission is not likely to be a problem. (However, protection of the data and ensuring individuals' privacy remains an important concern for the evaluators.)

If evaluators are not able to obtain data on individual clients because of privacy concerns, the evaluators can, as a fallback option, request outcome data for groups of clients, not outcome information on individual clients. Such protected access can break an impasse, especially if the agency can be paid for the time involved in providing the needed data. Such data, however, cannot be linked to other information on those clients. The evaluators would only have data on how many clients had particular outcome levels.

Sometimes, evaluators are concerned with measuring the impact of a program in a particular small location, such as a neighborhood. Individual identifiers such as a client's address might be desired for the evaluation. However, such spatial data might compromise the confidentiality of individual households. If evaluators are unable to obtain spatial data at the address level, they can ask that the address information on the individual record be replaced with a code representing a larger area, such as a census tract or county. Recoding individual addresses at a somewhat larger jurisdictional area preserves the confidentiality of the individual record, but still provides the evaluator with a spatial indicator for the evaluation.

If an agency contracts with another organization to deliver the service being evaluated, the contractor may resist access to its records on individual clients. In such situations, the evaluators should attempt to obtain voluntary compliance by working with the contractor. Organizations that anticipate such evaluations of services provided by contractors might state in the contract that the contractor must provide particular outcome information.

Data Quality Control Processes

Data errors can occur at any point in record keeping. To help maintain data quality, evaluators should consider the data checks for reasonableness and the staff training set out in the following sections.

Data Checks for Reasonableness

As noted earlier, the widespread use of computers and the availability of inexpensive software have greatly simplified the process of checking data for certain types of errors. Such procedures are particularly important when many people are engaged in data collection or data entry and many pieces of data are involved. Information that comes to the evaluators in the form of computer tapes can have many inaccuracies, such as missing, inaccurate, or contradictory data due to either entry errors or errors in the original data collection. Evaluators will generally need to clean the data—that is, check them for reasonableness—before making computations, whether the data checks are managed by computer or done manually. Such checks could include the following:

- Identify ranges of possible values for each data element, and check to see whether any of the data fall outside those ranges. For example, an entry of 120 for a person's age would be flagged, either manually or by computer. Also, where applicable, make sure the computer or manual data processors can distinguish between such entries as the number zero, "not applicable," and "don't know."
- Check consistency across data elements. With computers, elaborate checks can be made. For example, persons above certain ages are not normally employed in full-time positions. A computer could readily check for such problems. In an examination of drug-testing programs, evaluators found clients in the database who had been given the same identification number and birthday but were of different races or sexes. The evaluators went back to the original data source to correct what they found to be data entry errors.
- Look for missing data, flagging these instances so that decisions can be made about how to deal with them.

Staffing Considerations

Evaluators, whether undertaking in-depth program evaluations or helping agencies to develop ongoing performance measurement systems, should ensure that staff collecting the data are given sufficient instruction and training about what to look for. If different people collect information on the same elements, they should be trained to collect comparable data and identify differences that occur. They should be instructed to bring problems to the attention of the evaluation team for decisions on how to handle differences in data definitions.

One approach to alleviating data collection problems is to have data collectors specialize. For example, one person can be assigned responsibility for gathering specific data elements from agency records at all sites. This option, however, will not always be feasible.

Other Suggestions for Obtaining Data from Agency Records

The quality of data can be enhanced by actions taken prior to, during, and after the initial information has been obtained from the fieldwork. The following sections offer suggestions for data quality assurance steps in each of these three phases:

Before Field Data Collection Begins

- Become acquainted with the agency staff who originally collected the data. When evaluators are seeking data from people they do not know, making these individuals' acquaintance can be very helpful in gaining assistance and information throughout the data-gathering effort. In small agencies, typically only a few people have access to the information needed for the evaluation. These persons tend to be overburdened with multiple responsibilities. If the evaluator is able to describe the potential usefulness of the efforts, so that an investment of time will be useful to people in these positions, data requests are likely to meet less resistance.
- Try to deal directly with those who are most familiar with the data records. If evaluators need access to agency records, they should learn how the files are organized. They should ask those familiar with the records to identify possible problems, such as changes in definitions that have occurred over time, problems in obtaining the needed data, and likely reliability and validity problems. This effort gives evaluators a

sense of whether their data plans are reasonable, helps them anticipate problems, and helps them assess what information they can most likely obtain.

- When asking an agency to provide data rather than requesting access to agency files, make the task as easy as possible for the agency staff by following such steps as these:

  Give the agency as much advance notice as possible.

  Put the request in writing, and provide clear, full descriptions of the data needed.

  Explain to the agency people why the data are needed, but be flexible. The agency staff may be aware of problems with specific data items and be able to suggest suitable alternatives.

- Request samples of the data formats and definitions before going into the field in order to gain a better perspective on what data are available.

- In some cases, it may be necessary and appropriate to compensate the agency for the extra time and effort required to generate the requested information. This might occur, for example, if the information in the format and detail that the evaluators want requires major new computer runs on the agency's databases, or the evaluators cannot gain direct access to data files on individuals but are willing to use data without individual identifiers if agency employees are willing to transcribe the data from the records.

In the Field

- Whether collecting completed agency reports or extracting data from agency files, talk, if feasible, with the persons who provided the data and know something of its content. Ask about data definitions, their limitations, and especially any problems in how the data have been obtained. Even if the evaluators believe they have obtained such information before the start of field data collection, they should check again while in the field.

- Learn the form and detail in which the data are available. Data collectors will need to decide whether to forgo some of the information they wanted, try to obtain data not currently in the desired form or detail, or accept the less-than-ideal data situation.

- For each item of data collected, identify the periods of time covered by that item. Frequently, items of data apply to different time periods, requiring evaluators to make adjustments—or at least to identify the discrepancies in their reports. For example, data for some elements may refer to calendar years, data for others to fiscal years, and data for yet others to school years.

- Check to make sure that the data obtained from the agency are complete for the time period. If, for example, records of individuals who have dropped out of a given program are included in one data file but omitted from another, a simple comparison of outcomes related to the given program would likely be invalid.

- For data elements intended to cover specific geographical areas, identify what areas apply to each data element. Some outcome data, for example, might be reported by organizational unit coverage (such as police precincts, fire districts, regional districts, and offices). Other outcome data might be reported by census tracts or by neighborhood. This diversity may or may not present problems for the evaluation. Also, the geographical boundaries may have changed over the time period covered by the evaluation. Evaluators need to know the extent of such problems so they can make decisions on ways to make adjustments—or at least report them.

After Initial Data Have Been Obtained

- Determine, for each data element, how missing or incomplete data should be handled. Decisions to drop a certain element or case or to make a specific adjustment should be reached, when possible, prior to data analysis.
- Check for illogical, inconsistent data. Where appropriate, ask the data source for the correct data.
- Send data back to originators for verification—in situations when the originators are likely to be able and willing to make such verification.
- Thank agency sources for their assistance. Let them know that their help has been valuable and appreciated.
- Document and provide appropriate caveats in the evaluation report. The evaluators should provide their best judgments on the effects of these data problems on the findings.

Conclusion

Agency records will likely be a major source of important data for many, if not most, evaluations. At the very least, evaluators are likely to need to identify from records the amount of work that is the subject of the evaluation (for example, the number of clients or work elements). Inevitably, evaluators will find less than perfect data from agency records. Whether these data come from the agency in which the program is located, another agency, a contractor, or another jurisdiction, the evaluators need to ensure that they know the definitions and content of the various data elements being collected. The evaluators will need to ascertain that the data they use are sufficiently comparable for them to compare different groups or the same group across time.

Evaluators should be aware that obtaining data from agency records will present unexpected difficulties. The challenge is to make needed adjustments that do not compromise the overall quality of the evaluation.

References

Allison, P. D. *Missing Data.* Thousand Oaks, CA: Sage, 2001.

Coalition for Evidence-Based Policy. "Rigorous Program Evaluation on a Budget: How Low-Cost Randomized Controlled Trials Are Possibly in Many Areas of Social Policy. Washington, DC: Author, March 2012.

Corporation for National and Community Service. "AmeriCorps Program Applicant Performance Measurement Toolkit." [www.projectstar.organization]. August 23, 2006.

Elder, G. H., Jr., Pavalko, E. K., and Clipp, E. C. *Working with Archival Data: Studying Lives.* Thousand Oaks, CA: Sage, 1993.

Little, R.J.A., and Rubin, D. B. *Statistical Analysis with Missing Data* (2nd ed.). Hoboken, NJ: Wiley, 2002.

Nachmias, C., and Nachmias, D. *Research Methods in the Social Sciences* (7th ed.). New York: Worth, 2007.

Olson, J. A. *Linkages with Data from Social Security Administrative Records in the Health and Retirement Study.* Washington, DC: Social Security Administration, August 1999.

Rossi, P. H., Freeman, H. E., and Lipsey, M. W. *Evaluation: A Systematic Approach* (6th ed.). Thousand Oaks, CA: Sage, 1998.

Singleton, R., Jr., and Straits, B. C. *Approaches to Social Research* (5th ed.). New York: Oxford University Press, 2010.

U.S. Department of Education, Division of Adult Education and Literacy. *Measures and Methods for the National Reporting System for Adult Education—Implementation Guidelines.* Washington, DC: U.S. Government Printing Office, June 2007.

U.S. Department of Health and Human Services. "Protection of Human Subjects." *Code of Federal Regulations*, 45 (January 15, 2009), part 46.111(a)(7).

Webb, E., Campbell, D. T., Schwartz, R. D., and Sechrest, L. *Unobtrusive Measures: Nonreactive Research in the Social Sciences.* Skokie, IL: Rand McNally, 1966.

CHAPTER FOURTEEN

USING SURVEYS

Kathryn E. Newcomer, Timothy Triplett

L istening to citizens, program beneficiaries, public and nonprofit program managers and employees, elected and appointed officials, relevant substantive experts, and other stakeholders is frequently necessary to evaluate program delivery and results, whether for ad hoc evaluations or for ongoing monitoring of service. Reaching the appropriate respondents to learn about their experiences and measure their attitudes and opinions can be challenging. Capturing information reliably and efficiently through surveying is rewarding.

Surveying a representative and sufficiently large number of target respondents has been affected both positively and negatively by recent advances in technology and survey research methods. Advances in telecommunications technology have changed telephone use patterns in ways that directly affect surveying. Answering machines and caller ID are ubiquitous in homes and in offices and present a new hurdle for telephone surveying. And the increased use of cell phones, with a related decline in the importance of residential phones, presents another potential obstacle to reaching respondents. This has contributed in many instances to more reliance on mailed questionnaires, perhaps in combination with other modes of administration. Moreover, much surveying can now be done through the web (as described in Chapter Eighteen).

The availability of the Internet has provided new means of reaching respondents. Surveys increasingly are being administered by e-mail. With rising Internet literacy rates, respondents can also be asked to traverse the Internet to websites that present surveys in graphically attractive and enticing formats.

Advances in computer technology also have provided streamlined and cost-efficient means for inputting data collected from respondents in person or by phone and web directly into computers to facilitate analysis. Handheld computers and computer-assisted telephone surveying methodologies have reduced survey costs while adding greater flexibility in designing survey instruments.

New technologies such as smartphones and other handheld mobile devices and social media platforms, are changing ways in which people both access and share information about opinions, attitudes, and behaviors. Survey practitioners are increasingly looking at adopting new data collection tools to take advantage of the increasing numbers of people who use smart phones or connect through online social media either as a way of augmenting traditional data collection or for some populations as a completely alternative mode of collecting survey information.

Surveying the public for commercial purposes has increased as the technological advances have reduced costs. The result is a much more skeptical public that is reluctant to answer questions by any survey mode. Americans have tired of marketers' interrupting their leisure time, and they share concerns about the invasion of their privacy. The technological advances that have made it faster and cheaper to obtain data from the public have raised levels of cynicism among the public about surveying. Concern with response rates, or the proportion of those surveyed who responded, plagues evaluators. Creativity in boosting response rates and in examining limitations introduced by rates lower than desired is more essential than ever before.

Survey research methodologies have improved over the past two decades, bolstered by both technological advances and learning through expanded experience. The number of survey research firms has increased dramatically to meet increased demands from both private and public sector clients. Levi Strauss, General Motors, and Victoria's Secret rely on survey data, as do the U.S. Census, Internal Revenue Service, and the United Way. Surveying has become a growth industry. There are now many options for surveying support available to private, public, and nonprofit organizations.

In addition, survey researchers have become more skilled in their craft. Survey research has become a discipline whose practitioners are more knowledgeable and skilled in statistical and technological methods than ever before. Options for survey modes and sampling strategies have increased along with choices for analysis and reporting.

This chapter clarifies the options available and provides practical guidance for program managers, evaluators, and others who choose to survey relevant target populations to help them learn about program performance and results.

Planning the Survey

Before you can begin designing survey instruments, developing sampling plans, and deciding on data collection strategies, you need to establish evaluation questions.

Establish Evaluation Questions

A survey design matrix is especially useful in planning a survey. It arrays the design choices, such as data collection mode, sampling, and questions, that are made to address your survey objectives. Table 14.1 lists the types of categories of design choices that may be made in a design matrix and also lists criteria for making each set of choices. Exhibit 14.1 provides a sample design matrix to illustrate how these categories and criteria may be used in planning a specific survey. When completed, a design matrix summarizes virtually all of the design decisions in a succinct format that facilitates communication among and between policy or program staff and evaluators. In order to design a survey, define one or more evaluation questions in terms of your specific information needs or issues to be addressed. Formulating specific evaluation questions will help you determine whom you need to interview, help you write good survey questions, and provide a solid foundation for presenting the results. The evaluation questions should be clear and understandable and produce useful information. In addition, the questions should be objective, neutrally stated, and specific in terms of time frame and unit of analysis (for example, persons, classrooms, or larger entities).

Determine Whether a Survey Is Necessary and Feasible

Once you have established evaluation questions, you should decide, first, whether a survey is necessary, and second, whether surveys are within your time and budget constraints and will address your evaluation objectives. A survey may not be necessary if the answers to your evaluation questions can be obtained from information that has already been collected. For example, college students often complain about being asked to complete a survey that consists of questions that they already had to answer when they registered for classes. An important part of the planning stage is searching for and reviewing surveys and other information that address issues related to your objectives. You probably will not find the precise information you need to answer your evaluation questions, but any similar surveys you find will be extremely helpful

TABLE 14.1. CATEGORIES AND CRITERIA FOR A SURVEY DESIGN MATRIX.

Evaluation Questions	Information Source	Sampling	Data Collection	Survey Questions	Pretesting	Data Quality Assurance	Presentation Format
Identify the questions to be addressed by the data collection methods that are: Specific in terms of concepts, time frame, and unit of analysis Clear and understandable by both involved stakeholders and "cold readers" Objective and neutrally stated Appropriately framed in terms of scope and time frame Likely to produce information of interest and usefulness to the audience (client)	Specify target respondents who: Possess relevant knowledge or perceptions relevant to addressing the research questions Are accessible Are representative of the population to which generalization is desired Provide multiple and complementary perspectives to answer questions	Design a means of selecting respondents from the targeted respondents that: Allows generalization to the desired population Allows an appropriate amount of subgroup analysis Does not have too large a sampling error	Select modes of data collection that will: Ensure that collected directly and adequately address the evaluation questions Are reliably implemented Permit sufficient ability to probe accuracy of responses Achieve sufficient response rates Provide findings within the time available Are within budget	Craft questions to be used in survey mode that: Address one or more of the evaluation questions Are clear, understandable, and easy for respondents to answer Permit adequate generalizability of findings Permit adequate opportunity for desired quantitative analysis Are appropriate for your mode of data collection	Design a means of pretesting survey questions and procedures that will: Provide feedback to clarify all wording in questions Identify any unanswerable questions Reveal any assumptions made about respondents' willingness or ability to answer questions that are not supported	Devise procedures to continually obtain feedback on data collection processes and wording of survey questions that: Provide feedback to clarify wording in questions Reveal inconsistencies in data collection procedures or coding Improve interviewers' skills	Plan for analysis of the data obtained through the surveying that: Clearly displays the data that address the evaluation questions Permits a sufficient level of disaggregation to be useful for the audiences (clients)

EXHIBIT 14.1. EXAMPLE OF A SURVEY DESIGN MATRIX.

Evaluation Question	Information Source	Sampling	Data Collection Mode
Over the past twelve months, how well is Legal Aid Services meeting the needs of those eligible for services in the community?	Beneficiaries who have been represented by the Legal Aid attorneysApplicants for services who were deniedPotential beneficiaries who did not apply for Legal Aid Services but would have been eligible	A systematic random sample of names taken off agency records with potential stratification by gender, race, and crimeA systematic random sample of those who represented themselves in court taken from court records	Mail survey with monetary incentivesAnalysis of archival records indicating reasons for denial[a]Mode will depend on availability of contact information

Survey Questions

For Service Recipients: How satisfied were you with . . .

	Not satisfied		Extremely satisfied	Not applicable
a. Responsiveness of your attorney to your questions?	1	2	3	NA
b. Effectiveness of the representation afforded you by your attorney?	1	2	3	NA
c. Amount of time your attorney devoted to your case?	1	2	3	NA
d. Ease of obtaining legal representation?	1	2	3	NA
e. Courteousness of the Legal Services staff?	1	2	3	NA
f. Timeliness of the response of the Legal Services staff to your request for assistance?	1	2	3	NA

[a]A more expensive analysis would entail following up with court records to track the experience of applicants who were denied and locate them for subsequent contact.

EXHIBIT 14.1. EXAMPLE OF A SURVEY DESIGN MATRIX. (*Continued*)

For Potential Beneficiaries who did not apply: How important were each of the following reasons that you did not seek assistance from Legal Aid Services?

	Not satisfied		Extremely satisfied	Not applicable
a. Did not think I would qualify.	1	2	3	NA
b. Did not think I had enough time.	1	2	3	NA
c. Heard unfavorable reviews from friends or acquaintances.	1	2	3	NA
d. Never heard of this service.	1	2	3	NA

Pretesting	Data Quality Assurance	Presentation Format
Mail survey of a small systematic sample.	Write clear introduction that assures respondents of the anonymity of their responses.Send a pilot survey to reveal any problems beforehand. Train coders before they access records.	A table that arrays percentage frequencies for respondents broken out by key demographic characteristics.

in designing your own survey. The second reason for not conducting a survey is that obtaining the information you need would take too long or cost too much. Suppose you want to find out whether the number of homeless shelters is adequate and whether the shelters are located in appropriate areas. Given the difficulty of reaching and communicating with homeless people, a survey to collect this information would certainly be expensive and take a long time, and even with enough time and resources, this information still may not be attainable.

Determine the Population of Interest

As you establish your evaluation questions, you are also deciding on your population of interest: individuals or an organization or group (for example, school superintendents, principals, or state school officials). If the population of interest is an organization or group, you also need to think about who within this group would be the most knowledgeable and most able to provide information for the group. In some situations, surveys of several different groups of respondents may be necessary to address the evaluation questions. Besides identifying the population of interest, you also must consider whether there are any groups or individuals within this population to exclude because of their lack of pertinent experience. For instance, you might exclude part-time workers from an employee survey, businesses with fewer than five employees from a business study, or graduating seniors from a survey about future student housing needs. Usually, you exclude groups or individuals who you believe would not contribute useful information, but you also should consider limiting your population to save time and money. Limiting the population geographically is often done to save money. For instance, to save money, Alaska and Hawaii are often excluded in nationwide surveys. (Such exclusions should be made clear when reporting the findings.)

After defining the population of interest, consider whether there is anyone else to obtain information from. For instance, had we limited the population of interest to individuals who had been represented by legal aid attorneys in the sample survey design matrix in Exhibit 14.1, we would not have fully answered our evaluation question. To fully understand how effective legal aid services are in meeting the needs of the community, we need to expand the population of interest to include individuals who potentially could have used legal aid services as well as those who were denied services.

Decide on the Analysis Plan

Think about the analysis plan. How likely are you to analyze any subgroups within your population? If you plan on analyzing a group that constitutes a very small portion of your population of interest, the survey design will probably include oversampling this group. Careful consideration of the sorts of disaggregation that may be desirable for data analysis is needed from the start, for by the time report preparation begins, it is probably too late to boost subgroup sample sizes.

Decide on a Plan for Collecting the Data

The next important decision will be how to collect the data. Table 14.2 lists the advantages and disadvantages of the most common modes of data collection. Much of the work involved in preparing the survey instrument depends on

TABLE 14.2. COMPARISON OF SURVEY MODES.

Criteria	Mail	Internet	Telephone	In Person[a]
Quality of data				
Ability to locate respondent	High	*Low*[b]	Medium	High
Ability to probe	Low	Low	Medium	*High*
Response rates	Low-medium	Low-medium	Medium	*High*
Protect respondent's anonymity	High	Medium-high	Medium	Low
Ability to ask about sensitive topics	High	Medium-high	Medium	*Low*
Ability to interview less educated	Low-medium	Low	Medium-high	High
Quality of recorded response	Low-medium	Medium	High	High
Question complexity	*Low*	Medium	Medium	*High*
Opportunities for analyses				
Ability to use larger scales	High	High	Low	Medium
How quickly you can post results	Low	*High*	Medium-high	Low
Ability to collect anecdotes	Low	Low	Medium	*High*
Number of questions asked	*Low*	Low-medium	Medium	High
Ability to adjust for nonresponse	Medium	*Low*	Medium	High
Ability to add sample frame data	High	Low	Medium	High
Resources required				
Time required for preparation	*Low*	Medium	High	High
Time required for collection	High	*Low*	Medium	High
Expertise required for design	Medium	*High*	Medium	Medium
Survey research expertise	Medium	Medium	Medium-high	High
Staffing requirements	Low	Low	High	High
Equipment requirements	*Low*	Medium	Medium	Medium
Travel requirements	Low	Low	Medium	*High*
Costs per survey	Low	Low-medium[c]	Medium-high	High

[a]If it is appropriate to ask clients to complete the survey at an agency's facility, the ratings will not be as low (or costs as high).
[b]Italic font indicates a particularly strong advantage or disadvantage.
[c]Costs for e-mail- and web-based surveys decrease as sample size increases.

the mode of data collection. Therefore, a decision on which data collection mode to use should be made early on, so that there is enough time left in the schedule for preparing the survey instrument.

Mail Surveys.   Even with the increasing number of e-mail and web surveys, traditional mail surveys are still a popular form of data collection. The three distinct advantages of mail surveys are that they are relatively inexpensive, a complete list of addresses is usually obtainable, and they yield less response bias when the questions are sensitive. Some disadvantages of mail surveys are comparatively lower response rates, a response bias toward more educated respondents, higher nonresponse rates for individual questions, and the questionnaire needs to be short, with minimal or no skip patterns (that is, instructions that ask respondents to ignore certain questions).

Telephone Surveys.   Telephone surveys have been very popular because they often yield high response rates and less item nonresponse, provide more control of the question ordering, allow the use of longer questions and skip patterns, and allow callers to ask respondents to recall information during the interview. Some disadvantages of telephone surveys are that they are relatively more expensive, it may be more time consuming to write and test questions for them, and there is more bias when asking for sensitive or personal information. Higher cooperation rates and the ability to reach people by telephone have been two major advantages of telephone surveys, but these advantages are now on the decline. When the phone rang forty years ago, no one assumed the person on the other end of the line was going to try to sell him or her something. Twenty years ago, the only way to know who was calling was to say, "Hello." Today, many people screen their calls with caller ID, an answering machine, or a privacy manager. These changes explain in part why there are no longer big differences in response rates between a properly administered household mail survey and a telephone survey. In addition to falling response rates, it is becoming more difficult to contact people by telephone because of the decline in the proportion of households and persons within households that use landline telephones (Blumberg and Luke, 2013). This difficulty in reaching people by phone is particularly problematic for surveys that need to reach low-income or young adults. However, if the population being surveyed has a strong interest or feels some ethical obligation to respond when contacted personally, telephone surveys may still be a good choice. For instance, response rates among college students are often two to three times higher on telephone surveys than on mail surveys.

Face-to-Face Surveys. The oldest method, face-to-face surveys, still yields the highest response rates and is the best method for asking open-ended questions (questions that do not limit responses to predefined response options) or questions requiring visual aids. However, these surveys are usually expensive, require longer testing and data collection periods, and are inappropriate for surveys that include sensitive questions. In addition, sampling usually involves interviewers conducting several interviews in a small geographical area, which can create a clustering effect that will decrease the precision of some estimates. These surveys are appropriate for captive audiences, such as institutionalized clients.

Web Surveys. Web surveys are still a relatively new mode of survey data collection. However, there has been a recent proliferation in their use, which has paralleled the dramatic worldwide growth of Internet access. The lower cost of web surveys relative to telephone or face-to-face interviews has been another important reason behind the increased use of web surveys. Web surveys can take advantage of the established HTML and Java script standards that make it possible for survey designers to create complex questionnaires that can handle skip patterns and recall information from earlier questions. In addition, web surveys can provide enticing graphics or visual aids to help guide respondents. Although there is some concern with providing information over the Internet, the data are actually more secure than information provided by e-mail, and people are starting to understand this better, as evidenced by the increasing willingness of people to complete forms and make purchases on the Internet. In fact, now that almost everyone with e-mail access has access to a web browser, sending a short e-mail message about the survey with a link to the questionnaire has for the most part replaced e-mail as a mode of data collection. Web surveys used as the lone mode of data collection do not seem to have resolved the problem of falling survey response rates, but web surveys may improve response rates when used in combination with another mode of data collection. Also, web surveys are currently limited to populations that use the Internet, but that population continues to grow and there are now organizations (such as the GFKKnowledge Panel and Harris Interactive) that are conducting national studies that are representative of the nation by providing free web access to randomly selected respondents.

Mixed-Mode Surveys. Given the difficulties in persuading people to respond to surveys, survey practitioners have increasingly been offering people various ways of responding. There are many programs for which using a combination of data collection modes will increase participation. For instance, when conducting a job satisfaction survey, you may be able to collect most responses using the web, but for employees who do not use a computer, you may need to call them or provide them with a paper survey. The downside with mixed-mode surveys is that they cost more to design and you have to be careful that the mode of data collection does not influence the results. In general, survey results do not vary when self-administration modes of data collection, such as mail or web surveys, are combined, but results for interviewer-administered modes of data collection (phone or face-to-face) have been known to differ from the results collected through self-administered modes of data collection. A popular book that describes how to design mixed-mode surveys is *Internet, Mail, and Mixed-Mode Surveys: The Tailored Design Method* (Dillman, Smyth, and Christian, 2014).

Other Methods. There are many other ways to conduct surveys. You may use pencil-and-paper questionnaires when you have a captive audience—for instance, asking people to complete a survey at the end of a meeting, surveying students in the classroom, or having clients complete a survey while they fill out required forms. It is often possible to bolster the response rate by taking advantage of a captive audience.

Until recently, e-mail was seen as a good alternative to mail for conducting surveys with populations for whom you could obtain e-mail addresses. You can collect the data faster and potentially more efficiently through e-mail. However, confidentiality concerns about who has access to e-mail messages, filters and firewalls that prevent unsolicited e-mail, and increases in computer viruses sent by e-mail are all contributing to a declining interest in e-mail surveys.

The emergence of hand-held and mobile devices that often have a number of integrated features such as voice, photography, video, text, email, GPS, apps, and other features has given survey practitioners new measurement tools to study public opinion, attitudes, and behaviors. For instance, for travel surveys a GPS application can keep track of a person's time spent at different locations, which may be a good alternative to having a person fill out a survey travel diary or least aid the person in accurately filling out a diary.

Another important point is that, if you plan to compare results with a previous survey, try to use the same mode of data collection; using a different mode of data collection could introduce some unintentional bias.

Identify Who Will Conduct the Survey

While deliberating on the most desirable mode of data collection, you will also be considering whether to conduct the survey in-house or contract it out. Box 14.1 identifies some factors to consider in making this decision. The most common reason people choose to conduct their own survey is to save money. However, when you factor in all the hours staff spend working on the project, you may be surprised how little you actually save by not contracting out. Much of this chapter is written with the assumption that you plan to collect your own data, but the information in this chapter is almost equally important to those who select and work with contractors. If you are planning to contract out, Box 14.2 provides useful tips. In general, it is much easier to collect your data when you choose a self-administered mode of data collection, such as mail surveys, because interviewer-administered surveys have much higher start-up costs. For outcome-monitoring purposes, it is typically the agency that regularly surveys clients to obtain useful feedback about program operations and to estimate program outcomes. The less costly and easier to administer surveys will be especially appropriate for these purposes.

Box 14.1. When Should You Contract Out?

Do you have staff to perform all required work?

- Do staff have the needed expertise for survey design?
- Are staff skilled and available for interviewing?
- Do staff have the requisite expertise for analysis of the survey findings?
- Are staff available and skilled enough to write the report and prepare the graphics needed to support the findings in the report?
- Would the results benefit if you were able to state that the data were collected by an independent contractor?

Is there adequate technological support to support the survey?

- Do you have adequate hardware and software capabilities to collect data?
- Do you have the type of hardware and software needed to analyze the data?

Can staff complete the survey in time?

- How quickly do you need the data reported?

Box 14.2. Who Will Be the Right Consultant or Contractor for You?

Does the consultant have enough relevant experience?

- How much experience does the consultant have with the service delivery or policy being addressed in the survey?
- How much experience does the consultant have with the survey mode you think you want?

What is the quality of the consultant's communication skills?

- How compatible is the consultant's communications style with yours?
- How clearly does the consultant communicate orally and in writing?
- How responsive is the consultant in reacting to your requests and suggestions?
- How accessible is the consultant in communicating with all relevant stakeholders involved with the survey project?
- What do previous clients say about the consultant's communications skills in their recommendations?

What is the quality of the consultant's written reports?

- How clearly written are the consultant's previous reports?
- How effective are the presentations of graphics and analyses provided by the consultant in previous reports?

Is the consultant in your price range?

- How competitive is the cost estimate the consultant provides?
- How responsive is the consultant when asked to unbundle the tasks he or she will provide to reduce costs?
- Is the consultant willing to allow your staff to perform some tasks to reduce costs?

Decide on the Timing of the Data Collection

You need to decide when would be a good time to collect your data. Think about collecting during a time when reaching your population is least difficult. Often you should avoid conducting surveys around the holidays or during the summer months when people may be on vacation. However, if your project involves recalling an event, the survey needs to occur shortly after the event. Although surveys are often scheduled to accommodate important meetings or presentations, the quality of the survey will benefit from placing a higher priority on accommodating the respondents. For many customer surveys, especially for outcome monitoring, it is often most useful to collect data continuously, say at a fixed period of time after each client has completed services (such as at three, six, nine, or twelve months after departure). A continuous data collection process avoids seasonal or other fluctuations in satisfaction that often occur over time. If all clients are to be covered, you avoid worries about sampling, the subject of the next section.

Select the Sample

The first question should be: Do I need to try to interview everyone, or should I select a sample of the population to interview? If the population of interest is quite large, then you almost certainly need to select a sample. However, even if you think that you can survey all customers, selecting a relatively small number of respondents may provide reasonably precise estimates of the entire population at a much reduced cost. For routine outcome monitoring, many benefits accrue to covering all clients if the number is not too large. However, many one-time studies end up spending too much money trying to interview everyone, when they would have been able to get better estimates by spending more resources on getting a high response rate from a sample of the population. In general, sample sizes of one thousand, five hundred, or even two hundred or fewer can provide sufficient precision as long as the sample has been selected at random from the overall population. An introductory statistics book and online references can provide further guidance on the relation between sample size and precision.

If you are planning to conduct a separate analysis on a subgroup of the population, you may need to choose a larger overall random sample or select at random additional respondents who meet the definition of the subgroup you want to analyze. How many interviews you need to complete depends on a number of things (for example, types of analyses planned, variability of key variables, total population size), but most of all it depends on how much precision is needed for the study. Although the goal should always be to achieve the highest-quality project possible, most surveys do not need the same level of precision. That is why many successful surveys have published results based on sample sizes of five hundred or fewer.

Table 14.3 provides an overview of the various sampling options to consider. One of these options is what is usually described as a *convenience*

TABLE 14.3. SAMPLING OPTIONS.

	Description	Types of Studies	Analysis Concerns
Census	Interviewing the entire population	Small populations; e-mail and web surveys where most of the costs are incurred in designing the survey.	Possibly need some nonresponse weights adjustment, but usually no weighting is needed.
Simple random sample	Every person in the population has an equal chance of being chosen.	Studies where it is possible to obtain a list of all eligible and a census is too expensive or unnecessary.	Possibly need some nonresponse weights adjustment, but often a weighting adjustment is not needed.
Stratified random sample	Every person in the population has an equal chance of being chosen; sample is sorted by key variables before the sample is selected. For example, if the list includes postal code and gender, you could stratify (sort) it first by postal code and then within postal code by gender.	Studies where it is possible to obtain a list and the list contains useful information about the respondents.	Possibly need some nonresponse weights adjustment or some adjustment due to having differential response rates in the different subgroups.
Stratified with unequal probability of selection	Every person in the population has a known probability of selection; however, certain groups of people have a greater or lesser chance of being sampled.	Studies where you want to make sure to collect enough interviews with specific groups within the population in order to perform separate analysis on those groups.	In order to look at the population as a whole, you will need to weight respondents by the inverse of their probability of selection. In addition, you may need to do two or more nonresponse adjustments: one for the overall sample and one for each of the groups specifically oversampled. The key here is to use a weight variable when analyzing the overall population, but no weight or only a nonresponse adjustment weight is needed for analyzing the groups you oversampled.

(Continued)

TABLE 14.3. SAMPLING OPTIONS. (*Continued*)

	Description	Types of Studies	Analysis Concerns
Multistage sample design	Multistage sample designs are usually very complex and require the assistance of a sampling statistician. For these studies, you would be advised to have the data collected by a survey shop.	These are usually large household surveys where you want to speak with is often unknown until after information about the household has been obtained.	Requires both sample design weights and post-stratification weights. Also, estimates will be subject to design effects. To correctly estimate the variance of the measurements, you need to use special data techniques.
Convenience sample	Sampling populations at a place where they can be easily reached—for example, homeless in homeless shelters, drug users at drug treatment clinics.	Hard-to-locate populations; limited budget.	Should not generalize your results to the population as a whole.

sample, meaning that it relies on contacting population members who are easily located and willing to participate. Convenience samples are not recommended for evaluations that involve making an inference about the population as whole, but they can be justified when trying to interview hard-to-find populations or when the evaluation objective is not to produce estimates but rather to learn more about some of the key issues. As discussed in Chapter Twenty-Three, statistically significant findings that are generalizable to whole client populations require probability samples, but some evaluation questions may not require this level of coverage. For example, investigations of specific problems with program implementation or service quality may require only targeted surveys.

Design the Survey Instrument

You want both good, relevant answers to your questions and a high response rate. Accomplishing these two important objectives requires:

- Designing the survey and formulating the questions with the target respondents in mind;
- Writing extremely compelling introductions to get your foot in the door;

- Wording questions so they are easy for the respondents to answer and so they provide pertinent data for the intended users of the results; and
- Pretesting and continually reassessing the usefulness of the instrument in obtaining accurate and useful data.

Consider the Target Respondents

Before writing survey questions, think about the target respondents. Many characteristics of target respondents are especially pertinent to survey layout and question considerations. Think about how receptive the respondents will be to being surveyed, how much they know about the subject matter, and how sensitive they may feel about the questions asked.

The educational background of the target respondents will affect the sophistication of the terms you choose to use in the survey. Writing questions directed to scientists and engineers presents different challenges from writing questions directed to recipients of food stamps. Other demographic characteristics of the target respondents are also pertinent here, such as their age and primary language spoken.

The receptivity of the target respondents to answering questions about the issues may also reflect whether or not they have the desired information, how easy it is for them to get the information requested, and how willing they are to part with the information. You need to think through any assumptions you make about the knowledge or experience the target respondents have that is relevant to their ability to answer the questions. For example, evaluators may assume that target respondents are more familiar with service delivery procedures or with an agency's acronyms than they may actually be. Or evaluators may be overly optimistic in assuming that respondents can provide reliable information about their experiences, such as reporting how many hours they watch television. Memories are fleeting, and respondents' abilities to recall experiences or impressions may not be sufficient to provide accurate data.

Evaluators have to anticipate how receptive target respondents will be to the questions asked of them. The order of the questions should reflect how respondents are likely to perceive the intrusiveness or sensitivity of the questions. Typically, surveys start with straightforward, factual questions that are extremely easy to answer and inoffensive. The questions then move toward more sensitive areas, such as requesting respondents to evaluate services, and end with requests for demographic information that will help to disaggregate responses. For more information about the importance of understanding your respondent and asking sensitive questions, see Tourangeau, Rips, and Rasinski (2001), *The Psychology of Survey Responses.*

Get a Foot in the Door

The introduction to a survey conducted by any mode is critical. The right introduction will boost the likelihood that the respondents will participate. Introductions are more likely to be effective in convincing the respondent to answer questions when they explain the following information:

Box 14.3. Tips on Incentives

- Incentives improve response rates for all modes of data collection.
- Incentives are more effective with self-administered surveys.
- Prepaid incentives are more effective with mail surveys than are promised incentives.
- Response rate gains are the same when using either prepaid or promised incentives with telephone or face-to-face surveys.
- Money is more effective than gifts (equal in value) for all modes of data collection.
- A positive linear relationship exists between money and response rate.
- On average, there is a one-third percentage point gain in response rate per dollar spent on incentives in telephone surveys.
- On mail surveys, incentives have been found to increase response rates as much as 20 percentage points.
- The more burdensome a survey is, the more effective incentives are.

- The purpose of the survey
- The identity of the people or organizations who will use the information provided (such as a city council to improve city services)
- The identity of the people or organizations who are funding or sponsoring the survey
- The benefits the respondent will enjoy by participating in the survey

Providing incentives to participate, such as enclosing money in mail surveys or promising that money or in-kind awards will be sent to respondents, will help to convince respondents to participate, as described in Box 14.3 (Singer, 2002).

Craft Good Questions

Questions are only as good as respondents find them to be. They need to be clear to respondents and answerable by them. Crafting questions should be undertaken with the target respondents in mind. You must anticipate target respondents' receptivity to different sorts of question formats and their willingness to volunteer responses to open-ended questions. Asking open-ended questions works best in face-to-face interviews. Most questions in all other surveys should provide easy-to-understand options for the respondent to select.

A first step in formulating questions should be to look for questions on the intended topic that have been used before—in a previous survey or in customer surveys in another governmental jurisdiction, for example. Of course, just because the questions have been used previously does not mean they are ideal, but they do present options to consider and perhaps pretest. When used in outcome monitoring, questions should be asked with the same wording from year to year.

A second step in question preparation is to estimate the total number of questions that can feasibly be asked and the number of questions needed to address all the evaluation questions. Because asking too many questions will hurt the response rate, the need to ask more questions must be balanced against the negative impact a lengthier survey may have in discouraging respondents. For mail surveys, try to limit the questions to the number that will fit on perhaps two to four pages.

When evaluators are asking respondents to give their opinions or evaluations of services, they typically use answer scales. Using a numerical scale in which only the end points are defined (such as a 1 to 7 scale, where 1 equals *not at all useful* and 7 equals *extremely useful*) is preferable to using adjectives (such as *poor, fair,* and *above average*), because numbers are less fraught with connotations that vary across respondents. Box 14.4 contains tips for writing questions that will obtain reliable answers from respondents.

One question that typically arises about the use of scales to measure respondents' perceptions is whether to provide a middle value. In other words, some experts advocate forcing respondents to choose a positive or negative response rather than giving them a midpoint (neutral response), such as 3 on a 1 to 5 scale. The view against providing a middle, or neutral value is based in large part on the fear that too many respondents will prefer it. Our own experience is that offering midpoints does not lead respondents to rely overly on them. In fact, we advocate the use of an odd-numbered scale, such as 1 to 5 or 1 to 7. Focus group feedback on sample questions may help you to develop an appropriate scale (see Chapter Twenty for more information on focus groups). However, once you decide what scale to use, stick with it for the entire survey to provide a consistent metric for respondents. A good rule of thumb in formulating questions is to provide a thorough and mutually exclusive list of options for respondents to consider or rate, rather than asking them to volunteer responses. For example, rather than using an open-ended question to ask respondents what they liked about a training course or an encounter with an emergency squad, it is preferable to provide a list of program or service aspects that has been developed and refined through pretesting and to ask respondents to evaluate each aspect on the list. Question sequencing is also important, and developing effective lead questions is critical. Tips on sequencing appear in Box 14.5.

Box 14.4. Wording Questions to Measure Attitudes and Perceptions Reliably

- Use scales with numbers, not fuzzy adjectives, for respondents to assess their attitude.

Example: On a scale from 1 to 7, where 1 is *not at all clear* and 7 is *extremely clear*, how clear were the instructions in the manual?

1	2	3	4	5	6	7	NA

- Ask respondents to rate each factor that you want to evaluate rather than asking them to rank a list of factors (from first to last). (Provide terms only at the extreme ends of a scale unless you are asking respondents to compare two options. An example of the latter would be a scale of 1 to 7 where 1 is *online version more useful*, 4 is *versions are equally useful*, and 7 is *text version more useful*.)

Example: Please rate the usefulness of each of the following sources in helping you select a graduate program on a scale from 1 to 7, where 1 is *not useful at all* and 7 is *extremely useful*:

a. Website	1	2	3	4	5	6	7	NA
b. Written brochure	1	2	3	4	5	6	7	NA
c. Campus visit	1	2	3	4	5	6	7	NA
d. Interview with faculty member	1	2	3	4	5	6	7	NA
e. Calls from current students	1	2	3	4	5	6	7	NA
f. Any other useful sources; please specify	1	2	3	4	5	6	7	NA

- Keep the questions brief. Rather than confuse respondents with long statements, break up inquiries into clear components.

(Continued)

Example: On a scale from 1 to 3, where 1 is *not at all satisfied* and 3 is *extremely satisfied*, how satisfied were you with:

a. The clarity of the written training materials?	1	2	3	NA
b. The availability of the trainer for consultation outside class?	1	2	3	NA
c. The trainer's knowledge of the materials he or she covered?	1	2	3	NA

- Provide definitions in the survey instrument for any terms or concepts that may be vague or not understood in the same manner by all respondents. For example, *team building* may mean different things to different respondents.
- Use easy to answer, closed-ended questions. Because respondents will not likely spend much time answering open-ended questions by mail, e-mail, or the web, ask only a few open-ended questions, ones that will provide especially helpful information.
- Select the length of the scales based on the respondents' ability to discriminate, and then use the same scale for all questions in the survey. For example, engineers should be comfortable with longer scales, such as 1 to 7 or 1 to 10, but elderly recipients of Meals on Wheels might feel more comfortable answering 3-point scales.
- Ask an open-ended question at the end that requests respondents to identify an additional issue, factor, or quality (or whatever else is relevant) that was not addressed in the survey.

Box 14.5. Tips on Question Sequencing

- Ask more specific items first. For example, suppose you were asking people to rate community recycling services and garbage collection. People's rating of garbage collection is likely to be influenced by the recycling services provided. Asking, "How would you rate recycling services in your community?" before asking, "How would you rate garbage collection in your community?" cues the respondents that you want them to consider garbage collection separately from the recycling services.
- Consider a lead-in statement for items in which there is likely to be an order effect in either direction. For example, let's say that a respondent is trying to evaluate how well the police, the courts, and local leaders have been doing in preventing crime in the community. No matter what order you choose, there is likely to be some order effect, so you could use a lead-in statement similar to the following: "Now I'd like you to tell me how effective the police, the courts, and local leaders have been in preventing crime in your community. First, how effective. . . ."

Ease of answering from the respondents' point of view should be a driving principle, no matter what sort of question format is used. Box 14.6 lists the most common mistakes evaluators make in writing survey questions. Well-written questions do not make any of these mistakes.

Instructions should be given to respondents about how many responses to provide for each question and which option to select if they feel they cannot or should not answer a question due to lack of knowledge or experience. Box 14.7 lists some findings about respondents' reactions to "no opinion" or "don't know" options (see also Krosnick and others, 2002; McClendon and Alwin, 1993).

Box 14.6. Common Mistakes in Writing Questions

- The question asks about more than one thing.
- Some of the terms used are not familiar to some respondents.
- The response options are not exhaustive and mutually exclusive.
- The questions with scales do not offer balanced alternatives.
- The information asked for is redundant because it can be obtained from another source.
- Not all respondents will have the same interpretation of the question.
- The time frame is not clearly stated or is not reasonable for recall questions.
- There will be little variation in response because almost everyone will provide the same answer.
- The question contains a double negative.
- The question asks respondents to rank too many items or to do some other difficult task.
- The possible answers include an unnecessary "don't know," "no opinion," or neutral option.
- The intervals for numerical response options are not reasonable.
- The wording seems to advocate a particular answer (that is, it leads the respondents).

Box 14.7. Considerations for the "No Opinion" or "Don't Know" Option

- Less-educated respondents are more likely to choose this category.
- Offering this option increases the likelihood of other item nonresponse.
- Studies have shown that including these items does not improve the consistency of respondents' attitudes over time.
- For questions that require some thought, these items discourage respondents from thinking about the issue.
- Respondents who do not have clearly formulated opinions usually lean in one direction or the other.
- Recent cognitive studies have shown that respondents who choose these options could, if encouraged, provide substantive answers.

Pretest

Pretesting a survey instrument with a representative sample of the population of target respondents is essential. The questions, mode of administration, and procedures should be the same in the pretest as planned for the survey. Even if questions are borrowed from previous studies or other agencies or jurisdictions, the questions should be asked of a set of the target respondents to ensure clarity and understandability. Often more than one pretest is necessary; in general, the final pretest should look as much like the actual survey as possible. Cognitive interviewing presents another tool to use in pretesting, and is especially helpful when developing new questions. Please see Exhibit 14.2 for more on cognitive interviewing.

A good-sized sample for a pretest is generally twenty to twenty-five completed interviews or written surveys, with more needed for questionnaires that have lots of skip patterns. When possible, we recommend that with questionnaires administered by interviewers, you record the pretest interviews; this will allow you and others to carefully evaluate the respondents' understanding of the questions. Also, if the total population is very small, you will probably need to include the findings from the pretest sample in the analysis, noting the changes that were made as a result of the pretest. However, if the overall population is large enough, we recommend not including the findings from the pretest sample in the analysis results.

Focus groups of target respondents are useful in identifying pertinent aspects of experiences or services that should be addressed in surveys. A group of target respondents can help evaluators to operationalize what *quality* means in a specific type of service or program, for example. (Focus groups are discussed in Chapter Twenty.)

Collect Data from Respondents

Persuading respondents to complete the survey is a vital part of the survey process. If you do not follow up on all the planning and design with a good data collection effort, you will negate your preparation work. Moreover, designing a good and flexible data collection operation can overcome some preparation oversights.

Mail Surveys

For optimal response rates on mail surveys, the tailored design method (Dillman, Smyth, and Christian, 2014) remains the most popular mail survey

EXHIBIT 14.2. A TOOL FOR TESTING SURVEY QUESTIONS: COGNITIVE INTERVIEWING

Cognitive Interviewing Defined

Cognitive interviewing is a qualitative process of studying the mental processes experienced by individuals. Cognitive Interviews are usually employed as part of or prior to survey pretesting, and help evaluators better understand how respondents interact with an instrument and identify potential issues (Willis, 2005).

Evaluators can use different cognitive interviewing techniques depending on their objective(s). Two primary cognitive interviewing techniques are the "think-aloud" method (Ericsson and Simon, 1980) and verbal probing technique (Drennan, 2002). In the think-aloud method, participants complete the survey instrument while vocalizing their thought processes. This helps evaluators better understand how respondents will perceive the question and identify any misunderstandings (Ericsson and Simon, 1980). Evaluators using verbal probing technique administer the survey instrument to test subjects without commentary, and then ask probing questions after the respondent has completed the instrument (Willis, DeMaio, and Harris-Kojetin, 1999).

Objectives of Cognitive Interviewing

Evaluators can use cognitive interviews as a part of survey pretesting to accomplish two objectives. First, evaluators can use cognitive interviewing to identify problems with the survey instrument (Collins, 2003). Cognitive interviewing detect both overt and covert issues, including hidden subtext and times which have multiple interpretations. Moreover, cognitive interviewing can help determine the prevalence and severity of any errors (Blair and Conrad, 2011).

Second, cognitive interviewing can help assess and minimize the likelihood of response error by examining self-report capacity. For example, cognitive interviewing can help identify ways of phrasing questions which will provide the most accurate information. Using cognitive modeling in conjunction with cognitive interviewing, evaluators can better understand how respondents lose information, and can develop strategies to minimize the impact of any losses on the validity of survey data collected (Willis, 2005).

Limitations of Cognitive Interviewing

While cognitive interviewing can help evaluators identify problems with the survey instrument and assess the likelihood of response error, cognitive interviewing has its own set of limitations. Cognitive interviewing is both expensive and time consuming. Additionally, the sample size needs to be large enough to detect issues with the survey instrument; without an adequate sample size, serious issues may escape detection (Blair and Conrad, 2011). Moreover, even when cognitive interviewing successfully identifies a problem, it does not develop a solution (Collins, 2003).

EXHIBIT 14.2. A TOOL FOR TESTING SURVEY QUESTIONS: COGNITIVE INTERVIEWING. *(Continued)*

Other Steps to Strengthen Survey Pretesting

To strengthen the value of cognitive interviews or pretest interviews, the evaluator should try to record these interviews so multiple evaluators can assist in identifying potential problems and this will also provide the cognitive interviewer more time to assess the interview. Conducting cognitive interviews is one of many ways to test a survey instrument and, when used in conjunction with other pretesting efforts, it often helps evaluators gain a more comprehensive understanding of the survey instrument (Drennan, 2002).Cognitive interviewing can provide insight into how respondents will perceive and interact with a survey, but does not answer a host of other important questions about the respondents' experience. For example, evaluators should also be attentive to survey length, appropriateness, and formatting (for example, does the survey display accurately on the respondents' devices). Cognitive interviewing does not necessarily cover these aspects of the survey, which can also impact instrument reliability, validity, and response rate.

---

procedure. It calls for the following series of steps to achieve a satisfactory response rate:

1. Include in the first mailing a questionnaire, a separate cover letter, and a postage-paid return envelope (a stamp appeals more to respondents than a business permit).
2. Approximately ten days later, send the entire sample a reminder postcard that emphasizes the importance of the study and thanks people who have already responded.
3. About two weeks later, mail all nonrespondents another questionnaire, with a new, shorter cover letter. If the survey is anonymous, mail all potential respondents another questionnaire.

If you have enough funds, you may increase your response rate by using monetary incentives, using Express Mail, or sending a postcard announcing the survey prior to the first mailing. If you can afford it, you should also consider calling the nonrespondents and asking them to return their questionnaires. In many agencies, such as health and human service agencies, staff should be asked to encourage clients to complete the questionnaire.

If you are sending the questionnaire via e-mail, the methodology is similar except that your follow-up contacts should occur as soon as you notice a significant decline in the number of people responding.

Web Surveys

The number of web surveys being designed and implemented is increasing at a fast pace. They are cheaper and give the designer more flexibility in designing the survey, because the computer can handle skip patterns and process information on the fly. Most web surveys send potential respondents an e-mail that contains a description of the study and a web link to the server on which the survey resides. For web surveys that rely on an e-mail invitation to participate, your contact procedures are similar to the procedures used in conducting a mail survey. The initial e-mail invitation should include a description of the study and the web link, and it should be followed by a couple of short e-mail reminders. One major difference is the timing of the mailings. With e-mail, most people who are going to respond will do so the same day they receive the e-mail. Hence, instead of waiting ten days to send a reminder, it is best to send the reminder just after you see a significant decline in return responses (usually three to four days). After the reminder is sent, there should be some increase in returns. Once these returns significantly decline, a final reminder should be sent to nonrespondents. Try to send your e-mails at times when people are most likely to receive them; so avoid weekends. Keep the e-mail message short so that it is easy for the respondent to see the web link, and it is preferable to have an embedded password in the link so that each person can be connected to his or her own unique questionnaire without having to be given a password and log-in. Also make sure the web link fits on one line; longer links make it difficult for some respondents to click the link from within their web browsers. Send nonrespondents' follow-up e-mails at different times and on different days of the week than the initial mailing was sent. Finally, it is very useful to have someone with name recognition to send out a global e-mail announcement just prior to the start of data collection, explaining the importance of the study.

Currently, there is much exploratory research being conducted on the best ways of designing web surveys. Although you need access to a web server and probably some technical support, there are now many software applications that make it easy for a novice to design a web survey; among them are EZ-Survey, SurveyGizmo, SurveySaid, SumQuest, Remark Web Survey, SurveyMonkey, QuestionPro, Qualtrics, Zoomerang, and Snap Survey Software. Chapter Eighteen discusses using these various survey firms. In addition, before designing a web survey, you should browse the web to examine survey samples, and you should also check out the "WebSurvey Methodology" website (www.websm.org/). In addition, read the current literature about designing web surveys (Coupler, 2008; Dillman, Smyth, and Christian, 2014). One thing is certain: with Internet access increasing, web surveys are going to be an increasingly important mode of data collection.

In-Person Surveys

Face-to-face, or in-person, interviewing is the oldest form of data collection. Face-to-face interviewing also still provides the highest response rate. It works best for both open-ended questions and longer surveys. In addition, the sampling frame bias is usually lowest for face-to-face studies. Ease of administration is greatest if target respondents are together at a facility, such as a recreation center or hospital, and they can be interviewed or given pencil-and-paper questionnaires to complete. Usually, though, interviewing in person requires that interviewers travel to a place (usually a home or office) where the respondent can be interviewed. Thus, the cost of conducting face-to-face interviews makes this mode of data collection impractical for most survey studies. In addition to cost, two other disadvantages of face-to-face interviewing are that respondents do not usually report sensitive behavior in the presence of an interviewer, and it takes much longer to complete the survey study (Fowler, 2014). In addition, gaining access to respondents in their homes may be difficult due to respondents' fear of allowing a stranger into their home or agency fears of danger to the interviewers. The use of handheld computers using computer-assisted personal interviewing (CAPI) software can mitigate the challenges of collecting sensitive information by letting the respondents directly input their responses. However, even though the use of newer technology and CAPI procedures reduces the time it takes to retrieve information from the interviewers, the field periods for personal interviewing still remain longer than they are for the other modes of data collection.

Telephone Surveys

Because of the cost of face-to-face interviewing and the difficulty in obtaining good response rates on mail surveys, telephone surveys have been very popular over the last twenty years. Although they are still a viable mode of collecting survey data, changing technology, such as answering machines, cell phones, and call screening, has made it more difficult to achieve high response rates on telephone surveys. Nevertheless, for some populations acceptable response rates of over 75 percent can still be achieved using the telephone as the mode of data collection.

Now there is added importance in scheduling enough time to make multiple calls at varying times and days of the week. Most survey methodologists agree that, for household surveys, up to fifteen to twenty call attempts at varied times of the day is an optimal level of effort. After that, response rate gains for additional calls are very small relative to the added costs. Also, if you reach individuals on their cell phones, before starting the interview make sure that they are at a safe place and not, for instance, driving a car. A major difference between conducting telephone (and face-to-face) surveys and self-administered surveys (mail, e-mail, and web) is the need to recruit and train interviewers to ask the questions.

Train Interviewers

Recruiting and training face-to-face and telephone interviewers is time-consuming and difficult. For most good survey shops, maintaining a core staff of good interviewers is a high priority. The fact that a survey shop already has an available group of interviewers is probably one of the most important considerations when deciding whether to contract out data collection (budget probably being the most important). What makes recruiting and training interviewers especially difficult is that there are lots of people who are just not good at interviewing.

In general, it helps to have a mature-sounding voice and be female; however, there have been many successful male interviewers and young interviewers. For many studies, you may need to choose interviewers who have characteristics similar to the respondents. For instance, it is not advisable to have men ask women questions about domestic violence programs, and when surveying in populations whose first language is not English, having interviewers with relevant language abilities may be necessary. Usually, people with high levels of enthusiasm tend to be most successful at getting others to respond to surveys, but their enthusiasm sometimes biases the actual interview, especially when they are asking sensitive questions. Screening potential interviewers on the phone to assess the clarity of their speech before deciding whether training them to be interviewers is worthwhile. Even with this prescreening, often as many as half of the individuals who start out in training will not make it as useful interviewers.

Interviewer training should be broken into two separate sessions: a general training session and then a specific training session. The general training should cover the basics, such as reading verbatim, neutral probing, dealing with difficult respondents, and learning the computer-assisted telephone interviewing (CATI or CAPI) system if the interviewer will be using the computer. Although experienced interviewers may not need to attend this training, it is often a good refresher for them.

Specific training, which, again, should occur after general training, primarily consists of taking the interviewers through the survey instrument question by question. It is also important during the specific training to provide interviewers with information about the purpose of the survey. A lot of information is passed along to the interviewer during a good training session; therefore, interviewers should also be provided with a training manual that they can use as a reference. It is easy to locate good examples of interviewer training manuals by searching the web with the key phrase "survey interviewer training manual."

After the general and specific training, most survey shops have new interviewers conduct live practice calls before conducting interviews with respondents who were selected to be included in the final sample. This procedure helps protect the quality of the study because you will be able to assess whether a new interviewer is able to do the job before he or she begins calling actual respondents. It is very important to remove interviewers early on when they are having problems. Some people do not make good interviewers, and it is better to catch the problem early rather than deal with a bigger problem later. Although retraining is an option, it is usually less effective than replacing an interviewer with a new person.

If you plan to try to recontact respondents who initially refuse, provide special refusal conversion training. This has been found to help interviewers who are asked to try to convert refusals. Putting one's foot in the door, rather than conducting the interview, is emphasized during the refusal conversion training.

Employ Quality Control

Although no interviewer training is needed for mail, web, and e-mail surveys, you will have to train someone to monitor and track the processes and to institute quality control measures. For traditional mail surveys, this person should be detail oriented and carefully check a random sample of the mailing before sending it out. On days when mailings are being sent out, things are generally quite hectic; having a person in charge of quality control at this time will go a long way toward avoiding embarrassing mistakes, such as enclosing cover letters that do not match the label or not stuffing the envelopes correctly.

For e-mail and web surveys, it is important to find someone who is competent in using the e-mail system and also has experience using distribution lists. In addition, with web and e-mail surveys, someone must be available for a few days after each mailing who can answer e-mail questions, check address problems, and track the number of completed interviews that have been submitted or returned. Unlike in traditional mail studies, it has been found that a majority of people who participate in e-mail and web surveys do so shortly after receiving the e-mail survey or the e-mail that provides a link to the web survey. Because of this quick response time, consider creating smaller distribution lists and sending out the survey in batches. For example, if you are conducting a job satisfaction survey, the employer may not appreciate having all employees completing a survey at the same time. It should be noted that with both mail and e-mail surveys, it is essential to track returned surveys if second or third mailings are to be used.

Monitoring telephone interviews is a standard quality control practice. Most survey shops aim to monitor 10 to 20 percent of all interviewers' work, with more frequent monitoring at the beginning of the project. The person responsible for monitoring should try to listen in on various parts of the survey, especially to hear how well the interviewer performs on the introduction. In addition, a senior person may call a sample of respondents to validate responses to key questions. Monitoring telephone interviews requires a centralized phone facility with proper equipment. Also, most centralized phone surveys will be conducted using a CATI system that makes it easy to monitor interviewer quality by producing separate reports by interview on items such as the number of call attempts, number of interviews completed, number of refusals, average length of interviews, and item response rates.

If you do not have proper monitoring equipment, consider using some callback verification as a quality control alternative. Callback verification involves having a supervisor contact a respondent who was recently interviewed to verify that the interview was completed and to ask the respondent if he or she experienced any problems with the interviewer or the survey. Although evaluators generally think of monitoring and callback verification as tools to catch and solve data collection problems, it is equally as important to provide interviewers with immediate and positive feedback. For face-to-face interviewing, a combination of callback verification and having someone observe the interview is the best strategy, because monitoring at random is operationally more difficult for in-person interviewing.

Good record keeping and tracking relevant information during data collection are underappreciated but important parts of the survey process. Proper tracking and recording procedures always yield higher response rates, in addition to demonstrating a high level of professionalism to both respondents and audience.

For all types of surveys, but especially telephone and face-to-face interviews, good record keeping is essential because a respondent is often

EXHIBIT 14.3. SAMPLE TELEPHONE OR IN-PERSON CONTACT RECORD SHEET.

Case ID: 10001 Phone Number: (301) 555–9999

Interviewer ID:	Interview Date	Interview Time Start	Interview Time End	Outcome Code	Comments
414	Mon 03/13	7:30 PM		Callback	Will be home this weekend
523	Sat 03/18	5:05 PM	5:23 PM	Complete	

unavailable to complete the interview during the first contact attempt. The timing of contact attempts is critical in completing telephone and face-to-face interviews. Most computer-assisted telephone interviewing (CATI) and computer-assisted personal interviewing (CAPI) software includes features that keep track of previous call attempts and schedule future call attempts. If you are not using computer-assisted software, have interviewers fill out information about all contacts on a contact record sheet (see Exhibit 14.3). In addition to maintaining information on the date, time, and result of each contact attempt, the interviewer should record his or her initials (or ID number) and provide any comments that may be useful in future contact attempts.

For mail, web, and e-mail surveys, keeping track of when all mailings or e-mailings were sent, including postcard reminders, and when completed surveys were returned is an important part of the data collection process. This can be accomplished manually or, preferably, with standard spreadsheet or database software that allows you to manage and update mailing lists so that people who complete the survey can be excluded from follow-up mailings. For e-mail or web surveys, it is important to have the program automatically send a thank-you reply acknowledging receipt of the survey. For traditional mail surveys, a thank-you postcard is especially useful for populations you are likely to survey again. With web, e-mail, and mail surveys, use tracking to determine when to send the next reminder. For nonrespondents, send reminder e-mails at a different time of day and on a different day of the week from the original mailings.

Also, if most of the e-mail addresses in the sample are work addresses, do not send the e-mail out on Friday afternoon or on Saturday, Sunday, or Monday morning.

Because it is becoming increasingly difficult to reach respondents, many survey designs now use combinations of ways through which respondents can respond (telephone, mail, web or e-mail). With mixed-mode data collection efforts, a record of both when and what method has already been offered must be carefully kept.

Response Rates

Getting people to respond to the survey is the main goal of the data collection process. If everyone you are trying to contact is eligible to complete the survey, the response rate is the total number of people interviewed divided by the total number of people you attempted to interview (anyone ineligible to complete the study should be removed from the denominator). The lower the response rate is, the more likely the study is to be vulnerable to nonresponse bias. Unlike sampling error, the effect that nonresponse error has on the quality of the survey is not easy to quantify because evaluators do not know whether the nonrespondents differ from the respondents in terms of how they would have responded to the survey. The book titled *Survey Nonresponse* (Groves, Dillman, Eltinge, and Little, 2001) received the 2011 American Association for Public Opinion Research lifetime achievement research award and provides a compendium of research on survey nonresponse.

Although there is no such thing as an official acceptable response rate, response rates are the industry standard by which people judge the quality of a survey. Surveys that achieve a response rate of 70 percent or higher are generally thought of as being high-quality surveys, and nonresponse is not usually a concern. Studies that have response rates between 50 and 70 percent can use some nonresponse weighting adjustment to reduce potential nonresponse bias. Nonresponse adjustments usually involve weighting the data set to increase the overall impact of the data collected from people who have characteristics similar to the nonrespondents. For example, if you are attempting to measure employee satisfaction but, while collecting your data, you find that support staff are less likely to participate, you can reduce the potential nonresponse bias in the measurement by increasing the weighting factor for the support staff who did complete the survey. The adjustments apply to responses aggregated over different client groups and do not help in reducing errors due to nonresponses among individual client groups. Typically, adjustments are not made for small agency surveys, especially for local and nonprofit service providers.

Even if the budget is tight, try not to cut back on efforts to achieve a higher response rate. Reducing sample size or questionnaire length is usually a more appropriate way of trying to save money than reducing the level of contact effort during data collection. A low response rate often negates what may have been on the whole good survey design work.

The most important factor in achieving good response rates is making additional contact attempts. Most telephone and in-person interviews are not completed on the first call attempt. With household telephone surveys that rely on calling randomly selected telephone numbers, the average number of call attempts needed to complete an interview has risen to over five. Telephone studies that make fewer than five call attempts are not likely to achieve a 50 percent response rate. For mail, e-mail, and web surveys, a single mailing often yields a very low response rate. The standard is two or three mailings, with at least two mailings having a postcard or e-mail message sent a few days after the initial mailing to remind people to participate. Of course, the more professional the survey looks or sounds, the more likely it is that a respondent will decide to participate. A good introduction is particularly important for interviewer-administered surveys, and a strong cover letter and an attractive instrument design are key to gaining cooperation on self-administered surveys. For surveys by agencies of their own clients, if the agency has established a reasonable level of trust with clients, the key problem will be gaining contacts with clients, not client refusals to respond.

Besides the overall response rate, you should be concerned with item nonresponse. During data collection, it is very important (especially at the beginning) to check the quality of the respondents' answers. This usually is referred to as performing *data checks*. Data checks performed during data collection often uncover interviewer problems, procedural problems, or questionnaire problems. Also, during interviewer-administered data collection, routinely asking interviewers about what things are not working well often help detect problems. Although it may be too late to fix problems that are discovered during data collection, the damage can often be contained or minimized during data analysis.

Prepare Data for Analysis

Interview-administered and web surveys that use CATI and CAPI have the distinct advantage of providing a useful data file immediately after the data have been collected. For mail and paper surveys, a coder must enter the data into a data file. To reduce entry errors, it is recommended that at least 5 percent of a coder's work be checked for accuracy. If you find lots of errors during the checking, you may need to retrain the coder or there may be something wrong with the coding procedures. If the project has enough funding, consider doing double entry and fixing all errors found through checking discrepancies between the two data files. Regardless of how data were entered, by a coder, a respondent, or an interviewer, you will usually find yourself needing to fix or change entries for some answer responses. Never alter the original raw data file. It is better to make all edits and corrections and fix input errors using the statistical software package you plan to use for the analysis, thus creating an edited version of the original data file, preserving the original data file, and also being able to keep a record of all edits made.

"Backcoding" is a special type of data editing that involves giving a coder some rules for interpreting a respondent's open-ended response to a question that included "other" as a response category and asked the respondent to specify. Sometimes when a respondent has a series of response options that includes an "anything else" or "other" to be specified option, the respondent chooses "anything else" or "other," but then provides an answer that is equivalent to an existing response option. For instance, a respondent asked, "Do you consider yourself white, black, Asian, or some other race?" may record "African American" under "other." Backcoding procedures would most likely change the respondent's answer from "other" to "black."

To categorize responses to an open-ended question, break the task down into three distinct tasks: develop categories, code the responses, and enter the data with an identification variable so the new variable can be merged into the existing data set.

In some situations, you may want to weight the responses of subgroups of respondents. There are two main reasons to include a weight variable in the data file: the sample design was not a random sample or the selection was random, but the final sample of respondents significantly differs on key characteristics from the overall population you are trying to generalize to. If you need to weight for both of these reasons, create a weight that corrects for the sample design and, then, using this weight, adjust the sample to match the key characteristics of the population. For example, consider a study of engineers where you purposely gave women twice the chance of selection to ensure that enough interviews would be completed with women. Comparing men and women would not require using a weight. However, to calculate the overall percentage of engineers giving a particular response, you would need to weight women's responses by one-half. Suppose also that when you look at the weighted estimates, you realize that nuclear engineers were far less likely to complete the survey. If having too few nuclear engineers affects the result, adjust the weight (increasing the weight for nuclear engineers and reducing it for all other engineers) so that, in the weighted estimates, the proportion of nuclear engineers in the sample is the same as the proportion of nuclear engineers in the overall population.

Present Survey Findings

The most important objective when reporting findings is to present the data in a format that is accessible and clear for the intended audience. Knowing the audience is key. You need to anticipate:

- What the audience is most interested in seeing;
- How much and what sort of disaggregation of responses the audience will want;
- How sophisticated an analysis the audience expects and needs; and
- How long a report (or briefing) the audience will prefer.

As you decide which data to report and how to report them, think about the audience's priorities and then remember that less is better and clarity is essential when planning a presentation. (See Box 14.8 for tips on preparing tables for your report.)

Box 14.8. Tips on Designing Effective Tables

Less is better:

- Consolidate by grouping related questions together to minimize the total number of tables.
- Reduce the number of entries in each table: for example, report only the percentage of yes (or no) responses, or report only the percentage of agree (or disagree) responses.
- When reporting on the statistical significance of the findings, report only whether the results were or were not statistically significant at the level selected, rather than giving values for the statistical test.

Clarity is essential:

- Give each table a clear, descriptive title that identifies the variables that are related in the table.
- Label each variable with sufficient detail for your audience.
- Provide the exact wording of the question at issue in the first table in which the question appears.
- When collapsing a variable, clarify which values are in each group, rather than just labeling values as high or low.

- Provide the number responding to the particular items in each table, because the number may vary from table to table.
- Specify which units are in the denominator when reporting percentages, such as percentages "of those responding."
- When a measure of the strength of the relationship between a pair of variables is provided, briefly define it the first time it is provided, in a footnote to the table.
- When providing data from another source to compare to your survey data, identify that source with sufficient documentation in a footnote to the table.

The priorities of the audience should drive decisions on what to include and in what order findings should be presented. The first table should present demographic or relevant background on the people or jurisdictions responding to the survey. This table might be titled something like "Profile of the Sample." Comparable data on the general population's demographics should be arranged in this table as well (if they are available), so that the relative representativeness of the sample can be conveyed to the audience. Decisions on what to include in the profile table should reflect the audience's interests. Sometimes, for example, the answer to a key question, such as whether a jurisdiction has adopted an innovative tax or regulation, might be included in the first table.

Basic contingency tables that present percentages of units selecting each response for questions in the survey are the most user-friendly mode of presentation (see Tables 14.4 and 14.5). The percentages should be disaggregated according to respondent characteristics that are of interest to the audience. These characteristics might be simply demographic differences, such as levels of education or geographical location, or they might be behavioral factors, such as frequency of contacts with an office or with a specific service.

It is crucial to report response rates, and even the rates among subgroups, if relevant, no matter how you selected the sample. Sampling error is only one source of error and not necessarily the major one; thus analysis of the impact of nonrespondents is always required. When response rates are less than 70 percent, extra effort should be undertaken to ensure that there is no evidence of nonresponse bias. Only if assurances are sufficient to convince the most critical audience that the sample is fairly representative of the target population should statistical significance tests be used. The most common test used in contingency tables is the chi-square test. It simply reports whether the differences between subgroups are statistically significant (and thus generalizable to the target population) given the decision rule used, such as a 95 or 99 percent confidence level, rather than reporting actual values of a statistic such as the chi

TABLE 14.4. CONTINGENCY TABLE PRESENTING SURVEY FINDINGS.

Level of Satisfaction with Legal Aid Services by Type of Criminal Prosecution

How satisfied were you with the responsiveness of your attorney to your questions?	Drug Charges (N = 352)	Misdemeanor (N = 85)	Theft/Robbery (N = 122)
Not satisfied	5	8	10
Somewhat satisfied	10	12	18
Extremely satisfied	85	80	72
	100%	100%	100%

Note: The differences found in satisfaction levels across the subgroups divided by type of crime are statistically significant at a 95 percent level of confidence. However, this does not preclude nonsampling errors. One source of nonsampling error is nonresponse bias. In this case, only 63 percent of the sample responded. Also, totals may not add up to 100 percent due to rounding in this and all subsequent tables.

TABLE 14.5. CONTINGENCY TABLE CONSOLIDATING MULTIPLE VARIABLES.

Proportion of Respondents Who Are Satisfied with Legal Aid Services by Type of Criminal Prosecution

Proportion of Respondents Reporting Somewhat or Extremely Satisfied (2 or 3 on a 1 to 3 scale) with:	Drug Charges (N = 352)	Misdemeanor (N = 85)	Theft/Robbery (N = 122)
Responsiveness of your attorney to your questions	95%	92%	90%
Effectiveness of the representation afforded you by your attorney	90%	83%	88%
Amount of time your attorney devoted to your case	88%	81%	78%
Ease of obtaining legal representation	85%	84%	86%
Courteousness of the Legal Services staff	95%	94%	93%
Timeliness of the response of the Legal Services staff to your request for assistance	84%	80%	72%

square. (See Chapter Twenty-Three for more guidance on statistical analyses of survey data.)

Although the actual number of tables and amount of analysis reported should be limited by the targeted length of a presentation, the data should be analyzed from many different angles. Thorough analysis of the data means that many more tables are produced and reviewed than are reported. Simply searching for interesting relationships should not be frowned on. Sometimes the most interesting findings are not anticipated.

In addition to reporting the survey data in a user-friendly format, information on the methodology used to obtain the data is also extremely important. A "Scope and Methods" section should be included (possibly as an appendix) to describe the decisions you made and the reasoning behind them regarding sampling, wording of questions, and other pertinent decisions that may affect interpretation. It is also important to be explicit about how response rates were computed. Sufficient detail on the number of mailings sent and on means used to test the generalizability of the results should be given. The key is to provide clear, understandable background information on the methodology without overwhelming and boring the audience.

Conclusion

There are many options for surveying stakeholders in public and nonprofit programs. Certain aspects of survey methodology have remained constant and are likely to remain so into the future, whereas others continue to change. Principles of survey design, protection of confidentiality, sampling protocols, data analysis approaches, and audience-oriented presentation skills are fairly impervious to change. Technological improvements in means for reaching and encouraging respondents and for capturing data continue to modify the ways in which evaluators conduct surveys.

The keys to obtaining valid, useful data about programs are to rigorously plan and pretest the survey and the sampling strategy, and then meticulously oversee data collection and analytical processes. Many key decisions are made during the design phase that can make or break the entire endeavor. Careful consideration of the relative advantages and disadvantages of different survey modes, types of incentives, and types of questions to employ is essential. And then open discussion about the decisions made and the rationales underlying them is necessary for strengthening the legitimacy and credibility of the findings. As technological innovations open yet more choices, the key is to systematically weigh the options and choose wisely to provide the most valid and reliable information possible.

References

Blumberg, S. J., and Luke, J. V. *Wireless Substitution: Early Release of Estimates from the National Health Interview Survey, July–December 2012.* Atlanta, GA: National Center for Health Statistics, 2013. www.cdc.gov/nchs/data/nhis/earlyrelease/wireless201306.pdf.

Blair, J., and Conrad, F. "Sample Size for Cognitive Interview Pretesting." *Public Opinion Quarterly,* 2011, *75*(4), 636–658.

Collins, D. "Pretesting Survey Instruments: An Overview of Cognitive Methods." *Quality of Life Research,* 2003, *12,* 229–238.

Couper, M. P. *Designing Effective Web Surveys.* New York: Cambridge University Press, 2008.

Dillman, D. A., Smyth, J. D., and Christian, L. M. *Internet, Mail, and Mixed-Mode Surveys: The Tailored Design Method* (4th ed.). Hoboken, NJ: Wiley, 2014.

Drennan, J. "Cognitive Interviewing: Verbal Data in the Design and Pretesting of Questionnaires." *Journal of Advanced Nursing,* 2003, *42*(1), 57–63.

Ericsson, K. A., & Simon, H. A. "Verbal Reports as Data." *Psychological Review,* 1980, *87,* 215–250.

Fowler, F. J. *Survey Research Methods* (5th ed.). Thousand Oaks, CA: Sage, 2014.

Groves, Robert M., Dillman, Don, Eltinge, John L., and Little, Roderick J. A. *Survey Nonresponse.* Hoboken, NJ: Wiley, 2001.

Krosnick, J. A., and others. "The Impact of 'No Opinion' Response Options on Data Quality: Non-Attitude Reduction or an Invitation to Satisfice?" *Public Opinion Quarterly,* 2002, *66*(3), 371–403.

McClendon, M. J., and Alwin, D. F. "No Opinion Filters and Attitude Measurement Reliability." *Sociological Methods and Research,* 1993, *20,* 60–103.

Singer, E. "The Use of Incentives to Reduce Nonresponse in Household Surveys." In R. M. Groves, D. Dillman, J. L. Eltinge, and R.J.A. Little (eds.), *Survey Nonresponse.* Hoboken, N.J.: Wiley, 2002.

Tourangeau, Roger, Rips, Lance J., and Rasinski, Kenneth. *The Psychology of Survey Responses.* New York: Cambridge University Press, 2000.

Willis, G. *Cognitive Interviewing: A Tool for Improving Questionnaire Design.* Thousand Oaks, CA: Sage, 2005.

Willis, G., DeMaio, T., & Harris-Kojetin, B. "Is the Bandwagon Headed to the Methodological Promised Land? Evaluation of the Validity of Cognitive Interviewing Techniques." In M. Sirken, D. Herrmann, S. Schechter, N. Schwarz, J. Tanur, and R. Tourangeau (eds.), *Cognition and Survey Research.* Hoboken, NJ: Wiley, 1999.

CHAPTER FIFTEEN

ROLE PLAYING[*]

Claudia L. Aranda, Diane K. Levy, Sierra Stoney

Role playing is a research methodology used to directly observe a transaction. Studies using the method, also referred to as testing or audit studies, involve individuals trained to act as bona fide customers or clients. Role players gather detailed information of a transaction and document the experience in a manner to support empirical analysis. Role playing can take a number of forms and be used to answer questions pertaining to the quality of services provided by government agencies and private businesses and whether there are systematic differences in customer treatment. Although the method can be a complex and costly undertaking and raises ethical and legal issues that researchers must consider, it can provide information and insight difficult to access with other research tools. In this chapter, we review elements of the role playing methodology, provide examples of how it can be used for different types of research efforts, discuss key elements of implementation and data analysis, and address ethical considerations and limitations.

What Is Role Playing?

Role playing as a research methodology developed from participant-observer methods used by anthropologists (Erstad, 1998). It is well known for its use in

*This chapter draws from Chapter 11 in the second edition of the *Handbook of Practical Program Evaluation*. In particular, the authors acknowledge the contribution of Margery Austin Turner to the Statistical Analysis section.

federally funded, national studies of housing discrimination against racial and ethnic minorities that have been conducted since the 1970s. The method is flexible, as evidenced by the diversity of purposes for which it has been used, ranging from evaluations of customer service quality in fast-food restaurants to rigorous studies of discrimination against protected classes of renters and homebuyers in housing markets across the United States (Erstad, 1998; Turner, Santos, Levy, Wissoker, Aranda, and Pitingolo, 2013).

Role-playing studies can be conducted in person or remotely through Internet- or telephone-based interactions. In either scenario, the role player carefully observes how the role-play subject responds to inquiries and provides other information or treatment. Studies conducted in person allow the role player to observe characteristics and actions of the test subject and, most importantly, allow the test subject to observe the role player, thereby increasing the likelihood that the subject's treatment of the tester is based on an accurate identification of the tester's pertinent characteristic (the role player's gender, race, and so forth).

Some studies incorporate both in-person and remote test approaches to evaluate multiple levels of service. For example, researchers assessed the information provided to customers inquiring about emergency contraception by telephone and in person. This dual approach allowed researchers to collect a large number of observations and to determine whether there were differences in the amount and type of information provided to role players based on method of contact (French and Kaunitz, 2007).

The method can be structured for implementation with single testers, matched tester pairs, or with three or more matched testers. For the sake of brevity, we refer to single- and paired-test structures in this chapter. Single-tester role playing is used to collect information related to a specific event or behavior for which comparative information is unnecessary. For example, a study to assess an agency's response time to telephone calls can be carried out with a single-tester structure for information gathering.

Matched pair role playing is used when the objective is to learn about differential treatment of people based on a certain characteristic, such as age, gender, race or ethnicity, disability, and so on. The unique strength of paired role playing is its ability to measure treatment of one tester against a counterfactual. Testers of a pair are matched to the greatest extent possible on all characteristics but the one of interest. For example, a study of differential treatment based on ambulatory disability would match role players on age, gender, race and ethnicity, and assigned income, but one tester of each pair would use a wheelchair and the other tester would be ambulatory. Such role plays generate comparative data collected by the individual matched testers that are used to analyze the prevalence and forms of differential treatment. Without a reference point, there is no way to determine whether the observed treatment of the two role players differs based on the characteristic of interest.

Diversity of Uses

The role-play methodology can be used for a number of research purposes. Evaluation studies range from smaller, exploratory efforts that shed light on an issue to studies that produce statistical estimates of treatment. Evaluations can be used to strengthen support for a policy intervention or gauge the impact of an existing policy. Monitoring studies assess behaviors and identify areas for improvement. Enforcement studies gather evidence that can be used to enforce rules or laws and identify how best to target other enforcement efforts.

Evaluation

Evaluation studies conducted for exploratory purposes can use role playing to gain understanding of an issue or to test research protocols. Because such smaller studies are not intended to produce generalizable results, they can be completed with a small number of tests using semi-structured protocols that allow for the discovery of issues or protocol challenges that might be unanticipated. During the exploratory phase of a study on housing discrimination against persons with disabilities, researchers conducted a small number of tests in which persons with mental and physical disabilities utilized a wide range of testing approaches (Turner, Herbig, Kaye, Fenderson, and Levy, 2005). The exploratory tests confirmed what protocols were capable of being implemented across many tests as well as which specific populations could be the focus of the subsequent pilot phase of the study.

Evaluation studies also can measure the prevalence of behaviors or treatment. To produce generalizable results, such studies require a fairly large number of tests based on a representative sample of the target subject. Data collection protocols must be highly structured and relatively inflexible to enable role players to implement them consistently across all tests. Report forms role players use to record collected information provide researchers with data that can be analyzed statistically to identify patterns in treatment and to produce rigorous findings. Qualitative analysis of the role players' experiences can illustrate nuances in treatment that are not otherwise captured in quantitative data.

Studies using the role play methodology for evaluation purposes include a series of nationwide paired testing studies of housing discrimination based on race and ethnicity. These studies, sponsored by the Department of Housing and Urban Development since the late 1970s, have produced estimates of discrimination in the rental and sales markets. Results have shed light on the changes in the incidence and the forms of discrimination over time (Turner, Santos, Levy, Wissoker, Aranda, and Pitingolo, 2013). Other examples include a study on whether equally qualified women and men were treated differently when applying for the same restaurant position. The researchers hired people to pose as applicants for server positions. The role players sent similar resumes to restaurants and documented their experiences during the job application process. Analysts compared differences by sex in who received an interview, who was offered employment, and the starting wages. The statistically significant results found that male role players were more likely to receive job offers from high-end restaurants, whereas female role players were somewhat more likely to receive job offers from low-cost restaurants (Neumark, Bank, and Van Nort, 1996). (See also, Bone, Christensen, and Williams, 2014, for a study of differential treatment based on race and ethnicity in the commercial loan market; Vilnai-Yavetz and Gilboa, 2014, for a study on how customer service representatives in retail facilities treated customers based on their attire.)

Monitoring

Monitoring studies assess the extent to which behaviors change over time. This use of role playing relies on two or more interactions with representatives of the monitored entity to support analysis of information collected at different points in time. Role-play protocols, similar to those used in evaluation studies, must be relatively inflexible and implemented consistently over time to increase the comparability of the information collected.

Examples of monitoring studies include a project examining the effectiveness of customer service training on service quality. Role players posing as prospective patients contacted a health clinic twice by telephone. The first contact took place prior to the onset of customer service training; data from this contact provided a baseline for customer service performance. After the training, role players contacted the clinic again using the same protocol they used during the initial contact. Researchers' analysis of role players' responses on standardized data collection forms found that the training program improved service quality (Granatino, Verkamp, and Parker, 2013). Latham, Ford, and Tzabbar (2012) studied a role-playing program used by a restaurant to provide its managers with information they could use to train and coach wait staff. People were hired to visit the restaurant multiple times over a period of forty months. Feedback from these role players was studied to determine whether staff service quality improved over time.

Enforcement

When used for enforcement purposes, role playing gathers evidence of patterns of improper or prohibited practices that can be used to reinforce best practices or to bring suit if the practices are unlawful. Role play for enforcement targets entities or locations where improper behavior is suspected, which is one of the features that distinguishes this use of the methodology from role playing for evaluation research. Multiple tests of a single entity verify that observed violations are not random. Protocols need to be flexible to respond to the circumstances of a particular situation and role players are instructed to document more detailed, nuanced information than they would gather for a research study.

Role playing has been an effective approach to increasing retailer compliance with the federal requirement to verify the age of customers purchasing tobacco products. Although U.S. law prohibits the sale of such products to anyone under the age of eighteen, not all retailers conduct age checks. Krevor, Ponicki, Grube, and DeJong (2011) wanted to determine whether providing feedback on incidents of violation would result in fewer violations. Role players were hired to attempt purchase of tobacco products without valid identification. Researchers provided feedback to retailers that were found to violate the law and saw the rates of compliance increase over time.

Fair housing organizations and federal agencies charged with the enforcement of fair housing laws use role-playing methods to target housing providers suspected of discriminating against certain home-seekers. These entities often initiate paired tests after receiving complaints of unfair treatment by a person looking to rent or buy housing. Using people hired to conduct role playing, fair housing entities structure matched paired tests to determine whether discrimination is taking place and, if it is, to compile evidence that will be admissible in a court of law.

Sampling

Representativeness

During the initial design phase of a role-playing study, researchers must make the important determination of which types of transactions will have the opportunity to be included in the sample. Ultimately, the extent to which the sample is representative will have implications for how the findings of the study may be applied to a larger set of transactions. For example, in a study evaluating the quality of information given to seventeen-year-old women inquiring about emergency contraception in five states, the researchers selected a major city within each state as their focus. All of the commercial pharmacies in each city were included in the sample. The findings of the study illustrate the diversity of experiences of young women seeking emergency contraception, but cannot be used for statistical inference. By limiting the sample to a single city within five states, the researchers constrained their universe to metropolitan areas within these states (Wilkinson, Vargas, Fahey, Suther, and Silverstein, 2014).

The Housing Discrimination Study 2012, which aimed to produce statistically valid and precise national estimates of discrimination, could not include all possible interactions with housing providers in all metropolitan areas nationwide. The study limited the universe of possible housing providers to those that advertise online. Researchers sampled advertisements from multiple websites in proportion to the geographic distribution of the rental housing in the study's twenty-eight metropolitan areas. The populations of the selected study sites represented 88 percent of all black and Hispanic households in the United States and 90 percent of Asian rental households (Turner, Santos, Levy, Wissoker, Aranda, and Pitingolo, 2013).

When deciding which metropolitan areas will be included in a role-play study, researchers must determine whether prospective sites will need to reach a minimum population threshold in order to be considered. If the intended role players will have relatively uncommon characteristics, repeated tests in a geographic area with a small population will have a higher risk of detection. Selecting metropolitan areas with larger populations might make tests seem less conspicuous, but also might make test results less generalizable. Ultimately, a balance must be achieved between reducing the risk of disclosure by eliminating particular metropolitan areas from testing while retaining sufficient numbers of areas to avert the risk of noncoverage bias (Turner, Santos, Levy, Wissoker, Aranda, and Pitingolo, 2013).

Sample Size

The ideal sample size will depend on the objective of the study, the intended precision of the results, and the extent to which the findings for particular subgroups will need to be assessed. Research conducted for enforcement purposes may not require more than a few tests and compliance monitoring typically requires fewer tests to detect actionable violations. Likewise, role playing conducted for exploratory purposes also might not require more than a small number of tests to learn what researchers need to know about a population or a protocol issue. Evaluation studies require larger samples in order to generate valid, statistically significant results. Sample sizes are most commonly limited by the maximum number of tests that reasonably can be conducted within the project timeline and budget.

Selecting the Sample

For most evaluation studies, the researchers need to establish a method for selecting an unbiased, random sample from the full universe of transactions, where each entity has a positive probability of being included in the sample. When developing a sampling approach, the researcher should attempt to mimic how the transaction naturally occurs in the marketplace to the greatest extent possible. For example, in order to evaluate the differences in accessibility to specialty medical services for children depending on whether they have public insurance, Bisgaier and Rhodes (2011) compiled a list of clinics in Cook County, Illinois, using lists of physicians who had submitted specialty claims for children. By drawing a random sample from this list, the researchers could be confident that their sample would consist only of clinics that would expect calls from parents seeking specialty medical services for their children.

Evaluators also need to decide upon exclusion criteria that, once a random sample is selected, could cause a transaction or test site to be omitted. In the Housing Discrimination Study 2012, once the advertisements were drawn through a random selection process, project staff determined whether the housing had any of the carefully pre-determined set of characteristics that would merit its exclusion. For example, if the selected housing would not be covered by the Fair Housing Act, such as an owner-occupied building with fewer than four units, it was ruled ineligible for testing. Particularly when a study includes multiple sites with multiple test managers, significant oversight is necessary to help ensure that the application of the criteria determining which transactions will be included in the sample is done consistently and without any selection bias.

In other evaluations, however, a random sample might not be feasible given the research objectives, as was the case in Galster, Wissoker, and Zimmerman's 2001 matched pair study of discrimination in home insurance. In addition to matching testers on observable characteristics, the researchers also matched neighborhoods and homes on characteristics relevant to actuarial evaluation. The only observable difference in matched neighborhoods was the racial/ethnic composition of residents. The researchers evaluated differences in matched testers' interactions with local home insurance agencies. Because the researchers were required to match both the testers and the specific test sites given the study objectives, the sample could not be randomized at any point. For this reason and also because the study focused on local insurance agencies, the findings could not be generalized to represent the home insurance market broadly.

Data Collection Instruments

Determining Which Elements of Role Playing to Document

Given the research question to be answered, a researcher should explicitly identify actions or behaviors of interest and develop specific questions pertaining to whether these actions occurred during a test. In addition to data directly relating to the research question, additional information that might affect observed differences in the transaction should be included. For instance, the demographic characteristics of a housing provider, such as their age or gender, might be related to their treatment of a prospective renter; including this information in the data collection instrument will allow the researcher to explore these possibilities. Once the researcher has developed a list of relevant information to be gathered from the role-play tests, these items can be organized into a data collection instrument to be used by the role player.

A 2010 study of quality of information provided via telephone to teens by South Bronx medical practices simplified the data collection process for role players by incorporating flexibility into data collection forms. The researchers wanted to know whether medical centers provided information on four topics, and allowed role players to choose from a finite set of responses to indicate how (or if) the medical center provided the information. Additionally, the role player was asked for a subjective evaluation of the medical center staff's demeanor. The four questions were organized and presented to the role player in the order in which they were expected to arise during a test (Alberti, Steinberg, Khan, Abdullah, and Begdell, 2010).

Data Collection Forms

Because evaluation studies aim to generate results that can be aggregated across many tests, data collection forms require predefined, closed-ended responses that can be consistently compared across tests. Analysts may also find it useful to include open-ended questions that provide an opportunity for qualitative analysis. Open-ended formats also give role players an opportunity to include information that might turn out to be common among tests, but which was not anticipated by the researcher. Understanding the specific causes for observed differences, which are collected through open-ended documentation, is essential for effective enforcement, public education efforts, and training in the sector under study.

For example, in a study on housing discrimination against people using wheelchairs, each role player in a test pair completed a narrative, which provided a detailed, chronological account of their interaction with a housing provider (Levy, Turner, Santos, Wissoker, Aranda, Pitingolo, and Ho, 2014). Role players using wheelchairs each asked for reasonable modifications to improve the accessibility of the housing units. Although statistical analyses produced estimates for those requests that were approved or denied, and those which received no definitive answer, the qualitative analysis of the narratives helped capture the range of responses included in each category. While some housing providers did tentatively agree to the modification requests, they required extensive documentation before final approval. The narratives also showed that many housing providers were unfamiliar with the process for approving modification requests or did not know their official policy of what might be permissible. This finding suggested that more education on the Fair Housing Act, the Americans with Disabilities Act, and other relevant law could help housing providers be more responsive to the requests of prospective renters. Without the qualitative data provided by the tester narratives, such an important conclusion might not have been reached.

Open-ended questions and comprehensive narratives also can be critical tools during exploratory research. During the exploratory phase of a pilot study on discrimination against persons who are deaf or hard of hearing, researchers implemented two distinct testing scenarios (Turner, Herbig, Kaye, Fenderson, and Levy, 2005). The first required testers to use a telephone relay service (TTY) to contact a housing provider while the second had testers conduct in-person visits to obtain information about available housing. The thorough descriptions of each interaction with an agent helped researchers determine that while both approaches were feasible, deaf testers conducting in-person tests had difficulty gaining access to buildings with intercom systems. The note-taking process also was awkward, and testers had difficulty writing legible notes. The remote testing also provided the most efficient, cost-effective protocol since testers did not need to travel to meet with housing providers. Ultimately, the national study sponsored by HUD and conducted in 2014 utilized remote testing (with three different telephone relay systems) to estimate the incidence of discrimination against home-seekers who are deaf and hard of hearing (Levy, Turner, Santos, Wissoker, Aranda, Pitingolo, and Ho, 2014). The lessons learned during the 2005 pilot study, many of which were gleaned from the transcripts from relay calls as well as the tester narratives, helped determine the data collection procedures and tester protocols that were implemented in the national study.

In some circumstances, a researcher might find it useful to document role-play interactions independently, instead of assigning the role player with the task. An evaluation of health services directed to youth in Tanzania, for example, recorded transactions between teenage role players and clinic staff. The role players were trained to ask about specific health services, and the researchers later interpreted and coded the transactions. However labor intensive the process was for the researchers, this method of documentation provides more reliable data than if the role players had reported their experiences themselves (Renju, Andrew, Nyalali, Kishamawe, Kato, Changalucha, and Obasi, 2010). Researchers that choose to audio or video record role-play transactions should be mindful of the federal and state laws that may limit the ability to do so without appropriate consent. (Eleven U.S. states currently require the consent of every party to a phone call or in-person conversation in order to make the recording lawful.)

Given the wide array of available online tools, researchers developing a role-play evaluation should consider the benefits of a centralized data collection system. Testers will be able to complete test forms immediately following a transaction, and project managers will be able to monitor incoming data in real time. Project staff can assess tester adherence to reporting requirements and track progress toward study targets. Online forms also can help improve the quality of the data testers obtain—required fields can be created to ensure testers answer specific questions and in particular formats before being able to save a test form, helping reduce the amount of data cleaning that will be necessary and ensuring vital data is captured. Whatever data collection system is used, researchers should establish a detailed data security plan to help prevent any breaches in data confidentiality.

Recruiting, Selecting, and Training Role Players

One of the most important steps in implementing a successful role-play study is the meticulous recruitment, selection, and training of role players. Regardless of the specific characteristics that role players must have for a particular research study, the most successful candidates for any study will possess the ability to (1) maintain confidentiality about their roles and the study as a whole; (2) remain objective about the subject matter and the individuals being studied; and (3) be credible in each and every portrayal. If role players are not able to consistently achieve these objectives, they could place the entire study at risk.

Determining Key Characteristics for Role Players

Role players should be selected based on the characteristics that are relevant to the treatment or service provision being evaluated. In many cases, the role players' most important characteristics will be determined by the research objective but evaluators also will need to determine which bona fide characteristics are required and which will be assigned. In the Housing Discrimination Studies on race and ethnicity, role players were matched on their gender and relative age but were assigned a set of household and financial characteristics, including income, occupation, marital status, and family size. Testers were always unambiguously well-qualified for the housing they were seeking, and the minority testers were slightly better qualified overall relative to their match. In addition to conveying their true gender and age, role players were required to have the same racial and/or ethnic background that was being evaluated in the particular transaction. It should also be noted that, unlike some enforcement organizations, which only use role players who are obviously of their race/ethnicity, Housing Discrimination Study 2012 included a diverse pool of Hispanic, Black, and Asian role players whose racial/ethnic identifiability was assessed by third-party raters after data collection had ended. So, although role players need to convey fictitious information, researchers must decide where the line between reality and role playing must be drawn.

Douglas and Douglas (2007) encountered recruitment dilemmas in their feasibility analysis of the possibility of using "mystery students" to evaluate lecturer quality. While non-current students might prove to be more objective evaluators, their sudden appearance in the classroom may seem conspicuous to lecturers or other students. Moreover, non-current students, without the context of the prior lectures and written materials, might not be the best judge of lecture quality, and test reports would need to be limited to rigidly defined criteria. Current students would be more familiar with subjective indicators of lecture quality but might be biased observers; they also risk being detected if employed for analyses of different lecturers at too frequent intervals.

Matched pair studies (as compared with single tester studies) can present a more complicated recruitment and selection process because any individual role player cannot be used if one or more appropriate matches cannot be identified. In addition to matching a tester on observable characteristics, researchers must consider other, intangible traits, such as a person's overall demeanor, that might introduce unwanted variables if the traits are not present in both testers within the pair. For remote testing, where the role playing will take place online or over the telephone, the matching process is simpler. If the tester will only be perceived by their voice, there is greater flexibility in the matching of pairs.

Recruiting and Selecting Role Players

Assembling a robust and committed tester pool is one of the most important steps researchers can take to help ensure the success of an evaluation. Organizations that specialize in conducting role-play studies often will draw from their current tester pool or solicit informal referrals from within their existing networks of social service agencies, community groups, non-profit organizations, and universities. When conducting recruitment outreach, it is important to use general terms about hiring research assistants in order to avoid detection. More generally, advertising is discouraged because it could threaten the confidentiality of the evaluation. Because testing requires secrecy to avoid detection, any advertising done by researchers should be part of a careful, comprehensive strategy that avoids using terms that might disclose the sensitive nature of the work.

When meeting and identifying prospective role players, researchers should consider the additional traits that will affect the quality of information the role player will be able to obtain and report, such as their reliability and capacity to adhere to the research protocols. During an in-person interview with each prospective tester, researchers should ask specific questions related to the tasks they will be required to complete. Information gathered from the interview and from an application form should provide answers to the following types of questions:

- Does the applicant or anyone in the applicant's family work for the sector being studied? If so, the applicant might have a conflict of interest and their objectivity as a researcher may be compromised. Ask about conflicts of interest up-front to avoid inadvertently disclosing study details to a person who could violate the study's confidentiality, either intentionally or unintentionally.
- Does the applicant oppose role-play studies in general for ethical reasons? The researcher should avoid hiring an applicant who expresses opinions that suggest the applicant will have difficulty following instructions or being objective.
- Does the applicant express any aversion to offering information about him- or herself that is not entirely truthful as part of a research project?

- Does the applicant express doubt about his or her ability to be convincing in acting a role or seem reluctant to provide untruthful information in a role-play situation?
- Has the applicant been in the news frequently or have a high-profile job? If yes, the person is not a good role-play candidate.
- Is there anything about the applicant's statements that suggests the applicant will not be able to report his or her test experiences in an accurate, complete, and objective manner?

It is often possible to glean insights about applicants and how they might perform as role players from listening to the questions they ask and the comments they offer during the interview. The applicants' interactions with researchers during the interview also provide information about their personality, objectivity, reliability, cooperativeness, and ability to be matched with other testers.

Training Role Players

An essential step in preparing role players for the demands of consistently executing detailed protocols is a comprehensive training program, which includes a training session and the completion of a practice assignment. During the training session, researchers explain the entire data collection process in great detail; they present protocols and role-play guidelines, review forms, and discuss potentially problematic scenarios. Because the success of paired role play depends on consistency in behavior across a pair of role players, general codes of conduct must be discussed, including guidance on what should be worn during in-person testing. Role players should receive instruction on which behaviors might lead to detection or otherwise compromise the validity of the study results. The training also operates as a forum for discussing any questions role players might have prior to their first experience collecting data. During the Housing Discrimination Study 2012, in-person trainings were presented by research staff who integrated short film clips, participatory role plays, and interactive quizzes to increase tester engagement while reinforcing key protocols and guidelines. By presenting the testing procedures using a variety of formats, researchers help increase the probability that role players will retain the specific (and numerous) protocols.

It is good procedure to include at least one practice role play as part of any training program. Role players conduct a "practice" assignment as they would a "real" one but the information collected is not used for analysis. Role players meet with their coordinators during a "briefing" to review their assignment, review protocols and ask questions. Testers then conduct a test in-person or remotely, depending on the study, and complete data collection forms. Whether or not testers will be required to prepare a narrative for the real tests, they should write one as part of the practice test. During a "debriefing," coordinators thoroughly review all of the forms and the narrative to check for any protocol errors and to confirm the forms accurately reflect what transpired. Any errors or omissions should be addressed immediately. When training role players for a new project, coordinators should work closely with testers before and after their tests to ensure they have followed all protocols and have written comprehensive narratives. By making this initial investment of time during the training phase of the project, researchers will increase significantly the quality of the tests and the collected data.

Implementing Role Playing

Management and Quality Control

The proper implementation of the data collection phase of a role-play study requires extensive oversight to ensure high standards are achieved. It is crucial to have a management structure in place with ongoing and careful oversight so that researchers can identify and swiftly address any potential problems. The extent of the management structure will depend on the scope of the study. For a local study with a small team of testers, one coordinator probably can provide sufficient oversight to ensure consistent, high-quality work. The coordinator is responsible for managing role players, creating test assignments, enforcing protocols, and reviewing all completed test forms for completeness and accuracy. If the study includes remote testing, local managers could choose to review role players' performance directly. For example, in a telephone study evaluating the quality of information provided to teens by medical practices, researchers managed role player performance by observing calls (Alberti, Steinberg, Khan, Abdulah, and Bedell, 2010). A separate telephone study, which analyzed adolescent experiences when accessing emergency contraception, managed data quality by having two researchers independently code recorded interactions between role players and pharmacists. This approach removed role players' reporting responsibility and prevented variation in judgment across role players from biasing the data quality (Wilkinson, Vargas, Fahey, Suther, and Silverstein, 2014).

For a study taking place over multiple regions, a central manager might oversee several local coordinators to ensure that the testing protocol and standards are followed consistently in all study sites. The central manager reviews all forms submitted by local coordinators and requests clarification as needed. Large-scale or national studies likely will require several central managers, in which case a single director oversees all managers.

Cost Considerations

A number of design choices made in a role-play study can have significant implications for the overall cost of its completion. The type of interaction being simulated obviously has an impact on how much it will cost. An evaluation that can be completed entirely by telephone or online will require a much smaller project budget than a study requiring in-person visits. In many cases, cost considerations determine the type of test pursued and limit the sample size available. In-person tests are also exposed to greater risk of price volatility, which may lead to budget adjustments during testing. For example, a rise in gas prices during the testing period of an in-person study can result in an unexpected increase in the amount of funding needed to cover tester travel expenses.

Practical Problems (and Solutions)

Role-Player Attrition

For any role-play study, researchers should expect attrition among testers. Researchers should consider recruiting up to 20 percent more role players at the beginning of the study than might be needed. Without a sufficiently large pool of role players at the outset, coordinators likely will need to resume recruitment in the midst of data collection efforts, which can prove costly in time and budget resources. Once new role players are recruited, of course, they must be trained and conduct a practice test. For multi-site studies, in particular, the challenge of conducting repeated training sessions for each site can significantly constrain staff time and project resources.

Detection

One of the greatest challenges to the success of a role-play study is the possibility that its existence will become known to the test subjects. Once the confidentiality of the study is compromised, subjects might alter their behavior significantly, which affects data quality and the credibility of the results. At every turn, coordinators must reinforce with testers the importance of maintaining confidentiality and guarding against detection. In the era of social media, maintaining confidentiality about anything is exceptionally challenging; role-play studies can be one tweet or Facebook post away from being irrevocably exposed. Researchers should explicitly bar testers and project staff from sharing information about the role-play study on any social media. Coordinators should monitor social media accounts throughout the data collection period to check and enforce compliance.

Coordinators can help prevent disclosure by assigning role players credible characteristics on every test. They must work closely with role players and confirm that, for each assignment, testers are comfortable with each of their profile characteristics. If a role player will not be able to speak confidently about his or her assigned occupation or remember the name of the spouse assigned, he or she may place the study at risk with deficient portrayals.

Depending on the subject being evaluated, role players could be assigned to visit multiple offices owned or operated by a single company, which could increase the likelihood of detection. In the Housing Discrimination Study 2012, researchers encountered management companies that owned many rental properties. It was a significant concern that role players who visited more than one property owned by the same company would be detected because of the common practice for the individual complexes to keep a log of visits by prospective tenants. As a result, coordinators kept detailed records of which role players had visited properties owned by large, multi-property companies in order to avoid detection.

Design Efficiencies

Role-play studies requiring multiple stages of contact with a subject might include opportunities for efficiency gains. For example, if a role player must first contact a subject by telephone before meeting for an in-person test, the preliminary phone call can be treated as a telephone test, which concludes with obtaining an appointment. Documenting the details of the telephone interaction provides researchers with more information on the transaction overall at a relatively low cost. Role plays with two or more stages also support analysis of the marginal benefit of an in-person visit relative to the outcomes measured at the initial telephone stage. Researchers can contrast the number and quality of outcome measures between telephone and in-person tests while maximizing the utility of the integrated design.

Statistical Analysis

Role playing is a powerful methodology because its results are intuitively clear and compelling to nontechnical audiences. The public can understand findings that minors attempting to buy cigarettes were successful in three of every five establishments they visited, or that information provided by a tourist bureau was accurate 85 percent of the time. Paired role playing is particularly effective because its results directly document unfair differences in treatment. In the study of hiring discrimination against African Americans, 20 percent of the time that young African American men applied for entry-level jobs, they were unable to advance as far in the hiring process as equally qualified white applicants (Turner, Fix, and Struyk, 1991). This kind of result and the individual case examples that can accompany it are clear and convincing to policymakers and to the general public.

Analysis of outcomes using simple role playing in an evaluation of program performance does not present any special statistical challenges. However, analyzing data from paired role playing requires considerable caution. This section focuses on three key issues to address at the data analysis stage for paired role playing: basic measures of differential treatment, procedures for testing the statistical significance of these measures, and the issue of random systematic factors that contribute to the differences in observed treatment. All three of these issues apply specifically to analysis of paired outcomes. Analysis of results from nonpaired role playing is straightforward and can be accomplished with conventional measures and statistical tests.

Measuring Differences in Treatment

The key building block for analysis of data from paired role playing is a case-by-case determination of whether the two members of each pair were treated the same or differently and, if there was a difference, which person was favored. In this analysis, the unit of observation is the pair, and variables are constructed from the experience of the two testers to measure relative outcomes.

To illustrate, in the studies of employment discrimination, analysts determined how far in the hiring process each applicant was able to progress. Specifically, was the tester able to submit an application (Stage 1)? Was the tester granted a formal interview (Stage 2)? And did the tester receive a job offer (Stage 3)? Then outcomes for the two members of each pair were brought together to determine whether one tester advanced further than the other. A test was classified as white favored (if a white partner advanced to a higher stage than the African American partner), African American favored (if the African American partner advanced farther), or no difference (if they both testers reached the same stage). Finally, results were tabulated across tests to report the share of cases in which the white advanced further than an equally qualified African American and the share in which the African American advanced further. Analysis can also be conducted using the individual testers' experience as the unit of observation and comparing the overall outcomes for testers of one type to the overall outcomes for testers of the other type. For example, in the Hispanic-Anglo hiring discrimination study, analysts found that the Hispanic applicants received formal interviews 48 percent of the time they applied for entry-level jobs, compared to 64 percent for the white applicants (Cross, Kenney, Mell, and Zimmermann, 1990).

Sometimes it is difficult to decide whether the two members of a pair actually have been treated differently or whether the differences are so negligible that they should be ignored. To illustrate, the housing discrimination study focused on the racial and ethnic composition of neighborhoods where African American and white tester pairs were shown houses in order to determine whether African American home-seekers were being steered away from predominantly white neighborhoods (or vice versa) (Turner, Struyk, and Yinger, 1991). For each tester, analysts calculated the average percentage African American residing in neighborhoods where houses were shown. In other words, if a person were shown three houses—one in a neighborhood that was 10 percent African American, one in a neighborhood that was 13 percent African American, and one in a neighborhood that was 5 percent African American—the average racial composition for houses shown to this partner was 9.3 percent African American. Next, average neighborhood characteristics were compared for the two members of each pair to determine whether the African American partner was shown houses in more predominantly African American neighborhoods than the white partner.

At this stage, a threshold was established to define a non-negligible difference in neighborhood composition. Analysts decided that small differences in average racial composition were not meaningful from a policy perspective and should not be counted as steering. If an African American was shown houses in neighborhoods averaging 3 percent African American, while the white partner was shown houses in neighborhoods averaging 2.5 percent African American, it would be imprudent to classify this difference as a case of racial steering. In the housing discrimination study, analysts classified a pair's experience as steering only if the difference in neighborhood racial composition exceeded a threshold of 5 percentage points. Thresholds also were defined for differences in average per capita income and differences in average house values.

Results like those outlined above represent the share of cases in which two comparable testers of a pair received different treatment. In other words, they reflect the incidence of differential—or unequal—treatment. For many forms of treatment, this is the most logical measure. If the treatment of concern is categorical, then tester pairs are either treated the same or one of them is favored over the other, with no degrees of difference. Examples of such categorical outcomes include the following:

- Did an applicant receive a job offer?
- Did a loan office provide information about mortgage products?
- Was an advertised apartment available for rent?
- Did a taxi driver stop to pick up the passenger?

Other outcomes, however, may vary in terms of degree:

- What hourly wage was the applicant offered?
- What loan amount was the home-buyer quoted?
- How many apartments were made available for consideration?
- How long did the passenger have to wait for a taxi?

The incidence of differential treatment can certainly be calculated for continuous outcome measures, possibly using thresholds like those discussed in the racial steering example. In addition, analysts can compute the severity of differential treatment for continuous outcome variables.

Severity measures reflect the magnitude of differences in outcomes between test partners. They are constructed by (1) calculating the average value of a given treatment measure across all tester pairs of each type and (2) comparing the averages for two types of test partners. To illustrate, Table 15.1 presents several measures of the severity of discrimination in housing. On average, white homebuyers were told about 2.3 possible houses per visit to a real estate agent, compared to an average of 1.8 possible houses shown or recommended to their African American counterparts. Thus, the severity of discrimination can be expressed as 0.5 houses on average per visit—or as 21

TABLE 15.1. MEASURES OF THE SEVERITY OF DISCRIMINATION IN HOUSING FROM A STUDY USING PAIRED ROLE PLAYERS.

	Difference[a]	Percentage Difference[b]
African American and White Homebuyers	0.476	20.8
Hispanic and Anglo Homebuyers	0.522	22.1
African American and White Renters	0.404	24.5
Hispanic and Anglo Renters	0.176	10.9

[a]Average number of houses shown or recommended to the white tester minus the average number shown or recommended to the African American or Hispanic tester.
[b]Difference in houses shown or recommended as a percentage of the number shown or recommended to the majority auditor.
Source: Turner, Struyk, and Yinger, 1991.

percent fewer houses for African American homebuyers than for comparable whites.

In presenting measures of the differential outcomes, it is important to recognize that the average outcome measures incorporate cases in which (1) no differences in treatment occurred, (2) one type of partner was favored, and (3) the other type of partner was favored. Thus, this type of severity measure reflects the average difference in treatment across all cases, including those in which no difference was recorded. This measure indicates how big an impact differential treatment has on overall outcomes, not how severe the differences are when they do occur. Alternatively, severity measures can be constructed for the subset of cases in which one teammate was favored over the other to reflect how severe differential treatment is when it does occur (Yinger, 1991).

Tests of Statistical Significance

In studies that are based on a probability sample of encounters and whose goal is to describe the total universe of such encounters, the next important analysis step is to test the statistical significance of incidence and severity measures. Suppose that in a sample of one hundred cases, members of Group A receive more favorable treatment than their Group B partners fifteen times, members of Group B receive more favorable treatment than their Group A partners five times, and partners (A and B) were treated equally eighty times. Can the analyst reasonably conclude that Group A is consistently favored over Group B in the universe of all such transactions, or is there a real chance that this result is idiosyncratic—that another sample would have shown no such difference in treatment?

In more formal terms, one must test the null hypothesis that the incidence of preferential treatment for Group A (I_a– 15 percent in the example above) is actually zero. This hypothesis can be tested with a standard t statistic, which is calculated by dividing the incidence of preferential treatment by its standard error and determining from a table of t statistics how likely it is that the resulting ratio could occur by chance. Analysts typically reject the null hypothesis if there is a 5 percent chance or less that the observed results could occur when there is no real difference for the population as a whole. Sometimes a more rigorous statistical standard is applied, requiring a 1 percent chance or less. In matched paired role-playing studies, there are three possible outcomes for any test. Specifically, the analyst needs to test (1) the hypothesis that the incidence of group A being favored (I_a) is zero, (2) the hypothesis that the incidence of group B being favored (I_b) is zero, and (3) the hypothesis that both are treated equally. Some researchers might also test whether the difference between I_a

and I_b is zero. In the example, these would mean testing the hypothesis that 15 percent A favored is significantly different from 5 percent B favored.

Similar tests of statistical significance need to be conducted for measures of the severity of differential treatment. In this case, the appropriate measure is a difference-of-means test, which also produces a standard t statistic. Again, the observed difference in outcomes (D) is divided by its standard error, and a table of t statistics is used to determine whether the resulting ratio could reasonably have occurred by chance. If not, the analyst can reject the null hypothesis that D is equal to zero in the population as a whole.

Systematic Versus Random Differences in Treatment

In addition to statistical significance tests, an analyst must be aware of the distinction between systematic and random differences in treatment. Differential treatment of paired testers can occur for both systematic and random reasons. To illustrate, suppose a landlord showed one apartment to a white tester but no apartments to the African American partner, so that the case was classified as white favored for the outcome measure. This unfavorable treatment of the African American tester might have occurred for systematic reasons: perhaps the landlord wants to keep African Americans out of the building because he considers them poor tenants or because he fears that he will lose white tenants. But the same unfavorable treatment might have resulted from random factors. Perhaps the landlord received a call between the visits from the two testers indicating that a tenant had been found for the apartment. Or perhaps the agent felt tired or ill at the time of the African American tester's visit. Any number of random events might result in the differential treatment of two customers—differential treatment unrelated to race.

Simple measures of the incidence of differential treatment inevitably include some cases in which the majority role player was favored because of systematic discrimination and some in which the tester was favored for random reasons. In fact, the share of cases with white-favored outcomes might over- or understate the true incidence of systematically unfavorable treatment of African Americans, and there is no foolproof mathematical or statistical procedure for disentangling the random and systematic components of these measures.

One strategy for estimating systematic discrimination, that is, to remove the cases where nondiscriminatory random events are responsible for differences in treatment, is to subtract the incidence of African American–favored treatment from the incidence of white-favored treatment to produce a net measure. This approach essentially assumes that all cases of African American–favored treatment are attributable to random factors—that systematic discrimination never favors African Americans—and that random white-favored treatment occurs just as frequently as random African American–favored treatment. If these assumptions hold, the net measure subtracts differences due to random factors from the total incidence of white-favored treatment.

However, it seems unlikely that all African American–favored treatment is the result of random factors; sometimes African Americans might be systematically favored on the basis of their race or ethnicity. For example, an African American landlord might prefer to rent to families of her own race or a real estate agent might provide African American customers with extra assistance. Other instances of African American–favored treatment might reflect a form of race-based steering in which white customers are discouraged from considering units in African American neighborhoods or developments. The net measure subtracts not only random differences but some systematic differences, and therefore it probably understates the frequency of systematic differences. Thus, net measures provide lower-bound estimates of systematic discrimination and reflect the extent to which the differential treatment that occurs (some systematically and some randomly) is more likely to favor whites than African Americans.

Advanced statistical procedures can offer some insight into the relative importance of random and systematic differences in treatment in a paired role-playing study. For example, multivariate regression or logistical analysis can be used to quantify the independent impact of various observed factors on treatment outcomes and to estimate the residual role of random factors (Yinger, 1991). However, these procedures are technically complex and must be tailored to the circumstances of a particular data set.

It might also be possible to observe empirically differences in treatment between paired testers of the same race. If same-race testers are carefully matched and follow the protocols of a conventional paired test, any differences in treatment that are observed between them must reflect random factors (both observable and unobservable). A national study using role playing to measure racial and ethnic discrimination in housing experimented with three-part tests, including tests involving visits by two whites and an African American as well as tests involving two African Americans and a white tester. Analysis of these "triad" tests suggests that the incidence of same-race differences in treatment is generally not significantly different from the incidence of African American–favored treatment. In other words African American–favored treatment may be a reasonable proxy for random differences in treatment, and the net measure may provide a good estimate of systematic discrimination.

However, because sample sizes were small, these results should be interpreted cautiously (Turner and Ross, 2003).

Researchers continue to explore the issue of random and systematic contributions to observed differences in treatment and to refine statistical and other procedures for disentangling the effects of random factors. In the meantime, simple measures of the incidence of differential treatment are straightforward and informative. It is reasonable to report that, for example, African American job applicants receive less favorable treatment than comparable whites 20 percent of the time. Although not all of these cases of unfavorable treatment necessarily reflect systematic discrimination, they do reflect the incidence of unequal treatment. At the same time, it would make sense to report the incidence of white-favored outcomes. If the limitations of these simple measures are understood and the potential role of random factors is acknowledged, then complex statistical adjustments might not be necessary.

Expanding Applications for Role Playing

Innovative Applications for Role Playing

Role playing can be used to study a variety of transactions in a natural manner that provides researchers relatively unbiased data. Numerous studies of housing rental and sales, mortgage lending, insurance, and employment markets have been conducted. More recently, the role–play methodology has been used to study transactions in the medical and public services sectors both within and beyond the United States. These studies help extend the methodology to new settings and expand the possibilities for how it can be structured.

In the healthcare sector, remote role-play studies are being used to determine whether patients experience differences in access to care based on whether they have public or private insurance. This work has grown, in part, from a role-playing program established by the U.S. Department of Health and Human Services in 2011 to measure access to primary care following passage of the Affordable Care Act (Rhodes and Miller 2012). Studies have tended to focus on patient access to specialty care services, such as gastroenterology or dermatology (Bisgaier and Rhodes 2011; Chaudhry, Armbrecht, Shin, Matula, Caffney, Varade, Jones, and Siegfried, 2013; Patel, Naher, Murray, and Salner, 2013). Role playing also has been used to study the accuracy of information provided by pharmacy staff, and compliance with new healthcare policy rules (French and Kaunitz 2007; Wilkinson, Vargas, Fahey, Suther, and Silverstein, 2014). Findings from these studies point to changes in clinic or pharmacy practices that could measurably improve the experiences of patients seeking care.

Researchers assessing development initiatives have used members of the target population as role players. Leon, Brambila, De La Cruz, Garcia Colindres, Morales, and Vasquez (2005) studied whether healthcare practitioners in Guatemala were adhering to a program designed to provide female patients with appropriate contraception options. By assigning role players comparable profiles, the researchers were able to determine whether they received appropriate reproductive healthcare information. Role players also documented the length of their visit. Researchers analyzed data on visit length to assess the program intervention's effect on time spent with clients.

Renju, Andrew, Nyalali, Kishamawe, Kato, Changalucha, and Obasi (2010) used role playing to study the results of a policy intervention in Tanzania meant to make health services more "youth-friendly." Role players collected information by covertly audio-recording transactions with healthcare providers. Researchers analyzed the recordings and debriefed testers after each test to gather subjective descriptions and impressions of the experience. Role players' descriptions of the transactions provided nuanced details about the conditions in which transactions took place and the effects on "clients" in ways that standard report forms or even analysis of audio recordings could not capture.

Role-play studies are used by public organizations to audit the quality of service delivery and even teaching. For example, the state of Georgia established a program based on role playing that provided third-party evaluations of routine customer-service transactions with local governments (Bradbury and Milford, 2003). Researchers in Great Britain used role playing to evaluate faculty classroom performance in public institutions of higher education (Douglas and Douglas, 2007). People hired to pose as students collected information that was analyzed and provided to individual faculty members as part of an evaluation. Faculty members were aware of the study but not aware of the role players' identities. Douglas and Douglas discuss the necessity of establishing objective performance standards for assessing or measuring behaviors in public service delivery and education sectors.

Ethical and Legal Issues

Critics of the role-play methodology have raised ethical and legal objections, arguing that it deceives or entraps research subjects, imposes costs of interacting with a fictitious customer or client, and invades the privacy rights of the person or office being tested (see Edley, 1993). While these concerns are valid, convincing arguments have been made that role playing, particularly in the form of paired testing, often is the best or only feasible method for detecting and measuring treatment, and that the benefits outweigh the drawbacks. Carefully designed and responsible studies limit transactions to the minimum amount of time necessary for role players to collect information. Also, most studies involve responding to offers that are publicly advertised, such as advertisements for available housing or jobs, or engaging with businesses or service providers that are subject to laws or regulations barring discrimination. In these studies, there is no lure for test subjects to act any differently from the way they would otherwise act (Fix and Struyk, 1993; Rhodes and Miller, 2012). After considering the criticisms of role playing and weighing them against the benefits, the U.S. Supreme Court ruled in *Havens Realty Corp. v. Coleman* that evidence of discrimination gathered through paired testing is admissible in court (Turner, Santos, Levy, Wissoker, Aranda, and Pitingolo, 2013).

By making contact information publicly available, test subjects are inviting members of the public to call or visit for information. It is recognized in many settings that inquiries do not always indicate a commitment on behalf of the customer or client. When conducting research in a sector with limited goods or services, responsible researchers train role players to be noncommittal in their expression of interest so that agents will not withhold goods or services from actual customers.

It is neither necessary nor appropriate to obtain the consent of the tested businesses, agencies, or agents, particularly if studies do not collect any private or sensitive data about or from them. Role players are tasked with observing subjects' behavior during a transaction. Moreover, obtaining the consent of tested agencies or agents would invalidate results because agents would be aware of the role play and might alter their behavior. Subjects of role-playing studies conducted for research purposes can be protected from public disclosure by requiring all researchers, research coordinators, and staff to sign nondisclosure or confidentiality agreements; and by omitting names, addresses, or other identifying information on subjects from reports or shared data files.

Test subjects may consider role-play testing to be ethically inappropriate if they believe they are being deceived by a role player with ulterior intentions. Indeed, if an evaluation study suggests that a particular agency is in violation of an enforceable regulation, the agency might face a legal risk. However, the possibility that a complaint will be brought on the basis of the research tests can be minimized in a number of ways if the aim of the study is to collect objective data for research purposes. All testers and affiliated organizations must temporarily suspend their legal rights to file a complaint based on testing conducted as part of an objective research study. Also, researchers contractually can commit not to use the research tests as evidence in any enforcement action, although it may use these tests to decide how and where to target subsequent enforcement testing. Role-playing studies conducted for monitoring or enforcement purposes, however, are intended to identify subjects who are not following procedures or are breaking the law. In these types of studies, researchers must establish data-use parameters at the onset to ensure results are used in accordance with the study purpose.

Role players themselves face risks that need to be addressed. They can be exposed to emotionally or psychologically painful experiences during study transactions or even physical threats. For example, role players participating in research on differential treatment of maligned populations could find themselves in situations where they experience explicit discrimination or even threats of physical harm. In addition to training role players to be objective observers of agent behavior and appropriately compensating them for their time, researchers need to develop safety protocols and ensure support systems are in place. Training for staff and role players should include how to respond to safety issues that might arise during a transaction and the supports available for role players.

Limitations of Role Playing

The role-playing methodology can be a very effective research approach but it has significant limitations. Depending on the size of the study, role playing can be expensive—it is labor intensive whether used for evaluation, monitoring, or enforcement research. Budget might constrain sample sizes, which will affect the generalizability of evaluation findings. Studies conducted remotely are less costly than in-person studies, which can translate to the ability to conduct a larger number of interactions, but costs for other components of such studies still add up. Even when conducted for monitoring or enforcement research for which large sample sizes might not be necessary, effective training and oversight of role players, data collection, and reporting processes can be costly.

Another limitation is that most data collected through role playing is captured during early stages of transactions. What might happen in later stages of transactions is more difficult or impossible to capture with this methodology. For example, role players can inquire about available housing for rent or for sale, but cannot submit a rental application or enter into a purchase agreement to capture treatment post-application or after move-in. To move beyond the inquiry stage, role players would need to submit (false) information about themselves and sign documents that could be legally binding. Agent review of qualifications, including role players' credit scores in this example, would uncover the home-seekers' role as a tester.

Role-playing studies in other sectors can move through an entire transaction. For example, role players participating in a study of service provision in a restaurant could be seated, place an order, and pay for food and beverage, assuming the study is structured and budgeted to support these actions. In this type of study, role players can complete the transaction without having to submit or sign any documents that could lead to charges of fraudulent activity.

Research design can introduce limitations that affect findings. Studies that assign tester characteristics must decide whether role players will be well qualified or less well qualified for the good or service. For example, role players participating in housing discrimination studies can be assigned income that makes them well qualified to rent or purchase an advertised unit or marginally qualified. Research protocols that assign role players characteristics that ensure they are well qualified to receive the service or to afford the housing lead to findings relevant for well-qualified customers, but do not inform about the experiences of average customers. In this regard, the results likely will be conservative estimates of treatment because role players' assigned qualifications make them attractive customers.

Conclusion

Role playing is a flexible methodology that can be used in a variety of settings and for different research purposes. Role players collect information on the quality of services they are offered or the information provided by test subjects to assess differential treatment of population groups, to monitor program implementation, or to support enforcement of laws and regulations. The methodology can be implemented by single-tester role players or testers matched in teams of two or more. Role-playing studies that are well designed and implemented can produce results that are easily understood by the public, trusted by policymakers, and useful to program evaluators.

References

Alberti, P. M., Steinberg, A. B., Khan, E. H., Abdullah, R. B., and Bedell, J. F. "Barriers at the Frontline: Assessing and Improving the Teen Friendliness of South Bronx Medical Practices." *Public Health Reports*, 2010, *125*(4), 611–614.

Ayres, Ian, and Siegelman, Peter. "Race and Gender Discrimination in Bargaining for a New Car." *The American Economic Review*, 1995, *85*(3).

Bertrand, Marianne, and Mullainathan, Sendhil. "Are Emily and Greg More Employable Than Lakisha and Jamal? A Field Experiment on Labor Market Discrimination." *American Economic Review*, 2004, *94*(4).

Bisgaier, Joanna, and Rhodes, Karin, V. "Auditing Access to Specialty Care for Children with Public Insurance." *The New England Journal of Medicine*, 2011, *364*.

Bone, Sterling A., Christensen, Glenn L., and Williams, Jerome D. "Rejected, Shackled, and Alone: The Impact of Systemic Restricted Choice on Minority Consumers' Construction of Self." *Journal of Consumer Research*, 2014, *41*.

Bradbury, Mark D., and Milford, Richard L. "Measuring Customer Service: Georgia's Local Government Mystery Shopper Program." *State and Local Government Review*, 2003, *35*(3).

Brandon, Robert, and Campbell, Randall C. "Being New-Customer Friendly: Determinants of Service Perceptions in Retail Banking." *The International Journal of Bank Marketing*. 2007, *25*(1).

Chaudhry, Sophia B., Ambrecht, Eric S., Shin, Yoon, Matula, Sarah, Caffney, Charles, Varade, Reena, Jones, Lisa, and Siegfried, Elaine. "Pediatric Access to Dermatologists: Medicaid Versus Private Insurance." *Journal of the American Academy of Dermatology*, 2013, *68*(5).

Cross, Harry, Kenney, Genevieve M., Mell, Jane, and Zimmermann, Wendy. *Differential Treatment of Hispanic and Anglo Job Seekers*. Washington, DC: Urban Institute Press, 1990.

Douglas, Alex, and Douglas, Jacqueline. "Campus Spies? Using Mystery Students to Evaluate University Performance." *Educational Research*, 2007, *48*(1).

Edley, C. "Implications of Empirical Studies on Race Discrimination." In M. Fix and R. Struyk (eds.), *Clear and Convincing Evidence: Testing for Discrimination in America*. Washington, DC: Urban Institute Press, 1993.

Erstad, Margaret. "Mystery Shopping Programmes and Human Resource Management." *International Journal of Contemporary Hospitality Management*, 1998, *10*(1).

Fix, Michael, and Struyk, Raymond J. (eds.). *Clear and Convincing Evidence: Measurement of Discrimination in America*. Washington, DC: Urban Institute Press, 1993.

French, Amy C., and Kaunitz, Andrew M. "Pharmacy Access to Emergency Hormonal Contraception in the Healthcare Industry: A Secret Shopper Survey." *Contraception*, 2007, *75*.

Galster, George, Wissoker, Douglas, and Zimmermann, Wendy. "Testing for Discrimination in Home Insurance: Results from New York City and Phoenix." *Urban Studies*, 2001, *38*(1).

Granatino, Rachel, Verkamp, Jamie, and Parker, R. Stephen. "The Use of Secret Shopping as a Method of Increasing Engagement in the Healthcare Industry: A Case Study." *International Journal of Healthcare Management*, 2013, *6*(2).

Krevor, Brad S., Ponicki, William R., Grube, Joel W., and DeJong, William. "The Impact of Mystery Shopper Reports on Age Verification for Tobacco Purchases." *Journal of Health Communication*, 2011, *16*, 820–830.

Latham, Gary P., Ford, Robert C., and Tzabbar, Danny. "Enhancing Employee and Organizational Performance Through Coaching Based on Mystery Shopper Feedback: A Quasi-Experimental Study." *Human Resource Management*, 2012, *51*(2).

Leon, Federico R., Brambila, C., De La Cruz, M., Garcia Colindres, J., Morales, C., and Vasquez, B. "Provider Compliance with the Balance Counseling Strategy in Guatemala." *Studies in Family Planning*, 2005, *36*(2).

Levy, Diane K., Turner, Margery Austin, Santos, Rob, Wissoker, Doug, Aranda, Claudia L., Pitingolo, Rob, and Ho, Helen. "Discrimination in the Rental Housing Market Against People Who Are Deaf and People Who Use Wheelchairs: National Study Findings." Report prepared for the U.S. Department of Housing and Urban Development, Washington, D.C., 2014.

Neumark, David, Bank, Roy J., and Van Nort, Kyle D. "Sex Discrimination in Restaurant Hiring: An Audit Study." *The Quarterly Journal of Economics*, 1996, *111*(3).

Patel, Vatsal B., Nahar, Richa, Murray, Betty, and Salner, Andrew L. "Exploring Implications of Medicaid Participation and Wait Times for Colorectal Screening on Early Detection Efforts in Connecticut—A Secret-Shopper Survey." *Connecticut Medicine*, 2013, *77*(4).

Renju, Jenny, Andrew, Bahati, Nyalali, Kija, Kishamawe, Coleman, Kato, Charles, Changalucha, John, and Obasi, Angela. "A Process Evaluation of the Scale Up of Youth-Friendly Health Services Initiative in Northern Tanzania." *Journal of the International AIDS Society*, 2010, *13*.

Rhodes, Karin V., and Miller, Franklin G. "Simulated Patient Studies: An Ethical Analysis." *The Milbank Quarterly*, 2012, *90*(4).

Riach, P. A. and Rich, J. "Field Experiments of Discrimination in the Market Place." *The Economic Journal*, 2002, *122*(4).

Saunders, Cynthia M. "Effectiveness of Toll-Free Line for Public Insurance Programs." *Evaluation & the Health Professions*, 2005, *28*(1).

Turner, Margery Austin, Fix, Michael, and Struyk, Ray J. *Opportunities Denied, Opportunities Diminished: Racial Discrimination in Hiring*. Washington, DC: The Urban Institute Press, 1990.

Turner, Margery Austin, Herbig, Carla, Kaye, Deborah, Fenderson, Julie, and Levy, Diane K. *Discrimination Against Persons with Disabilities: Barriers at Every Step*. Washington, DC: U.S. Department of Housing and Urban Development, 2005.

Turner, Margery Austin, and Ross, Stephen. *Discrimination Against African Americans and Hispanics: Supplemental Results from Phase II of HDS 2000*. Washington, DC: U.S. Department of Housing and Urban Development, 2003.

Turner, Margery Austin, Santos, Rob, Levy, Diane K., Wissoker, Doug, Aranda, Claudia L., and Pitingolo, Rob. *Housing Discrimination Against Racial and Ethnic Minorities 2012*. Washington, DC: U.S. Department of Housing and Urban Development, 2013.

Turner, Margery Austin, Struyk, Ray J., and Yinger, John. *Housing Discrimination Study Synthesis*. Washington, DC: U.S. Department of Housing and Urban Development, 1991.

Vilnai-Yavetz, Iris, and Gilboa, Shaked. "The Cost (and the Value) of Customer Attire: Linking High- and Low-End Dress Styles to Service Quality and Prices Offered by Service Employees." *Service Business*, 2014, *8*(2).

Wilkinson, Tracey A., Vargas, Gabriela, Fahey, Nisha, Suther, Emily, and Silverstein, Michael. "'I'll See What I Can Do': What Adolescents Experience When Requesting Emergency Contraception." *Journal of Adolescent Health*, 2014, *54*.

Yinger, John. *Housing Discrimination Study: Incidence and Severity of Unfavorable Treatment*. Washington, DC: U.S. Department of Housing and Urban Development, 1991.

CHAPTER SIXTEEN

USING RATINGS BY TRAINED OBSERVERS

Barbara J. Cohn Berman, Verna Vasquez

When evaluating a program involves rigorously assessing conditions or behaviors that can be classified, counted, or rated by using one's eyes, ears, and sometimes other senses, observer ratings can serve as an effective evaluative tool. This technique is used by governments, nonprofit organizations, community groups, and academic institutions in the United States and in many other places.

The observation approach may be used both for one-time, *ad hoc* program evaluation and for tracking outcomes on a regular basis. Collecting information using this method often relies on volunteer efforts or the use of existing personnel, thereby becoming a relatively low-cost effort.

In this chapter, after noting a variety of circumstances that lend themselves to the use of this method, we provide a list of threshold questions to help you determine if this method is right for your needs and if so, what you need to get started. We then set forth examples of trained observation initiatives that have used trained volunteers, others that involve current employees to do the work, and still others that engage observers from outside the organization being rated. In some situations, we may find that all three types of observers may need to be involved. We also include examples that rate not only visible conditions but those that rate more subtle but still observable *interactions*. The examples cited here come from various places in the United States and abroad—local, nationwide, and international.

We go on to describe ways to help ensure the quality of the data obtained and some advantages of this method. We close with a summary of key steps in implementing trained observer programs and of the method's limitations.[1]

Uses for Trained Observer Ratings

The following program evaluation tasks lend themselves to the trained observer method:

- Evaluating government's effectiveness in maintaining streets from the perspective of residents
- Comparing the effectiveness of private contractors with that of municipal forces in providing park maintenance services or roadway repairs or in maintaining streetlights
- Assessing the difference between in-person requests and telephone requests for service with regard to the accessibility, courtesy, and responsiveness of public agencies
- Assessing the physical condition of part or all aspects of a public school, and subsequently evaluating the effectiveness of policies and programs undertaken to address the needs identified
- Assessing the physical conditions encountered by passengers in trains and busses
- Assessing physical conditions in nursing homes, public housing, or hospitals
- Evaluating interactions between teachers and students; judges and jurors; medical students, and physicians and patients[1]

This method can also be used for non-evaluative purposes. For example, in 2014, as the Ebola virus epidemic threatened the United States, the Centers for Disease Control and Prevention issued guidelines for trained observers to monitor all health care workers treating patients with Ebola to assure compliance with every step in the process of donning and doffing of protective gear and equipment, thereby guarding health care workers from contracting and spreading the virus themselves (www.cdc.gov/vhf/ebola/hcp/ppe-training).

---

[1]For more detail on trained observer rating scales and procedures, see the chapter, "Trained Observer Ratings," by John Greiner that appeared in the second edition of this volume. Julie Brenman reported on several examples of trained observer applications in the third edition of this volume, some of which are repeated here.

Is a Trained Observer Method Appropriate for Your Needs?

Below and in Box 16.1, we identify key questions that should be addressed before adopting a trained observer process. Answering these questions will also help you determine the appropriate design for a successful trained observer initiative.

As its name implies, this method is useful for studying factors that are observable and clearly discernible. The first matter to be addressed, then, is whether the purpose of your proposed evaluation involves observable phenomena, in whole or in part. Only if the program you are evaluating involves phenomena observable by one or more senses should you consider adopting a trained observer initiative and go on to address the remaining questions in Box 16.1.

Box 16.1. Questions to Address Before Adopting and Designing Trained Observer Programs

- What do you want to know? What conditions, characteristics, or behavior need to be evaluated? Are they visually identifiable? Audible if relevant? Discernible by other senses?
- What characteristics do you want to rate: Is the condition present or not? How many? How good? How smooth? How serious? Clean? Polite? Responsive?
- Who will be the audience for your findings and report(s)? What information will the users of the information need?
- How much information or detail do you need?
- Is special expertise or access required?
- What do you want to do with the information? Provide a one-time assessment? Use it as a baseline for future assessments? Compare one site with other sites? Compare one period in time with another?
- What type of training and supervision is required to assure consistent and accurate findings?
- Do you have the resources:
  - To train and supervise the project?
  - To do the observations and record them?
  - To collate the findings and generate reports?
  - To follow up when necessary?
- Will your findings require subsequent action? By whom? When?

What Do You Want to Know?

The clearer you are at the outset about what information you need, the better the observations will be. A good working knowledge of the subject under study is necessary so that you are familiar beforehand with the various possibilities that may be observed.

Specificity is important. It is not sufficient, for example, to have raters report that a neighborhood is "dirty," because that is a subjective term that needs to be further defined for it to be a verifiable and remediable finding. For your evaluation to be truly useful, you will want information about what was observed: Uncollected household garbage? Litter, as you have defined it? Leaves? Weeds? Bulk items such as mattresses or refrigerators? Unswept sidewalks? And you have to specify when and where it was observed as well as which streets were observed.

Anchoring your rating scale is essential so that each rating is abundantly clear and one rating is not confused with another. Rating scales often need to categorize the quantity and/or quality of the observations: Did the litter occupy the entire block? Was it a major concentration—as you have defined that term? Was it only one or two pieces on a block? Were no items observed? Were any observed items hazardous?

Will Your Findings Require Subsequent Action?

An advantage of a trained observer process is that the information can be used not only for one-time evaluation and accountability purposes but also to trigger corrective actions for problems identified by the observer. If the observations are the first step in a process that requires, for example, a subsequent examination by an expert or by a government agency, you will have to devise a recording and referral process to track the timing of observations and subsequent actions taken after the problems have been referred for correction. Be sure from the outset that you are collecting information that will include all necessary identifiers—precise location, correct nomenclature, and so forth.

What Do You Want to Do with the Information?

Knowing how you will use the information collected will help you make good decisions about how you will collect, store, and analyze it. If the project is a one-time effort, a simple collation or database can suffice. If you will be comparing changes over time or with other places, a more complex and hardy system will be needed.

Considering, addressing, planning, and pretesting for all of these factors in the planning stage of a trained observer effort will help ensure that you gather what you need.

What You Will Need to Start

Trained observer projects need the following:

- A form to be used by observers to record the information being observed. The form may be electronic and part of a program on a handheld or other type of computer, or it may be on paper.
- Clear definitions of what is to be captured, including pictures or videos, when appropriate, for each rating along the rating scale to be used.
- Clear instructions about where the ratings should take place, including a map or floor plan.
- Uniform training materials and presentation(s)—to be given to all observers and supervisors.
- Assembled materials and equipment.
- A room or quiet space for training observers and supervisors.
- A cadre of potential observers who are willing, able, and available to do the work.
- Explicit expectations—what is required of the observers in terms of attendance, schedule, and so forth.
- A contact sheet with the names of all observers and supervisors and ways to reach each of them.
- Instructions for emergencies.
- A trial run to assure that the observers are implementing the instructions and to respond to questions of clarification they may have.
- A work schedule.
- Plans for collating the observations, storing the data, and producing reports.
- One or more project supervisors to oversee all aspects of the program.

All of the materials listed here must be pretested to determine whether the instructions are understandable to the potential observers, if the work can be conducted in the environment in which observations will be made, and if, indeed, the information required will be captured. The pretesting will inform you of what, if anything, needs revision or clarification.

Decisions About Ratings and Sampling

Evaluators must select a rating methodology that is appropriate for the things that need to be evaluated. These methods can range from a simple two-point, *yes/no* or *present/not present* rating to grading (*A, B, C, and so on*) to other more complex scales. Later in this chapter we provide examples of each.

Evaluators also need to determine whether a sample or full inventory is necessary. This decision will depend on how precise the findings need to be, how diverse the matters under observation are known to be, and the resources available to do the ratings.

Examples of Trained Observer Programs

Several trained observer programs are described in the following section, starting with instances where trained, interested, non-expert volunteers do the observations. We follow with cases in which concerned organizations train some of their existing personnel to serve as observers, applying their already honed skills to this initiative. In the next set of examples, experts from outside the organization have conducted observations. The last grouping involves evaluating not just visible phenomena but interactive behavior.

Some of the programs are run at the local level, some are national, others operate internationally. Many of these initiatives are not legally mandated; thus their longevity and permanence varies. One administration or community may expand the effort, another change or curtail it only to be revived, in some cases, in a revised manner, later on.

Volunteers as Trained Observers

Keep America Beautiful [KAB].   KAB is a national nonprofit organization that strives to engage individuals to take greater responsibility for improving their community environments. Their Litter Index is a tool that allows quick and reliable visual assessment of intentional or unintentional pollution resulting from consumer waste products being carelessly handled or improperly disposed. The Litter Index is designed to be a low cost commonsense tool that could be deployed by volunteers. After a year and a half of research, the model was field-tested, and has been in use for more than fifteen years. It identifies cigarette butts, paper, aluminum cans, old mattresses, and tires. The data obtained can be used by elected officials to determine the types of community improvement programs needed to address existing conditions and achieve long-term sustainable results.

Their scale ranges from 1 (*no litter*) to 4 (*extremely littered*), with the ratings tied to the amount of litter visible as well as to the effort that would be required to clean it up:

1. *No litter.* Virtually no litter is seen in the subarea. One would have to look hard to find it; maybe one or two items in a city block that could easily be picked up by one person.
2. *Slightly littered.* A small amount of litter is obvious, but it would take one or two people only a short time to pick it up. The eye is not continually grabbed by the litter.
3. *Littered.* Considerable litter can be readily seen throughout the subarea and will likely need a concentrated cleanup effort. There is enough litter here that it obviously needs to be addressed.
4. *Extremely littered.* A continuous amount of litter is the first thing noticed. There might be major illegal dump sites that would require equipment and extra manpower. There is a strong impression of a lack of concern about litter.

KAB's certified affiliated organizations use trained volunteers as observers to apply the Litter Index annually in their communities. After selected members receive training from the national office, local organizations conduct a forty-five- to sixty-minute training session for the volunteers. The training includes visual, auditory, and kinesthetic experiences, including a video. After conducting a sample site observation, volunteers are sent into the community to rate specific areas.

KAB's Litter Index surveys are consistent in that a standard kit including a manual, score sheet, and the video is provided to all affiliates. Communities have some flexibility in customizing the survey for their individual needs. Most affiliate organizations have used a pencil-and-paper method for collecting survey results; some have used handheld computers.

The Litter Index helps identify what is effective—and what is not—in bringing positive change to littering attitudes and behaviors and related community improvements. Consistent use on an annual basis can track progress in reducing litter and quantitatively demonstrate community improvement. (For more information see kab.org.)

Computerized Neighborhood Environment Tracking [ComNET]. ComNET is a program conceived and operated by the authors and their staff while at the Center on Government Performance (CGP) of Fund for the City of New York.

ComNET began in 1998, has been used in over 135 areas in seven cities, and has spawned offshoots, some under different names, in California, Connecticut, North Carolina, Iowa, Massachusetts, and elsewhere. ComNET has been described as one of the first programs in which a nonprofit organization used handheld computers (Wallace, 2001).

CGP identified, through focus groups and community meetings, a core list of street features and associated problems that are of concern to neighborhood residents and businesspeople and that are able to be rated by trained observers (see Exhibit 16.1 for a partial list). Local groups determine which street features and conditions they want to capture, on a present/not present scale, and which streets they want to survey. Carefully designed route maps are prepared to avoid overlapping or omission of streets during the surveying.

A two-hour training session for the observers (called *surveyors*) covers issues such as safety, terms, and definitions, how to look at a street, and how to use the software and handheld computer provided to them—both designed for ease of use while in the field. Slides of typical conditions in the area to be surveyed are shown to help the surveyors recognize the conditions they are studying. The training also includes hands-on practice time under supervision. By the end of the training, surveyors have learned to recognize the conditions and know the correct terms for each.

They walk in teams on the predetermined routes and enter on the handhelds the problems they see and where the problems are located. To simplify the work of the surveyors, the streets to be surveyed and the features and problems of interest in each locale are pre-entered into the handhelds. Surveyors enter the block they are rating by simply clicking on the pre-entered list in a drop-down window, to show the cross-streets and the direction in which they are moving. The raters then enter, from a drop-down window, each street feature and problem observed and exactly where it is—in front of, on, next to, or across from a specific address on the block—so that the entry can be verified and the condition can be found and corrected. This precision also allows maps of the findings to be created later.

A digital camera is integrated into the handheld computer, enabling surveyors to take pictures of offending conditions, when necessary. The software links the photograph with the rating entry and is stored in a web-enabled database for later analysis and report production.

ComNET's database, known as *ComNET Connection*, was designed to provide quality control checks. The database alerts users through highlighting when duplicate entries are present, when conflicting entries are made, and when a survey remains "open" for longer than, say, twenty weeks, raising the question of the timeliness of survey data. Supervisors can review and check the

EXHIBIT 16.1. EXAMPLES OF LOCAL STREET CONDITIONS RATEABLE BY TRAINED OBSERVERS–A "PRESENT-NOT PRESENT" SCALE (PARTIAL LIST).

Building, Vacant
Bills/Stickers Posted
Dumping (Large Items)
Graffiti
Unsecured
Other

Bus Stop/Shelter
Bills/Stickers Posted
Broken Glass
Graffiti
Litter
Scratchiti
Other

Catch Basin/Sewer
Clogged/Ponding
Grate Broken
Litter
Not Level With Roadway
Under Construction/Repairs
Vermin
Other

Curb Cut - Pedestrian Ramp
Broken
Missing
Not Level With Roadway
Other

Lamppost
Base Plate Missing
Base Plate Unattached/Open
Bent
Bills/Stickers Posted
Broken Glass
Bulb Out
Chain, Abandoned
Exposed Wiring
Fallen
Graffiti
Incomplete Installation
Leaning
Peeling/Scraped Paint

Lot-Vacant
Bills/Stickers Posted
Dumping (Large Items)
Fence Broken
Graffiti
Litter
Ponding
Rat Holes
Vermin
Weeds
Other

Roadway
Bollard Damaged
Bump/Hummock
Cave-In
Cobbles/Bricks Defects
Cross Hatching Faded
Litter
Metal Plate Not Level With Roadway
Open Street Cut
Ponding
Pothole
Snow and Ice Not Removed
Under Construction/Repairs
Uneven Patching
Other

Roadway Utility Cover
Broken
Missing
Not Level With Roadway
Under Construction/Repairs
Other

Sidewalk
A-Frame Sign Blocking
Broken Glass
Dumping (Large Items)
Gum/Gum Residue, Significant
Litter
Pavers Cracked/Damaged
Pavers Loose
Pavers Missing
Ponding

Snow and Ice Not Removed
Stained Heavily
Trip Hazard
Under Construction/Repairs
Weeds
Other

Sign (Bus, Streetname or Traffic)
Bent
Bills/Stickers Posted
Chain, Abandoned
Faded
Fallen
Graffiti
Hanging/Bolt Missing
Maps/Schedules Missing
Missing
Not Readable
Obscured
Peeling/Scraped Paint
Pole Fallen
Pole Leaning
Other

Traffic/Pedestrian Light
Bills/Stickers Posted
Broken Glass
Graffiti
Incomplete Installation
Missing
Not Operating
Peeling/Scraped Paint
Unsecured
Other

Tree
Dead
Debris in Tree
Roots Trip Hazard
Other

Waste Basket
Bent
Missing
Overflowing
Other

Source: Fund for City of New York, Center on Government Performance, 2010.

highlighted data before they become part of the database that produces final reports.

Surveyors have consisted of local residents of all ages, teams of local business people, business improvement district and local development corporation staff, high schoolers (during the school year as part of their curriculum, in after-school programs, or in summer youth programs); youths teamed with seniors; interns; and college and graduate school students. At times, government staff have joined the surveyor team. We discourage sole surveyors because having at least two people on any given route provides a greater measure of safety and quality control since all team members have to agree before an entry is made.

Groups have presented the program's findings to government agencies that are responsible for ameliorating serious conditions, to the local legislature, community boards, borough presidents and other officials. Some findings have influenced governments to provide additional resources and funding. Groups have also decided which conditions they can correct themselves, such as removing graffiti and painting scarred lampposts (see www.fcny.org/cmgp/comnet).

In addition to its original purpose, ComNET procedures and technology have been adapted in some of the following ways:

- By a university to compare two neighborhoods in terms of their differences in "walkability," opportunities to engage in physical fitness, and observations of people exercising in various ways
- By a business improvement district to monitor their contractors who are responsible for maintaining privately owned street furniture
- By an industrial business zone to evaluate physical conditions in the industrial park
- By a business improvement district to track the illegal use of parking permits in its business area
- By a volunteer parks association to monitor and report on conditions in a local park
- By local government to monitor community improvement efforts funded by the government

ComNET2Go. In keeping with the desire to stay abreast of technological and other developments, a newer addition to the ComNET initiative is *"Com-NET2Go"* which adapts the ComNET purpose for use on local surveyors' own mobile devices, enabling them to capture and track street level problems in their neighborhood, confirm their entries by seeing them on a map, attach a picture of the condition and send the material captured directly to the Com-NET database. They can then see and use summary reports, interactive maps and produce reports from the ComNET2Go database.

Building Government-Community Relationships and Repairing Neighbor-hoods in Durham, North Carolina.

We include this program here because, although local government sponsored, it relies on neighborhood volunteers to conduct the observations and then to set their priorities while working with government staff to foster better communication between government and the people it serves. Wishing to improve relationships with its neighborhood residents, the government of the City of Durham pilot tested and then put into operation its trained observer program inviting, through press releases, government TV, and list servs and at community meetings, community organizations to participate. Once a community organization decided to conduct a survey, city staff provided technical assistance to the team through a two-hour surveyor training session. Then, survey teams of three or four people, accompanied by at least one city employee, surveyed a four- to six-block route predetermined by the team. Street-level environmental data were collected in a uniform and verifiable manner, using a handheld computer. The survey results were uploaded to the database for review by the community surveyors.

The next step in Durham's program involved a prioritization session in which the community members, in the presence of city staff, ranked the problems in terms of their importance to the community. The citizen input during the prioritization session is important, because what seems important to city government is not always the top priority of citizens. City personnel provided explanations and a time frame for when and how the neighborhood priorities could and would be addressed.

Based on questionnaire results and follow-up calls to citizens, survey teams have stated that both community appearance and communication with government have improved. They report that 93 percent of all priority service requests created since the program's inception have either been closed successfully and/or have been assessed by the appropriate department, to be addressed when resources become available. Tracking progress provides additional feedback so that government and the community are in closer communication.

Apparently, the program has visibly improved conditions in Durham's neighborhoods. Perhaps more important, the process also created a positive relationship between the community volunteers and city staff. By knowing who is responsible, seeing that repairs are being or will be made, and taking ownership for fixing some problems themselves, Durham residents have more confidence in their government and pride in their neighborhood (Reinstein, Birth, and Brenman, n.d.)

Employees as Trained Observers

Measuring Street Cleanliness—A Forty-Year-Old Program Using a Photographic Scale.   Operated by New York City's Mayor's Office of Operations, the Scorecard Cleanliness Program has been described by Harry Hatry, a pioneer in the field of performance measurement and trained observation, as "probably the longest running trained observer operation in the world" (Hatry, 2006, p. 100). Created in the 1970s at the Fund for the City of New York with the assistance of the Urban Institute, Scorecard evaluates the effectiveness of programs of the City's Department of Sanitation in keeping the city's roadways and sidewalks clean. To assure the credibility of the ratings, the trained observers are employees of the Mayor's Office of Operations, not employees of the Department of Sanitation.

Observers are trained in the use of a series of photographs that depict, on a point scale, a range of the cleanliness observed on the city's streets, ranging from "a clean street with no litter," to a street where "litter is very highly concentrated in a straight line along and over the curb." The scale levels are grouped into three categories: acceptably clean, not acceptably clean, and filthy.

A sample consisting of 6,900 blockfaces drawn from all sanitation districts in the city is inspected twice a month. Inspectors ride these blocks in a car, rating the streets, and entering their scores on computers. For quality control purposes, the inspectors' assignments are varied from month to month, as is the time of day, the day of the week, and the week of the month that inspections are conducted. In a central database, the findings are weighted by street mileage, with longer sections having more weight in determining district, borough, and citywide scores. Monthly reports are made available to the Department of Sanitation, the Mayor's Office of Operations, community districts, borough offices, business improvement districts, and the City's budget office. The findings are available to the public on the city's website and appear in the charter-mandated Mayor's Management Report, issued twice a year. In addition to its public reporting function, Scorecard ratings are a performance management tool for the Department of Sanitation in directing its resources.

Reporting On and Curtailing Littering in Scotland.   In its Environmental Protection Act of 1990, the government of Scotland enacted a wide-ranging and highly detailed piece of legislation addressing many environmental issues, including controlling and ameliorating litter throughout the country. It placed the responsibility for keeping public spaces free of refuse and litter primarily on its thirty-two local authorities, providing them with mandated directions, including a nationwide Code of Practice, penalties, and an appeals process. The full details of this ambitious legislation and program are too great to include here. We distill below excerpts relevant to this chapter and recommend readers to consult several websites for further information and illumination. (See Exhibit 16.2 and the indented material below.)

A picture scale is used to illustrate and delineate the grades. Standards are set for different land use categories such as town centers, beaches, and schools. A Local Environmental Audit and Management System (LEAMS) is structured "so that all authorities carry out the same monitoring" to ensure that results can be compared among authorities.

All local authorities receive training first on the legislation, the LEAMS process, methodology to conduct litter surveys by trained city employees and how to use data from the surveys. Each local authority is to conduct bi-monthly surveys within their area, covering "a random minimum sample of 2 percent of the streets and other relevant sites."

The following criteria are assessed during each of the surveys:

- Cleanliness grade
- Litter bins (count of bins and count of overflowing bins)
- Types of litter
- Sources of litter

EXHIBIT 16.2. USING GRADES TO REPORT ON STREET LITTER THROUGHOUT SCOTLAND.

"Litter is anything that is thrown down, dropped, or deposited and left that causes defacement in a public place by any person. This accords with the popular interpretation that, 'litter is waste in the wrong place'."

Grades of Cleanliness

The Code of Practice is based on the concept of four standards, or grades, of cleanliness:

Grade A: no litter or refuse

Grade B: predominantly free of litter and refuse, apart from a few small items

Grade C: consistent distribution of litter and refuse with minor accumulations

Grade D: heavily littered with significant accumulations.

Source: Code of Practice on Litter and Refuse Issued Under Section 89 of the Environmental Protection Act 1990. www.scotland.gov.uk/Publications/2006/12/13125718/4; www.scotland.gov.uk/Publications/2006/12/13125718/6

- Adverse environmental quality indicators, such as dog fouling, graffiti, or weed growth
- Any other comments that may be useful for the site

A data summary sheet is completed following each of the surveys to keep a record of the survey findings. Every six months each local authority carries out a minimum 2 percent sample survey *within another local authority area* [emphasis ours]. This process allows for independent audits to be carried out and allows an exchange of information and best practice to take place.

An annual validation survey is carried out by Keep Scotland Beautiful, an independent public charity, also assessing a minimum 2 percent sample survey within each of the local authority areas, providing an external, independent evaluation.

As part of the Cleanliness Index Monitoring System, further larger surveys are conducted looking at a minimum of 10 percent of the sites in each land use category and geographical area to provide a fully representative sample. More detailed surveys can be conducted to give more in-depth data into local conditions (www.scotland.gov.uk; www.keep scotlandbeatiful.org).

Other participant observer programs aimed at street cleanliness have been carried out in the Republic of Georgia, working with the Urban Institute, where youth volunteers have used photographic rating scales and presented the results to the local government in a public meeting.

A Government Mandated and Run Program in San Francisco.

A voter initiative passed in 2003 included a provision to establish objective standards for park and street maintenance, giving responsibility for the effort jointly to the city controller and the departments of Recreation and Parks and Public Works. In partial response to the voter initiative, San Francisco's government has established a parks inspection program, summarized below.

San Francisco has over 200 parks. Each park is inspected five times per year—four times by the Recreation and Parks Department and once by the controller's audit staff. Annual training lasting a few hours is provided to all inspectors from both departments and includes an in-field demonstration. As new staff members join the program, managers provide training.

During the inspections, which typically take one and one-half to two hours, staff review fourteen features in the parks, such as lawns, trees, restrooms, and play areas. Dozens of conditions relevant to each feature are reviewed, including cleanliness, presence of graffiti, signage, structural integrity, and functionality of structures. Observations are also made about the presence of park staff and other concerns, such as the presence of homeless people. The inspectors use a paper checklist to conduct the review. Manually entering the inspection data is labor-intensive, but tight budgets have not allowed the purchase of handheld devices to record the results. The controller's staff conducts a re-inspection for quality control purposes on a sample of the inspections conducted by its staff.

The program serves two primary purposes: to provide information for a public scorecard and to assist in operational decisions. The Controller's Office analyzes the inspection results and includes the results in an annual report. The average scores recorded by the Recreation and Parks Department have typically been higher than the Controller's Office scores, but the trend scores over time have been consistent. In the annual report the controller includes information on management practices that could be improved. The Recreation and Parks Department has used the inspection information to modify the allocation of resources, such as reducing maintenance staff time spent on fields in order to increase time spent maintaining restrooms or, on a larger scale, shifting resources from one park district to another. Over time, the park grades have improved, and the disparity between high-performing and low-performing parks has decreased. (See City and County of San Francisco, Office of the Controller, www.sfcontroller.org, for more information.)

Other government inspections and inspectors utilize the trained observation method, be they inspecting physical conditions in hospitals, nursing homes, restaurants, schools, construction sites, or other places where conditions are prescribed and proscribed and public interest is at stake.

Outsiders Running Trained Observer Programs

The New York City ComNET program described earlier was conceived and run by a nonprofit organization. Two other examples of programs that rely solely on outside assessors follow.

The Worcester Regional Research Bureau [WRRB].[2]   This is an independent organization founded in 1985 by Worcester, Massachusetts, businesspeople who felt the need for an organization to conduct independent, nonpartisan research on public policy and make recommendations for more effective and efficient municipal government.

---

[2] *Note:* Some of the material in this section is drawn from Schaefer, 2008.

WRRB implemented biennial, technologically assisted surveys of the physical conditions of Worcester's most socioeconomically challenged neighborhoods, in which almost one-third of the city's residents live. The surveys in fifteen neighborhoods enabled residents and officials to identify and document specific problems affecting residents' quality of life—such as potholes, faded crosswalks, abandoned vehicles, illegal dumping, and overgrown vegetation. Once neighborhoods possessed this inventory, they had both a "punch list" of problems and also a baseline for gauging changes over time.

Before employing the system and technology, WRRB engaged in extended discussion with neighborhood associations on how to define neighborhood boundaries and on selecting the more than 275 specific conditions to be observed. The second step was to create detailed maps for each neighborhood that was to be surveyed, along with the routes to be followed, and then to program handheld computers with those streets and the physical features and conditions to be recorded.

This effort led to a long list of quantitative and qualitative improvements in Worcester:

- Residents had long complained of a perceived increase in abandoned vehicles; the surveys made it possible to document the extent of the problem and pinpoint the exact location of every vehicle.
- The quantitative evidence swayed political priorities and gave funding to areas with documented needs.
- WRRB's follow-up dispelled the perception that some neighborhoods get favored treatment from municipal government, because they found similar resolution rates for problems across neighborhoods.
- This process led residents to take on more responsibility for physical deficiencies in their neighborhood.
- Finally, the program helped to break down some of the traditional town-and-gown barriers between Worcester and its institutions of higher education. WRRB teamed up with Holy Cross College to incorporate the ratings into the service-learning component of that institution's curriculum.

New Yorkers for Parks [NY4P].   This is an independent advocacy organization that promotes action and policies to ensure quality parks and adequate recreational opportunities for all New York City's residents. The organization developed a Report Card on Parks, an independent annual assessment of the conditions of small neighborhood parks.

Park surveys were conducted every summer by teams of trained nongovernmental surveyors with handheld computers and digital cameras to rate park conditions. The rating methodology was developed through focus group research and interviews with parks users. Their report card has rated major areas such as active recreation space, passive green space, playgrounds, sitting areas, bathrooms, drinking fountains, and pathways. They assign a letter grade from A to F to each. Surveyors complete an electronic questionnaire for each park feature and document its condition with photographs. These survey instruments contain an average of twelve "yes" or "no" questions that are designed in a way that does not leave much room for interpretation—such as, "Can the water fountain be turned on?" or "Is there litter on the ground within a three-foot radius of the park bench?"

With the help of a professional statistician, the answers are converted to numerical scores, weighted, and averaged to arrive at the final numerical and letter grades for the park. The surveyors (staff members and graduate student interns) are trained to distinguish, carefully and accurately, service areas and park features, to rate park features, and to fill out the survey forms. All survey results and photo documentation are stored in a central database, and when photo documentation does not correlate with recorded conditions, experienced surveyors revisit the park. The findings are posted on the organization's website.

Observing and Rating Interactions

Many important functions are performed in the public and nonprofit sectors that involve verbal communication with the public. The way in which interactions are conducted and unfold are critical to the effectiveness of the function and the desired outcomes. Designing fair, objective, consistent evaluation tools, standards and procedures to observe critical interactions are challenging and often require special expertise to operate successfully. Some of these initiatives continue to be reviewed and assessed. Nonetheless, the need for trained observations of interactions is compelling. Three areas where such programs have been undertaken are explored below.

Evaluating Teachers by Observing Them in the Classroom. Assessing and improving the effectiveness of public school education is an abiding national concern and priority. Typically, if teachers' performance is evaluated at all, it has been linked to how well their students score on standardized tests—a connection that is imperfect. Yet, the role of the teacher in influencing students' education is significant and uncontroversial. Although not as easily quantifiable as test scores, classroom observations have been regarded as another method of evaluating some aspects of teacher effectiveness and its impact on student learning. We report on one such initiative here that has been recognized for its progress.

The Cincinnati Public Schools Teacher Evaluation System (TES)[3] in Ohio has been regarded as a model evaluation program for classroom observations. TES was developed from efforts begun in 1998 by a joint effort of the teachers' union and school district administration after the previous contract negotiations called for a new teacher evaluation system. Over the following years, the system was developed, piloted and revised.

Highlights of the way the Cincinnati system operates include:

- All new teachers must undergo a thorough evaluation in their first year of teaching
- Teachers are evaluated in their fourth year and then every five years after that.
- When a teacher is being evaluated, the process evolves over the course of one year.
- During their evaluation period, at least four classroom observations must be made of the teacher.

At least three of the four classroom observations are done by a highly trained peer evaluator external to the school and once by a local school administrator[4] (Kane, Taylor, Tyler, and Wooten, 2011).

Peer evaluators are chosen from lead teachers—experienced classroom teachers who had high ratings from their own evaluations and choose to work for the TES program. Peer evaluators work as full-time evaluators for three years[5] (Kane, Taylor, Tyler, and Wooten, 2011).

Cincinnati TES divides the skills and responsibilities required of an effective teacher into four domains,[6] two of which—Creating an Environment for Learning, and Teaching for Learning—lend themselves to classroom observation. Cincinnati TES was developed from, among other things, the work of

---

[3]More detailed information about the Cincinnati Public Schools Teacher Evaluation System can be found at www.cps-k12.org/about-cps/tes.

[4]"Evaluating Teacher Effectiveness," By Thomas J. Kane, Eric S. Taylor, John H. Tyler and Amy L. Wooten. Education Next, Summer 2011, Volume 11, Number 3.

[5]"Evaluating Teacher Effectiveness," By Thomas J. Kane, Eric S. Taylor, John H. Tyler and Amy L. Wooten. Education Next, Summer 2011, Volume 11, Number 3.

[6]Cincinnati TES was developed from, among other things, the work of educator Charlotte Danielson and framework and standards described in her book, *Enhancing Professional Practice: A Framework for Teaching.*

EXHIBIT 16.3. EXAMPLES OF PEER EVALUATION STANDARDS FOR CLASSROOM TEACHERS IN CINCINNATI, OHIO.

Domain 2: Creating an Environment for Learning

Standard 2.1 The teacher creates an inclusive and caring environment in which each individual is respected and valued.

Standard 2.2 The teacher establishes effective routines and procedures, maintains a safe and orderly environment, and manages transitions to maximize instructional time.

Standard 2.3 The teacher manages and monitors student behavior to maximize instructional time.

Domain 3: Teaching for Learning

Standard 3.1 The teacher communicates standards-based instructional objectives, high expectations, instructive directions, procedures, and assessment criteria.

Standard 3.2 The teacher demonstrates content knowledge by using content specific instructional strategies.

Standard 3.3 The teacher uses standards-based instructional activities that promote conceptual understanding, extend student thinking, and monitors/adjusts instruction to meet individual needs.

Standard 3.4 The teacher engages students in discourse and uses thought-provoking questions aligned with the lesson objectives to explore and extend content knowledge.

Standard 3.5 The teacher provides timely, constructive feedback to students about their progress toward the learning objectives, using a variety of methods and corrects student errors/misconceptions.

Source: Cincinnati Public Schools Teacher Evaluation System.

educator Charlotte Danielson and framework and standards described in her book, *Enhancing Professional Practice: A Framework for Teaching.*

A domain is further defined by a set of standards. Each standard is then anchored and comprised of elements that are specifically judged and scored by evaluators. For each element, evaluators apply the following rating scale: "Distinguished," "Proficient," "Basic," or "Unsatisfactory." Exhibit 16.3 below displays the standards in Domains 2 and 3.

Exhibit 16.4 shows, as an example, the next layer in the TES rating protocol: three elements included under Standard 3.3, this time with the scoring guide for each element using their four-point scale rating of "Distinguished," "Proficient," "Basic," or "Unsatisfactory."

Their four-point scale is more informative than the commonly used binary ratings of "satisfactory" or "unsatisfactory." TES provides specific feedback to

EXHIBIT 16.4. SCORING GUIDE USING FOUR-POINT SCALE FOR EVALUATING TEACHERS.

Domain 3: Teaching for Student Learning

Standard 3.3: The teacher uses standards-based instructional activities that promote conceptual understanding, extend student thinking, and monitors/adjusts instruction to meet individual needs.

Elements	Distinguished (4)	Proficient (3)	Basic (2)	Unsatisfactory (1)
A. ConceptualUnderstanding	Teacher uses challenging,*standards-based activities at the appropriate cognitive level that promote conceptual understanding and meet individual needs.	Teacher uses challenging *standards-based activities at the appropriate cognitive level that promote conceptual understanding.	Teacher uses *standards-based activities at the appropriate cognitive level that do not promote conceptual understanding.-or-• Teacher uses *standards-based activities at the inappropriate cognitive level that promote conceptual understanding.	Teacher uses *standards-based activities at the inappropriatecognitive level that do not promote conceptual understanding.-or-Teacher does not use *standards-based activities.-or-Teacher uses inappropriate activities.

(Continued)

EXHIBIT 16.4. SCORING GUIDE USING FOUR-POINT SCALE FOR EVALUATING TEACHERS. (Continued)

Elements	Distinguished (4)	Proficient (3)	Basic (2)	Unsatisfactory (1)
B. Extension of Thinking	Teacher creates situations that challenge students to think independently, creatively or critically about the content being taught, to reflect on their understanding and to consider new possibilities.	Teacher creates situations that challenge students to think independently, and creatively or critically about the content being taught.	Teacher creates situations that challenge students to think about the content being taught.	Teacher creates situations that do not challenge students to think about the content.
C. Monitoring, Adjusting and Student Engagement	Teacher invites input from students in order to monitor and adjust instruction /activities/pacing to respond to differences in student needs. - or-The instruction and activities address the needs of the students.Teacher pursues the active engagement of all students.	Teacher monitors and adjusts instruc-tion/activities/pacing to respond to differences in student needs. Teacher pursues the active engagement of all students.	Teacher has difficulty monitoring or adjusting instruction/activities /pacing to respond to differences in student needs.Teacher pursues the active engagement of all students.	Teacher fails to monitor or adjust instruc-tion/activities/pacing to respond to differences in student needs. Teacher does not pursue the active engagement of all students.

Source: Cincinnati Public Schools Teacher Evaluation System.

the teacher being evaluated and enables the evaluator to distinguish exceptional teachers from the good, acceptable and truly poor ones.

Cincinnati acknowledges that having an evaluation system is not an end in itself. Its essential goals are to develop new teachers, reward those teachers who do an exceptional job and help those teachers that have low ratings develop their strategies for more effective teaching.

Evaluating the Performance of Judges in Their Courtrooms. Having confidence in our judicial system's fairness and proper operations, including being able to understand its sometimes complex operations, is essential to our democracy. While criteria for the selection of judges is explicit in many places and procedures within the courtroom are set forth in laws and precedent, systematic evaluation of the interactions of judges in the courtroom, if done at all, is undertaken in various ways by state or local bar associations or specialized nonprofit organizations. An example of a long-standing program that has involved trained members of the public to do this work follows.

The Fund for Modern Courts was founded in 1955 as a private, nonprofit, nonpartisan organization with a mission to improve the administration of justice in the State of New York. It boasts at having more than 600 citizen court monitors in sixteen counties throughout the state who observe and report on many matters involving court operations. Their reports of the findings of their monitors are released to the judiciary and the public and appear on The Fund for Modern Court's website. The aim is to obtain tangible improvements in the court system, to improve the public's understanding of court processes and to inform court personnel of the public's perspectives regarding the court's work.

Of particular relevance here are the "yes/no" questions their monitors are required to answer as they report on their observations of what occurs in a Family Court courtroom, as shown in Exhibit 16.5.

Observing and Rating Medical Students' Interactions. The Objective Structured Clinical Examination [OSCE], in widespread use in medical schools, tests medical students' skills and knowledge in a clinical setting. It evaluates future physicians' communication and physical examination skills, application of medical procedures and knowledge, interpretation and diagnostic abilities, and other relevant competencies targeted to the whole range of medical specialties.

A typical OSCE exam involves each contender moving through a series of stations, with each station run by one or more different impartial expert examiners. During a five- to fifteen-minute period at each station, the candidate is asked to respond to standardized questions related to an actual or simulated

EXHIBIT 16.5. YES/NO QUESTIONS EVALUATING JUDICIAL PERFORMANCE IN A COURTROOM.

Overall Courtroom Management/Professionalism			Notes
1. Judge waited for the parties and their attorneys to be seated before he/she began the case.	Yes	No	
2. Judge had each party and their attorney(s), if any, provide their names and relationship to the case.	Yes	No	
3. Judge began the proceedings by clearly reviewing a brief history of the case.	Yes	No	
4. Judge began the proceedings by clearly presenting the specific issues before him/her on that day.	Yes	No	
5. Judge fully explained the proceedings in an understandable manner.	Yes	No	
6. Judge clearly read/explained the charges to the parties.	Yes	No	
7. Judge spoke in "plain English," that is, made the proceedings easy to follow while being thorough.	Yes	No	
8. Judge informed parties of their right to an attorney and how to obtain assistance (limited cases).	Yes	No	
9. Judge gave each party an opportunity to speak.	Yes	No	
10. Judge asked each party if they had any questions.	Yes	No	
11. Judge answered the questions presented by parties and/or attorney.	Yes	No	
12. Judge went over the settlement or order carefully with the parties.	Yes	No	
13. Case was adjourned.	Yes	No	
14. Court personnel were helpful and courteous.	Yes	No	
15. Court officer was present in the courtroom.	Yes	No	
Children: Juvenile Delinquency/PINS			
16. Children were represented by an attorney.	Yes	No	
17. Children were clearly explained their rights by the judge.	Yes	No	
18. Children were given an opportunity to ask questions.	Yes	No	
Children: Custody/Visitation/Abuse and Neglect			
19. Children were in the courtroom.	Yes	No	
20. Supervised visitation was ordered (or continued).	Yes	No	
21. Judge ordered/allowed visits in a public place because supervisor was not available.	Yes	No	
22. Judge asked children questions in open court	Yes	No	

Source:http://moderncourts.org/programs/citizen-court-monitoring/

patient. All candidates rotate through the same stations and are judged by the same grading system—an effort to make the process as objective as possible. Scripts are developed and adhered to, thereby providing all students involved with the same information, directions and instructions, delivered in the same way. The results of the ratings provide the medical schools with information beyond traditional testing and evaluations by individual instructors about how their students can perform in practice. The results provide feedback to the medical students that, it is reported, help them hone their skills before they leave the medical school environment.

Below, in Exhibit 16.6, from the Medical Council of Canada, is an example of the factors examined by expert observers there, including communication skills and language fluency and the rating scale used when performing their Objective Structured Clinical Examination.

Presenting Findings for Trained Observations

When presenting findings, keep in mind:

- The purposes of work,
- The expected audiences and their expectations, and
- Anticipated and unanticipated results that need to be addressed.

Care should be taken to present findings in a clear and accessible manner, including displaying findings and explanations on a website when appropriate.

Findings from trained observer studies may be in the form of detailed spreadsheets, summary tables, bar, pie, and other charts, intensity and other maps, each accompanied by a narrative and explanatory footnotes, as necessary. If using a database for the collection of the data, the database software may have the capacity to produce some or all of the desired tables and charts, eliminating the time and expense of designing them. As with all new programs, and ongoing ones, we recommend that you pre-test proposed reports' format and content with typical expected users and periodically get feedback and consider suggestions for improvements to be sure that the reports meet users' needs.

Exhibit 16.7 displays a table of ratings of acceptably clean streets in part of one community district (out of fifty-nine districts in New York City). It is excerpted from a report in the form of a table showing ratings found through trained observation of the cleanliness of New York City's streets. It appears on the city's website. The full report enables comparisons among community

EXHIBIT 16.6. EXAMPLES OF RATING SCALES ITEMS.

NAC Examiner Competency Descriptors

Unacceptable as compared to a recent graduate from a Canadian medical school	Borderline unacceptable as compared to a recent graduate from a Canadian medical school	Borderline acceptable as compared to a recent graduate from a Canadian medical school	Acceptable as compared to a recent graduate from a Canadian medical school	Above the level expected of a recent graduate from a Canadian medical school
○	○	○	●	○
○	○	○		○

The following are descriptors of *acceptable* performance levels per competency.

History Taking
Expectations: Acquires from the patient, family, or other source a chronologic, medically logical description of pertinent events. Acquires information in sufficient breadth and depth to permit a clear definition of the patient's problem(s).

Physical Examination
Expectations: Elicits physical findings in an efficient logical sequence that documents the presence or absence of abnormalities and supports a definition of the patient's problem. Sensitive to the patient's comfort and modesty; explains actions to the patient.

Organization
Expectations: Approach is coherent and succinct.

Communication Skills
Expectations: Uses a patient-focused approach. Shows respect, establishes trust; attends to patient's needs of comfort, modesty, confidentiality, information. Provides appropriate, clear information and confirms patient's understanding throughout clinical encounter. Uses repetition and summarizes to confirm and/or reinforce information, and encourages questions. Shares thinking when appropriate. Asks about patient's support system, if appropriate. If applicable, negotiates a mutually acceptable plan of management and treatment. Demonstrates appropriate nonverbal communications (eye contact, gesture, posture, use of silence).

(Continued)

EXHIBIT 16.6. EXAMPLES OF RATING SCALES ITEMS. (Continued)

Language Fluency
Expectations: Please rate the candidate's overall speaking skills/quality of spoken English. Speaks clearly (appropriate volume and rate) with clear pronunciation; accent did not hinder interaction. Speaks directly to person addressed using appropriate eye contact. Provides easily understood instructions, comments and questions. Uses understandable terms for body parts and functions. Uses appropriate choice of words and expressions for the context (for example, giving bad news). Avoids the use of jargon/slang. Uses logical flow of words, phrases, and sentences and appropriate verb tenses to convey intended meaning.

Diagnosis
Expectations: Discriminates important from unimportant information and reaches a reasonable differential diagnosis and/or diagnosis.

Data Interpretation
Expectations: Appropriately interprets investigative data in the context of the patient problem.

Investigations
Expectations: Selects appropriate laboratory or diagnostic studies to elucidate or confirm the diagnosis; takes into consideration risks and benefits.

Therapeutics and Management
Expectations: Discusses therapeutic management (including but not limited to pharmacotherapy, adverse effects and patient safety, disease prevention and health promotion), when appropriate. Selects appropriate treatments (including monitoring, counseling, follow-up); considers risks of therapy and instructs the patient accordingly.

Source: http://mcc.ca/wp-content/uploads/OSCE-Booklet-2014.pdf

EXHIBIT 16.7. SAMPLE REPORT FROM TRAINED OBSERVER RATINGS.

Monthly SCORECARD Community Board Report–June 2014
Percent of Acceptably Clean Streets–Brooklyn

Community Board	Cleaning Section	Acceptable Streets %	Acceptable Streets %—Previous Month	Acceptable Streets %—Year Ago
1	BKN011	91.8	100.0	80.0
	BKN012	82.5	83.3	68.3
	BKN013	83.3	81.0	92.7
	BKN014	61.0	85.4	53.3
	BKN015	90.2	89.5	95.0
	1 Total	**83.2**	**88**	**80.4**
2	BKN021	89.6	100.0	91.7
	BKN022	90.2	84.0	96.0
	BKN023	91.8	100.0	98.0
	BKN024	87.8	88.5	96.2
	2 Total	89.6	93.5	94.9

Source: New York City Mayor's Office of Operations, 2014.

districts further disaggregated by smaller cleaning sections. It also compares ratings over time, by current month, previous month, and the year before.

Figure 16.1 is an intensity map that pinpoints the locations of graffiti found when surveyors walked streets and, also, by using different sized dots, tells the reader about the degree of concentration of problems at particular locations, thereby providing information that can lead to decisions about where action is most sorely needed.

Quality Control

Since trained observer ratings rely on human senses, a well-designed, clearly defined observation instrument combined with effective quality-control procedures are necessary to minimize the subjective nature of the ratings and ensure valid, reliable results.

FIGURE 16.1. INTENSITY MAP OF TRAINED OBSERVER RATINGS

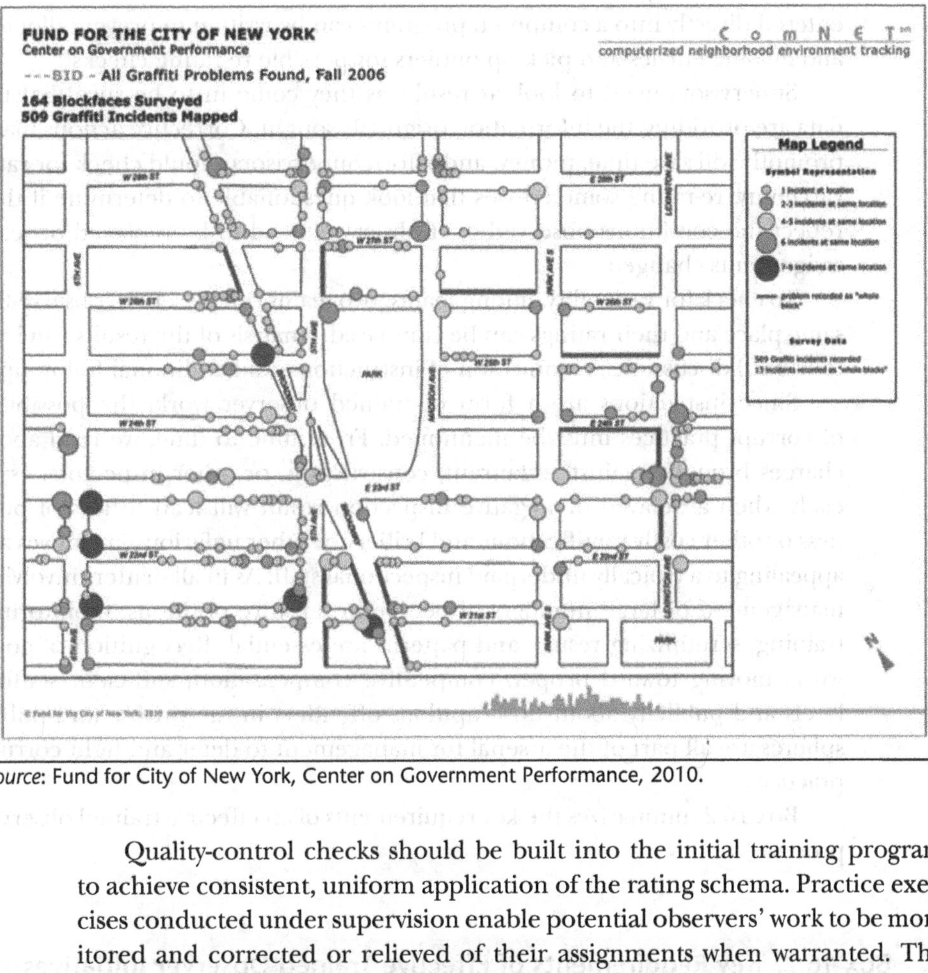

Source: Fund for City of New York, Center on Government Performance, 2010.

Quality-control checks should be built into the initial training program to achieve consistent, uniform application of the rating schema. Practice exercises conducted under supervision enable potential observers' work to be monitored and corrected or relieved of their assignments when warranted. The practice session also provides supervisors with ideas about how forms and instructions may need to be modified and retested.

Conducting a training or review session immediately before the observations take place is highly recommended so that surveyors can apply what they have learned right away. Gaps in time between training and the survey execution can result in poor-quality observations and incorrect data entry.

The use of observer teams is recommended so that at least two people agree that a condition or practice or interaction exists and then agree on its rating. Ratings by one person alone may be problematic if, for example, the person has a particular axe to grind or a conscious or unconscious bias.

It is also recommended that a supervisor or another person knowledgeable in the ratings check a sample of each observer's work. If the ratings are entered directly into a computer, programs can be written to prevent illogical and missing entries and pick up outliers for possible re-rating checks.

Supervisors need to look at results as they come in to be sure that the data are providing the information originally sought. Corrective actions made promptly will save time, money, and effort. Supervisors should check for rater variability, re-rating some entries that look questionable to determine if they reflect the conditions observed or if observers need to be replaced or team assignments changed.

To check for variability among teams, two teams can be sent to observe the same place and their ratings can be compared. Analysis of the results can lead to fruitful discussions, clarification of instructions, and additional follow-up.

Since inspections are a form of trained observer work, the possibility of corrupt practices must be mentioned. From time to time, we read about charges brought against restaurant, construction, or other inspectors, especially when a delayed or negative inspection result will lead to loss of business or other costly ramifications and bribery or other nefarious incentives are appealing to a typically underpaid inspectional staff. As in all matters involving management of large numbers of people in sensitive positions, monitoring, training, scrutinizing results and patterns are essential. Recognition of good work, moving toward proper, competitive compensation, sufficient staffing levels and publicity about unscrupulous offenders in the private and public spheres are all part of the arsenal for management to deter and fight corrupt practices.

Box 16.2 summarizes the key requirements of an effective trained observer process.

Box 16.2. Key Requirements of Effective Trained Observer Initiatives

- Clarity of purpose
- Clarity of definitions
- Consistency of definitions
- Pretesting of instruments and definitions
- Consistent training of observers
- Vigilant supervision
- Quality checking of procedures and data collected
- Verification
- Clear, understandable, useful reports

Using Technology or Paper?

Many of the examples cited in this chapter relied on computers to enter the results of the observation as it was being made to collate the results and produce reports. The technology, when correctly designed, helps assure consistency of reporting, enables faster detection of errors, and saves countless hours or longer of interpreting or misinterpreting handwritten notes. Moreover, the manual collating and summarizing of findings alone can be a tedious and daunting task. Often, projects are aborted before the collation of data is completed because of inadequate personnel to sort, check the work, and produce reports.

On the other hand, obtaining the technology can be costly and time-consuming during the initial development period and the necessary funding may be unavailable. In some situations, observers may be unfamiliar, uneasy, unable, and/or unwilling to use technology. If so, we must keep in mind that research was conducted before the age of technological developments. Planning in these situations involves larger staffing and allowing more time to get the job done. Vigilance in planning, quality control, training, field work, report production, and other requirements previously noted are required.

Benefits of the Trained Observer Approach

Lower Costs

When trained volunteers are used to conduct the ratings, the cost is relatively low compared to involving consultants or specialists. And when the volunteers are familiar with what is being observed, or are even users, they will have a perspective, and an eye for detail, that an outsider may not. For example, when neighborhood people observe the streets, they see things such as trip hazards that others may not notice. As long as volunteers can do the work and can remain true to the instructions and have no biases, this approach is extremely beneficial. Some costs are involved nonetheless, including material, equipment, space for training, printing of directions, and identifications. Supervisors may need a stipend or more compensation. Local organizations may provide no-cost, loaned equipment, access to a confidential database or space to do the collating and report production to avoid additional expenses.

When employees are the observers, the costs are also minimized and depend on how long employees are diverted from other duties and the relative importance of the other duties. Further advantages include the likelihood that the employer will be able to provide the necessary space and equipment and the observers will be knowledgeable in whatever specialty is relevant to the observations. Note that careful training in the specifics of the work at hand for the observation project, quality checks, and supervision are still essential.

The Only Direct Way

When what you need to evaluate is obtainable only by seeing it, hearing it, or applying other senses singly or in combination, the trained observer method is a direct hit. Other methods of inquiry, at best, are indirect surrogates. Asking elementary school students to evaluate their teacher's performance by answering survey questions may yield interesting results. Those results, however, will be a far cry from an impartial experienced teacher observing, first hand, how the teacher relates to students and students respond, the body language of both, the overall atmosphere and structure in the classroom, ease of communication, and so on. Similarly, sending a robot to check on progress and safety on a construction site may miss information about staffing credentials, strength tests, absences of critical personnel, and a myriad of other relevant matters that a trained inspector at the site would pick up.

Trained observers may be the only, if not the best, source to identify and capture measurable but subtle interactions and interpersonal behavior and factors that can lead to actionable results.

Conclusion

The trained observer technique can play a major role in program monitoring and in in-depth program evaluation. Trained observer ratings can serve to rigorously compare and assess differences in service quality and conditions over time or provide an accurate picture on a one-time or *ad hoc* basis. Indeed, trained observer ratings are a version of the kinds of systematic inspections already used in connection with government services, such as building or food inspection programs.

Although many applications of trained observer ratings have focused on streetscape conditions and facilities maintenance, the technique can be applied to a wide variety of conditions and outcomes—from assessing how crowded a bus is to observing the post-treatment behavior of mental health patients.

One must keep in mind that trained observer ratings are usually practical only for assessing characteristics that can be readily and directly sensed or experienced by the rater. Moreover, considerable care must be exercised to ensure that the inherent subjectivity of the rating process does not impair the precision, repeatability, and inter-rater comparability of the results. And one must keep in mind that the very fact that someone is observing an interaction, for example, may, in fact, alter that interaction.

Most of these concerns can be addressed through careful design and implementation of the rating procedures—by appropriately selecting the characteristics to be graded; systematically developing the rating scales; maximizing the use of available technology; carefully choosing, training, and supervising the raters on a timely basis; ensuring adequate quality control throughout the process; and properly analyzing the results. The importance of investing adequate time and resources on quality control cannot be overemphasized.

All told, careful planning and execution elevate trained observer ratings to a valid, systematic measurement technique capable of providing useful evaluative information for program managers, elected officials, and the general public.

Box 16.3 distills the steps involved in operating an effective trained observer initiative:

Box 16.3. Operating Trained Observer Initiatives: Step by Step

1. Determine what you are evaluating and what you intend to do with the results of the evaluation.
2. Develop one or more survey instruments.
3. Field-test the survey instrument(s).
4. Train participants to conduct the survey.
5. Conduct the survey.
6. Repeat a sampling of the survey for quality control.
7. Analyze the results of the survey.
8. Develop a clear, easy-to-understand report and presentation about the findings (develop multiple reports and presentations if needed for multiple audiences).
9. Communicate the results to relevant audiences.
10. If this is an ongoing endeavor, engage in continuous improvement by consulting with observers, users of the findings, and developers of new technology and methods.

References

City and County of San Francisco, Office of the Controller. http://sfcontroller.org.
City of Durham, North Carolina, Department of Neighborhood Improvement Services. www.durhamnc.gov/departments/manager/strategic/comnet_index.cfm.

Hatry, Harry P. *Performance Measurement: Getting Results* (2nd ed.). Washington, DC: The Urban Institute Press, 2006.

Kane, Thomas J., Taylor, Eric S., Tyler, John H., and Wooten, Amy L. "Evaluating Teacher Effectiveness." *Education Next*, Summer 2011, *11*(3).

Keep America Beautiful. "The KAB Litter Index." www.kab.org.

Mark, K. "Experience with Trained Observers in Transition and Developing Countries: Citizen Engagement in Monitoring Results." In P. de Lancer Julnes and others (eds.), *International Handbook of Practice-Based Performance Management.* Thousand Oaks, CA: Sage, 2008.

New York City Mayor's Office of Operations. "Monthly Scorecard Community Board Report." www.nyc.gov/html/ops/

Reinstein, J., Birth, T., and Brenman, J. "ComNET: Repairing Neighborhoods and Building Relationships in Durham, NC." www.ci.durham.nc.us/departments/manager/strategic/pdf/in_this_issue.pdf, n.d.

Schaefer, R.R. "Starting Performance Measurement from Outside Government in Worcester." *National Civic Review*, 2008, *97*(1), 41–45.

Wallace, N. "Good Works in the Palm of a Hand." *Chronicle of Philanthropy*, Sept. 20, 2001, pp. 41–43.

CHAPTER SEVENTEEN

COLLECTING DATA IN THE FIELD

Demetra Smith Nightingale, Shelli Balter Rossman

There is much interest among policymakers, public officials, the media, and the general public in understanding what actually occurs in programs at the ground level and learning what kinds of services or programs seem to work best for different target groups or in different localities. Evaluators are often called on to examine how local programs or agencies operate and how services are delivered. The inquiry might be part of a multifaceted formal evaluation, or it might occur independently as a self-contained study. The focus of analysis might be one program in a single location or several programs in multiple locations, and the study might be cross-sectional (conducted at one point in time) or longitudinal (addressing operations over a period of time). In addition to formal evaluations, federal and state officials and program managers routinely visit local programs to get a better sense of operational realities. Public officials with monitoring responsibilities, for example, visit programs to review specific issues.

Many public and non-profit program evaluations are field based to some extent, meaning that researchers generally collect some information at locations where programs are operating. The field location may be a federal, state, or local agency office, a nonprofit organization, or the office or facility of a public or private operator or provider of services. While on site, evaluators systematically collect information by observing program activities or through surveys; focus groups with participants; interviews with officials, staff, or other stakeholders; and retrieving data from management systems or case file reviews. There are many strategies and various methods for analyzing the qualitative and quantitative data collected. Among the more common types of studies or activities, for example, are single-site case studies, organizational studies, and thematic cross-site comparative studies. Field-based data collection is also frequently used in process studies, implementation analyses, or organizational assessments, as well as outcome and net-impact evaluations.

Other chapters in this volume describe specific data collection methods such as questionnaires, focus groups, and interviews; designs such as case studies, implementation analysis, and logic models; and quantitative and qualitative analytical methods and tools that typically use data collected in the field. This chapter covers some of these topics and complements other chapters by focusing directly on the rationales for collecting data in the field, the different models and conceptual frameworks that can guide field studies, and the procedures and logistics associated with collecting and maintaining data and ensuring quality control. Examples presented include multisite studies that are part of formal evaluations, as well as separate process studies and less extensive efforts that are more appropriate for routine program monitoring and oversight.

Objectives of Field Studies

The details of fieldwork depend on the objectives of the data collection, which are based on the overall purposes of the study or project within which the fieldwork occurs. It is important to fully understand what the fieldwork is intended to achieve, how it fits into the conceptual framework of the evaluation as a whole, and the categories of information it is expected to collect.

The objectives of the fieldwork determine both the focus (priorities) and the scope (intensity) of the data collection activity. At least two types of fieldwork studies are common: program management projects and program evaluation. Box 17.1 displays some examples of objectives from field-based studies that address issues that are related to both management (e.g., program performance, service delivery assessment) and evaluation (e.g., implementation and process analysis) objectives.

Box 17.1. Examples of Field Research Study Objectives

Objectives for a Multisite Adult Drug Court Evaluation (Rossman and Roman, 2004)

National web-based survey objective	Document extant adult drug court models as context for selecting representative sites to participate in impact evaluation.

Process evaluation objective	Document and assess drug court implementation practices—including courtroom observation, procedural manuals and participant records reviews, and staff and stakeholder interviews and focus groups—in twenty-three adult drug court sites.
Impact evaluation objective	Compare relapse and recidivism and also psychosocial outcomes of drug court participants to outcomes of a comparison group of offenders with similar drug and crime histories in six non-drug court jurisdictions.
Cost-benefit analysis objective	Determine drug court costs and benefits as compared to "business as usual" in criminal justice responses to substance abuse offenders.

Objectives for an Implementation Evaluation of Welfare-to-Work Programs in New York City (Nightingale, Pindus, Kramer, Trutko, Mikelson, and Egner, 2002)

| Performance analysis objective | Examine program participation and outcomes over eight years. |
| Implementation analysis objectives | Describe the organization, management, and service delivery procedures in local welfare offices and in programs under contract to serve welfare recipients. Identify policy, bureaucratic, and political factors that influence the way local programs are structured and managed. |

Objectives for a Program Outcome Evaluation of a Child Support Enforcement Collections System (Holcomb and Nightingale, 1989)

| Performance analysis objective | Estimate the impact of the information clearinghouse in five demonstration states on child support collections and government savings. |
| Implementation analysis objectives | Document and assess how the clearinghouse was planned, implemented, and operated. Assess the feasibility of implementing and operating an automated clearinghouse by identifying problems encountered and solutions applied. Identify differences in the clearinghouse across the five demonstration states and reasons for the differences. |

(Continued)

Objectives for an Impact Evaluation of an Aftercare Program for Substance Abusers (Rossman, Roman, Buck, and Morley, 1999)

Impact analysis objective	Compare substance abuse relapse and criminal recidivism of offenders randomly assigned to receive program services (Opportunity to Succeed [OPTS] clients) to the same outcomes for offenders not enrolled in the program.
Implementation analysis objectives	Document and assess the implementation of collaboration between probation and parole entities and service providers.
	Document and assess the nature and extent of case management and core services (substance abuse treatment, employment, housing, medical and mental health treatment, and family support) provided to OPTS clients.

Program Management Fieldwork Model

Federal, state, and local program managers routinely conduct monitoring reviews that involve field visits, reviews of records, interviews, and observations. The topics or issues reviewed depend on the needs of management (such as determining compliance with regulations or improving program performance). Analysis may be quantitative or qualitative, ideally based on predetermined management standards or criteria. The fieldwork is usually conducted by managers or staff of public agencies. However, in some cases, contractors may be engaged to carry out the management review: for example, as part of a performance monitoring project or an assessment of technical assistance needs. The review may involve obtaining management data from computerized or hard copy case files or data in a management information reporting system. The results, typically presented in site reports, may lead to recommendations for corrective action or performance improvement.

Program Evaluation Fieldwork Model

Evaluators ideally collect information on predetermined topics. The classification of topics is based on the overall evaluation project and its objectives. Various data collection methods might be used, including interviews, surveys, focus groups, observations, statistical compilations, and record reviews. Standard social science principles (such as validity, reliability, and objectivity) must be considered in developing the fieldwork plan. The fieldwork and the evaluation are based on theoretical models and hypotheses. Both qualitative and quantitative analysis may be conducted. Individuals who have academic or professional training in research or evaluation usually conduct the fieldwork. Evaluators can be staff of public agencies or researchers from outside research organizations or universities. The results of the work are presented in project reports and often are integrated into other components of a larger or multi-component evaluation.

Each of these and other fieldwork models—or reasons for conducting the study—can potentially involve similar types of data collection methods, but each is based on somewhat different professional practices and experience. The important point is that the specific objectives of the fieldwork set boundaries or standards for the data collection effort. Although it is not essential that a study have a clearly defined fieldwork model, one usually exists, even if it is unstated. The fieldwork model heavily influences specific details about how the fieldwork is designed, the types of data collection instruments used, the professional backgrounds of data collectors and analysts, and the types of quality control and analytical methods employed. These issues are discussed in the sections that follow.

Thus, fieldwork is conducted for at least two purposes:

- To describe what happens at the level being examined (local office, local program, local agency, local community, state office, state agency, and so on) by collecting information about procedures and data on activities, services, institutional features, outcomes.
- To explain why the situations are as they are.

The specific objectives of a fieldwork effort usually fall under one or both of these two general purposes. Before researchers design the details of the fieldwork, it is critical that they articulate clearly and specifically the evaluation questions and issues that relate to the fieldwork portion of the study. Some field studies have very specific objectives, even though the overall evaluation may address broader issues. In contrast, some field-based components of evaluations are called on to address broader program issues, while other components focus on specific questions.

For example, in most large-scale program evaluations that estimate client impacts at the individual level (such as the effect a program has on individuals' employment or educational achievement), an implementation analysis component of an evaluation may involve field data collection to document and investigate in detail specific characteristics of the program being evaluated, such as organizational structure, intake procedures, management functions, and staff job satisfaction. A complementary impact analysis component the evaluation would focus on statistically estimating the change in individual outcomes. Thus, many program participant impact evaluations commonly include process analysis or implementation analysis components with fieldwork to document specific details of a program. The qualitative program descriptors collected in the field can then be transformed into quantitative program variables and incorporated into statistical analyses of program impacts on individual clients to explain the impact findings more fully.

In most evaluations, it is necessary to build the fieldwork design around the basic evaluation questions. Some evaluations attempt to understand variations in performance. An early institutional analysis of the Work Incentive Program (WIN) for welfare recipients, for example, was designed to examine the organizational, managerial, and service delivery characteristics of high- and low-performing state and local programs to determine what seemed to be related to differences in performance (Mitchell, Chadwin, and Nightingale, 1979). The resulting information was used to develop performance improvement strategies for the program nationally. The study had two components: a quantitative analysis of program performance and a more qualitative analysis of features of high- and low-performing programs. The second component relied heavily on information obtained by teams of evaluators who conducted fieldwork in forty-three local communities. Other field-based studies are designed to document variation across sites or identify potentially promising approaches. A study of the implementation of expanded summer jobs programs for youth conducted fieldwork in twenty sites to identify potentially promising approaches that could be of interest to other localities (Bellotti, Rosenberg, Sattar, Esposito, and Ziegler, 2010). These types of issues determine several aspects of the design of the fieldwork.

Design Issues

When the evaluation questions, objectives, and issues of interest have been clearly specified, the evaluators need to make a number of design decisions:

- Determine an appropriate method for guiding the data collection and subsequent analysis.
- Select sites.
- Decide which types of data collection instruments to use and then develop them.
- Identify and select respondents.

These decisions depend greatly on any cost and time constraints that may exist. Evaluations addressing similar or even identical questions may use different fieldwork designs reflecting different cost and time constraints.

Frameworks for Guiding Data Collection

It is sometimes tempting to attempt to examine all aspects of an agency or program using unstructured data collection methods—often described as "getting into the field and finding out what is going on." Even though one might obtain a valuable sense of "what is going on" from a study like this, it is not based on a conceptual framework, it lacks methodological rigor, and the credibility of findings reported may be compromised.

However, one of the greatest pitfalls in conducting field-based studies is the risk associated with collecting too much information; not only can this consume resources unnecessarily, but also analysts can easily become overwhelmed with mounds of qualitative and quantitative information: field notes, interview transcripts, focus group reports, management reports, and site reports, among other data. Unless the data collection stage is well organized, the analysis will be very difficult and subject to problems of accuracy and reliability. To avoid subsequent analytical problems, it is important to use or develop guidelines or a framework at the beginning to help focus the study.

Just as there is no common set of research questions that field-based studies are called on to address, neither is there a common framework used to guide the data collection—in other words, there is no cookie-cutter framework that can be adopted. Instead, the evaluators must develop an overriding framework for each study. In some evaluations, the guidance can be based on the research questions, using them to structure the data collection. Many studies use graphic logic models to help structure data collection. In large-scale evaluations, more theoretical conceptual models often are used.

Research Questions.   Here is a sampling of the many types of research questions that might be addressed in studies that are likely to involve fieldwork:

- What are the major goals and assumptions underlying the policy that was adopted? What are the policy's underlying premises and assumptions? What is the policy intended to accomplish? How does this vary by level of program (for example, state, local)?

- What are the main program outcomes and performance of a program or policy? How are outcomes and performance measured? What are the priorities among measures? How consistent are the various outcome and performance criteria? What is the trend in performance over time or across sites?
- What are the organizational and service delivery structure and context in which the policy is operationalized? How is the organization structured? What are staff roles and responsibilities? What organizational arrangements and linkages are in place to deliver services? What types of interagency and interprogram interactions and collaborations are involved?
- How are key management functions carried out, and what role do they play in the program? How is program planning structured? Who is involved? What types of management information are used and for what purposes (planning, monitoring, performance analysis, performance improvement, evaluation, or something else)?
- Is the program following the formally established strategy? Are all the components implemented as required? Are all the components implemented efficiently? If linkages among components are necessary, are they all in place? Are some components weaker than others?
- Do programs deviate from the planned model? If so, what are the reasons for adaptations/deviations?
- How are services delivered, and how do clients flow through the service delivery system?

Research questions such as these are commonly posed to evaluators. A small-scale field-based evaluation might address one specific type of issue—for example, how key management functions, such as program planning, performance measurement, or staff development, are carried out in a particular program. The important dimensions of that general issue can be clarified in discussions with policymakers, program administrators, or agency officials before finalizing the actual data collection instruments. Then the evaluators can specify the types of questions or data items that will have to be collected and the types of respondents in the field who might be interviewed. Thus even small-scale studies focusing on one or just a few localities and on a few related issues should develop a data collection and fieldwork plan by carefully specifying the various dimensions of the evaluation questions at hand. The key point is that it is important to have a clear guide for collecting information in the field, even if the evaluation question seems simple and straightforward.

A study plan can help the evaluators maintain objectivity and avoid over-collection of information. A plan based on research questions should, at a minimum:

- Clarify each of the evaluation questions to be addressed in the study.
- Identify types of information required to address each question (for example, program procedure information, program data on outcomes, organizational information, staff perceptions on key issues, customer satisfaction).
- Specify data collection strategies to use to collect each item of information (for example, management information data, staff surveys, administrator interviews, and customer or user surveys).

Logic Models.   At a somewhat higher level of methodological sophistication, such as an evaluation that involves fieldwork to multiple sites, evaluators often benefit from preparing a diagrammatic or graphic model to specify the key dimensions of the issue being addressed and how different dimensions or factors relate to each other and to the research questions and evaluation outcomes. Flowcharts and logic models have long been used by public administrators to plan and develop programs, specifying program components, client-flow procedures, management activities, and program outcomes. (See Chapter Three for more detail on logic models and their use in evaluations.) Logic models are used for developing programs and delivery systems to improve the quality of services, such as to ensure that mental health service treatments or interventions are appropriate and consistent with clinical practice (Hernandez, 2000). Decision points and action sequences are included in models, and some models indicate when different levels of a program or organization interact around a particular activity or service. Carefully developed logic models have the potential to improve service provision or program management because the model, or plan, incorporates a theoretical understanding of how different actions or steps interact to produce certain outcomes.

Just as flow models have been routinely used in program planning development and administration, they are now increasingly used for program evaluations of management issues, as a complement to individual impact evaluations, and for addressing other issues that involve sequential phenomena (Abbott, 1995). Logic models can help focus the topics that should be included in field interviews, for example, documenting the organizational units, the sequencing of activities, and outcome or performance measures. In formative evaluations, if outcomes are less than acceptable, staff and managers can use the logic model to diagnose problem points and suggest improvement strategies.

Implementation Models.   Large-scale evaluations of public programs generally include implementation analysis components in addition to individual impact analysis, cost-benefit analysis, and program outcome analysis. Program implementation components of large evaluations often focus on the details of program processes: understanding the internal dynamics and structure of a program, the organizational context in which the program operates, the ways clients enter and move through the program, and the ways the program is structured and managed. Describing and analyzing the process involves delineating program services or client activities into discrete components, documenting how these components fit together in terms of client flow, and obtaining a variety of perspectives from people inside and outside the program on the strengths and weaknesses of the various components. Process analysis is considered a subcategory of implementation analysis, focusing on the specific procedures (such as provision of services and client flow) that occur at the operational service delivery level.

Using graphic depictions similar to logic models, program implementation and process studies that are embedded into comprehensive evaluations often use conceptual framework models to guide the development of hypotheses, data collection, and analysis. Implementation analysis draws from many academic disciplines, especially those related to organizational behavior, social networks, economic behavior, and group dynamics.

Implementation studies of many human services programs, such as welfare-to-work programs, employment services, social services, and programs for formerly incarcerated individuals, draw extensively from organizational theory and systems theory to build a conceptual framework that defines the various categories of information that will be collected in the field. Figure 17.1 shows a simplified depiction of an implementation framework used in impact evaluations, documenting and assessing factors that influence program outcomes (Rossman, Roman, Buck, and Morley, 1999).

The general premise is that some factors (such as the economy, funding levels, or political priorities) totally outside the control of managers and administrators affect how a program is structured and designed. The decisions about structure, design, and operations in turn influence the nature of service delivery and, ultimately, program outcomes.

Evaluating the implementation of a program or policy therefore requires documenting each factor or component that is hypothesized to influence outcomes. A carefully specified framework that defines the factors in each category can form the basis for organizing data collection instruments and analysis to explain how a program operates.

FIGURE 17.1. SIMPLIFIED COMPONENTS OF AN IMPLEMENTATION ANALYSIS CONCEPTUAL FRAMEWORK.

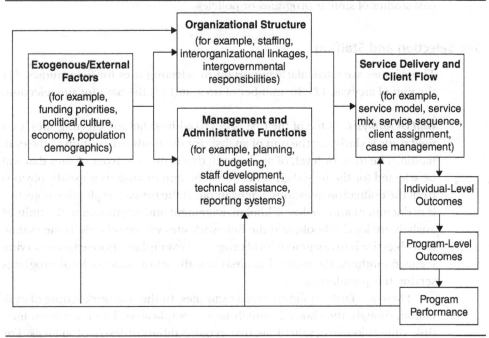

Source: Rossman, Roman, Buck, and Morley, 1999.

Large implementation studies based on theoretical understanding of how organizations and programs operate stand in contrast to less formal efforts that do not use formal fieldwork protocols and involve visiting a few convenient sites, meeting with local administrators, touring a program, and possibly speaking with clients. Some theoretical models from certain disciplines such as economics or sociology can be adapted to serve as conceptual frameworks for field studies. Systems theory and program logic models can also be used to establish conceptual frameworks for field-based studies.

Program implementation is complex. To fully understand what is happening in a program, the evaluator must examine it from different perspectives and view each component of the program both separately and as part of the whole entity. Without a guiding framework, it is very easy to become overwhelmed in the details and lose track of the program as a whole. Conceptual models and frameworks help the evaluator stay organized and avoid information overload. There is no one standard conceptual framework. Each study requires developing a framework that draws on relevant intellectual theory from established academic disciplines or on accumulated knowledge from past studies of similar programs or policies.

Site Selection and Staffing

Three issues are particularly important in selecting sites for field studies: (1) the unit of analysis, (2) the number of sites, and (3) the basis for site selection.

Unit of Analysis. One of the first issues to address before selecting sites for a field study is clarifying the unit of analysis for the fieldwork portion of the evaluation. The unit, or level, of analysis will determine the types of sites that will be selected for the field data collection. The unit of analysis is usually obvious from the evaluation questions. For example, if the primary evaluation objective is to document and analyze school management and organization, the units of analysis are local schools, and the fieldwork sites will be schools. If the evaluation objective is to document local programs' exemplary approaches to serving teenage mothers, the units of analysis and the study sites are local programs serving this population.

These are fairly straightforward examples. In the real work setting of evaluation, though, the choice is usually more complicated. There are often multiple dimensions to evaluations that require different levels of analysis. For instance, if the evaluation objective is to determine how teenage mothers feel about their circumstances and the services available to them, these mothers are the units of analysis. But the evaluators must decide how—that is, from what source—to identify the mothers: schools, hospitals, local programs, welfare rolls, or cities or states. These then also become units of analysis. The final analysis might focus on mothers served by local programs in general or on each local program (with the mothers each of them serve) or on both levels of analysis. Thus, if evaluators want to be able to discuss individual programs in their analysis, they should consider this when selecting the sites where the fieldwork is to be conducted—for example, a city, a neighborhood, or one or more institutions or programs serving the city or neighborhood.

Multiple levels of analysis are common in program organizational evaluations, that is, evaluations not focusing just on individuals. In a national evaluation of coordination between welfare programs and job training programs, for example, a number of units of analysis are possible: local communities (within which all job training and welfare programs would be examined), states (within which all job training and welfare programs would be examined), one or more specific job training programs (which could be examined at the state or local level), or one or more specific welfare programs (which could be examined at the state or local level). Evaluators often also look at different partnership configurations and interorganizational arrangements as the unit of analysis. For example, job training programs often collaborate with social services or public welfare programs).

The unit of analysis for fieldwork studies should be obvious given the overall evaluation questions specified in the study design. Common units of analysis in evaluations are local programs, local offices, individual local facilities (such as libraries or schools or other public agencies), cities, neighborhoods, institutions, and states.

Number of Sites. Once it is clear what units of analysis should be used, the evaluators must decide how many sites to include. The final decision on how many sites to include in the field study depends heavily on the analytical requirements of the specific impact evaluation being conducted, the resources available, and the staffing required. For example, if an evaluation is estimating the nationwide impact of a large program, sampling statisticians may determine that a particular number of sites must be included in the study to ensure that the findings are generalizable to the nation as a whole. The fieldwork component would then also have to include a certain number of sites (either all sites in the overall evaluation or a subsample of sites, based on the statistical sampling parameters). In most field studies, decisions about staffing and site selection are made simultaneously.

Four main factors affect the resource levels required for fieldwork:

- Travel distance.
- Length of time on site.
- Level of evaluation staff required.
- Number of evaluation staff required.

The importance of each of these items varies somewhat in different studies. Travel times, for example, may be associated with cost, but sometimes distance alone does not equate to higher costs. Traveling from the east coast to the west coast may cost less and take less time than traveling from either coast to the northern plains. The cost of each of these factors will also be governed by the intensity of data collection. If the field efforts are exploratory, involving unstructured data collection activities, such as discussions with key officials or staff in a program, then each site visit can probably be limited to a short period of time—one or two days—when one evaluator works alone. That person should be fairly senior to ensure that the exploration is as comprehensive as possible. At the other extreme, an evaluation that involves collecting detailed descriptions of program operations by surveying or interviewing a number of staff in each site will require more days on-site, probably more than one staff person, and a longer period of time.

Most large federally sponsored program evaluations now include an implementation, or process, analysis component. Typically, the fieldwork design involves a team of two evaluators, with one fairly senior and the other either a midlevel evaluator or a research assistant. The two-person team is on-site for three to five days, depending on the size of the site or city and the scope of the inquiry. Two-person teams have proved to be effective for collecting accurate data and, subsequently, analyzing and interpreting the information. The evaluation team can discuss issues and share contextual insights while in the field that greatly strengthen the overall quality of information.

Tight resources may preclude having two-person teams. There are lower-cost staffing configurations that may be fully satisfactory for some less-intensive field-based studies, such as program reviews, survey administration, or collection of routine statistical data. As an example, one public official (such as a state program monitor or program administrator, or a federal inspector or monitor, or an evaluator) can visit a local program for just one day and collect a substantial amount of information. The on-site time can be spent efficiently, using carefully developed data collection instruments, scheduling activities in advance, and following field protocol established before the visit.

Many different activities might be carried out while on site to obtain the information and data specified in the study design based on the objectives and conceptual plan. Site visits can be demanding, and caution should be exercised to avoid placing too high a workload burden on the field staff. To provide a rough estimate of the staff resources required on site, two trained evaluators working together can be expected to accomplish any one of the following types of activities in one day:

- Each person can usually conduct three or four one-hour interviews with staff, administrators, or community officials, allowing time for preparing for each interview and reviewing notes before starting the next interview.
- The team together can conduct two or three (depending on the study) focus groups lasting one to two hours each.
- Each evaluator can administer six forty-five-minute, in-person questionnaires.

- The team can review case records. A typical single welfare case record review, for example, takes between fifteen and forty-five minutes, depending on the size of the file and what information needs to be extracted from the files.
- The team can perform a well-planned combination of two activities, such as one or two in-person interviews and one focus group session, during the same day.

Evaluations generally involve using multiple data collection methods on site, such as trained observer ratings or statistical data collection from management information systems. Thus, the resources devoted to each site visit depend on the mix of activities to be conducted. Fieldwork can become quite expensive. For example, on-site fieldwork that involves collecting data on programs in ten cities, each in a different state, using a two-person team (one senior evaluator and one midlevel evaluator) on site for one week per city, would require about one hundred person-days, at a cost of between $100,000 to $150,000 for labor, travel, per diem, and expenses. An additional one hundred to two hundred person-days would be required for previsit preparations and post-visit report writing. Some data collection activities may have additional costs; focus groups, for example, often involve costs for providing individual financial incentives, or reimbursing participants for travel expenses, or arranging for refreshments to motivate participation.

Basis for Site Selection

When there are several possible units of analysis, decisions about site selection are typically based on how the information acquired in the fieldwork will be used by the evaluators. If the purpose is to prepare case studies, each of which can stand on its own, it is not necessary to select sites that are all of the same type. An examination of coordination, for instance, could include one or more local communities and also one or more states. If the purpose is more analytical—perhaps to examine factors that encourage or discourage coordination between two programs—then the evaluators should select sites that represent as broad a range as possible of the various types of programs and situations, perhaps including programs of varying sizes and in both urban and rural locations or programs serving populations with different demographic characteristics.

The sample of sites for fieldwork can be selected in a number of ways. At one extreme, the sampling method may be random, using standard probability sampling techniques. This requires identifying a universe of possible sites, clustering or stratifying the sites on the basis of some criteria, and then randomly selecting within the strata or clusters. At the other extreme, the site selection process can be purely purposive, with specific sites or specific types of sites chosen, such as small rural sites with high-poverty populations or award-winning programs that are considered exemplary or large programs in high-growth economic labor markets.

Site selection for most field studies usually falls somewhere between these extremes. Evaluators examining exemplary program models might choose sites based on some feature of the program that is of particular interest—the specific populations served, unique locations, innovative program models, and special organizational structure—and choose randomly from among sites meeting those criteria.

In large part, the selection of sites depends on whether the findings from the field are intended to be representative of some larger group of programs or sites or whether they are to be used for stand-alone case studies. If the data and information from the field sites are to be generalized to a larger group of sites or programs, the selected sites should be as representative as possible of the population of sites from which the sample is drawn. If the information is to be used primarily for descriptive case studies and is intended to be illustrative only, then purposive sampling is sufficient.

Even if evaluators choose sites purposively, the selection should still be based on clear guidelines and criteria. In many cases these resemble the types of criteria used to select sites by random stratification or clustering. Examples of selection criteria include level of program performance, rural versus urban location, level of client income, level of client ethnic concentrations, labor market conditions, and geographical location.

In some field studies, site selection might evolve through the evaluators' soliciting interest from local jurisdictions, programs, or agencies. One Urban Institute study was designed to develop and then evaluate a management-oriented performance improvement model in state Work Incentive Programs serving welfare recipients (Nightingale and Ferry, 1982). The study could include only two states, and the following conditions were used to select them:

- The state agency had to have a strong potential for improvement while not currently performing at full capacity.
- The program administrators at the state level had to express a deep commitment to improving their operations.

- State officials had to be willing to participate actively in developing and implementing improvement strategies by making key staff available for the duration of the two-year project.

In the selection process, the evaluators compiled information showing how well each candidate state met these three criteria. The information was obtained through reviews of program performance reports and conversations with key state administrators.

There are no hard-and-fast rules about how to select sites for fieldwork studies. Site selection evolves from the general evaluation objectives. The evaluator must decide whether sites should represent maximum variation or maximum similarity. Regardless of how scientific the site selection process is, evaluators must have pre-established criteria that can also be used subsequently when reporting the implications of the findings. The selection of sites should be based on the objectives of the evaluation, but the final decisions must also consider the staffing that will be required and all costs at each site.

Types and Scope of Instruments

Except in the most exploratory type of fieldwork, evaluators will need to use one or more data collection instruments. At a minimum, the evaluation will need a field data collection guide that includes instructions for obtaining information from interviews, observations, surveys, case reviews, and focus groups. Instruments vary from highly structured to very unstructured.

The structured types of data collection instruments are best known and include surveys, questionnaires, tests, and data coding sheets. Structured instruments have specific items, questions, or codes that data collectors must use in recording information. The least structured evaluations may have no formal data collection instruments. Between are the semi-structured data collection instruments, which consist of topical areas or subject categories, along with questions that the interviewer may use, as well as suggested wording for asking about key issues. (See Chapter Nineteen for a more detailed discussion of semi-structured interviews.)

Field Visit Protocol

Fieldwork projects require careful attention to many procedural and logistical details before, during, and after the site visits. This section discusses the protocol—the critical procedures—that should be developed for a field visit.

Field evaluators should be fully trained on these details. Procedures should be followed precisely to ensure that the information collected is of high quality, the different evaluators collect information in a comparable manner, the fieldwork is minimally intrusive, and confidentiality and other human subjects protections are maintained to the maximum extent possible.

Previsit Preparations

The successful completion of the on-site portion of an evaluation that includes fieldwork depends critically on careful preparation before the site visit. Evaluators should not underestimate the importance of the previsit activities. Previsit preparations include a variety of activities, from setting up site-specific files of existing materials to handling logistical arrangements and recruiting and training field staff.

During the early stages of planning an evaluation, materials should be assembled from a variety of sources, such as government program files, agency and program Internet websites, grant applications, existing databases, or site narratives from prior field trips or evaluation files. Where feasible, these materials should be organized into files associated with each of the designated field sites. A log of contacts (such as phone conversations with the key contact person or program director in each site) can also be included in each site's master file or folder. A log of contacts is especially important in studies that will be conducted over a long period of time and those involving several researchers because it serves as the official record for the study. For evaluations in which many documents are being collected from each site, attach a checklist of materials requested to the site's master folder or file. The materials should be checked off as they are received. Follow-up requests should be made and noted on the log. All files and contacts must be carefully documented to allow the evaluation to be completed efficiently regardless of changes that might occur within the project (for example, if the evaluation team changes due to turnover or if evaluator assignments change).

Site Clearances.   Initial contact with field sites should identify any constraints that might affect scheduling or data collection. For example, to gain entry into schools and speak to teachers and staff, evaluators may need to obtain clearances from high levels in an agency, or there may be other evaluations under way in the same site that might require coordinating schedules. Similarly, to conduct interviews in jails or prisons, permissions need to be obtained from facility directors, and should cover such issues as interviewer dress codes, whether electronic equipment such as smart phones and laptops are permitted, and interview space that permits confidential exchanges outside the line-of-sight of facility staff. If entry clearance or interview authorizations are needed, the evaluator should clarify who is responsible for obtaining approvals (that is, the evaluator or the contact person in the agency), whose permission must be sought, and what information is needed to facilitate the process. Scheduling must be sufficiently flexible to accommodate delays due to bureaucratic obstacles; at the same time, planning should include actions that can be taken to minimize schedule slippage.

Scheduling Visits and Interviews.   Several factors, including travel distance and level of staffing required, affect site scheduling. Early communication should identify primary contact persons at selected sites who can serve as liaisons to the evaluation and tentative dates or time periods or possible alternative schedules for the visit. This scheduling will permit advance planning of logistics, such as travel reservations and field staffing assignments. Economies of scale in both travel and staffing costs can often be achieved when visits to geographically close sites can be scheduled together.

Information packages should be assembled and sent to the local contact person to provide background about the evaluation. These should include:

- An overview of the evaluation objectives and of the scope of each field visit.
- Assurances that confidentiality procedures will be followed (for either individuals interviewed or for the site as a whole, depending on the study).
- A sample schedule that the evaluation team would like to follow, identifying those individuals the team wants to interview or meet with, for how long, and the times each day that the field evaluation team members will be available.

Either the field visit team or the designated site contact person can schedule the interviews. The division of responsibility should be clearly established as soon as possible. During that discussion, the evaluators should review with the contact person the list of potential respondents, verifying that appropriate categories of staff have been identified and identifying other persons who may also be important to interview. Usually, the initial interview in a site should be with the key contact person, who can provide an overview of the system.

Evaluators must decide whether they will conduct individual or group interviews and determine the appropriate setting for conducting the interviews. If interview topics are sensitive or there is a need to ensure individuals' confidentiality, one-on-one interviews rather than group interviews should be planned, with private rooms secured for each session. Even when confidentiality is not an issue, reasonable efforts should be made to secure quiet, unobtrusive settings for interviewing in order to minimize distractions, which can reduce the quality of responses.

Once the field visit has been scheduled, personnel at the site should be notified by phone, mail, or e-mail of the dates for the visit and the time scheduled for the interviews. Several days prior to the visit, contact should be made with the key contact person and possibly with each respondent to reconfirm plans, review the proposed agenda, and ensure the scheduling of the interviews.

Defining Information Needs. Evaluators often collect program materials, agency reports, and other documents related to the study site. It is important to request copies of relevant reports in advance of the actual visit. During the initial telephone conversations regarding the site visit schedule, for example, evaluators should ask about reports, organizational charts, procedure manuals, and other program descriptions, and request copies for review before the visit. If the evaluators intend to collect copies of records or documents while on site, they should discuss their needs in advance with the key contact person or respondents and encourage site personnel to assemble the information before the visit. This is especially helpful when a large number of documents or files are needed or when the site has limited resources, such as a small number of staff or limited access to duplicating equipment, that might make it difficult to compile requested information.

If the evaluation is assessing processes fidelity, or analysing outcomes associated with promising or "best" practices or curriculum-based programming, evaluators should request that training and quality assurance materials, as well as the practice protocols or curricula, available for on-site review, if it is not feasible to obtain copies in advance.

Staffing Assignments. Decisions about the division of labor should be made as early as possible so that field staff know which sites they will cover, which interviews they will be responsible for conducting, and the specific issues they will be exploring. Once field assignments are established, staff should review materials already on hand, such as organizational charts, management information reports, grant applications, program planning documents, and fiscal forms. At the same time, staff should review the research instruments/protocols and the checklist of requested documents, noting which materials still need to be collected, either in advance or when on-site.

The issue of field staff safety bears special mention. Both real and perceived risks of working in some communities (such as high-crime neighborhoods) can make it difficult to hire qualified researchers to staff certain projects. It is crucial to consider the kinds of actions that may be taken to ensure staff safety. Here are some helpful strategies:

- Use two-person teams for site visits in high-risk areas, possibly including someone on the team who is familiar with the local situation.
- Schedule interviews only in public locations, such as public offices, libraries, fast-food restaurants, or other well-lit, high-traffic facilities.
- Train staff to take appropriate logistical precautions (such as having a clear set of directions and a map, a sufficient quantity of gas, accessible cell phones preprogrammed with key contact information and local numbers for assistance, and knowledge of public transportation options or how to arrange for taxicabs).
- Prepare field evaluators to watch out for their own safety. Teach them the kinds of situations to avoid (such as parking in isolated locations, walking a long distance in unfamiliar territory, and publicly displaying large amounts of cash or expensive jewelry).

Project Orientation.   Unless the fieldwork is of very short duration or involves fewer than three field researchers, the team should prepare a document specifying procedures that field data collection staff are to follow. Such a document is helpful for both previsit training of the teams and for use as a reference while in the field.

The project field documents should review the following topics:

- The overall objectives of the evaluation and the specific purpose of the field visits.
- Human subject protections and data security, including the provisions of an institutional review board (IRB) plan if such a review was required.
- Item-by-item instructions for administering instruments, including definitions of terms used in the project.
- Advice on how to gain respondent cooperation and, when necessary, procedures appropriate to obtaining informed consent.
- Confidentiality requirements, including privacy during interviews.
- Procedures for conducting interviews, and circumstances under which interviews should be terminated and contingency plans for such emergencies should hold sway (e.g., if an interviewer perceives the respondent is

under the influence of drugs or alcohol, or is showing signs of mental or physical distress).

- Other procedures for collecting data, such as carrying out structured observations, distributing or administering questionnaires, or auditing records.
- Data storage, maintenance, and security procedures.
- Quality control procedures, including instructions on when additional follow up is recommended for clarification, and how to edit field notes.
- Administrative requirements, such as accounting and reporting procedures for dispensing incentives or submitting expense reports, obtaining reimbursement for travel, per diem rates, and so on.
- Recommendations for managing time while on site.

Training. Training for field teams should cover all aspects of the field visits, including going over the instruments and all procedures in detail. Another important topic to include in the training is how to gain and maintain respondent cooperation. The level of cooperation secured will be partially dependent on the interviewer's ability to listen to the respondent, being aware of any sensitivities or anxieties the respondent might have, and responding appropriately to place the respondent at ease.

Before going into the field themselves or sending staff there, evaluators should consider the kinds of issues or resistance that respondents may raise. Training should incorporate answers to anticipated questions and should include having team members practice appropriate responses to likely situations or procedures to follow in the case of unforeseen events that could pose a threat to data collection. In large evaluations, these mock interviews are sometimes videotaped to provide immediate and forceful feedback to the interviewers.

Site Packets. Before the field trip, research staff should review the planned on-site procedures to assess their need for supplies and equipment, such as writing implements, notepads, electronic devices, and other office supplies that they should bring. We have found that two long (one hour) or three short interviews can be recorded in a notebook the size of a journalist's notebook (about six by eight inches). Staff should plan to take a few extra notebooks on each field visit to avoid running out. Similarly, if staff plan to use laptops to record information, preparation should include sufficiently long electric cords to charge devices during interviews and back-up paper and writing implements in the event of electronic failure.

If visits to several sites are linked or researchers anticipate collecting large amounts of bulky material, it may be desirable to bring along prepaid mailing labels and envelopes to send completed materials back to the home office. Because data, such as interview responses, may not be replaceable if lost, it is probably wise to use courier-type delivery services, which have sophisticated tracking capabilities, virtually guaranteeing that packages will not be lost. Electronically recorded information should be backed up each day, if not after each interview. Where confidentiality is a concern, arrangements should be made in advance to transmit these data using secure procedures (e.g., secure file transfer protocol or SFTP).

On-Site Procedures

Information on important on-site activities for which evaluators must be prepared should be included in the field visit protocol (procedures) developed before conducting the site visits.

Maintaining the Schedule and Interviewing Protocol. It is not possible to guarantee a particular response rate in advance. However, with appropriate planning and effort (such as careful scheduling, following guidelines for encouraging respondent cooperation, and having contingency plans for various situations), the team should be able to achieve a high interview completion rate, approaching 100 percent of those scheduled in advance. Professional demeanor and ability to conduct interviews without exhibiting judgment or excessive sympathy or emotion are particularly important.

If a respondent is reluctant to cooperate, field staff should attempt to convert reticence into cooperation. A first step is to ascertain whether the respondent has concerns or questions about the study or the interview that can be resolved, thus permitting the interview to proceed. For example, the timing may be inconvenient, in which case rescheduling the interview might resolve the impasse. In some cases, a rescheduled interview can be completed later in the visit or, if necessary, at a later time by telephone or videoconferencing. If this does not succeed, it may be best to allow another interviewer or the evaluation supervisor to attempt the interview at a future time.

A pilot test, or pretest, should be conducted in at least one site to try out all instruments and procedures. This will help to identify revisions or corrections that are needed. In most evaluations, the pilot site can also be part of the formal field evaluation because most of the same information will be collected.

Collecting and Recording Information. Field evaluators should be given materials that both help them to explain the purpose of the study to respondents and permit them to move efficiently through the planned interview. Each interview should begin with a brief introduction to the project. (An example is provided in Box 17.2.) Each respondent must understand the project and the purpose of the interview. Explaining the project takes only one or two minutes and is one of the most important parts of the interview. In these first few minutes, the interviewer should establish a rapport that places the respondent at ease.

Box 17.2. Sample Introduction and Statement of Confidentiality

"It is very important for us to learn how the Program for Family Independence operates here, problems or issues you have identified, and suggestions for how a program like this should be run. This is a new program, and it is essential to document its implementation and ongoing development.

"We need your cooperation to do this, since you know the most about welfare and employment and training problems and the problems that must be overcome. We are not employees of any state agency, nor are we auditors. We will be submitting reports to the state legislature, but in these reports, no one will be able to identify what any particular individual told us. We pledge confidentiality. The sources of our interview information will not be divulged to anyone else here in this office, city, or state. No names will be included in our reports.

"Do you have any questions before we begin?"

Immediately after the introduction, the interviewer should address confidentiality (also shown in Box 17.2). If the respondent's name is going to be included in a report, that must be explained at the time of the interview. If all information is to be confidential, meaning no names will be included in the report and no findings will be attributed to anyone by name, that needs to be explained. Confidential interviews are more likely than "public" interviews to produce rich detail—if the respondent understands the confidentiality pledge and believes that the interviewer will abide by the pledge. This is true even when the information being requested is not sensitive.

The evaluation should establish procedures for handling and storing the information collected in an interview, particularly if it is confidential. The procedures for maintaining confidentiality may range from not entering respondents' names into any databases that are constructed to devising systems of randomly generated identification numbers maintained in secured computer files.

After the introduction it is helpful to break the ice with an initial question designed to obtain background information on the respondent and ease into the interview. This can include asking the respondent his or her official job title, length of time employed with this agency, and what he or she did before this job. After this, the evaluator should move into the substance of the interview.

There are several ways to record the information from an interview: audio- or videotaping, taking notes by hand and transcribing the information into a notebook or directly onto interview forms, or using an electronic portable notebook or tablet, where notes can be written in longhand onto the electronic pad and later converted into a standard word processing format. Many evaluators now use laptop or tablet computers pre-loaded with data collection instruments, and type responses directly into such forms in appropriate places. Electronic pens are also available, allowing field teams to record notes that convert directly as a word processing document.

There are pros and cons associated with each approach, and the decision about which to use is generally a matter of personal preference. Subsequent analysis of information is generally accomplished more easily when interview notes (whether initially obtained through longhand notes or electronic methods) are transcribed into standard word processing following an established outline or topic format.

Daily Reviews.   After the day's data collection is completed, evaluators should review the material gathered to add subject codes, respondent codes, site codes, or other explanatory details where needed. The material should be cleaned and clarified to be sure it is legible and meaningful to other members of the evaluation team. For example, only agreed-on abbreviations or those defined in the interviewer comments or other notes should be used.

Some evaluators choose to dictate each day's interview notes or reflections on other materials into a tape recorder. The tapes can later be transcribed for analysis or preparation of site reports. Some electronic pens also have audio recording capabilities in addition to electronic text conversion. The taping process also allows the evaluators opportunities to review the day's information carefully.

If there is more than one evaluator on site, the members of the evaluator team should briefly review their respective notes, data, and experiences to identify possible areas of inconsistency, issues that may have been missed totally (such as a question none of the respondents was able to answer well because it was outside all respondents' scope of responsibility), or areas that need further clarification or detail. The end-of-day debriefings afford valuable exchanges of information that can be helpful later in the analysis. The team may want to record those sessions.

When an interview is finished, the respondent may express interest in knowing what the evaluators are finding. Similarly, when all data collection is completed at a site, an administrator may want to discuss with the evaluators the findings or conclusions they have drawn. Evaluators will naturally be thinking about preliminary findings before they leave the site, but they should not attempt to draw conclusions or make recommendations while in the field. Later phases of the evaluation (after the site visits) should be devoted to analysis. It is very tempting to provide immediate feedback but also extremely risky, so it should be avoided. Evaluators should be prepared to respond politely to such requests by explaining that they have accumulated a large amount of information and material that will have to be carefully reviewed and analyzed before it can be reported. This response may make the evaluator slightly uncomfortable, but it is much better than realizing later that he or she has given a program official partial or incorrect findings. To soften the exchange, evaluators can briefly review with the site principals what the researchers plan going forward (e.g., when follow-up visits will occur, when a draft report is anticipated, whether sites will be given the opportunity to review and comment on draft materials, and when and how final reporting is expected to be made public).

Data Maintenance and Analysis

Once field data have been amassed, they can be used to generate several types of summaries, such as quantitative frequencies, trends, contingencies, and intensities. In addition, qualitative information can provide rich anecdotal evidence.

Most important when observation or semi-structured interviews are used, evaluators need to decide how to systematically summarize the large quantity of information collected. Analyzing qualitative data is roughly equivalent to performing analysis of more structured data collection methods such as surveys, in which the documents under scrutiny are the records of interview responses. Such analysis involves organizing the data into relevant sets of content or issue categories or topics and sets of response alternatives for each content or issue category.

Even when data sets are derived from semi-structured, open-ended instruments, evaluators should identify preliminary categories of possible responses prior to data collection. This structure provides guidelines that help to orient the data collection efforts. For example, anticipating certain themes and possible responses can help field staff determine whether observations, interviews, or record extractions are achieving the evaluation objectives or whether evaluators need to probe further. Usually, preliminary categories or topics can be proposed during the fieldwork planning stage, based on the evaluation questions or hypotheses. Often the range of response alternatives can also be anticipated. However, these predetermined coding possibilities should be viewed flexibly because new themes and insights are likely to emerge during the data collection, or some anticipated topics and responses may never materialize.

One approach to data organizing is to have field evaluators sort the information for each identified research topic or category, using the response alternatives postulated prior to actual data collection. The coding scheme is then finalized in light of feedback from field staff about categories or response alternatives they have identified that do not fit the data. Adjustments can be made by expanding or collapsing the initial choices of topics or responses. As analysts sort the data, they can also flag any anecdotes or quotations that might enrich the final report.

A more rigorous (but also more costly) approach to analyzing qualitative interview notes, if resources are sufficient, is to divide the analysts into two teams to review a sample of observations, interviews, or extracted records independently. Each team develops a set of content categories and response alternatives for each category based on the data sources. The teams convene as a single group to discuss and merge the categories and responses. Once consensus is achieved, the data can be split into subsamples. Each team receives one subsample, which team members code using the agreed-on scheme; then the teams exchange samples and repeat the categorization process. This approach tests both intracoder reliability (the degree of consistency with which a coder interprets similar responses) and intercoder reliability (the degree of consistency in interpretation among different coders).

If consistency in coding is unacceptably low, there are several options for improving reliability:

- Categories can be tightened and redefined to reduce the chances for miscoding.
- A training session can be held to increase intercoder reliability by making coders more familiar with the categorization system.
- Instead of having analysts code every item for a series of observations or interviews, each analyst can be assigned responsibility for coding the same set of questions or topics for all observations or interviews, thus becoming

the coding specialist for specific items, and thereby increasing intracoding reliability.

The data maintenance approaches described above refer to situations when the information collected in the field is manually sorted and coded. Researchers can use electronic tools instead of, or in combination with, manual procedures. Technology is rapidly developing, and there are various creative electronic tools for recording, coding, sorting, and analyzing field data and notes. For instance, there are many content analysis software programs that can be used to generate lists of unique words or phrases in one or more documents, as well as enumerate the frequency of occurrence. These and other programs have streamlined qualitative data analyses.

Conclusion

The fieldwork portion of an evaluation provides an opportunity to collect rich detail that can augment more quantitative data that are included in the evaluation. Too often, fieldwork is approached in an informal or haphazard manner that results in massive amounts of notes and other information that cannot be easily analyzed. Evaluators should pay careful attention to developing fieldwork procedures, designing fieldwork data collection instruments, and preparing plans for managing and analyzing the information collected. Carefully implemented, fieldwork data collection can produce valid and credible information that cannot be obtained from other sources.

References

Abbott, A. "Sequence Analysis: New Methods for Old Ideas." *Annual Review of Sociology*, 1995, *21*, 93–113.

Bellotti, J., Rosenberg, L., Sattar, S., Esposito, A. M., and Ziegler, J. *"Reinvesting in America's Youth: Lessons from the 2009 Recovery Act Summer Youth Employment Initiative."* Princeton, NJ: Mathematica Policy Research, 2010.

Hernandez, M. "Using Logic Models and Program Theory to Build Outcome Accountability." *Education and Treatment of Children*, 2000, *23*, 24–40.

Holcomb, P., and Nightingale, D. S. *Evaluation of the Western Interstate Child Support Enforcement Clearinghouse.* Washington, DC: Urban Institute, 1989.

Mitchell, J. J., Chadwin, M. L., and Nightingale, D. S. *Implementing Welfare Employment Programs: An Institutional Analysis of the Work Incentive Program.* Washington, DC: Urban Institute, 1979.

Nightingale, D. S., and Ferry, D. *Assessment of the Joint Federal-State Performance Improvement Projects in the Work Incentive Program.* Washington, DC: Urban Institute, 1982.

Nightingale, D. S., Pindus, N., Kramer, F., Trutko, J., Mikelson, K., and Egner, M. *Work and Welfare Reform in New York City During the Giuliani Administration.* Washington, DC: Urban Institute, 2002.

Rossman, S. B., and Roman, J. "Issues in Designing the National Evaluation of Drug Courts." Presentation at the American Society of Criminology, Nashville, Tennessee, November 18, 2004.

Rossman, S. B., Roman, C. R., Buck, J., and Morley, E. *Impact of the Opportunity to Succeed (OPTS) Aftercare Program for Substance Abusing Felons.* Washington, DC: Urban Institute, 1999.

Further Reading

Century, J., Rudnick, M., and Freeman, C. "A Framework for Measuring Fidelity of Implementation: A Foundation for Shared Language and Accumulation of Knowledge. *American Journal of Evaluation,* June 2010, *31*(2), 199–218.

Holcomb, P., and Nightingale, D. S. "Conceptual Underpinnings of Implementation Analysis." In T. Corbett and M. C. Lennon (eds.), *Policy into Action: Implementation Research and Welfare Reform.* Washington, DC: Urban Institute Press, 2003.

U.S. Agency for International Development. "Manual for the Implementation of USAID Poverty Assessment Tools." www.povertytools.org/USAID_documents/Manual/USAID_PAT_Implementation_Manual_205-6-2011.pdf. May 2011.

U.S. Department of Labor, Clearinghouse for Labor Evaluation and Research (CLEAR). "Operational Guidelines for Reviewing Implementation Studies." http://clear.dol.gov/sites/default/files/CLEAR_Operational_Implementation_Study_Guidelines.pdf. June 12, 2014.

Werner, A. *A Guide to Implementation Research.* Washington, DC: Urban Institute Press, 2004.

CHAPTER EIGHTEEN

USING THE INTERNET

William C. Adams

In the twenty-first century we are living our lives—acquiring and exchanging both personal and professional information—via the Internet to a degree that was unimaginable not so many years ago. Program evaluations are no exception. This chapter discusses how the Internet can be used in three ways: to conduct electronic literature reviews, to administer online surveys, and to post research.

Using the Internet for Literature Reviews

In Chapter Twenty-Five, Robert Boruch, Anthony Petrosino, and Claire Morgan offer a compelling case for the utility of highly systematic literature reviews, including meta-analyses, as opposed to the rambling narratives of the old-fashioned, nonreplicable, impressionistic lit reviews. This chapter now turns to a subsidiary undertaking: using the Internet to conduct some of that research. Boruch, Petrosino, and Morgan argue persuasively against relying totally on electronic searches and point out additional avenues to pursue. Nevertheless, a year spent in dusty library stacks is unlikely to accomplish as much as a day of electronic searches, so the latter approach does merit extra attention.

Rather than discuss web research in general, the topic here is on the heart of the literature review: locating prior research about the type of program to be evaluated. In addition, the intention is to be highly selective and blatantly judgmental, rather than print yet another long, indiscriminate list of links.

As you begin the literature review, be sure to maintain a thorough record of exactly how you conduct electronic searches. Keep a list of which search engines and databases you use, with precisely which search terms, along with any other tweaks, such as limiting the time period or types of publications searched. Why bother? So you won't waste time later repeating any searches; you may think you will remember specific terms and the like, but a week later you won't. If you later discover a better search term, thanks to your log you can retrace your steps with precision. Records will also permit documenting in your final report the dazzling degree to which you systematically explored and scrutinized prior studies on this topic. Otherwise, critics may fear that you just selectively cited a few convenient sources.

The great electronic chasm between the haves and the have-nots is between researchers in universities and large public policy institutions with access to vast online libraries versus those who lack such access. It is not impossible for those outside the password walls of institutional access to conduct online research, but it is not easy and will entail fees to read many published articles. Large municipal public libraries ordinarily do not subscribe to academic databases and e-journals. It may be less expensive just to enroll in a yoga class at a large public university in order to gain full access to all databases and full-text articles (plus stretching is healthy after all that time at the computer). Nevertheless, let's first consider a few key avenues open to everyone.

The Campbell and Cochrane Collaborations

One extraordinary gold mine is The Campbell Collaboration (campbell collaboration.org), which regularly assembles updated, systematic reviews (essentially meta-analyses) of studies of the impact of interventions and policy trials in the fields of education, social welfare, psychology, and criminal justice, plus some coverage of a few related areas. You can strike it rich here if you find a meta-analysis on the type of program you wish to evaluate. Are you assessing a correctional boot camp? The Campbell Collaboration offers a rigorous review of thirty-two studies of such programs. Are you examining the impact of a neighborhood watch program? Read its analysis of forty-three such evaluations. The Cochrane Collaboration (cochrane.org) is comparable to the Campbell site but assembles the findings of medical treatments and interventions. The online libraries at both sites are easy to use and free to access. See Chapter Twenty-Five for additional background on these two remarkable enterprises.

Google, Bing, and Yahoo!

Their names may sound childish, but the major search engines scan incredible volumes of material in an instant. However, one drawback is the huge number of links they collect. For example, a single search for "correctional," "boot camp," and "evaluation" yielded 200,000 hits on Google (google.com) and 88,000 hits on both Bing (bing.com) and Yahoo! (search.yahoo.com), which now share the same search engine. Trawling through many thousands of hits is tedious and laborious. Narrowing search terms and mastering advanced search techniques can help, but rarely cull the output nearly as much as needed. Recall that the thorough researchers at the Campbell Collaboration had successfully amassed only forty-three serious evaluations of correctional boot camps.

The big search engines are sufficiently effective to lure us into thinking we have conducted a thorough search if we plow through the first dozen pages until the links start becoming less relevant. On the test topic of correctional boot camp evaluations, the first few pages of the searches do reveal some serious evaluations, many of them posted online by the National Institute of Corrections or by state governments. However, they still fail to cite many of the noteworthy studies tracked down by the Campbell Collaboration. Moreover, the big-name search engines do not search the so-called "gray literature" (discussed later in this chapter). And some of their promising links have a price tag. One early boot camp link was to a sagepub.com page with a tempting but vague abstract; without institutional access, you must pay $30 to access the article, which might prove to be a costly disappointment.

Google Scholar

This free search engine (scholar.google.com) conducts full-text searches of many academic journals that are available in electronic form, both those that are free and those that are not free to read without payment or institutional access. Google Scholar also searches dissertations and theses, along with reports of many public policy think tanks. Although controversial (How could anything so effortless possibly be scholarly?), this new resource is gaining increasing respect. It has dramatically expanded its journal coverage, as most major publishers have now granted permission, has added full-text searches of the many volumes archived in Google Books (most traditional book searches rely on keywords alone, not full text), and ranks the results in order of relevancy (unlike some licensed library databases).

One recent study (Howland, Wright, Boughan, and Roberts, 2009, published in *College and Research Libraries* journal, of all places) concluded that Google Scholar was actually superior to the leading complex, proprietary library search engines. Unfortunately, Google Scholar does not yet publish a list of all its searched journals or the years they are indexed, thus precluding clarity about just how exhaustive its searches are. Anyone can use Google Scholar to search, but if you are also logged in to your library and you have chosen that library in your Google Scholar "preferences," you can link directly to the full text of many publications. Also, be sure to examine the options facilitated by the "advanced search" page. Running the prior boot camp search identified over 9,000 academic sources.

ProQuest, PAIS, and ArticlesPlus

Compared to open Internet search engines like Google Scholar, the advantages of proprietary, subscription databases are that, to date, they still cover more journals, are explicit about the journals and time periods searched, and offer more advanced (although sometimes complex) search options. Traditionally, PAIS International (csa.com/factsheets/pais-set-c.php) was the premier database for public policy and broader social research areas that now merges. PAIS is now under the umbrella of ProQuest Central (proquest.com), which consolidates numerous strong databases. Every year progress is made toward merging the previously fragmented academic databases into a unified and simplified interface. Many larger academic libraries now use a consolidation program called ArticlesPlus powered by a ProQuest-owned search engine. This trend ought to reduce the headaches suffered by reference librarians around the world. Access will continue to be exclusively through subscribing libraries.

WorldCat

Using your library's online catalog, which ideally is plugged into WorldCat and thereby canvasses over 10,000 libraries worldwide, to look for relevant books is an obvious step. However, remember that these are not full-text searches of every word in every book; you are at the mercy of how well your search terms match the assigned keywords. A book with relevant information may not feature your search terms among its relatively few keywords. Again, Google Scholar's search of the entire text of books (not just keywords) is of special value, even if it does not yet include every book on the planet.

WorldCat can be used free of charge online at worldcat.org. Repeating the boot camp evaluation search, WorldCat returned 400 items, most highly relevant, including 169 books, 217 articles, and nine thesis and dissertations.

PolicyFile

Efforts have been underway to gain online access to more of the so-called gray literature, documents from channels that have traditionally been difficult or impossible to obtain. The gray is fading fast as more and more government agencies, nonprofits, and private groups are now putting their documents online and in databases and as ProQuest, Google Scholar, and others scramble to be as inclusive as possible. Nevertheless, some dim corners remain. One good resource for scouring at least some of the gray literature is PolicyFile.com, because it compiles reports, papers, and other output from over 350 public policy think tanks and other research institutes, university centers, advocacy groups, and other nongovernment organizations. It usually links to full-text documents and is updated weekly, although its keyword search is not optimal and it is not available outside subscribing library portals.

CRS and GAO Reports

In the "light gray" area, studies prepared for Congress by the respected Congressional Research Service are not automatically made available to the public. Of the CRS studies that are released, many are posted at opencrs.com by a public interest group. An alternative is to query a major search engine with: "CRS Report for Congress" and crs.gov plus your topic. Another important agency of Congress, the U.S. Government Accountability Office, usually posts its many investigations of policy implementation and budgeting atgao.gov.

Government Publications

To search the thousands of publications issued by the federal government—whether online and only in print—the best single source is the U.S. Government Printing Office (catalog.gpo.gov). For online resources for local, state, and federal governments, go to search.USA.gov (formerly FirstGov.gov) and then to "Advanced Search" and screen for federal only, state only, or a particular state or territory.

The laws that are the basis for the current federal policy or program you may be evaluating can be found (by searching the text or by using the popular names of laws) in the *U.S. Code*, the "consolidation and codification" of federal laws at uscode.house.gov. Rules, regulations, and proposed and amended rules promulgated by federal departments and agencies, along with Executive Orders of the President, are published in the *Federal Register* (federalregister.gov). The final rules are later codified in the *Code of Federal Regulations* (ecfr.gov). Online access to state laws and regulations varies by state.

Public Policy Research Institutes

Increasingly, think tanks are making their studies, or at least abstracts, available online, so they can be found by using the various searches described previously. However, there is still no definitive compendium of the output of the many hundreds of think tanks; indeed, there is no definitive online list of the think tanks themselves, due in part to the blurry boundary lines among advocacy groups, consulting firms, and think tanks as well as to their sheer number. One recent effort (gotothinktank.com/rankings) found nearly 7,000 worldwide, including 1,800 in the United States, and also attempted to rank the leading think tanks, with the Brookings Institution (brookings.edu) and the RAND Corporation (rand.org) topping the list for domestic policy. Excluding foreign policy think tanks, others in the top twenty were the Heritage Foundation (heritage.org), the American Enterprise Institute (aei.org), the Cato Institute (cato.org), Pew Research Institute (pewresearch.org), the Hoover Institution (hoover.org), the Center for American Program (americanprogress.org), the Hudson Institute (hudson.org), and the Urban Institute (urban.org). Outside the United States, most of the top-ranked think tanks focus on international relations; one highly ranked exception was the Fraser Institute (fraserinstitute.org) in Canada.

The recommendations given in this chapter are not presented as the sole sites deserving exploration. If more resources and time are available, numerous other sites can be examined. However, these suggestions have proven to be especially worthwhile starting points.

Conducting Surveys on the Internet

Using the Internet to sample a cross-section of the general public presents enormous hurdles to obtaining tolerable response rates from a genuinely representative pool. Some valiant efforts are being made, but this particular challenge is beyond the scope of this chapter. In evaluation research, however, we are almost always surveying not the mass public but targeted groups, such as staff administrators of a program; the recipients, clients, or customers of the program; and perhaps members of a matched comparison group or randomized control group. For such specific groups the Internet might be ideal. In Chapter Fourteen, Kathryn Newcomer and Timothy Triplett summarize the advantages of Internet surveys as including

Cost
- Relatively low cost per survey
- No large staff required
- Low or no travel requirements

Speed
- Quick distribution and relatively rapid data collection
- Rapid time for quantitative analysis

Candor
- High sense of respondent confidentiality
- Appropriate for fairly sensitive questions

Format
- Layout suitable for longer scales

In addition, Internet surveys have some valuable advantages in terms of accuracy. Responses automatically go to a database, thereby eliminating transcription errors. When only one answer is appropriate, use of "radio buttons" can prevent multiple responses. Important questions can be programmed to be required, so respondents cannot omit them.

In sum, Internet surveys can be a bargain, are relatively fast, encourage candor, and reduce certain errors. That combination of efficiency and effectiveness is extremely attractive. However, Internet surveys are not without disadvantages. In particular, as Newcomer and Triplett point out, those contemplating Internet surveys must be aware of the following drawbacks:

Potentially Limited Completion Rates
- Less suitable for surveying less educated and low-income populations
- Difficulty in locating targeted respondents (unless an accurate list of their e-mails is available)
- Difficulty in obtaining high response rates (unless the topic is of special interest and the survey is very well designed)

Limited Follow-Up
- Inability to do ad hoc probing
- Difficulty in collecting anecdotes

Limited Length
- Need to limit the overall length of the instrument

If length is the only concern, one simple solution is to carefully split the mass of questions into two (or even three) separate surveys and randomly assign respondents to one of the versions. However, two other concerns—obtaining a representative final sample and a respectable response rate from the intended group—can be a fatal flaw. Consequently, stay away from Internet surveys if one or more of the following situations apply:

1. A nontrivial portion of your target sample is less educated.
2. A nontrivial portion of your target sample is unlikely to be already using the Internet.
3. Accurate e-mail addresses are not available for a nontrivial portion of your target sample.
4. The topic of your survey is unlikely to generate enough interest to motivate most of your target sample to respond online.

In any of these four situations, some form of telephone or in-person interviews may be required (or perhaps a mail survey) instead of an online survey. Otherwise, if your target population is at least fairly educated and likely to use the Internet, and e-mail addresses are available for this population, then the key remaining drawbacks concern flexibility (inability to do ad hoc probing and collect anecdotes) and length. If your project does require extended, probing interviews—with everyone surveyed—then the concise, structured format of an Internet survey will not be suitable.

When long, probing surveys of everyone are not mandatory, one option to consider is the dual-method strategy of conducting Internet surveys of most people supplemented by a smaller number of in-person, semi-structured interviews (see Chapter Nineteen) that can last longer and probe for details and examples. This solution merges the breadth of an Internet survey (large scale, less expensive, rapid) with the depth of semi-structured interviews in person (albeit this solution is more expensive and more time-consuming per interview).

Now, assuming that your endeavor meets the criteria of having an appropriate, reachable target audience and being able to use a structured (not overly long) format for all or many of those target respondents, let's turn to the steps of conducting an Internet survey.

Getting Started: Drafting Questions

Whether or not you plan to outsource the online survey, it is a good idea to draft the questions first. Doing so can confirm whether the questions are, in fact, suitable for the limited length and structured format of an Internet survey. (This step also reduces the cost of the contract by doing much of the initial "heavy lifting" on the questionnaire.) At the outset, don't agonize over the precise wording of every question or the exact sequence of the questions. They can be edited and rearranged later. Instead, prepare a list of all the issues the instrument ought to address and ruthlessly cull the list to identify the ones that are essential for this particular study.

Assuming that this process confirms that list of necessary questions is not too long or too open-ended for the Internet, you can proceed to refine the draft questionnaire by polishing the wording of individual questions and arraying them into a smooth whole. With Internet surveys, developing the questionnaire is the most time-consuming part of the whole survey process. Of course, the substantive design is critical for all kind of surveys, but with Internet surveys the subsequent execution is relatively fast and easy, so allocate a generous amount of time to craft a deft, disciplined instrument.

Before turning to unique aspects of Internet questionnaires, let's briefly review a basic issue common to all surveys, regardless of the medium, aiming for crisp, clear, neutral questions. The art of writing questions involves a number of key do's and don'ts. Ten of those major guidelines and ways to address them are summarized in Table 18.1.

After the individual questions have been drafted, it is time to sort them into a progression that flows logically and smoothly. The classic approach is as follows:

- Start with a brief engaging introduction.
- Follow with easy to answer, nonthreatening, closed-ended initial questions.
- Insert short transition statements when shifting from one topic to another.
- Try to minimize the risk that question order may influence and bias subsequent items.
- Use only a limited number of carefully chosen open-ended questions, if any.
- Position the more sensitive questions later in the survey.

- Conclude with demographics (those inescapably prying and revealing queries into age, marital status, education, income, and so forth) and use the broadest usable ranges rather than exact amounts in order to be less intrusive (for example, ask the respondent to select an age group rather than to give an exact age).
- Eliminate nonvital questions to create the shortest possible survey (thereby increasing the ultimate response rate).

TABLE 18.1. TIPS FOR QUESTION WRITING.

Principle	Ways to Check the Principle
Keep questions as short as possible.	See whether you must take more than one breath to finish reading the question aloud.
Focus on a single issue; avoid double-barreled questions.	Scan for the dangerous word "and."
Use everyday vocabulary familiar to the respondents.	Search for uncommon and long words, along with strings of long words that create dense wording.
Frame questions positively; especially avoid double negatives.	Look for negative words like not and never.
Use unbiased language; also avoid inserting an implied justification for a particular answer (if justifications are given, they should be given for all answers and be balanced).	Find people with diverse opinions, politics, and backgrounds to critique the wording.
Pose response options that are exclusive and exhaustive (unless asking for multiple responses, as in "check all that apply").	Scrutinize all options to make sure every possible answer falls into a single, clear category.
Offer concrete rather than vague options whenever possible.	Look for vague options and substitute specific ones (for example, ask "how many times the past month?" rather than "often, sometimes, seldom, or never?").
Do not ask about things too obscure, detailed, or long ago for people to recall.	Err on the side of caution because people often guess instead of admitting they do not know or remember.
Check out skip patterns thoroughly.	Check that the jumps flow properly.
Ask only questions essential to the research.	Think through the final data analysis in advance to identify superfluous questions.

The artistry required for a well-crafted survey cannot be entirely reduced to a list of rules, however. The process takes time and involves considerable trial and error, which is why extensive pretesting is so important. Allocate adequate time for several iterations of pretesting the draft initially with colleagues, later with people who are similar in background to the ultimate target group, and finally with a small pilot study, if possible. The number of iterations and pretests required will vary depending on the instrument's length, the difficulty of the topics, the target audience, and the time and resources available. Don't forget to test the online layout with different browsers and different operating systems and on both Macs and PCs. Also, be sure to optimize the layout for tablets, if not cell phones. Questionnaires can be edited eternally without ever satisfying all critics, but at some point the feedback will attest to reasonably worthy text and layout.

Validating Respondent Representation

Many of the points mentioned earlier (especially keeping the questionnaire concise) and later (such as using effective initial contacts and adopting a simple, professional-looking layout) are intended to improve the response rate. All these elements have a cumulative, crucial impact, and even with an Internet-using target group, you must not naïvely assume that most people you e-mail will drop what they are doing and eagerly fill out your online survey. If the response rate is low and does not adequately represent the population to which you wish to generalize, your efforts will have been largely wasted.

This concern is not confined to Internet surveys, to be sure. With any type of survey, evaluators must be concerned about how representative participants are of the group surveyed. How much overall damage did nonresponse bias (due to refusals, unsuccessful contact attempts, and all other reasons) do to the final results? The higher the response rate the better, but how can evaluators assess representativeness? The most straightforward way is to add several questions that will allow you to contrast characteristics of the survey respondents to known characteristics of the target group. If reliable records show, for example, proportions in terms of gender, age groups, and employment status for your total target group, you can then gather that same information in the questionnaire. Although this validation approach (focusing on demographics not attitudinal factors) is not perfect, it offers a practical means to compare respondents to the overall target group that was sampled.

Using Unique Aspects of Online Survey Design

Because the Internet is a visual medium, the format and layout of an online survey have more in common with a self-administered paper instrument, such as a mail survey, than they do with the aural medium of a telephone survey or in-person interview. Moreover, the programmable and interactive aspects of the computer interface add some unique issues. As a consequence, several special design considerations are worth noting:

1. Unless the survey is remarkably short, putting all of it on a single web page can damage the response rate. When people must hit the "page down" key repeatedly to see the entire mass of questions, completing the survey can look like a far greater chore than it really is. To avoid this threat, sort questions into groups of similar topics that do not fill much more than one computer screen at a time. A traditional-sized screen (or a screen and a half) looks manageable and not too onerous.

2. When using these page breaks, be sure to add a progress bar to the bottom of the screen to show respondents visually that they are advancing rapidly to the end and their task is not endless; otherwise, they quickly begin to fear the worst. (One early study suggested that when the progress indicator barely moves it has a negative effect, but the solution is to shorten the survey not get rid of the progress bar.)

3. When clustering questions on a page, look for opportunities to employ consistent answer categories, such as the Likert *strongly agree* to *strongly disagree* rating scale or a 1 to 10 scale that can be displayed on a compact grid on the right-hand side of the screen. This design condenses the layout so the survey does not seem nearly as long as it would with every question spread out separately. To be sure, a mass of many dozens of items in an enormous matrix can be daunting, too, so in that case divide the items into several more modestly sized matrices on different pages.

4. Exploit the web interface to insert skip patterns as needed. Usually self-administered surveys are designed to minimize if not completely avoid skip patterns (that is, the "go-to" instructions to jump over questions that do not apply), because so many respondents ignore skip directions. However, online surveys can be constructed to employ contingency questions flawlessly. For example, if someone clicks that she did not attend training sessions, the next screen can be set to leap past all follow-up inquiries about those sessions.

5. Employ web programming that allows special features not available to printed surveys. In addition to the skip function just noted, these include requiring the answers to key questions (not necessarily every question), automatically rotating items in a series (to avoid advantaging the first or last item in a list), and using drop-down menus (selectively) to avoid cluttering the screen with long lists. At the same time, do not overuse drop-down menus; it's better for respondents to see a grid of Likert options than to have to click on a drop-down menu each time to obtain the choices.

6. For open-ended questions, tell respondents how many characters are available for the answer and provide a box that exact size that allows text wrapping. Although participants may be more willing to type answers to open-ended questions than to write them by hand, the number of open-ended questions should still be kept to a minimum because composing even short essays is viewed as burdensome by many respondents and can damage response rates. (Analysis of open-ended answers is also quite time-consuming.)

7. Enable respondents to report problems and ask questions. Even if everything runs smoothly, the mere availability of a helpline phone number and e-mail address adds a receptive, open feeling to the communications.

8. One more general factor about Internet surveys ought to be mentioned. Because Internet users are now exposed to so many high-powered, elaborately designed websites, expectations for the appearance of professional sites have soared. Layouts that were acceptable a few years ago look hopelessly amateurish today. Consequently, the online display of your survey matters. If it looks unprofessional and sloppy, regardless of the elegance of the actual prose, it may not be taken as seriously as you would wish by potential participants. Not surprisingly, completion rates are higher for attractively designed online surveys (Dillman, 2000).

Outsourcing Online Survey Research

Most of the many hundreds of survey research companies in the developed world have added web surveys to their repertoire. So if you decide to outsource the project, the planet will be full of eager bidders. Extensive lists of companies can be found at the websites of GreenBook (greenbook.org), a subsidiary of the New York American Marketing Association, and of the American Association for Public Opinion Research (aapor.org/find). However, why outsource something that is not terribly difficult or expensive to do in-house thanks to the many web services that take care of all the mechanics for you? Online companies will host your survey at their website; have online software that streamlines converting your text into a handsome HTML layout; have ready formatting for virtually every type of poll question imaginable (Likert items, semantic differentials, multiple-response, open-ended, you name it); facilitate special features such as password protection, contingency question skips, and sending e-mail reminders to the people who have not yet participated or opted out; and at the end, download your data in spreadsheet and other formats along with ready-made graphics of your frequency distributions. Remarkably, at least to date, this panoply of services has been reasonably priced.

As of mid-2014, the leading online survey company was SurveyMonkey (surveymonkey.com), ranking in the top (most accessed) 1,000 websites worldwide according to the Alexa ranking of web traffic, far surpassing its competitors. Another four survey companies were ranked among the top 100,000 sites: QuestionPro (questionpro.com), SurveyGizmo (surveygizmo.com), FreeOnlineSurveys (freeonlinesurveys.com), and KeySurvey (keysurvey.com). Rounding out the list of companies falling into Alexa's top one million websites were eSurveysPro, Survs, SurveyConsole, SurveyMethods, KwikSurveys, Demographix, LimeService, 2ask.net, and SurveyShack. Along with these companies, over two dozen additional rivals were also identified and, although they may or may not have fine products, they had not yet attained as much web traffic. (This list omits companies that do not host online surveys, that emphasize small polling widgets to embed in blogs and elsewhere, and that only design mini-apps for Twitter and cell phone polls.)

Clearly, lots of web entrepreneurs are fighting for a piece of what must be a rather large market. All that competition must be helping to keep prices down. When investigating alternatives, note that almost all companies allow the use of their service for free on scaled-down bases (fewer questions or fewer respondents) or grant a free trial period, so you can explore their interfaces and options rather than speculate. Most have discounted rates for nonprofit organizations too. With paid access, most allow unlimited use and an unlimited number of respondents. Consider that extraordinary implication for scalability: As long as you have the e-mail list, you can survey 10,000 people for the same total cost as surveying 100.

Most major companies have customizable templates and over a dozen pre-programmed question types, allow incorporating your logo, permit randomizing of response options, allow skip or branch logic, offer progress bars, provide thank-you pages that can be tailored, support multiple languages, allow launching the survey directly from a link in the contact e-mail, will schedule optional follow-up reminders, offer a variety of downloadable survey reports (including cross-tabulations and filtering), and export to Excel, SPSS, and PDF formats. Some, but not all, can automatically meet accessibility standards of Section 508 of the Rehabilitation Act (section508.gov). Unlimited annual usage of these impressive services is available for only a few hundred dollars.

Contacting Respondents

Should you sample a random portion or survey everyone in the target group? With other types of surveys, considerations of time and money can be decisive in making this choice. When you survey via the Internet, however, your costs and calendar will be the same regardless of the number surveyed, assuming that your e-mail list is in computer-readable form. In the rare event that you need to conduct frequent surveys of the same target group, you might alternately survey subsets of the group to avoid survey fatigue, which would soon damage response rates. For sampling, the usual practices for simple, stratified, and multistage samples outlined in Chapter Fourteen apply. Otherwise, go for it and survey everyone in the target group; this will make the results more definitive, may actually be easier than having to draw a sample, and increases the power of any statistical significance tests.

As with all survey modes, it helps to have publicized and legitimized the forthcoming survey so that people are expecting it. Advance notice through multiple channels increases response rates, so seek opportunities for notices in newsletters, blurbs on organizational websites, memos from organizational leaders, and even postcards.

As they do with other survey types, many potential respondents will make an immediate cost-benefit decision about whether to complete your online survey, so the first impression is crucial. The usual cover letter strategies apply to the introductory e-mail, too: emphasize positive motivations by telling the potential respondents that the research is important and their opinions are valued, and minimize negative concerns with assurances of confidentiality and the brevity of the instrument. Then, if the e-mail recipients are persuaded to click on the link to the survey, the first screen they see must be especially welcoming, interesting, uncluttered, professional, and easy to use.

If many thousands of people are contacted, you may want to stagger the e-mail invitations so as not to risk flooding the web server and freezing the interactive program, although if the e-mails are sent late in the evening people will typically log on and reply at different times throughout the following morning and day anyway. When the reply stream slows to a trickle (or the poll popcorn begins to stop popping), following up with a reminder e-mail will boost incoming replies again. Most online services let you limit reminders to those who have not responded, but it is less brazen to say, ambiguously, "if you haven't yet had a chance to participate." Most services also respectfully allow individuals to "opt out" upon receiving the first e-mail; thus, they can avoid harassing these individuals with reminders if they have definitely refused to participate.

Most online services allow you to password protect your survey as well as to prevent one person (from the same computer IP address) responding more than once. Some allow you to require clicking in the e-mail on a complex URL code that can be used only once and thus works the same as sending a password. (If passwords are used, avoid using letter l, digit 1, letter O, and digit 0.)

If a screening question is placed early in your survey, be gentle with those who do not pass the qualifying hurdles. Consider even sending them to a few additional dummy questions, rather than ejecting them abruptly at the start. Speaking of politeness, the concluding thank-you screen is an occasion to expand a statement of gratitude to a couple of sentences, not just two words. By participating in your online survey, those civic-minded respondents have saved you thousands of dollars and weeks or months of work and let you turn sooner to analyzing the results. (See Chapter Twenty-Two for a review of quantitative data analysis.)

If you are interested in further reading about Internet surveys, two good sources are a RAND monograph (Schonlau, Fricker, and Elliott, 2002) that can be downloaded for free (rand.org/pubs/monograph_reports/MR1480) and the latest book by prolific survey research guru Don Dillman (Dillman, Smyth, and Christian, 2014).

Putting Your Program Evaluation on the Web

These days every organization is expected to have a website, and every activity of any consequence is expected to be on a page at that website. Can anything today have credibility, legitimacy, and standing without a web presence? Indeed, it now seems vaguely suspicious for any allegedly serious enterprise to be absent from the Internet. Be that as it may, to date the web visibility of program evaluations hinges mainly on whether the research is in progress or has already been completed. Studies that have been completed usually have far greater Internet prominence than studies that are still under way.

Turning first to the uneven status of web coverage of current research, a few university-based research institutes do list summaries of current as well as completed research projects, including the funding, research goals, time period, and principal investigators, often with links to the principal investigator's résumé. For example, see the Institute of Public Policy at George Washington University (gwu.edu/~gwipp/); the Evaluation, Assessment and Policy Connections Unit at the University of North Carolina (unc.edu/depts/ed/evap/projects.html); the Harvard Family Research Project at Harvard University (hfrp.org/evaluation/projects); the Sar Levitan Center for Social Policy Studies at Johns Hopkins University (levitancenter.org/initiatives.html); the Food Policy Institute at Rutgers University (foodpolicy.rutgers.edu/

research.asp); and the Institute for Social Research at the University of Michigan (isr.umich.edu/home/projects).

In contrast to these cases, many university research institutes only summarize their general areas of specializations. And even though they may provide links to completed reports, many do not identify current research projects. Most major think tanks, despite or because of a staggering number of ongoing projects, also rarely list them online. For example, the RAND Corporation is one of the largest, often with more than one thousand projects underway at single time but few are listed online. RAND is not alone. It is difficult to find information about current projects at the elaborate websites of most other large research organizations, such as the Urban Institute, the Research Triangle Institute, and Mathematica Policy Research, Inc.

So should you post information about your ongoing program evaluation study on your organization's website, including the scope and basic research questions, funding source, time period, principal investigators, and even other members of the research team? Why bother? The potential value of a good online summary, besides showing off the prowess of your organization, is that you have a URL to put on your business card, in an e-mail, or in a cover letter as a convenient reference for more information that you can easily transmit to potential new hires, survey respondents, or others who will be contacted about your study. Once research has been completed and as long as the findings are not proprietary, the widespread and constructive practice is now to post the completed report, in PDF format, on a website, whether it was conducted at a university institute, a think tank, government agency, or other research organization. The result is a wealth of publicly available studies representing an enormous expenditure of time, talent, and money. Having exploited the Internet to conduct an extensive, systematic literature review, and then perhaps having used its electronic magic to disseminate, collect, and tally surveys, putting the final product of these labors online is only fitting.

References

Dillman, D. A. *Mail and Internet Surveys: The Tailored Design Method* (2nd ed.). Hoboken, NJ: Wiley, 2000.

Dillman, D. A., Smyth, J. D., and Christian, L. M. *Internet, Mail, and Mixed-Mode Surveys: The Tailored Design Method* (4th ed.). Hoboken, NJ: Wiley, 2014.

Howland, J. L., Wright, T. C., Boughan, R. A., and Roberts, B. C. "How Scholarly Is Google Scholar? A Comparison of Google Scholar to Library Databases." *College and Research Libraries*, 2009, *70*, 227–232.

Schonlau, M., Fricker, R. D., and Elliott, M. N. *Conducting Research Surveys via E-Mail and the Web.* Santa Monica, CA: RAND Corporation, 2002. rand.org/pubs/monograph_reports/MR1480.html.

Further Reading

Andrews, D., Nonnecke, B., and Preece, J. "Electronic Survey Methodology: A Case Study in Reaching Hard to Involve Internet Users." *International Journal of Human-Computer Interaction*, 2003, *16*, 185–210.

Lucas, W. A., and Adams, W. C. *An Assessment of Telephone Survey Methods.* Santa Monica, CA: RAND Corporation, 1977.

CHAPTER NINETEEN

CONDUCTING SEMI-STRUCTURED INTERVIEWS

William C. Adams

How do we ask people for information? At one extreme is using a battery of identical, mostly closed-ended questions. These highly structured surveys, typically with large samples, can be administered many ways (phone, mail, Internet, in person; see Chapters Fourteen and Eighteen). At the opposite extreme is the fluid inquiry of focus groups (see Chapter Twenty). Compared to surveys, a focus group engages far fewer people (an optimum of ten to twelve per session) for a much longer period (up to two hours) with an elastic agenda of open-ended questions that allow extended probing. Making up in depth what they lack in breadth, focus groups enable the moderator not only to pursue detailed inquiry into existing opinions but also to obtain reactions to new ideas and conduct group brainstorming, if desired.

Another approach falls between standardized, mostly closed-ended surveys of individuals and free form, open-ended sessions with groups. This intermediate method pulls elements from both but puts them into a distinctive package. Curiously, this methodology does not have a consensus name. Lewis Dexter (1970) called it *elite interviewing*, although that label may erroneously suggest talking only with high-status respondents. Robert Merton (1956) termed it the *focused interview*, although that phrase now risks confusion with *focus group*. Cultural anthropologists speak more narrowly of the *ethnographic interview*. Sociologists sometimes refer to *depth interviewing*. Due to the approach's many open-ended questions, the term *qualitative interviewing* may also be used. However, the name that appears to be currently garnering a majority of usage is not crisp, clever, or inventive but it is simple and descriptive: the *semi-structured interview*. That is the term used in the chapter. Let's call it *SSI* for short.

Conducted conversationally with one respondent at a time, the SSI employs a blend of closed- and open-ended questions, often accompanied by follow-up *why* or *how* questions. The dialogue can meander around the topics on the agenda—rather than adhering slavishly to verbatim questions as in a standardized survey—and may delve into totally unforeseen issues. Relaxed, engaging, in-person SSIs can be longer than telephone surveys, although they seldom last as long as focus groups. About one hour is considered a reasonable maximum length for SSIs in order to minimize fatigue for both interviewer and respondent.

Disadvantages and Advantages of SSIs

Before going into more detail about semi-structured interviews, let's first consider their disadvantages, in case you may then decide to skip the rest of this chapter. SSIs are time-consuming, labor intensive, and require interviewer sophistication. Interviewers need to be smart, sensitive, poised, and nimble, as well as knowledgeable about the relevant substantive issues. The process of preparing for the interviews, setting up the interviews, conducting the interviews, and analyzing the interviews is not nearly as quick and easy as you might think. The time and effort required to do all of it right is considerable. SSIs usually entail the arduous task of analyzing a huge volume of notes and sometimes many hours of transcripts.

Another drawback—unless you are just interviewing members of a small group (such as the board of a nonprofit organization or top program administrators)—is that, without an enormous outlay of time and personnel, SSIs are unlikely to encompass a large enough sample to yield precision of the "plus or minus *n* percent" variety. Consequently, for many purposes, a standardized survey of six hundred clients would be superior to attempting six hundred one-hour SSIs. For some other purposes, four focus groups with ten people each would be much more efficient than conducting forty individual SSIs. Yet, despite the disadvantages and costs of SSIs, they offer some extraordinary benefits as well.

Semi-structured interviews are superbly suited for a number of valuable tasks, particularly when more than a few of the open-ended questions require follow-up queries. Especially consider employing SSIs in the following situations:

- If you need to ask probing, open-ended questions and want to know the independent thoughts of each individual in a group
- If you need to ask probing, open-ended questions on topics that your respondents might not be candid about if sitting with peers in a focus group
- If you need to conduct a formative program evaluation and want one-on-one interviews with key program managers, staff, and front-line service providers
- If you are examining uncharted territory with unknown but potential momentous issues and your interviewers need maximum latitude to spot useful leads and pursue them

In mixed methods research, SSIs can be useful as an adjunct to supplement and add depth to other approaches. For example:

- If you need to conduct some in-depth reconnaissance before designing a large-scale survey, configuring a focus group agenda, or constructing an overall research strategy
- If, after drafting a standardized survey questionnaire, you discover that important questions cannot be effectively addressed without more open-ended questions and extended probing
- If you want to explore "puzzles" that emerge (or remain) after you have analyzed survey or even focus group findings

The people who may be appropriate for SSIs can run the gamut of those involved in the program being evaluated. For convenience, let's put them into three general groups:

1. Program recipients (or beneficiaries, clients, customers, members, constituents, or audience—preferred term will vary)
2. Interested parties (contributors, suppliers, any other stakeholders who are neither direct recipients nor program administrators, plus others in proximity who may be affected in collateral ways)
3. Administration (front-line service delivery people, other staff, top managers, program board members, whether salaried or volunteer)

If one or more of the SSI situations listed previously applies to one or more of these three general SSI-appropriate groups—and if you have adroit and well-spoken interviewers available who can be adequately educated on the program at hand—then semi-structured interviews would be the methodology of choice.

Designing and Conducting SSIs

Assuming that this methodology is your choice, let's proceed to consider practical steps for designing and conducting semi-structured interviews: selecting and recruiting the respondents, drafting the questions and interview guide, techniques for this type of interviewing, and analyzing the information gathered.

Selecting Respondents and Arranging Interviews

Chapter Seventeen offers detailed advice on preparing for site visits, making staff assignments, training field teams, and carrying out other practical administration steps for collecting data in the field. However, a few basic elements important to SSIs should be mentioned here. Having identified at the outset the target group or groups for SSIs, how do researchers then select respondents from among the target group? If the group is a large one, researchers ordinarily choose to interview a manageable random sample or a stratified random sample (as defined in Chapter Fourteen). If the group is not so large and resources permit, it may be possible to interview virtually everyone, such as all key administrators and all program board members. Even if time and resources do not allow conducting a large numbers of SSIs, it is still important to get the perspectives of more than just a few people.

Respondents ought to have been identified and appointments set up before interviewers arrive at the site. If staff members of an organization are being interviewed, ordinarily, top managers will assist in setting up the interviews, greatly simplifying the process. If a sample is being drawn from a roster (stratified perhaps to include set numbers of managers, supervisors, and various categories of staff members), the evaluators convey the names of the chosen individuals to the managers, rather than letting the managers personally pick which staff members are heard. Sometimes, researchers must telephone those chosen to request and schedule each individual appointment. Rather than making a "cold call," researchers should send a short letter of introduction in advance, noting the importance of the individual's advice and citing the project's endorsement by the top administrator. This can add legitimacy and save time that would otherwise have to be spent explaining and justifying the research. That advance letter can pave the way for the subsequent phone call to arrange the meeting.

Approaches vary when interviewing program beneficiaries (rather than program workers), depending on who the beneficiaries are and their relationship to the program. If possible, they should be chosen randomly (incorporating stratification when certain subgroups are targeted) to eliminate the biasing effect of convenience samples. Sometimes the program staff is best positioned to set up the interviews, or at least make the introductions. Other times researchers may obtain a list from which to sample and contact the potential respondents.

Prospective respondents will probably want to know how much of their precious time you covet, and that can be the trickiest single issue in obtaining the interview. Proposing too long a period can prompt an outright refusal. Conversely, if an unrealistically short period is requested, respondents may depart after the allotted time, even if key agenda items are far from finished; the interviewer also risks appearing to have been deceptive or foolish or both. So here are a few ideas to consider. Pretesting the interview should yield a rough idea of how long the questions will take. You can initially mention that time ("It shouldn't take much longer than . . ..") . Then, if things are going well but slowly during the actual interview, ask permission for "just a few more questions" to finish the core questions and perhaps cover some of the second tier of topics. A late afternoon session may have the advantage of not running up against another meeting. Regardless of the time and place, the most important element—aside from respondents' actually consenting to be interviewed—is the content of those interviews. The development of appropriate and well-crafted interview guides is essential.

Drafting Questions and the Interview Guide

Questionnaire is not the best term for the compilation of SSI questions, because that word connotes a fixed instrument to be read verbatim, rather than the flexible, interactive approach of SSI questions. Instead, you must create the agenda for the *interview guide*, the outline of planned topics, and questions to be addressed, arrayed in their tentative order. Of course, if SSIs are going to be conducted with different groups, a guide will have to be tailored to each group. Consider the following recommendations when constructing an SSI guide:

1. At the outset, be sure to budget enough time to carefully draft, edit, pretest, and polish the interview questions and guide, allowing time for several iterations and feedback from colleagues. If possible, pilot tests with a few intended respondents (or people similar to them) can be the final step in refining the guide.

2. Don't try to cram too many issues into the agenda, but if the list of potential topics is long, decide in advance which ones are critical and which ones are

optional. Once the top priorities are clear, put those questions in bold. Classify the second and third tiers of questions to be raised if time allows, but decide in advance which questions are vital and which ones are lagniappes. In theory, SSIs can be somewhat lengthy, but that does not mean that busy respondents are going to want to dedicate hours to talk. As part of rigorously editing the draft questions, be sure to omit questions asking for simple facts that can be retrieved from an organization's website, published material, or available records (unless perhaps you want to assess someone's understanding of those facts).

3. Don't forget that closed-ended questions can be ideal gateways to open-ended probing. For example, after asking, "In your judgment, was this program change a major improvement, minor improvement, or not an improvement?" the interviewer could follow up by asking, "Why is that?" or "Why do you feel that way?" and continue with additional probing as needed. Compared to using a broad start (such as, "What did you think about this program change?"), the beauty of incorporating a closed-ended query first is that it dramatically streamlines the summary analysis to have some firm quantitative points of reference (for example, "Ten of the twelve board members called the change a 'major improvement' and cited these reasons. . . .").

4. When potential respondents do not speak English, careful translations and bilingual interviewers will be required. Even if the respondents do speak English, don't assume it's exactly the same language spoken by university-trained researchers. Communication can fail when we blithely assume that everybody shares our vocabulary, acronyms, and lingo. In designing an SSI, use the everyday words of the target groups, while taking care not to talk down to them as well. It may be useful to make adjustments to question wording after the first round of interviewing.

5. Think through the extent to which the draft questions may evoke pressure to give socially acceptable answers. Might recipients worry that their eligibility could be jeopardized by what they say? If so, along with assurances of confidentiality, look for ways to remove any stigma that might attach to certain answers. One tactic for showing nonjudgmental acceptance is to insert a prefatory comment such as "some people tell us [*a particular opinion about an issue*]," before asking, "How do you see this issue?" This suggests that answers like the one cited would not surprise or disturb the interviewer. Administrators themselves may feel an urge, conscious or otherwise, to circle the wagons and put the best possible face on a less than ideal program situation. Rather than asking them to identify what is "bad," ask about "areas that need improvement" to help minimize defensiveness.

6. The agenda for a semi-structured interview is never carved in stone. If a conversation unexpectedly turns from the first to the fourth topic, by all means, reorder the topics on the fly and return later to pick up the ones that were skipped. Nevertheless, when drafting the tentative question order, try to anticipate the most likely and smoothest sequence. These time-tested guidelines can help the agenda fall into place:

   • After customary pleasantries, as the actual interview begins, start with a few extra easy, even throwaway questions to start a comfortable chat before the more serious inquires begin. To break the ice, respondents might be asked how long they have lived in the city or worked in the program, for example.

   • After establishing some rapport, turn next to more directly relevant but still nonthreatening questions.

   • When introducing critique questions, consider putting positive inquiries first: "What are the good things about X?" or "What do you like about it?" Starting with positives allows those people who might be reluctant to voice criticisms to share their complaints later because they already offered some praise. Another advantage of this approach is that some people, once they adopt a harsh critical tone, find it difficult to say anything good, as if they fear they would be contradicting themselves or minimizing the seriousness of their grievance.

   • After looking at the positive sides of a topic, turn next to its drawbacks, disadvantages, disappointments, or areas that need improvement, always taking a neutral, nonjudgmental tone. (There will be more information about tone and delivery later in this chapter.)

   • The most potentially embarrassing, controversial, or awkward questions should come toward the end. By this point the interviewer is no longer a stranger but a pleasant, nonargumentative professional who seems genuinely interested in the respondent's opinions. Now respondents are wishing that their kids, spouse, or co-workers showed as much respect and attentiveness to their thoughtful opinions. So at this stage, more sensitive questions can be introduced, along with reminders of confidentiality as needed.

   • Why are demographic questions best saved until the end? For many people, few topics are more delicate or possibly painful than their current marital status, their age, their amount of education, their income, and so forth. These questions raise fundamental identity issues in a way that mere opinion questions do not. Revealing one's personal profile, even in confidence, can still feel like a privacy intrusion. Be sure to scrutinize the typical laundry list of demographic questions to omit all that are not essential for this specific program evaluation. Refusals can be minimized by asking about the broadest usable categories, instead of exact amounts (for example, asking respondents to select from among large income ranges rather than prying for precise annual income). A few demographic variables, such as gender, often race, and perhaps general age group, can be coded by the interviewer without needing to ask.

- To end on a substantive note, consider concluding by returning to a short, easy, program-related question, perhaps about the future.

Once developed, the interview guide, no matter how extensive its preparation, should still be considered a work in progress. It remains subject to change for this reason: in the field, as feedback quickly begins to accumulate, adjustments will need to be made (Galletta, 2013). Perhaps the sequence of questions will have to be rethought, the way certain issues are posed will have to be recast, and some unanticipated issues will emerge that seem sufficiently important that they should be added to all subsequent interviews. Agile researchers will exploit these new insights to rapidly refine the interview guide and will actually have planned for this possibility at three stages—after the first interview, after the first round of interviews, and periodically thereafter.

After the first interview, reassess everything. What works well, and what needs to be modified? Some questions and topics may need to be added or subtracted, expanded or condensed, recast or reordered. If more than one interviewer is working on the project, have the most experienced and knowledgeable person conduct the first interview; then he or she can brief the others and take the lead in refining the questions and agenda. After everyone on the team has conducted an interview, schedule another opportunity to share tips and experiences as well as to modify the questions as needed. Thereafter, periodic, even daily if feasible, sessions allow the team members to continue to review their work to identify any areas for which adjustments should be made and to ensure that their individual approaches are not diverging too much.

Decisions on modifying the interview guide in the field are necessary judgment calls. If, for example, one respondent volunteers a surprising and troublesome problem that seems potentially quite threatening to the effective execution of the program under study, should subsequent respondents be asked pointedly about that issue if they fail to volunteer it? Adding it to the guide might be the safest strategy. If feedback from the next rounds of interviews consistently dismisses that particular concern, it might then be taken back off the guide and the initial response treated as an outlier. Ongoing reassessments of the interview guide, particularly during the early waves of interviewing, let researchers catch areas for improvement early, avoiding the need to repeat numerous interviews.

During the course of their interviews, some respondents (program administrators, for example) may refer to certain documents that the interviewers may not yet have. Interviewers should keep a list of any such documents that are of interest (and not subject to privacy restrictions) so these items can be collected immediately after the interview if possible or, if not, then sent by e-mail or mail. The post-interview thank-you note can serve as a convenient vehicle for a reminder.

Starting the Interview

Interviewers should establish a positive first impression. They should dress professionally—men with ties even on Fridays—although slightly more casual attire is preferable when the respondents are economically disadvantaged. They should always arrive early and review the agenda, having allowed time for potential travel delays and getting lost, rather than risk arriving even one minute late. Thanking the respondent for the meeting and offering a business card can add to professional credibility.

To record or not to record, that is a key judgment call. A small digital recorder, if permission is granted, allows the interviewer to be more actively engaged in the conversation as well as to ponder the best next question instead of having to concentrate on writing down answers. However, if the topics covered are at all sensitive, respondents may be inhibited by a recording device, even if complete confidentiality if promised and consent is given; some people forget the recorder is running, but others stay wary. If the machine option does seem acceptable, bring a small, unobtrusive digital recorder (or a microcassette tape recorder) that has been verified as working properly and is ready to use, so no fumbling is required. After gaining permission, switch it on and say something like this, "OK, [*respondent name*], thanks for letting me record this," to document the confirmation of consent. Be fully prepared, in case the respondent declines, to nonchalantly switch to taking notes.

If the interview is not recorded electronically, alternatives for taking notes include booklets, legal pads, electronic tablets, laptop computers, or smaller notebook computers. The interview guide can be produced in a number of layouts: bound as a booklet (with enough blank space between items for writing out the answers), put into a condensed format (perhaps even one page, so you can see everything at a glance, with answers recorded separately), or even printed on five-by-eight-inch index cards that can be shuffled as needs dictate in the conversation. In any layout, it can be helpful to use a large font, with priority questions in boldface or color coded. One additional strategy should be considered if resources permit and a recorder is not used: a two-person team. Using a division of labor, one person can take the lead in asking questions and ensuring that all key topics are addressed, while the other person, who does not have to be mum, concentrates on taking notes.

When taking notes, interviewers should do the best they can with their own shorthand systems. They should use quotation marks when writing verbatim phrases. Many notes will be paraphrases and should be treated as such when writing the report, but it is important to write down word-for-word and put quotation marks around any particularly valuable or memorable comments. Put any interviewer observations (for example, of respondent laughter, nervousness, or anger) in square brackets. If needed, it is fine, even flattering, for interviewers to ask respondents to pause for a moment in order to finish writing down an important comment. Immediately after the interview, interviewers should be able to rush to a computer to clarify and expand their scribbles and, while the chat is fresh, add any other key remarks that they recall but did not write down at the time.

At the start of the interview, the matter of confidentiality must be addressed clearly. If the respondent is going to be quoted by name in the report, that must be explained and consent obtained. However, unless there is some compelling reason to do otherwise, confidential interviews are generally better because they are more likely to elicit candid answers. If that route is taken, it is worth explaining and emphasizing confidentiality to the respondent in the initial invitation and at the start of the interview. For example:

> We're trying to learn how the XYZ program operates and get your suggestions on how it can be improved. We're not auditors and we're not employees of any government agency. We're independent. Nothing you say today will be quoted with your name. We'll be submitting a report, but no confidential names will be mentioned. Do you have any questions about our pledge of confidentiality?

If later, when writing the report, some observation stands out as so brilliant that you really ought to give credit to that person, contact him or her to ask permission. Likewise, if a valuable comment obviously must have been voiced by a particular person, he or she might be asked, "May I quote you on that by name?" during the interview, or the evaluator might go back later to ask permission, so as not to violate the confidentiality promise. The evaluation should also establish procedures for handling and storing the information collected, especially if it is confidential. Procedures may range from not entering respondents' names into any project databases to randomly generating identification numbers maintained in encrypted computer files.

Polishing Interview Techniques

Preparation is vital. Interviewers should know the questions thoroughly, understand the purpose of each question and the overall priority level of each question in the overall research scheme. When asking questions, tone is extremely important. SSI interviewers should take a casual, conversational approach that is pleasant, neutral, and professional, neither overly cold nor overly familiar. In this relaxed, comfortable setting, probing is accomplished without the interviewer sounding astonished by anything said, interested but not shocked.

Not all SSI practitioners agree about the exact persona that the interviewer should adapt. Some advise interviewers to "appear slightly dim and agreeable" (McCracken, 1988, p. 38), so that respondents won't feel threatened. Even though being sensitive to people's feelings is certainly a good idea, too much playing dumb might make respondents decide they are wasting their time and should not bother getting into complex discussions with such a clueless interviewer. The opposite extreme, a superior, all-knowing stance, seems likely to be off-putting and counterproductive as well. Probably the best balance is to appear generally knowledgeable, in a humble, open-minded way, but not to pose as more expert than the respondent (Leech, 2002). In that vein, interviewers should not debate with or contradict a respondent; interviewers must be sure they understand his or her views. They should maintain that calm, nonreactive demeanor, even when faced with a respondent whose personality or comments are offensive.

From time to time, it can be constructive to restate concisely in one or two sentences, using mainly the respondent's own words, what was just said. This technique of active listening reinforces that the interviewer is indeed intently interested and can ensure that the interviewer does, in fact, understand a point. After any unrecognized lingo or acronyms, interviewers should not apologize, but just repeat the mystery word in a questioning tone.

Prompting respondents to elaborate can be done in many ways besides just asking, "Why is that?" "Could you expand on that?" or "Anything else?" Sometimes a simple "yes?" with a pause, repeating a key word, or even nodding in silence is sufficient to signal that the interviewer would like to hear more. A tilted head can also be a green light for more detail. Avoid asking, "What do you mean?" because that accuses the respondent of failing to communicate. Asking for an elaboration or for an example is better. However, if something is unclear, do not hesitate to obtain a clarification. In the give-and-take of the conversation, take care not to interrupt and be overly controlling. Even when respondents drift into irrelevant territory, wait until they finish before making a soft segue back to a priority topic.

Sometimes, even if the recorder is running, it may be helpful to jot down an occasional note or star something on the agenda to return to later. Interviewers should be sufficiently familiar with the general questions that they do not have to bury their heads in the text to read each question verbatim. A glance down at the text should be sufficient. Because the actual conversation may diverge from the original order on the agenda, the interviewer must be flexible and ready with subtle improvisations to weave back to other issues. Entirely unexpected but promising avenues of interest may open up, and, if so, interviewers should feel empowered to pursue them. Such developments should be promptly shared with colleagues to determine whether those new topics should be explicitly added to the agenda or if the agenda order should be revised. After conducting numerous interviews, interviewers may sometimes find that answers begin to seem predictable. They have to remain alert, however, for different nuances in the answers that may be worth exploring or at least noting in the report.

Near the end of each session, nothing is wrong with asking for a moment to review the agenda guide to ensure that no key questions were missed. If time is running out, the interviewer will have to make a quick decision about whether to omit some of the remaining questions (and which ones), to ask to extend the visit a bit longer, or to request a short follow-up meeting at a later date. At the conclusion of the interview, the interviewer should thank the respondent cordially and confidently (not apologetically) for helpful comments. Before the day is out, the interviewer should send a short thank-you e-mail or, to be more traditional, a handwritten note; this extra expression of appreciation makes a difference in how respondents remember the experience and the people involved.

Other important tasks should also be completed daily. Interview notes should be cleaned and clarified so they will make sense to other members of the research team (and to the original interviewer a few weeks later). If notes were handwritten, they should be entered into a computer right away, and even if a small computer was used to take raw notes, these notes still have to be reviewed and edited while fresh. Maintain a master list of any abbreviations used in the interview summaries. Even if the session was recorded, some additional documentation (date, time, site codes, and so forth) should be filed. To save time, some interviewers prefer to dictate their elaboration of their hand-written notes; the dictation then must be transcribed later.

Analyzing and Reporting SSIs

Once the SSIs have been completed, the next step is to explore the results. As something of a hybrid between a standardized survey and a focus group, semi-structured interviews are suitable for a report that is a hybrid, too. If, as recommended, a few closed-ended questions were employed, there will be some hard numbers to cite, maybe suitable for a few simple tables and graphs. Percentages can be brought to life by the follow-up responses to open-ended questions. Look for ways to consolidate themes found in multiple answers and to supplement them with well-chosen, illustrative quotations. This aspect of the SSI report resembles a focus group report. (For a published example of a report of focus group findings, see Adams, 2005, Chapter 8.) For example, if roughly three out of four program administrators complained they were bur-dened by mountains of paperwork, quote some comments to make this issue vivid and explain it in more detail. Ordinarily, omit the highly unrepresenta-tive outliers, unless for some reason a particular comment, even if rare, should be conveyed to decision makers.

The time involved and method chosen for analyzing the open-ended ques-tions will depend heavily on the number of people interviewed and the num-ber of topics addressed. Summarizing a dozen SSIs of top managers will not be onerous, but systematically assessing SSIs of several hundred program ben-eficiaries will be a challenge. For more advice about the analysis phase, see Chapter Twenty-Two, which explains in detail the techniques that can be used in coding open-ended answers, along with the software programs that assist in the process. A judicious appraisal of the findings should yield a depth of understanding about the issues at hand beyond that possible from the alterna-tive survey techniques alone. All in all, effectively conducted semi-structured interviews, even though labor intensive, should be worth the effort in terms of the insights and information gained.

References

Adams, W. C. *Election Night News and Voter Turnout: Solving the Projection Puzzle.* Boulder, CO: Lynn Rienner, 2005.

Dexter, L. A. *Elite and Specialized Interviewing.* Evanston, IL: Northwestern University Press, 1970.

Galletta, A. M. *Mastering the Semi-Structured Interview and Beyond.* New York: NYU Press, 2013.

Leech, B. L. "Asking Questions: Techniques for Semistructured Interviews." *PS: Political Science & Politics,* 2002, *35*, 665–668.

McCracken, G. *The Long Interview.* Thousand Oaks, CA: Sage, 1988.

Merton, R. K. *The Focused Interview.* New York: The Free Press, 1956.

CHAPTER TWENTY

FOCUS GROUP INTERVIEWING

Richard A. Krueger, Mary Anne Casey

Consider advertising, public relations, and product testing. Companies spend millions of dollars annually on focus groups to test, introduce, and market consumer products. But there is another side of focus group interviewing that receives less publicity—its use as a research and evaluation strategy for public, not-for-profit, academic, and religious organizations.

This chapter discusses using focus groups as a component of an evaluation strategy. It focuses on both the benefits and the limitations of using this method and also offers suggestions for the effective use of focus group interviewing in an evaluation.

A focus group is a planned discussion led by a moderator who guides a small group of participants through a set of carefully sequenced (focused) questions in a permissive and nonthreatening conversation. The goal is not to reach agreement but to gain participant insights on the topic of discussion.

Focus groups are a wonderful method for gathering information for formative and summative evaluations. But don't limit your use of focus groups to the time after a program is implemented or completed. Focus group interviews are also valuable for gathering information in the design phases of programs, policies, and even evaluations. Here are some examples of the ways focus groups have been used.

Examples of Focus Group Use

To Assess Needs and Assets

A land grant university wanted to expand its outreach programs to minority ethnic and cultural groups in the state. It conducted focus groups to listen to these residents to determine what types of outreach programs would be most beneficial to their communities. Focus groups were held in various locations and in different languages to gather insights of local residents. With this information, the university then designed effective ways of delivering services, classes, and other opportunities.

To Design an Intervention

A state public health agency teamed with a local school district to design a program to increase the amount of fruits and vegetables that grade school students ate while at school. The team conducted focus groups with students, parents, teachers, and the food service staff to identify barriers to eating fruits and vegetables and to identify motivators for eating more fruits and vegetables. The team used the focus group findings to design a program that increased kids' motivation to eat fruits and vegetables and decreased the barriers.

To Evaluate Policy Options

When a state department of natural resources contemplated changes in hunting regulations, it conducted focus groups with hunters to get feedback on the changes. How easy are the potential regulations to understand? Do they make sense to hunters? How easy will the new regulations be to enforce? Answers to these questions helped policymakers craft regulations that were easier for hunters to understand and more efficient for game wardens to enforce.

To Pilot-Test Data Collection Instruments

A year after the completion of a smoking cessation study, we were asked to conduct focus groups with participants to evaluate the program. Although participants were extremely positive about the smoking cessation program, they complained consistently and with much passion about the telephone surveys used to collect participant data (even though we never asked about the telephone interviews). Participants said the telephone surveys were tedious and frustrating because the response categories changed frequently and, without visual cues, the participants couldn't remember which response category to use. Some said they became so frustrated they didn't take the survey seriously. Had focus groups been used to test the data collection instrument and process, we might have identified this problem and gotten better compliance and data.

To Understand Quantitative Findings

A health care system monitored its performance using a quantitative data collection system. As the health care system grew, ratings from staff declined. Administrators didn't know how to interpret the lower scores or how to reverse them. All they knew was that the scores were down and they wanted them back up. An outside organization conducted focus groups with staff, asking them to help the administration understand the drop in ratings and how the scores might be improved.

To Monitor and Evaluate Agency Operation

A federal agency regularly uses focus groups to monitor the employee climate, to canvass employees about human resource systems, to evaluate the promotion and recognition systems, and to improve cooperative efforts within the agency and with other federal agencies. Focus groups have helped the agency identify key factors that improved morale, streamlined the promotion process, and improved collaboration at all levels.

Of course, as mentioned, focus groups can also be used in formative and summative evaluations. They have been used to find out what's working, what's not working, and how programs can be improved. And they have been used to gather perceptions of program outcomes.

Focus groups may be conducted with:

- Potential participants, participants who completed a program, and participants who didn't complete a program
- Policymakers, administrators, staff, and others who want the evaluation findings for decision making
- Frontline people who will be asked to collect and provide evaluation data
- Experts in evaluation

Focus groups with decisions makers might identify gaps between the data that are currently available for decision making and the data that are needed. Focus groups with those who must provide the data might focus on how to get useful, credible data without overburdening frontline workers. Focus groups with evaluation experts might concentrate on how to create a cost-effective system that can provide the data decision makers need.

Characteristics of Focus Group Interviews

A focus group is not just any group where people get together to talk about a topic. Focus groups have certain characteristics. It is surprising how many people (experts and novices alike) do not clearly distinguish between a group discussion and a focus group.

Drawing on the pioneering work of Robert Merton, academics who study focus group research, and professionals who conduct focus group research, here are the core features that make focus groups distinctive.

The Questions Are Focused

The questions used in a focus group interview are carefully sequenced so that they focus more and more specifically on the key topic of the study. That is, the questions progressively direct participants into discussing the topic in greater detail and more depth. In other interview environments, the researcher might ask the most important questions first or use an informal, unstructured approach to interviewing. These strategies are not used in focus group interviews.

There Is No Push for Agreement or Consensus

Focus groups are distinctive in that the goal is not to reach consensus or to discover a single solution. Other group processes, such as the nominal group process or the Delphi method, are intended to push the group toward agreement. Although agreement can be a worthy goal, it is not the intent of the focus group. Focus groups are conducted to gather the range of opinions and experiences. The moderator doesn't pressure participants to come to agreement. Indeed, we have gained valuable insights in focus groups even from individuals who have described unique perceptions or experiences. One way to think of the distinction between different types of groups is to identify where the decisions are made. In focus group studies the decision-making process occurs after all focus groups have been completed. Focus group participants often offer recommendations, but these are used as input into the decision-making process by those who sponsor the study. By contrast, in a nominal group process the group is encouraged to make a decision at the conclusion of the discussion.

The Environment Is Permissive and Nonthreatening

The focus group environment should be comfortable. The moderator must be perceived as a person who is open to hearing anything. The moderator lays out the ground rules and states that participants may have differing opinions and that there are no wrong answers. All views are welcome, and if at times the group seems to be rushing toward agreement, the moderator might ask if there are opposing views. The focus group offers an honoring environment where individuals feel their views will be respected. The participants are assured that their names will not be used in any reports. The goal is to make people as comfortable as possible so they are willing to say what they think and describe how they feel. Focus groups are often held in places that are convenient for and familiar to the participants. The moderator welcomes participants and makes them feel comfortable and appreciated.

The Participants Are Homogeneous

People are invited to a particular focus group because they have something in common. They might all live in the same neighborhood, belong to the same organization, or have experienced a new program. Or they might have demographic factors in common that are important to the study (such as age, gender, race, or ethnicity). Focus groups use a homogeneous, purposeful sample composed of information-rich participants. This homogeneity fosters a sense of commonality that results in greater sharing of insights.

Sometimes there is confusion about homogeneous sampling because the participants are rarely completely homogeneous. What homogeneity means in this context is that the participants have something in common that relates to the topic of conversation. For example, in a study involving parents in a local school, the basis of homogeneity is that they are parents and they have children attending a particular school. Those same parents might be of different races or ethnic backgrounds, different occupations, or different ages or be different on other factors. The emphasis on homogeneity gives individuals comfort that they have something in common with other participants and this fosters sharing.

The Group Size Is Reasonable

The size of a focus group can range from as few as four or five to as many as a dozen people. The most workable size depends on the background of the participants, the complexity of the topic, and the expertise of the moderator.

Larger groups of nine to twelve participants tend to work better when working with consumer topics that do not evoke strong attachments. Smaller groups of five to eight are recommended for topics that might be seen as sensitive or personal or when the participants have considerable expertise or experience with the topic. The danger of the larger group is that it results in trivial responses, shortened answers, and less elaboration on critical details simply because of time constraints. In a focus group of a given length, each of six people can talk twice as long as each of twelve people can. The richness of the focus group is in the details and the explanations of the comments. This elaboration comes from having adequate time for participants to talk.

Patterns and Trends Are Examined Across Groups

Seldom would we conduct just one focus group. The rule of thumb is to hold three or four groups with each type of participant for which you want to analyze results. Therefore, if you want to compare and contrast the ways that men and women view a particular topic, you would conduct three to four groups with men and three to four groups with women.

The Group Is Guided by a Skillful Moderator

Skillful moderators make facilitation look easy. They are friendly, open, and engage with participants before the group starts, making people feel welcome and comfortable. They give a thorough introduction, helping people to feel they have enough information to trust the process. They move smoothly from one question to another. They have a set of questions and they get through all the questions in the allotted time. They get people to share their views freely. And they know just when to probe for additional insights. Typically, you want a moderator to ask the question, then sit back and listen. Let the participants interact. Let them have a conversation about the question. A focus group is working well when participants begin to build on each other's comments rather than continually responding directly to the moderator. The moderator begins to play a less central role as participants share experiences, debate ideas, and offer opinions. Some groups arrive at this point quickly. Others never reach this point.

The Analysis Fits the Study

One of the most time-consuming aspects of focus group research is the analysis. This is the process of identifying trends and patterns across groups and deriving meaning. In some situations it can involve audio recordings, transcripts, and content analysis of the exact words of participants. In other situations the analysis might be based on observation, field notes, and the memories of the research team. The rigor and intensity of the analysis has to fit the circumstances of the study. The critical factor in all analysis is that the process be systematic and verifiable. It should be systematic in that it follows a prescribed plan in a consistent way that fits the situation. It should be verifiable in that it leaves a trail of evidence that others can review.

Responsibilities

Evaluators must ensure that a variety of responsibilities are met when conducting a focus group study:

- Planning
- Developing questions
- Recruiting
- Moderating and capturing the data
- Analyzing and reporting

A key role is the study team leader, sometimes called the *principal investigator* (PI), who takes on the overall leadership of the study. The PI coordinates the budget, the timeline, the evaluation team, and the overall project. In most studies the PI assumes one or more of the responsibilities just listed. One person can complete all these tasks. However, we prefer working with a small team of perhaps two to four people who divide the responsibilities. These team members work together to complete the study, but individuals take primary responsibility for certain tasks. For example, one person may take primary responsibility for organizing—planning the study and developing questions—but the plan and the questions are usually stronger when that person involves others in the planning and question development. Or the team might involve multiple moderators who speak different languages or both men and women moderators, depending on what types of people the evaluators wants to listen to. We also often include a representative of the program or the client on the study team. We describe these tasks and roles in the following pages.

Planning

The main challenge during the planning stage is to come up with a study design that will answer the questions you have within the constraints of your timeline and budget. You and your team must be clear about the purpose of the study. You must decide whether focus group interviewing is an appropriate method for your study. If focus groups are appropriate, you must decide how many groups you will do and to whom you want to listen.

First Steps

The following sections offer a guide for the first steps in planning your focus group study.

1. Decide Whether Focus Groups Are Appropriate.   Focus groups work particularly well for:

- Understanding how people see needs and assets in their lives and communities.
- Understanding how people think or feel about something, such as an idea, a behavior, a product, or a service.
- Pilot-testing things, such as ideas, campaigns, surveys, or products. Focus groups can be used to get reactions to plans before big amounts of money are spent in implementation.
- Evaluating how programs or products are working and how they might be improved.

Focus group interviews are not meant to be used as:

- A process for getting people to come to consensus.
- A way to teach knowledge or skills.
- A test of knowledge or skills.

Also, if you answer yes to any of the following questions, you will likely need to consider other methods to use in conjunction with or instead of focus group interviews.

- *Do you need statistical data?* Focus groups cannot provide statistical data to project to a population. The number of people listened to is too small.

- *Will harm come to the people sharing their ideas?* Although you can promise that you will keep information shared in the group confidential, you cannot guarantee that participants in the group will keep the information confidential. If harm may come to people who openly share in the group, choose another method, such as individual interviews.
- *Are people polarized by your topic?* People are very passionate about and polarized by some topics. In the United States, abortion, race, gay marriage, and the environment are topics that people have a hard time discussing with others who hold opposing views. Emotions run high, so it is difficult to conduct a focus group that contains people holding strong opposing views.
- *Is there a better, more efficient way to get the information?*

2. Clarify the Purpose of the Study.   Sometimes study team members disagree about the type of information they want to obtain through the study and what they will do with the information once they have it. Having a clear purpose makes planning, conducting the groups, analyzing, and reporting simpler.

3. Decide What Types of People to Listen to—the Information Rich.   What types of people have the experiences or characteristics that will enable them to provide input on the study topic? Michael Quinn Patton (2014) calls these individuals "information-rich" cases. They may not be the most highly educated or the most influential, but they are the people who know something about what you want to know about. For example, young people who drop out of school know a lot about what it might take to keep young people in school. Teachers, counselors, and parents can give you different perspectives.

   Consider listening to:

- Those most affected by the change or program
- Those who must support the change or program before it can happen
- Employees (both frontline staff and managers) who must implement the change
- Government leaders or elected officials
- Influentials—respected people who may not hold an official office

4. Listen to the Information Rich.   Find a few people like the people you want to invite to the focus groups. (For example, in the study just described you might look for a few young people who have dropped out of school.) Tell them about the study. Ask for their advice. Find out things such as these: Who can ask these kinds of questions (who can moderate)? What type of moderator would people feel comfortable with? Where might the groups be held? What days or times might work well for people? How do you find people with the characteristics you are looking for? What will it take to get people to come to the focus group?

5. Plan to Conduct the Focus Groups in Stages.   When conducting focus group studies, we often find that the first few focus groups give us important clues about what lies ahead. This valuable information can be lost if all groups are conducted without reflection and feedback. We suggest that you plan to pause, analyze, and reflect after the first or second focus group. This means you transcribe early results, closely examine the data and consider whether adjustments are needed. Look over your data and think about whether your questions are being adequately answered. Are these first focus groups yielding insight or do you need to fine-tune the questions, the participant selection, or the assumptions undergirding your study? Too often, studies are conducted in one fell swoop, without reflection and without fine tuning. Consequently, they miss important opportunities to improve the study.

6. Put Your Thoughts in Writing.   Develop a written plan. Developing this plan forces you to arrange your ideas in a logical order and also allows others to review your plan and offer comments. Your written plan ought to include a statement of purpose, number of groups, characteristics of information-rich participants, list of potential questions, and a timeline and a budget.

Sampling and Number of Groups

The basic strategy is to conduct three or four focus groups with each participant category that is of interest to you. So, if you want to evaluate a special education program and want to compare student, parent, and teacher reactions to the program, you might plan three or four focus groups with students, three or four groups with parents, and three or four groups with teachers. If you are hearing new information after the third or fourth group with one participant category, you might continue conducting focus groups until you have achieved redundancy.

Do not use a statistical formula for determining sample size. Instead, use the concept called *redundancy,* or *theoretical saturation.* With redundancy, or theoretical saturation, the researcher continues interviewing until no new insights are presented. In effect, the researcher has exhausted the range of views on the topic. Continuing the interviews after reaching theoretical saturation will only yield more of what the researcher already knows. This tends to occur after three or four groups with one participant type.

Developing Questions

There are several challenges when developing questions. Try to

- Develop questions that address the purpose of your study. Although that sounds obvious, some study teams get swept away dreaming up questions that would be fun to ask or nice to know the answer to but that don't address the purpose of the study.
- Identify questions that will produce information useful to the decision makers.
- Write your questions so they are conversational and easy for the participants to understand. Use words the participants would use.
- Aim for the right number of questions—not too many or too few. Usually, a set of ten to fourteen questions is appropriate for a two-hour focus group.
- Sequence the questions so that early questions set the stage for the conversation and later questions focus on the most important topics.
- Phrase questions so they are open-ended. Don't ask questions that can be answered with one word.
- Include some questions that get participants actively involved by listing, sorting, arranging, drawing, or some other activity.

Developing the Questioning Route

A *questioning route* is a set of questions developed for one or more focus groups. For a two-hour focus group, plan to use ten to fourteen questions, written in a conversational style. Follow these five steps to develop a questioning route.

1. Hold a Brainstorming Session.   Invite four to six people who are familiar with the study to a one- or two-hour meeting. These people might be colleagues, members of the research team, or the individuals representing the client who is requesting the evaluation. Ask these people to generate questions that could be asked in the study. Try to use the procedures of brainstorming. Questions might be briefly discussed, but don't get stuck debating the merits of a single question. Have one person record all these questions.

2. Use the Brainstorming Questions to Draft a Questioning Route.   Groups are good at brainstorming, but aren't efficient at developing questioning routes. Have one person use the questions generated in the meeting as the basis for developing a questioning route. Start by selecting key questions, questions that best address the study purpose and seem most likely to provide useful information. These are the heart of the focus group. Then add beginning questions and ending questions. Rephrase the questions using the ideas throughout this chapter. Then sequence the questions in a logical flow from general to specific. Say the questions out loud. Are they easy to ask? Do they seem like questions the target audience will be able to answer?

There is no magic to having about ten to fourteen questions. But beginning focus group researchers often develop questioning routes with twenty to thirty questions—far too many. The result? You will end up with superficial data because participants will not have enough time to go into depth on any of the questions. Once you have a draft questioning route, you can estimate how much time you think the group should spend on each question. Not all questions deserve the same amount of consideration. Some questions are simpler or less important than others and can be easily covered in five minutes. Some key questions may be complex or include activities. A key question might take up fifteen to twenty minutes. Once you have estimated times for each of the questions, you can add up the total to determine whether you should add or delete questions.

3. Send the Draft Questioning Route Out for Feedback.   Send the draft to the brainstorming team and ask: Will these questions elicit the information we need? What have we missed? What can be deleted? Are these the words participants would use? Does the flow make sense? Revise the questioning route based on the team's feedback.

Remember, the same questions are asked in all the interviews with each type of participant. However, if separate groups are going to be conducted, for example, with teachers, parents, and students, a slightly different questioning route might be used for each of these types of participants (for example, you might ask students a question that you don't want to ask parents or teachers). Keep a core set of questions the same in each questioning route so responses can be compared across audiences.

Examples of Questioning Routes

Here are three examples of questioning routes for different situations. The first one includes an introductory statement as well as a list of questions.

For Pilot-Testing New Materials

Take a few moments and look over the materials. They include a brief description of a program and examples of handouts that participants would get.

1. What do you like the best about the materials?
2. What do you like the least about the materials?

3. If you could change one thing about the materials, what would it be?
4. What would get you to participate in this program? (Under what conditions would you participate?)
5. Suppose that you were trying to encourage a friend to participate in this program. What would you say?
6. What advice do you have for us as we introduce this new program?

For Formative Program Evaluation

1. Tell us how you participated in the program.
2. What did you like the best about the program? (What has been most helpful to you?)
3. What did you like the least about the program? (What was least helpful to you?)
4. What are the important accomplishments of the program?
5. What are the biggest weaknesses of the program?
6. What should be changed?
7. What should be continued and kept the same?
8. What other advice do you have about the program?

For Evaluating Services for Children

1. Introduce yourself and tell us how you learned about these services.
2. Think back to when you first became involved with these services. What were your first impressions of the services?
3. What has been particularly helpful about the services your family has received?
4. What has been disappointing about the services?
5. What has your child liked about the experience?
6. What has your child not liked about the experience?
7. Some of you may have had experiences with other services for your child. How does this approach compare with other services you've experienced? Is it any different? How so?
8. What would make the services work better?
9. Is your child any different because he or she has received these services? If so, how?
10. Is your family life any different because you received these services? How?
11. If you had a chance to give advice to the director of this program, what would you say?
12. Based on your experiences, would you recommend these services to other parents?

Recruiting

When you have your plan and you know the questions you are going to ask, the next challenge is to find the right people and persuade them to attend the focus groups.

The first step is to identify as precisely as possible the characteristics of information-rich participants. A basic principle of focus group interviewing is that the researcher controls attendance. You do not invite people simply because they are interested in attending. You invite people because they meet the *screens*, or qualifications, for the study. You invite people who have experienced something specific or who have common characteristics. For example, they may have participated in a community program that you are evaluating, or they may be residents in the community and you are doing a needs assessment of the community, or they may be farmers who have adopted improved agricultural practices.

One of the challenges of focus group interviewing is how to persuade people who may be uninterested in your study to participate. They may be apathetic, indifferent, or even consider the topic to be irrelevant. At times, you will want to involve people who are not initially interested in participating. If you limit your study to only those who show interest in the topic, you might obtain biased results. To be successful, think about your recruiting procedure as well as the incentives to participate.

The Recruiting Procedure

There are two distinct qualities of successful recruiting. First, the process is personalized. This means that each invited person feels that he or she has been personally asked to attend and share his or her opinions. Second, the invitation process is repetitive. Invitations are given not just once but two or three times. Here are the steps in a typical process of recruiting.

1. Set Focus Group Dates, Times, and Locations.   Most groups with adults are scheduled for two hours. Focus groups with children are usually shorter. Don't schedule more than two groups in one day unless you have multiple moderators available.

2. Recruit Participants.   Recruit participants via telephone or in person. This allows you to respond immediately to questions or concerns about the study. Before beginning the recruiting, be clear about how you are going to describe the study. People will want to know the purpose of the discussion, who wants the information, what the sponsor of the study is going to do with the information, why they are being asked to participate ("Why me?"), and how you found their names.

Usually, you shouldn't invite people to a "focus group." That term could be intimidating. Instead, you could say you are inviting a few people together to talk about the topic. Don't use jargon in the invitation. You want it to sound as though it will be an easy, comfortable, interesting conversation.

Think about who should offer the invitation. Will people be more willing to participate if someone from their community invites them than they would be if a stranger invites them? Or would people feel honored to be invited by the head of a local organization? People are usually more likely to say yes if someone they know and respect invites them to participate. If that isn't possible, it helps to be able to refer to a person they know and respect and to identify that person as supporting the study. For example, it often helps to say, "The president of the chamber of commerce [*or the community health nurse or some other person they know and respect*] said you might be able to help us. We are inviting some people to get together to talk about [*name of topic*]."

3. Send a Personalized Letter.   Soon after the person has agreed to participate, send him or her a personalized letter. Don't use a generic salutation, such as "Dear Friend." This letter should thank the person for agreeing to participate and confirm the date, time, and place.

4. Send a Reminder.   Phone or contact each person the day before the focus group to remind him or her of the group: "I'm looking forward to seeing you tomorrow at. . . ."

Finding a Pool of Participants

Typically, you will find a pool of people who meet your selection requirements and then you will randomly select individuals to invite from that pool. For example, you might invite every fifth name on a list or every tenth person who enters a store. Here are several different ways to find a pool:

- Find a list of people who fit your selection criteria. Think about who might have such a list. It might be a list of program participants or employees or parents.
- Piggyback on another event that attracts the type of people you want. Do farmers in a certain area get together for a specific event, for example?

- Recruit on location. For instance, invite every fifth person who arrives at a clinic.
- Ask for nominations. Ask key people, like elders, educators, or service providers, for names of people who fit the selection criteria.
- Build snowball samples. Once you find some people who fit the selection criteria, ask them for names of other people who fit the selection criteria.

Getting People to Attend—Incentives

First, think about what might make it hard for people to attend. Try to eliminate these things. If appropriate, provide transportation and child care.

Then, think about what might entice people to participate. Ask a few people who are like the people you are trying to attract what it will take to get them to show up. Here are things that have been used to encourage people to participate:

- Money. (We will pay you.)
- Food. (There will be something to eat.)
- Gifts. (We have a gift for you.)
- Compliment or honor. (We value your insights about the program.)
- Enjoyment. (You will have a nice time.)
- Community. (Your participation will help the community.)
- Location. (The location is familiar, easy to get to, and comfortable.)

Consider Your Recruiting Assets

Nonprofit, educational, public and similar organizations have unique assets, which can be valuable when recruiting. In many cases, these organizations have developed a positive reputation and image among those they want to recruit. Regularly, they can recruit and get people to attend without tangible incentives. One of the most overlooked assets is the special invitation to participate from an influential person with the organization. Don't ask the most recently hired employee to make the recruiting contacts. Instead, seek out a senior member of the organization whose name is recognized and respected by the potential attendees. When he or she makes a phone call to invite a participant, the potential attendee often sees it as an honor. If these senior people aren't available, then an alternative is for someone else to make the invitation in their name.

Moderating

The challenge of moderating is to help participants feel comfortable enough to share, in the presence of the rest of the group, what they think and how they feel. They must trust the moderator, the process, and the sponsoring organization and also that the results will be used in a positive way. The moderator must know when to wait for more information and when to move on. The moderator must be able to control dominant speakers and encourage hesitant participants. The moderator must respect the participants, listen to what they have to say, and thank them for their views even when he or she may personally disagree.

Moderator Skills

The moderator should have enough knowledge about the topic to understand what the participants are saying. He or she does not need to be an expert on the topic but should understand common terms that will be used in the discussion.

It sometimes helps to have a moderator who looks like the participants. This can make the participants more comfortable and give the impression that "this person will understand what I have to say." Consider such things as gender, age, and race and ethnicity. For some topics these things may not matter, but for other topics they are very important. For example, women may be more willing to talk about breastfeeding with a woman than a man. Also remember that the moderator should be fluent in the participants' language.

Here are other things the moderator should do:

Be Mentally Prepared
- Be alert and free from distractions. Arrive early so you are relaxed and ready to listen.
- Have the discipline to listen. Often beginning moderators are delighted that people are talking, and they don't notice that the participants are not really answering the question. As you listen, ask yourself, are they really answering the question? If not, refocus their attention on the question.
- Be familiar with the questioning route. Know which questions are the most important. Know which questions can be dropped if you are running out of time.

Work with an Assistant Moderator
- An assistant moderator improves the quality of the groups.

- On one level, the assistant helps by taking care of details (such as seeing to the refreshments, monitoring the recording equipment, or dealing with latecomers).
- On a more important level, the assistant helps to ensure the quality of the analysis by taking careful notes, summarizing the discussion at the end, and acting as another set of eyes and ears for analysis.

Polish Your Hosting Skills

- When conducting focus groups, act like the host. This means greeting people when they arrive, introducing them to other participants, providing beverages or snacks, and making the participants feel welcomed. Too often, the evaluator forgets to smile or welcome people and the environment changes to apprehension or, worse, drudgery. Focus groups are a social experience and people must feel comfortable and valued before they will share quality data.
- Create a warm and friendly environment. While you are waiting for participants, engage those who arrive first in small talk—informal discussions on topics of casual importance. These informal conversations that occur before the focus group help participants get a sense of you as the moderator. The small talk should put participants at ease and foster conversations among the participants even before the focus group begins. Think of this time before the focus group as what good hosts do when guests arrive at their homes—they welcome them in, introduce them to the others already there, and discuss an easy, upbeat topic.
- Small talk topics should be easy to talk about. It might be what is happening locally (if it is off the topic of the focus group). If you are new to the area, ask participants about the weather, or geography, or transportation, or places to eat, or their families. Your job is to make people feel welcome and comfortable.

Record the Discussion

- It is impossible to remember everything that is said in a focus group. The group's dialogue can be recorded in several ways, such as in field notes, by audio recording, or on a laptop computer.
- Digital audio recorders provide excellent sound quality, the ability to quickly locate comments, and the ability to regulate playback speed and background noise.
- Video recording of focus groups is regularly done in market research focus group facilities where cameras are placed behind one-way mirrors or mounted inconspicuously in the room. However, these video cameras can

be problematic in evaluation focus groups because of topic sensitivity, the need for confidentiality, and participant comfort. As a result, we avoid video recording evaluation focus groups.

Give a Short and Smooth Introduction

- Welcome everyone.
- Give an overview of the topic.
- Provide any ground rules for the discussion.
- Ask the first question.

Use Pauses and Probes to Draw Out More Responses

- Be comfortable with using a five-second pause. Beginning moderators are sometimes uncomfortable with silence. However, pauses encourage people to add to the conversation.
- Use probes to get more detail. Usually more detailed information is more useful. Consider these probes:
  "Would you explain further?"
  "Can you give an example?"
  "I don't understand."
  "Tell me more."

Control Reactions to Participants

- Don't lead participants by giving verbal or nonverbal clues as to what you like or don't like. The moderator should avoid showing signs of approval or disapproval. For example, it is often tempting for the moderator to give a broad smile and nod his or her head when hearing certain comments. Participants quickly spot this behavior and then assume that more of these "approved" comments are wanted.
- Avoid verbal cues like "that's good" or "excellent."
- Don't correct participants during the group. If they share information that is harmful, offer the correct information at the end of the group.
- Do not become defensive if participants tell you they think your program is horrible. Instead, try to get information that will help you understand their perspective.

Use Subtle Group Control

- Your job is not to make sure everyone speaks the same amount in a group. But everyone should have the opportunity to share. Some people will have more to say. If they are answering the question and giving new and useful information we let them continue.

- Control dominant talkers by thanking them for their input and asking for others to share. Remind the group that it is important to hear from everyone.
- Call on quiet participants. They are often reflective thinkers and have wonderful things to offer. Invite them to share by saying something like this: "Maria, I don't want to leave you out of the discussion. What would you like to add?"

Use an Appropriate Conclusion

- Summarize the key points of the discussion and ask for confirmation. Usually, the assistant moderator does this. (Do not summarize the entire focus group. Instead, summarize three to five of the most important points.)
- Review the purpose and ask whether anything has been missed.
- Thank the participants, distribute any incentive, and conclude the session.

Analysis

The analyst must take the focus group data and find what is meaningful to the purpose of the study. One of the skills that beginning analysts must learn is to match the level of analysis to the problem at hand. Not all studies require the same level of analysis. It helps to break the analysis into doable chunks so the analyst is not overwhelmed by the task. The analyst must look for the major themes that cut across groups and those gems that might have been mentioned by only a few people. The analyst can only do this by being clearly grounded in the purpose of the study.

Use a Systematic Analysis Process

Focus group analysis should be systematic. There is no single best way, but rather many possible ways to have a systematic process. Being systematic simply means that the analyst has a protocol that follows a predetermined and verifiable set of steps. Here is an example of a systematic analysis process that we have used often. Notice that the process begins while the first group is still being conducted and continues after the last focus group is completed. (See Box 20.1 for additional analysis tips.)

1. Start the Process While Still in the Group
   - Listen for vague or inconsistent comments and probe for understanding.
   - Consider asking each participant a final preference question.

- Offer an oral summary of key findings and ask if the summary is correct.
2. Continue the Process Immediately After the Group
    - Draw a diagram of the seating arrangement.
    - Spot-check the audio recording to ensure that the machine picked up the discussion. If the recorder didn't work, immediately take time to expand your notes. Recreate as much of the discussion as possible.
    - Turn the audio recorder back on. Record the observations of the moderator and assistant moderator. Discuss and describe such things as these:

        What seemed to be the key themes of this discussion?
        What was surprising?
        How did this group compare with prior groups?
        Does anything need to be changed before the next group?
        What hunches, interpretations, and ideas did the discussion produce?

    - Label, date, and file field notes, digital files, and other materials.
3. Analyze the Responses from Each Group Soon After Their Completion
    - Option 1: Transcript-based analysis

        Make a backup copy of the audio recording and send a copy to the transcriber if a transcript is needed.
        Listen to the audio recording, review the field notes, and read the transcript.
        Use the transcript (along with the other group transcripts) as the basis for the next steps.

    - Option 2: Analysis without a transcript

        Prepare a summary of the individual focus group in a question-by-question format with amplifying quotes.
        Share the summary with other researchers who were present at the focus groups so they can verify its accuracy.
        Use the summary (along with other group summaries) as the basis for the next steps.

4. Analyze the Series of Focus Groups Within Days of the Last Group's Completion
    - Analyze groups by categories (for example, first analyze the parent groups, then analyze the teacher groups, then analyze the student groups).
    - Analyze groups across categories (for example, compare and contrast the parent groups with the teacher and the student groups).
    - Look for emerging themes by question and then overall.

- Identify areas where there is agreement and disagreement, both within each focus group and across the series of focus groups.
- Consider developing diagrams of the analysis that depict flow, sequence, structure, or other factors of interest.
- Describe findings and use quotes from participants to illustrate.

5. Finally, Prepare the Report
   - Decide whether to use narrative style or bulleted list style.
   - Decide whether the report should be organized by question or by theme.
   - Use a few quotes from participants to illustrate each important point.
   - Share the draft report with other study team members for verification.
   - Revise in light of the feedback and finalize report.

Box 20.1. Tips for Focus Group Analysis

When analyzing focus group data consider the following:

Frequency
Frequency tells you how often a comment was made. But frequency alone does not tell you how many different people made this particular comment. Indeed, you might have ten similar comments that were all spoken by the same person. Do not assume that frequency is an indicator of importance. Some analysts count up how many times certain things were said and believe that those discussed most often are more important. This is not necessarily true.

Extensiveness
Extensiveness tells you how many different people made a particular comment. This measure gives you a sense of the degree of agreement on a topic. Unfortunately, it is impossible to determine extensiveness using only the transcript unless names are attached to comments. If you were present in the focus group you will have a sense of the degree of extensiveness and this can be captured in the field notes. Usually, extensiveness is a more useful concept in focus group analysis than frequency.

Intensity
Occasionally, participants talk about a topic with a special intensity or depth of feeling. Sometimes the participants will use words that connote intensity or tell you directly about their strength of feeling. Intensity may be difficult to spot with transcripts alone because vocal tone, speed, and emphasis on certain words also communicate intensity. Individuals will differ in how they display strength of feeling, and for some it will be speed or excitement in the voice, whereas others will speak slowly and deliberately. Some may cry. Some may bang their fists on the table. Pay particular attention to what is said with passion or intensity.

(Continued)

Specificity

Responses that are specific and based on experiences should be given more weight than responses that are vague and impersonal. To what degree can the respondent provide details when asked a follow-up probe? Greater attention is often placed on responses that are in the first person as opposed to hypothetical, third-person answers. For example, "I feel the new practice is important. I used it and I haven't smoked in a year," has more weight than, "These practices are good and people should use them."

Finding Big Ideas

One of the traps of analysis is focusing so much on the detail that you miss the big ideas. Step back from the discussions by allowing an extra day or two for big ideas to percolate. For example, after finishing the analysis the researcher might set the report aside for a brief period and then jot down the three or four most important findings. Assistant moderators or others skilled in qualitative analysis might review the process and verify the big ideas.

Important Comments That Don't Reoccur

In most qualitative analysis, we are looking for themes and patterns that reoccur within or across cases. In a focus group, we listen to see if others offer similar or complimentary views and, if so, we place emphasis on that data. But in focus group research, we occasionally find that important and insightful comments may not reoccur. A visionary individual may see relationships or consequences that are not apparent to others. Or an individual may have an unique experience. In a recent study, two focus groups were conducted with church members about tithing. In the first focus group, there was strong agreement that all members should be encouraged to give a specified percent of their income to the church. In the second focus group, the same pattern emerged until one woman spoke up and told about her financial difficulties. She valued the congregational community and wanted to remain in the church but she was a single mother and a required donation was beyond her reach. She cried as she told her story of financial struggle. The views of one person had a profound impact on other members of the focus group and on the church's decision.

The Analyst Should Be Present in the Focus Groups

We recommend that the person responsible for analysis attend the focus groups. Some analysts wrongly assume that they can do quality analysis by merely examining transcripts. Transcript analysis without actually attending the focus groups is not recommended and can lead to serious errors in analysis. By being present at the groups the analyst can get a sense of the conversation, the difference between frequency and extensiveness, the presence of emotions or intense feelings and the overall energy of the group. The analyst could serve either as the moderator or as a note taker.

Try the Classic Analysis Strategy: Long Tables, Scissors, and Colored Marking Pens

If you have not analyzed focus group data before, you may want to try this strategy. It offers a concrete way of categorizing and "seeing" the data. After you understand this method, it is easier to understand how the analysis process can be accomplished using computer software.

Equipment Needed
Two copies of all transcripts
Scissors
Tape
Lots of room, long tables, and possibly flip chart stands
Large sheets of paper (flip chart paper, newsprint paper, and so forth)
Colored marking pens
Sticky notes

Box 20.2. Tip for Preparing and Managing Transcripts

Consider printing transcripts on different colors of paper and color-coding by audience type, category, and so forth. For example, transcripts for groups of teenagers might be on blue paper and those for groups of parents on green paper. In addition, use a marker to draw one line down the right margin of each page of, for example, the transcript for the first parent group, two lines down each page of the transcript for the second parent group, and three lines down each page of the transcript for the third parent group, and so on. This way, once you have all the transcripts cut up, you can easily see that a participant response on green paper with two lines down the side came from the second parent group. Do this for each category of groups. To take this even a step further, most word processing programs allow you to easily number each line of a transcript. If you are uncertain about how to do this on your software just go to your "Help" icon and enter "Add line numbers."

---

1. Prepare the Transcripts for Analysis. You will save time and agony later if you are careful in preparing the focus group transcripts (also see the tip in Box 20.2). Be sure they follow a consistent style (for example, with comments single-spaced and a double-space between comments by different speakers.

The comments of the moderator should be made easily identifiable by bolding, caps, or underlining.

2. Make Two Copies of Each Transcript.   One copy will be cut up and the other one will be left intact for later reference.

3. Arrange Transcripts in an Order.   The most useful order for the transcripts could be the sequence in which the groups were conducted, but more likely it will be by categories of participants or by some demographic screening characteristic of participants (users, nonusers, and employees, or teens, young adults, and older adults, and so on). This arrangement helps you be alert to changes that may be occurring from one group to another.

4. Read all Transcripts at One Sitting.   This quick reading is just to remind you of the whole scope and to refresh your memory of where information is located, what information is missing, and what information occurs in abundance.

5. Prepare Large Sheets of Paper.   Use a large sheet of paper for each question. Place the large sheets on chart stands, on a long table, or even on the floor. Write one of the questions at the top of each sheet.

6. Cut and Tape.   Start with the first question you want to analyze. Read each quote, and answer these questions:

a. Did the participant answer the question that was asked?
>   IF YES → Go to question c.
>   DON'T KNOW → Set it aside and review it later.
>   NO → Go to question b.
>> (If you are undecided or unclear about any answers, then take the conservative approach and save the comments for later review.)
b. Does the comment answer a different question in the focus group?
>   IF YES → Move quote to that question.
>   IF NO → Put in discard pile (but don't throw the discard pile away until you are done with analysis).
>> (*Caution:* Don't assume that answers will follow the questions. Occasionally, participants will provide answers to questions asked earlier or to questions that have not yet been asked. When this occurs, move the answer to the appropriate location.)

c. Does the comment say something of importance about the topic?

    IF YES → Tape it to the newsprint under the appropriate question.

       (Or if you are working on a horizontal surface, just start a pile.)

    IF NO → Put in discard pile.

       (*Tip:* Don't use a lot of tape because you will want to move the quotes around later.)

d. Is it like something that has been said earlier?

    IF YES → Start grouping like quotes together. Basically, you are making piles (categories) of like things.

    IF NO → Start a separate pile.

       You are constantly comparing and making decisions. Is this similar to or different from other things?

When you are done categorizing the quotes from the first question, move to the second. After you've cut up all the transcripts and have your initial categories, you're ready to begin analysis of specific questions. Make sure you have all the quotes that say similar things together. Rearrange until you're satisfied. You might have categories and subcategories. You may get so many quotes about one thing that you make subcategories. Or you may decide to combine categories. You may want to talk with someone else about how you are categorizing certain things. When you've finished arranging quotes into categories, you are ready for the next step.

7. Write a Statement About Each Question. Review the quotes that are arranged by categories on the question sheet and prepare a paragraph that describes participant reactions to the question. The form of the description will vary depending on the content of the responses. For example, you might be able to compare and contrast differing categories, you might find a major theme and a minor theme, or you might find it useful to discuss the variability of the comments or even the passion or intensity of the comments. After writing this overview paragraph you may need to prepare several additional paragraphs to describe subsets of views or to elaborate on selected topics. Compare and contrast the ways in which different audiences (such as parents, teachers, and students) answered the question. (If you color-coded the transcripts, you can easily use the colors to help you "see" how the different audiences answered the questions.) When you are finished, go on to the next question.

8. Take a Break. Get away from the process for a while. Refocus on the big picture. Think about what prompted the study. It's easy to get sidetracked into

TABLE 20.1. COMMON CHALLENGES AND SOLUTION STRATEGIES IN FOCUS GROUP INTERVIEWS.

Challenges	Solution Strategies
Making participants feel comfortable and getting them to talk to one another. Beginning moderators tend to approach focus groups like individual interviews, expecting answers from individual participants but not encouraging interaction among them.	Even before the focus group begins encourage participants to talk to each other. In the focus group tell them it is OK to talk to each other. Use questions that elicit conversation and opinions instead of factual information. Use pauses to elicit conversation. Invite participants to comment on the ideas of others.
Recruiting. This is often the greatest challenge for those starting out with focus groups. It is especially difficult when you are recruiting individuals with no connection or allegiance to the topic or sponsor.	Successful recruiting is personalized and repetitive. Think about who should extend the invitation to participate and practice the recruitment invitation so that it flows smoothly and comfortably. Also, think about the array of incentives that prompt people to actually attend. In evaluation focus groups, cash incentives are sometimes effective, but don't overlook the persuasive appeal of nontangible factors.
Developing questions. This takes time and effort. Good questions are essential for successful focus groups.	Several heads are better than one. Work with others when developing your questions. Consider brainstorming to identify possibilities. Anticipate that you will have several drafts. Invite review by colleagues and potential participants.
Selecting the right level of analysis for the study. Analysis strategies are on a continuum; different strategies require different amounts of time and reflect differing degrees of rigor.	Don't be trapped by having only one way to do the analysis. Some situations demand more rigor, and in those cases you might use complete transcripts and even qualitative analysis software. But in other situations you may need a faster process that is based on careful field notes and uses oral summaries, participant response forms, or other strategies.

areas of minor importance. Be open to alternative views. Be skeptical. Look over the pile of unused quotes. Think of the big picture.

9. Prepare the Report. After you prepare the report with the paragraphs you have written for each question and the big ideas that emerged from the study, invite research colleagues to review your work and offer feedback.

Addressing Challenges in Focus Group Interviews

When using focus groups for evaluation purposes there are some challenges. We list the frequent challenges along with potential solution strategies in Table 20.1

Conclusion

Focus group interviews can provide valuable insights in program evaluation. They can be used alone or in combination with other evaluation methods. Results from focus groups are particularly valuable because they provide insights into the logic and rationale for certain behaviors, explain why these behaviors take place, how a program or issue is perceived, or the barriers or concerns of key stakeholders, and because these answers are presented in the words and logic of the people closest to the program. Focus groups look easy, especially when conducted by a skilled moderator, but they can be challenging to plan, conduct, and analyze.

Successful focus group studies are grounded on five key steps: planning, developing questions, recruiting, moderating, and analyzing. Each of these steps is critical to success. Those who seek to have successful focus groups should be attentive to performing each step with care, thought, and skill. Those who seek to develop skills would benefit from reading the literature on focus groups (see the Further Reading section for some suggestions), observing experts conduct focus groups, practicing the key skills, and seeking feedback.

Reference

Patton, M. Q. *Qualitative Evaluation and Research Methods* (4th ed.). Thousand Oaks, CA: Sage, 2014.

Further Reading

Bystedt, J., Lynn, S., and Potts, D. *Moderating to the Max.* Ithaca, NY: Paramount, 2003.
Hennink, M. M. *International Focus Group Research: A Handbook for the Health and Social Sciences.* New York: Cambridge University Press, 2007.
Krueger, R. A. *Analyzing and Reporting Focus Group Results.* Thousand Oaks, CA: Sage, 1998.
Krueger, R. A. *Developing Questions for Focus Groups.* Thousand Oaks, CA: Sage, 1998.
Krueger, R. A., and Casey, M. A. *Focus Groups: A Practical Guide for Applied Research.* Thousand Oaks, CA: Sage, 2015.

Krueger, R. A., and King, J. A. *Involving Community Members in Focus Groups.* Thousand Oaks, CA: Sage, 1998.

Merton, R. K., Fiske, M., and Kendall, P. L. *The Focused Interview.* New York: The Free Press, 1956.

Morgan, D. L. *Focus Groups as Qualitative Research.* Thousand Oaks, CA: Sage, 1997.

Morgan, D. L., and Krueger, R. A. (Eds.). *The Focus Group Kit.* Thousand Oaks, CA: Sage, 1998.

CHAPTER TWENTY-ONE

USING STORIES IN EVALUATION

Richard A. Krueger

Study the writing of authors who are successfully translating research for the public: Malcolm Gladwell (*Blink, Outliers, The Tipping Point*), Daniel Goleman (*Emotional Intelligence, Ecological Intelligence*), or Dacher Keltner (*Born to Be Good: The Science of a Meaningful Life*). Each of these books begins with a story. Each book is packed with stories to illustrate points, to make concepts memorable, and to keep the reader engaged. They are the kind of stories that you want to retell—to your partner over dinner or your colleague over coffee. Or look at the Tuesday Science Times section of the *New York Times*. Reporters and columnists consistently use stories about individuals to explain the latest research findings. The writers who best translate research findings use stories. Evaluators can learn from these examples.

I believe in the power of stories. I have spent much of my career listening to people tell their stories in focus groups and individual interviews. People's stories have made me laugh, made me cry, made me angry, and kept me awake. Quantitative data have never once led me to shed a tear or spend a sleepless night. Numbers may appeal to my head, but they don't grab my heart. I believe that if you want people to do something with your evaluation findings, you have to snatch their attention, and one way to do that is through stories.

Stories can help evaluators capture their audience's attention, communicate emotions, illustrate key points or themes, and make findings memorable. This chapter offers suggestions on how to use established qualitative research principles to collect stories for evaluation studies.

In this chapter, I'll describe:

- How stories can be used in evaluation projects
- An overview of critical steps
- Strategies used by storytellers to communicate their stories
- Challenges in using stories and how to avoid them

How Stories Enrich Evaluations

Stories give researchers new ways to understand people and situations and tools for communicating these understandings to others (Box 21.1).

Box 21.1. Story Example: Understanding Others

In a recent study, two focus groups were conducted with church members about stewardship. In the first focus group, there was strong agreement that all members should be encouraged to give a specified percent of their income to the church. In the second focus group, the same pattern emerged, until one woman spoke up and told her story. She valued the congregational community and wanted to remain in the church but she was a single mother and the required donation was beyond her reach. Tears came to her eyes as she told of financial struggle. She was supporting both her mother and her child. She was employed but had to carefully budget her money. Her story was heart-felt and sincere and touched the others in the group. The others hadn't realized that some in the congregation were facing serious financial problems. Upon hearing of her experiences, the group reversed their opinion of required tithing.

They Help Us Understand

Stories provide insights that can't be found through quantitative data. A story helps us understand motivation, values, emotions, interests, and factors that influence behavior. Stories can give us clues about why an event might occur or how something happens.

Stories help us interpret quantitative data. Stories can also be used to amplify and communicate quantitative data. For example, a monitoring system might detect a change in outcomes, but what prompted the change usually can't be found in quantified data. Stories from clients and staff can help us understand factors that change lives and influence people.

They Help Us Share What We Learned

Stories help communicate evaluation findings. Evidence suggests that people have an easier time remembering a story than recalling numerical data. The story is sticky, but numbers quickly fade away. Evaluation data are hard to remember. The story provides a framework that helps the reader or listener remember salient facts.

Stories help communicate emotions. Statistical and survey data tend to dwell on the cold hard facts. Stories are different. They show us the challenges people face, how people feel, and how they respond to situations. Stories tug at our hearts and affect our outlook. Evaluators tend to be apprehensive about emotional messages for valid reasons. Emotional messages can ignore important facts, be fabrications, or overlook empirical data. But instead of avoiding these emotional messages, this chapter suggests combining the emotional aspect of stories with empirical data to address the concerns of both the heart and the head. Stories make quantitative data more credible. A story personalizes the data and takes the information out of the abstract and into a specific situation. A story connects with people because human beings have a natural curiosity about each other, and when the data are coupled with a story, then the logic and description are more credible.

Because stories are memorable, believable, and convey emotions, they can influence people in a way that numbers don't. Stories have an impressive ability to provoke and elicit action. Individuals and groups take action, organize, vote, and talk to others because of stories they hear, not because of survey results or statistical analysis.

A Definition of an Evaluation Story

An *evaluation story* is a brief narrative account of someone's experience with a program, event, or activity that is collected using sound research methods. The purpose of collecting the story is to gain insight into someone's experience or to shed light on an evaluation topic. These stories can vary in length from a few sentences to several pages and provide insights on a topic designated by the evaluator. Single stories can be useful and provide valuable insights, but multiple stories have an added benefit because they can shed light on patterns and trends. Evaluation stories are gathered using accepted qualitative research methods. Some researchers dismiss stories as unreliable or idiosyncratic or simply anecdotes. Using accepted research protocol gives the stories more credibility.

The evaluation story is a result of disciplined inquiry. The evaluation story is not an accidental event or a serendipitous description. Instead, it is the result of deliberate actions taken by the evaluator with attention to the principles of qualitative inquiry. The evaluator uses a systematic and verifiable collection process. As a result, these stories qualify as evidence useful in an evaluation study. They can be used to supplement quantitative data or the stories can stand alone. Box 21.2 presents an example of a story that I and other researchers gathered in a recent evaluation.

Here are the key factors that differentiate the evaluation story from other stories. The evaluation story:

- Is a deliberate, planned effort using systematic procedures
- Identifies the source of each story
- Verifies stories with the storyteller or others familiar with the story
- Includes a description of how the stories were captured and handled using accepted research protocol
- Includes a statement by the evaluator about the degree to which the story represents other individuals with similar circumstances

---

Box 21.2. Story Example: Medical Mistakes

We were conducting an evaluation of patient safety in a large medical system. Our goal was to uncover the barriers that deterred the hospital staff from disclosing mistakes. It was a sensitive topic. With some frequency, front-line staff contended that hospital management sent mixed signals. One participant told this story:

I enjoy hang gliding. We've got some terrific places to hang glide in this area. When we do it, we do it as a group. We gather at the top of a mountain and then one person sails off alone while the others watch. We call this person the "wind dummy." Everyone's eyes are on this first person. We watch how the updrafts and crosswinds affect the glide. We are attentive to the turbulence and watch for any difficulties encountered by the wind dummy. When this first person has completed the sail, then the rest of us take off, incorporating the lessons we learned from watching the wind dummy. The same is true here at the hospital. We watch what happens when someone reports a medical mistake. If that person crashes and burns, then the rest of us change our behavior accordingly.

How Stories Can Be Used in Evaluation Studies

Here are six major ways evaluators can use stories:

1. To illustrate other data
2. To complement quantitative methods
3. To reveal patterns and trends
4. To document organizational success
5. To inform future research
6. To motivate or change behavior

In the first strategy, the evaluator begins with existing quantitative data. It could consist of census data, official documents, or other research or evaluation findings. These sources provide the evaluator with insights and clues about story themes. For example, Paul Nyhan is a reporter for the *Seattle Post-Intelligencer* and is nationally known for his powerful stories on poverty. In an interview on National Public Radio, Nyhan was asked to describe how he uses stories in his reporting. He said he begins by carefully studying census data, labor statistics, and other sources that shed light on the area he is examining. He is looking for "something surprising, something unusual" in the data that will attract the attention of his readers. Armed with an unusual or surprising statistic, he will spend months seeking stories that illustrate and explain these data. For example, in reviewing data, he discovered that the percentage of poor kids receiving a four-year degree has barely budged in the past thirty years, but the percentage of college graduates from middle-class environments has risen steadily (see Nyhan, 2005). Nyhan wondered, "How do you explain this statistic?" He spent two months talking to high school students in low-income environments looking for stories that illustrate why a kid with an A or B average chooses not to attend college.

Stories can be used to complement and augment quantitative data. By using quantitative methods, evaluators can make statements that would not be possible with stories alone. These statements tell us how often, how many, or to what extent key factors in the story might occur. When surveys and stories are used together in this second strategy, one of the issues to consider is which data to collect first. One style is to begin with stories, identify the patterns that emerge across these stories, and then use surveys as a follow-up method. The survey produces the measures that couldn't be detected with the stories alone. The benefit of collecting stories first is that they inform the design of the survey, so that the survey questions are more relevant and applicable.

The Department of Veterans Affairs had a year-long leadership institute for staff taking on top jobs in the organization. At the end of the year, participants were asked to take ten minutes to tell their fellow participants a story about what they had learned and how it was of benefit to the organization or patients of the VA medical system. The presentations were videotaped, transcribed, and analyzed. Several themes emerged. A follow-up survey was designed to quantify the extent to which these things happened. In the follow-up survey with the fifty-plus participants, my colleagues and I were able to gain quantitative measures of hours worked, levels of satisfaction with various working conditions, and the cost savings resulting from innovations. In this study, the stories guided the follow-up survey.

Reversing the sequence also has merit. Robert Brinkerhoff, in his book *Telling Training's Story* (2006), suggests beginning with a survey and using the survey to identify stories of success. In this situation, the survey helps identify types of stories that will be of greatest interest. Brinkerhoff indicates that training almost never helps 100 percent of the participants to be successful. The survey gives the evaluator an idea of the percentage of success, and the stories describe the nature of the success.

A third strategy is to assemble a collection of stories on a designated theme and then look for patterns and themes. The process begins with the identification of a topic or a question. Stories are collected that fit the topic or question, and analysis is conducted to identify patterns across the stories. What do the stories have in common? How are they different from each other? The collection of stories provides insight for evaluators.

When the University of Minnesota Extension Service listened to stories from their customers, they detected a pattern that later influenced policy. When asked to describe examples of successful experiences, the customers told stories of many different experiences. At first, there didn't seem to be a pattern in the answers. But when enough stories were accumulated, a pattern emerged. The pattern was in the process of receiving help from the extension service. Customers said: "I had a problem; I didn't know how to solve it. I asked an extension worker for help. That person gave me a solution strategy. I applied the solution and it was successful, and now I am grateful for the help I received." What was most distinctive was the type of help. It was personal help from a known individual. The study occurred at a time when the organization was considering a restructuring that would save money by having people find solutions on the Internet instead of with local experts. It seemed unwise to eliminate the key elements that made the organization successful. Box 21.3 presents another example of finding a theme in stories.

Box 21.3. Story Example: ECHO

ECHO is a Christian nonprofit organization that provides support to people working on hunger issues in developing countries. When ECHO staff describe what ECHO does, they often talk about their tree nursery, their seed bank, their team of people who answer technical questions, and their interns who spend a year learning about tropical agriculture: they tended to focus on the scientific, technical features. My colleagues and I gathered stories about ECHO's impact in Haiti from Haitians who had long-term experiences with the organization. We analyzed the stories and found three themes: that ECHO helps cultivate crops, ECHO helps cultivate people, and ECHO helps cultivate visions. Although ECHO staff focused on the technical skills—cultivating crops—they didn't notice that they were also cultivating social skills like networking, community development, and leadership. And they didn't realize that this was changing people's visions of what was possible for Haiti or for themselves. These staff people were changing the hopes and aspirations of people.

A board member said the stories helped the people of ECHO to reframe how they think about what they are doing: "It is the difference between believing you are laying bricks or believing you are building a Cathedral."

A fourth strategy is to capture success stories to depict program outcomes and shed light on the processes that brought about those outcomes.

There are two ways organizations use these stories—for evaluation and marketing. This can be a rub for evaluators who believe that focusing only on success is limiting or feel they are being manipulated to serve the marketing department. Be clear about how decision-makers intend to use these stories and be ready to have conversations about the advantages and disadvantages of gathering stories for evaluation versus marketing.

Success stories are framed in different ways. In one version, the organization is the "hero" of the story. For example, "The university has developed a new early apple variety that is generating X dollars for the state." But most readers don't care about organizations; they care about people. Stories about organizations often come off as insincere, shallow, and contrived.

A better way to tell success stories is to make the client or customer the hero. The apple story is more powerful if it features a grower. "Andy Smith of River Bluff Orchards, which was devastated by September frosts, says a new, early apple variety developed by the university will help him expand his growing season and help keep him in business." In this version, the organization (or a staff member) is the "guide" that helps clients reach their goals. The plot centers on how an individual accomplishes an important goal and moves to a higher level. The story is told from a customer's perspective.

Some "success" stories emphasize a certain component of the total experience:

- A customer describes challenges he or she faced before participating in the program.
- Customers describe how a program helped them change.
- Customers describe how they are different because of a program.
- A staff member describes how customers are helped.
- A staff member describes factors that prevent customers from receiving help.
- A customer doesn't achieve success, but learns an important lesson.

The power of these stories is that they can depict the yearnings, frustrations, and feelings of accomplishment that are difficult to communicate in other forms of data.

A fifth strategy is to use stories to inform future research or evaluation. Occasionally, stories emerge that describe rare events or anomalies. These stories don't fit neatly into other categories. They don't occur with sufficient frequency to allow for pattern identification or content analysis, and yet the stories can inform and enlighten evaluators or researchers. These stories are in a special class because they help us see an issue, a paradox, a dilemma, or a concern. Much of scientific research is based on predictable repetition. But some events are neither predictable nor repetitive, and consequently, they tend to be set aside by researchers when using traditional scientific methods. The work of Elizabeth Mayer in her book *Extraordinary Knowing* (2007) illustrates the conundrum that traditional science has with these stories.

Sometimes a rare event can influence policy. Some colleagues and I were conducting a study on the treatment of veterans suffering from post-traumatic stress disorder. We listened to scores of stories from veterans and family members, and one story was significantly different. A father told a story of his son, a veteran, who would have occasional episodes that, if left untreated, would sometimes escalate to violent behavior. The father could identify the early symptoms and would then take his son to the local veteran's hospital for treatment. The father said that sometimes all the beds in the mental health unit at the hospital were full, and then he was told to take his son to the county jail. The father said that it didn't seem right to take his son to the jail because he wasn't a criminal, he was sick. We heard this story only once, but when we relayed it to officials at the VA medical headquarters, they issued an immediate directive to all VA hospitals in the country mentioning the story and instructing hospital staff that they always have space for PTSD patients and the event in the story should never, ever happen again. Sometimes a unique or rare story reveals an important finding.

A sixth strategy is to use stories to motivate or change behavior. Stories influence people. They change how we think, how we behave, and how we feel toward others. When someone tells a story of how they overcame a barrier and made changes, that story can inspire others to make difficult choices. Researchers and evaluators have begun to use stories as an intervention in health care. Dr. Thomas Houston and his colleagues used stories as an intervention for controlling high blood pressure and found that the stories increased healthy behaviors. Dr. Irene Sia is using stories with recent immigrants to control type 2 diabetes. Local residents describe how they made healthy changes. The hope is the stories inspire and motivate others to make changes. These researchers are discovering that stories influence behavior when two factors are present: the story is told by a community member and the story content describes practical action steps that result in better health.

Table 21.1 compares six story strategies. The evaluator is likely to use differing procedures depending on the purpose of the story process. In some situations, a random sample might be appropriate, but in other cases the random sample can be inefficient and ineffective.

An Overview of Critical Steps

It is important for the evaluator to be careful and thoughtful about the collection of stories. Qualitative evaluation is sometimes discounted because it seems natural and commonplace. It is not intrusive and burdensome to the participants as are written tests, lab exams, or physical measurements. But this naturalness is a result of thoughtful planning. In fact, qualitative evaluation requires the same attention to detail and discipline as quantitative evaluation procedures. But the procedures are different and must be spelled out for the benefit of evaluation colleagues and those who read and use the evaluation reports. Having a written plan allows colleagues to review and critique the effort. It allows improvements to be made, and it ensures that the data gathering, handling, and analysis are consistent and reflect prevailing standards of quality. The credibility of the study will depend on both the story and the process of obtaining the story. The story conveys the message, but it is the process of collecting the story that shows that the story is unbiased, credible, and worthy of consideration. This planning process helps ensure that the evaluation follows accepted protocol.

TABLE 21.1. COMPARING STRATEGIES FOR USING STORIES IN EVALUATION.

	Illustrating Evaluation Data	Complement Surveys	Identifying Patterns	Document Success or Outcomes	Inform Future Research	Motivate or Change Behavior
Objective	Locate a story that illustrates a point uncovered in secondary data	a. Illustrate or amplify a point from a survey b. Provide insight for developing a survey	Discover patterns across a group of stories	Document the success or accomplishments of an organization	Create awareness and insight about people and their experiences	Using stories to motivate people to change behavior
When to Use	Effective for illustrating human aspects of secondary data	Program evaluation, evaluations within organizations or communities	Needs assessment, program monitoring, process evaluation, development of logic models	Use when evidence of accountability is needed or when questions arise about the organization's purpose	These stories are usually not sought out, but arise while searching for stories for other purposes	When evaluating the effectiveness of an intervention in medicine or public health

(Continued)

TABLE 21.1. COMPARING STRATEGIES FOR USING STORIES IN EVALUATION. (Continued)

	Illustrating Evaluation Data	Complement Surveys	Identifying Patterns	Document Success or Outcomes	Inform Future Research	Motivate or Change Behavior
Sampling	Purposeful – typical cases	Random sample or entire population if small	Purposeful (information rich cases)	Purposeful and sometimes random to show extent of success	Varies	Purposeful – from within the target community
Locating the Stories	Nominations, referrals, local contacts, organizational records, and more	a. Stories requested using survey instrument b. Inviting all participants to submit their stories c. Information-rich sample	Purposeful sample of Information-rich cases	Nominations, referrals, and respondents to surveys	Referrals from local sources or key informants	Referrals from local sources or key informants
Analysis Strategy	Obtain a close fit between secondary data and story characteristics	a. Analyze survey and request stories that fit survey data b. Constant comparative identifying patterns	Constant comparative identifying patterns	Stories can be treated as separate cases or for a pattern if multiple cases exist	Stories are treated as separate cases with little or no analysis	Those receiving stories are compared to a control group

Decide on the Evaluation Question or the Topic

Begin by deciding on the question or topic that will guide the entire evaluation. Selecting the question or topic helps the evaluator narrow the field of inquiry. Instead of gathering any and all stories, the evaluator focuses on stories related to a particular question or topic. This topic helps the evaluator focus his or her efforts on finding specific stories, identifying potential storytellers, and formulating specific questions that will elicit the stories. A topic could be examples of success, changes made by clients, things staff do that improve the organization, or things teachers do that change the lives of students. Think of the topic as the fence that keeps in the stories. When you hear a story that fits the topic or addresses the guiding question, it goes into the corral. You will also hear many stories that don't address the topic or the evaluation question, and you will place them elsewhere or set them aside for now. Too many stories make data handling and analysis more difficult and increase costs.

Decide How You Will Use Stories in the Evaluation

Will you use stories to illustrate secondary data? Will you collect stories before or after collecting quantitative data? Will you amass a collection of stories to analyze for patterns and trends? Or will you use stories to provide insights on rare occurrences? You may wish to review Table 21.1 for suggestions on when to use different story strategies.

Decide on a Sampling Strategy

Sampling is important because it affects statements about the representativeness of the stories. Will you gather stories from the entire target population? This is possible and preferred when evaluating a program with a small number of participants. Or will you use a random sample for efficiency and to capture a cross-section of people? Or will you seek information-rich cases and use a purposeful (nonrandom) sample in order to capture insights from a particular group of people? Each of these is an appropriate strategy, but the evaluator must describe why a particular strategy was used and be ready to make a statement about the degree to which the stories represent the experiences of others.

Select a Method for Gathering Stories

Stories can be difficult and labor-intensive to acquire. On a few occasions, you might be able to ask for stories submitted in writing, but more typically, someone will need to go directly to each person and listen to stories over a period of time. Poor-quality stories can be obtained quickly. But great stories take time, patience, and feedback loops. Be ready to invest time to obtain quality. The story collection process might involve having a number of people who purposefully collect stories, or it might involve a strategy of encouraging staff or community members to submit stories. At this planning stage, the evaluator must be eminently practical and thoughtful about how to capture quality stories from the right people with a minimum of time and effort.

Stories can be gathered in a variety of ways. Individual and small-group interviews are often the primary methods. The small focus group has been particularly effective because the stories told help others recall their own stories. I and other researchers have used a variety of other strategies such as site visits, individual reflection and writing, colleagues sharing stories with each other, supervisors asking subordinates to share a story at an upcoming meeting, telephone interviews, and more.

Develop Questions to Elicit Stories and Guide the Storytellers

Getting a story out of a person is harder than it seems. Asking someone to tell you a story will often result in a blank look and a statement that he or she has no stories to tell. So consider questions that encourage people to tell you how something happened, what was meaningful, or what didn't work. Then use probes to gain additional insights as to how he or she felt and other details needed to complete each story.

Decide How You Will Capture the Stories

Most evaluators capture data in a variety of ways. Often, they combine field notes with audio recordings. In some situations, after an initial interview, we have asked for a second interview so we could video certain stories. Consider augmenting the notes and recording with photographs.

Collect the Stories

Collecting the stories sometimes takes more time and effort than you would imagine. Some people you interview will be natural storytellers. They will give you details and images. They will describe their emotions. Their stories will make sense and fit together. You will immediately understand how the story fits your topic and its significance. Other people may not understand what you are looking for. Or they may be reluctant to tell their stories. Or they may remember only bits and pieces. Or they will talk in generalities, which aren't as useful as details. Or dates and details won't seem to jibe. Stay at it. Sometimes my colleagues and I will ask a question several times to see whether it takes the storyteller further each time. Sometimes we will go back to a storyteller to gather more information. In other situations, we seek information from others, such as the storyteller's family members or colleagues.

Decide How to Present the Stories

Stories can emerge from many different environments. Some stories might be written by the storyteller and presented in a careful and logical order. More often, stories are told orally and the flow is haphazard. Occasionally, the story-teller begins at the end, then goes back and fills in earlier aspects of the story. Or the teller might omit critical facts that seem obvious to him or her. When a person is the originator of the story he or she is telling, the story often comes out in pieces and fragments and sometimes not even in chronological order. It may come out in pieces during a two-hour interview or a two-day site visit. It will include incomplete sentences, thoughts, and switchbacks. Not all the data collected can or should be shared in a report. The evaluator needs to assemble the story in writing and put it into a logical and coherent order. But evaluators must be careful to preserve the intent and key elements of the story. Direct quotes and dialogue are included. The evaluator also makes a decision at this point about the framework for the story. Should the story be told in the format originally used or be revised into a different format for clarity and evaluation needs?

Having a consistent outline for stories can greatly simplify the analysis process because then all the stories have a similar structure, and this facilitates comparability. The traditional *story outline* consists of four basic parts. They are the:

- *Background.* Introduce the environment and situation.
- *Problem.* Describe the challenges or problems.
- *Resolution.* Describe how obstacles were overcome (or not).
- *Purpose.* Review the reason for the story.

Analyze the Stories

If you gather a collection of stories, look for patterns and themes that reoccur across the stories. Select labels for these patterns and themes. Identify those stories that you plan to use in your report. In this step, you may need to edit the stories again, using a consistent story outline and including dialogue and emotions, as described in the later section on strategies of expert storytellers.

Verify the Stories You Will Use in Your Reports

A verification process helps ensure that the story as documented and written by the evaluator accurately describes what was intended by the storyteller. Once the story is transferred into a written format, it is presented back to the storyteller for verification. "Is this your story?" "Does it present the story in the way you had intended?" "What changes, if any, would you recommend?" This step ensures that the written story is an accurate rendition of the actual experience.

Decide on the Level of Confidentiality

Not all stories should be retold! Occasionally, the evaluator will hear stories that are sensitive, embarrassing, or uncomfortable. Some stories might relate to undesirable, inappropriate, or illegal behavior. The fact that the evaluator has heard a story doesn't mean the story should be retold. In effect, the evaluator doesn't "own" the story until the storyteller gives it to the evaluator. Interestingly, the storyteller might not be aware of, or sensitive to, the need for confidentiality until the story has been told. I encourage evaluators to ask for permission to use a story and to inquire about the desired level of confidentiality. When permission isn't available, as in cases where the storyteller is repeating someone else's story and the original source of the story is unknown, the evaluator must be cautious and aware of the ethical, moral, and social consequences of releasing the story.

When my colleagues and I first began collecting stories, we thought that confidentiality would take the form of the two levels regularly used by journalists: on the record and off the record. When we encountered the actual stories of people, we found that this two-level system wasn't adequate and we evolved a four-level system:

Level 1: Report story and reveal source.

Level 2: Report story without revealing source.

Level 3: Report general concept, but not details of the story or source.

Level 4: Don't report story, concept, or source.

We prefer Level 1 stories because they offer the greatest flexibility. At Level 1 we can capture audio or video stories in addition to the written stories. The presence of the name adds credibility to the story. Moreover, by citing the source, the researcher is honoring the storyteller and acknowledging his or her contribution.

Some storytellers might be reluctant to have their names attached. They might not like the publicity, or they may perceive that the story might reflect negatively on an individual or the organization. In these Level 2 situations, we follow the traditional promises of confidentiality; that is, we promise that the evaluation team will not reveal the names or details that might reveal the source of the story.

Level 3 stories occur rarely. In these situations, the storyteller may feel that the story itself will reveal the storyteller. For example, if the story is on wrongdoing within an organization, there may be only a few people who are aware of the event and telling the story would compromise their confidentiality. So the storyteller might feel that, if the story were to be told to others, he or she would be identified. In these situations, we agree not to use the story and instead describe it in general terms that mask the identity of the storyteller.

When it comes to Level 4 stories, the storyteller has considerable concerns about the consequences of having the story retold. In some situations the concern is that the story will identify the storyteller, but there might be other concerns as well. Sometimes the concern is to protect the organization, the community, or a family, and the story has been told only to provide background and offer insight for the evaluator. A storyteller might be reluctant to share a story for a number of reasons: fear, embarrassment, propriety, modesty, and so forth. Stories told at this level tie the hands of the evaluator and make it more difficult for the evaluator to communicate the findings of the study. Sensitivity is needed with these stories, and sometimes the evaluator can make modifications that allow the story to be moved to a less problematic level.

Describe Representativeness

Evaluators need to be mindful of common questions asked about stories, such as: "Is this story typical?" or "How often do stories like this occur?" This concern makes evaluation and research stories a bit different from other types of stories. The listener often wants to place the story into a larger context and know whether it was typical or an anomaly.

The evaluator should anticipate these questions and be ready to make a statement. The response could take several forms. One approach is to give an overview of the methodology. You might describe how you obtained the story, the number of stories that were collected, and whether this story fit a pattern. Did the storyteller indicate that this story was similar to that of others? Or did experts indicate that the story was similar or different from stories they've heard from this audience? Or how do the demographic characteristics of the storyteller compare to those of the target audience?

If the issue of representativeness is important, the evaluator can conduct a follow-up survey with the target population. This survey can provide insight as to how often others have experienced certain elements of the story. In some situations, this follow-up survey can provide additional insights, such as the consequences, the follow-up actions taken, or how others have coped with similar situations.

Deal with the Concept of Truth

The evaluator cannot determine the truth of a story. In the process of telling stories, sometimes an individual embellishes or adds to the actual details. As people say, the fish that got away gets larger as the angler gets farther from the lake. For a variety of reasons, stories are changed. Sometimes the change is intentional in order to provide background, context, or entertainment. The storyteller might add, omit, or rearrange the facts to make the story more interesting. In other situations, the storyteller might not recall important facts or may choose to invent details. So the storyteller might be unaware or unconcerned that the story has changed. But the evaluator should be attentive to this issue and be cautious about stories that change or seem to be fabrications.

Motivational speakers routinely tell stories to illuminate, inspire, and entertain. They are less concerned with whether these stories are factual and more concerned with how each story influences the audience. Evaluators are different. The evaluator has to be prepared to make a statement about how the story was collected and to provide insight about the truthfulness of the story.

The evaluator can do a number of things to make this task manageable. First, it must be understood that in most cases the evaluator cannot prove the truthfulness of the story. But the evaluator can report what is known about the storyteller and the story itself. The evaluator ought to be able to make a statement about the truthfulness of the story. This statement might simply be: "The storyteller said the story was her own personal experience." "The storyteller said it was true." Or "Others verified the story and said that it was a true account." Or "I was told the story, but I do not know whether it is true." What is important is that the researcher has thought about this issue and can make a statement.

This means that the evaluator must be attentive when the story is first told. In many situations, the storyteller is telling about a personal experience and it is assumed to be true. But if the story is about another person, then the researcher might ask for more information about the story. Did the storyteller know the person involved in the story? How did the storyteller hear the story? By asking a few questions, the researcher seeks to determine the degree of confidence he or she can have that the story is factual.

Document Your Strategy

The process of collecting, handling, and analyzing stories ought to be transparent. Evaluators must describe their protocol, have processes where others can see and understand how the stories are handled, and use care in providing the proper level of confidentiality. How did the evaluator go about soliciting stories? Who was invited to share a story? What were the criteria for selecting those individuals?

Unfortunately, sometimes evaluators do not provide adequate documentation on their methods and decisions, and this can lead to suspicions of bias or omission of critical data. Transparency should be achieved by providing details to interested parties before, during, and after the stories are collected. To protect the confidentiality of the storytellers, the evaluator might consider two levels of transparency. One level, which is available only to other evaluators on the study team, allows access to confidential data on the characteristics of the storyteller and details surrounding the story. The second level is intended for other interested parties, including the public, and has access to the story materials and reports in a manner respectful of the confidentiality wishes of the storyteller.

Strategies of Expert Storytellers: Presenting the Story Effectively

Storytellers have been around for a long time. Over the centuries they have developed certain strategies that make their stories effective. When rewriting and retelling evaluation stories, include these elements to make the stories work. Here are eight elements suggested by such masters of storytelling as Joseph Campbell (1949), Jon Franklin (1986), Andy Goodman (2009), Doug Lipman (1999), Richard Maxwell and Robert Dickman (2007), and John Walsh (2003).

1. Stories Are About a Person, Not an Organization

One of the big mistakes researchers make in evaluation studies is focusing on the organization or program instead of the people. Stories should be about people and, more precisely, about a person. Tell your audience about the individual, not the crowd, the program, the organization, the corporation, or the community. Tell them how that individual feels, thinks, and acts. Stories are rooted in emotions. Emotions interest an audience. Organizations don't have emotions. As a result, organizational stories often fall flat.

2. Stories Have a Hero, an Obstacle, a Struggle, and a Resolution

Stories often have a plot. A person is the center of action—a hero. This person has a problem or an obstacle he or she wants to overcome. It might be a goal he wants to attain, or a dilemma, or a person who gets in the hero's way. The hero takes some action or struggles in some way. Then there is an outcome or resolution and the story concludes with a message learned from the experience. Many stories have these ingredients. Consider including them in your evaluation story.

3. Set the Stage for the Story

Stories begin with important background information that sets the stage and helps the listener understand the context. This background gives the audience insight about what has happened previously, the context of the story, or other critical factors that make the story important. This information prepares the reader or listener to receive the message of the story. It may be as short as a phrase or a sentence or as long as a paragraph.

4. The Story Unfolds

As the story begins, the tension starts to develop. The key actors are identified, and the hero takes action. Remember, the story is not about policies, procedures, or organizational events. It is about a person who is doing something that makes a difference.

5. Emotions Are Described

The listener or reader wants to know how the hero feels. Tell your audience what the hero was thinking and how that influenced his or her action. Use descriptive language to convey feelings.

6. Dialogue Adds Richness

As the story unfolds, certain elements add richness. Include short conversations or insightful quotes from the key players. Consider repeating an especially important quote, and if repeating it orally, say it a bit slower to capture the meaning of the statement.

7. Suspense and Surprise Add Interest

Expert storytellers use suspense and surprise to hold the attention of the audience. These elements delight the listener and make the story memorable. The suspense is deliberate, to maintain the attention of the listener, and the surprise evokes humor, relief, or resolution to the conflict.

8. Key Message Is Revealed

Finally, the story concludes with the key message. This is the reason for the story. The statement must be short and memorable. Consider saying it twice for emphasis. For example, in the story about medical mistakes in Box 21.2, the final sentence of the story was: "We watch what happens when someone reports a medical mistake. If they crash and burn, then the rest of us change our behavior accordingly." You might repeat the last sentence for emphasis: "If they crash and burn, then the rest of us change our behavior accordingly."

These eight elements are often used by expert storytellers. They add interest and power to the story. Evaluators ought to consider these best practices and incorporate these elements in their evaluation stories.

Challenges in Using Stories and How to Manage Them

Using stories is easier if you can anticipate the typical difficulties and plan accordingly. Here are some of the challenges that I and other researchers have encountered.

Using stories often takes more time than anticipated. Not every person has a story and not every story can be used for evaluation purposes. It takes considerable time to seek out the stories, and to edit them and convert them into written form.

Stories are dismissed as "mere anecdotes." Be ready to explain why the story is relevant, why decision-makers should pay attention to the story, and why the story has meaning. Describe the process used in obtaining the story, handling the story, and verifying the story and what the story represents. Describe how the story is a product of disciplined inquiry.

It takes skill to find the stories—to actually get them out of people. There is an art to getting others to tell their stories. Some are reluctant or hesitant to share their experiences, and others might not think they even have a story to tell. Still others can't remember. The evaluator in search of stories needs to make people feel comfortable and respected, to engage people in conversation, ask interesting questions, listen attentively, and probe carefully. Interestingly, my colleagues and I have found that it is better to avoid asking for a "story" because it locks up people's memory. Instead, you can ask people to "tell me about. . . ."

Sometimes the evaluator's search may not find meaningful stories. Sometimes people are unable to remember stories, and sometimes there just are no stories of interest. Don't expect that there will be stories for every program or activity.

It often takes editing to develop powerful and memorable stories. When in search of stories, you will find that some are irrelevant, many are trivial, and a few hold promise. Often stories that show promise require editing to sharpen the point. Anticipate that the editing will continue until the story effectively and clearly conveys the point of the storyteller. Expect to invest time in such editing. It has been my observation that researchers aren't natural storytellers. Training and practice in storytelling can be helpful.

There is a temptation to focus on success stories. Lately, there has been a push to gather success stories to depict program outcomes. Program managers tend to overvalue these stories and overlook stories of lessons learned. The problem with success stories is that the organization might acquire an unrealistic view of the frequency and magnitude of success. The intent of the organizational manager might be to convey the success of the organization, but the public might regard the story with skepticism.

A Final Thought

Searching for stories is like looking for fossils. You suspect that they are out there, but you don't know exactly where to look. To find them you don't look just anywhere; rather, you go to places where fossils are likely to be found. It is not a random search but rather a purposeful effort. The fossils are rare and it takes effort to locate them. It takes talent and skill to recognize the fossil, understand its significance, and explain its importance to others. Others might have walked by the fossil many times and not recognized its value. The goal is not so much to collect as many fossils as possible but rather to find meaningful fossils that shed light on a species or provide rich insight.

Conclusion

The use of stories in evaluation studies offers considerable potential. Stories are memorable and convey emotions. People have a natural interest in stories. Stories can be used in a variety of ways; evaluators might offer a series of stories on a theme, use stories before or after a survey, or use a story to illustrate data obtained in other ways or to describe a unique or rare event. Evaluators must attend to the story-collection process to make stories credible in the evaluation environment. In addition, evaluators can learn critical elements from professional storytellers that will help them communicate effectively.

References

Brinkerhoff, R. O. *Telling Training's Story*. San Francisco, CA: Berrett-Koehler, 2006.

Campbell, J. *The Hero with a Thousand Faces*. Princeton, NJ: Princeton University Press, 1949.

Franklin, J. *Writing for Story*. New York: Plume, 1986.

Goodman, A. "Telling Stories." *BoardSource*, Mar.–Apr. 2009, *18*(2), 2–3.

Houston, T. K., Allison, J. J., Sussman, M., Horn, W., Holt, C. L., Trobaugh, J., Sales, M., et al. "Culturally Appropriate Storytelling to Improve Blood Pressure." *Annals of Internal Medicine*, 2011, *154*(2), 77–84.

Lipman, D. *Improving Your Storytelling*. Little Rock, AK: August House, 1999.

Mayer, E. L. *Extraordinary Knowing*. New York: Bantam, 2007.

Maxwell, R., and Dickman, R. *The Elements of Persuasion*. New York: HarperCollins, 2007.

Nyhan, P. "College Divide Threatens to Keep the Poor in Poverty." *Seattle Post-Intelligencer*. Sept. 27, 2005.

Walsh, J. *The Art of Storytelling*. Chicago, IL: Moody, 2003.

Further Reading

Patton, M. Q. *Qualitative Research and Evaluation Methods* (4th ed.). Thousand Oaks, CA: Sage, 2014.

PART THREE

DATA ANALYSIS

The time to think about how data will be analyzed and reported is early in evaluation planning. Conceptualizing what the audience for an evaluation will desire in terms of analytical sophistication and precision can help evaluators select among the many techniques available. Mapping out what the end product should look like provides some of the structure needed to guide planning of analysis procedures.

Constraints on evaluators' choices among analytical options go beyond what their clients will expect in reports, however. Time and resources will affect the types of data collected and, thus, the sorts of analytical techniques that can be used. In many cases, evaluators must rely on data that others have collected or on the formats that others prefer for further data collection efforts. Evaluators' skills in effectively applying and reporting analytical techniques may also limit the possibilities for analysis of evaluation data.

The Chapters

The chapters in Part Three present techniques for analyzing data collected in evaluation efforts. The four chapters cover (1) analysis and interpretation of data collected through qualitative data collection techniques such as interviews and site visits; (2) selection, application, and reporting of quantitative statistical techniques, including regression analysis; (3) the use of cost-effectiveness and cost-benefit techniques in program evaluation; and (4) analysis and synthesis of previously conducted evaluations.

The authors of these chapters describe analytical techniques in nontechnical terms to clarify the relative advantages and disadvantages of the various options. In each chapter the authors describe the purpose of the analytical strategies and the types of evaluation questions that are most amenable to the application of each strategy, the assumptions or requirements of the data and the data collection methods that must be met to use each analytical technique effectively, the sorts of information that should be provided in reports about application of each technique, and the possible limitations that may accompany application of the techniques.

Delwyn Goodrick and Patricia Rogers, in Chapter Twenty-Two, discuss strategies for analyzing qualitative data collected through observation, examination of documents, and interviews. They provide a useful overview of four sets of methods for qualitative data analysis: enumerative, descriptive, hermeneutic, and explanatory.

Data analysis activities discussed include performing content analysis, abstracting and transforming raw data during the data collection process, developing data displays organizing the data, and drawing and verifying conclusions during and after data collection. The authors explain how to accomplish each of these qualitative data analysis activities and list references that provide further guidance. The authors also suggest several approaches that evaluators can use to strengthen the credibility, generalizability, and objectivity of qualitative evaluation efforts—for example, triangulation, peer debriefing, informant feedback, and using auditors to assess the evaluation process and product.

Kathryn Newcomer and Dylan Conger, in Chapter Twenty-Three, describe a variety of statistical techniques available to evaluators. They identify the most important issues that evaluators should address when applying statistical techniques to strengthen the conclusions drawn from the findings. They describe basic distinctions among statistical techniques, outline procedures for drawing samples and applying statistical tools, provide criteria for evaluators to use in choosing among the data analysis techniques available, and offer guidance on reporting statistics appropriately and clearly. Illustrations of the application of the chi-square test and the t test are provided. They also demonstrate how regression analysis can be applied to evaluate the results of a program. They introduce the basic regression model and define all the basic concepts in clear terms. In addition, they offer guidance on using data visualization to report quantitative data analyses.

Stephanie Riegg Cellini and James Kee, in Chapter Twenty-Four, offer guidance on the application of cost-effectiveness and benefit-cost techniques in program evaluation. They outline opportunities to apply the various options, along with the issues evaluators must address should they select one of these techniques. The authors provide guidance to evaluators as they describe cost-effectiveness analysis and its capabilities, differentiate among the various types of benefits and costs that should be arrayed in any benefit-cost analysis, offer suggestions on the valuation and measurement of benefits and costs, identify common problems in cost-effectiveness and benefit-cost analyses, and provide guidance on presenting information to decision makers.

And in Chapter Twenty-Five, Robert Boruch, Anthony Petrosino, and Claire Morgan describe how to systematically review and analyze the results of previously conducted evaluations. They clarify the differences in the analytical methods used in three types of summaries: meta-analyses, systematic reviews, and research syntheses. They discuss the benefits that can be derived from employing all three approaches, noting in general that careful use of these techniques can help evaluators determine where good evidence has been produced on the effects of interventions, where good evidence is absent, and where the evidence is ambiguous. They offer practical advice on the logistics and resources required and the potential obstacles encountered with each approach. They also identify many valuable resources.

The chapter authors in Part Three carefully delineate the issues evaluators should address as they select analytical techniques and report the results of analyses. They discuss factors affecting such decisions and the potential threats to the validity of results provided in evaluation reports. Replicability with the assurance of consistent results is the hallmark of valid and appropriate data analysis. Evaluators need to acknowledge analytical choices and unanticipated obstacles to help ensure that results are interpreted appropriately.

CHAPTER TWENTY-TWO

QUALITATIVE DATA ANALYSIS

Delwyn Goodrick, Patricia J. Rogers

Most evaluations include some qualitative (non-numeric) material, such as open-ended responses in questionnaires, interview data—in the form of transcripts, notes, audio or video tapes—and textual data from existing documentation, such as policy documents and meeting minutes. Many evaluations also include visual types of qualitative data, such as photographs and images, and newer forms of qualitative products include materials generated in social media, such as tweets and posts. Some evaluations use solely qualitative data to draw conclusions, some use qualitative data in a supplementary role to complement quantitative data, and some give equal weight to qualitative and quantitative data in an integrated mixed-method approach.

Qualitative data allow readers to gain an understanding that goes beyond descriptive and inferential statistics. For example, although it may be useful to incorporate a count of how many young people in a mentoring program gained new skills, a more comprehensive understanding of the program is achieved from paying attention to how the young people describe their experience of learning new skills, and the way they connect their participation in the program with these outcomes. Qualitative data can provide deep insights into how programs or policies work or fail to work and more compelling accounts of the reasons for success and failure.

The value of qualitative data in program evaluation is well established. It can be challenging, however, to know what to do with the data generated from qualitative approaches, particularly for the evaluator who has little experience with qualitative data analysis. Within the constraints of tight timelines, evaluators must make sense of the material, analyze and synthesize it, and communicate the findings to others in ways that are clear, informative, credible, and useful.

This chapter provides an overview of four different ways to analyze qualitative data and provides advice about how to choose methods of analysis that address the purpose of the evaluation. It provides particular advice on how to code qualitative data in ways that are suit the type of analysis needed.

Types of Evaluation and Analytic Purpose

Evaluations are organized around key evaluation questions, and a particular form of analysis may address one or more of these questions. Qualitative data can be used across the full spectrum of evaluation types, such as needs assessment, program theory, process, and impact evaluation. While less common, qualitative data can be used in performance monitoring and economic evaluation.

Qualitative data can complement quantitative data, or can stand alone. Table 22.1 outlines the respective use of qualitative and quantitative data according to the type of evaluation being conducted.

Coding Data

Qualitative data analysis often involves sorting data into categories and labeling the categories. These categories are sometimes referred to as codes, nodes, or tags.

The coding process can be done in various ways, from structured processes with codes assigned a priori and applied to the data, to emergent coding frameworks that identify codes directly from the data. There are many options that may be undertaken in coding. Evaluators must think critically about these options and make reasoned choices. Particular methods of analysis may require formalized coding strategies. In later sections of this chapter we talk about different ways of coding data that suit the type of analysis being undertaken

Box 22.1 provides a definition of the distinctions we make between coding and categorizing processes.

TABLE 22.1. USES OF QUALITATIVE AND QUANTITATIVE DATA IN DIFFERENT TYPES OF EVALUATION.

Type of Evaluation	Common Uses of Qualitative Data	Common Uses of Quantitative Data
Needs Assessment/Situation Analysis (including strengths as well as needs)	In-depth understanding of people's experiences and needs Evocative description of people's situations Identification and documentation of problems and resources through photography or stories	Measuring the extent of needs and resources through social indicators and population surveys
Program Theory	Stakeholders' mental models of how programs or policies work Qualitative evidence (discrete or synthesized) from impact evaluations about effective programs and causal mechanisms	Quantitative evidence (discrete or synthesized) from impact evaluations about effective programs and causal mechanisms
Process Evaluation	Documenting the processes and implementation context of an innovation so it can be reproduced Periodic discussion and reflection on how things are going and how they might be improved Checking compliance with best practice/ quality standards using expert or peer review	Checking compliance with best practice/ quality standards using standardized measures of standardized processes
Performance Monitoring	Collection and review of qualitative performance measures Monitoring qualitative indicators over time	Collection and review of predetermined quantitative performance measures and indicators
Impact Evaluation	Exploration of a range of impacts (including unintended and unanticipated) and what they mean to participants Research designs that use historical information for causal attribution Values clarification, concept mapping of what is valued Realist synthesis of diverse evidence	Standardized impact measures and experimental and quasi-experimental research designs Statistical meta-analysis of effect sizes

TABLE 22.1. USES OF QUALITATIVE AND QUANTITATIVE DATA IN DIFFERENT TYPES OF EVALUATION. *(Continued)*

Type of Evaluation	Common Uses of Qualitative Data	Common Uses of Quantitative Data
Economic Evaluation	Documenting the costs and benefits incurred by all groups (including negative outcomes) that cannot be quantified or monetized. Exploring what is valued by different groups	Quantifying costs and benefits and calculating the ratio of costs to benefits, or the cost for achieving a given level of effectiveness.

Box 22.1. Coding vs. Categorizing

- A **code** is a descriptive word or phrase that is intended to describe a fragment of data. For example, a segment of interview text could include multiple codes, participant role, length of time in the program, excitement about the program.
- A **category** is formed from the review of a cluster of codes. A category incorporates a collection of codes that relate to the same issue, topic, or feature in the data. For example, coded segments that relate to a participant's view of the program could be clustered together and examined. They could be further categorized as positive perceptions and negative perceptions and information sorted into each category. Categories can be theory led and developed a priori to be applied to the data or generated from an examination of the data (emergent or empirical categories). In evaluation, there is likely to be a combination of a priori and empirical categories based on the program theory or conceptual framework of the program being evaluated
- A **theme** is the outcome of categorizing and reflection by the evaluator on salient patterns in the data. Themes can be identified a priori (theory led) or inductively generated from examination of the data corpus. Themes are not a restatement of the key questions asked in an interview. "Perceptions of the program" is not a theme, and it is misleading to indicate that thematic analysis was undertaken if the evaluator has merely organized data under headings. Themes are often at a higher level of abstraction referring beyond what participants' stated to the meanings derived from the comparison of participant interviews. For example, "being invisible" may be identified as a theme that was drawn from an analysis of participants' stories or patterns noted in the data, but it may be that no participant actually used the term "invisible."

Analysis, including the coding processes that form part of it, requires hard thinking and dedicated space and time. It is difficult to retain the focus you will need if your analytic efforts are constantly being interrupted. Set clear time aside for coding and analysis. You will be more likely to have analytic breakthroughs when you persevere with the hard cognitive work of coding and analysis and limit interruptions.

Analysis and writing go hand in hand, so begin writing early. It may be useful to develop a working draft of the key evaluation questions and the relevant material/data that will address these questions. It is important to go back to the original data collection matrix to re-orient yourself to the intended purpose of the interviews (or other qualitative material that have been collected) and their relationship to the key evaluation questions.

The questions below (adapted from Baptiste, 2001) may assist decisions about coding and categorization processes.

Coding

1. When will I begin coding? Will I collect all the data and then start coding, or will I code as I collect data?
2. Will I use a software package or code manually?
3. Would it be useful to develop a number of categories (based on key evaluation questions or program theory) to assist in initial classification before I begin analysis, or will I rely on developing categories from the data as I review it?
4. Will it be useful to code by proceeding through each transcript or record, or would it be preferable to code in parallel (classifying and comparing responses to the same question across transcripts or records, or across stakeholder groups?
5. How detailed should the coding be? Will I code every data element that seems of interest or only code those directly related to the evaluation question.
6. How will the reliability of team coding be assessed? Will inter rater reliability be calculated or, will we adopt more interpretive processes to discuss and review coding structures?

Categorizing

1. How will I cluster codes into categories?
2. Is there an appropriate balance of categories? Is the level of categorization useful in informing analysis rather than being overwhelming?
3. Have I classified all the relevant data, or been overly selective in what I have classified?
4. Is each category linked to data elements and codes? Is there evidence for classification as a category? What are my decision rules?
5. Do my memos link codes and categories back to the context?

6. How will I move from categories to themes? How will I ensure I adequately link categories and themes to ensure that the written account is not fragmented?

Overview of Qualitative Analytic Methods

Across the wide range of methods for analyzing qualitative data, we have identified a useful heuristic to classify different methods. Each method of analysis has a primary focus and purpose. *Enumerative methods* turn qualitative data into numbers by sorting the data into a coding framework, tallying the data, and then developing categories. *Descriptive methods* show how concepts and entities are related by displaying them in tables or diagrams. *Hermeneutic methods* focus on identifying and eliciting manifest and latent meanings in the data. *Explanatory methods* generate and test theories about cause and effect relationships. An evaluation might use a number of these methods for analyzing different data or for analyzing the same data in different ways.

As the use of qualitative approaches has grown, there has been a corresponding growth in the nomenclature used to define and describe the methods, and variants in application and use of the methods across disciplines. The boundaries between the methods is not sharp, but we believe that the classification is helpful in making sense of the variety of potential strategies to analyze data, and that this classification can inform decisions about the most appropriate ones to address evaluation questions.

Table 22.2 shows examples of methods in each group according to purpose; methods in bold are discussed in more detail in later sections of this chapter. While there is overlap of methods across purposes, for example matrix displays may also be used for hermeneutic and explanatory purposes, we classify the methods by their primary use as documented in the literature and in evaluation studies.

In the sections that follow, we discuss the purpose of each method, and provide a description of an example that uses a particular method. We provide more detail about hermeneutic methods and explanatory methods. We focus on these, as hermeneutic methods are a common priority in qualitative evaluation contexts. Explanatory methods are also highlighted, as qualitative comparative analysis is gaining popularity in program evaluation to address causal evaluation questions, but there is limited information on the method in evaluation contexts.

Enumerative Methods

Overview   Enumerative methods focus on categorizing qualitative materials so that they can be analyzed quantitatively. As for any analysis method, these

TABLE 22.2. FOUR GROUPS OF METHODS FOR ANALYSIS OF QUALITATIVE DATA.

Primary Purpose	Description	Examples of Methods
Enumerative	Summarizing data in terms of discrete and often a priori categories that can be displayed and analyzed quantitatively	**Classical Content Analysis (Krippendorf, 2013)** Word count Cultural domain analysis (pile sorts, free lists) (Spradley, 1980) Ethnographic decision models (Gladwin, 1989)
Descriptive	Describing how concepts and issues are related	**Matrix Displays (Miles, Huberman, and Saldana, 2014)** Timelines Concept maps/mind maps (Trochim, 1989) Template/framework analysis (Crabtree and Miller, 1999; Ritchie and Spencer, 1994)
Hermeneutic	Identifying or eliciting meanings, patterns and themes	**Thematic Analysis (Boyatzis, 1998)** Constant Comparative method (Strauss and Corbin, 1998) Thematic narrative analysis (Riessman, 2008) Framework analysis (Ritchie and Spencer, 1994) Discourse analysis (Wetherell, Taylor, and Yates, 2001) Qualitative content analysis (Schreier, 2012)
Explanatory	Generating and testing causal explanations	**Qualitative Comparative Analysis (Ragin, 1987)** Process Tracing (Collier, 2011)

methods are only appropriate for particular purposes and for particular types of data. While these methods can highlight patterns in data, they are a good option for analysis of open-ended survey questions and/or analysis of existing documentation or program records. This method can be used to analyze existing data (such as project documentation) or data created for an evaluation (such as transcripts of interviews). Enumeration is not recommended when the data is rich or detailed, as it tends to be overly reductionist and can decontextualize or distort the meaning.

Example Enumerative Method: Classical Content Analysis Classic content analysis is an example of an enumerative method of analysis, often used to analyze existing textual material such as newspaper reports or social media. Content analysis can involve examining the data for:

- Presence of absence of particular words, phrases, concepts, indicative of knowledge or awareness,
- Frequency in which an idea or concept is used, which may indicate importance or emphasis,
- The number of favorable and unfavorable words assigned to the idea, which may be evidence of attitudes about the program,
- .The nature of qualifications made in the text that may point to intensity or uncertainty of beliefs and motivations, and
- The frequency of co-occurrence of two ideas, which may indicate associations between particular concepts or ideas. (Krippendorf, 2013)

The key steps to classical content analysis are presented below.

1. Clarify the purpose for using content analysis.
2. Determine the population and sample of texts/documents that will be analyzed. Sometimes it is possible to access and analyze an entire population (for example, all documented policies, or all tweets with a particular hashtag) and other times a random or purposeful sample is used.
3. Identify the unit of analysis to be categorized. The unit can be an entire document or a section of a document, depending on how it is to be analyzed. For example, is the purpose to identify what percentage of policy documents referred to a specific issue? Or to count how many times a particular policy issue was referenced?
4. Develop an initial coding framework This may be deductively driven (categories are developed from an existing conceptual framework derived from previous research or policy documents) or inductively generated (categories are identified from text statements present in the material). An initial draft can be developed and then modified as new issues arise when coding and categorizing. Formal decision rules for coding should be developed to ensure common definitional criteria are adopted and to maximize the reliability of coding processes. It may be helpful to develop a codebook for this purpose.
5. Test and revise the coding system. In classical content analysis inter-rater reliability can be calculated for teams involved in coding. Each member of the team is asked to code segments of text, and the coded segments are then compared for consistency across team members or raters. Further

training or testing is performed until sufficient reliability is attained. While there is no established standard of reliability in content analysis Krippendorf suggests that tentative conclusions are possible with a reliability coefficient between .67 and .80. In more interpretive approaches to inter-coder reliability, a co-efficient need not be calculated, but agreements and disagreements in coding should be discussed and addressed. This process of checking the reliability of coding is known as consensual coding.

6. Code the data set. Apply the coding scheme to the data, identifying any issues arising where the codebook has to be modified. While the coding framework informs coding and classification, it is important to be open to other codes that emerge from the subsequent review of materials.

7. Summarize and present the findings. Once the data have been satisfactorily coded, the frequencies can be analyzed using various quantitative analysis methods, including frequency tables, graphs, univariate, bivariate, and multivariate statistics. If a random sample has been drawn, and an adequate response rate achieved, inferential statistics can be used to infer the characteristics of the population of documents, people or sites from which the sample has been drawn.

Good reporting of enumerative analysis includes transparency about the categories that have been used, and documentation of what has been coded under each category.

Application

An experimental project by the United Nations Global Pulse Lab, in conjunction with the Indonesian government, UNICEF, and the World Food Program, explored whether tweets could be used to provide real-time warnings of increases in food prices (UN Global Pulse, 2014). The dataset included all publicly available tweets from March 2011 to April 2013 (Figure 22.1), which were mined using the social media monitoring platform, ForSight. Tweets in Bahasa, Indonesia, were selected and then screened to only include those that included the keywords "harga" (price) and "naik" (rise) along with one or more food commodities. These 113,386 tweets were then classified as being either positive, negative, confused, or no emotion, initially manually and then by an algorithm. The monthly totals were compared to the official prices (for calibration) and the daily totals were graphed and compared to historical events and information from key informants. The trial showed that the tweets provided reliable evidence of increases in beef and chicken but not onions—giving agencies early warning of potential crises in food security.

FIGURE 22.1. DAILY TWEETS ABOUT FOOD PRICE RISES (MARCH 2011–APRIL 2013).

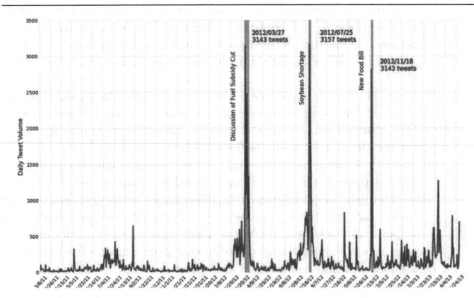

Enumerative analysis of the data was appropriate for this example because the purpose was to understand frequency, and the comparisons with official prices and local information showed that the data could usefully be analyzed in this way. A small set of keywords consistently identified the tweets of interest, and the high usage of Twitter among Internet users in Indonesia (Semiocast, 2012) meant there was adequate data about changes in food prices

Other trials have not always been so successful. Whereas initial analysis of reports of influenza symptoms on twitter had shown good correlation with actual reported cases, and provided early warning before official data were available (Paul and Dredze, 2011), later analysis of Google searches for the Google Flu Trends website overestimated incidence because the algorithms did not take account of heightened media coverage of flu outbreaks, so that searches were a poor indicator of incidence (Claburn, 2013).

When These Methods Are Appropriate

Enumerative methods are appropriate when the purpose of the analysis is to understand frequency. The sampling strategy and data collection process needs to have been designed for this purpose. These methods are also useful for categorizing open-ended responses on surveys. Frequency counts of the most or least identified topics will provide an indication of the prevalence of a topic. The evaluator still needs to pay attention to issues of survey quality, ensuring that the analysis is combined with a discussion of response rate and proportion of respondents that provided open ended responses.

Enumeration is not appropriate for analyzing data from a focus group discussion, where the purpose has been to explore different dimensions, not to calculate frequencies. Even reporting results in terms of "most people said." is not appropriate when the sample has been drawn for maximum diversity not for representativeness.

The categories must be able to be consistently and defensibly defined. Conclusions about what is the most common response will depend in part on how the responses are categorized. A broader category, for example, coding Greek and Italian responses under European, will appear to have a higher frequency than more specific categorization, for example by country. The evaluator must be confident about having coded the text accurately, which may require existing cultural knowledge or a review of the coding by content experts.

Enumerative approaches will be suitable if the evaluator has a large amount of qualitative data and clear categories for enumeration. The method can be persuasive to audiences interested in the salience and frequency of particular comments. The clear decision rules about categorization and the identification of discrete labels for enumeration mean the process is replicable.

Enumerative methods may also be potentially useful when the evaluation has generated thin data across a number of dimensions. In some cases, enumerative techniques may be the only possible option. For example, Del was asked to analyze interviews conducted by doctors with other doctors who had completed a quality improvement initiative. Following a review of the data, it was clear that most of the questions were closed-ended (for example, Did the initiative improve your practice?) or scaled (To what extent do you think that. . .?), to which the interviewee had responded with dichotomous answers. The only reasonable option for analysis was to count the frequencies of responses to particular questions and groups of questions and display these with illustrative quotes, where these were available. We believe that it would be unwise to rely on these methods if the evaluation data is rich and detailed, for example, when you have collected narratives or stories of change or have lengthy descriptive interviews, and your purpose is to elaborate the meanings.

The use of enumeration of qualitative data can be controversial in evaluation contexts. It is sometimes used when it is not appropriate—and some qualitative evaluators do not see them as being appropriate at all for analyzing qualitative data. It is understandable therefore that the conditions for their use need to be clearly assessed and justified for their use (see, for example, Patton's [2014] rumination 'Keep qualitative data qualitative').

One of the cautions when using these approaches is that they presume decisions about the frequency and concordance of words/terms can be determined by the evaluator. There may be little opportunity to check the meaning with evaluation participants. Counting words or terms can also be misleading, as participants will have a range of ways of expressing their views and use vocabulary that fits their intention, but that may be interpreted very differently by the evaluator. For example, if a participant describes a program as "wicked," does this communicate enthusiastic approval or strong disapproval, and does the participant's age suggest the meaning intended? It may require specialist knowledge to understand the intended meaning of participant statements. If this knowledge is not present in the evaluation team, some form of checking will be needed. (We discuss member checking or respondent validation in a later section.)

Evaluators using enumerative methods of data analysis tend to privilege quality criteria that are associated with traditional scientific criteria such as inter-rater reliability of coding of units that will be enumerated and independence of coding and assessment process.

Descriptive Methods

Overview.   Descriptive methods of analysis focus on summarizing the information into a form that can then be compared and contrasted. We acknowledge that there is no such thing as pure description, but the function and form of these types of methods is to provide a strong descriptive account of materials gathered during an evaluation. While enumerative methods are descriptive, our classification of these methods as descriptive indicates that the intended focus and product is not enumeration.

Description is at the heart of good analysis and interpretation. As evaluators we must adequately describe the available data that has formed the basis of evaluative interpretations, conclusions, and judgments. Descriptive methods can be valuable for recording and analyzing fieldwork observations and interview and focus group data.

Example of Descriptive Method: Matrix Displays.   A common analytic choice often associated with descriptive methods in evaluation is matrix displays.

Matrix displays can be used for descriptive, hermeneutic, and explanatory purposes, but our focus here on their use for describing and displaying qualitative data.

Miles, Huberman, and Saldana (2014) outlined a range of displays, with the most common being identified as either a matrix (table) or network and relational diagrams.

Matrices are formed by intersecting variables or labels of interest and presenting these in a table. The evaluator identifies the dimensions for comparison and then uses the data to populate the cells. Cells in the matrix can be raw data or summaries of statements. Matrices may allow comparisons across evaluation participants or sites, and can be used to organize and display data by type (that is, interviews, observations). For example, in a role-ordered matrix, the row headings may be the stakeholder role (nurse, surgeon, social worker) with the columns indicating responses to structured or semi-structured interview questions. In a time-ordered matrix, the evaluator may classify data according to the program timeframe to show change or progress over time in several sites implementing a new program. It is clear that some form of coding and categorizing is required to determine the content of the cells.

Network models or diagrams display and organize observations, data, or events in relationship to each other. Hierarchical tree diagrams can depict relationships among particular concepts or dimensions. These types of diagrams emphasize the power of visual displays in contributing to understanding. When included in evaluation reports, they assist readers in making the links between the evidence collected and key claims.

Steps to Develop Matrix Displays

1. Clarify the purpose for using matrix displays or network diagrams.
2. Assess the data types and sources available and consider the way these data types and sources can be displayed. Matrices can be developed during data collection in the form of templates that can be filled in by the evaluation team, or be developed post–data collection to display and summarize key findings.
3. Identify categorization and classification options. Identify the type of matrix that will be most useful given the evaluation context and the key evaluation questions. The evaluator may initially develop matrices that summarize findings from different data types (interview or focus groups) or sources (sites or participants). Frequency/occurrence matrices and binary dichotomous matrices for key issues (yes/no; high/low) may also be useful organization schemas.

4. Define the format for display. In general, a landscape presentation of a matrix is easier to read than a portrait version. Matrices work best with a readable number of rows and columns, ideally fewer than twenty. If the evaluation includes a range of sites or a large number of people, you will have to identify ways to cluster and reduce the dimensions further, for example, by type of school (primary schools and secondary schools, rather than individual schools) or role of informant (director, manager, employee, rather than individual). In this way, data from a larger range of stakeholders can be represented in the matrix. Select column and row labels to allow comparison within and between cells and begin filling in the cells. Gaps in cells may indicate missing data if the summary was based on structured or standardized interviews.

5. Compare and contrast both within columns and across rows to form propositions. In this step the matrix is used to inform description and to explore relationships between dimensions.

6. Use a range of matrices to support description and analysis. Often more than one matrix will be appropriate, particularly if there is an interest in more layered analysis.

7. Present findings with reference to the matrices or diagrams.

The evaluator may elect to include one or two matrices in the report to provide evidence for evaluation claims, or to illustrate the categorization process. Some evaluators use matrices to make the process of description, analysis, and interpretation transparent: the reader can trace the interpretations back to the descriptive matrices included in the report (or in a technical appendix) that accompanies the report. This may be particularly important when findings are controversial or there are mixed stakeholder perspectives about the value of the program. Avoid the use of too many diagrams or tables in final reports, as they may detract from key messages and overwhelm the reader.

Application

An example of a role-ordered matrix is presented in Table 22.3. This matrix was presented at the end of a narrative section as a qualitative summary of key points and issues raised by stakeholders about a quality improvement program for breast disease services. The columns indicate the dimensions summarized in the matrix. The rows represent a summary of the perspectives shared by various stakeholder groups.

TABLE 22.3. SUMMARY MATRIX: PERSPECTIVES AND EXAMPLES OF QUOTES.

Stakeholder Group	Perspective on the Program	Example Quotes
Consumers	Favorable about the program, but unsure about evidence of change Questioned the expenditure on funding, especially non-tangibles Unsure about others' acknowledgement of their role in direction of the program Tended to highlight and profile visible (tangible) outputs of the program (e.g., the hand-held record)	"It's a really vital thing to do and it will improve services, especially for rural women." "Our involvement [in the program] is often tokenistic." "There needs to be a broader consumer base to draw on. I feel I am the token consumer voice."
Radiologists/ Oncologists	Saw value in the initiatives undertaken in the program, but concerned about the inequity of service delivery to other cancer groups	"I see a lot of cancer patients, and every one of my cancer patients has the same problem. It's just happens that one of them . . . the breast cancer group . . . gets the golden run." "The rest of the cancer community may be affronted if more money is given to breast cancer and the rest are ignored."
Specialist Breast Surgeons/ Breast Care Nurses/ Nursing Managers/ Clinical Coordinators	Saw value in the program Many stakeholders across these groups highlighted specific changes in practice they attributed to the program Concern about sustainability and transferability of the model to other cancers	"The institution sees breast cancer as a growth area, as a high profile area that is worthwhile to be involved in. They see it as a program that can be generalized to other cancers." "I see it as a model that could be readily transferred to other cancer groups."

When These Methods Are Appropriate

Matrices are commonly used in evaluation as a way to bring together salient information from across cases or across data types in one format. During the analysis process, they provide a structured, visual display of data that allows the evaluator to compare and contrast information, identify patterns, and explore outliers. In evaluation, the progressive use of matrix displays will lead to propositions that can be tested in further stages of data collection.

In written reports, we have found that evaluation audiences appreciate the inclusion of a summary table and may often prefer this form of representation to a lot of freestanding text or narrative description. They want to quickly grasp the key points.

Evaluators who adopt descriptive methods are often driven by pragmatic concerns about coding and classification. Classifications that make sense to the evaluation purpose and for presentation enhance their credibility to evaluation audiences.

Hermeneutic Methods

Overview.   Hermeneutic methods often involve an iterative process between data collection and analysis and acknowledge the role of the evaluator and their observations as part of the data corpus. These approaches attempt to generate manifest and latent meanings inherent in qualitative data by some process of coding and labeling. Manifest meanings are visible, descriptive labels that appear in the data. Latent meanings are underlying meanings, gleaned from an iterative process of examining the material, looking for similarities and differences, and identifying themes.

Some hermeneutic methods, such as narrative analysis, eschew formal coding in favor of case-based knowledge and holistic accounts. Evaluators from these traditions contend that the process of coding fragments the data and strips meaning from the context in which it was produced.

Most often, evaluators who utilize qualitative methods will draw on hermeneutic processes, in recognition of the value of rich data and the role of the evaluator in generating interpretations and judgments from the material. The processes associated with textual analysis in the qualitative evaluation literature also tends to emphasize these approaches. The popularity of hermeneutic methods reflects the paradigmatic commitments of many evaluators, influenced by interpretive frames of reference that emphasize a nuanced, contextualized response to textual and visual materials.

Example of Hermeneutic Method: Thematic Analysis.   A common type of analysis associated with hermeneutic methods is thematic analysis. One of the features of thematic analysis is iterations of analysis over time. The evaluator moves back and forth among data, classification, and writing about data. The first stage of analysis is often used to inform further data collection. In this case, the evaluator will return to the field to gather more data.

Thematic analysis can be deductively or inductively driven, that is, the evaluator can assign data to categories from existing program theory or according to key evaluation questions. More commonly, thematic data analysis is associated with inductive reasoning, in which the evaluator reviews the material and generates organizing categories that adequately summarize the content. In practice, we believe that inductive, deductive, and retroductive reasoning are at play in analysis of materials generated within an evaluation context. Broadly speaking, induction entails using observations from data gathering to infer to a general conclusion. Deduction involves developing a hypothesized statement and looking for evidence in the study.

In retroduction, conclusions or claims are made and then an assiduous search for confirming and disconfirming evidence is undertaken. The reasoning is based on trying to answer the question, "How did this come about?" While retroduction sounds similar to deduction, the conclusion must follow from the premises.

The evaluator has collected the information from participants to answer particular key evaluation questions. These orient the categorization and classification of data. While the evaluator should remain open to categories inherent in the data, more often than not a combination of strategies is required.

Thematic analysis broadly involves the following eight steps:

1. Clarify the purpose for using thematic analysis.
2. Focus the analysis process by revisiting the key evaluation questions that framed data collection.
3. Familiarize yourself with the materials to be analyzed. The task in this first step is to organize existing material. The material may include transcripts from individual or focus group interviews, documents, observational notes and evaluation reflections, and/or materials produced by the participants (diaries, drawings). The evaluator may have a partial data set that will be analyzed to inform further stages of data collection, or may have a complete data set.
4. Undertake first-level or open coding. First-level coding involves reviewing the material and assigning labels or tags to text, video, or observation segments. The purpose is to descriptively capture what the individual or group is talking about or what is occurring. The coding process, whether formal or informal, is a data reduction process. Its purpose is to tag text or material in order to allow classification of data into a smaller, more refined set of labels. Coding is a common strategy in developing broader category clusters.
5. Do second-level/pattern coding and categorizing of the material. This step involves looking for patterns within the material and across other materials

that have been coded. Similarities and differences are explored and these are used to assign categories. At this stage, the evaluator may have up to thirty or more categories. Categories can also be identified from program theory and used to classify evaluation materials, but the evaluator should ensure that they remain open to other categories evident in the data.

6. Write a memo about relationships and connections derived from the coding and categorization process. Writing or diagramming assists the evaluator in forming propositions. The evaluator may also explore the connectedness among data elements, even when these elements are not directly comparable in terms of similarities or differences. Memos are a powerful strategy that draws on the interpretive skills of the evaluator.

7. Elaborate a limited set of themes. Identify both manifest and latent themes with example quotes. A manifest theme may be the reference to an experience that the majority or all of the participants discussed. For example, most participants may have expressed fear and anxiety about participating in the new program. A latent theme is generated by the evaluator and is often developed from exploration of a broader corpus of data. The evaluator may search the transcript for particular word choices used by the participants, level of emotion expressed, comments that were emphasized in some way (for example, the most important thing you need to know about this program is that . . .) sideline or off the record comments, unexpected or unanticipated comments that surprised the interviewer/evaluator, or things that were not said during the interview. The evaluator's observations during site visits or during the data collection process may contribute to identification of latent themes. A careful audit trail must be maintained to ensure the process of developing themes is transparent.

8. Begin writing about categories and their relationship to codes and emerging insights from the analysis process. While this is defined here as the final step, in practice, writing is a way of finding out (Richardson, 2007) and occurs throughout the process, during stages of writing memos and in drafting of reports. Test propositions by referring back to the data. Diagram relationships using matrix displays and network diagrams or mind maps, and identify example quotes to illustrate the key claims about the program.

Other hermeneutic forms do not privilege coding as described above. For example, narrative approaches in evaluation often seek to retain the sequential and storied elements of an interview and eschew the fragmentation that occurs with formal coding and classification. In narrative analysis, some kind of categorization process is evident, but formal coding may not be. Clearly, the analyst is making decisions about which elements (or categories of meaning) to present.

Seidman (2005) noted the importance of creating profiles from interviews to maintain the coherence of the account from the participants' perspective. Michael Patton (2015) has also written about the value of creating case profiles to make sense of data.

Application

A thematic analysis was adopted to understand the experiences of early years educators involved in a coaching program. The evaluation included a combination of qualitative (interviews and focus groups) and quantitative methods (a statewide survey).

Full transcripts of interviews with coaches and educators were prepared and used as the basis of analysis. Transcripts were sorted by perspective (coaches and educators) about the contribution of the program to observed outcomes. Transcripts from each group were read and notations made in the right-hand margin in the form of categories relating to their experience and to the key evaluation questions. For example, positive views of the program, negative views of the program. Illustrative quotes that exemplified the categories were highlighted. In the left margin, the evaluator made comments about issues to follow up or other evaluation information (links between survey information and interviews). Memos about each transcript were made, and a collation of categories and related codes was recorded. A within-case analysis was undertaken (within each stakeholder group) and a summary made of the key findings associated with key evaluation questions. A cross-case analysis (of comments made by coaches and educators) was then undertaken to identify salient program variables that may have contributed to outcomes. Illustrative quotes provided evidence for evaluation claims, and this information was combined with the available quantitative data (a statewide survey) to answer evaluation questions.

When These Methods Are Appropriate

Hermeneutic approaches are valuable if the evaluator has access to rich data in the source of interview transcripts or comprehensive notes of observations at site visits. But the downside is that hermeneutic methods often require the investment of more time than enumerative or descriptive methods. The evaluator needs to organize the data, identify codes and categories, and compare and contrast segments of the data to identify patterns and themes, often returning to the data to generate and test these propositions.

One of the key features of hermeneutic methods is the maintenance of the depth and detail of the data collected. There is likely to be fuller coverage of the available data, rather than selective coding of pieces or sections deemed to be most closely tied to the evaluation questions.

In larger studies, time may prohibit the inductive identification of codes and categories. Under these circumstances, the evaluator may decide to inductively code and categorize a proportion of the materials and then apply this coding and categorizing system to the remaining set. The evaluator should still retain an openness to new or emergent codes that are not captured by the existing classification system.

Those evaluators that use hermeneutic methods often privilege constructivist criteria such as trustworthiness and authenticity, rather than traditional validity (truth value) criteria. Specific strategies, such as reflexivity, triangulation, and respondent validation may be adopted. Those evaluators that hold a critical or social change perspective, may focus on a more explicit set of relational and ethical criteria (Abma and Widdershoven, 2011; Lather, 1993) that involve an assessment of the consequences of the findings, the capacity of those involved to take meaningful action, and the explication of values across a range of stakeholder groups.

Explanatory Methods

Overview. Explanatory methods of analysis focus on generating and testing causal claims from data and are particularly relevant to address outcome evaluation questions. In impact evaluations, clients want to know whether the program worked, and if so, how it worked to produce outcomes and impacts.

Most evaluation clients want to understand the contribution of projects to the larger program of effort, or they seek transferable lessons from implementation of projects in an array of contexts. Others want to understand what programmatic factors in what combination contributed to the observed outcomes so they can make decisions about future funding. For example, do the support resources and professional development workshops together foster improved knowledge and skills of welfare workers, or would the professional development workshops be sufficient on their own to generate improvements?

These are causal or explanatory questions. They require analysis that can link proposed causal mechanisms to specific outcomes. In traditional terms, the role of causal analysis has been limited exclusively to the use of experimental or quasi-experimental designs. Yet, most evaluators are called upon to address these questions when these designs are not relevant (for example, quality improvement programs implemented across a state or borough, or when implementation has already occurred). Other techniques will be required to address these questions.

There is growing interest in alternatives to experimentation for strengthening causal inferences, and a number of promising strategies are available utilizing qualitative data in small n studies. Process tracing and qualitative comparative analysis are two potential strategies that may contribute to plausible causal claims. In this section we focus on qualitative comparative analysis as a promising analytic method for addressing explanatory claims in evaluation contexts.

Example of Explanatory Method: Qualitative Comparative Analysis.   Qualitative comparative analysis (QCA) is a systematic comparative approach that maintains a focus on the richness and context of cases. Charles Ragin (1987), a political scientist, pioneered the use of the method arguing for its relevance in determining causal claims in small n studies. Between five to fifty cases or more are appropriate for QCA.

Essentially, QCA examines the combinations of factors that are associated with a particular outcome using a minimization algorithm generated from comparing and contrasting causal conditions and their relationships to an outcome of interest.

There are two types of QCA: crisp set qca and fuzzy set qca. In crisp set qca, each individual condition identified for each case (school, program, and so forth) is classified with an 0 or 1 to indicate absence or presence, respectively, of this condition. Fuzzy set qca allows levels of presence or absence (for example, .25, .50, .75).

Broadly, the QCA method involves the following steps:

1. Clarify the purpose and appropriateness of using qualitative comparative analysis
2. Identify the outcome of interest and the relevant conditions that may be associated with the outcome. This is a critical stage and must be strongly informed by theory. The evaluator can draw upon program theory or policy documentation or consultations with stakeholders to identify a limited number of conditions.
3. Develop a truth table and classify cases as rows and conditions as columns. A truth table is a matrix that includes various combinations of conditions and the outcome. Each identified causal condition is categorized in the truth table by its presence or absence (crisp set) or by the level of presence

or absence (fuzzy set) in relation to the outcome. We acknowledge that there may be some loss of data precision in this step, but the formalization of decision rules about classification is helpful in generating and testing propositions. Criteria for classification must be transparent. This process also enables to evaluator to examine patterns among causal conditions and their relationship to the outcome of interest. An example of a truth table is presented in Table 22.4.

4. Using the software of choice (for example, NVivo [QSR]) Tosmana [Cronqvist, 2006]), compare the constellations and interactions among conditions and the outcome.

The output provides the minimization algorithm, using Boolean logic (or + / and x) that identifies the specific combination of variables that are sufficient for occurrence or non-occurrence of the outcome. The notion of equifinality is important here. QCA is based on a conception that it is possible that an outcome can be achieved from different patterns of causal conditions and that a causal condition (for example, clarity of partnership roles) may have a different influence on an outcome, depending on the context. The evaluator can explore which conditions are necessary for outcome success. While this method appears to have much in common with regression analyses, there is a substantive difference in underlying philosophy. QCA depends on deep case knowledge to generate causal claims and is based on analyses of set-theoretic relationships, not variable-oriented relationships.

5. Explore contradictory configurations for cases to generate a richer knowledge of the cases and their contexts. The evaluator may explore the cases involved in the contradictory configuration. Decisions about exclusion of these contradictions will need to be made and be justified clearly in the evaluation report. Interpret the minimal formulas to develop a comprehensive narrative about the causal conditions that contributed to program outcomes in particular contexts. Use case-based knowledge to ground propositions about the relationship between particular conditions and the outcomes of interest.

Application

Befani, Ledermann, and Sager (2007), used QCA in an evaluation of the effects of the Swiss Environmental Impact Assessment (EIA). The EIA is a regulatory structure that ensures infrastructure projects address environmental

TABLE 22.4. SIMPLE EXAMPLE OF A TRUTH TABLE.

Case	Clarity of Partnership Roles	Grants (High Grant Success)	Registration High	Broker Stable (Service of Broker)	Community Plan in Place	Community Development Activity High	Outcome (Success)
1 Urban	1	1	1	0	1	1	1
2 Urban	1	0	0	0	1	1	0
3 Rural	1	0	1	1	1	1	1
4 Rural	1	1	0	1	0	0	0
5 Urban	0	0	1	1	0	0	0
6 Urban	0	0	1	0	1	0	0
7 Rural	1	1	0	1	1	1	1

standards. After reviewing theory and existing studies, the team identified plausible configurations of conditions that may trigger outcomes within particular contexts. In essence they developed a program theory about the ways in which an outcome of success or failure may occur. Conditions were assigned a value of 1 if they were present and 0 if they were absent. Case studies were then undertaken to ensure thorough knowledge of the cases, and to generate a truth table of conditions and trajectories of outcomes (failure or success). QCA was then performed with the use of fuzzy set QCA (fs/QCA). The output from these analyses led the authors to a series of propositions about the influence of the policy context on outcomes. The authors argued that the application of QCA was consistent with their adoption of a realist evaluation framework and that the process involved necessary iterations among theory, data, and propositions.

When These Methods Are Appropriate

Explanatory methods may be valuable in impact evaluations. Qualitative comparative analysis holds much promise for evaluators who seek to maintain a close and rich understanding of the context of particular cases, but are also interested in testable patterns within and across cases. Given the central role of the truth table and the minimization formula, it is important to use software that supports these processes. Specific software developed for QCA may be used (for example, Tosmana) or generic theory testing software such as NVivo can be used to organize and classify the data.

Evaluators who adopt explanatory approaches such as QCA will tend to draw on traditional scientific criteria, but while traditional canons of reliability and validity are held, they are reinscribed in meaning. Advocates of QCA adapt the traditional criteria to reflect the importance of case knowledge, emergence and iteration, and interrelationships between observed outcomes and configurations of conditions that are associated with those outcomes. Given the inherent interest in causal mechanisms and context, QCA will be relevant to evaluators who practice realist evaluation

Framing Analytic Choices

We have presented a typology of four purposes of qualitative data analysis and focused in on one method that is closely associated with the purpose, enumerative, descriptive, hermeneutic, and explanatory. We have argued that it is better to choose data analysis methods that fit the purpose of the analysis, the context of the evaluation, and the technical requirements of the process rather than privilege one method. Evaluators have a range of analysis options that can be used and, ideally, using more than one method (analytic triangulation) may strengthen the plausibility and persuasiveness of evaluation claims.

Choice of analytic method will be influenced by the nature of the data, purpose, and desired product. For some audiences, a numeric summary of the material gathered by frequency may be preferred. For other audiences, the use of rich illustrative quotes will be favored. Or the evaluator may choose a combination of strategies to portray the findings and provide warrants for key claims.

Some analysis and presentational strategies require particular kinds of data. For example, there may be limited value in applying narrative methods of analysis if the evaluation has only generated short, very structured interview material. Narrative approaches often utilize free-flowing conversation, rather than information presented in a structured question-and-answer format. Similarly, it may not be appropriate to quantify material that was designed to illuminate or illustrate an issue or to use semi-structured or open-guide interviews when individuals are not asked to share insights on a particular issue. We are not implying that the evaluator cannot transform this material into another type of product, but caution that the evaluator be aware of strengths and limitations of particular techniques according to available data.

Potential data analysis options should be anticipated before any data are collected, to ensure that there is alignment between type of information required, scope of data, and purpose. As analysis of qualitative data is often undertaken concurrently with data collection, the evaluator can rehearse data analysis and display options to maximize communicative power.

How Can Software Help?

Many different computer packages facilitate the coding and analysis process. These can be categorized into four groups:

- Word processing and spreadsheet software, such as Word and Excel, which can be used for simple coding and analysis
- Specialized qualitative data analysis software, such as NVivo, HyperResearch, MaxQDA, and Atlas-TI
- Machine learning software, such as MonkeyLearn
- Visual analysis software that produces word cloud or network diagrams of text

Word processing and spreadsheet software can be useful for simple analysis of small quantities of data where there is not the time or budget to buy and learn specialist software. Text (such as the answers to an open-ended question) is put into cells, one cell per response. A label is given to each of these and it is typed into an adjoining cell. The data can then be sorted and the coding checked for consistency. Using a spreadsheet such as Excel makes it possible to use pivot tables to produce summary statistics, such as counts for each code and cross-tabulations with other variables, such as gender.

Specialist qualitative data analysis software do not automatically analyze the data, but provide structures for organizing, classifying, and storing information. They can do some autocoding, for example, doing a text search and creating a category of all text that includes that code, or putting all the responses to a particular questionnaire item or interview question into a category for further analysis. Many packages allow versions of coding to be stored for later retrieval, which can be helpful in tracking movement in the sophistication of the analysis and allow documentation that justifies the links among data, evidence, and evaluation claims.

Specialist software is recommended where this is a large volume of data and analysis (for example, multiple stakeholder groups, or thirty or more cases), and where there is the time and money to buy and learn how to use it. Software facilitates the efficiency and tracking of the coding and retrieval process. The most common error in using this type of software is to become stuck at the coding stage, creating and using an impractical number of codes. For evaluations, in most cases it is more useful to do an initial cycle of coding, analysis, and reporting and then return to the data with more questions and do further coding. This reduces the risk of not producing a useful report.

Machine learning software is designed to learn how to classify data. For example, a sample of hotel reviews can be classified as either "positive" or "negative." The software will identify predictive words and phrases (for example, "disgusting" or "worst hotel") and show the degree of success in predicting the classification based on these words. If the level is not sufficiently high, further training with more data can be undertaken. Once an acceptable level has been reached, the software can be used to automatically code data. This type of software is most appropriate when there is a large quantity of data (for example, using a web scraper to take data from reviews or social media) and a simple classification needed (for example, positive or negative).

Visual analysis software can produce a word cloud, where the size of a word reflects its frequency, and word network diagrams, which show how words are connected in the text. While word clouds have become increasingly popular as a quick way of sharing some analysis, they are often not very helpful. For example, doing a word cloud of book titles, speeches, or newspaper reports will have all the risks of simple enumeration previously discussed. Even if words such as "the" and "and" are excluded, word clouds don't deal with synonyms well. They can be useful when the data have been collected in the form of a single word summary.

Software developments are ongoing and rapid. The CAQDAS website (http://www.surrey.ac.uk/sociology/research/researchcentres/caqdas/index.htm) offers regular updates on software developments. While multiple texts on the attributes and use of software are available, many of these do not frame the discussion of software in relation to qualitative research and evaluation practices. Two notable exceptions are Kurkkartz (2014) and Richards (2009). These texts discuss analytic practices and profile the use of specific packages, MaxQDA and NVivo, respectively.

Given the range of software available, St. John and Johnson (2000, p. 397) have identified questions that researchers or evaluators might ask themselves when choosing a package, including the following:

- "What are the advantages and disadvantages of this package for my research?
- What purpose will this package serve for this research project?
- Will this package handle the type of data I intend to collect?
- Will this package enable flexible handling of data for this project? ...
- Will this package enable me to interact with and reduce data in a way that is consistent with my methods?"

Who Does the Analysis?

In larger evaluations, we may be working as part of a team. Team members may be assigned different tasks such as data collection or instrument design across all sites, or be responsible for collating and analyzing all information from a project site with the expectation that the information will inform cross-site analysis. There are distinct advantages of analyzing with others, most notably the presence of critical friends to challenge and test assumptions and claims and as a form of triangulation in the analysis process. However, if there is a lack of clarity about processes of analysis and how the team will discuss coding and categorizing processes, the resulting product can be very messy. We recommend that teams discuss analysis options and clarify processes that will be adopted prior to data collection. Review and discuss initial coding with team members of a small subset of the data before proceeding to analyze the whole data set.

Co-analysis can also be undertaken with clients as a form of early data rehearsal or as a way to identify implications of the data. This may be particularly fruitful when the evaluator does not have substantive knowledge base about the evaluand. Good interpretations occur within a framework of context and descriptive detail. For example, Del undertook an evaluation of a statewide coaching program (2013) for early year professionals. She did not have a background or substantive experience with early years services. Initial propositions were discussed with a reference group, including experienced early years coaches and program funders who had considerable experience in early education and care. Interpretations were reviewed by drawing on the evidence collected in conjunction with the substantive content knowledge base shared by the coaches and funders.

High Quality Qualitative Data Analysis

We have argued that methods of analysis should reflect the purpose of the analysis and the intended product required. Good quality analysis of qualitative data requires clarity about which standards will be used to judge the quality and effective strategies to meet these standards.

In this section we focus particularly on the issue of the quality of inferences—a reframing of the standard of accuracy to be more appropriate across the different approaches to qualitative data analysis. Traditionally, the terms "validity" or "trustworthiness" have been used to denote an empiricist or interpretivist orientation to evaluation with an associated series of procedures that evaluators may adopt. The mixed method literature has moved toward the term "inference quality." Rather than remain tangled in the debates about the most appropriate terminology for quality and given that most evaluations adopt multiple methods, this term seems appropriate as an umbrella term.

Depending on the paradigmatic stance of the evaluator and the intended users of the evaluation, there can be quite different standards for what is considered to be high-quality inference in qualitative data analysis. Constructivist evaluators may highlight the value of member checking or respondent validation and triangulation. Evaluators who adopt a critical change focus to guide their work (Mertens, 2009; Wadsworth, 2011), may draw more on strategies that engage with issues of power and diversity and advocate relational criteria such as authenticity and reciprocity.

Program Evaluation Standards and Quality criteria for QDA

The five high-level evaluation standards—utility, accuracy, feasibility, propriety, and accountability—provide a useful reference point for thinking about the quality of qualitative data analysis. While the accuracy standard seems most closely associated with quality of data analysis, the standards broaden consideration of analysis as purely a technical activity.

Utility is about usefulness and fit for purpose. Analysis methods must be selected that fit the purpose and intended product required. In some cases, we may select matrix displays to guide analysis and use these in a written report to substantiate the claims we make. Matrix displays can summarize the evidence in a format that is readily understandable to the client. Evaluators may combine criteria or choose dimensions that reflect the intended purpose of the analysis.

The second standard is *accuracy*. Accuracy applied to qualitative analysis means that the evaluator will pay attention to issues of validity and trustworthiness of inferences generated from the analysis process. The considerations of analytic rigor will differ depending on analytic method. For example, inter-rater reliability may be a preferred strategy in classical content analysis to strengthen rigor, but it may be rejected as a concept of relevance to a constructivist or critical/transformative evaluator. For example, interpretive differences between evaluators do not mean that one evaluator is wrong, just as a high inter-rater reliability coefficient does not confer correctness or accuracy.

A number of strategies are adopted by evaluators to strengthen inferences from qualitative data. In descriptive and hermeneutic methods of analysis, evaluators are likely to draw from the trustworthiness criteria developed by Lincoln and Guba (1985) A transformative evaluator may find the authenticity criteria associated with collaborative and participatory approaches more relevant as a guide to strengthen inference quality. Those evaluators adopting explanatory methods will likely be influenced by criteria such as pattern matching and assessing alternative explanations.

While there is some overlap among the strategies for supporting accuracy of inferences and acknowledging the interpretive basis of qualitative data analysis, the evaluator must be able to defend decisions. Evaluators may combine criteria or choose dimensions that reflect the intended purpose of the analysis, but it will be important to maintain consistency between the techniques adopted and the evaluators' perspective. For example, many advocates of thematic analysis undertaken from a hermeneutic perspective would eschew the calculation of inter-rater reliability, especially if the interviews were unstructured or narrative accounts. Inter-rater reliability confers confidence in the reader that two or more analysts have coded consistently, which communicates a message to evaluation audiences that the higher level of agreement means that the coding is not only consistent, but right. For many interpretivist evaluators, inter-rater reliability is a superficial technique that does not add value and does not recognize the inherent intersubjective nature of qualitative methods. This does not presume that all classifications are equally valid, but rather challenges the conception that reliability is a precursor to accuracy.

The interpretive strategies outlined below in italics are not designed to be used as a checklist, as some will be more relevant than others in differing evaluation contexts and for differing analytic purposes.

Trustworthiness strategies include activities that are concerned with the depth of evidence gathered such as *prolonged engagement*. In an evaluation context, this strategy may lead evaluators to question whether their exposure to the program and to data collection opportunities provided a sufficient basis to make particular claims about implementation and outcomes. A second strategy is *triangulation*. Evaluators may be more confident in the credibility of their claims if there is corroboration of evidence across data sources, methods, theories, or analysis processes. It is important, however, to be aware that divergent evidence may also be useful in encouraging the evaluator to test assumptions and to more deeply consider alternate explanations. *Peer debriefing* with other team members, evaluation advisory groups, and those not directly involved in the evaluation can help the evaluator avoid blind spots and can assist the evaluator to make defensible claims.

A fourth strategy is to review *negative cases*. The evaluator pays attention to cases that do not support or, indeed, contradict patterns in the data. In the evaluation of a training program, the evaluator may seek out those participants who did not complete the program, rather than relying only on those participants who do complete. The evaluator may return to participants to discuss interpretations through a *member checking* or *respondent validation* process. Participants may be asked to review interpretations and/or provide additional information to sharpen interpretations. In some collaborative evaluation approaches, this process is explicitly built into the evaluation from the planning stages. Methodological accountability is supported through strategies such as reflexivity and audit processes. *Reflexivity* means that evaluators critically assess their role in data collection and analysis, their potential influence on participants, and the values that have shaped their interpretations.

An *audit trail* is a useful strategy to strengthen the rigor of claims. Evaluators have to document their data collection processes and decisions and ensure transparency in linkages among data collection, analysis, and evaluation claims so that these can be reviewed and assessed by others. Evaluators adopting participatory or transformative evaluation approaches are likely to draw on trustworthiness strategies, but supplement these with attention to authenticity criteria that acknowledge issues of participant access, voice, power, and representation.

Feasibility is an evaluation standard that relates to prudence of processes and procedures. In a data analysis context, this means that methods should be selected that are appropriate to the budget and timeframe available for the evaluation. Hermeneutic and explanatory methods are likely to take much longer and entail more iterations than enumerative or descriptive options. The evaluator must consider the feasibility of methods at several stages of the evaluation, balancing attention to information needs, rigor, and timelines.

Propriety in the evaluation standards refers to the need for evaluations to be ethical and legally appropriate. The depth and rich detail of qualitative data means that the evaluator must carefully consider how best to protect the identity of participants and respect their rights within the evaluation and in the written presentation of the evaluation report. The evaluator must have appropriate processes in place to ensure raw data files are appropriately stored and that pseudonyms, if appropriate, are applied. Inessential details within the context of the evaluation (such as number of siblings or age) can be modified to further protect identification. If modifications are made in this way to protect participants, this should be declared in the method section of the evaluation report.

Accountability is the fifth evaluation standard. In program evaluation, this is most closely associated with meta-evaluation. In the context of data analysis, accountability means that the evaluator documents purposes, decision rules, and processes and ensures that a clear argument is made for the selection of particular analytic approaches. In the spirit of transparency and accountability, the evaluator should ensure that materials that form the basis of the analysis are available for secondary review if required, as long as appropriate ethical issues regarding access to primary data have been addressed.

The standards can sometimes be in tension, so consideration has to be given to the appropriate level of trade-offs. For example, achieving a high standard of accuracy is constrained by the need to be timely (utility standard), cost-effective (feasibility standard), and not excessively burdensome on respondents (propriety standard).

Table 22.5 summarizes the application of the evaluation standards to qualitative data analysis processes. The strategies are suitable for all methods of analysis discussed in this chapter, with particular strategies associated with particular methods where relevant.

TABLE 22.5. EVALUATION STANDARDS AND STRATEGIES TO MAXIMIZE INFERENCE QUALITY.

Evaluation Standards	Qualitative Data Analysis Principles	Strategies to Consider
Utility	Data analysis decisions should be fit for purpose and relevant to client needs	Potential data analysis methods should be identified before data collection begins and then reviewed throughout the evaluation Requirements for each type of analysis method should be made explicit Strengths and limitations of analytic methods should inform selection
Accuracy	The analysis process should be rigorous and transparent according to method	Enumerative Inter-rater reliability, documentation Descriptive/hermeneutic: Use relevant strategies to support inferences such as peer debriefing, member checking, negative case analysis, reflexivity, triangulation, audit trail Hermeneutic/explanatory Pattern matching, ruling out alternative explanations
Feasibility	The choice of analysis method should be feasible given purpose, resources, and timeframes	Identify data requirements for analysis purpose and build in time/cost to evaluation budget
Propriety	Analysis processes should protect the rights of participants	Discuss limits of confidentiality with participants and client Define likely risks of analysis processes
Accountability	Analysis processes should be documented and linkages among data, analysis, interpretation, and reporting should be explicit	Agree on procedures for secondary review/peer review of analysis

Conclusion

Qualitative data make a powerful contribution to research and program evaluation. Techniques for the effective gathering of such data are important, and many texts detail these processes well. Similarly, methods of data analysis have been described, but have not themselves been amenable to analysis for their suitability for purpose. This has often resulted in analyses that are overly shallow or descriptive analyses that undermine the value of the information generated.

In this chapter, we have argued that decisions about analytic techniques be considered early in an evaluation, and that these decisions will be informed by a range of practical considerations, such as audience, time and resource constraints, and the type of data available. Whatever approach or range of approaches are adopted to code or summarize, classify, analyze, and synthesize qualitative data, there is a need to make sure the processes are transparent and traceable. This is not for the purpose of replicability, but for the justification of claims that arise from purpose of the analysis.

We have presented a typology of purposes and outlined an example of a key analysis method for each purpose. The typology is presented as a heuristic, not intended to be prescriptive, as this would negate the value of deliberative decisions based on an appreciation of the specific context. Evaluators may combine purposes and methods in a single evaluation or mix analytic methods to challenge existing insights or to generate new ideas.

An overview of quality criteria for assessing and strengthening data analysis was provided that builds on substantive guidance provided by the program evaluation standards. The warrants for claims evaluators make must be based on strong, clear synthesis of evidence. Evaluators require a rigorous set of methods for making sense of qualitative data and for assessing its appropriateness. This chapter has reinforced the value of systematic analysis, creativity, and the important of transparency of these processes to the evaluation profession and to evaluation clients.

A quote by Janice Morse (1994) provides a fitting conclusion that captures the technical and creative elements of good qualitative data analysis:

> Data analysis is a process that requires astute questioning, a relentless search for answers, active observation, and accurate recall. It is a process of piecing together data, of making the invisible obvious, of recognizing the significant from the insignificant, of linking seemingly unrelated facts logically, of fitting categories one with another, and of attributing consequences to antecedents. It is a process of conjecture and verification, of correction and modification, of suggestion and defense. It is a creative process of organizing data so that the analytic scheme will appear obvious. (p. 25)

References

Abma, T., and Widdershoven, G.A.M. "Evaluation as a Relationally Responsive Practice." In
   N. Denzin and Y. Lincoln (eds.), *Handbook of Qualitative Research* (4th ed.). Thousand
   Oaks, CA: Sage, 2011.

Baptiste, Ian. "Qualitative Data Analysis: Common Phases, Strategic Differences." *Forum
   Qualitative Sozialforschung/Forum: Qualitative Social Research* [Online Journal], September
   2001, *2*(3). Available at www.qualitative-research.net/fqs-texte/3-01/3-01baptiste-e.htm

Bazeley, P. *Qualitative Data Analysis: Practical Strategies.* London: Sage, 2013.

Befani, B., Ledermann, S., and Sager, F. "Realistic Evaluation and QCA Conceptual
   Parallels and an Empirical Application." *Evaluation*, 2007, *13*(2), 171–192.

Boyatzis, R. E. *Transforming Qualitative Information: Thematic Analysis and Code Development.*
   Thousand Oaks, CA: Sage, 1998.

Claburn, T. "How Google Flu Trends Blew It." *InformationWeek*, September 25, 2013.

Collier, D. "Understanding Process Tracing." *Political Science and Politics*, 2011, *44*(4),
   823–830.

Crabtree, B. F., and Miller, W. L. *Doing Qualitative Research.* Thousand Oaks, CA: Sage, 1999.

Cronqvist, L. *Tosmana–Tool for Small N Analysis* (version 1.254). Marburg, Germany:
   University of Marburg, 2006.

Gladwin, C. H. *Ethnographic Decision Tree Modeling.* Thousand Oaks, CA: Sage, 1989.

Kuckkartz, U. *Qualitative Text Analysis: A Guide to Methods, Practice, and Using Software.*
   Thousand Oaks, CA: Sage, 2014.

Krippendorf, K. *Content Analysis: An Introduction to the Methodology* (3rd ed.). Thousand
   Oaks, CA: Sage, 2013.

Lather, Patti. "Fertile Obsession: Validity After Poststructuralism." *The Sociological Quarterly*,
   1993, *34*(4), 673–693.

Lincoln, Y., and Guba, E. *Naturalistic Inquiry.* Thousand Oaks, CA: Sage, 1985.

Mertens, D. *Transformative Research and Evaluation.* New York: Guilford Press, 2009.

Miles, M. B., Huberman, A. M., and Saldana, J. *Qualitative Data Analysis: A Sourcebook of New
   Methods* (3rd ed.). Thousand Oaks, CA: Sage, 2014.

Morse, J. "Emerging from the Data: The Cognitive Processes of Analysis in Qualitative
   Inquiry." In J. M. Morse (ed.), *Critical Issues in Qualitative Research Methods (22–43).*
   Thousand Oaks, CA: Sage, 1994

Patton, M. Q. (2015). *Qualitative Research and Evaluation Methods* (4th ed.). Thousand Oaks,
   CA: Sage, 2015.

Paul, M. J., and Dredze, M. "You Are What You Tweet: Analyzing Twitter for Public Health."
   ICWSM, International Conference on Weblogs and Social Media, 265–272, July 2011.

Ragin, C. *The Comparative Method. Moving Beyond Qualitative and Quantitative Strategies.*
   Berkeley, CA: University of California Press, 1987.

Richards, L. *Handling Qualitative Data: A Practical Guide* (2nd ed.). London: Sage, 2009.

Richardson, Laurel, and St Pierre, E. "Writing: A Method of Inquiry" (959–978). In N.
   Denzin and Y. Lincoln (eds.), *The Sage Handbook of Qualitative Research* (3rd ed.).
   Thousand Oaks, CA: Sage: 2005.

Riessman, C. K. *Narrative Methods for the Human Sciences.* Thousand Oaks, CA: Sage, 2008.

Ritchie, J., and Spencer, L. "Qualitative Data Analysis for Applied Policy Research." In A.
   Bryman and R. G. Burgess (eds.), *Analyzing Qualitative Data* (173–194). London:
   Routledge, 1994.

Schreier, M. *Qualitative Content Analysis in Practice.* Thousand Oaks, CA: Sage, 2012.

Seidman, I. *Interviewing as Qualitative Research: A Guide for Researchers in Education and the Social Sciences.* New York: Teachers College Press, Columbia University, 2005.

Semiocast. "Geolocation Analysis of Twitter Accounts and Tweets by Semiocast." http://semiocast.com/en/publications/2012_07_30_Twitter_reaches_half_a_billion _accounts_140m_in_the_US, 2012.

Spradley, J. *Participant Observation.* New York: Holt, Rinehart and Winston, 1980.

St. John, W., and Johnson, P. "The Pros and Cons of Data Analysis Software for Qualitative Analysis." *Journal of Nursing Scholarship,* 2000, *32*(4), 393–397.

Strauss, A., and Corbin, J. *Basics of Qualitative Research: Techniques and Procedures for Developing Grounded Theory.* Thousand Oaks, CA: Sage, 1998.

Trochim, W. "Outcome Pattern Matching and Program Theory." *Evaluation and Program Planning,* 1989, *12*(4), 355–366.

UN Global Pulse. *Mining Indonesian Tweets to Understand Food Prices.* New York: UN Global Pulse. www.unglobalpulse.org/sites/default/files/Global-Pulse-Mining-Indonesian-Tweets-Food-Price-Crises%20copy.pdf, 2014.

Vogt, W. P., Vogt., E. R., Gardner, D. C., and Haeffele, L. M. *Selecting the Right Analyses for Your Data: Quantitative, Qualitative and Mixed Methods.* New York: The Guilford Press, 2014.

Wadsworth, Y. *Everyday Evaluation on the Run: The User-Friendly Introductory Guide to Effective Evaluation* (4th ed.). Sydney, Australia: Allen and Unwin, 2011.

Wetherell, M., Taylor, S., and Yates, S. J. (eds.). *Discourse as Data: A Guide for Analysis.* London: Sage, 2001.

CHAPTER TWENTY-THREE

USING STATISTICS IN EVALUATION

Kathryn E. Newcomer, Dylan Conger

S tatistics are used in a variety of ways to support evaluation endeavors. The manner in which program and pertinent contextual factors are measured greatly affects the sorts of analytical techniques and statistical tests that are available for use.

A key distinction affecting choices of statistical tools is the level of measurement used for coding the phenomena of interest. In 1946, Stevens identified four levels of measurement: *nominal, ordinal, interval,* and *ratio.* These levels have been used to describe empirical data ever since. Under Stevens's taxonomy, nominal-level measurement entails simply attaching numbers to data for purposes of assigning them to groups with no order (for instance, assigning members in an evaluation of a job skills training program to the program group or the comparison group). Ordinal-level variables bear some ordered relationship to one another. For example, participants in the program might be "satisfied," "neutral," or "dissatisfied" with the services they received. Interval and ratio variables reflect an underlying numerical continuum where the distance between each value is equal (for instance, the program administrators might be interested in measuring program and comparison group members' hourly wages, in dollars, following the intervention). Ratio measures differ from interval measures only in the assumption of a meaningful zero point.

An enduring legacy of the Stevens taxonomy is the need to match the level of measurement to the analytical technique; it is frequently the case that the selection of the appropriate analytical technique is virtually pro forma once the levels of measurement of the key variables in the analysis have been established. In practical applications of statistics, other considerations, such as the audience's comfort level, also merit attention. Matching analytical techniques to the level of measurement, the audience, and evaluation questions is yet another challenge for evaluators.

Other chapters in this volume have referred to statistical decisions, such as determining an adequate sample size and selecting an appropriate measure of a program effect. This chapter offers more background for such decision making and guidance for selecting and understanding statistical techniques.

Descriptive Statistics: Simple Measures Used in Evaluations

When any phenomena are counted, the numbers can be tabulated according to a variety of procedures. If the resulting statistics, such as averages, are used to describe a group of items, the figures presented are called *descriptive* statistics. We focus here on two types of descriptive statistics: those intended to summarize information on a single variable (*univariate* statistics) and those intended to describe the relationship between two variables (*bivariate* statistics).

Univariate Statistics

Nominal variables are most easily summarized by frequency counts and percentages. For instance, the nominal variable "employment" is best summarized by the number and percentage of program group participants who are employed. Interval and ratio variables are better summarized with means and medians; for instance, the average and median wages of study participants. Ordinally measured outcome variables can be treated in a number of ways. Often evaluators will collapse the variable into two or three groups to simplify analyses. For instance, if program participants are asked in a survey to rank the services on a 5-point scale from *very unsatisfied* (1) to *very satisfied* (5), often the best summary measures to present are the percentages of participants who report that they are at least satisfied (a value of 4 or 5). Another summary measure that might be useful is the mean or median satisfaction score (with 3 capturing a neutral stance). When an ordinal scale contains fewer than five values, it is probably best to treat the scale as a nominal measure. Even if the scale contains five or more values, it is best first to examine the observed frequencies and then determine whether the range in the actual responses is sufficient for the scale to be treated as an interval measure. For example, if the vast majority of clients rated services 4 or 5 on a 5-point scale, the measure should probably not be treated as if it were interval.

Bivariate Statistics

Bivariate statistics are used to understand the relationship between two variables. In program evaluation, a basic question is whether participating in the program (the first variable) had the intended effect on the outcome of interest (the second variable). Establishing causal relationships between programs and outcomes requires a strong research design (see Chapters Five, Six, and Seven for a discussion of the strengths and weaknesses of evaluation designs), yet most designs begin with a simple measure of association between program participation and outcomes. There are many measures of association available to quantify the relationship between these two variables. We focus here on the two most commonly used measures in program evaluation: the difference between two percentages and the difference between two means (for more discussion of other measures, such as the Pearson's r correlation coefficient, see any standard statistics textbook; a list of some of these works is provided in the Further Reading section). Later in this chapter, we discuss regression analysis and slope coefficients, which are a natural extension of the differences between percentages and means.

Which difference the program evaluator chooses will be driven by the way that the outcome variable is measured. If the outcome variable is a nominal variable (for example, whether the study participant obtained a job within six months), the most straightforward measure of program effect is the difference between program and comparison group members in the percentages who obtained a job. Consider a study of a job training program with 100 program group members and 100 comparison group members. The evaluators examine the employment of both groups six months after the program group finishes the treatment and finds that sixty program group members obtained a job, while only forty comparison group members obtained a job. A straightforward measure of the relationship between program participation and employment is the difference between the employment percentages, in this example, 20 percentage points (60 percent – 40 percent).

If the outcome measure is the wages earned six months later (an interval variable), a simple summary measure would be the difference in the mean wages of the two groups. For instance, if the program group earns $10 an hour on average and the comparison group earns $7 an hour on average, the difference in the means is $3 an hour.

Relationships between nominal and ordinal variables are often best shown through the use of *cross-tabs* or *contingency tables*. Table 23.1 provides an example of the relationship between two ordinal variables: the level of participation (also referred to as program "dosage") of homeless clients in an art class

TABLE 23.1. EXAMPLE OF A CONTINGENCY TABLE WITH TWO ORDINAL VARIABLES: REPORTED INCIDENCE OF BOUTS OF DEPRESSION BY PARTICIPATION IN MORNING ART CLASSES.

	Level of Participation of Homeless Clients in Art Class		
	Never Participated in After-Breakfast Art Class	Participated in After-Breakfast Art Classes About Once a Week	Participated in After-Breakfast Art Classes Two or Three Times a Week
Reported number of bouts of depression			
More than once a week	53	33	29
At least weekly	21	33	33
Never	26	33	38
	100%	99%	100%

Note: Totals may not add up to 100 percent due to rounding.

and the reported incidence of bouts of depression. The evaluators are looking for signs that homeless persons who participated in the art classes have lower levels of depression, and that the higher the level of participation, the larger the drop in depression (also referred to as "dosage-response"). Such signs are found in the table. For instance, 53 percent of those who never participated in the program report depression more than once a week, compared to only 33 percent of those who participated once a week, and 29 percent of those who participated two or three times a week. One simple statement of estimated program impact would be that there is a 20 percentage point difference between nonparticipants and once-a-week participants in the experience of depression each week.

It is important to note that the numbers reported in Table 23.1 are descriptive statistics that have been calculated from a sample, not a population. Whether the differences shown in the table (for instance, the 20 percentage point gap) would have been found if data on the entire homeless population were available is a matter for inferential statistics, a subject we turn to next.

Inferential Statistics: From Samples to Populations

In many situations, the population of program recipients, or even service providers, is so large that to survey the entire population would be too costly.

Instead, a sample is drawn from the population, with the hope of generalizing the results to the population. When sample statistics are computed with the intention of generalizing from the sample to the population from which the sample was drawn, the statistics are referred to as *inferential* statistics. In this section, we offer tips on drawing samples and explain the two basic applications of inferential statistics: hypothesis testing and confidence intervals.

Sampling Tips

If statistics are to be generalized with confidence, the evaluator must ensure that the sample is drawn appropriately. If a group of units is selected in a systematic fashion so that the probability for each unit to be selected from the larger population is known, the group can be referred to as a *probability sample*. In lay terms, the ideal sample is selected so that all members of the population have an equal chance of being selected and so that nothing about them would change their probability of being selected. Four principles should guide evaluators when they select samples:

- The population of interest must be reasonably known and identifiable. This criterion presents a challenge for evaluators when records are not comprehensive. Therefore, evaluators should make efforts to ascertain whether the reason that information is missing also reveals a source of bias.
- A sampling technique should be used in which the probability for selecting any unit in the population can be calculated (*probability sampling*). Evaluators should use a sampling technique such as using random numbers to select units (*random sampling*), perhaps using the tables of random numbers found in textbooks or in statistical software, or selecting every *n*th unit in the population (*systematic sampling*). When there are specific subgroups within the population of particular interest, the evaluators may divide the population into such subgroups and apply probability sampling techniques within each of the subgroups, an approach called *stratified sampling*.
- A sample should be drawn that is of appropriate size relative to the size of the population to which generalization is desired. Basic statistics textbooks and software provide formulas that can be applied to identify appropriate sample sizes as long as the evaluators can specify how much confidence they wish to have in the results and the amount of error they are willing to accept.
- Even though probability sampling is applied, evaluators should examine a sample to ensure that it is truly representative of the population to which the

evaluators hope to generalize on variables of critical interest, such as demographic characteristics like gender and race. Probability sampling can help rule out chance variation that may conceal true relationships or impede accurate identification of program effects, but it cannot guarantee that the sample contains certain units or people in the same proportion as they exist in the population of interest.

When the data collection strategies make the use of probability sampling techniques impossible, as when evaluators do not have access to the full population, using statistics for inferential purposes may be problematic. In such cases, statistics should not be generalized from the sample to the population; evaluators should take even greater care to test the representativeness of the sample and identify sources of bias that render the sample unlike the population from which it was drawn. The statistics might then be used for inferential purposes with explicit recognition that the statistical inferences are not as valid as the numerical representation of confidence indicates.

Statistical Hypothesis Testing

The primary application of inferential statistics is statistical *hypothesis testing*. The process of hypothesis testing involves stating a hypothesis about a relationship between two variables in the population (for example, that participating in the training program increases earnings) and then using sample data to test that hypothesis. The actual test is conducted using a theoretical distribution known as the *sampling distribution*. The sampling distribution is the distribution of all possible sample outcomes that an evaluator would generate if she sampled from the population an infinite number of times. The evaluator cannot generate this distribution (she has the resources for only one sample), but fortunately, hundreds of years of statistical probability theory have resulted in some well-known properties of the sampling distribution. These properties allow evaluators to make educated guesses about populations by using the information on only one sample, provided it is randomly drawn. A full treatment of this distribution is beyond the scope of this chapter, but several good texts provide more detail (see, for example, Healey, 2006; additional texts are listed in the Further Reading section).

As described previously, the two most basic measures of bivariate relationships are the difference between two proportions and the difference between two means. Correspondingly, there are two primary inferential statistical tests that allow one to make statements about these differences in the population using sample statistics: the chi-square and the t test. We explain these two tests briefly in this section and offer more complete examples in Appendixes 23A and 23B. To lead up to our discussion of these two tests, we first provide an overview of hypothesis testing, including the concepts of false negatives and false positives, statistical confidence levels, and confidence intervals, all of which form the basis of statistical hypothesis tests.

The first step to statistical hypothesis testing is to identify the relationship between any two variables of interest. For two variables, a *null hypothesis* is stated. The null hypothesis in program evaluation is typically that the program has no effect in achieving the intended outcome. For example, "access to home health aides does not affect medical costs for emergency care" might be a null hypothesis for an evaluation of a home health aide program (from here forward, all reference to program "effect" assumes a very strong causal design). The alternative (or research) hypothesis is that the program does have the intended effect. The next step in the test is to determine whether this null hypothesis can be rejected or not rejected. When the null hypothesis is not rejected, the interpretation is that the sample data do not permit the evaluator to conclude that the program had the intended effect in the population.

If the program truly has no effect and the null is not rejected, there is no problem. Similarly, if the program has the intended effect and the test data demonstrate this, again there is no problem. Problems arise when there is a discrepancy between the true relationship in the population and the test results from the sample; in that case an erroneous conclusion can be drawn. If the true situation is that the program does not have the desired effect but the statistics calculated suggest that it does, an error called a *false positive*, or *type I error*, is committed. If the true situation is that the program does have the desired effect but the test data suggest that it does not, a *false negative*, or *type II error*, is committed.

It is difficult to protect equally against both types of errors, so the costs of committing each should be considered and attention paid to avoiding the more costly one. In some cases a false positive may be more costly to the public than a false negative. For example, when evaluators make a false-positive conclusion that a costly teenage pregnancy prevention program is effective when it really is not, the result may be that future funding is wasted on an ineffective program. A false-negative conclusion that an effective airline regulation is not working when it is may mean that this useful regulation is not reauthorized. In any case, aspects of the evaluation design that may make either a false positive or a false negative more likely should be carefully considered. Table 23.2 identifies design features that may make an evaluation vulnerable to either a false-positive or a false-negative finding. Evaluators should weigh

TABLE 23.2. EVALUATION DESIGN FEATURES LIKELY TO GENERATE FALSE POSITIVES OR FALSE NEGATIVES.

Design Features	Raises the Likelihood of False Positives	Raises the Likelihood of False Negatives
1. Threats to validity:		
a. The sample is made up of volunteers.	X	
b. The same instrument is used to assess participants at pretest and posttest. For instance, the same questions appear on pre- and posttest surveys.	X	
c. Experimental mortality—only the more motivated group members remain in the program to be measured.	X	
d. Hawthorne effect—the program participants are aware they are being measured and change their behavior in the desired direction.	X	
e. The program is new and program staff or participants are more motivated than they might be later in the life of the program.	X	
f. Control or comparison group members try to compensate for their failure to receive treatment.		X
g. Staff fear harm to the control group and try to compensate by providing more help to them.		X
2. Other design characteristics:		
a. The sample size is too small.		X
b. The time period for measurement is too short.		X
c. Control group members receive "treatment" from other sources.		X
d. The program is not fully implemented.		X

the consequences of committing both false-positive and false-negative errors and then identify ways in which they might minimize the more costly error.

Any measurement precaution that helps protect the evaluator from committing a false negative increases the statistical power of the test—the capability of a statistical test to accurately detect *effects* or differences between groups. Once the relative costs of committing a false positive and a false negative are considered, evaluators can develop a decision rule that reflects the level of confidence they wish to have in their decision to generalize the existence of relationships found in their sample to the population. Because the probabilities of committing a false positive and a false negative are inversely related, the more evaluators protect against one type of error, the more vulnerable the test will be to the opposite error.

Selecting a Statistical Confidence Level

A quantified decision rule for specifying how much evidence is needed to generalize results also indicates how confident the evaluator wishes to be that a false positive will not occur. This decision rule provides the confidence level for the test.

The confidence level reflects the amount of evidence evaluators want to have to ensure that they are correct in concluding that the program does produce the observed effect. In the social sciences and public affairs research, a 95 percent confidence level is conventionally used as a decision rule for testing statistical hypotheses. The null hypothesis to be tested is that the treatment does not have the intended effect. If the findings are sufficiently deviant from what the probability tables predict they would be if the null were true, the null hypothesis is rejected. This decision allows the evaluator to generalize the program effects found in the sample to the population from which the sample was drawn, with the confidence that over the long run a test of this type should result in a false-positive error only five times out of one hundred.

For some public program purposes, the 95 percent confidence level may be excessive. Conclusions for which evaluators are 80 percent or 90 percent confident may be adequate and will reduce the size of the sample needed, thereby reducing cost. When the costs to the public of committing a false negative are high—if, for example, an evaluation obtaining data from a very small sample risks judging an effective airline safety program to be ineffective—it may be appropriate to go beyond convention and use even an 80 percent confidence level. Although such a figure indicates that the risks of committing a false positive are greater than typically accepted, this lower confidence level helps hedge against making a false-negative error and dooming a program because the data do not seem to indicate that the program is effective.

Conducting a test that achieves significance at the 95 percent confidence level is typically interpreted in either of the following ways:

- One would obtain findings like this only five times out of one hundred samples if the null hypothesis (of no effect) was really true.
- One can be 95 percent confident that the sample findings were not simply the result of random variation.

When the null hypothesis is rejected (using the 95 percent decision rule), it is appropriate to state that the relationship in the sample data is "statistically significant at a confidence level of 95 percent." Concluding that a relationship between two variables is statistically significant tells the audience that following conventional statistical hypothesis testing procedures, the relationship found in the sample reflects a real relationship in the population from which the sample was drawn. However, generalizing a relationship can be subject to many other threats, such as a selection bias, perhaps due to the evaluator's not being able to obtain data on some of those in the sample (for example, because they refused to complete surveys) or due to those in the sample being volunteers. Even if the numbers demonstrate that the findings are statistically significant at the 95 percent confidence level, other problems with the representativeness of the sample may render the generalization of a relationship between two variables inappropriate.

Using a Confidence Interval to Convey Results

When the magnitude of a program effect (or the relationship between two variables) is given, the results should be reported as a confidence interval. The confidence interval is a range of most likely values of the population mean given the sample values. For example, an evaluator might report that "the proportion of clients still receiving welfare benefits was 5 to 10 percentage points lower for those who had completed the job training program compared to those who did not complete the training." Confidence intervals are one way to report the critical information on uncertainty (along with standard errors, margin of error, or p-values).

Reporting of both statistical significance and the size of program effects should be clear. Both findings should be reported and interpreted for the audience. For example, a difference between treatment and control groups may be minuscule yet be statistically significant at a specified confidence level, usually due to a very large sample size. Will policymakers care if a new program raises third graders' reading scores by 0.2 percent? Probably not; it is too small a gain if the program is at all costly.

Testing Statistical Significance for Nominal- and Ordinal-Level Variables: The Chi-Square Test

Now that we have laid the groundwork for hypothesis testing, we describe two tests in greater detail. The first is the *chi-square test*, a test that is used to test for relationships between nominal- and ordinal-level variables. The chi-square test provides an approach for testing the statistical significance of relationships between variables with any number of categories.

The chi-square test can be used in any situation in which evaluators are interested in the relationship between two nominal-level variables. In

TABLE 23.3. CONTINGENCY TABLE: PARTICIPANTS' PREFERENCES FOR YMCA PROGRAMMING BY GENDER OF CHILD.

Reported Favorite Type of YMCA Programming	All ($n = 50$)	Observed Boys ($n = 22$)	Observed Girls ($n = 28$)	Expected Boys ($n = 22$)	Expected Girls ($n = 28$)
Science and technology	18%	27%	11%	18%	18%
Sports	28%	45%	14%	28%	28%
Creative and performing arts	54%	27%	75%	54%	54%
Total	100%	99%	100%	100%	100%

Note: Totals may not add up to 100 percent due to rounding.

fact, although the most typical application of the chi-square test pertains to nominal-level scales, chi-square tests are frequently also used with ordinal scales and sometimes even with collapsed interval and ratio scales (although more powerful tests are available and would generally be preferred over chi-square in such cases).

The logic behind the chi-square test is that it compares a set of observed frequencies (or proportions) to frequencies (proportions) that would be expected under a certain set of assumptions. Suppose evaluators interviewed children participating in YMCA youth programs as part of an analysis to help the YMCA target programming more effectively. Although the sample of respondents is not totally random, because there were virtually no refusals, the evaluators assume they can apply chi-square to test whether they can generalize their findings for differences in programming preferences between the boys and the girls they interviewed to all target participants (whom they did not interview). Their sample has fifty participants. They decide to use the conventional decision rule of 95 percent. Thus the null hypothesis being tested is *gender has no effect on programming preferences.* And the alternative hypothesis is *gender does affect programming preferences.*

Table 23.3 shows the observed programming preferences for the entire sample of children and for boys and girls separately. For instance, 18 percent of all children sampled rank science and technology highest, with boys ranking it higher than girls do, 27 percent and 11 percent, respectively. Recall the simple bivariate measure here: a gender difference of 16 percentage points in preferences for science and technology. The inferential question is whether (and more specifically, the probability that) this difference of 16 percentage points could have been drawn from a population where the true difference is

TABLE 23.4. PARTICIPANTS' PREFERENCES FOR YMCA PROGRAMMING BY GENDER OF CHILD.

Reported Favorite Type of YMCA Programming	Boys ($n = 22$)	Girls ($n = 28$)
Science and technology	27.3	10.7
Sports	45.5	14.3
Creative and performing arts	27.3	75.0
	100.1%	100%

Note: Chi-square is statistically significant at the 95 percent confidence level; totals may not add up to 100 percent due to rounding.

zero. Thus the chi-square test compares the sample distributions shown on the left side of the table to the distributions that would be observed if there were no difference between boys and girls in preferences. These expected differences are shown in the last two columns of the table. Not coincidentally, the preferences among boys and girls are the same in the expected distribution (hence, a gender difference of zero). The chi-square test generates the chi-square statistic, which summarizes the difference between the observed and expected distributions. If they are far enough apart, then the probability that a sample difference of this size could have come from a population where the real difference is zero will be very low (say less than 0.05), and the null hypothesis can be rejected with 95 percent confidence.

Appendix 23A provides more detail on how this test is conducted using a commonly used software program—Statistical Package for the Social Sciences (SPSS). Table 23.4 provides an example of how the data and results of the chi-square test might be displayed in an evaluation report.

Chi-square results do not tell us how strongly two variables are related. Measures of the strength of the relationship, such as the percentage point difference between categories, should be used along with chi-square to address the magnitude of the relationship analyzed.

Testing Statistical Significance of Difference of Means: The *t* Test

The second most commonly used hypothesis test is the *t* test, which allows researchers to test for the difference between two means. The null hypothesis in this test is often that the difference between the two means is zero. The alternative is that the difference is non-zero, and the test is set up to determine whether the zero-difference hypothesis can be rejected.

TABLE 23.5. REPORTED NUMBER OF YEARS PARTICIPATING IN YMCA PROGRAMS BY GENDER OF CHILD AND BY FAVORITE TYPE OF PROGRAMMING.

	N	Mean Reported Number of Years Participating in YMCA Programs	Is *t* Test of Difference in Means Statistically Significant at 95%?
Total sample			
Boys	22	4.1	No
Girls	28	5.6	
Among those whose favorite programs are science and technology			
Boys	6	2	Yes
Girls	3	7	
Among those whose favorite programs are sports			
Boys	10	5.8	No
Girls	4	8	
Among those whose favorite programs are creative and performing arts			
Boys	6	3.3	No
Girls	21	4.6	

Let's return to the example of the YMCA program. Suppose the evaluators want to know whether there is a difference between boys and girls in the number of years in which they participate in the YMCA programs. Thus, the dependent variable is the number of years in which the children report having participated in the YMCA programs, and the independent variable is gender (boys versus girls). The null hypothesis is *gender is not associated with the length of time (in years) participants attend YMCA programs.* And the alternative hypothesis is *gender does affect the length of time (in years) participants attend YMCA programs.* The mean years of participation for boys is 4.09 and the mean years for girls is 5.61, a difference of 1.52 years. Similar to the chi-square test, the *t* test asks what the probability is that the difference of means observed in this sample could have been drawn from a population where the true difference of means is zero. As explained earlier, the *t* test can be conducted using any confidence level. The 95 percent level is the default in most fields. Yet the sensitivity of the test can be increased with a higher risk of false significance, such as 90 percent. Given that the stakes for a false negative are not high here (that is, if there is truly a difference in the population yet the *t* test fails to reject the null), sticking with the default 95 percent decision rule is recommended.

Appendix 23B provides the results of the *t* test for this example. Table 23.5 provides an example of how this information might be conveyed in an evaluation report. In addition to providing the difference between means for the overall sample, Table 23.5 provides the difference between means among youths with different program preferences.

By looking within program preference selections, the analysis essentially examines the relationship between gender and years, controlling for program preferences. In the next section we discuss another way to examine relationships between two variables, controlling for others; the technique is regression analysis.

Regression Analysis

Regression analysis is an extraordinarily powerful tool that finds frequent use in evaluation and applied research. Regression analysis is used to describe relationships, test theories, and make predictions with data from experimental or observational studies, linear or nonlinear relationships, and continuous or categorical predictors. Regression is a natural extension of the simple bivariate relationships described earlier, and yet it offers much more, including the ability to control for the influence of other variables and the flexibility to model nonlinear relationships among variables. The user must select specific regression models that are appropriate to the data and research questions. Many excellent books provide extended discussion of regression analysis (again, Healey, 2006, is an example; others are listed in the Further Reading section). In this chapter we focus on concepts, vocabulary, computer commands and output, and presenting results to a nontechnical audience in the context of basic applications relevant to evaluation.

Introduction to the Multiple Regression Model

Many practical questions involve the relationship between a dependent or criterion variable of interest (call it Y) and a set of k independent variables or potential predictor variables (call them $X_1, X_2, X_3, \ldots, Xk$), where the scores on all variables are measured for N cases. For example, evaluators might be interested in predicting performance (Y) using information on years of experience (X_1), an aptitude test (X_2), and participation in a training program (X_3). A multiple regression equation for predicting Y can be expressed as follows:

$$\hat{Y} = \hat{B}_{0X_2} + \hat{B}_1 X_1 + \hat{B}_2 + \hat{B}_3 X_3.$$

To apply the equation, each X score for an individual case is multiplied by the corresponding value, the products are added together, and the constant is added to the sum. The result is $Y\hat{\ }$, the predicted Y value for the individual case. is called the intercept because it is where the regression line *intercepts* Y when $X = 0$; it is the predicted value of Y when all the X's are zero. In this example, B_0 is the predicted performance for someone with zero years of experience, a zero on the aptitude test, and no participation in a training program. All the other B's (known as *slope coefficients*) tell us how much Y changes when one of the X's is increased by one unit and the other X's are held constant. For instance, is the change in Y that is predicted when years of experience increases by one year. If X_3 is coded as 1 for people who participated in the training program and 0 for people who do not (the comparison group), then tells us the predicted performance difference between people who do and do not participate in the program, holding years of experience and aptitude constant. More specifically, is the *adjusted difference of means* between program and comparison group members.

Can performance be predicted better than chance using this regression equation? Does the training program improve evaluators' ability to predict performance, or can they do as well with only the first two predictors? Could evaluators improve prediction by including an additional variable? Is the relationship between performance and years of experience linear, or is the relationship curvilinear? Is the relationship between aptitude and performance stronger or weaker for people who participated in the training program? Regression models can be designed to address these questions and more.

To provide an example of regression analysis, let's return to the example of the relationship between gender and years of program participation. To simplify our explanation of regression, we have the dependent variable as years and only one independent variable; the variable *FEMALE* is a nominal variable equal to 1 if the child is female and 0 if the child is male. A variable that takes on values of only 0 or 1 is called a *dummy* or *indicator* variable. With dummy-coded group membership as the independent variable and the dependent variable in a regression analysis, we obtain the following results:

$$\hat{Y}EARS = 4.59 + 1.52FEMALE$$

This means that the predicted years of experience 5 4.59 1 1.52 * *FEMALE*. Thus, when *FEMALE* = 0, the predicted years is 4.59. When *FEMALE* = 1, the predicted years is 4.59 1 (1.52 * 1) = 5.61. Not coincidentally, these are the same means (and difference of means) discussed in explaining the t test.

If there is no significant difference between the group means in the population, then *FEMALE* is not a useful predictor of the *YEARS*, and the slope () in a sample would not differ significantly from zero. In the regression equation, a t test can also be used to test for the statistical significance of the B's.

We can compare this test to the standard independent samples t test. The t test is based on the assumptions that samples are randomly selected from the populations of interest, that the residuals (errors in prediction) are reasonably normally distributed, and that the variance of these errors is about the same at each level of X. The test results, conclusions, and assumptions for the regression analysis are identical to those from the t test analysis.

Tips on Pulling It All Together: Practical Significance

The terms *significance* and *statistical significance* are conventionally reserved for the judgment that sample results showing a relationship between variables can be generalized to the population from which the sample was drawn. A separate judgment should be made regarding the magnitude of the effect that is being measured. In fact the presentation and terminology used should clarify that two separate judgments are made: whether the sample data can be generalized and whether the size of the effect is slight, moderate, or strong. Judgments about the size of the effect reflect what the evaluators view as the practical importance of the measured effect. For example, if a new mathematics curriculum in a high school appears to raise students' achievement scores by 1 percent, then even if the large sample drawn indicates that the effect is statistically significant, the size of the impact of the curriculum may seem inconsequential.

There are no standards available for evaluators to use when interpreting the magnitude of the observed effect (or the observed relationship between two or more measures). For example, most statistics measuring the magnitude of relationships between measures range from 0 to 1, or –1 to 11, and the closer to 1 (or –1) a number falls, the stronger the relationship is. There are no conventionally accepted rules to indicate what number is high enough to call "high." The best way to evaluate such numbers is to compare them to appropriate referents, such as comparable figures for previous years, other administrative units, or comparable programs. Indeed, one useful benchmark for determining the importance of the effect of a particular intervention is to compare it to the effect of the best alternative interventions. Appropriate and meaningful comparisons are absolutely essential to lend credibility to measures of magnitude. Statistical tests of the strength of the relationship between two variables are available that reflect how the two variables are measured and whether the analyst can convincingly argue that one of the variables is associated with the other.

Selecting Appropriate Statistics

Evaluators should use a number of criteria to ensure selecting the most appropriate statistics in a particular situation. The three categories of criteria that evaluators should use in deciding which statistical technique will be most appropriate are presented in Box 23.1. The substantive questions identified to guide an evaluation, the data collection decisions made about how to measure the phenomena of interest, and the type of audience the evaluator is addressing all affect selection of statistical techniques.

Box 23.1. Criteria for Selecting Appropriate Data Analysis Techniques

Question-Related Criteria
- Is generalization from the sample to the population desired?
- Is the causal relationship between an alleged cause and alleged effect of interest? Is it an impact question?
- Does the question (or statutory or regulatory document) contain quantitative criteria to which results can be compared?

Measurement-Related Criteria
- At what level of measurement were the variables measured: nominal (for example, gender), ordinal (for example, attitudes measured with Likert-type scales), or interval (for example, income)?
- Were multiple indicators used to measure key variables?
- What are the sample sizes in pertinent subgroups?
- How many observations were recorded for the respondents: one, two (for example, preprogram and postprogram), or more (time-series)?
- Are the samples independent or related? That is, was the sample measured at two or more points in time (related)?
- What is the distribution of each of the variables of interest, such as bimodal or normal?
- How much precision was incorporated in the measures?
- Are there outliers affecting calculation of statistics: that is, extremely high or low values that skew the mean and other statistics?

Audience-Related Criteria
- Will the audience understand sophisticated analytical techniques, such as multiple regression?

- Will graphic presentations of data (such as bar charts) be more appropriate than tables filled with numbers?
- How much precision does the audience want in numerical estimates?
- Will audience members be satisfied with graphs depicting trends, or will they desire more sophisticated analyses, such as regressions?
- Will the audience members understand the difference between statistical significance and the practical importance of numerical findings?

Sample data are usually selected with the intention of generalizing results to the population from which the sample units were drawn. Statistics that allow such generalizations include chi-square and t. Which of these statistics is selected depends on how the variables were measured. Chi-square can be used no matter how the variables are measured, but the t test requires that the dependent variable (typically the program effect) be measured at the interval or ratio level—for example, an unemployment rate or income. Appendix 23B provides an illustration of applying the t test using SPSS software.

No matter which analytical technique is selected, both the statistic used to assess statistical significance and the magnitude of an effect or the strength of the relationships analyzed should be reported. Table 23.6 displays objectives evaluators may have in analyzing data and the statistical techniques frequently used to address those objectives.

Selecting Techniques to Sort Measures or Units

When multiple indicators have been used to measure a phenomenon of interest, such as a program effect, there are two basic *situations*—one in which criteria for measuring effect are set for the evaluators before they collect any data and one in which they are uncertain. The approach devolves from the situation.

When criteria for measuring a program effect, such as quality of services, are set for evaluators, the measures used may simply be aggregated. A summary index can be used that weights different measures and then sums the total.

When evaluators are unsure of the basic factors that best express the criterion of interest, they can use analytical techniques that sort through the indicators to identify covariation that might permit the creation of indices. *Factor analysis* is the technique most frequently used for such data-reduction purposes. The logic supporting factor analysis is that there are underlying factors that explain the observed variation in the indicators. The correlations

TABLE 23.6. MATCHING STATISTICAL TECHNIQUES TO ANALYTICAL OBJECTIVES.

Objective of the Analysis	How the Variables Are Measured	Appropriate Technique	Appropriate Test for Statistical Significance	Appropriate Measure of Magnitude
To compare a sample distribution to a population distribution	Nominal/ordinal	Frequency counts	Chi-square	Differences in column percentages
	Interval	Means and mediansStandard deviations/interquartile range	Chi-square	Difference in column percentages
To analyze a relationship between two variables	Nominal/ordinal	Contingency tables	Chi-square	See Table 2 and difference in column percentages
	Interval	Contingency tables	Chi-square	Difference in column percentages
		Test of differences of means or proportions	t	Difference in means
To reduce the number of variables through identifying factors that explain variation in a larger set of variables	Interval	Factor analysis	NA	Pearson's correlations; Eigenvalues
To sort units into similar clusters or groupings	Nominal/ordinal/interval	Cluster analysis; discriminant function analysis	F, Wilks' lambda	Canonical/correlation coefficient[2]
To predict or estimate program impact	Nominal/ordinal dependent variable	Log linear regression	t and F	Odds estimates
	Interval dependent variable	Regression	t and F	R^2, beta weights
To describe or predict a trend in a series of data collected over time	Dummy (0,1) or interval independent variables but interval dependent variable	Regression	t and F	R^2, beta weights

among the indicators are examined to identify patterns suggesting independent groups of covarying measures that might actually be reflecting more fundamental factors. For example, an evaluation of air controllers' responses to new regulations might start with a set of forty-five indicators but, with factor analysis, the number might be reduced to five basic concerns.

Sometimes, evaluators wish to sort units such as delivery sites into groups to identify characteristics of high or low performers. If the criterion on which the units are evaluated as low and high is known beforehand, *discriminant function analysis* can be used to identify the other characteristics of the units that will best predict which units will score high on the criterion measure. Discriminant function analysis is similar to regression in that it identifies linear combinations (models) of other variables that best predict the groupings—of high and low performers, for example. To illustrate, suppose evaluators were trying to identify key characteristics of parolees who commit crimes versus those who do not commit crimes after release. Discriminant function analysis might allow evaluators to use five indicators describing the parolees to identify characteristics most likely to predict recidivism.

When the criterion on which units are to be disaggregated is not known beforehand, *cluster analysis* can be used to identify similar groupings. Cluster analysis differs from factor analysis in that the objective is to group objects, typically people or units, rather than to identify groupings among variables. Characteristics of programs such as the level of administrative workload and other contextual characteristics might be used to identify clusters. An evaluator of an interjurisdictional program, such as legal services to the poor, might be interested in identifying clusters of offices that appear to operate under many of the same constraints. In this case, cluster analysis might be applied to identify characteristics that seem to differentiate most consistently across the offices. (See Hair, Anderson, Tatham, and Black, 1998, for more on factor analysis, discriminant function analysis, and cluster analysis.)

Other Factors Affecting Selection of Statistical Techniques

In addition to considering how statistics will be used in an evaluation, evaluators must consider other criteria when selecting a statistical technique. Sample size, for instance, may have a dramatic effect on an analysis; a small sample may fail to demonstrate an effect for a program, and preclude any further analysis of subgroup differences.

In addition to the actual size of a sample, the number of observations recorded for the units of interest is pertinent when evaluators are choosing statistical techniques. For example, when two or more observations are taken on the same units, change over time may be analyzed, and the notion of related samples is introduced, leading to the selection of statistics created just for such situations. When many observations are available on a specific phenomenon, such as traffic fatalities over a series of years or infant mortality rates for specific jurisdictions over a period of years, time-series techniques employing regression may be applied.

Before employing any statistical technique, evaluators should examine the distribution of the units along each of the variables or measures. Such basic frequency analysis will indicate how much the units vary on each of the variables. For example, if race is of interest in an analysis of the impact of a management training course on managers, and only two of fifty-six training participants are minority group members, it will be impossible to use race as a variable in any analysis. If age of program participants is of interest in an evaluation but a sample contains only fifteen- and sixteen-year-olds, the low variation on age rules out many analytical techniques. When a variable is measured at the interval level but the sample range is very narrow, the techniques available are limited to those appropriate for ordinal variables.

Similarly, if measurement was intended to be expressed in intervals but responses indicate that respondents could not make such fine differentiations, then techniques requiring interval measures are again ruled out. For example, survey questions asking researchers to report the percentages of their time devoted to each of three areas—research, administration, and teaching—are intended to yield interval measures given in percentages. However, if almost all respondents respond "about half" or "about one-third" to these questions, this level of precision suggests that these variables should be analyzed as ordinal, not interval, measures.

The question of how to handle outliers frequently arises. Basic statistics such as the mean and standard deviation can be skewed by extreme values (outliers). It may be tempting to report statistics without the inflating effect of units that vary wildly from most other units. One option is to select statistics that are not affected by outliers, such as a median in place of a mean or an interquartile range (the interval capturing the middle 50 percent of the scores) in place of a standard deviation. When applying more sophisticated techniques, such as regression, a good option is to conduct and report analyses both with and without outliers.

Evaluators should ascertain whether highly sophisticated techniques with numerical statistics will be accessible and desirable for their clients. Anticipating clients' preferences may automatically disqualify some techniques. For example, instead of inserting an SPSS printout (like Exhibits 23A.1 and 23B.1) in an evaluation report or appendix, present a more user-friendly version of the same data (like Tables 23.4 and 23.5). Evaluators who are not trained in statistics should employ a statistician to help them make decisions about specific statistical techniques. The most frequently used statistical software packages—SPSS, SAS, and STATA—are user friendly and well documented, but they do not obviate the need for consulting a statistician.

Reporting Statistics Appropriately

Clarity is essential when statistical results are reported. The level of detail provided is again contingent on clients' expectations and preferences. Box 23.2 contains a number of suggestions for reporting statistical analyses. Box 23.3 (with Figures 23.1 and 23.2) provides guidance on using data visualization techniques when reporting statistics.

The degree to which the tables and graphs providing statistical results are user friendly is also important. To assist readers, consolidation of numerous analyses is helpful. Abbreviations, acronyms, and software jargon are often confusing to readers. Complete information about how variables were measured should accompany tables, with sufficient information to allow the reader to assess the adequacy of measurements used.

Box 23.2. Tips for Presenting Data Analyses

Identify Contents of All Tables and Figures Clearly
- Use the title to identify the variables or measures used.
- Label all variables or measures with adequate detail.
- Provide the exact wording of the relevant questions on the table or figure.
- Identify program components and program results (alleged causes and alleged effects).

Indicate Use of Decision Rules in Analysis
- State whether a category for missing or inapplicable responses is included in the analysis.
- If values of variables were collapsed to create fewer categories, such as "Low" and "High," state where the cutoffs were made.
- If the term *average* or *midpoint* is used, state whether this means *mean* or *median*.

Consolidate Analyses Whenever Possible
- Present only the percentage reporting yes for questions to which the only response possible is yes or no.

(Continued)

- Present in one table the percentages for a series of substantively related questions.
- Collapse responses to contrast agrees versus disagrees, omitting unsure responses if appropriate.

Do Not Abbreviate
- Do not present the shortened table and figure titles or labels used during data processing.
- Do not use acronyms.
- Do not use statistical symbols to represent statistics.

Provide Basic Information About Measurement of Variables
- Give the minimum and maximum value for each variable used.
- Give the sample size (or number of respondents reporting) for each variable displayed in a table or figure.
- Provide complete information about the scale or measurement mechanism used—for example, "scale ran from 1 (meaning Not at All Relevant) to 5 (meaning Completely Relevant)."

Present Appropriate Percentages
- Provide percentages, not raw figures.
- Clearly identify the base from which percentages were calculated.
- Calculate percentages on the appropriate base, for example, "85 percent of the treatment group scored high on the criterion," not, "32 percent of those scoring high were in the treatment group."

Present Information on Statistical Significance Clearly
- Present the confidence level used in each table, such as 90 percent or 95 percent.
- Be consistent in reporting confidence levels across all tables in a report.
- Show which statistics were statistically significant through the use of asterisks with clear legends.
- Do not present raw values of statistics, such as chi-square, and expect readers to calculate statistical significance.

Present Information on the Magnitude of Relationships Clearly
- Distinguish between statistics showing the statistical significance of relationships and statistics measuring the strength of relationships or the magnitude of effects.
- Present the confidence interval or error band around measures of strength or magnitude in a user-friendly manner: for example, "Program participants' scores were from 20 percent to 24 percent higher than those of the comparison group."

- Comment on the importance of the magnitude of the relationship or effect as well as noting whether it was statistically significant.

Use Graphics to Present Analytical Findings Clearly
- Use zero as the starting point for axes in graphs.
- Use appropriate scales, so that figures will not be unduly distorted.
- Use colors or patterns (for example, stripes) whenever possible to present more than one line on the graph.
- Label lines on the graph, not in the legend.
- Do not use more than four patterns or colors to represent groups if possible.

A good reality test of completeness is for the evaluators to examine the statistics reported and the explanatory information provided and then to ask themselves whether an analyst outside the project could write a report from these statistics without needing any additional data. Replicability is a hallmark of accuracy and thoroughness for any analysis.

The last step in completing a thorough analysis of quantitative data is to report any threats to the statistical validity of the information provided. Common weaknesses are samples that are too small and application of techniques without meeting all assumptions or criteria appropriate for their use. The challenge for the evaluator is to provide a user-friendly explanation of all decisions made and a critical assessment of the statistical accuracy that the test can reasonably be expected to provide. (Chapter Twenty-Six provides guidance on acknowledgment of threats to validity.)

Box 23.3. Data Visualization

The goal of data visualization is to succinctly convey a message about the content being presented, not to demonstrate the author's expertise in data visualization. In order to be effective, data visualization should:

1. Be Understandable
- Design tables and figures to be clear for all of the report's audiences.
- Report only needed statistics so that tables and figures are not unnecessarily complex.
- Include interpretation of data and statistics so that readers do not need to perform calculations to understand the data.

(Continued)

2. Be Free Standing
- Include enough information so that tables and figures do not require additional explanation.
- Explain measurement processes (e.g. original question wording should be provided).
- Do not rely on color coding and/or acronyms that will not be clear to the audience.
- Tables and figures should be readable, even if the report is photocopied in black and white.

3. Support the Key Message(s)
- Design tables and figures with similar font, color, and placement as the rest of the report.
- Place tables and figures adjacent to the text that references them.
- Use graphics and figures to emphasize key takeaways.

(See Evergreen, 2014, for more on data visualization.)

TABLE 23.7. PERCENTAGE OF INDIVIDUALS WHO REPORTED FEELING COMFORTABLE DESIGNING CHARTS AND TABLES BY YEAR.

	2008	2009	2010	2011	2012	2013	2014
Overall (n = 1500)	15%	14%	16%	12%	11%	64%	75%
Data analysts (n = 100)	80%	82%	81%	80%	79%	92%	91%
Program staff (n = 1400)	10%	9%	11%	7%	6%	62%	74%

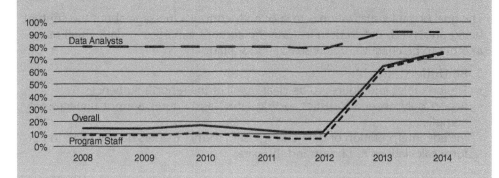

TABLE 23.8. HOW EFFECTIVE WAS THE LECTURE AT TEACHING YOU ABOUT DATA VISUALIZATION? BY GENDER.

	Men(n = 400)	Women(n = 350)
Not at all effective – 0	7%	10%
1	13%	15%
Somewhat effective – 2	25%	37%
3	35%	23%
Very effective – 4	20%	15%

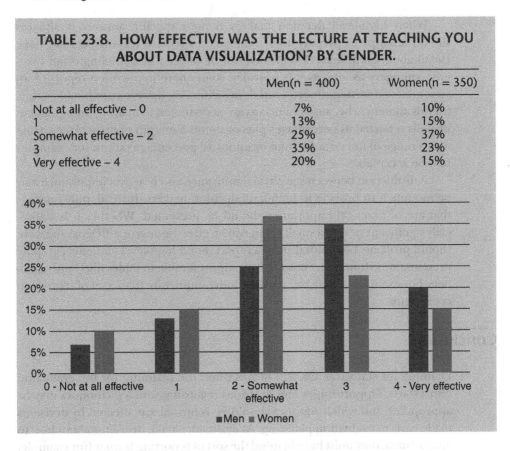

Reporting Statistical Results to High-Level Public Officials

The advice offered here for reporting statistical results applies in most situations. However, reports for high-level officials, such as mayors and legislators, present a special case. Typically, these clients are not concerned with technical issues such as statistical confidence and confidence intervals. In fact, they may not want to hear evaluators' findings diluted by statements specifying that the numbers may (or may not) fall within a range.

The unique challenge to evaluators reporting directly to the highest-level decision makers is to convey the tentative nature of statistical results accurately without excessive hedging. Certainty is simply not part of a statistician's vocabulary; statistical inference offers best estimates, not specific answers.

When high-level decision makers request specific answers, evaluators should attempt to prepare their audience to receive less-than-certain data. Detail about confidence levels need not be offered in a briefing or an executive summary as long as it is provided somewhere in a written report or an appendix to a written report. Confidence intervals, however, are not too exotic for this audience, because politicians are accustomed to hearing their popularity polls reported as percentages plus or minus a margin of error. An estimate with a range of uncertainty (plus or minus 10 percentage points, for example) may be acceptable.

A distinction between statistical significance and practical importance may be too much to provide to high-level decision makers. Instead, only findings that are of practical importance should be presented. Whether it is statistically significant or not, a small change in an effectiveness or efficiency measure should probably be omitted from a report. For a high-level audience, graphic presentations showing trends are typically preferable to tables filled with numbers. For example, a time trend will be more impressive than a set of regression coefficients.

Conclusion

Planning for statistical analyses begins when the planning for the evaluation effort starts. Opportunities and decisions regarding which techniques may be appropriate and which statistics should be reported are affected by decisions made early in evaluation planning. As evaluators make decisions about how to analyze data, they must have in mind the sort of reporting format (for example, highly quantitative? or rich in detail?) that their clients will want in an analytical report. In addition to clients' expectations, the questions that are addressed, the measurement decisions made, and the need to depend on samples to generalize quantitative results to larger populations all shape evaluators' decision making regarding statistics. Statistics never speak for themselves, but evaluators must take great care to ensure that they speak with statistics accurately and clearly.

Appendix 23A: An Application of the Chi-Square Statistic Calculated with SPSS

The Problem. Recall the problem explained in the text. Evaluators interviewed children participating in YMCA youth programs as part of an analysis intended to help the YMCA target programming more effectively. Although the sample of respondents is not totally random, because there were virtually no refusals, the evaluators assume they can apply chi-square to test whether they can generalize their findings for differences in programming preferences between the boys and the girls they interviewed to all target participants (whom they did not interview). Their sample has fifty participants. They decided to use the conventional decision rule of 95 percent. Thus the null hypothesis being tested is *gender has no effect on programming preferences.* And the alternative hypothesis is *gender does affect programming preferences.*

Exhibit 23A.1 provides the computer printout produced by SPSS to analyze the relationship between program participants' preferences and gender. The printout provides the results of the chi-square test along with some other measures of association. The SPSS printout produces too much information, and you would not want to provide all of it to readers. The essential data are presented more clearly in Table 23.4.

The Solution. A chi-square of statistical significance can be calculated for these data. The chi-square tests the null hypothesis that there is no difference in YMCA program preferences expressed by boys and girls. Calculation of chi-square first involved computing what would have been the expected frequencies in the table if the null hypothesis were true, then comparing these expected frequencies with the observed frequencies. A chi-square distribution can be consulted to identify the value of chi-square that would be needed to reject the null hypothesis and allow 95 percent confidence in this conclusion. To use a chi-square table, one must calculate the degrees of freedom; for the chi-square, this number is calculated as (the number of rows in the table − 1) multiplied by (the number of columns in the table − 1). For the problem at hand, the degrees of freedom is $(3-1)$ multiplied by $(2-1)$, or 2. For a 95 percent confidence level and 2 degrees of freedom, a chi-square table indicates 5.99 as the number that must be exceeded in order for the null hypothesis (that there is no generalizable difference between the preferences for the groups) to be rejected. Thus the decision rule for this problem is as follows: if the calculated chi-square exceeds 5.99, the null hypothesis of no difference in the program preferences of boys and girls will be rejected.

The following are the steps in testing the hypothesis of no relationship between gender and program preferences:

Step 1. Compute chi-square (see the Exhibit 23A.1). Chi-square is the sum of the squared difference between the expected frequency and the observed frequency divided by the expected frequency for each cell.

Step 2. Compare the computed chi-square (shown as the Pearson chi-square) to the decision rule set earlier. In this example, the

EXHIBIT 23A.1. SPSS PRINTOUT OF ANALYSIS OF THE RELATIONSHIP BETWEEN YMCA PROGRAM PREFERENCES AND GENDER

Gender of Child * Favorite Type of Programming Cross-Tabulation

Favorite Type of Programming

			Science and Technology	Sports	Creative and Performing Arts	Total
Gender of Child	Male	Count	6	10	6	22
		% within Gender of Child	27.30%	45.50%	27.30%	100.00%
		% within Favorite Type of Programming	66.70%	71.40%	22.20%	44.00%
		% of Total	12.00%	20.00%	12.00%	44.00%
	Female	Count	3	4	21	28
		% within Gender of Child	10.70%	14.30%	75.00%	100.00%
		% within Favorite Type of Programming	33.30%	28.60%	77.80%	56.00%
		% of Total	6.00%	20.00%	42.00%	56.00%
Total		Count	9	14	27	50
		% within Gender of Child	18.00%	28.00%	54.00%	100.00%
		% within Favorite Type of Programming	100.00%	100.00%	100.00%	100.00%
		% of Total	18.00%	28.00%	54.00%	100.00%

EXHIBIT 23A.1. SPSS PRINTOUT OF ANALYSIS OF THE RELATIONSHIP BETWEEN YMCA PROGRAM PREFERENCES AND GENDER *(Continued)*

Case Processing Summary

Cases

	Valid		Missing		Total	
	N	Percent	N	Percent	N	Percent
Gender of Child *Favorite Type of Programming	50	100.00%	0	0%	50	100.00%

Chi-Square Tests

	Value	Df	Asymp. Sig. (2-sided)	Exact Sig. (2-sided)
Pearson Chi-Square	11.348*	2	0.003	
Likelihood Ratio	11.780	2	0.003	
McNemar Test				b
N of Valid Cases	50			

*1 cells (16.7%) have expected count less than 5. The minimum expected count is 3.96.

computed chi-square of 11.348 is greater than 5.99, so evaluators can reject the null hypothesis of no difference between the boys' and girls' program preferences.

Step 3. To convey the finding in an appropriate manner, the evaluators would use wording such as this: "Based on our sample of fifty participants, there was a difference between the boys and girls in terms of their program preferences, and this difference in the sample is large enough for us to conclude that differences exist in the population at the 95 percent confidence level." Note that a generalization of gender-based differences from the sample to the population, the alternative

TABLE 23A.1. EFFECT OF SAMPLE SIZE ON CHI-SQUARE.

Rearrested Within Twelve Months of Release	Prisoner Served Full Sentence	Prisoner Released into Halfway House Six Months Prior to End of Sentence
Yes	63.3	58.6
No	36.7	41.4
	100%	100%
Sample Size	x^2	**Significance**
100	.1984	NS
2000	3.97	.05
3500	7.00	.01

hypothesis, is supported. In fact, boys were more than twice as likely as girls to identify science and technology and sports programs as their favorite programs, whereas girls were almost three times as likely as boys to select creative and performing arts as their favorite YMCA program.

The chi-square test requires expected frequencies that are not very small. The reason for this is that chi-square tests the underlying probabilities in each cell, and when the expected cell frequencies fall, these probabilities cannot be estimated with sufficient precision. Because the formula for computation of chi-square includes the expected value of the cell frequency in the denominator, the chi-square value would be overestimated if this value were too small, resulting in the rejection of the null hypothesis.

To avoid incorrect inferences from the chi-square test, a commonly applied (albeit possibly too conservative) general rule is that an expected frequency less than 5 in a cell is too small to use. Conservatively, when the contingency table contains more than one cell with an expected frequency less than 5, it is often appropriate to combine them to get an expected frequency of 5 or more. However, in doing so, the number of categories will be reduced, resulting in less information.

The chi-square test is also quite sensitive to the sample size. Table 23A.1 illustrates the impact of sample size on chi-square. Notice in the lower half of the table that the chi-square value (x^2) increases as the sample size increases, so that samples of 2,000 and above render the results statistically significant (note that the significance column provides probabilities that are at or below .05) but a sample size of 100 renders results that are not statistically significant (NS).

TABLE 23A.2. EFFECT OF COLLAPSING TABLES ON CHI-SQUARE.

Level of Medicare Patient Satisfaction with Facility	Location of Procedure	
	Outpatient Clinics ($N = 100$)	Hospitals ($N = 100$)
1 Not at all satisfied	10	12
2	10	13
3	12	9
4	25	28
5 Extremely satisfied	43	38
	100%	100%

With 5 rows and 2 columns, x^2 would have to exceed 9.50 for the significance level to fall below .05.

1,2	20	25
3, 4, 5	80	75
	100%	100%

With 2 rows and 2 columns, x^2 would have to exceed 3.84 for the significance level to fall below .05.

Note for Appendix 23A

Running Crosstabs. To develop a contingency table in SPSS, select Analyze from the top pull-down menu. From there, select Descriptive Statistics, followed by Crosstabs. Choose the appropriate variables for the "row" and "column" categories. Clicking on Statistics allows you to identify how you will measure statistical significance (in this case, we have used chi-square). Clicking on Cells will allow you to decide how the data will be displayed (here we have selected Rows, Columns, and Totals). Click on OK to run the crosstabs.

Similarly, Table 23A.2 illustrates that the same data are more likely to produce statistically significant findings when the number of cells in the table is reduced.

Appendix 23B: An Application of the *t* Test

The Problem. The interview data from YMCA program participants discussed in Appendix 23B are again analyzed. The evaluators want to know if there is a difference in the number of years boys and girls participate in the YMCA programs, and they also want to know if the difference is the same or not depending on which programs the boys and girls prefer. Thus the dependent variable is the number of years the children report having participated in the YMCA programs, and the independent variable is gender (boys versus girls). In addition, a third variable, called the *control variable*, is introduced to see whether the original relationship between gender and years of participation changes in relation to programming preferences. The null hypothesis is *gender does not affect the length of time (in years) participants attend YMCA programs, even when controlling for their preferred programs.* And the alternative hypothesis is *gender does affect the length of time (in years) participants attend YMCA programs, even when controlling for preferred programs.*

The Data. The SPSS printout for the *t* test appears in Exhibit 23B.1. Again, for presentation purposes, you would not provide all the data reported on the SPSS output. Table 23.5 provides the essential data from the four *t* tests performed: one for the entire sample and one for each of the three categories of "favorite program."

The Solution. The *t* test of statistical significance can be calculated for these data. This technique tests the null hypothesis that there is no difference between boys and girls in the number of years they have participated in YMCA programs. A *t* distribution can be used to identify the value that the observed *t* statistic should exceed to support the conclusion that the observed difference in the two sample means is large enough to generalize to the population from which the program participants were drawn. In other words, if the null hypothesis is rejected in this sample, the evaluators may generalize the difference they observed to the larger population using an appropriate vehicle, such as a confidence interval placed around the observed difference, to convey their best estimate of the difference in years one might expect in the population to which they wish to generalize.

In consulting a table showing the *t* distribution, one first must calculate the degrees of freedom for this problem, which are computed as the size of the sample in group 1 minus one plus the size of the sample in group 2 minus one. In this example the degrees of freedom equal $(22 - 1)$ 1 $(28 - 1)$, or 48. As the evaluators wish to test for a significant difference in either direction and they have chosen a 95 percent decision rule, the value of observed *t* must exceed 2.00 or be less than –2.00 to demonstrate statistical significance. Thus the decision rule for this problem is the following: if the calculated *t* statistic exceeds 2.0 or is less than –2.0, then the null hypothesis that there is no difference between boys' and girls' mean years in YMCA programs will be rejected.

The steps in conducting the *t* test for this problem are as follows:

Step 1. Calculate *t.* Here *t* equals the difference of the means for the two groups divided by the joint standard error. SPSS allows evaluators to test whether they can assume that the variance in the dependent variable is equal in the two groups, using the F test, which is a statistical test commonly used to test the equivalence of variances in two or more groups. Here the F is not statistically significant, so evaluators can use the t value where the variances are assumed to be equal.

Step 2. Compare the computed t statistic to the decision rule set earlier. In this case, the t statistic equals -1.8, which does not exceed the criterion level specified in the decision rule. Thus the null hypothesis cannot be rejected.

Step 3. To convey the findings appropriately, evaluators can start by stating:

Based on our sample of 50 YMCA participants, there is insufficient evidence to say there is a statistically significant difference in the number of years boys and girls have participated in YMCA programs: that is, we cannot generalize a relationship between gender and years of participation to the population. When we examine the t tests for the three subgroups, we find we can reject the null at a 95 percent confidence level only for participants who prefer science and technology. Because we rejected the null hypothesis of no difference for that group, the next question to be addressed is this: How big is the difference between the groups? To address this question, we may use the standard formula for a confidence interval to place around the observed difference between the means reported for the two groups. The observed difference is 5 years. The interval to be placed around this value is the joint standard error multiplied by the t value for a 95 percent confidence level for this problem. Thus, the interval will be 3 to 7 years.

Note for Appendix 23B

Running a t *Test Analysis.* To run t tests, select Analyze, then Compare Means, and then Independent Samples T-Test from the menu at the top of the screen. Choose the appropriate variables for Test Variable and Grouping Variable. The grouping variable will need to be a dichotomous variable that you define in the space provided (in this example the grouping variable is gender). Select OK to run the t test.

Running a t *Test with Controls.* Before following the t test directions, you will need to split the file, which will allow the data to be analyzed within specified categories (in our example, we have split the file by program preferences). Select Data and then Split File from the top of the computer screen. Select Organize Output by Groups and define which groups you would like to use in organizing the data from the menu on the left. When you are finished, select OK to run the t test.

EXHIBIT 23B.1. SPSS PRINTOUT FOR A *t* TEST OF THE DIFFERENCE IN YEARS OF PARTICIPATION BETWEEN BOYS AND GIRLS, CONTROLLING FOR PROGRAM PREFERENCES

Independent Samples Test

	Levene's Test for Equality of Variances		*t*-test for Equality of Means					95% Confidence Interval of the Difference	
	F	Sig.	t	df	Sig. (2-tailed)	Mean Difference	Std. Error Difference	Lower	Upper
Number of Years Participating in the YMCA Programs — Equal variances assumed	0.287	0.595	21.798	48	0.078	21.5162	0.84325	23.21170	0.17923
Equal variances not assumed			21.816	46.684	0.076	21.5162	0.83515	23.19664	0.16417

Group Statistics

Gender of Child	N	Mean	Std. Deviation	Std. Error Mean
Number of Years Participating in YMCA Program — Male	22	4.0909	2.82690	0.60270
Female	28	5.6071	3.05916	0.57813

t-Tests with Controls Favorite Type of Programming = Science and Technology

Group Statistics

Gender of Child	N	Mean	Std. Deviation	Std. Error Mean
Number of Years Participating in YMCA Program — Male	6	2.0000	0.63246	0.25820
Female	3	7.0000	2.00000	1.15470

EXHIBIT 23B.1. SPSS PRINTOUT FOR A *t* TEST OF THE DIFFERENCE IN YEARS OF PARTICIPATION BETWEEN BOYS AND GIRLS, CONTROLLING FOR PROGRAM PREFERENCES *(Continued)*

Independent Samples Test

		Levene's Test for Equality of Variances		t-test for Equality of Means					95% Confidence Interval of the Difference	
		F	Sig.	t	df	Sig. (2-tailed)	Mean Difference	Std. Error Difference	Lower	Upper
Number of Years Participating in the YMCA Programs	Equal variances assumed	3.500	.104	25.916	7	.001	25.0000	0.84515	26.99847	23.00153
	Equal variances not assumed			24.226	2.203	.044	25.0000	1.18322	29.66718	2.33282

Independent Samples Test

		Levene's Test for Equality of Variances		t-test for Equality of Means					95% Confidence Interval of the Difference	
		F	Sig.	t	df	Sig. (2-tailed)	Mean Difference	Std. Error Difference	Lower	Upper
Number of Years Participating in the YMCA Programs	Equal variances assumed	.158	.698	21.075	12	.304	22.2000	2.04654	26.65903	2.25903
	Equal variances not assumed			2.951	4.492	.390	22.2000	2.31325	28.35441	3.95441

EXHIBIT 23B.1. SPSS PRINTOUT FOR A *t* TEST OF THE DIFFERENCE IN YEARS OF PARTICIPATION BETWEEN BOYS AND GIRLS, CONTROLLING FOR PROGRAM PREFERENCES (*Continued*)

Favorite Type of Programming = Sports Group Statistics

	Gender of Child	N	Mean	Std. Deviation	Std. Error Mean
Number of Years Participating in YMCA Program	Male	10	5.8000	3.19026	1.00885
	Female	4	4.16333	2.08167	

Favorite Type of Programming = Creative and Performing Arts Group Statistics

	Gender of Child	N	Mean	Std. Deviation	Std. Error Mean
Number of Years Participating in YMCA Program	Male	6	3.3333	1.75119	.71492
	Female	21	2.78345	.60740	

Independent Samples Test

		Levene's Test for Equality of Variances		t-test for Equality of Means					95% Confidence Interval of the Difference	
		F	Sig.	t	df	Sig. (2-tailed)	Mean Difference	Std. Error Difference	Lower	Upper
Number of Years Participating in the YMCA Programs	Equal variances assumed	2.101	.160	21.340	25	.192	21.6190	1.20814	24.10725	.86915
	Equal variances not assumed			21.726	13.115	.108	21.6190	.93811	23.64390	.40580

Here is another way to say all of this:

We can then conclude that based on this sample of 50 participants, using a 95 percent confidence level, among participants who prefer science and technology programs, girls have participated 3 to 7 years longer than boys in these programs.

In this example, a relationship between gender and length of participation is statistically significant for only one of the three subgroups, indicating that, at least based on the numbers, the relationship is not generalizable to the broader population, and the magnitude of the observed difference in years is large enough for evaluators to suggest that there is a difference in boys' and girls' participation time only for those who prefer the science and technology programs. And there are other questions that evaluators should ask about the findings. For example, how comfortable do they feel that the sample truly represents all YMCA program participants? With such a small sample, and with a statistically significant difference in only one subgroup that has a really small sample size, they would definitely want to be cautious in presenting their findings.

References

Evergreen, S. *Presenting Data Effectively: Communicating Your Findings for Maximum Impact.* Thousand Oaks, CA: Sage, 2013.

Hair, J. F., Anderson, R. E., Tatham, R. L., and Black, W. C. *Multivariate Data Analysis.* Upper Saddle River, NJ: Prentice Hall, 1998.

Healey, J. *Statistics: A Tool for Social Research* (2nd ed.). Belmont, CA: Wadsworth, 2006.

Stevens, S. S. "On the Theory of Scales of Measurement." *Science*, 1946, *103*, 677–680.

Further Reading

Textbooks

Anderson, A.J.B. *Interpreting Data.* New York: Chapman & Hall, 1989.

Bohrnstedt, G. W., and Knoke, D. *Statistics for Social Data Analysis.* Itasca, IL: Peacock, 1982.

Foreman, E. K. "Survey Sampling Principles." D. B. Owen and others (eds.), Vol. 120: *Statistics: Textbooks and Monographs.* New York: Dekker, 1991.

Goodman, L. A. *Analyzing Qualitative/Categorical Data* (J. Magidson, ed.). Lanham, MD.: University Press of America, 1978.

Groninger, L. D. *Beginning Statistics Within a Research Context.* New York: HarperCollins, 1990.

Hedderson, J. *SPSS/PC 1 Made Simple.* Belmont, CA: Wadsworth, 1990.

Loether, H. J., and McTavish, D. G. *Descriptive and Inferential Statistics: An Introduction* (4th ed.). Boston, MA: Allyn & Bacon, 1992.

Meier, K. J., and Brudney, J. L. *Applied Statistics for Public Administration* (2nd ed.). Boston, MA: Duxbury Press, 1987.

Renner, T. *Statistics Unraveled: A Practical Guide to Using Data in Decision Making.* Washington, DC: International City Management Association, 1988.

Siegel, S. *Nonparametric Statistics for the Behavioral Sciences* (rev. ed.). New York: McGraw-Hill, 1988.

Walsh, A. *Statistics for the Social Sciences: With Computer Applications.* New York: HarperCollins, 1990.

Welch, S., and Comer, J. *Quantitative Methods for Public Administration* (2nd ed.). Chicago, IL: Dorsey, 1988.

Special Topics

Achen, C. H. *Interpreting and Using Regression.* Sage University Paper series on Quantitative Applications in the Social Sciences, series no. 07–029. Thousand Oaks, CA: Sage, 1982.

Asher, H. B. *Causal Modeling.* Sage University Paper series on Quantitative Applications in the Social Sciences, series no. 07–003. Thousand Oaks, CA: Sage, 1976.

Berry, W. D., and Feldman, S. *Multiple Regression in Practice.* Sage University Paper series on Quantitative Applications in the Social Sciences, series no. 07–050. Thousand Oaks, CA: Sage, 1985.

Cohen, J. *Statistical Power Analysis for the Behavioral Sciences.* New York: Academic Press, 1977.

Converse, J. M., and Presser, S. *Survey Questions: Handcrafting the Standardized Questionnaire.* Sage University Paper series on Quantitative Applications in the Social Sciences, series no. 07–063. Thousand Oaks, CA: Sage, 1986.

Edwards, W., and Newman, J. R. *Multiattribute Evaluation.* Sage University Paper series on Quantitative Applications in the Social Sciences, series no. 07–026. Thousand Oaks, CA: Sage, 1982.

Hartwig, F., and Dearing, B. E. *Exploring Data Analysis.* Sage University Paper series on Quantitative Applications in the Social Sciences, series no. 07–016. Thousand Oaks, CA: Sage, 1979.

Henkel, R. E. *Tests of Significance.* Sage University Paper series on Quantitative Applications in the Social Sciences, series no. 07–004. Thousand Oaks, CA: Sage, 1976.

Hildebrand, D. K., Laing, J. D., and Rosenthal, H. *Analysis of Ordinal Data.* Sage University Paper series on Quantitative Applications in the Social Sciences, series no. 07–008. Thousand Oaks, CA: Sage, 1977.

Klecka, W. R. *Discriminant Analysis.* Sage University Paper series on Quantitative Applications in the Social Sciences, series no. 07–019. Thousand Oaks, CA: Sage, 1980.

Levine, M. S. *Canonical Analysis and Factor Comparison.* Sage University Paper series on Quantitative Applications in the Social Sciences, series no. 07–006. Thousand Oaks, Calif.: Sage, 1977.

Lewis-Beck, M. S. *Applied Regression: An Introduction.* Sage University Paper series on Quantitative Applications in the Social Sciences, series no. 07–022. Thousand Oaks, CA: Sage, 1980.

Lodge, M. *Magnitude Scaling: Quantitative Measurement of Opinions.* Sage University Paper series on Quantitative Applications in the Social Sciences, series no. 07–025. Thousand Oaks, CA: Sage, 1981.

McDowall, D., McCleary, R., Meidinger, E. E., and Hay, R. A., Jr. *Interrupted Time Series Analysis.* Sage University Paper series on Quantitative Applications in the Social Sciences, series no. 07–021. Thousand Oaks, CA: Sage, 1980.

Ostrom, C. W., Jr. *Time Series Analysis: Regression Techniques.* Sage University Paper series on Quantitative Applications in the Social Sciences, series no. 07–009. Thousand Oaks, CA: Sage, 1978.

Reynolds, H. T. *Analysis of Nominal Data.* Sage University Paper series on Quantitative Applications in the Social Sciences, series no. 07–007. Thousand Oaks, CA: Sage, 1977.

Schrodt, P. A. *Microcomputer Methods for Social Scientists.* Sage University Paper series on Quantitative Applications in the Social Sciences, series no. 07–040. Thousand Oaks, CA: Sage, 1984.

Wildt, A. R., and Ahtola, O. T. *Analysis of Covariance.* Sage University Paper series on Quantitative Applications in the Social Sciences, series no. 07–012. Thousand Oaks, CA: Sage, 1978.

Statistical Software

Minitab, Inc. *Minitab Reference Manual for DOS, Release 8.* State College, PA: Minitab, 1991.

Norusis, M. J. *SPSS/PC 1 Studentware.* Chicago, IL: SPSS, 1990.

Norusis, M. J. and SPSS, Inc. *SPSS/PC 1 4.0 Base Manual.* Chicago, IL: SPSS, 1990.

Norusis, M. J. and SPSS, Inc. *SPSS/PC 1 4.0 Statistics.* Chicago, IL: SPSS, 1990.

SAS Institute, Inc. *SAS User's Guide: Basics* (Version 5 ed.). Cary, NC: SAS Institute, 1985.

SAS Institute, Inc. *SAS User's Guide: Statistics* (Version 5 ed.). Cary, NC: SAS Institute, 1985.

Stata Corporation. *Stata Release 8.* College Station, TX: Stata Corporation, 2003.

CHAPTER TWENTY-FOUR

COST-EFFECTIVENESS AND COST-BENEFIT ANALYSIS

Stephanie Riegg Cellini, James Edwin Kee

B oth cost-benefit analysis (CBA) and cost-effectiveness analysis (CEA) are useful tools for program evaluation. Cost-effectiveness analysis is a technique that relates the costs of a program to its key outcomes or benefits. Cost-benefit analysis takes that process one step further, attempting to compare costs with the dollar value of all (or most) of a program's many benefits. These seemingly straightforward analyses can be applied anytime before, after, or during a program implementation, and they can greatly assist decision makers in assessing a program's efficiency. However, the process of conducting a CBA or CEA is much more complicated than it may sound. In this chapter we provide an overview of both types of analyses, highlighting the inherent challenges in estimating and calculating program costs and benefits. We organize our discussion around practical steps that are common to both tools, highlighting differences as they arise. We begin with a simple description of each approach.

Cost-effectiveness analysis seeks to identify and monetize the costs of a program. It then relates these costs to specific measures of program effectiveness. One can obtain a program's cost-effectiveness (CE) ratio by dividing costs by what we term "units of effectiveness."

$$\text{Cost-Effectiveness Ratio} = \frac{\text{Total Cost}}{\text{Units of Effectiveness}} \qquad (24.1)$$

Units of effectiveness are simply a measure of any quantifiable outcome central to the program's objectives. In an example that we will use throughout the chapter, a dropout prevention program in a high school would likely consider the number of dropouts prevented to be the most important outcome. For a policy mandating air bags in cars, the number of lives saved would be an obvious unit of effectiveness. Using the formula above to divide costs by the number of lives saved, we could calculate a cost-effectiveness ratio, interpreted as "dollars per life saved." We could then compare this CE ratio to those of other transportation safety policies to determine which policy costs less per unit of outcome (in this case, lives saved). While it is typical to focus on one primary outcome in CEA, one could compute cost-effectiveness ratios for other outcomes of interest as well.

Like cost-effectiveness analysis, cost-benefit analysis also identifies and places dollar values on the costs of programs, but it goes further, weighing those costs against the dollar value of program benefits. Typically, one subtracts costs from benefits to obtain the net benefits of the policy (if the net benefits are negative, they are referred to as net costs):

$$\text{Net Benefits} = \text{Total Benefits} - \text{Total Costs} \qquad (24.2)$$

In this chapter we focus on social (or economic) cost-benefit and cost-effectiveness analyses, rather than financial analyses. A social CEA or CBA takes into account the costs and benefits—whether monetary or non-monetary—that accrue to everyone in society. Any negative impacts of a program are treated as costs and added to actual budgetary outlays in assessing the overall costs of a program, while positive impacts are counted as benefits. To assess the value to society, the analyst would consider all of the costs and benefits that accrue to taxpayers, neighbors, participants, competing organizations, or any number of other groups that are impacted by the program under study. In contrast, a financial CEA or CBA considers only the monetary costs and benefits accruing to a particular organization, and simply ignores the rest. While such an approach is sometimes useful for accounting and budgeting purposes, it is less useful in assessing a program's effectiveness. Nonetheless, the process we outline below can be easily applied to a financial CBA or CEA; the only difference is that a narrower set of costs and benefits are considered in the analysis.

The concepts and basic equations presented above are seemingly simple, yet obtaining accurate estimates of costs and benefits can be extremely challenging. Every analysis requires a host of assumptions, sometimes complicated calculations, and ultimately, the careful judgment of the analyst. We address

TABLE 24.1. STEPS IN COST-EFFECTIVENESS AND COST-BENEFIT ANALYSIS.

1. Set the framework for the analysis.
2. Decide whose costs and benefits should be recognized.
3. Identify and categorize costs and benefits.
4. Project costs and benefits over the life of the program, if applicable.
5. Monetize (place a dollar value on) costs.
6. Quantify benefits in terms of units of effectiveness (for CEA) or monetize benefits (for CBA).
7. Discount costs and benefits to obtain present values.
8. Compute a cost-effectiveness ratio (for CEA) or net present value (for CBA).
9. Perform sensitivity analysis.
10. Make a recommendation where appropriate.

these challenges as we discuss each of a ten step process in Table 24.1 below (adapted from Boardman, Greenberg, Vining, and Weimer, 2006).

To illustrate the ten-step process, we discuss the evaluation of a program to reduce the incidence of early high school dropouts, aimed at at-risk students. This is an important national issue that was a target of President Obama's initial speech to Congress and is being addressed in various ways in school districts across the United States. For some of the data, we will be drawing from a 2008 Ohio study by the Economics Center for Education Research. We encourage the use of spreadsheet software, such as Microsoft Excel, to allow the analyst to consider multiple assumptions about the valuation of costs and benefits.

Step 1: Set the Framework for the Analysis

The first question is: Will you undertake a CBA or a CEA? This will depend on what you want to know. Are you evaluating one program or comparing two or more? Does the program have multiple objectives or just one major focus? Box 24.1 provides an overview of the choice.

Box 24.1. Step 1 (Key Issue): Deciding on Cost-Benefit or Cost-Effectiveness Analysis

Cost-Benefit Analysis is most useful when you are analyzing a single program/policy to determine whether total benefits to society of the program exceed the costs; or when you are comparing alternative programs-especially those with different outcomes—to see which one achieves the greatest benefit to society. The major difficulty with CBA is that it is often difficult to place dollar values on all (or most) costs and benefits.

Cost-Effectiveness Analysis is most useful when you know the outcome you desire and you are determining which of a set of alternative programs/projects achieves the greatest outcome for the costs. It can also be useful in cases when major outcomes are either intangible or otherwise difficult to monetize. The major difficulty with CEA is that it provides no value for the output, leaving that to the subjective judgment to the policymaker.

We Recommend: While some view CBA as a superior technique, it is difficult and time-consuming. CEA may provide a good starting point by requiring the evaluator to identify the most important outcome and relate that outcome to the dollars spent on the project.

The Status Quo

No matter how many programs you are evaluating and whether you choose CEA or CBA, the step-by-step process outlined here is essentially the same. In considering each program or project, the analyst must always start by describing the *status quo*, or the state of the world in the absence of the program or policy. This scenario sets the baseline for the analysis. The only costs and benefits that should be considered in a CBA or CEA are those that would occur over and above those that would have occurred without any action (under the status quo). These are known as the marginal or incremental costs or benefits of a policy and these are what we seek to capture in our measures of total costs, total benefits, and units of effectiveness.

Timing

Both CBA and CEA can be performed at any point in the policymaking process. A CBA or CEA undertaken when a program is being considered is considered an *ex ante* (or prospective) analysis. This type of analysis is useful in considering whether a program should be undertaken or to compare alternative prospective programs aimed at common policy objectives. If an analysis is done at some point during implementation, it is considered an *in medias res* analysis (or current year or snapshot analysis). Such an analysis provides data on whether the program's current benefits are worth the costs. Finally, an *ex post* (or retrospective) analysis provides decision makers with total program costs and benefits upon the program's completion, to assist them in evaluating a program's overall success.

Each of these types of analyses has its usefulness, peculiarities, and issues. For example, in an *ex ante* analysis, the estimation of costs and benefits is most difficult because they have not yet occurred. In this case, the analysis will require a significant number of assumptions and may yield less accurate results. In contrast, in an *ex post* analysis costs and outcomes are largely known and can often be estimated accurately. Nonetheless, it can be difficult to determine which costs and benefits to attribute to the program because the observed outcomes may have been the result of programs or events other than the one being analyzed.[1]

Step 1: Dropout Prevention Program. In our illustration, we will examine a dropout prevention program that is currently implemented in just one high school. We assume that we have been tasked with evaluating the program's effectiveness for state policymakers interested in expanding it. The policymakers would like to know whether the costs of the program have been worth the results and they may be considering alternative programs to achieve the same objective. Because they will want to know both whether the program is better than nothing and how it compares to others, both CEA and CBA will be useful. For purposes of illustration, we present both analyses below.

The Dropout Prevention Program illustration involves the creation of a special academy aimed at students at risk of dropping out. The academy has access to space, teachers, and equipment. In order to create the program, a consultant was hired to train the teachers and provide a curriculum for the academy. One full-time teacher was hired to manage the academy, and three other teachers were paid extra compensation to work after school in the program. As an analyst you may be asked whether the current program—now completing its fifth year—has been worth the costs and whether it should be continued or expanded to a larger group of high schools.

In this example, the status quo would simply be described as all regular high school activities and programs that occurred before program implementation. Our analysis will thus count the incremental changes in costs, dropouts prevented, and other benefits that can reasonably be attributed to the program.

Step 2: Decide Whose Costs and Benefits Should Be Recognized

Almost every policy or program involves a broad range of stakeholders and every cost or benefit ultimately affects a particular group of people. For public programs, taxpayers may bear a large portion of the costs of a program, while the benefits may be concentrated on a few select groups (for example, program participants). In light of this, determining whose costs and benefits should "count" (or who should have standing) is an important consideration in CEA and CBA.

In a social CEA or CBA, the goal is to assess the impact of the policy on society as a whole, so the analyst must include all members of the relevant society in the analysis—one cannot simply pick and choose which stakeholders within society deserve standing. The key issue then becomes how to define "society." To maintain objectivity, society must be defined on a geographic basis. Typically, analysts choose to define society according to national, state, county, or city borders, but other geographic distinctions are also acceptable. Box 24.2 provides a summary of the factors to take into consideration when deciding on issues of standing.

Box 24.2. Step 2 (Key Issue): Whose Benefits and Costs Count?

A major issue for evaluators is determining the geographic scope of the analysis, e.g., should benefits and costs be aggregated at the national or state level? The narrower the geographic scope, the fewer costs and benefits will need to be counted. However, narrower geographic boundaries will miss any costs and benefits that may "spillover" to neighboring jurisdictions. It is often useful to identify these missing costs and benefits, even if you do not quantify or place a dollar value on them. Sometimes spillovers, such as air and water pollution, have broad negative impacts; at other times, projects such as mass transit have positive spillovers to neighboring jurisdictions and those benefits might be used to argue for a subsidy or other assistance from that jurisdiction.

We recommend: The analyst should base her definition of society on the jurisdiction that will bear the brunt of the costs and receive the majority of the benefits. This will be the primary concern to the policymakers of that jurisdiction. However, major spillovers (both costs and benefits) should at least be recognized and explained in the analysis. Policymakers might want greater information on those that are the most significant and/or have political implications. If spillovers are substantial the most useful approach might be to start with a broader geographic scope (for example, state), then look at the subset of costs and benefits accruing to smaller areas (for example, cities).

Step 2: Dropout Prevention Program. In the Dropout Prevention Program illustration, the state policymakers will likely want to consider the costs and benefits from the state's perspective. The decision may also depend on who is paying for the policy. In this case, we assume that the school district and state taxpayers foot the bill, so a state-level perspective can again be justified. We should therefore count all of the costs and benefits of the program that accrue to state residents. Defining "society" as the state will naturally include almost all stakeholders, as few costs and benefits of one high school's program are likely to spillover to neighboring states. Note, however, that if the school is near a state border causing costs and benefits to spill over to other jurisdictions, or if the program is paid for by federal taxpayers, the analyst might want to consider taking a broader regional or national perspective, or at least identify and discuss the nature of the spillovers.

Step 3: Identify and Categorize Costs and Benefits

In conducting a cost-effectiveness or cost-benefit analysis as part of a program evaluation, the third step is to identify and categorize as many of the known benefits and costs of the program as possible. While all costs and benefits cannot be known for certain, the analyst should make a reasonable effort to identify those that will have the most significant implications on the policy. Not all of these effects will require an evaluation in dollars. Small or negligible costs and benefits—those that will have little impact on the bottom line—are often ignored or just briefly discussed in the final analysis. Nonetheless, in the early stages of analysis, we recommend thinking broadly about possible costs and benefits.

When discussing costs and benefits, it is common to classify all negative impacts of a policy as costs and all positive impacts as benefits, whether these occur in implementation or as a consequence of a particular policy. However, one could instead frame the analysis as comparing inputs to outcomes. In this case, both the inputs and outcomes could be either positive or negative, but the same process applies. In identifying and classifying these costs and benefits, we suggest a framework in Box 24.3 based on Musgrave and Musgrave (1989), to divide them further into distinct categories: real versus transfers, direct and indirect, tangible and intangible, financial and social. Keep in mind that where to place a specific benefit or cost is sometimes debatable.

Box 24.3. Step 3 (Key Issue): Categorizing Costs and Benefits or Outputs/Outcomes

Real Benefits and Costs vs. Transfers. Real benefits and costs represent net gains or losses to society, whereas transfers merely alter the distribution of resources within the society (again, defined by geographic area). Real benefits include dollars saved and dollars earned, lives saved and lives enriched, increased earnings and decreased costs to the taxpayers, and time saved and increased quality of life. In contrast, some societal gains are directly offset by other losses and are considered transfers. For example, a local tax abatement program for the elderly will provide a tax-saving benefit to some but a cost (of equal amount) to others (higher taxes or lower services). Many government programs involve the subsidizing of one group by another in the society and thus should be clearly identified when possible. But from an overall societal perspective, transfers do not increase total welfare; they merely redistribute welfare within society.

Direct and Indirect Benefits and Costs. Direct benefits and costs are those that are closely related to the primary objective of the project. Direct costs include such costs as personnel, facilities, equipment and material, and administration. Indirect or secondary benefits and costs are by-products, multipliers, spillovers, or investment effects of the project or program. An often-cited example of indirect benefits from space exploration is the numerous spin-off technologies benefiting other industries. Indirect costs are intended (such as overhead) and unintended costs that occur as a result of a government action. For example, a dam built for agricultural purposes may flood an area used by hikers, who would lose the value of this recreation. This loss might be partially offset by indirect benefit gains to those using the lake created by the dam for recreation.

Tangible and Intangible Benefits and Costs. Tangible benefits and costs are those that the analyst can readily identify in unit terms (for CEA) and can convert to dollars for CBA. In contrast, intangible benefits and costs include such things as the value of wilderness or increased sense of community. It is especially difficult to place a dollar value on many intangible benefits. This is perhaps the most problematic area of cost-benefit analysis and why cost-effectiveness analysis is considered more appropriate for some types of programs.

Financial and Social Benefits and Costs. We believe it is important to identify those costs that are financial, that is, are cash outlays of the organization considering the program or project, and those costs that are social, that is, they are not cash outlays, but represent real benefits and costs to society. For example, salaries and benefits paid by an agency for a government regulatory program are a fiscal cost; the effects of those regulations on business and the public are social benefits and costs.

Step 3: Dropout Prevention Program

Costs.   Using the framework suggested above, we illustrate in Table 24.2 various cost categories of the Dropout Prevention Program.

Benefits.   The benefits of the Dropout Prevention Program accrue mainly to those attending the program. It is well known that high school graduates, on

TABLE 24.2. DROPOUT PREVENTION PROGRAM COST BREAKDOWN.

Cost to Program Participants

Opportunity cost to students participating in the after-school program, for example, loss of wages from a part-time job (indirect, tangible, social)

Costs to Society (Including School)

One-Time or Up-Front Costs (We describe the timing of costs further in Step 4 below.)

Cost of a consultant who provided teacher training and information on how to set up the academy (direct, tangible, fiscal)

Computer software purchased for use in the program (direct, tangible, fiscal)

Ongoing Investment Costs

Use of existing classroom facilities (direct, tangible, social)

Purchase of computers for use in the academy (direct, tangible, fiscal)

Academic texts that are used for more than one year (direct, tangible, fiscal)

Recurring Costs

Full-time salaries and benefits of teachers dedicated to the academy (direct, tangible, fiscal)

Part-time salaries and benefits for teachers receiving extra compen-sation for after-class programs associated with the academy (direct, tangible, fiscal)

Extra maintenance costs associated with after-school use of the facilities (indirect, tangible, fiscal)

Materials and supplies, including workbooks and other material used up during the program (direct, tangible, fiscal)

Travel expenditures for field trips (direct, tangible, fiscal)

Overhead costs, such as general supervision and finance (indirect, tangible, fiscal)

Increased insurance (indirect, tangible, fiscal)

Cost of volunteers (indirect, tangible or intangible, social)

Opportunity cost to parents; for example loss of time in transporting students (indirect, tangible, social)

---

average, earn more than high school dropouts and there is less unemployment among high school graduates. There would be some indirect fiscal benefits for taxpayers: less dependency on government subsidies and increases in taxes paid by the high school graduates. Though indirect (not the primary reason for the program), they provide fiscal benefits to government and society. Table 24.3 contains a summary of the benefits:

TABLE 24.3. BENEFITS OF A DROPOUT PREVENTION PROGRAM.

Benefits to Program Participants:

Higher lifetime earnings (direct, tangible, social)
Less taxes
Less transfer payments
Greater self-esteem (indirect, intangible, social)

Benefits to Society in General:

Decrease in government subsidies (welfare, healthcare, etc.) (indirect, tangible, fiscal)

Increase in taxes paid by program participants (indirect, tangible, fiscal)

Decrease in crime and other social problems (indirect, tangible/intangible, both fiscal and social)

Step 4: Project Cost and Benefits Over the Life of the Program, If Applicable

After identifying and categorizing costs and benefits, the next step involves thinking about the timeframe for your analysis and how the costs and benefits will change over time. CEAs and CBAs may be conducted over any length of time, and time is typically measured in years, although the analyst can also use any other unit of time that seems reasonable. Most cost-benefit and cost-effectiveness analyses consider a timeframe in the range of five to fifty years, but in some cases the analyst may decide that just one year is sufficient to assess costs and benefits. If this is the case, the analyst can skip this step.

If you have settled on a timeframe with more than one time period, you typically start with the first year of the program and track down information on the costs and benefits that accrue in that year (we describe how to place dollar values on costs and benefits further in the next steps). For an *ex ante* analysis, you will then have to predict the impacts over the life of the project: Will each cost or benefit remain the same each year or will it increase, decrease, or disappear in each subsequent year? If there are changes over time, will costs or benefits increase smoothly (for example, at 2 percent per year) or change at irregular intervals (for example, appear for five years during construction then disappear thereafter). For an *ex poste* analysis, much of this information may be known, particularly if actual costs and outcomes have been reported annually. It may help to consider whether costs and benefits are one-time (or up-front), accruing only in the first year, or whether they are recurring costs or benefits that occur every year. A final category of costs are ongoing investment costs: one-time investments that are used continually. Box 24.4 contains a summary of the issue of an appropriate timeframe. We provide details on how to place dollar values on these costs and benefits in the next sections.

> **Box 24.4. Step 4 (Key Issue): Considering Costs Over the Life of the Project**
>
> You may decide to evaluate the costs and benefits accruing over one year, five years, fifty years, or even an infinite number of years. The key to deciding on a timeframe is assessing the "useful life" of the program. The term comes from infrastructure projects, such as buildings or highways that need replacement or substantial maintenance after some typical length of time (perhaps twenty years). In the case of program evaluation, a program that requires Congressional reauthorization in five years suggests that a five-year analysis may be a logical timeframe.
>
> **We Recommend:** We suggest using a length of time that is sufficient to capture most costs and benefits of the program. It may be that the costs accrue over a shorter period of time than the benefits. The reverse could be true, if state action creates negative actions (such as pollution) that might extend over many years.

Step 4: Dropout Prevention Program. One challenge to the analyst in the Dropout Prevention Program is that the program's fiscal costs are mostly upfront, while the benefits (both fiscal and social) accrue over a long period of time; in the case of the participants, their increased earnings over a lifetime. Thus, it is appropriate to examine the total costs of the program over its first five-year period of operations; but benefits will need to be analyzed over an extended period of time. We choose thirty years to capture most of the benefits from increased earnings, tax savings, and other long-term benefits.

Step 5: Monetizing (Putting a Dollar Value on) Costs

After identifying all costs and benefits and considering how they change over the time period you study, the next step in both CEA and CBA is to assign each cost a dollar value. Critics of cost-benefit analysis and even cost-effectiveness analysis often ask why monetization is necessary—particularly for intangible costs or benefits. The idea is simply that we want to put all or most costs and benefits (in the case of CBA) in the same units for easier addition and comparison. Since dollars are a common measure of value that people generally understand, they are preferred to other measures.

For each cost (or benefit) that we seek to place a dollar value on, it is important to clearly state its nature, how it is measured, and any assumptions made in the calculations. Those assumptions must be made clear to decision makers and subjected to a sensitivity analysis (described in Step 9) to determine to what extent the outcome of the analysis is controlled by the assumptions made.

Budgetary/Accounting Costs. Accounting or budgetary information typically would provide data on teachers' salaries, capital costs and materials, and other expenditures used in a program. Nevertheless, some costs will not be as easily identified from project documents but must be developed using best estimates. Economists focus on the concept of "opportunity cost": if a resource is used for one thing, it cannot be used for something else.

Cost of Capital. The cost of capital assets should be spread out over their expected useful life. Normally, the asset (less its final salvage value) is depreciated equally per year over the life of the asset (straight-line depreciation). In addition to depreciation, the government loses the opportunity to use the money that is tied up in the undepreciated asset. This opportunity cost is expressed as an interest (generally, the cost of capital to the jurisdiction) rate times the undepreciated portion of the asset. Spreadsheets and numerical tables provide an amortization or annualized cost of depreciation plus interest (see Levin and McEwan, 2001). In Excel, the payment (PMT) function can compute this value for you once you add the interest rate (r), time period or number of payments (nper), and the initial capital cost (pv).

Sunk Costs. Sunk costs are defined as investments previously made in a program or project, such as original research and development costs, as compared to ongoing costs. In an *ex post* evaluation of total benefits and costs of a program, the evaluator will consider all previous costs. However, when recommending future action on a program or project, sunk costs should be ignored, because they have no impact on the marginal costs and benefits of the continuation of the project or program.

Indirect Costs.   *Overhead.* Many institutions employ a standard indirect cost allocation figure on top of their direct costs, often computed at 30 to 60 percent of the total direct costs or a subset of direct costs, such as personnel expenditures. The major controversy with indirect cost allocations is whether a specific program really adds marginal cost to the overhead agencies. Rather than estimating an overhead rate, an evaluator might use a method called activity-based costing (ABC). In this method, overhead costs are allocated based on certain cost drivers. For example, if a proposed program was going to use summer help and involve significant personnel actions, then the additional cost assigned to the project would be the additional costs to the personnel or human resource office, perhaps as a function of program employees versus total employees. Box 24.5 discusses how to handle certain non-monetary indirect costs that are sometimes controversial.

Box 24.5. Step 5 (Key Issue) Dealing with Non-Monetary Costs

Costs to the Private Sector

Government often shifts costs to the private sector, especially in regulatory activity. When the Environmental Protection Agency mandates the installation of scrubbers on electric utilities or the purchase of higher-cost low-sulfur coal in order to reduce acid rain (as legislated in the 1991 Clean Air Act), the costs of the program are not just the regulatory agencies' costs of enforcement of the new requirements. The costs to the electric utilities, which will likely be passed forward to the consumers of the utilities' power, must also be considered.

Costs to Participants and Volunteers

The cost to participants and volunteers should also be considered. Although these are not cash outlays, they are considered real social costs of the program. For example, in the Dropout Prevention Program illustration, the academy operates after school. For the students involved, this represents an opportunity cost for their time that might be used for part-time employment. This program, and many government programs, uses the services of volunteers. Volunteers can provide a real benefit to a program and may relieve the agency from spending money for part-time staff. Levin and McEwan (2001) argue that the value can be determined by estimating the market value of the services that a volunteer provides. This approach seems correct where the volunteer has specific skills and the agency would otherwise have to employ someone of the same skills. Otherwise, the cost might be viewed as the opportunity cost to the volunteer. On the other hand, volunteers also may gain something by volunteering—a sense of civic virtue or new knowledge, for example—that may outweigh or simply cancel out the opportunity cost.

We Recommend: Indirect costs to the private sector and to participants and volunteers are controversial and their valuation sometimes problematic. Because of this, it is useful to separate costs (and benefits) to various groups, for example, costs to participants, costs to government, and costs to others in society. In this fashion, the decision maker can more readily determine the most important costs to consider.

Step 5: Dropout Prevention Program. For both cost-effectiveness analysis and cost-benefit analysis, the evaluator must estimate and monetize total costs of the program, including both fiscal and social costs. For example, if the academy uses dedicated classroom space, whether during the school day or after school, there is no cash outlay for the school, but the classroom use would represent an opportunity cost. That is, the use of this space for the academy means it cannot be used for other educational activities. Should the evaluator place a dollar value on that opportunity cost? If the school could rent the space for other after-school activities, then the opportunity cost would be measured by the rental income forgone. If the classrooms would otherwise be vacant, then the opportunity cost for the space would be zero. Some additional cost would have to be assigned to the program for the additional maintenance cost of the facility caused by the extra use. This incremental cost should be charged to the program by the analyst.

In the Dropout Prevention Program illustration, the cost of computers and textbooks that have a useful life of more than one year should be amortized over the expected life of the asset. Computers typically would be amortized over a five-year period and textbooks over three years. Thus, the purchase of ten computers in Year 1 of the project at $2,000 per computer would cost $20,000; however, the actual costs per year assigned to the program would be the depreciation (over five years) plus the interest cost on the undepreciated portion. This number can be annualized by using Excel's payment function. In this case, the interest rate is assumed to be 5 percent (cost of capital for the school or state), the capital cost is $20,000, and the time period is five years. This leads to an annual cost of $4,619 for the computers. Similarly, the textbooks with a cost of $1,000 and a useful life of three years would have an annual cost of $367. Table 24.4 provides a typical breakdown and estimate of costs and Table 24.5 displays those costs over a five-year period.

Table 24.5 examines the costs of the program over its first five years with fifty participants in each year. Note that even where the analyst chooses to not include a dollar value of the cost, it should be indicated and considered.

TABLE 24.4. COSTING AN EXISTING DROPOUT PREVENTION PROGRAM.

Financial Costs (to the School)	Estimate and Method of Valuation
Up-front costs: Use of consultants and computer software	Actual costs of program in its first year-Assume $3,000 for consultants and $500 for software.
Capital expenses: Purchase of material with use longer than one year—computers and texts	These costs are generally spread out over their useful life—for computers and texts, three to five years. Assume ten computers at $2,000 for five years (annual cost: $4,619) and 20 texts at $50 with a three-year life (annual cost: $387).
Salaries: Both full-time and part-time salaries include annual costs plus benefits.	Assume one full-time faculty at $35,000 plus 30 percent benefits ($10,500); plus three part-time faculty—nine months at $2,000 per month plus benefits (part-time benefits are lower, assume, 10 percent). Annual cost: $104,900.
Maintenance: Extra costs of maintaining facilities after normal hours; may include energy cost, janitorial, and maintenance.	These would be the marginal costs incurred over what the costs would have been without the program. Assume $1,000 a month for nine months. Annual cost: $9,000.
Materials and supplies: Paper, pencils, chalk, etc.	Annual costs: Assume $100 per participant, with fifty participants. Annual cost: $5,000.
Travel: Cost of buses for field trips, car mileage, etc.	Annual assumed costs: $3,000.
Overhead: Administrative, including any costs of supervision; insurance.	Appropriate measure is marginal cost; for example, if insurance went up because of the new program or cost of auditing program increased cost of annual audit. Annual assumed costs: $1,000.
Social Costs	**Estimate and Method of Valuation**
Facilities: Use of classroom after school	Opportunity cost of classroom use. Assume there is no other use: $0.
Participants' cost: Opportunity cost of students' time.	Although this is a non-budget cost, it represents a real cost to participants ($1,700 per participant).
Parents' cost: Opportunity cost of parents' time.	Parents may take time off from work or may incur additional transportation costs. If this is the case, their average wage should be used to value this cost (we have assumed no cost).
Volunteers' cost: Opportunity cost of volunteers' time.	This one is controversial and we have assumed benefits are equal to the cost: $0.

Cost data are important; they can, for example, provide information on exactly how much money is spent annually. In the Dropout Prevention Program, fifty students participate at an annual cost (in Year 5) of $127,887 to the school and $220,037 when adding costs to participants. The total cost to society over all five years is $1.1 million.

TABLE 24.5. DROPOUT PREVENTION PROGRAM LIFETIME COSTS, IN CONSTANT DOLLARS.

	Year 1	Year 2	Year 3	Year 4	Year 5	Total
Fiscal costs to the school						
Up-front cost						
Consultants	$3,000					$3,000
Software	$500					$500
Capital expenses						
Classroom	$0	$0	$0	$0	$0	$0
Computers	$4,619	$4,619	$4,619	$4,619	$4,619	$23,097
Texts	$367	$367	$367	$367	$367	$1,836
Salaries						
Full time	$45,500	$45,500	$45,500	$45,500	$45,500	$227,500
Part time	$59,400	$59,400	$59,400	$59,400	$59,400	$297,000
Maintenance	$9,000	$9,000	$9,000	$9,000	$9,000	$45,000
Materials and supplies	$5,000	$5,000	$5,000	$5,000	$5,000	$25,000
Travel	$3,000	$3,000	$3,000	$3,000	$3,000	$15,000
Overhead						
Administrative	$500	$500	$500	$500	$500	$2,500
Insurance	$500	$500	$500	$500	$500	$2,500
Total cost to school	$131,387	$127,887	$127,887	$127,887	$127,887	$642,934
Social costs to others						
Participants	$92,150	$92,150	$92,150	$92,150	$92,150	$460,750
Parents	$0	$0	$0	$0	$0	$0
Total costs to others	$92,150	$92,150	$92,150	$92,150	$92,150	$460,750
TOTAL COSTS	$223,527	$220,037	$220,037	$220,037	$220,037	$1,103,684

Step 6: Quantify (for CEA) and Monetize (for CBA) Benefits

While the cost calculations described above for CEA and CBA are identical, the benefit calculations diverge. In the case of CEA, we typically quantify only the most important benefit to get the "units of effectiveness" in Equation (24.1). If more than one benefit is deemed important, separate cost-effectiveness ratios for an additional outcome or two are sometimes calculated and discussed. In CBA, however, we not only quantify benefits, but we also ascribe dollar values to them. Further, we do this for all benefits (or as many as possible), not only the most important.

Quantifying Benefits (for CEA)

For CEA, the task is seemingly straightforward. We must first identify the most important benefit by which we wish to measure success of the program. Measures of effectiveness are idiosyncratic to each program. In all cases, they must be related to the objectives of the program. Levin and McEwan (2001) provide a number of examples of effectiveness measures from various studies. A program with the objective of improving the functioning of disabled infants and toddlers was estimated based on behavioral tests, and a Brazilian program to improve achievement in elementary schools on test scores in basic skills in Portuguese and mathematics. Since one of CEA's strengths is its ability to provide comparisons with other programs, the measure of effectiveness should be a benefit that has direct comparisons to other programs.

The next task is to quantify the benefit in terms of units of effectiveness. The idea is to count only the units of effectiveness that are attributable to the program, or the causal effects of the program over and above the status quo. In a safety program, the analyst might need to estimate the number of lives saved. For educational programs, the difference in test scores between participants and non-participants provides the relevant quantification of units of effectiveness, though experimental or quasi-experimental estimates of participants' test score gains would be preferable, if available.

Step 6: Dropout Prevention Program, CEA. Cost-effectiveness analysis of the Dropout Prevention Program simplifies the task of relating costs to benefits because it does not require converting all benefits into dollars. The key is whether there is one measure of benefit or effectiveness that can serve as a surrogate for program success. In the case of the Dropout Prevention Program, the program has several benefits—potential dropouts who now graduate will lead more productive lives, earn higher wages, have less reliance on government assistance (such as welfare programs), and perhaps exhibit fewer criminal and other negative behaviors. But since the program's goal is to prevent dropouts, the obvious measure of effectiveness for a CEA is simply the number of dropouts prevented. This can be measured using either the actual decrease in the number of dropouts or the increase in number of students graduating. All other benefits are left out of the CEA, but we return to them in our CBA below.

In an *ex post* analysis to determine the number of dropouts prevented as a result of the program, an analyst would examine data on dropouts for at-risk high school students. In the example, the analyst determines that of fifty at-risk high school students, twenty typically drop out before graduation. However, those enrolled in the Dropout Prevention Program were more likely to

TABLE 24.6. DROPOUT PREVENTION PROGRAM COST-EFFECTIVENESS ANALYSIS.

Year	1	2	3	4	5	Total
Dropouts per 50 at-risk students	20	20	20	20	20	100
Dropouts per 50 participants	17	15	13	12	12	69
Dropouts prevented	3	5	7	8	8	31
Fiscal costs to school	$131,387	$127,887	$127,887	$127,887	$127,887	$642,934
Fiscal costs per dropout prevented	$43,796	$25,577	$18,270	$15,986	$15,986	$20,740
Total cost to society (including participants costs)	$223,527	$220,037	$220,037	$220,037	$220,037	$1,103,684
Total cost per dropout prevented	$75,509	$44,007	$31,434	$27,505	$27,505	$35,603

stay in school. Data indicate that over the five years of the program, of 250 participants, sixty-nine dropped out before graduation compared to the expected 100 with no program. Thus, the number of dropouts prevented by the program can be estimated at 31.[2]

The analyst can now compare the thirty-one dropouts prevented with the program cost. Those costs can be displayed (in Table 24.6) on an annual basis and totaled over the five years. Over the five-year period, total costs per dropout prevented are approximately $35,600 of which the school spent about $20,000 per dropout prevented (or per additional student who graduated). First year costs to the school were higher and they gradually declined to about $16,000 per dropout prevented in Year 5. This information provides important data for the principal, school board, and state policymakers; and the question is now whether the result (preventing a dropout) is worth $16,000 to the taxpayers or $35,600 to society. This figure also can be compared with other programs that achieved the same goal.

Monetizing Benefits (for CBA)

For a CBA, our ideal goal is to calculate a dollar value for every major output or benefit. The more complex the program objectives (for example, urban renewal), typically the more difficult the benefit analysis is because it often involves multiple objectives aimed at different beneficiary groups (business interests, the poor, the middle class, and many others). Further, while some outcomes may be monetized using the approaches described for costs in Step 5, most benefits are more complicated to place a dollar value on and some of the methods used are controversial. We describe several of the most common challenges and techniques below.

Non-Market Goods and Services. Unlike the majority of costs, many social benefits are not reflected or easily estimated using market prices or budgets. Most economists argue that market prices are a good valuation of a benefit, as they reveal a person's true preference or "willingness to pay" for a product or service.[3] Unlike in business, however, for most government programs, the recipients are not fully paying for the benefits received; therefore, the evaluator must make an alternative assessment of value. These valuations are often referred to as "shadow prices" and can be obtained using a variety of methods. One of the most straightforward is to use prices in a similar private market to assign a dollar value to a public good. For example, to monetize the benefit of a free public swimming pool, one might use the fees that people pay for a similar swimming experience in a private pool—multiplying these fees by the number of patrons at the public pool.

Cost Avoidance. Cost avoidance or cost savings are also benefits. Thus, an anticrime program analyst could measure dollars saved from avoided burglaries. A health program analyst could measure avoided costs of medical care and lost productivity. To estimate the amount of cost avoidance, the evaluator would likely rely on historical data and trends before and after implementation of the government program and estimate the effect of the program on other government spending and the general public.

Time Saved. Time saved is a tangible benefit. However, measurement of its dollar value is more subjective. Each person may value his or her time differently. A common method of estimating the value of time is by using the economists' theory of labor-leisure trade-off. When people have control over the hours they are working, they will work (including overtime) until their subjective value of one hour of leisure is equal to the income they would gain from one more hour of work—their after-tax wage rate. The idea, then, is that the wage rate reflects the value of an hour of time to the individual. Further, if labor markets operate efficiently, a person's wage also reflects the value to society of his time, as this is what his time is worth to an employer.

Increased Productivity.   Increased productivity is a common objective of many government investment programs—both capital investments, such as roads, bridges, water projects, and other infrastructure developments, and human capital investments, such as education and job training. These benefits might be measured in increased profits or wages.

Property Values.   Increased property values may or may not be a benefit, depending on the geographical scope of the analysis. The narrower the scope, the more likely it is that increased property values will be a real benefit of the project. If property values increase in a neighborhood because of a new community park, from the neighborhood's perspective, this would be considered a benefit. In a CBA from the city's perspective, however, this benefit might be offset by losses in property values in other areas of the city farther from the park that are now relatively less desirable. It is only if demand is fueled by new residents from outside the jurisdiction that the benefits should be counted.

Taxes.   Taxes are sometimes thought of as a benefit, and from a fiscal or budgetary perspective they are important, especially if the program or project is designed to produce revenues equal to expenditures. But from a societal perspective, taxes are transfers: the gain to the government is a loss to the individual paying the taxes. The individual does gain from the services that the government provides with taxes but loses dollars that could have been spent on private purchases. Economists also believe that there is some "deadweight loss" associated with taxes, due to the market distortions that they create, but it is usually left out of CBAs.

Value of the Environment.   Many projects—particularly those that affect the environment—provide recreational activities such as hiking, fishing, or swimming. In this case, one must calculate recreational values. These values are typically based on the concept of willingness to pay. The evaluator first must determine the number of people who have visited a particular recreational area and then attempt to value each "user day" of recreation.

One approach is asking recreational users what they would be willing to pay to use a particular recreational area (a park, wilderness, or something else). This survey technique, known as contingent valuation, has several problems. One of the most significant problems is that respondents may answer strategically. If they think they may have to pay to use a favorite park, they may give a lower value than the true value to them. If they think the response may influence the continued provision of the recreation, they may place a higher value than their true value. In many cases, statements of willingness to pay have differed from actual behavior.

A second technique is to estimate what it costs users to travel to the recreation area—plane fares, rentals, gasoline, travel time, and so forth. This works best for recreational sites that draw visitors from a wide area, such as a national park. Finally, evaluators sometimes look at similar recreational experiences in the private sector. As described above, the value of a public swimming pool might be assessed using rates similar to the costs of similar private facilities in the area, adjusting for any difference in quality of the experience.

In addition, individuals typically value parks and other wilderness areas for more than just their direct recreational value. One indirect benefit of these areas is the option they provide for a future visit. This so-called "option value" can be thought of as a person's willingness to pay in order to maintain the option of visiting the area at some time in the future. To calculate this value, analysts often use recreation values multiplied by the probability of a future visit. Even if a person does not intend to visit a wilderness area, he may simply value its existence. This "existence value" may derive from a concern for others who may want to use the area now or in the future (for example, saving the polar bears so that our grandchildren can see them), but it may also derive simply from the idea that plants and animals have a right to exist. Of course, putting a price tag on existence value is difficult, and surveys are about the only hope for ascertaining it.

Box 24.6 deals with perhaps the most difficult problem, putting a value on a human life.

Box 24.6. Step 6 (Key Issue): Valuing Life

Valuing Life

Lives saved is clearly a tangible benefit of a policy and the justification for many government health and safety programs. The value of a life may be of infinite value to the person whose life was saved and their loved ones. However, if the value of life is infinite, any project that leads to even a single life being saved should be undertaken. This leaves no sensible way to determine the admissibility of projects. The most common approach is to de-personalize the valuation of life. Ideally, we seek to use an average value for ANY human life whether old or young, rich or poor, in the CBA. This value is known as the Value of Statistical Life (VSL). To obtain this value, economists typically rely on a wage-risk trade-off method. This approach compares the wages received by individuals in high-risk jobs such as coalmining to those of individuals in similar, but lower-risk jobs. The idea is that the coal miner is trading some risk of death for a higher wage. Using this information, we can impute the coal miner's implied VSL and use it for all lives saved in the analysis.

We Recommend: While different studies still find different values for the VSL and some federal agencies require analysts to use a specific VSL for all of their CBAs, the generally accepted range is $3 million to $8 million (in 2009 dollars).

Chain Reaction Problem

A common error often made in benefit-cost analysis is to make the project or program appear successful by counting indirect benefits that arise from it while ignoring indirect costs. For example, if a government builds a road, the direct benefits are the reduction in transportation costs (time spent and fuel) for individuals and businesses. Profits of adjacent restaurants, motels, and gas stations may also increase due to the traffic. This may lead to increased profits in the local food, bed linen, and gasoline production businesses. Economist Harvey Rosen (2001) calls this the chain reaction game: if enough indirect effects are added to the benefit side, eventually a positive net present value can be obtained for practically any project.

Rosen notes that this process ignores the fact that there are likely losses as well as gains from building the road. Profits of train operators may decrease as some of their customers turn to cars for transportation, businesses in and around train stations may suffer lost profits, and increased auto use may bid up the price of gasoline, increasing costs to many gasoline consumers. At the very least, indirect costs must be counted as well as indirect gains. In many cases, these benefits and costs are often transfers, with the gains to some equaling the losses to others. While a detailed discussion of the complexities of such "secondary markets effects" is beyond the scope of this chapter, we refer the reader to Boardman, Greenberg, Vining, and Weimer (2006) and recommend restricting the analysis to the most significant indirect effects.

Step 6: Dropout Prevention Program, CBA. In the analysis of the Dropout Prevention Program, the analyst may want to undertake a CBA to assess the efficiency of the program or may want to compare this program with other options that produce dissimilar benefits, for example, expanding the advising and counseling program to assist students in gaining college admissions. Either way, the analyst will want to place dollar values on the benefits of the program and compare them to the costs. The major benefit of completing high school is to the participants themselves: an increase in lifetime earnings because of the diploma. To estimate this figure, an evaluator could compare the wages of individuals who have completed high school with those of similar individuals who have dropped out. These data are available from the U.S. Bureau of Labor Statistics. Alternatively, one could draw on a number of articles in the economics literature that have used quasi-experimental methods and other data sources to estimate the returns to schooling. For purposes of illustration, we use data from a University of Cincinnati study (Ramsey, Rexhausen, Dubey, and Yu, 2008) of the economic benefits of education. In Ohio, the median earnings of a high school dropout is $17,748 (with a 47.5 percent employment rate) compared to $26,207 (70.6 percent employed) for high school graduates. Thus, the earnings differential per graduate (wages plus employment rate) was $10,079 a year over the person's lifetime.

There are also indirect benefits to the rest of society as a result of an individual's completing high school. This includes less crime (and prison expenses), less government support (welfare and other transfers), and increased taxes paid to the government. Some of these benefits to the rest of society are costs to the participants. Thus, taxes gained by government are a cost to the participants (in effect, a transfer that is netted out of the analysis). We include taxes as negative benefits to the participants in the table below.

The analysis makes the assumption that lower crime costs are primarily a benefit to the rest of society (less detention and judicial system cost). This includes the "gain" to potential victims (they avoid a loss of their property), which might be offset somewhat by the "loss" to the participants (they lose the value of goods stolen and fenced). However, because criminals do not abide by the laws of society, the losses they suffer are typically not included in cost-benefit analyses.

It is clear that there are some benefits that are difficult to put a monetary value on. For example, the cost of stolen goods to victims does not cover the full cost of pain and suffering to the victims, but these costs may be difficult to place a dollar value on. Similarly, graduating from high school may create a self-confidence in the students that enhances their lives beyond lifetime earnings. In addition, better-educated citizens may benefit society in other nonmonetary ways. While we do not value these intangible benefits, a thorough cost-benefit analysis should acknowledge them.

Table 24.7 provides a breakdown of benefits to participants and others in society as identified by University of Cincinnati Economics Center (2008).

Although costs begin in Year 1 of the project, benefits do not occur until the students have actually graduated at the end of Year 1 or beginning in Year 2, although it is possible that some benefits (such as lower crime) might begin immediately. Furthermore, the benefits continue to occur over the graduates' lifetime, beyond the thirty years we focus on here. Nonetheless, our

TABLE 24.7. ESTIMATED BENEFITS OF DROPOUT PREVENTION PROGRAM.

	Annual Benefit Per Dropout Prevented	Thirty-Year Projection for Thirty-One Dropouts Prevented
Direct Benefits to Participants		
Increase in earnings	$10,079	$8,305,096
Less welfare payments	($564)	($1,845,760)
Less taxes	($2,240)	($464,736)
TOTAL TO PARTICIPANTS	$7,275	$5,994,600
Indirect Benefits to Others		
Increase in tax revenue	$564	$464,736
Reduction in welfare payments	$2,240	$1,845,760
Reduction in incarceration costs	$1,586	$1,306,864
TOTAL TO OTHERS	$4,390	$3,617,360
TOTAL BENEFITS	$23,330	$9,611,960

calculations reveal a total of approximately $9.6 million in benefits, although these benefits have not yet been discounted. We describe this important adjustment in the next step.

Step 7: Discount Costs and Benefits to Obtain Present Values

It is important to recognize that the school, by spending $642,934 on the Dropout Prevention Program, did not have those dollars to spend for other programs, and thus there is an additional opportunity cost that should be recognized in the analysis. The idea is that, even without inflation, $100 today is worth more to us than the same $100 promised to us one year from now, and much more than the same $100 promised to us in ten years. The reason is that the money has an opportunity cost. We could take the $100 today and invest it to receive more money in the future. Just how much we will receive will depend on the interest rate we obtain. The same is true of all costs and benefits. We value costs and benefits incurred today more than those that we may incur in the future.

In order to incorporate this concept, both cost-benefit and cost-effectiveness analysis convert all monetary values to their present value—or their equivalent value at the beginning of the project, in Year 1. Rather than an actual interest rate, in CEA and CBA we use what is known as a social discount rate (r) (e.g., .03 for 3 percent), to calculate the present value of costs and benefits. The social discount rate is meant to reflect the society's impatience or preference for consumption today compared to consumption in the future. We discuss the choice of the social discount rate further below.

In cost-effectiveness analysis, we take the present value of the costs of the project to use as the numerator in our cost-effectiveness ratio. To do this, we first aggregate the costs in each year, noting each year's costs as C_t, where t indicates the year from 1 to T (the last year of the analysis). The values in each year need to be converted to their Year 1 equivalent, and this is done by dividing C_t by $(1 + r)^{t-1}$. For example, using a 3 percent social discount rate, $1 million of costs accruing in Year 3, would be converted to present value by dividing $1 million by $(1.03)^2$. The result would be $942,596. Summing the present value of the costs in each year, we obtain the present value of the costs of the whole project (PVC):

$$PVC = C_1 + \frac{C_2}{(1+r)^1} + \frac{C_3}{(1+r)^2} + \cdots + \frac{C_T}{(1+r)^{T-1}} = \sum_{t=1}^{T} \frac{C_t}{(1+r)^{t-1}} \qquad (24.3)$$

The PVC is then used to calculate the CE ratio, as described in Step 8 below.

In cost-benefit analysis, the calculation is much the same. One simply takes the present value of the benefits and subtracts the present value of the costs. The final calculation is now referred to as the "net present value" (NPV), rather than net benefits. The formula becomes:

$$NPV = \sum_{t=1}^{T} \frac{(B_t)}{(1+r)^{t-1}} - \sum_{t=1}^{T} \frac{(C_t)}{(1+r)^{t-1}} \qquad (24.4)$$

Rather than calculate these formulae by hand, it is much easier to use Excel's NPV function. One simply inputs the interest rate (r) (e.g., .03) and the values to be discounted. Box 24.7 discusses the difficult question of which social discount rate to use.

Box 24.7. Step 7 (Key Issue): Choosing a Social Discount Rate

The choice of an appropriate discount rate is critical for the program evaluator using CEA or CBA; however, there is considerable debate as to the appropriate rate. For many years, the U.S. Office of Management and Budget (OMB) required a 7 percent discount rate for a base case CBA (OMB 1992). More recently, it advocated calculating net present value with both 7 and 3 percent rates (OMB 2003). In contrast, OMB's recommended discount rates for CEA are based on current interest rates, but vary depending on the time frame of the analysis (OMB 1992). For example, in the 2013 low rate environment, real discount rates ranged from –0.7 percent (for three-year projects) to 1.9 percent (for thirty-year projects) (OMB 2013). Most other sources suggest rates in the range of 2 to 8 percent, depending on the project and its length (Boardman, Greenberg, Vining, and Weimer, 2006; Treasury Board of Canada Secretariat, 2007) However, recently, some have argued for discount rates near 0 for longer-range projects affecting future generations (Stern 2006).

We Recommend: Unless your organization specifies a specific discount rate, we suggest using a base real discount rate of 2 to 3 percent, while testing for sensitivity of the project to higher rates of 5 to 7 percent.

Step 7: Dropout Prevention Program.   In the Dropout Prevention Program, the choice of an appropriate discount rate to obtain net present value is important because the costs are upfront and the benefits accrue over many years into the future. The higher the discount rate, the greater the adverse impact on long-term benefits. For this analysis, we have chosen a 3 percent discount rate for the baseline, and later explain how a change in the discount rate would affect the analysis (part of the sensitivity analysis).

Step 8: Compute Cost-Effectiveness Ratio (for CEA) or Net Present Value (for CBA)

Compute Cost-Effectiveness Ratio (for CEA)

This step finally brings together the present value of costs and units of effectiveness to calculate a CE ratio, where you have a single measure of program effectiveness. Rather than Total Costs (as in equation (24.1)), we substitute the present value of these costs (PVC) into our ratio (note, however, that often the term "Total Costs" is still used, but the present value is assumed):

$$\text{Cost-Effectiveness Ratio} = \frac{\text{PVC}}{\text{Units of Effectiveness}} \quad (24.5)$$

The result is expressed in "dollars per dropout prevented" or "dollars per life saved." When comparing multiple projects, you would calculate the CE ratio for each project separately.

A common alternative is to use the reciprocal of the standard CE ratio in program evaluation. That is, we could divide units of effectiveness by PVC. The ratio would then be interpreted as "dropouts prevented per dollar" or "lives saved per dollar." These, of course, would be quite small, so often evaluators scale the dollars up to interpret the results as "dropouts prevented per $1,000 dollars" or "lives saved per million dollars." The advantage of this approach is that it may be easier to evaluate programs within the context of a specific budget.

One caution when using CEA to compare projects is that ratios hide differences in scale. That is, if one project is ten times the cost of another with roughly ten times the units of effectiveness, the CE ratios of the two projects would look the same, while the actual costs and benefits differ tremendously. In light of this, CEA is most useful when comparing projects of similar sizes.

Calculate Net Present Value (for CBA)

For CBA, the most important calculation is the net present value (NPV), as shown in equation (24.4). The NPV can give the clearest answer to whether a project improves social welfare and should be reported in every CBA. There are, however, two alternative calculations that may be used to supplement the NPV calculation.

The first is the benefit-cost ratio, calculated by taking the NPV of the benefits and dividing them by the NPV of costs. Benefit-cost ratios are useful in two respects. First, they may make it easier to compare similar programs. Second, a decision maker can decide whether a specific benefit gained per dollar of cost is sufficient given other investment or budget alternatives. From an economic efficiency perspective, any program with benefits exceeding costs, or with a benefit-cost ratio of better than 1, would be considered an efficient allocation of resources. We caution, however, that decision makers should use benefit-cost ratios only when they are examining two similar projects in size and scope. Otherwise, CBA ratios can mask scale differences, just as in CEA, which may lead to a choice that does not provide the greatest net benefits to society.

The second alternative calculation is the return on investment. Unlike the private sector, government evaluators in the United States do not usually conduct economic rate of return (ERR) analysis (sometimes referred to as IRR, or internal rate of return). However, international organizations use it more frequently and it can easily be computed. The ERR/IRR is simply the discount rate that would yield total present value benefits equal to costs. The government agency or political decision maker can then assess the value of the project based on whether a certain percent rate of return is satisfactory given other opportunities the agency might have had in Year 1.

Box 24.8. Step 8 (Key Issue): How to Display Your Analysis

When providing a summary of your findings, it is most important to understand what it is that is expected of the evaluator. Are you comparing various programs based on their CEA or CBA or examining one program from various perspectives?

We recommend: Even where the goal is to develop dollar values on all costs and benefits, it may be useful to develop an interim measure of cost-effectiveness by relating costs to one or more measures of effectiveness. While this does not provide a dollar value on the benefits, it provides policymakers with important information on what they are receiving (in benefits or outcomes) for the dollars they are spending. However, where dollar values can be calculated on the benefits, providing information on the net present value of a project is likely to provide the most useful information to decision makers.

Step 8: Dropout Prevention Program. Table 24.8 provides a summary of our cost-benefit and cost-effectiveness analyses. It reports all benefits and costs in present value, using a 3 percent social discount rate. It also includes a breakdown of the benefits and costs for the participants and for the rest of society on an aggregate basis and on a per-dropout-prevented basis.

Whether viewed from the traditional societal perspective (participants and all others), or simply looking at the net benefits to each group separately, the

TABLE 24.8. DROPOUT PREVENTION PROGRAM: COST-BENEFIT AND COST-EFFECTIVENESS SUMMARY.

	Total	Per Dropout Prevented (31 total)
COSTS (PV at r = 3 percent):		
Fiscal costs to school	$606,754	$19,573
Social cost to participants	$434,681	$14,022
TOTAL COSTS	$1,041,435	$33,595
BENEFITS (PV at r = 3%)		
To Others	$2,301,360	$74,237
To Participants	$3,813,757	$123,024
TOTAL BENEFITS	$6,115,117	$197,262
NET PRESENT VALUE (NPV)	$5,073,682	$163,667
Benefit-Cost Ratio	5.87	

Dropout Prevention Program can be considered a success: benefits exceed the costs.

- The CEA ratio is the total cost to society ($1,041,435) divided by the number of dropouts prevented (thirty-one), about $33,600 per dropout prevented (the fiscal costs are about $19,600 per dropout prevented).
- The Net Present Value is substantial, over $5 Million, with $3.4 million accruing to the participants and $1.7 million to the rest of society.
- The PV of benefits ($6,115,117) divided by the PV of costs ($1,1041,435) yields a benefit-cost ratio of 5.87 to 1.

Step 9: Perform Sensitivity Analysis

As we have noted throughout the chapter, it is important for the program evaluator to test the sensitivity of the analysis to particular assumptions. The advantage of Excel and other spreadsheet programs is that they allow the evaluator to easily plug in a range of alternative assumptions and determine their impact on the analysis. There are two main types of sensitivity analysis—partial and extreme case. While other, more sophisticated methods (such as Monte Carlo simulations) are available, partial and extreme case sensitivity analyses remain the methods of choice for most analysts. Box 24.9 reviews the two main approaches to conducting a sensitivity analysis.

Box 24.9. Step 9 (Key Issue): Conducting a Sensitivity Analysis

Because CEAs and CBAs must rely on assumptions that are often "best guesses," it is critical that they contain an explicit sensitivity analysis that discusses key assumptions in the standard "base case" analysis and varies those assumptions to see how a change affects the analysis.

Partial Sensitivity Analysis: This approach varies one assumption (or one parameter or number) at a time, holding all else constant. For example, if the value of life plays an important role in your analysis, you might use an average value of $5 million for the value of statistical life (VSL) in your base case. Using partial sensitivity analysis you would then plug in a range of values for the VSL from $3 million to $9 million without changing any other assumptions and report the results. You would apply the same process for other uncertain parameters, returning each time to the base case figures for everything except the number in question.

Extreme Case Sensitivity Analysis: This approach varies all of the uncertain parameters simultaneously, picking the values for each parameter that yield either the best- or worst-case scenario. If a project looks good even under the worst case assumption, it strengthens the case to go forward. Similarly, if the project looks questionable under a best case scenario, it is unlikely to be successful.

We Recommend: Both approaches are useful. Partial sensitivity analysis is most useful when there are only a handful of critical assumptions, while extreme case is more useful in cases of greater uncertainty. The choice of which approach to use will depend upon the number and type of assumptions made as well as the expectations of policymakers.

Step 9: Dropout Prevention Program. In the Dropout Prevention Program, there are several uncertain assumptions and parameters. Among the most important to the bottom line are the number of dropouts prevented, the annual earnings gain for those who graduate, the foregone earnings of participants, and the social discount rate. Table 24.9 provides an example of a partial sensitivity analysis for the Dropout Prevention Program.

From this information, the decision maker can easily determine that the analysis is most sensitive to the discount rate; however, a small change in any of the assumptions would not have a dramatic impact on the analysis: none of the changes would bring the NPV of the program below 0.

Given the consistently positive net benefits of the partial sensitivity analysis, it may also be useful to undertake a worst case sensitivity analysis. Such an analysis will reveal if we can ever expect to see negative net benefits of the

TABLE 24.9. PARTIAL SENSITIVITY ANALYSIS OF THE DROPOUT PREVENTION PROGRAM.

Base Case Analysis: Net Present Value = $5 million

Key assumptions and base case parameters:

Thirty-one dropouts prevented over five years of program

Increased earnings of high school graduates at $10,079 a year

Opportunity costs to students in foregone earnings of $1,843 per participant

Social discount rate of 3 percent

Effect of changes in key assumptions on NPV:

One fewer/additional dropout prevented per year:+/–$0.7 million

Earnings of high school graduates $1,000 more/less than baseline:+/–$0.5 million

Eliminate opportunity cost to participants: +$0.4 million

Discount rate of 1 percent higher/lower than baseline:+/–$0.8 million

---

program. We now vary all of the uncertain parameters at the same time, pushing each to the most extreme (yet plausible) values that will yield the highest costs and lowest benefits. We recalculate net benefits with the following worst-case assumptions:

- Three fewer dropouts prevented per year (sixteen prevented over five years)
- Earnings of high school graduates $1,000 less than baseline ($9,079)
- Maximum opportunity cost to participants ($1,843 per participant)
- Social discount rate of 7 percent

Even in this worst case scenario, the net present value remains positive at $710,834.

Step 10: Make a Recommendation

The final step of cost-effectiveness and cost-benefit analysis, if appropriate, is making a policy recommendation. For cost-benefit analysis, if a program has a positive net present value (particularly after a worst-case sensitivity analysis), then one should (theoretically) implement the policy, as it would increase social welfare. If it has negative net present value, then the project should be rejected.

In cost-effectiveness analysis, there is no clear decision rule when evaluating one project. The policymaker must use his or her own judgment as to whether the cost per unit of effectiveness is sufficiently low to merit adoption. However, when two or more programs are evaluated against the same units of effectiveness, the policy with the lowest CE ratio should be implemented (assuming the projects are of roughly the same scale, as noted above).

These decision rules, while simple, should not be the only consideration in making a policy recommendation. There are several other important points to take into account.

The Black Box. The biggest danger in any such analysis is the black box syndrome. Instead of laying out the relevant issues, assumptions, and concerns, the analyst may be tempted to hide the messiness of the analysis from the decision maker, presenting a concise answer as to net benefits or costs or cost-effectiveness. However, two honest, careful analysts might arrive at opposite conclusions on the same set of facts if their assumptions about those data differ. A Scotsman once proclaimed that the "devil is in the detail," and it is the detail—the assumptions and the sensitivity of the analysis to those assumptions—that may be of most use to the decision maker in judging the value and usefulness of the evaluator's work. The best approach may be to provide a non-technical overview of the analysis and an appendix with the full technical details.

Equity Concerns. It is not just the total benefits and costs but also who benefits and who pays that are of concern to policymakers. It is not always easy to determine whether there are strong distributional consequences to the program, but when there are, they should be noted. Concerns over rising income inequality in the United States have made it common to give special consideration to distributional consequences in cases where low-income populations stand to gain or lose substantially. One approach to dealing with distributional issues is to weight the benefits and costs. For example, the analyst could weight a benefit or cost to a low-income family as twice the value of a similar benefit and cost to a middle-income family and three times as much as a similar benefit to an upper-income family. The issue is the appropriate weights—a subjective factor that is ultimately the judgment of policymakers. A less controversial alternative is simply to identify the costs and benefits to each significant group that is affected by the project. That approach is illustrated in the Dropout Prevention Program case above, where benefits are divided between participants and the rest of society.

Unquantifiables. No matter how creative the evaluator is, there will be some benefits and costs that defy quantification. Even if you can value the cost of an injury, that dollar figure will not fully capture the pain and suffering involved, and financial savings from burglaries prevented does not fully capture the sense of security that comes with crime prevention. In other cases, the analyst may not have the time or resources to quantify every cost and benefit, even if they could be valued. Box 24.10 discusses one approach to handling unquantifiables.

Box 24.10. Step 10 (Key Issue): Dealing with Intangibles and Unquantifiables in Your Recommendation

While it would be ideal if all benefits and costs could be measured and valued, the reality is that many program benefits and costs may be intangible or unquantifiable. If these effects are significant, they need to be highlighted by the evaluator.

(Continued)

Indirect methods of valuation: The best method for identifying issues surrounding unquantifiable benefits and costs is to relate them to the final dollar results. For example, if the analysis reveals net costs (or negative NPV) of $2 million but also identifies certain environmental benefits that could not be converted to dollars, then the analyst might highlight the question of whether the environmental benefits over the period studied would be enough to offset the $2 million in costs. By juxtaposing dollars against the unquantifiables, both the analyst and decision maker should then use their judgment in assessing the importance of these factors in the analysis.

Relating cost to intangible outcomes: If the major benefit of a project or program is to achieve some intangible benefit (such as improving visibility over the national parks through stricter environmental regulation), it may be best to treat the problem more as a cost-effectiveness issue, asking, for example: What is the marginal cost to increase park visibility from the current ten miles to twenty miles?

Step 10: Dropout Prevention Program. The high net benefits in the base case, the relative insensitivity of the results to changes in assumptions, and a worst case analysis that remains positive, all suggest that the program was a success and should be expanded to other schools in the state. The benefits to society outweigh the costs under a range of assumptions, suggesting that the program improves efficiency or overall social welfare. Before making the recommendation however, one should consider any unquantified costs or benefits that might change our results. For example, we did not include any negative psychological effects that participants may incur from stigma associated with the program. Still, unless these negative feelings cause students more than $5 million of harm total (or $100,000 per participant—which seems implausibly large), we have no reason to believe that omitting these effects will change our recommendation. A final consideration is equity. As this program potentially helps low-income students who are most at risk of dropping out, equity is likely enhanced, providing one more reason to recommend that the program be expanded.

The *ex post* CBA assesses the success of the program to date—or for the thirty years we analyze. But if policymakers are considering whether or not to continue the program after the first five years have elapsed, in an *in medias res* evaluation, other considerations might also need to be taken into account. By Year 5, the program is costing $127,887 a year and is preventing eight dropouts a year for a fiscal cost to society per dropout prevented of $15,986 (see Table 24.6). At this point, certain costs incurred by the school (for example, the original cost of consultants) are now sunk costs, that is, funds have already been spent and resources used. They have no relevance for decisions about whether to continue the project. Thus, the previously spent funds on start-up and on capital costs are not considered by the agency in deciding whether to continue the project. The state policymakers are concerned only with the program's current and future costs and expected continued benefits. The considerations might include whether more funding will be needed to modify the program in the future, whether new equipment will be needed, and whether there will still be a need or demand for this program in the future. Thus, the program's continuation faces a different analysis from an *ex post* analysis of the project's net benefits. One of the challenges for the analyst is determining whether the projections of costs and benefits are realistic.

The cost-benefit illustration reinforces an important distinction for the analyst: the difference between total and marginal (or incremental) benefits and costs. In assessing the overall efficiency of a proposed or existing project, a policymaker should consider the total costs of getting the program or project started through its operation's cycle. But at any point when an agency is deciding whether to continue or discontinue a project or program, it should consider only its marginal costs and benefits—those that will accrue over and above the status quo at that point in time

Conclusion

Cost-benefit and cost-effectiveness analyses are not panaceas that will provide decision makers with the answer to a policy problem. Indeed, both techniques may be more of an art than a science. With a host of considerations and sometimes controversial assumptions, the process is far more complicated and potentially more biased than many realize. However, much can be learned about a project in creating a framework to consider benefits and costs: simply attempting to identify them, measure them, and value them can provide important information for the decision maker. Adding a thorough sensitivity analysis and a clear explanation of each assumption and estimate, CEA and CBA can be extremely effective tools in program evaluation. Box 24.11 lists some recent CEAs and CBAs that provide additional illustrations of the two techniques.

Box 24.11. Selected Applications and Critiques of CEA and CBA

Belfield, Clive R., Nores, Milagros, Barnett, Steve, and Schweinhart, Lawrence. "The High/Scope Perry Preschool Program: Cost-Benefit Analysis Using Data from the Age 40 Follow-Up." *Journal of Human Resources,* 2006, XLI(1), 162–190.

(Continued)

Chen, Greg, and Warburton, Rebecca N. "Do Speed Cameras Produce Net Benefits? Evidence from British Columbia, Canada." *Journal of Policy Analysis and Management,* 2006, *25*(3), 661–678.

General Accountability Office. "Clean Air Act: Observations on EPA's Cost-Benefit Analysis of its Mercury Control Options." GAO-05-252, 2005.

KPMG Foundation. "The Long-Term Costs of Literacy Difficulties."www.kpmg.co.uk/pubs/beforepdf.cfm?PubID=1890. December 2006.

Landau, Steve, and Weisbrod, Glen. *Effective Practices for Preparing Airport Improvement Program Benefit-Cost Analysis.* Transportation Research Board of the National Academies, Airport Cooperative Research Program, Synthesis 13, 2009.

Levin, Henry M., Belfield, Clive, Muennig, Peter, and Rouse, Cecilia. "The Costs and Benefits of an Excellent Education for All of America's Children." New York: Center for Benefit-Cost Studies on Education at Teacher's College, Columbia University, 2007.

Mandelblatt, Jeanne, Saha, Somnath, Teutsch, Steven, Hoerger, Tom, Siu, Albert L., Atkins, David, Klein, Jonathan, and Helfand, Mark. "The Cost-Effectiveness of Screening Mammography Beyond Age 65." *Annals of Internal Medicine,* 2003, *139*(10), 835–842.

Paltiel, David A., Weinstein, Milton C., Kimmel, April D., Seage, George R., III, Losina, Elena, Zhang, Hong, Freedberg, Kenneth A., and Walensky, Rochelle P. "Expanded Screening for HIV in the United States—An Analysis of Cost-Effectiveness." *New England Journal of Medicine,* 2005, *352,* 586–595.

Russell, Louise B., Gold, Marthe R., Siegel, Joanna E., Daniels, Norman, and Weinstein, Milton C. 1996. "The Role of Cost-Effectiveness Analysis in Health and Medicine." *Journal of the American Medical Association,* 1996, *276*(14),1172–1177.

Salt Lake City Million Solar Roofs Partnership. "Memorandum of Support, Rocky Mountain Power's Proposed Pilot Solar Initiative." www.psc.state.ut.us/utilities/electric/07docs/.../53801CorresSLC.doc. 2007.

Schwindt, Richard, Vining, Aidan, and Globerman, Steven. "Net Loss: A Cost-Benefit Analysis of the Canadian Pacific Salmon Fishery." *Journal of Policy Analysis and Management,* 2000, *19*(1), 23–45.

Siegfried, John, and Zimbalist, Andrew. "The Economics of Sports Facilities and Their Communities." *Journal of Economic Perspectives,*2000, *14*(3).

Stern, Nicholas. The Stern Review Report on the Economics of Climate Change. London, UK: HM Treasury, 2006.

Washington State Institute for Public Policy. *Benefit-Cost Results and Technical Manual.* www.wsipp.wa.gov/BenefitCost.

Weimer, David (Ed). *Cost-Benefit Analysis and Public Policy.* New York: Wiley-Blackwell, 2008.

Wiseman, Virginia, Kim, Michelle, Mutabingwa, Theonest K., and Whitty, Christopher J. M. "Cost-Effectiveness Study of Three Antimalarial Drug Combinations in Tanzania." *Public Library of Science Medicine,* 2006, 3(10). www.plosmedicine.org/article/info:doi/10.1371/journal.pmed.0030373.

Notes

1. Note that in CBA and CEA, the term "outcome" is typically used to refer to the causal impacts of a policy or program, rather than broader "program outcomes," described in other chapters of this volume. As discussed above, the analyst should seek to ascertain the causal impacts of a policy—those over and above the status quo that would not have occurred in the absence of the policy. Experimental and quasi-experimental methods are best suited to obtain causal effects, though they are difficult to implement in the context of a CBA or CEA. However, if experimental or quasi-experimental estimates are available on a particular cost or benefit, they should certainly be used.

2. Again, we point out that experimental or quasi-experimental estimates that control for differences between participating and non-participating students would yield more accurate estimates. However, in most CBAs and CEAs, these types of estimates are well beyond the scope of the study.

3. Technically, market values reveal a person's minimum willingness to pay for a product. An individual may well value the product more. Ideally, we would like to measure this additional "consumer surplus," but it is difficult to do in practice.

References

Boardman, A. A., Greenberg, D. H., Vining, A. R., and Weimer, D. L. *Cost-Benefit Analysis: Concepts and Practice* (3rd ed.). Upper Saddle River, NJ: Prentice Hall, 2006.

Levin, H. M., and McEwan, P. J. *Cost-Effectiveness Analysis* (2nd ed.). Thousand Oaks, CA: Sage, 2001.

Musgrave, R., and Musgrave, P. *Public Finance in Theory and Practice.* New York: McGraw-Hill, 1989.

Office of Management and Budget. *Circular A-4.* Washington, DC, 2003. www.whitehouse.gov/omb/circulars_a004_a-4/

Office of Management and Budget. *Circular A-94, Revised.* Washington, DC, 1992.,www.whitehouse.gov/omb/circulars_a094ˉ8.

Office of Management and Budget. *Circular A-94, Appendix C, Revised December 2013.* Washington, DC, 2013. www.whitehouse.gov/omb/circulars_a094/a94_appx-c/.

Ramsey, B. B., Rexhausen, J., Dubey, A., and Yu, L. *An Evaluation of the Economic Benefits of High School Education.* Cincinnati, OH: University of Cincinnati: Economics Center for Education and Research, 2008.

Rosen, H. S. *Public Finance* (6th ed.). Homewood, IL: Irwin, 2001.

Stern, N. *The Stern Review Report on the Economics of Climate Change.* London, UK: HM Treasury, October 30, 2006.

Treasury Board of Canada Secretariat. *Canadian Regulatory Cost-Benefit Analysis Guide.* www.tbs-sct.gc.ca/rtrap-parfa/analys/analystb-eng.asp. 2007.

CHAPTER TWENTY-FIVE

META-ANALYSES, SYSTEMATIC REVIEWS, AND EVALUATION SYNTHESES*

Robert Boruch, Anthony Petrosino, Claire Morgan

What is a *meta-analysis?* A *systematic review?* An *evaluation synthesis?* A variety of phrases are used to describe scientifically disciplined approaches to searching literatures, assembling studies for review, and analyzing, interpreting, and reporting the results. Here, we adopt the definitions given by Chalmers, Hedges, and Cooper (2002). A *systematic review* involves the application of strategies that limit bias in the assembly, critical appraisal, and synthesis of all relevant studies on a specific topic. *Meta-analysis* is the statistical synthesis of data from separate but similar (that is, comparable) studies, leading to a quantitative summary of the pooled results. *Evaluation synthesis* is an attempt to "integrate empirical evaluations for the purpose of creating generalizations . . . [in a way that] is initially nonjudgmental vis-a-vis the outcomes of the synthesis and intends to be exhaustive in the coverage of the database" (Cooper, Hedges, and Valentine, 2009, pp. 5, 19).

The word *bias*, as seen in the definition of systematic review and implied in the other definitions, has a basic meaning of "systematic error introduced into sampling or testing by selecting or encouraging one outcome or answer

*Work on the topic discussed in this chapter has been funded by the Institute for Education Sciences, the research arm of the U.S. Department of Education. The views expressed here do not necessarily reflect the views of funding organizations.

over others" (as stated in *Merriam-Webster's Collegiate Dictionary*) but exists in many forms. Identifying and depending only on reports that suit the reviewer's ideological or theoretical preference is an obvious source of bias, for example. The tactic has been exploited shamelessly in political, professional, and even ostensibly dispassionate arenas, such as the university. Paying attention only to reports that are published in refereed academic journals also implies a biased sample of pertinent reports: those not published in such journals are ignored or not identified. Bias also refers to the study design for each study in an assembly of studies and, in particular, bias in the statistical estimates of an intervention's effect that is produced by each design. Randomized trials, for instance, when they are carried out well, produce statistically unbiased estimates of the relative effect of an intervention. The statistical bias in estimates of effect produced by alternative approaches, such as a before-after evaluation, cannot always be identified, much less estimated.

Simple definitions are necessary but not sufficient. There is a science to reviewing research, including meta-analyses. The rationales, principles, and procedures used and the scientific standards of evidence employed have to be made clear.

Why Be Conscientious in Reviewing Studies of Intervention Effects?

Any college student or professor, legislative staffer or public lobbyist, journalist, or thoughtful citizen can do a Google, Bing, or other Internet search on phrases such as "what works." Our rudimentary search on just these terms in July 2014 yielded a staggering two billion hits in .05 seconds. Obviously, more careful and systematic procedures are necessary to reduce this volume and focus exclusively on those studies that directly bear on the effectiveness of an intervention. The following gives some other reasons to justify conscientious review procedures in synthesizing evaluations.

Multiple Evaluations Versus a Single Evaluation

Other things being equal, examining multiple, independent, and high-quality evaluations of an intervention or a class of interventions is a better way to understand the intervention's effects than examining one evaluation. Findings from a single study done in one place, by one team, and with one actualization of the intervention, for instance, usually cannot easily be generalized to other settings, other teams, or other actualizations. Replication or a near-replication is important for supporting statements about how often, to what degree, and in what circumstances the intervention works. Meta-analyses, systematic reviews, and evaluation syntheses try to get beyond the single study, if indeed there are more studies to examine.

For instance, Petrosino, Turpin-Petrosino, and Guckenburg (2010) examined the effects of juvenile system processing on delinquency. Less serious juvenile offenders can be handled with considerable discretion. Juvenile system practitioners can opt to bring the child formally through the juvenile justice system (official processing), divert the child out of the system to a program or service, or release the child to parents or guardians with no further action. To some observers' surprise, at least twenty-nine randomized trials have been mounted since 1972 that have compared assignment of juveniles to an "official" system processing condition (that is, petitioned before the court, appearance before a judge, case moving forward in the system) with at least one release or diversion program condition.

Across these twenty-nine experiments, there is considerable variation. The selective reader could cite any single study—or selective number of studies—as "evidence" for a position that processing has a "deterrent" effect and reduces subsequent delinquency. Indeed, about ten studies show positive results for processing. Relying on a selective gathering of evidence might lead decision makers to opt for processing juvenile offenders formally through the court system as a deterrent measure.

The totality of the evidence reviewed by Petrosino and his colleagues, however, paints a different picture. Figure 25.1 presents the effect sizes for juvenile system processing versus a diversion program or release condition. (In this review, standardized difference [Std. Mean Diff.] refers to the difference between the outcomes for the treatment and control group divided by the standard deviation.) In this instance the assembly of evidence suggests that across all twenty-nine studies, the effect size was –.11. Although this is a negative effect, indicating that processing led to an increase in delinquency, this would be considered by most readers to be a small effect size. But keep in mind that juvenile system processing is a more expensive option for most jurisdictions than simple release and likely more expensive than almost all but the most intensive diversion programs. If there is no deterrent impact of official judicial processing but in fact a small negative effect, and if it is a more expensive option, a judge, citizen, or policymaker could clearly ask if it would be better to divert or release less serious juvenile offenders.

Identifying High-Quality Evidence

The best high-quality systematic reviews, meta-analyses, and evaluation syntheses identify high-quality evidence that has been produced on the effects of
interventions and where such evidence is unavailable. The review discussed
in the previous section is an illustration of this. It identifies the dependable
grounds on which decisions can be made to adopt, avoid, or improve the intervention. As will be discussed below, to be determined of high quality and worthy of inclusion in a systematic review, the evidence must meet transparent
inclusion criteria identified by the researchers. An example of how important
it can be to establish the absence of high-quality evidence can be found in a
review conducted by Fisher, Montgomery, and Gardner (2008). These investigators conducted a systematic review of research on the effects of providing employment or educational opportunities (that is of "opportunities provision") to prevent gang involvement. They searched widely for dependable evidence from experimental and quasi-experimental studies that tested the provision of opportunities to actual or prospective gang members in the interest of
preventing or reducing participation in gangs. They did not find a single study
meeting their eligibility criteria. The value of such a systematic review lies in
establishing that *no* high-quality evaluations have been carried out on a particular topic. Such a review establishes the need for funding primary evaluation
studies that test promising interventions.

Governments and non-governmental aid organizations often want evidence to show where their funding can be most effectively allocated. Recently,
for example, some multinational organizations that are concerned about the
availability of quality evidence for low-income countries have begun to fund
production of such evidence in the interest of better interventions and decision making. The International Initiative for Impact Evaluation (3ie), for
instance, promotes rigorous studies, particularly randomized controlled trials, in the developing nation context. This organization also sponsors systematic reviews—*synthetic reviews* in the organization's vernacular. With 3ie's
support, Petrosino, Morgan, Fronius, Tanner-Smith, and Boruch (2014) conducted systematic searches to identify experimental and quasi-experimental
studies that tested the impact of an intervention on school enrollment, attendance, dropout rates, and the like, in developing countries. The project initially identified some high-quality evidence (seventy-six eligible studies), and
a large number of studies that either did not use an experimental or quasi-
experimental design or did not include an outcome measure of school enrollment. This kind of mapping has benefits for decision making not only about
what programming to implement but also where future studies are likely to be

FIGURE 25.1. PROCESSING EFFECTS ON PREVALENCE: FIRST EFFECTS

Study Name	Outcome	Std. Mean Diff.	Lower Limit	Upper Limit	p-Value
Patrick & Marsh (2005)	First Effect-P	0.28	-0.30	0.86	0.34
Severy & Whitaker (1982)	First Effect-P	0.10	-0.08	0.27	0.30
Klein (1986)	First Effect-P	-0.48	-0.84	-0.12	0.01
Smith et al. (1979)	First Effect-P	0.00	-0.61	0.61	1.00
Baron & Feeney (1976) 602	First Effect-P	-0.43	-0.76	-0.10	0.01
Baron and Feeney (1976) 601	First Effect-P	-0.25	-0.38	-0.12	0.00
Dunford et al. (1982) KC	First Effect-P	0.09	-0.22	0.40	0.55
Dunford et al. (1982) NY	First Effect-P	-0.32	-0.61	-0.03	0.03
Dunford et al. (1982) FL	First Effect-P	0.10	-0.22	0.42	0.56
Koch (1985)	First Effect-P	-0.2	-0.82	0.27	0.32
Blakely (1981)	First Effect-P	0.07	-1.03	1.16	0.91
Davidson II et al. (1987)	First Effect-P	-0.23	-0.72	0.27	0.37
Davidson II et al. (1980)	First Effect-P	-0.94	-1.44	-0.43	0.00
Quay and Love (1977)	First Effect-P	-0.24	-0.47	-0.02	0.03
Bauer et al. (1980)	First Effect-P	-0.51	-1.18	0.16	0.13
Quincy (1981)	First Effect-P	-0.47	-0.90	-0.04	0.03
Hintzen et al. (1979)	First Effect-P	1.00	0.11	1.99	0.03
Smith et al. (2004)	First Effect-P	-0.05	-0.34	0.24	0.73
Povitsky Stickle et al. (2008)	First Effect-P	0.16	-0.31	0.63	0.50
University Associates (1986) OTSEGO	First Effect-P	-0.19	-1.28	0.90	0.73
University Associates (1986) BAY	First Effect-P	-0.03	-0.42	0.37	0.89
University Associates (1986) KALAMAZOO	First Effect-P	0.03	-0.25	0.31	0.84
University Associates (1986) DETROIT	First Effect-P	-0.05	-0.34	0.24	0.73
Curran et al. (1977)	First Effect-P	-0.64	-0.82	-0.45	0.00
Sherman et al. (2000) JPP	First Effect-P	0.65	0.22	1.08	0.00
McCold and Wachtel (1998)	First Effect-P	0.368	-0.01	0.74	0.06
True (1973)	First Effect-P	0.68	-0.54	1.91	0.28
		-0.11	-0.24	0.02	0.10

Source: Petrosino, Turpin-Petrosino, and Guckenburg, 2010.

informative and should be initiated. The credibility of such a map depends heavily on conscientious and well-documented searches for published and unpublished reports on the topic of interest.

Going Beyond the Flaws in Conventional Literature Reviews

Few of us are without sin, of commission or omission, in reviewing a body of literature. We fail at times by relying on machine-based (keyword) searches when it is known that visually inspecting each journal volume's contents (i.e., hand searches) is superior. We also often rely on traditionally-published literature when other sources of reports are increasing available and just as important. We often fail to understand systematic review or meta-analysis in basic scientific terms: framing a question properly, identifying a target population of studies, sampling the studies well, and analyzing the results properly. When we do literature reviews, we may fail to make our standards of evidence and procedures explicit. The modern approaches to reviews assist us in being scientifically virtuous, or at least in understanding what virtue is.

Farrington and Petrosino (2000) have contrasted the imperfections of "common reviews of the literature" with the quality of the reviews produced by organizations such as the international Cochrane and Campbell Collaborations. They point out that on the one hand, common literature reviews are usually one-off exercises that fail to be updated or to exploit new technologies of searching, reviewing, and summarizing studies. The Cochrane and Campbell Collaborations, on the other hand, capitalize on contemporary technical methods and attempts to periodically update reviews. Farrington and Petrosino remind us that conventional reviews are usually based on one country's research and on English language publications, whereas organizations such as Cochrane and Campbell are international. Common reviews often do not present explicit details on such important components as what literature will be included, how it will be assessed, and criteria for determining success of an intervention. Cochrane and Campbell Collaboration reviews stress explicit and transparent methods, including an externally peer-reviewed and electronically published protocol or plan for the review. Finally, these authors point out that conventional reviews are published in a variety of outlets that each have their own jargon and standards of evidence, which presents substantial difficulties for policy people, practitioners, and researchers who work across disciplines. The purpose of organizations such as Cochrane and Campbell Collaboration is to provide an electronically accessible data base of high-quality, uniformly structured, systematic reviews and evaluation syntheses.

How Are the Best Approaches to Systematic Reviews Employed at Their Best?

Doing serious scientific research in the context of systematic reviews is hard work. Easing the burden without degrading the quality of the product is a good idea. A fine aspiration at least.

Practical Advice: Read or Take a Course

Evaluators and other applied researchers who know nothing about a systematic review can learn by reading a good one. Since 1993, the most uniform of and transparent of the genre in health care have been produced by the Cochrane Collaboration (www.cochrane.org). More recent parallel efforts in the social sector are being produced by the Campbell Collaboration (www.campbellcollaboration.org). Both rely heavily on voluntary efforts. In education in the United States, the What Works Clearinghouse (WWC) has been well funded to produce remarkably detailed reviews of particular curriculum packages that can withstand the legal threats of commercial publishers and package developers. Smaller but equally noble efforts have been mounted by the Coalition for Evidence-Based Policy, and by Robert Slavin in his "Best Evidence for Education (BEE)."

These are among the best partly because they get well beyond the flaws of run-of-the-mill literature reviews. They depend on organizational innovations and technology, including transparent standards of evidence on effects of interventions.

Perish the thought of reading or taking a course for those who prefer only Google. But people who are serious in their interest might read a book. A comprehensive handling of advances in the area is edited by Cooper, Hedges, and Valentine (2009). Their book requires stamina but is mighty thorough.

Short courses on systematic reviews, meta-analysis, and the activities they require, such as hand searches of journals and adherence to explicit standards, are valuable. The Cochrane Collaboration and Campbell Collaboration offer these at annual meetings and at other times. The WWC has developed training courses for reviewing education evaluations (http://whatworks.ed.gov). Among other organizations, the Society for Prevention Research has initiated presentation on the topic at its annual meeting. Academic institutions, such as the Evidence for Policy and Practice Information and Coordinating Centre (EPPI Centre) at the University of London, now offer programs and courses in research synthesis.

Practical Advice: Contribute to a Meta-Analysis, Systematic Review, or Evaluation Synthesis

Conducting a meta-analysis, systematic review, or evaluation synthesis that is governed by high standards can be demanding. The opportunities for voluntary contributions are ample; for example, the Cochrane and Campbell Collaborations seek such voluntary efforts (e.g., as authors, reviewers, passing along eligible studies). For the opportunities in the international Campbell Collaboration more generally, see http://campbellcolaboration.org. In Copenhagen, SFI Campbell (formerly the Nordic Campbell Centre), which "works with evidence and measuring of effects of social welfare interventions," (www.sfi.dk/Default.aspx?ID=432), provides seed money to talented people who want to contribute to systematic reviews that are far better, and more demanding, than the more common reviews of literature. Nowadays, substantial numbers of good reviews are produced through government agencies, such as the WWC, and through contracts with or grants to organizations whose staff and consultants produce the reviews. These arrangements typically depend on salaried professional staff rather than volunteers.

Producing a Meta-Analysis, Systematic Review, Evaluation Synthesis

The major steps in a systematic review, meta-analysis, or evaluation synthesis are easy to lay out. However, they are not easy to take, just as the analogous steps in field evaluations and other applied research are not easy. The simplified list in the following section capitalizes on the guidelines of the Quality of Reporting of Meta-analyses (QUOROM) group (Moher and others, 1999) and on Cooper, Hedges, and Valentine (2009), the Campbell and Cochrane Collaborations, the WWC, and other sources.

Specify the Topic Area. In the WWC, for instance, specifying the topic means identifying (Gersten and Hitchcock, 2009):

1. A rationale for addressing the problem
2. The specific question(s) that will be addressed
3. The relevant outcome variables
4. The relevant target populations and subpopulations of interest
5. The relevant class of interventions that address the problem

Reviewers proposing new topics for review in the Campbell Collaboration must fill out a title registration page containing such information. This is done to enhance transparency and uniformity as well as to avoid duplication of effort.

As important, authors of proposed reviews must indicate what types of studies are going to be reviewed and the relevant outcomes and the targeted populations of interest. For example, in the Petrosino, Morgan, Fronius, Tanner-Smith, and Boruch (2014) review on the effects of school enrollment strategies in developing nations, the research team specified that it would examine evaluations of school enrollment policies and practices based on randomized trials or rigorous quasi-experimental designs. The team also required that eligible studies report at least one outcome of enrollment, attendance, or dropout and that these studies be conducted in developing nations with primary and secondary school students.

Develop a Management Strategy and Procedures.   Managing a single systematic review, meta-analysis, or evaluation synthesis requires a strategy that does not differ *in principle* from the management requirements of a field study. This includes identifying who will do what tasks, when, with what resources, and under what ground rules. A plan for conducting the review is required by the Campbell and Cochrane Collaborations and by funding agencies, such as the Institute for Education Sciences and 3ie, that support such syntheses. This protocol lays out the plan for the review and indicates the timeline for completing the review and submitting deliverables such as the final review draft. Such protocols, especially when published electronically by organizations like the Campbell and Cochrane Collaborations, also provide a level of transparency in that one can determine if and how review teams deviated from the plan.

The time required and difficulty encountered in doing a review, and the funding and other resources needed to complete one, are influenced heavily by the size and complexity of the studies that will be included. A review that does not find any eligible studies will of course be substantially cheaper and quicker than a review including hundreds of studies.

Specify the Search Strategy.   Specifying what literatures will be searched, how, and with what resources is crucial. The best reviews are exhaustive, and usually exhausting, in searching for reports published in peer-reviewed social science journals or issued by organizations with high-quality editorial screening, or both. Doing both is better, at least in the United States, where some evaluation organizations have external peer review systems with standards that get beyond those of some professional journals. Will evaluations that are relevant but not reported widely also be included in the systematic review? Many organizations, for-profit and otherwise, for instance, do not publish articles in peer-reviewed

TABLE 25.1. SYSTEMATIC REVIEW SEARCH STRATEGIES.

Conduct electronic searches of bibliographic databases using specified keywords
and strings
Conduct online "hand searches" of relevant journals
Examine online holdings of relevant organizations and research firms
Scan the references of each retrieved report
Contact researchers working in the topic area

journals. Unless they put a report on an easily accessed website, that report might not be uncovered. Evaluation reports by school district research offices, and by vendors of educational software and curriculum packages are not circulated widely, if at all. The systematic review team has to decide whether to survey these and how to do so. The Institute for Education Science's WWC, for example, posts the topical protocol for each review that is planned on its public website. The WWC tells the formal WWC Network about each, so as to invite people to submit studies that seem pertinent for inclusion in a particular review. Surveying researchers in the field, as Waddington, Snilstveit, White, and Fewtrell (2009) did, is one approach reviewers have used in an attempt to identify what is referred to as *grey* or *fugitive* literature that might otherwise remain stuck in file drawers.

Researchers may undertake online "hand searches" of certain peer-reviewed journals, knowing that such a search yields a far more reliable and complete assembly of relevant studies than a search engine. The best systematic reviews undertaken under the guidelines of the Campbell and Cochrane Collaborations, the WWC, and others make plain what literatures have been covered in the search. For example, a review of studies of the effect of water, sanitation, and hygiene practices intended to combat diarrhea in developing nations (Waddington, Snilstveit, White, and Fewtrell, 2009) searched ten electronic bibliographical databases, contacted key scholars working in the area, and conducted specialized searches of the Web sites of approximately twenty-five leading international organizations, such as the International Federation of the Red Cross and Red Crescent Societies. The searches yielded 76 experimental and quasi-experimental impact studies that appeared dependable for estimating the effects of the interventions.

Table 25.1 outlines search strategies commonly undertaken in a thorough systematic review. Beyond identifying the target for the literature search, the way the search is conducted has to be specified. What keywords, constructed how and why, will be used with what electronic search engine and with what electronic databases? Randomized trials, for instance, are sometimes hard to locate given that relevant keywords often do not appear in a journal article's

TABLE 25.2. EXAMPLES OF INCLUSION CRITERIA
FOR SYSTEMATIC REVIEWS.

Was the evaluation conducted in the region or with the population of interest?

Does the evaluation include the outcome measure(s) of interest?

Was the evaluation conducted during the timeframe of interest?

Does the evaluation report on construct validity that ties the outcome variable to interventions?

Does the evaluation employ a design that permits unbiased and relatively unequivocal estimates of the intervention's effects

Does the evaluation report sufficient information to estimate effect sizes?

Does the evaluation meet methodological quality criteria, e.g.: Was the intervention implemented with fidelity? Were there selection bias or attrition issues?

---

abstract or title. Consequently, trying out different words in each database may be warranted. In searching for study trials in the crime and justice arena, Petrosino's (1995) search suggested that the following keywords had a high yield: *random, experiment, controlled, evaluation, impact, effect,* and *outcome.* Depending on the vernacular employed in the discipline, databases, search engines, and so on, another researcher's list could be appreciably different from this. The aforementioned water sanitation review (Waddington, Snilstveit, White, and Fewtrell, 2009) reported that good success arose in part from pairing terms such as *sanitation, water quality, water quantity,* and *hygiene* with *diarrhea.*

Develop Inclusion and Exclusion Criteria for Studies in the Review. This step focuses on identifying the studies that will be regarded as potentially legitimate data for a systematic review. Efforts to make inclusion standards uniform, explicit, and scientific in orientation have been made by the Cochrane Collaboration, the Campbell Collaboration, the Coalition for Evidence-Based Policy, and the WWC, among others. Table 25.2 shows some examples of questions to ask when evaluating a study for inclusion in a systematic review.

Once a study is tentatively included, more detailed questions on implementation fidelity, rates of missing data and loss of participants or attrition from study samples quality of measurement, and so on are posed. In the WWC, for example, data drawn from study reports are coded, preferably by two independent coders, so as to permit further determinations about how much one can depend on the study at hand. For instance, a randomized trial or quasi-experiment with a 30 percent difference in the attrition rates for the intervention and the control groups would be ruled out as a dependable resource by reviewers who understand how vulnerable this difference in attrition rate renders the study's results. An exception may be made if evidence can be produced to argue that plausible biases are negligible.

Under the WWC standards, a study is rejected from a systematic review if it (1) fails to report on construct validity that ties the outcome variable to interventions, (2) fails to employ an evaluation design that permits unbiased and relatively unequivocal estimates of the intervention's effects, (3) does not test the intervention on appropriate target populations, or (4) fails to report information sufficient to estimate effect sizes. Studies that do report information in all these areas are tentatively included in the review.

As the definitions given earlier suggest, inclusion criteria in systematic reviews focus on eliminating biased estimates of the effects of interventions. Generalizing from the studies at hand is often subordinate to the aim to eliminate biases from the studies being examined. Nonetheless, when a systematic review includes a number of studies conducted in a wide range of jurisdictions (including multinational settings, on occasion), conducted over a long time period, and using various measurement outcomes of a construct, the findings can be construed as having higher external validity than findings from single studies. Various advanced statistical methods can help one understand the assumptions underlying such generalizations.

Reviewers are often surprised, despite the number of publications on studies conducted in a field, at the number of studies that do not meet the eligibility criteria for dependability of the evidence. For example, a U.S. Government Accountability Office (GAO) review of sixty-one studies of interventions for the low-income participants in the Special Supplemental Nutrition Program for Women, Infants, and Children (WIC) depended heavily on only 37, which were declared "relatively credible" (Hunt, 1997, p. 41). Mark Lipsey's review of studies on juvenile delinquency prevention and treatment programs initially amassed more than 8,000 citations, and after screening depended on 443 that met the researchers' standard for good design and execution (Hunt, 1997, p. 129). In a review of effects of a marital and family therapy, "a year and a half of such efforts netted [William] Shadish a haul of roughly two thousand references" (Hunt, 1997, p. 45). About 160 of these met high standards of evidence and were included in the review. Gersten and Hitchcock (2009) identified 700 publications related to English-language learners and interventions for them, and covered just two dependable evaluations in their WWC review.

Develop a Scheme for Coding Studies and Their Properties. Evaluation syntheses, systematic reviews, and meta-analyses direct one's attention to an assembly of studies. The assembly is often a mob. The implication is that reports on evaluations of the effects of interventions, when included in a disciplined review, need to be construed as objects for interrogation and categorized in a variety of ways. As David Wilson (2009) put it, coding for a systematic review

TABLE 25.3. EXAMPLES OF VARIABLES TO CODE IN INCLUDED EVALUATIONS.

Characteristics of Intervention	Characteristics of Study Population	Characteristics of Study Methods
Description of intervention		
Detailed descriptions of the intervention and control condition, including the "dosage" of the treatment being implemented, and the number of participants assigned to each group	Detail about the type of participants in the trials	
Whether the program experienced significant implementation and fidelity problems	Setting and context in which trial was conducted	Information about randomization or quasi-experimental assignment
Issues with crossovers (persons receiving a condition they were not assigned to)		Level of assignment and whether the study included multiple analyses at different levels
		How the groups were equated and whether any problems with equating were reported
		Loss of participants due to attrition or database matching issues and whether the attrition differentially affected the groups
		Selection bias (e.g., breakdowns in randomization or unusual unequal distributions in groups)

is akin to "interviewing the studies." In best practice, coding and abstraction of each study considered for a systematic review involves development of coding schema, training of coders, and the use of at least two independent coders (double coding) so as to provide reliability checks. The codes address details of the intervention, characteristics of the samples used in the study, definitions of specific outcomes, dose levels, and so on. Table 25.3 lists examples of variables that could be included in a coding instrument.

Consider an example. Wilson, Lipsey, and Soydan's (2003) award-winning review of the effect of mainstream delinquency programs on minority youths is based on the double coding of about 150 features of each study in the review. The authors' early attention to detail in coding permitted their later research on subsamples of minority youths in evaluations that included small to moderately sized subsamples. Coding categories in this review were similar to those used in Cochrane, Campbell, and WWC reviews, at least with respect to the evaluation's design; for example, randomized trials are distinguished routinely from nonrandomized trials. Codes identify detailed features of the interventions, such as the kinds of staff delivering the treatment, the format (group versus individual), the site, and so on.

A review may have to discard studies following the detailed coding of reports. Upon closer inspection, for instance, some studies originally thought to be eligible may be put aside because they do not provide the necessary data for meta-analysis. To judge from Gersten and Hitchcock's (2009) examination of the flaws in reporting, common problems are that the published reports do not provide any quantitative data to permit the computation of an effect size or do not analyze data correctly and do not provide enough information to correct the original analysis.

Compute Effect Size Estimates, Code Them, and Estimate Their Variances. An *effect size* in any science is estimated relative to some basis for comparison, reference, or benchmark. In a two-arm, randomized controlled trial, for instance, the common estimate of effect size involves computing the difference between mean outcomes for the two interventions being compared, and then dividing this difference by the square root of a pooled estimate of variance within the intervention groups. Odds ratios are common in the health sector and are being used more often in meta-analyses of social interventions (Cooper, Hedges, and Valentine, 2009). Neither of these statistical indicators of effect size or odds ratios is easily understandable to many people. Consequently, graphic portrayals that meet good statistical standards, such as the example in Figure 25.1, are now common. The technology and the art of portraying results in numbers, prose, and charts are still developing and deserve serious research on how people understand and value the portrayals (Boruch and Rui, 2008).

Impact evaluation reports do not always contain sufficient information for the reviewer to estimate effect size. This may lead to a study being eliminated from a review. However, many procedures have been developed that permit estimates of effect size to be computed from minimal data, such as the actual statistical test value (t, F, or chi-square distributions) or the statistical probability that the observed result occurred by chance. Lipsey and Wilson (2001), among others, make such conversion procedures readily available in their texts. Helpful software programs have been developed to assist researchers in computation of effect sizes and analysis of samples; one such is

Comprehensive Meta-Analysis Version 2.0 (see Borenstein, Hedges, Higgins, and Rothstein, 2005).

Develop an Analysis Strategy. The purpose of systematic review, meta-analysis, and evaluation synthesis is to reach conclusions based on a summary of results from an assembly of studies. Analysis steps are put simply in the following paragraphs:

First, arrange your thinking about the data at hand (studies of interventions) in terms of the studies' target populations, samples observed and samples not observed, and the effect sizes produced. Ensure that these effect sizes are constructed so as to make their interpretation plain. And ensure that outliers and artifacts of particular studies are identified and taken into account.

Second, focus attention on the distributions of the effect sizes. For instance, any given randomized trial on an intervention produces an effect size for which a confidence interval can be constructed. Other studies you have included will also produce effect sizes, each of which associated with a confidence interval. All these effects can be plotted out in a chart of the distribution of effect sizes. Systematic reviews under the definition given earlier typically include such a chart. A meta-analysis involves combination of effect sizes, and (often) the analysis of effect sizes as a function of the coded characteristics of the studies that are included in the review.

Describing the effects sizes and their distribution for an assembly of interventions in a class is essential for a high-quality review. Petrosino, Turpin-Petrosino, and Guckenburg (2010) did so in their review of juvenile system processing (Figure 25.1). This satisfies the interest of some readers who want to know whether an intervention resulted in doing some good, relative to high standards of evidence, and whether it did no good, relative to the same standards.

Beyond this, sophisticated statistical machinery and substantive understanding might be brought to bear on the question: What seems to "explain" the variation in effect sizes among studies that were reviewed? For instance, one may examine effect sizes for the studies as a statistical function of characteristics of study design, such as whether the design is a randomized trial or not, sample size, and so on. One may examine effect sizes as a function of coded characteristics of the intervention. Lösel and Beelman (2003), for instance, undertook a meta-analysis of eighty-four reports on randomized trials that were designed to estimate the effect of child skills training on antisocial behavior. They depended on different kinds of statistical models to understand the relationship between effect sizes (dependent variable) and characteristics of each study, the characteristics of the interventions, and the characteristics of the children in each study sample. For example, studies with smaller samples tended to be associated with larger effect sizes. Treatment dosage appeared not to be related to effect size. Interventions administered by study authors or research staff or supervised students were associated with larger effect sizes.

As Berk (2007) and others point out, statistical modeling in this meta-analytic context has the same merits and shortcomings as those of model-based analyses of data from passive observational studies. That is, the studies in a systematic review are units of observation; they are observed passively by the reviewer. The observations are the results of a kind of survey. Conventional regression analyses of effect size then can help to illustrate relationships. But misspecification of the regression model, unobserved variables that are related to variables in the model (i.e., *confounders*), and relations among the independent variables usually do not permit unequivocal statements about what *causes* the effect size to vary.

Interpret and Report the Results.   In the best systematic reviews, reports of at least two kinds are produced. The first is exquisitely detailed and contains all the scientific information sufficient for an independent analyst or scientist to conduct an identical review, that is, to replicate. As a practical matter, such detailed reviews are published in electronic libraries, and unlike hard-copy reports and research journals, have no page limitations. In the best, the topical coverage is uniform and standards are uniformly transparent, to make it easy for readers to move from one systematic review to the next. The Cochrane Collaboration, Campbell Collaboration, and WWC products have this character.

A second kind of report, a summary in hard-copy or electronic form, is crucial to users of evaluations who are not themselves researchers. Users such as policy decision makers and other practitioners typically value a summary that is uniform from one review to another and in language that is as plain as possible. The Cochrane Collaboration's reviews in recent years have included such summaries. The WWC produces these routinely and not without serious effort.

In the most sophisticated production of systematic reviews, reporting may involve the engagement of networks of users who were parties to a review's production, networks of potential users who might repackage and distribute the results, information brokers, and so on. The hard problem is developing networks of users and information brokers. The Institute of Education Sciences has invested resources in developing a network to ensure that products of the WWC are understood and influenced by a network of potential users. The practical advice on this is to engage potential users at the front end.

There is a third kind of report that is not yet common. It involves publication of all micro-records from all studies that are covered in a systematic review. Such a report, compiled with good definitions and numbers, would permit secondary analysis of micro-records by anyone with access to a spreadsheet and a way of importing files. This opportunity for transparency is part of the future.

What Resources Can Be Employed to Do the Job Well?

There are now many organizations that are conducting systematic reviews, and several, such as the Cochrane and Campbell Collaborations and the WWC, that are producing them on a grand scale. Besides these large-scale efforts, technological advances are improving the ability of researchers to identify, catalog, and analyze the results of separate but similar evaluation studies.

Independent International and Domestic Resources

The international Cochrane Collaboration was formed in 1993 to prepare, maintain, and make accessible systematic reviews of evaluations of the effects of health-related interventions. As of June 2014, the Cochrane Collaboration had produced over 6,000 completed systematic reviews based on explicit and uniform operating principles and transparent standards of evidence, with over 2,300 published protocols indicating current reviews in progress. The international Campbell Collaboration is the Cochrane Collaboration's young sibling. Created in 2000, its aims in its area of interest are identical to Cochrane's: to prepare, maintain, and make accessible systematic reviews of studies of the effects of interventions. This is to inform people about what works in the arenas of crime and justice, education, social welfare and international development. The *Cochrane Handbook for Systematic Reviews of Interventions* is used by both organizations to meet technical, quality control, and uniformity standards.

The Coalition for Evidence-Based Policy (www.coalition4evidence.org) has been remarkably influential, partly on account of its informed advocacy of randomized trials in the United States and partly on account of its efforts to identify top-tier programs in the United States that depend on basic standards of evidence (www.toptierevidence.org). The Best Evidence Encyclopedia (www.bestevidence.org) is a U.S.- and U.K.-based effort that uses some of the basic evidence standards for identifying dependable studies.

Among U.S. states, California's Evidence-Based Clearinghouse for Child Welfare (www.cachildwelfareclearinghouse.org) is a precedent. The Washington State Institute for Public Policy (www.wsipp.wa.gov) has been remarkable in uncovering and using systematic reviews of high-quality evidence and ensuring that such evidence gets to state legislators; its efforts get to a macro-level that involves reviews of many reviews. WSIPP also uses systematic reviews to estimate anticipated benefits from investing in particular programs, in their economic analyses (i.e., cost-benefit studies).

Government Organizations and Government-Sponsored Entities

In the United States, a variety of government organizations have undertaken systematic reviews of the applied research and evaluation literature or have provided funds to others to do so. Some of these organizations, such as the GAO, have helped to advance the state of the art since the 1980s (Cordray and Morphy, 2009). The U.S. Department of Education's What Works Clearinghouse has developed technical resources, such as uniform standards and procedures for determining whether each evaluation study in an assembly of studies can be used as a basis for a causal inference about an intervention's effect. It is moreover a remarkable source of guidance on technical issues in analysis of cluster randomized trials, statistical power analysis, and missing data analysis.

An initiative known as the Community Guide has been undertaken by the U.S. Centers for Disease Control and Prevention (www.thecommunityguide.org). The initiative's Task Force on Community Preventive Services conducts systematic reviews of research on the effects of interventions relevant to preventing health problems, including violence and injuries. For example, recent reviews focus on firearm laws, early childhood visitation programs, school-based violence prevention, reducing exposure to environmental tobacco smoke, and worksite obesity prevention programs.

Police agencies in the United Kingdom and private foundations such as the Jerry Lee Foundation in the United States have supported systematic reviews of evidence in crime prevention approaches such as closed circuit television. Farrington and his colleagues (2011) reports on sponsored projects in the context of the Campbell Collaboration's Crime and Justice Group. The Norwegian, Danish, and Swedish governments have sponsored systematic reviews in the education and social services sectors under the auspices of the Campbell Collaboration. Canada has supported systematic reviews under the same auspices in social welfare and under the auspices of the Cochrane Collaboration in health.

Technical Resources

Technical resources include the monographs, books, and software identified earlier. They include the technical guidance documents being produced by the WWC and at times by voluntary organizations such as the Cochrane and Campbell Collaborations. Because technology in design, execution, and analysis of studies changes with time and because there are changes in procedures used in identifying, assembling, and screening studies, the aspiring systematic reviewer has to pay attention to new developments. Younger people have stamina, and we wish them good luck on this account.

Web-oriented databases and search engines that furnish the ingredients for an evaluation synthesis are low cost and access to them is easy. PsychInfo and ERIC, for instance, are databases that are accessible in most research universities and many research and evaluation organizations. Each database is accessed by different vendors' search engines, however, and costs and benefits of these may differ appreciably.

The electronic search engines are sometimes less helpful than one might expect. For instance, they often do not search the full text of the evaluation report for the keywords. As a consequence, studies are missed. For instance, a PsychInfo search of abstracts from the *Journal of Educational Psychology* (1997–2000) for randomized trials yielded about thirty reports on trials. A search of the full text of the journal's contents for the same years yielded 100 trials (Turner and others, 2003). Machine-based searches of *American Education Research Journal* (1963–2000) yielded less than a third of the evaluations based on randomized trials in math and science education. To complicate matters, abstracts of articles in refereed journals on evaluation and applied research are not uniform. One technological advance that constitutes a resource in hand searches is the electronic publication of full texts of journal articles and books. This greatly facilitates full-text searches of course, including immediate demarcation and reproduction of pertinent reports or portions of them.

Resources and Issues for the Future: Scenarios

Part of the future lies in the reviewer's access to micro-records from each study that is used in a review. During the 1970s, for instance, evaluation studies of programs began to yield micro-record data that were made available at times for independent secondary analysis. Micro-records from evaluations of the effects of capital punishment on crime in the United States, from randomized trials on the effects of cultural enrichment programs on children in Colombian *barrios*, and from randomized trials on graduated taxation plans are among those that have been made accessible. These data have been reanalyzed to confirm earlier analyses, test new hypotheses, and for other reasons (Boruch, Wortman, and Cordray, 1981). In milestone studies, Mosteller (1995) and Krueger (1999) reanalyzed micro-records from the Tennessee Class Size randomized trial to verify earlier analyses by Finn and Achilles (1990) that had found that reducing class size had substantial effects on children's achievement. As a practical matter, the internet makes access to machine-readable micro-records on impact evaluations far more feasible than it has been. This in turn means that people who undertake systematic reviews, meta-analyses, and evaluation syntheses will be able to undertake deeper reviews that capitalize on micro-records rather than only on evaluation reports. The research literature on systematic reviews, meta-analysis, and research synthesis, however, is disconnected from the research literature on data sharing and secondary analysis of micro-records. Still to be worked out are ethical issues generated by using data collected from individuals for an earlier study they had consented to, for a different project.

To What End? Value Added and Usefulness

Systematic reviews have not only generated surprising results that countered widely believed notions, but they have also led to some important by-products.

Value Added: Surprises

What can evaluators and users of evaluations learn from a disciplined meta-analysis or systematic review? Surprises are important, as are independent confirmation of results of an earlier review.

Roberts and Kwan (2002) reviewed randomized trials on driver education programs to understand whether they worked. Given substantial investments in such programs in the United Kingdom, United States, and elsewhere, the public would expect that the programs would be found effective. Using Cochrane Collaboration standards and procedures, Roberts and Kwan found that the programs did not lead to lower accident rates among graduates of driver education programs. Because students got their licenses earlier than non-students as a consequence of graduating from these programs, their exposure risk was higher. This led to more accidents.

Shadish and others (1993) produced an award-winning systematic review showing that marital and family therapy, on average, placed about 70 percent of participants above the mean of control group members (50 percent base).

The origin of this review lay in serious doubts about the effectiveness of such therapy, including criticism of it by therapists whose work focused on individuals rather than couples or families. The doubts were put to rest, for a while at least, on scientific grounds.

Cooper, Robinson, and Patall (2006) examined a topic that brings anxiety, if not fear and loathing, to many parents, not to speak of children or teachers: homework. Their systematic review of studies of the effects of homework covered elementary, middle, and high school. It led to recommendations that in elementary school grades, one ought not to expect the homework assignments to yield better test scores. Rather, one should expect better study habits. It led to recommendations, based on reliable studies, that assignments for elementary school students ought to be short, and engage materials found at home. The academic benefits of homework kicked in at middle school and could be regarded as an extension to classroom and curriculum in high school. This review and the recommendations based on it have been featured in contemporary media, such as *The Wall Street Journal* and *The New York Times*, on TV shows, and in forums at the local school-level and national levels.

In the medical sector, Chalmers and others recognized that over a twenty-year period, over fifteen different approaches to handling acute myocardial infarction had been tested in randomized trials. Results varied. The main message, roughly speaking, was this: meta-analyses of diverse evaluative studies showed that anti-clotting drugs "almost certainly" reduced the risk of dying by 10 to 20 percent. Further, streptokinase is among these drugs, tested in over thirty trials. Over reported trials, cumulative odds ratios favor the interventions. Part of the surprise in this is that many physicians had paid no attention to the earlier evidence (Hunt, 1997).

Academic Disciplines, the Policy Sector, and Dependence on Systematic Reviews

An indicator of value added to the sciences is that meta-analyses and systematic reviews are undertaken in many disciplines, including agricultural sciences, physiological research, psychology, education, health research, and the physical sciences (see Chalmers, Hedges, and Cooper, 2002, and Cooper, Hedges, and Valentine, 2009, for specific references in each area). Recent workshops undertaken by the National Academy of Sciences (NAS), on field evaluation of methods and tools for intelligence and counterintelligence, made use of a Campbell Collaboration Crime and Justice Group review by Lum, Kennedy, and Sherley (2006), for instance.

To judge from Cordray and Morphy's (2009) empirical study and from deliberations of the Milbank Fund in the health sector, systematic reviews of the kinds discussed here are not well recognized and are infrequently used by policy-makers. Examples given earlier from the Washington State Institute for Public Policy and the U.S. Government Accountability Office are exceptional. Understanding how to ensure that policy people know about the evidence, understand it, have the capacity to use it, and are willing to use it in this context is as important as the challenge of encouraging use of dependable evidence in the policy sector more generally. John Graunt discussed the matter in the seventeenth century. (We will not tease the reader with a reference for this history. Unless asked.)

By-Products

Some by-products of organized efforts to produce systematic reviews are important. These include uniform transparent guidelines on classifying the quality of evaluations on the basis of their design and execution. Higher order guidelines make explicit the standards used in deciding whether an assembly of evaluations justifies a systematic review or meta-analysis. To take a simple example, the Campbell Collaboration and the Cochrane Collaboration require that each review make the standards explicit and, moreover, abide by Collaboration guidelines in doing so. Randomized trials are put high in the priority of designs that justify a causal inference. Simple before-after studies are low in priority unless some remarkable evidence or theory can be invoked to justify causal claims based on the results. To the extent that reviews and organizational efforts make standards of evidence explicit, we expect that the number of new studies that can sustain causal inferences will increase.

Another by-product is the development of better databases that can serve as the reservoir from which studies are drawn for systematic reviews. For instance, Medline searches routinely failed to identify *randomized trial* in that database until the 1990s. The Cochrane Collaboration's hand searches of journals revealed that these searches had a far higher yield of trials than Medline-based searches. Medline changed its database policy to ensure that randomized trials are more easily detectable to anyone, including Cochrane people who do reviews, trialists who are designing a study, and so on. For example, this effort resulted in adding, when applicable, the words "Randomized controlled trial" to the "publication type" heading for abstracts (Willis, 1995).

Organized networks to generate systematic reviews, supported by individual pro bono efforts, can be construed as another kind of product, notably social and intellectual capital. The Cochrane Collaboration has developed a network of over 10,000 people involved in health-related reviews in nearly thirty countries, for instance. Cochrane's sibling, the Campbell Collaboration, has involved people from ten to fifteen countries in annual meetings since 1999. The people in these networks include evaluators and other applied researchers, policymakers, and practitioners of other kinds.

Conclusion

The title of this chapter could easily have been "Try All Things and Hold Fast to That Which Is Good," exploiting one of St. Paul's letters to the Thessalonians. We can find similar ideas in medieval Arabic literature, notably Ibn Khaldun's *al Muqaddimah*, in the writings of nineteenth-century scientists and practitioners such as Florence Nightingale, and elsewhere.

People who today do systematic reviews stand on the shoulders of such colleagues in at least two respects. First, they, as their departed colleagues did, try to understand what is good. That is, they take seriously the question of what evidence justifies the claim that the intervention, program, or policy worked better than an alternative in a fair comparison. Second, contemporary systematic reviewers also try to bring order out of the chaos of publications in academic journals, the ill-disciplined issuances on websites, the declarations on television and in blogs, tweets, and technological whatnot. They do so in ways that make the processes and standards of evidence plain. Ibn Khaldun would have admired. Ditto for Florence. Maybe even Paul.

References

Berk, R. A. "Statistical Inference and Meta-analysis." *Journal of Experimental Criminology,* 2007, *3*(3), 247–270.

Borenstein, M., Hedges, L., Higgins, J., and Rothstein, H. *Comprehensive Meta-Analysis Version 2.* Englewood Cliffs, NJ: Biostat, 2005.

Boruch, R. F., and Rui, N. "From Randomized Controlled Trials to Evidence Grading Schemes." *Journal of Evidence Based Medicine,* 2008, *1,* 4–49.

Boruch, R. F., Wortman, P. M., and Cordray, D. S. (1981). *Reanalyzing Program Evaluations: Policies and Practices for Secondary Analysis of Social and Education Programs.* San Francisco, CA: Jossey-Bass.

Chalmers, I., Hedges, L. V., and Cooper, H. "A Brief History of Research Synthesis." *Education and the Health Professions,* 2002, *25*(1), 12–37.

Cooper, H., Robinson, J. C. and Patall, E. A. (2006). "Does Homework Improve Academic Achievement? A synthesis of Research, 1987–2003." *Review of Educational Research, 76,* 1–62.

Cooper, H., Hedges, L. V., and Valentine, J. (eds.). *The Handbook of Research Synthesis and Meta-Analysis* (2nd ed.). New York: Russell Sage Foundation, 2009.

Cordray, D. S., and Morphy, P. "Research Synthesis and Public Policy." In H. Cooper, L. V. Hedges, and J. Valentine (eds.), *The Handbook of Research Synthesis and Meta-Analysis.* New York: Russell Sage Foundation, 2009.

Farrington, D. P., and Petrosino, A. "Systematic Reviews of Criminological Interventions: The Campbell Collaboration and Crime and Justice Groups." *International Annals of Criminology,* 2000, *38,* 49–66.

Finn, J. D., and Achilles, C. M. "Answers and Questions About Class Size: A Statewide Experiment." *American Educational Research Journal,* 1990, *27*(3), 557–577.

Fisher, H., Montgomery, P., and Gardner, F. "Opportunities Provision for Preventing Youth Gang Involvement for Children and Young People (7–16)." *Cochrane Database of Systematic Reviews,* 2008, 2. [http://cochrane.org].

Gersten, R., and Hitchcock, J. "What Is Credible Evidence in Education? The Role of the What Works Clearinghouse in Informing the Process." In S. I. Donaldson, C. A. Christie, and M. M. Mark (eds.), *What Counts as Credible Evidence in Applied Research and Evaluation Practice?* Thousand Oaks, CA: Sage, 2009.

Gill, C. E. (forthcoming). "Missing Links: How Descriptive Validity Impacts the Policy Rel Rolled Trials in Criminology." *Journal of Experimental Criminology.*

Hunt, M. *How Science Takes Stock: The Story of Meta-Analysis.* New York: Russell Sage Foundation, 1997.

Krueger, A. B. "Experimental Estimates of Education Production Functions." *Quarterly Journal of Economics,* 1999, *114,* 497–532.

Lipsey, M. W., and Wilson, D. B. *Practical Meta-Analysis.* Thousand Oaks, CA: Sage, 2001.

Lösel, F., and Beelman, A. "Effects of Child Skills Training in Preventing Antisocial Behavior: A Systematic Review of Randomized Evaluations." *Annals of the American Academy of Political and Social Science,* May 2003, *587,* 84–109.

Lum, C., Kennedy, L. W., and Sherley, A. J. "The Effectiveness of Counter-Terrorism Strategies. *Campbell Systematic Reviews,* 2006, *2.*

Moher, D., and others, for the QUOROM Group. "Improving the Quality of Reports of Meta-Analyses of Randomized Controlled Trials: The QUOROM Statement." *Lancet,* 1999, *354,* 1896–1900.

Mosteller, F. "The Tennessee Study of Class Size in the Early School Grades." *The Future of Children,* 1995, *5*(2), 113–127.

Petrosino, A. "The Hunt for Randomized Experimental Reports: Document Search Efforts for a 'What Works' Meta-Analysis." *Journal of Crime and Justice,* 1995, *18*(2), 63–80.

Petrosino, A., Morgan, C., and Boruch, R. F. "School Enrollment Policies in Developing Nations (Protocol)." *Register of Interventions and Policy Evaluations.* Campbell Library. Oslo: Campbell Collaboration, 2010.

Petrosino, A., Morgan, C., Fronius, T., Tanner-Smith, E., and Boruch, R. F. "What Works in Developing Nations to Get Children into School or Keep Them There? A Systematic Review of Rigorous Impact Studies." *Research on Social Work Practice,* 2014, *25*(1), 44–60.

Petrosino, A., Turpin-Petrosino, C., and Guckenburg, S. "Formal System Processing: Effects on Delinquency (Review)." *Register of Interventions and Policy Evaluations.* Campbell Library. Oslo: Campbell Collaboration, 2010.

Roberts, I., and Kwan, I. "The Cochrane Injuries Group, Driver Education. School Based Driver Education for the Prevention of Traffic Crashes." *Cochrane Database of Systematic Reviews*, 2002, *4*. [http://cochrane.org].

Shadish, W. R., and others. "Effects of Family and Marital Psychotherapies: A Meta-Analysis." *Journal of Consulting and Clinical Psychology*, 1993, *61*(6), 992–1002

Turner, H., and others. "Populating International Register of Randomized Trials: C2-SPECTR." *Annals of the American Academy of Political and Social Science*, 2003, *589*, 203–223.

Waddington, H., Snilstveit, B., White, H., and Fewtrell, L. "Water, Sanitation, and Hygiene Interventions to Combat Childhood Diarrhea in Developing Countries." *3ie Synthetic Review 001*. New Delhi, India: International Initiative for Impact Evaluation, 2009.

Willis, J. "Changes to Publication Type (PT) Data." *NLM Technical Bulletin*, 1995, *286*, 19.

Wilson, D. "Missing a Critical Piece of the Pie: Simple Document Search Strategies Inadequate for Systematic Reviews." *Journal of Experimental Criminology*, 2009, *5*(4), 429–440.

Wilson, S. J., Lipsey, M. W., and Soydan, H. "Are Mainstream Programs for Juvenile Delinquency Less Effective with Minority Youth Than Majority Youth? A Meta-Analysis of Outcomes Research." *Research on Social Work Practice*, 2003, *13*(1), 3–26.

PART FOUR

USE OF EVALUATION

Program evaluation presents many challenges beyond the issues that arise in evaluation design, data collection, and data analysis. Evaluators should make all reasonable efforts to (1) gain and hold the interest, confidence, and support of policymakers, managers, and other intended users of evaluation information; (2) maintain the cooperation of program managers, staff, clients, and others who provide evaluation data; (3) present evaluation findings and improvement options clearly; and (4) stimulate the actions needed to improve public programs and communicate their value to policymakers and the public.

The six chapters in Part Four discuss problems that may be encountered in the evaluation process and ways to avoid those problems, the development of recommendations and preparation of evaluation reports, evaluation contracting, the use of evaluation in government and the politics of evaluation, and some emerging evaluation challenges and trends.

Evaluation leadership and management involve both art and science. Those in charge of evaluation programs and projects may face difficult challenges in producing credible findings and in getting their findings used by policymakers, managers, and other stakeholders. There is helpful guidance to enhance use in each of the chapters in this section.

The Chapters

Harry Hatry and Kathryn Newcomer, in Chapter Twenty-Six, provide a checklist to help evaluators and those reviewing evaluations to assess how potential pitfalls in planning and implementing evaluations may hinder the validity, reliability, and credibility of evaluation findings. Recognizing that all evaluations have limitations, the authors note that recognition and explanation of those limitations can add to the credibility of evaluation work.

George Grob, in Chapter Twenty-Seven, discusses how evaluators can develop recommendations, suggestions, and options that policymakers and managers will find helpful to improve policies and programs—and thus improve people's lives.

George Grob, in Chapter Twenty-Eight, discusses how evaluators can write evaluation reports that clearly convey the report's message and stimulate constructive action. He shows how evaluators can craft their core message, communicate their findings, and effectively but efficiently describe their methodology and its limitations.

James Bell, in Chapter Twenty-Nine, discusses how organizations can procure needed evaluation products and services. He shows how sponsors can develop feasible evaluation plans and well-defined requests for proposals (RFPs), find and select well-qualified contractors, monitor the contractor's progress, and ensure creation of high-quality, useful reports.

Joseph Wholey, in Chapter Thirty, discusses the use of evaluation in government and the politics of evaluation. He provides guidance for evaluators to overcome political and bureaucratic challenges, get their work used, and help improve policies and programs. Though the discussion focuses on the use of evaluation in government, much of the chapter applies to the nonprofit sector as well.

In the final chapter, the editors discuss quality control of the entire evaluation process, the selection and training of evaluators, and evaluation standards and ethics. They offer additional suggestions on increasing the use of evaluation findings to improve programs and discuss the relation between performance monitoring systems and evaluation studies. The editors conclude with their thoughts on likely trends in evaluation over the next decade.

CHAPTER TWENTY-SIX

PITFALLS IN EVALUATIONS*

Harry P. Hatry, Kathryn E. Newcomer

Two key issues in program evaluation are determining what the effects (outcomes) of the program have been over a specific period of time and determining the extent to which the specific program, rather than other factors, has caused those effects. Both issues are typically subject to considerable uncertainty, particularly given that the great majority of evaluations are not conducted under controlled laboratory conditions. Program effects are often unclear, are often ill defined, and can be quite messy to measure. Attributing effects to the specific program also presents considerable difficulties: outcomes can be affected by numerous other factors in addition to the program itself, and the effects of these external factors will generally be difficult to determine without careful analysis.

Strong methodological integrity is critical to support efforts to measure both the programs (treatments) and the outcomes (effects) in all evaluation projects. The integrity of evaluation findings rests on how well design and data collection choices strengthen the validity and reliability of the data. The best time to anticipate limitations to what we can conclude from evaluation work is when designing the research and developing the instruments. Unfortunately, we can never anticipate everything, and the best-laid plans may not work out.

When reporting findings, in addition to following the good advice given about design and data collection provided in this book, evaluators should

*This chapter draws material from Harry P. Hatry, "Pitfalls of Evaluation," in G. Majone and E. S. Quade (Eds.), *Pitfalls of Analysis* (Hoboken, NJ: Wiley, 1980).

carefully assess how pitfalls that occur in the conduct of the work may hinder the validity, reliability, and credibility of their findings and conclusions. This chapter provides a checklist of pitfalls to help evaluators or those reviewing evaluations assess how problems in planning and executing evaluations constrain what can be concluded about the programs studied. The implications of each pitfall for the validity, reliability, and credibility of the findings are identified. Many of these pitfalls are discussed in detail in various texts on program evaluation, such as the classic works by Riecken and Boruch (1974) and Shadish, Cook, and Campbell (2002).

The primary touchstones of methodological integrity discussed in social science methods texts are *measurement validity* (or *trustworthiness* and *authenticity* of measures for qualitative measurement) *generalizability or external validity* (or *transferability* for qualitative measurement), *internal validity (or confirmability* for qualitative measurement), *reliability* (or *auditability* for qualitative measurement), *and statistical conclusion validity* (O'Sullivan, Rassel, and Berner, 2003; Singleton, Straits, Straits, and McAllister, 1988; Stangor, 1998). We have added *credibility* to our list because evaluation findings are not likely to be used if program staff or funders do not find the findings believable. The definitions are set out in Box 26.1.

Box 26.1. The Touchstones of Methodological Integrity

Credibility. Are the evaluation findings and conclusions believable and legitimate to the intended audience? Evaluation findings are more likely to be accepted if the program stakeholders perceive the evaluation process and data to be legitimate and the recommendations to be feasible.

Generalizability or External Validity (Transferability). Are you able to generalize from the study results to the intended population? Evaluation findings are generalizable (or externally valid) when the evaluators can apply the findings to groups or contexts beyond those being studied.

Internal validity (Confirmability). Are you able to establish whether there is a causal relationship between a specified cause, such as a program, and the intended effect? Attributing program results to a program entails ensuring that changes in program outcomes covary with the program activities, that the program was implemented prior to the occurrence of outcomes, and that plausible rival explanations for the outcomes have been ruled out to the extent reasonable.

Measurement validity (Trustworthiness and Authenticity). Are you accurately measuring what you intend to measure? Measurement validity is concerned with the accuracy of measurement. The specific criteria for operationalizing concepts, such as program outputs and outcomes, should be logically related to the concepts of interest.

Reliability (Auditability). Will the measurement procedures produce similar results on repeated observations of the same condition or event? Measures are reliable to the extent that the criteria and questions consistently measure target behaviors or attitudes. Measurement procedures are reliable to the extent that they are consistently recording data.

Statistical conclusion validity. Do the numbers generated accurately estimate the size of a relationship between variables or the magnitude of a specific criterion measure? Numerical figures are valid if they are generated with appropriate statistical techniques supported by reasonable assumptions.

The pitfalls discussed in this chapter are arranged according to the time at which a pitfall generally occurs: before the beginning of data collection for the evaluation, during the process of data collection, or after the data have been collected (when findings are to be presented and use is to be made of the findings). A summary of the pitfalls and the methodological concerns each addresses is presented in Tables 26.1, 26.2, and 26.4.

Pitfalls Before Data Collection Begins

If the evaluation does not get off to a good start, the whole evaluation can be undermined.

Pitfall 1: Failure to Assess Whether the Program Is Evaluable

Not doing an assessment of the potential utility and evaluability of an evaluation candidate to ensure that it is likely that the program can be evaluated in sufficient time for the evaluation findings to be useful, and within available resources, can severely limit what can be learned. A program probably should not be subject to substantial program evaluation effort when:

- The program has vague objectives.
- The program objectives are reasonably clear but the current state of the art in measurement does not seem to permit meaningful measurement of impacts.
- The program's major impacts cannot be expected to show up until many years into the future, by which time the information is not likely to be useful (if, for example, all relevant important decisions will already have been made so that whatever is found cannot be acted on).

TABLE 26.1. PITFALLS OCCURRING BEFORE DATA COLLECTION BEGINS.

	Methodological Concerns					
	Measurement Validity/ Authenticity	Generalizability/ Transferability	Internal Validity/ Confirmability	Statistical Conclusion Validity	Reliability/ Auditability	Credibility
Program or Theory Feasibility						
1. Failure to assess whether the program is evaluable		X	X	X		X
2. Starting data collection too early in the life of a program		X	X	X		X
3. Failure to secure input from program managers and other stakeholders on appropriate evaluation criteria	X	X	X			X
4. Failure to clarify program managers' expectations about what can be learned from the evaluation						X
Preparation for Collection						
5. Failure to pretest data collection instruments appropriately	X	X	X	X	X	X
6. Use of inadequate indicators of program effects	X	X	X	X	X	X
7. Inadequately training data collectors	X	X	X	X	X	X

In many instances, evaluability problems can be alleviated, as Wholey discusses in Chapter Four, through use of an evaluability assessment. The evaluability assessment should be careful not to overreact to apparent hurdles. For example, with persistence, it is often possible to identify major specific objectives for programs that seem vague at first. It is often possible to obtain rough but adequate impact information about characteristics that at first glance appear to be too subjective (such as by using structured interviewing of systematic samples of clients on various aspects of program services). Often, even evaluations conducted over prolonged periods may be useful for decisions in later years even though they are not useful to the current funders or sponsors.

Proper evaluation requires adequate staff, money, and time, and the evaluation plan clearly needs to be compatible with the resources available.

However, although some corner-cutting and less sophisticated approaches can often be used when resources are scarce, too many such compromises can weaken an evaluation to the point where it is not worth doing.

Seldom discussed in the literature is the need to distinguish whether the program to be evaluated is under development or is operational. Evaluations of projects in a developmental stage in general seek less definite information on impacts and are likely to be more concerned with determining the characteristics of the preferred program and its basic feasibility. Ignoring this distinction appears to have resulted in inappropriate expectations and inappropriate evaluation designs in some instances, especially for U.S. federal agency evaluations.

Pitfall 2: Starting Data Collection Too Early in the Life of a Program

Not allowing enough time to assess stable program operations is a pitfall frequently encountered in the evaluation of new programs. There seems to be a chronic temptation to begin collecting program outcome data for evaluation as soon as the initial attempt at implementation begins. For many new programs, however, the shakedown period may last many months. During this time, program procedures stabilize, new people become adjusted to the new procedures, and the new program begins to operate under reasonably normal conditions. Thus, enough time should be allowed before beginning collection of the post-program data, and enough time after for an adequate test of the new program. Evaluation periods of less than a year may not provide enough program experience and data can be affected by seasonal differences. For example, tests of a new street repair procedure might not cover the special effects of the bad weather season. The appropriate timing will depend on the nature of the program and the setting into which it is introduced. To illustrate a likely typical timing, a minimum period of perhaps six months might be appropriate before the program is assumed to have been implemented, and at least one year of subsequent program operations should be covered by the evaluation.

Pitfall 3: Failure to Secure Input from Program Managers and Other Stakeholders on Appropriate Evaluation Criteria

A complaint sometimes voiced by program stakeholders about evaluation conclusions and recommendations is that the evaluators did not measure the right things. Evaluators should seek input from program staff, funders, and program clients to ensure that they employ criteria of both the program treatment and the more relevant program effects, or outcomes, that staff and funders consider relevant and legitimate.

As McLaughlin and Jordan describe in Chapter Three, logic modeling is a highly useful tool for involving program staff in identification of appropriate measures of program activities and short- and longer-term outcomes. Participation of program stakeholders before data collection in identification of what is most relevant to measure and what are the most accurate operational indicators to employ is critical in ensuring the findings will be deemed credible.

Pitfall 4: Failure to Clarify Program Managers' Expectations About What Can Be Learned from the Evaluation

Program staff are typically not receptive to evaluation and may need to be convinced that evaluation efforts can produce information useful to them. Evaluators may also find that program staff are leery of opening up programs to analysis of how they are working. Thus, one of the major obstacles to the undertaking and use of evaluation is that evaluators too often pay too little attention to helping program staff identify constructive ways in which programs can be improved. Unfortunately, identifying ways to improve is easier said than done. Usually a large number of factors, in addition to the program procedures, can affect program success. These include such elements as the quantity and quality of the staffing used to operate the program, the success in motivating the employees who will implement it, and the organizational structure in which the program operates. Program staff members often are in a particularly good position to obtain insights into reasons for problems. If the evaluators can draw on this understanding and act as a constructive force for program improvement, the credibility and utility of the evaluation function will increase over the long run. Then, perhaps, the innate hostility of program managers to being evaluated will be diminished.

Evaluations of any kind seldom give definitive, conclusive, unambiguous evidence of program success (or failure). Even with experimental designs, numerous problems inevitably arise in keeping the experiment uncontaminated and, subsequently, in extrapolating and generalizing the results beyond the experimental scope and time period. The evaluators should be careful to make it clear from the start to their customers, and to potential users of the evaluation findings, that such limitations exist. Unrealistic expectations by program managers about what they can learn from evaluation findings may discourage future evaluation support.

Pitfall 5: Failure to Pretest Data Collection Instruments Appropriately

An essential task for evaluators prior to beginning data collection is to pretest all collection instruments. Whether data are observational or perceptions, the instruments used to measure conditions, behaviors, or attitudes should be carefully tested to ensure they will capture the intended phenomena. As Berman and Vasquez describe (Chapter Sixteen) and Newcomer and Triplett emphasize (Chapter Fourteen), all instruments for recording data need to be pretested in the specific program context in which they will be applied.

Pitfall 6: Use of Inadequate Indicators of Program Effects

The credibility and usefulness of an evaluation can be called into considerable doubt if inadequate measures are used. Variations of this pitfall include limiting the assessment to only one criterion or a very few criteria when others are also relevant (perhaps because a decision has been made to evaluate only those criteria agreed on ahead of time with program officials) and neglecting possible unintended consequences of the program (sometimes beneficial and sometimes detrimental). For example, an evaluation of a program for placing mental patients in their own homes and communities rather than in government institutions should consider not only changes in the condition of the clients but also the effects on clients' families and the community into which the clients are transferred. Economic development programs sometimes have adverse effects on the environment, and environmental programs sometimes have adverse effects on economic development.

Before establishing the final evaluation criteria, evaluators should review the objectives of the program from the viewpoint of the agency installing the program and the clients of the program and look for significant effects that were not initially anticipated. Evaluators should strive to identify various perspectives on the objectives (both explicit and implicit) of the program to be evaluated. For example, opinions might be sought from supporters and opponents, program operators and clients, and budget officials and program managers. (This assumes that evaluators will have sufficient leeway from the sponsors of the evaluation to try to be comprehensive.)

An important variation of this pitfall is failure to assess the impact of the program on the various major client groups. Inevitably, programs have different effects on various groups, helping some groups significantly more than others and perhaps harming other groups. Insufficient identification of the effects on different groups of program recipients will hide such differences and prevent users of the evaluation findings from considering equity issues.

The lack of an assessment of program financial costs can also be an important omission. Evaluators often neglect costs, but such information can be of considerable use to funders.

Finally, when attitudinal data are being collected from program participants, care should be taken to word survey questions in a clear, unbiased manner to assess program effects fairly. Pretesting surveys and questionnaires should reduce the use of slanted questions. However, it is still possible that users of evaluation findings may view the questions as skewed in a way that either inflates or reduces effects. Guidance on question wording is provided by Newcomer and Triplett (Chapter Fourteen).

Pitfall 7: Inadequately Training Data Collectors

Regardless of the type of data collection employed in an evaluation, sufficient time must be given to training the evaluation staff used to visit sites, review files, or conduct interviews. The length of time needed for training, and the frequency of the retraining, will vary depending on the type of collection activity, as Nightingale and Rossman (Chapter Seventeen) and Berman and Vasquez (Chapter Sixteen) discuss. Typically, consultation among data collectors should continue throughout the collection phase of the evaluation. Initial training may not adequately anticipate all context-specific challenges for data collectors.

Pitfalls During Data Collection

A number of pitfalls can occur during an evaluation's operation (see Table 26.2).

Pitfall 8: Failure to Identify and Adjust for Changes in Data Collection Procedures That Occur During the Measurement Period

As discussed in Chapter Thirteen, evaluators need to look for changes in agency record keeping, such as changes in data element definition or data collection procedures that affect the relevant data. Data definitions and data collection procedures can change periodically and in the process cause important differences in the meaning of those data. Evaluators using data for which they themselves have not determined the data collection procedures should be careful to look for, and adjust for (if they can), such occurrences. As has been

TABLE 26.2. PITFALLS OCCURRING DURING DATA COLLECTION.

	Methodological Concerns					
	Measurement Validity/ Authenticity	Generalizability/ Transferabilty	Internal Validity (causal inference)/ Confirmability	Statistical Conclusion Validity	Reliability/ Auditability	Credi- bility
Research Procedures						
8. Failure to identify and adjust for changes in data collection procedures that occur during the measurement period	X	X	X	X	X	X
9. Collecting too much data and not allowing adequate time for analysis of the data collected			X			X
Measurement Constraints						
10. Inappropriate conceptualization or measurement of the intervention	X	X	X	X	X	X
11. Beginning observation when conditions (target behaviors) are at an extreme level		X	X	X		
Reactivity						
12. Inappropriate involvement of program providers in data collection	X	X	X	X	X	X
13. Overly intrusive data collection procedures that change behaviors of program staff or participants	X	X	X		X	
Composition of Sample						
14. Failure to account for drop-off in sample size due to attrition		X	X	X		X
15. Failure to draw a representative sample of program participants		X	X	X		X
16. Insufficient number of callbacks to boost response rates		X	X	X		X
Flawed Comparisons						
17. Failure to account for natural maturation among program participants		X	X			X
18. Failure to provide a comparison group		X	X			X
19. Failure to take into account key contextual factors (out of the control of program staff) that affect program outcomes			X			X
20. Failure to take into account the degree of difficulty of helping program participants		X	X			X

noted (Riecken and Boruch, 1974), "Too often a new program is accompanied by changes in record-keeping" (p. 107).

Pitfall 9: Collecting Too Many Data and Not Allowing Adequate Time for Analysis of the Data Collected

These two problems go hand in hand. They are all too prevalent when tight timetables exist for evaluations, which usually seems to be the case. The temptation seems to be prevalent to collect data on any characteristic of the client or situation that conceivably could be relevant and then not allow enough time for analysis of the data. The temptation to collect data is a difficult one to overcome, particularly given that it is not possible at the beginning of an evaluation to know which data will be useful in the study. The argument is often advanced that evaluators can always exclude data later. However, once collected, data pile up, with a pyramiding effect in terms of data processing and analysis effort (as well as adding to the costs of data collection).

Allowing enough time for data analysis is complicated by the tendency to impose overly tight deadlines for evaluations. When implementation difficulties delay the start of the program, when data come in later than anticipated, and when computer processing is later than promised, these delays all lead to squeezing the amount of time available for analysis before the deadline for the evaluation. To help alleviate these problems, schedule for unforeseen contingencies and include fewer data elements to be processed.

Pitfall 10: Inappropriate Conceptualization or Implementation of the Intervention

Adequately capturing program activities can be challenging due to fluctuations in program implementation that occur, which is frequently the case. The best-laid plans of evaluators may not come to fruition when they are placed in real-life settings. The longer the period of observation, the greater is the chance of deviation from the original intentions.

For example, in evaluations of neighborhood police teams, the assignment of teams to specific neighborhoods may depart from the plan if dispatchers assign those police officers too frequently to other neighborhoods. In some cases, if the program planners and evaluators watch carefully, such deviations can be corrected, but in other situations this may not be possible. Another example involves the difficulties of maintaining random assignment procedures in an experiment when assignments have to be made throughout the period by personnel other than the evaluation team. For example, in an experiment to test the effects of requiring appearances for moving traffic violations before a judge, the court clerk who had responsibility for the random assignments had firm ideas about the need for a court appearance for young drivers and did not adhere to the random assignment procedure (Conner, 1977). Random assignments of clients in controlled experiments may initially be done appropriately but subsequently be altered under the pressure of a heavy workload.

Because of such challenges to defining the treatment, it is important that the evaluators carefully monitor the program over the period of the evaluation. At the least they should check periodically to ascertain that no major departures from the plan have occurred during implementation. When substantial deviations occur, adjustments should be made (such as, in effect, beginning a "new" evaluation if a major overhaul of the program occurs during the evaluation). If such adjustments cannot be made satisfactorily and the changes are of major importance, the evaluation should be terminated, or at least the alterations should be explicitly considered when assessing the findings.

Pitfall 11: Beginning Observation When Conditions (Target Behaviors) Are at an Extreme Level or Not Adjusting for This

Timing is crucial in evaluation. Evaluators need to investigate, to the extent feasible, the target behavior among program participants (or communities) prior to implementation of the program treatment. When new program activities are introduced because conditions have risen to undesirably high levels (perhaps birthrates among unwed teenage mothers have soared) or undesirably low levels (perhaps the percentage of substance abuse treatment clients staying sober has plummeted), it is likely that program effects will be inflated. This "regression to the mean" phenomenon implies that if the target behaviors have risen (or fallen) to extreme levels, a natural shift toward improvement (or deterioration) can be expected even without the new program. Clients who at the outset have the greatest need (they may be in crisis situations) are likely to show a greater amount of improvement than others. Conversely, the less needy, most able clients may tend to show little, no, or even negative improvement, regardless of the program (Conner, 1977). For example, a program initiated because of a recent rash of problems, such as a high traffic fatality rate, might show an improvement merely because the chances of recurrence are small (Campbell and Ross, 1968).

Ways to alleviate this problem include projecting time trend lines and categorizing clients as to their degree of difficulty and then analyzing the outcomes for each level of difficulty. Such approaches enable better and fairer comparisons.

Pitfall 12: Inappropriate Involvement of Program Providers in Data Collection

This pitfall is well known but nevertheless often ignored. Government agencies with tight resources, especially subnational governments such as state and local governments in the United States, and small, nonprofit service providers, are particularly tempted to use program staff to provide ratings of program success.

It is desirable for any agency, as a matter of good management, to undertake some internal evaluation of its own programs. For example, mental health and social service agencies frequently use caseworkers' ratings to assess the progress of the caseworkers' clients. This procedure is reasonable when the information is solely for internal purposes, such as for use by the caseworkers themselves and their immediate supervisors. Such procedures, however, do not provide data on client improvement after clients have left the programs to determine the longer-term effects of the services, and such procedures seem to be expecting too much of human nature (asking employees to provide objective information that will be used to make judgments about continuation of their own programs).

Pitfall 13: Overly Intrusive Data Collection Procedures That Change Behaviors of Program Staff or Participants

When program staff or participants are aware that their program is being evaluated, they may behave differently than they do normally. The Hawthorne effect may mean that several providers or recipients act in ways that lead to overestimation of program effects. For example, program staff may try harder to ensure that a new program activity demonstrates positive results.

Program personnel who are handpicked to staff a new program may make the outcomes of the test unrepresentative and non-generalizable. Using specially chosen personnel may be appropriate in the developmental stages of a program, but it is to be avoided when the program is to be evaluated for its generalizability. For a representative test, personnel who would ordinarily be operating the program after the evaluation period should be used. Otherwise, any observed advantage to the treatment period might be due to the use of the special personnel.

Recipients of benefits who are aware that the program is being evaluated may provide overly positive feedback about services and effects or try harder to demonstrate their achievement of desired changes.

Pitfall 14: Failure to Account for Drop-Off in Sample Size Due to Attrition

For many social services, it is difficult to track program participants for an adequate length of time to assess intermediate or long-term program outcomes. Sometimes this pitfall occurs due to the transient nature of the target population, such as homeless people or youths released from juvenile detention centers. In some cases, follow-up efforts to survey program beneficiaries fail due to the provider's failure to maintain up-to-date contact information for those served. And in other cases, beneficiaries of services, such as mental health or reproductive health services, may refuse to acknowledge that they received the services. Small sample sizes may result from these obstacles, leading to less precision in the findings. Unrepresentative samples may also result that are skewed toward participants who are more motivated or stable. Evaluators need to acknowledge whatever *completion* rates occur and identify the implications.

Pitfall 15: Failure to Draw a Representative Sample of Program Participants

The inability to locate program beneficiaries at points of time some period after their receipt of services, or refusals from beneficiaries to be surveyed, present only two potential constraints on the representativeness of samples. Other flaws in sampling procedures may hinder efforts to generalize results, such as sampling in a way that omits or under-samples a key group, such as in telephone surveys: persons without phones; households that only have cell phones; those with unlisted telephone numbers; persons with answering machines; those living in trailers; those living in multiple dwelling units; or having more than one telephone number.

Survey procedures that are based solely on self-selection, such as placing survey questionnaires on tables or in tax bills, are likely to result in very low response rates and highly unrepresentative samples. The possibility that program participants who submit surveys or participate in interviews or focus groups differ from those who do not participate, in ways relevant to their responses, is virtually always a concern in evaluation work. Efforts to test for differences between sample respondents and those who choose not to participate in data collection efforts are necessary, yet not fully sufficient to eliminate suspicions of nonresponse biases.

Pitfall 16: Insufficient Number of Callbacks to Boost Response Rates

An inadequate number of callbacks or making calls during limited time periods in the day or in the week can result in too small and unrepresentative samples of program participants. Unfortunately, evaluation resources often are not sufficient to do all that is ideally desirable to reach participants. As noted in Chapter Fourteen, the increasing use of answering machines presents a new challenge to evaluators hoping to conduct telephone interviews as part of their research.

Pitfall 17: Failure to Account for Natural Maturation Among Program Participants

In some cases, *maturation* can occur, in which the participants served improve normally even without program intervention, perhaps because of aging. For example, as criminals, alcoholics, or drug addicts age, reductions in their adverse behavior may occur even without treatment programs. As another example, an evaluation of community alcoholic treatment centers included a follow-up eighteen months after intake of a comparison sample of persons who had an intake record but for whom only nominal treatment was provided (Armor, Polich, and Stambul, 1976). Of this group, a large percentage, 54 percent, were identified as being in remission even without more than normal treatment (compared to 67 percent of the treatment group).

Pitfall 18: Failure to Provide a Comparison Group

The lack of a comparison group or use of an inappropriate comparison group can distort the interpretation of evaluation findings. Even if randomized controlled experiments are used, examining groups that were not part of the intervention can often provide evidence about whether the outcomes were due to the program. In the classic evaluation of the Connecticut highway speeding crackdown, the large reduction in fatalities in Connecticut was compared with other nearby, and presumably similar, states to see if similar reductions had occurred (Campbell and Ross, 1968). Such a comparison helped rule out some other possible causes of reduced fatalities in Connecticut, such as special weather conditions in the region during the period or the introduction of safer automobiles.

An evaluation of community alcoholism treatment centers followed up not only those who received significant amounts of treatments but samples of two comparison groups: persons who had made only one visit to a treatment center and who received no further treatment and clients who had received minimal services (usually detoxification) but then left the center and never resumed contact. As noted in Pitfall 17, the evaluators identified 67 percent of all treated clients as being in remission at the time of an eighteen-month follow-up. But even the nominal treatment group showed a 54 percent remission rate. Thus, it appears likely that a substantial portion of the remission in the treatment group would have occurred without the program. Considering only the 67 percent would lead one to overstate the effects of the treatment.

Comparison groups should be used with considerable care. If the program's clients differ from the comparison group in some critical characteristic (such as the motivational levels of persons entering the program), differences in outcomes could be due to those characteristics and not to the program. Therefore it is important, when possible, to check the comparison groups for similarity of key characteristics. Unfortunately, opportunities to observe useful comparison groups are not always available.

Pitfall 19: Failure to Take into Account Key Contextual Factors (Out of the Control of Program Staff) That Can Affect Program Outcomes

A wide variety of possible circumstances or factors affect participants' behavior or other program effects and can lead to unrepresentative and misleading findings. For example, changes in the employment status of persons given training programs can occur because of changes in general economic conditions, regardless of participation in the training programs. The greater the number of different agencies, jurisdictions, and service providers involved in program implementation, the more opportunities there are for contextual factors to affect outcomes (U.S. General Accounting Office, 1998).

Pitfall 20: Failure to Take into Account the Degree of Difficulty of Helping Program Participants

Not explicitly considering and controlling for workload-client difficulty when assessing program results can lead to misinterpretation of what has occurred. The difficulty of the incoming workload can cause success (or failure) rates to be misleading (Hendricks, 2002). Higher success rates for programs that have a larger proportion of easier-to-help clients than other programs should not necessarily lead to labeling the programs as being more effective. Consider the hypothetical outcomes shown in Table 26.3.

Based on the totals alone, the results for Unit 1 appear superior because success was achieved in 60 percent of the cases as contrasted with 47 percent. Unit 2, however, shows a higher success rate for both high-difficulty clients (25 percent, compared to 0 percent for unit 1) and routine clients (80 percent,

TABLE 26.3. CONSIDERATION OF WORKLOAD DIFFICULTY.

	Unit 1	Unit 2
All cases	500	500
Number helped	300	235
Percentage helped	60%	47%
Difficult cases	100	300
Number helped	0	75
Percentage helped	0%	25%
Routine cases	400	200
Number helped	300	160
Percentage helped	75%	80%

Source: Adapted from Hatry, 1999, p. 112.

compared to 75 percent for unit 1). The overall higher success rate for the first unit stems from its having a larger proportion of clients with lower difficulty.

Thus, the difficulty of the incoming workload can be a major explanation for observed effects. In controlled experiments, even if workload difficulty is not explicitly controlled in making random assignments (such as by stratifying the sample), randomization would likely result in assigning similar proportions to each of the groups. Nevertheless the control and treated groups should be examined after they are chosen to determine if they are indeed sufficiently similar on difficulty.

Pitfalls After Data Collection

Even fine-quality evaluations can be wasted if care is not taken when reporting the findings (see Table 26.4).

Pitfall 21: Overemphasis on Statistical Significance and Under-emphasis on Practical Significance of Effect Size

Too narrow a focus on too much precision and too much reliance on statistical significance can lead to excessive costs in resource allocation (such as by encouraging the use of larger samples than needed at the expense of other evaluation tasks) and even to misleading findings. Statistical significance levels at the 95 to 99 percent significance levels will often be overkill for programs other than those with important safety or health elements. Typically, the information gathered in evaluations and other factors in making program decisions are not precise, and for most management decisions a high level of precision

TABLE 26.4. PITFALLS OCCURRING AFTER DATA COLLECTION ENDS.

	Methodological Concerns					
	Measurement Validity/ Authenticity	Generalizability/ Transferabilty	Internal Validity (causal inference)/ Confirmability	Statistical Conclusion Validity	Reliability/ Auditability	Credibility
Inappropriate Use of Analytical Techniques						
21. Overemphasis on statistical significance and under-emphasis on practical significance of effect size	X	X	X			X
22. Focusing only on overall results with inadequate attention to disaggregated results	X	X				X
Insufficient Link Between Data and Conclusions						
23. Generalizing beyond the confines of the sample or the limits of the program sites included in the study		X	X			X
24. Failure to acknowledge the effects of multiple program components	X		X			X
25. Failure to submit preliminary findings to key program staff for reality testing		X	X			X
26. Failure to adequately support conclusions with specific data						X
27. Poor presentation of evaluation findings						X

is not needed. "It doesn't pay to lavish time and money on being extremely precise in one feature if this is out of proportion with the exactness of the rest" (Herzog, 1959, p. 82).

Whatever the significance levels used, the use of statistical significance as the only criterion for detecting differences can be misleading to officials using the information. What may be a statistically significant finding (at a given significance level) can, particularly when very large samples are involved, suggest that important program effects have occurred even though the effects may be small in practical terms and may be unimportant to public officials. With large sample sizes, differences of even two or three percentage points between the outcomes of the treatment and comparison groups can be statistically significant, but they may not be significant to officials making decisions based on that information.

Good advice is to present the actual differences and the level of statistical significance, so that users of the information can judge for themselves. All too often, summaries of findings indicate whether findings are statistically significant without identifying the actual size of the program effects.

Pitfall 22: Focusing on Only the Overall (Average) Results with Inadequate Attention to Disaggregated Results

Examination of the aggregated data is useful for assessing a program's aggregate effect. However, in general, the analysis should not be limited to presenting the aggregate effects. It will often be highly useful to examine subsets of the data. For example, when a number of projects are included in the evaluation, the evaluators should consider whether certain projects or groups of projects tended to have greater effects than others. Variations in conditions among projects are likely, and an examination may be able to shed light on possible reasons for variations, possibly suggesting variations that should be considered further even when the overall program does not appear successful.

Some types of clients served by the program may be more (or less) successfully served than others, even though such differences were not anticipated in the original evaluation design. Therefore, in general, evaluators should examine various subgroups to detect whether some groups were substantially better (or worse) served than indicated by the aggregate figures. For example, a particular type of program may work well with more severe cases than with less severe cases or with older clients than with younger clients or with female clients than with male clients.

Sometimes subgroups to be followed up in the evaluation may be stratified at the beginning to ensure adequate consideration of different characteristics. If this is not done, an after-the-fact analysis of outcomes for various types of clients might not be possible if those subgroups are underrepresented in the sample.

Pitfall 23: Generalizing Beyond the Confines of the Sample or the Limits of the Program Sites Included in the Study

Even when the evaluation is well done and well controlled, there are numerous pitfalls in trying to generalize results to other sites or situations. "Too many social scientists expect single experiments to settle issues once and for all" (Campbell, 1969, p. 427). "The particular sample from which control and experimental group members are drawn . . . may be idiosyncratic in that other potential target populations are not represented. If the conditions . . . in the experiment . . . differ markedly from conditions which prevail in other populations, then it is reasonable to believe that additional testing of the program is required" (Riecken and Boruch, 1974, p. 144). There are several variations of this pitfall; recognizing them should temper statements about the generalizability of findings:

> The trial's results may represent only one sample point—that is, one trial under one set of conditions. Replication may be needed in other sites and at other times before one can state with confidence the general effectiveness of the program. Of course, to the extent that the initial trial covers a variety of sites and the evaluation of the program covers the entire target population, this will be of less concern. Often, however, there will be limitations on the size and coverage of the trial. Not all locations, not all potential client groups, and not all other potentially important conditions are likely to be covered.

Such limitations of the evaluation should be clearly stated in the findings. For example, the New Jersey Graduated Work Incentive experiment examined only one type of geographical location on the U.S. urban East Coast. It covered only male-headed households, and it varied only the level of income guaranteed and the tax rate (Roos, 1975). The applicability of the findings to other conditions would need to be judged accordingly. As another example, if a test of a new street-patching material happens to be undertaken during a year with an unusually low amount of rain, the validity of the findings would be in question for periods of normal rainfall.

A special variation of the overgeneralizing pitfall can occur when explicit or implicit statements are made about the particular characteristics of the intervention that "caused" the observed impacts. This problem arises particularly where only one site (and one set of program intervention characteristics) is used in the trial of the program. As discussed under Pitfall 10, it is vital that evaluators know what was actually implemented and that they be alert for features of the trial that appear to be significant in the program's apparent success or lack of it, even though they were not initially intended to be tested during the trial. For example, in evaluations of the effectiveness of social service casework, such characteristics as the particular technique used, the caseworker's personality, the amount of time spent with the client, and the caseworker's style could all affect the outcomes (Fischer, 1976).

Unless the evaluation procedures attempted to isolate these characteristics in the test, evaluators would be unable to generalize about the extent to which these characteristics affect the outcomes. They would not be able to state whether, for example, apparent successes (or failures) were the result of the techniques used or the caseworkers' style and personality. This might be less of a problem if a large number of sites and many different caseworkers were involved in the test. Otherwise there would be substantial ambiguity about what was driving the observed outcomes and what should be done about the program. The conclusion might be reached that casework is (or is not) effective, whereas what was actually evaluated was only one combination of casework characteristics.

Behavior may change when the novelty of a new program wears off (for either program operators or their clients). And client behavior may alter from that in trials undertaken on only part of the population when the program is established so that everyone can receive the program. For example, a program to determine the effects of the use of group homes rather than large institutions for caring for children with juvenile delinquency records might be tested in one or two locations. The finding might not be representative of other settings if the program's scale was expanded. For example, citizens might become antagonistic to a larger number of homes in their community. Or if the locations were chosen because of the communities' willingness to test the group homes, other communities might be more resistant.

Some groups may turn out not to have been covered by the evaluation. In some instances, this may have been part of the plan; in others, it may be unintentional. The evaluators should determine which types of clients were included and which were not. They should avoid attributing observed effects to those not covered in the evaluation unless a logical case can be made for it. Many evaluations will not be able to cover all the major target groups that were initially intended for coverage and are intended to be covered by the program after it goes into full-scale operation. If this is found to be the case, the findings should be qualified. The New Jersey Graduated Work Incentive experiment, as noted, was limited to male-headed households and those located in only one geographical location; thus its generalizability was limited.

Pitfall 24: Failure to Acknowledge the Effects of Multiple Program Components

In many areas of social services, program participants benefit from many activities. For example, in many homeless shelters, participants may receive meals, counseling, basic health services, shelter, and even religious guidance in faith-based organizations. They may also receive services from multiple agencies. For example, youths may receive messages regarding the effects of drug use and unsafe sex from many sources. The evaluation may attempt to isolate the effectiveness of the different program components, but sometimes this is too costly. Identifying other related services received by beneficiaries should be part of initial work. However, if it is beyond the scope of the evaluation to sort out their effects, subsequent generalizations about program effectiveness need to acknowledge the possible influence of these other services.

Pitfall 25: Failure to Submit Preliminary Findings to Key Program Staff for Reality Testing

Permitting key program personnel to review the findings before promulgation of the evaluation findings is generally a matter of courtesy and good practice. It also has an important technical purpose: to provide a review of the findings from a different perspective. This practice appears to be regularly followed by audit agencies in the United States and by many government-sponsored evaluators but is not always followed.

Program staff may be aware of situations and factors that the evaluators have missed, and they can often add considerable insight into the interpretation of the data, sometimes identifying misinterpretations and misunderstandings by the evaluators. Even when program managers are defensive and hostile, they may offer comments that will indicate that the evaluators have indeed made misinterpretations or even errors that should be corrected. In one evaluation in which one of the chapter authors was involved, drug treatment program personnel reviewing the draft report pointed out to the evaluation team that an important group of program clients had been left out, requiring the evaluators to follow up what would otherwise have been a neglected group of clients. Finally, the opportunity to suggest modifications may reduce defensiveness by program personnel, thereby enhancing the likelihood that the evaluation findings will be used.

Pitfall 26: Failure to Adequately Support Conclusions with Specific Data

In presenting the findings of an evaluation, whether orally or in writing, evaluators should be careful to clearly link objective findings and objective data to the conclusions offered. Program staff and others will be quick to question the nature of the supporting evidence for findings, especially when findings are not positive.

This caveat also applies to recommendations. The basis of each recommendation should be identified. When evaluators attempt to provide insights into why programs are not as effective as they might be and then provide recommendations to improve the program, there is a tendency not to distinguish those recommendations that follow from the major technical examination from recommendations that have emerged from the more subjective, qualitative insights the evaluators obtained during the technical evaluation. Preferably, such insights would be obtained through technical analyses. However, even when these are obtained through more qualitative means, it is important that evidence supporting recommendations be clearly presented.

Pitfall 27: Poor Presentation of Evaluation Findings

Program evaluation findings, whether presented orally or in writing, should be clear, concise, and intelligible to the users for whom the report is intended. This should not, however, be used as an excuse for not providing adequate technical backup (documentation) for findings. The technical evidence should be made available in writing, in either the body of the text, appendixes, or a separate volume, so that technical staffs of the program funders and other reviewers can examine for themselves the technical basis of the findings. (See Chapter Twenty-Eight for suggestions for effective report writing.)

In addition, pitfalls encountered throughout the evaluation process, even those identified too late during the process of evaluation to address fully, should be discussed. The amount of uncertainty in the findings should be identified not only when statistical analysis is used but in other instances as well. Information about the impact of pitfalls encountered by evaluators on the magnitude or relative certainty of program effects should be provided, even if only in the form of the evaluators' subjective judgments.

The widespread use of multiple methods to collect data during evaluation work has led to a proliferation of advice on how to integrate and report out findings from mixed methods (for example, see Creswell and Clark, 2011). All the pitfalls discussed here are applicable, but when multiple methods are employed it is also important to clarify the interpretive rigor, that is, the relationship of findings to the methods employed, any inconsistencies across methods found, and the credibility of the integrated findings (Creswell and Clark, 2011, p. 270).

Conclusion

The checklist of pitfalls provided here should not be considered to cover all pitfalls. There are always evaluation-specific problems that can confront evaluators. Focusing on how decisions made throughout the evaluation process affect the different kinds of validity, reliability, and credibility of findings and recommendations is essential. The care with which potential limitations are identified and explained serves to strengthen the credibility of the evaluator's methodological expertise. Recognizing pitfalls should not be considered a weakness but rather a strength of rigorous evaluation work.

References

Armor, D. J., Polich, J. M., and Stambul, H. B. *Alcoholism and Treatment.* Santa Monica, CA: RAND Corporation, 1976.

Campbell, D. T. "Reforms as Experiments." *American Psychologist,* 1969, *24,* 409–429.

Campbell, D. T., and Ross, H. L. "The Connecticut Crackdown on Speeding." *Law and Society Review,* 1968, *8,* 33–53.

Conner, R. F. "Selecting a Control Group: An Analysis of the Randomization Process in Twelve Social Reform Programs." *Evaluation Quarterly,* 1977, *1,* 195–244.

Creswell, J. W. and Clark, V.L.P. *Designing and Conducting Mixed Methods Research* (2nd ed.) Thousand Oaks, CA: Sage, 2011.

Fischer, J. *The Effectiveness of Social Casework.* Springfield, IL: Thomas, 1976.

Hatry, H. P. *Performance Measurement: Getting Results.* Washington, DC: Urban Institute Press, 1999.

Hendricks, M. "Outcome Measurement in the Nonprofit Sector: Recent Developments, Incentives and Challenges." In K. Newcomer, E. Jennings, Jr., C. Broom, and A. Lomax (eds.), *Meeting the Challenges of Performance-Oriented Government.* Washington, DC: American Society for Public Administration, 2002.

Herzog, E. *Some Guide Lines for Evaluative Research.* Washington, DC: U.S. Department of Health, Education, and Welfare, Welfare Administration, Children's Bureau, 1959.

O'Sullivan, E., Rassel, G., and Berner, M. *Research Methods for Public Administrators.* White Plains, NY: Longman, 2003.

Riecken, H. W., and Boruch, R. F. (eds.). *Social Experimentation: A Method for Planning and Evaluating Social Intervention.* New York: Academic Press, 1974.

Roos, N. P. "Contrasting Social Experimentation with Retrospective Evaluation: A Health Care Perspective." *Public Policy,* 1975, *23,* 241–257.

Shadish, W., Cook, T., and Campbell, D. *Experimental and Quasi-Experimental Designs for Generalized Causal Inference.* Boston, MA: Houghton Mifflin, 2002.

Singleton, R., Straits, B., Straits, M., and McAllister, R. *Approaches to Social Research.* New York: Oxford University Press, 1988.

Stangor, C. *Research Methods for the Behavioral Sciences.* Boston, MA: Houghton Mifflin, 1998.

U.S. General Accounting Office. *Managing for Results: Measuring Program Results That Are Under Limited Federal Control.* Washington, DC: U.S. Government Printing Office, 1998.

CHAPTER TWENTY-SEVEN

PROVIDING RECOMMENDATIONS, SUGGESTIONS, AND OPTIONS FOR IMPROVEMENT

George F. Grob

One of the most rewarding and challenging aspects of our work as evaluators is making recommendations. This is our opportunity to make the world better. It is both exhilarating and humbling that we have been hired for the express purpose of advising senior officials of our government or other organizations on how to improve important programs or services, even to improve peoples' lives.

But it is not easy. Every one of our studies examines difficult problems that creative members of our society have not yet solved. If the solutions were easy, we wouldn't be in business, because the solutions would already have been identified and adopted.

Still, we must deliver. Recommendations are our bottom line. Even though evaluators may be proud when they have completed their studies in a professionally acceptable manner, most evaluators I know would not be satisfied with that. They want their studies to make a difference. Sometimes that can be achieved with findings alone, but usually it also requires recommendations, suggestions, or options for program or policy change. Evaluators are happy when their recommendations are accepted and acted upon, and disappointed when they are rejected or ignored.

It is, therefore, worthwhile to reflect on what kinds of recommendations are expected of us, what kinds are acceptable, what kinds are not, and how we can systematically and prolifically crank out the appropriate kinds, difficult as that may be.

In this brief chapter, I will discuss when to make recommendations, principles to follow in doing so, and practical suggestions on how to come up with good recommendations. I will also take up the intriguing question of evaluator independence in formulating recommendations.

But First, an Important Distinction

The principles and effective practices of making recommendations depend on the circumstances under which they are proffered. There are too many such circumstances to consider here, but an important distinction is whether or not the evaluator is conducting a compliance review, especially when the compliance review involves a statutory or regulatory requirement for recommendations to be made and for the officials whose programs are being evaluated to publicly respond to the recommendations. This is often (although not always) the case for evaluators working for the U.S. Government Accountability Office (GAO) or in a federal, state, or local government inspector general (IG) office, audit agency, or other such office. This chapter will occasionally note whether a particular point is applicable or not to a compliance review.

When to Make Recommendations

As just noted, in the case of compliance reviews, the evaluator is usually required to make recommendations. That may also be the case when the evaluator is working as part of a special commission established to study a public problem and make recommendations to address it. Examples are congressionally mandated studies to investigate problems of child abuse, pollution of drinking water, emergency response readiness, access to health care, progress in improving elementary education, and the like. In most other cases, it is a matter of negotiation between the entity that commissions the evaluation and the evaluator whether recommendations are to be offered. For example, sometimes a contracted evaluator's role is defined as providing evidence, not recommendations. In other cases, the contractor may want options or recommendations. Furthermore, even if recommendations are requested, they may or may not be intended to be included in the formal, published evaluation report. Even then, unpublished recommendations may still be useful to the requestor. Evaluators may also offer recommendations, even if they are not requested to provide them.

Of course, there are cases when the evaluator is acting independently or on behalf of an independent group, such as a citizens' watch group. In those cases, no negotiations with the officials of the evaluated program are necessary or even appropriate. However, recommendations made in such cases are generally useful and productive only if they are made after consultations with program officials and stakeholders, as described later in this chapter.

Aiming for Acceptance and Appreciation

Recommendations will be appreciated if they are deemed helpful by officials of the evaluated program or higher-level or legislative branch officials. In the case of compliance reviews or when otherwise legally or administratively mandated, recommendations must be offered whether or not they are appreciated. However, the goal should be to offer recommendations that are appreciated, whether or not mandated. The effect the evaluator should aim for is for the program officials to say, "Thank you so much for your thoughtful recommendations. This is so helpful." The odds that the officials will act on the recommendations are much higher with that kind of reaction—again, whether or not recommendations are required, requested, or published.

As a reality check, the ambitious evaluator intent on reforming the world should recall that the officials requesting or receiving recommendations can seldom act on them alone. Most difficult problems require many people and organizations, such as higher-level officials, boards of governors, legislative bodies, or stakeholder groups, to embrace the recommendations before they can be implemented. Hence, the evaluator, in proposing recommendations, always has to be speaking to an audience much broader than the officials who administer the evaluated program.

Choosing Between *Recommendations* and *Suggestions*

When recommendations are not mandated, the evaluator might well consider offering suggestions for improvement rather than recommendations. In most cases there is no practical substantive difference in the content of the evaluator's advice, but what a difference a word makes!

The difference between *recommendations* and *suggestions* is that the former sounds more authoritative, compulsory, and imposing. In the case of a compliance review with findings of dire conditions or illegal activity, this is exactly what is needed. This is also true for a report from an official commission assigned to make recommendations to address a serious public problem. The requesting authority—for example, government legislature, president, governor, mayor, or foundation board of directors—wants public recommendations made by a competent and authoritative independent source. At the opposite end of the spectrum, especially when program officials are themselves seeking help in understanding and remedying ongoing problems that they already know and are worried about, the evaluator may want to offer *suggestions for improvement.* This term connotes something like, "I hope these ideas are helpful."

Whether the evaluator's advice is offered as recommendations or suggestions, it is usually helpful to offer options. Except in the case of compliance reviews (and sometimes even then), there is no single correct solution to a problem but a range of possibilities, each with its attendant advantages and disadvantages. Recall that if there were an obvious solution, it would have already been adopted. Furthermore, decisions are seldom made by one person. Usually, a combination of legislative and executive officials must agree on a solution before it is adopted. And these officials will generally seek solutions that are acceptable to key stakeholders. For this reason, the evaluator will be seen as far more helpful when he or she is offering a number of possible solutions and describing the pros and cons of each. This also greatly increases the odds of the evaluator's advice being accepted.

It is particularly useful to combine options with recommendations or suggestions for improvement. The way to do this is to make recommendations or suggestions for outcomes or improvements and then offer several options to achieve the higher level of performance. For example, a response to a finding that many eligible beneficiaries are not being enrolled in a program to provide important benefits to which they are entitled would be to make a recommendation that the organization increase the percentage of eligible beneficiaries enrolled in the program to 75 percent within three years, and to then offer options related to outreach, simplification of enrollment procedures, and targeting enrollment initiatives to neighborhoods with high concentrations of eligible persons, and the like.

Hallmarks of Effective Recommendations

Although evaluators' clients (such as government entities, foundations, nonprofit organizations, or advocacy groups) generally want evaluators to make recommendations, they do not want them to be capricious in doing so. They expect the evaluators' solutions to flow from their findings, to be analytically sound, and to be practical.

Compliance Reviews

In the case of compliance reviews, the link between the findings and recommendations must be clear and direct. This is both necessary and possible because compliance findings are subject to well-established rules of evidence. They tend to be very discrete, concrete, and highly focused, describing situations in which an organization has failed to comply with specific statutes, regulations, guidelines, or administrative requirements. The associated recommendations are straightforward, as described in Box 27.1.

Box 27.1. Recommendations for Compliance Reviews

- Comply with the appropriate statutory, regulatory, or administrative provisions.
- Repair the damage done (for example, return funds that were improperly spent).
- Take practical steps to avoid noncompliance in the future.
- Pay fines or comply with other penalties if legitimately imposed.

So direct is the connection between compliance findings and recommendations that the recommendations themselves can seldom be challenged. If the agency wishes to disagree with the recommendations, it must discredit the findings.

Other Evaluations

Of course, many (perhaps most) evaluations do not have findings of noncompliance. They may examine efficiency, effectiveness, cost-effectiveness, or causal impact of programs. Here the connection between findings and recommendations is less direct. There is much more room to argue about how efficient an operation can be, and there are many ways to achieve higher impact or more cost-effective results, each with its advantages and disadvantages, side-effects, and constituencies. Gone are the comforting, unambiguous statutory or regulatory requirements. The officials of the evaluated entity can deny that they have any obligation to implement recommendations not required by law, regulation, or administrative requirement. They cannot be compelled. Instead, they must be persuaded.

Unlike the typical case with the compliance review, there is not just one solution. Rather, there are many options, each with its relative merits. In some cases, solutions may not be found by achieving compliance with the law. In fact, recommendations may call for modifying or repealing a current statute or regulation. Although it would be unacceptable for a compliance review to offer dozens of expansive recommendations when what is so clearly called for is that the evaluated agency simply comply with the law or regulations, it would be equally unacceptable for a program evaluation to restrict itself to one or two narrow recommendations when looking at a complex problem that has not been solved by the best minds in the country, community, or organization.

Box 27.2. Recommendations That Solve Problems

- Ideally, eliminate the causes of the problems described in the findings.
- If that is not possible (as is usually the case), alleviate the bad effects.
- Offer proposals that
  - Are feasible, practical, and affordable.
  - Have minimally disruptive side-effects.

Box 27.3. Common Recommendation Mistakes

- Recommending actions outside the authority of the evaluated entity
- Recommending actions that are impractical or too expensive to implement (in the sense that their cost would exceed the authorized budget of the entity), without acknowledging that this is the case
- Making a single recommendation when many more options are available

---

Perhaps the best way for evaluators to think about their responsibility in developing recommendations is this. Evaluators' clients want solutions—the more the better. However, they want them to be reasoned, to be related to evaluation findings, and to be practical.

In essence then, for most evaluations other than compliance reviews, it is best to develop recommendations along the lines described in Box 27.2.

To better understand these principles, it may be beneficial to consider mistakes commonly made in first drafts of evaluation reports and needing to be corrected by more experienced and seasoned senior supervisory evaluators. Among the most common are those described in Box 27.3.

General Strategies for Developing Recommendations

When solving problems, it is best to begin by identifying a multitude of options. Start by being expansive. Initially, ignore the problem of financing. I will deal with that later in this chapter. It is relatively easy to narrow down a long list. It is far more difficult to create that list. This goal can be achieved, however, through proper technique and the participation of a broad group of thoughtful, reasonable, informed individuals.

Brainstorm

The technique to start with is that of brainstorming. There are so many good books on this subject, and various methods are so well-known and practiced in the field of evaluation that there is no need to elaborate on it here. Suffice it to say that it is essential to

- Involve several people with various perspectives.
- Be very open to new ideas.
- Be respectful of others.

Usually, the initial brainstorming is done by the evaluation team. However, it is appropriate at this stage and later stages (as discussed later) to draw others into the brainstorming, especially those in other, but related, disciplines and programs. The evaluation team itself may have been chosen for its familiarity with the program or for just the opposite reason, not just for its good judgment and general experience but for its cold and unimpassioned perspectives. Ultimately, both kinds of individuals—those familiar and those unfamiliar with the program—must be involved in formulating recommendations.

Vet Ideas Up the Chain of Command and into the World of Stakeholders

After an initial set of problem-solving ideas is developed by a core set of brainstormers, recommendations are naturally vetted up the chain of command of the evaluated program and among its key stakeholders. This will happen whether or not the evaluator intends it. Every person or organization that has a stake in the evaluated program will weigh in in increasingly public ways as the evaluator's report and recommendations are vetted up the program's chain of command and are published. There is no question that all these affected parties will weigh in and comment. It is only a question of when—before or after the evaluation report is published.

FIGURE 27.1. A NARROW AND FRUSTRATING INTERPRETATION OF THE REVIEW PROCESS.

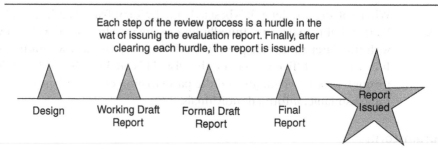

It typically is far better to involve all these program officials and stakeholders in advance of publishing the report, if practical. The reason for this is not just to avoid embarrassment but to corral good ideas. All these people and organizations care about the evaluated program and its effects on their constituencies. They want to solve the currently unsolved and important problem that is the subject of the evaluation. Many of them have really good ideas as to how to do that. The evaluation report, as it moves through the usual clearance process, serves as a magnet for attracting these good ideas. The evaluator becomes the grand coordinator of the enterprise of inviting these ideas, having them scrutinized, and then choosing the best ones to include in the evaluation report.

This way of looking at things runs contrary to the usual interpretation of the standard frustrating clearance process for evaluation reports, which is illustrated in Figure 27.1. The broader view sees the clearance process as a way to develop creative solutions that are likely to be accepted by program officials and stakeholders. This view is illustrated in Figure 27.2.

It is worth emphasizing here that the difference between the two approaches is entirely psychological. The steps, actions, and participants are the same. The key difference is how open the evaluation team is to the ideas that come pouring in—that is, encouraging and welcoming these ideas or being possessive and defensive about the recommendations that the team ultimately makes.

Start with the Findings

As noted earlier, the consumers of evaluation reports expect the recommendations or suggestions to flow from the findings. Thus, solutions have to address

FIGURE 27.2. A BROADER AND IMPROVEMENT-ORIENTED INTERPRETATION OF THE REVIEW PROCESS.

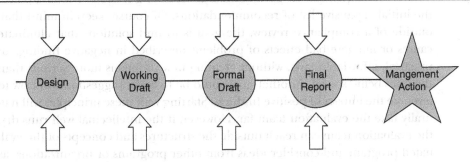

At each stage, insights of more and more experts are brought to bear on the study. The final report is only one step in a process resulting in action being taken to improve the program being evaluated.

the causes and effects of the problem being described in the report. Starting down this line of thinking will take the evaluator in the right direction to formulate recommendations fairly quickly.

It is also useful to note here that evaluations are not always, or at least not exclusively, about what is going wrong with a program. Evaluations can also reveal that a program is successful, or at least partially so. An evaluation may focus, for example, on a family of grants, such as grants made to states or to a set of other entities to run a particular program; the grant recipients may have been selected because they needed more assistance or because they are believed to serve as "demonstrations" of effective practices. Some of these grant recipients may be performing better than others. This is an ideal source of good recommendations (see Hendricks, 1994). The evaluator can suggest that all the grantees adopt at least some of the effective approaches of the successful grantees.

This approach is usually appreciated by decision makers, because the evaluation does not come across as a study commissioned just "to get them." To do this approach well, though, requires the evaluator to dig a bit deeper to understand just how the best practices of the successful grantees are achieved and the circumstances under which these grantees operate. This deeper analysis is not readily available to the other grantees, and they will be glad to receive it. In addition, these kinds of recommendations have a tendency to motivate the grant recipients to action. None of them want to think of themselves as being at the bottom of the performance list or want to stay there if they are.

Think Outside the Box

Several techniques can be used in the brainstorming session to come up with the initial expansive list of recommendations. Of course, keep in mind that, outside of a compliance review, the goal is to find solutions that eliminate causes or mitigate bad effects of problems described in negative findings in practical, affordable ways, without creating new problems more serious than the ones being solved. Another goal could be to make suggestions on how to leverage the impact of positive findings. Starting with these principles will naturally take the evaluation team far. However, if the intellectual well runs dry, the evaluation team can reach outside the structures and concepts of the evaluated program and consider ideas from other programs or organizations, as identified in Box 27.4.

Box 27.4. Consider What Other Organizations Do in Related Program Areas

- Federal departments or agencies
- State governments
- Local governments
- Large cities
- Counties
- Private sector
- Foundations
- Charities
- Religious organizations
- Accrediting organizations

The evaluated program probably uses a few of the standard governance functions to achieve its goals. The evaluation team can productively consider functions used in other programs, such as those listed in Box 27.5, and systematically consider whether any of these functions can be used or improved in the evaluated program.

In considering what other organizations do in related program areas and what processes they use to accomplish their goals, it is important to avoid doing so slavishly. No two environments are ever exactly like, and what one organization does may not work in another. Rather, it is best to initially cull lots of ideas from plausible sources simply to use them as mind joggers that expose ideas for further consideration and analysis. The evaluator will have to do the hard work of adapting the general approaches to the case at hand. The evaluator

Box 27.5. Consider Various Governance Functions

- Research and demonstration
- Discretionary or entitlement grants
- Public affairs initiative
- Planning
- Evaluation
- Accounting systems
- Quality assurance systems
- Interagency coordination
- Contracts

can begin narrowing the ideas by first considering programs that are similar to the one he or she is now evaluating, play similar roles in larger enterprises of which they are a part, use similar organizational structures to implement them, and so on.

It would also be useful to highlight the potential limitations associated with using such approaches. Being explicit about such limitations is important because it is natural for program proponents to resist outside ideas by pointing out such difference and limitations. Strangely, the evaluator's self-proclamation of such shortcomings lends greater credibility to the analogies. Also, it is better to first discuss such ideas with the evaluation client before putting them into a report. In fact, it may be more productive to just discuss them "offline," so to speak, and leave them out of the report. This shows great respect to the client and may well be more persuasive. It is healthy and productive to remember that the goal is to provide practical ideas that may lead to adoption of effective solutions by the evaluation client. The evaluator's sense of personal reward will be driven more by the adoption of the ideas than by their inclusion in a report.

Another technique is to make good use of the variation usually found in similar programs administered in several geographical or administrative areas. Such variation occurs, for example, with regard to the programs and administrative systems of areas identified in Box 27.6. Programs that make grants to many or all states will probably be handled somewhat differently in each state, some with more or some with less success than others. Similarly, programs are often administered through regional offices, some of whose administrative practices will be better or worse than others. Whenever such variation occurs, evaluators can make useful recommendations to require that all entities stop doing destructive things that they and others do or that they adopt the effective practices that the more successful ones are doing. Examination of these variances is also useful for demonstrating the feasibility of the recommended practices.

Box 27.6. Pick the Best Practices from Different Locations

- Cities
- States
- Regional offices
- Grantees within a single program

Consider the Problem of Financing the Recommendations

One of the most frustrating aspects of evaluators' work is that they find so many serious social problems that they can't solve. One common reason for this inability is the lack of funds available to address these problems. Unfortunately, it is generally not prudent for evaluators to recommend additional funding for particular programs.

Funding issues are the prerogative of policymakers, generally elected officials or boards of directors. It is a proper matter of public policy for our elected representatives to decide which of the many problems facing our society need to be addressed first and how much of our nation's resources should be devoted to each. With limited budgets, raising funds for one issue frequently requires decreasing funds for others. It is not for evaluators to decide such matters. Instead, the evaluator's job is to, in a nonpartisan way, serve up the facts and ideas that will enlighten the public debates that necessarily occur about the future directions of our social programs.

Even elected officials are constrained by available resources. For example, the current rules pertaining to federal congressional budget deliberations are that no new expansion can be approved for one program without identifying a comparable savings to pay for the expansion.

Nevertheless, there are ways to deal with the problem of financing, including those listed in Box 27.7. The best tactic is to suggest ways to save money by improving program efficiency. It is always worth making extra efforts to find such economies.

Narrow the List and Provide Options

Once the initial brainstorming is over, it is necessary to analyze the solutions to ensure that they would eliminate the cause of the problems or at least mitigate their effects, are feasible, and would not create additional problems. Analysis might also reveal whether there are additional advantages not originally identified. This analysis will weed out the impractical solutions and perhaps provide a basis for ranking or prioritizing the proposals.

Box 27.7. Financing Tactics

- Capitalize on options that do not require large expenditures, such as research and development projects.
- Provide self-financing through user fees.
- Require matching funds by grantees.
- Suggest offsetting savings, that is, make specific suggestions to reduce program costs.
- Use incentive funding, that is, suggest allocating a portion of program funds to be used as an incentive fund to be distributed among grantees according to how much effort they make, how efficiently they conduct their programs, or how successful they are.

One issue that sometimes arises is whether to include recommendations that seem to make sense but are so radical (in the sense that they are so different from current thinking on the topic) or so unlikely to be accepted that, even though they are valid, their inclusion might jeopardize the credibility of the entire report. There is no pat way to decide this. The best approach is to have an open discussion and let those in authority make a reasoned judgment on the matter.

Even after weeding out impractical ideas, the team may still find itself with many solutions. One way to handle this is to group them into categories, generalize their common thrust, and present them as options under a general recommendation, as discussed in the earlier section on options.

Take Ownership of the Recommendations

Throughout this chapter, I have emphasized the need to attract solutions from many sources. It makes perfect sense to include recommendations offered by others. In the end though, the evaluator in charge must take ownership of the recommendations, using only those that he or she is comfortable in advocating. For this reason, this chapter ends with a summary (in Box 27.8) of the most important principles that should govern the formulation of recommendations by evaluators.

Box 27.8. The Bottom Line

- Make sure the recommendations flow from the findings.
- Focus on solutions that
  - Address the causes of the problem or alleviate its effects,
  - Are feasible, practical, and affordable, and
  - Have minimally disruptive side-effects.
- Offer as many solutions as possible.
- Invite others to help find solutions.
- Take responsibility for the recommendations offered by the evaluation team.

Reference

Hendricks, M. "Making a Splash: Reporting Evaluation Results Effectively." In J. S. Wholey, H. P. Hatry, and K. E. Newcomer (eds.), *Handbook of Practical Program Evaluation*. San Francisco, CA: Jossey-Bass, 1994.

CHAPTER TWENTY-EIGHT

WRITING FOR IMPACT

George F. Grob

The objective of this chapter is to explain how to write compelling evaluation reports that convince readers of the findings and promote taking action in response. Evaluators take great pride in their work. What is especially rewarding for them is knowing that their studies make a difference, that positive changes will result from their clients' taking action based on their findings and recommendations. Of course, the best way to achieve such results is to produce rock-solid reports with strong evidence and practical advice. However, the way the reports are written also matters. That is what this chapter is all about—not just writing well, but also writing for impact.

Effective writing involves an interplay and command of three facets of communication:

- *The message:* what the writer wants people to remember after they have read the report
- *The audience:* individuals the writer wants to read or hear about the study
- *The medium:* the many factors that carry the message—words, pages, reports, typeface, graphics, paper, ink, color, computer screens, slides, newsletters, panel discussions, and the like

These three facets of effective writing are highly interrelated, but it is convenient to discuss them one at time.

The Message

The message is the most important of the three facets. This is what the writer wants people to remember—the core message and the related findings and recommendations.

The Mom Test

No report will matter much unless it passes what I call the *Mom Test*. Imagine that you have just finished nine months of work on an evaluation of community policing. You have delivered the report and are waiting to hear from the client, your hometown local government. You stop by to see your family while you are in town and bring with you a fresh printed copy, with its back spine as yet uncracked, and slide it across the table to your mother, who is serving your favorite cookies and home-brewed coffee. She looks at it lovingly and says: "We're all so proud, Chris. What does it say?" And you answer, "Mom, it says. . . ."

That's the Mom Test: being able to finish the sentence. You can add one more short sentences if you need to, but no more. You have to do it in a way that your mother can easily understand you. Your summary has to be simple but also specific, insightful, inspiring, and interesting, and it must elicit a response something like "Well, I sure hope they do something about it."

Here are some examples that pass the test:

"Police officers on the beat in a community make a big difference. Now is not the time to cut funding for them."

"Only 80 percent of children entering school in our town are fully inoculated against common childhood diseases. The average in our state is 90 percent."

"The reading improvement program started last year in our schools seems to be working. Reading levels are up significantly in every classroom where it was tried."

Do not misinterpret the Mom Test as an admonition to "dumb it down" so that even your mom can understand. Moms today are likely to be just as informed and intelligent as any policymaker or evaluator. The point is that it is necessary but difficult to boil a report down to its essence, and it will probably take you many tries to get it right.

Failure to pass the Mom Test is the most common and significant weakness in evaluation reports that fail to inspire action. The main reason for failing the test is not the difficulty of finding words to succinctly express the report's message. It is because there is no message. The author may have provided lots of findings and good recommendations, but no kernel, no unforgettable nub that attracts attention and compels the reader's interest. This point cannot be emphasized enough:

- An evaluation report can have impact only if readers can discern its main message.
- They can do so only if the evaluator expresses the message.
- The evaluator cannot express the message without having one.

Findings

Much more is needed to convey the results of an evaluation study than a simple one- or two-sentence main message. Clients and stakeholders expect to see detailed findings. From the perspective of writing for impact, the following principles should guide the formulation of findings:

- Tell them something they don't already know.
- Be reasonable.
- Be concise.

Most of an evaluator's clients and readers understand their own field of work very well. Still, they are hoping that an independent, creative, intelligent professional can help them find what has eluded them: new insights. Hence the first principle is to tell them something new. The reaction that evaluators want to obtain from other stakeholders is: "Thanks. This was helpful." Stakeholders who react that way will give the findings and recommendations serious attention, and the evaluators will make a difference. If stakeholders do not react this way, evaluators will harvest indifference at best and resistance at worst.

The principle of reasonableness does not mean "tell them what they want to hear." Clients can handle criticism. In fact, it is independence and professionalism that they most value in the evaluator. That is the reason they are willing to pay good money to obtain the evaluator's assistance. So evaluators should tell it like it is—but be measured and reasonable in doing so. Being reasonable means putting yourself in the shoes of your audience and stakeholders, trying to understand their constraints and opportunities. It also means avoiding extreme and unrealistic positions, using exaggerations and sarcastic language, and impugning the motives and character of others. And it also means being willing to listen to and consider what stakeholders have to say.

The third principle, conciseness, is the child of the Mom Test. Readers can remember about two to five key ideas, and no more. If there are too many findings to reduce to five, they can be grouped into no more than five categories. Then the writer can summarize the findings in each category into a single broad finding and let the detailed findings be part of the explanation of the broad ones.

Options and Recommendations

To have impact, an evaluator usually needs to offer solutions to the problems discussed in the findings, although there are some exceptions. For example, a finding might be so startling that just stating it and letting others deal with its consequences might be the most effective way to generate solutions. Or the study may find no problems to correct, just a big misunderstanding. But these are exceptions. Most of the time, recommendations are needed and appreciated. Here are a couple of principles to use in formulating them (also see Chapter Twenty-Seven).

- *Be practical.* Temporarily step into your clients' shoes while formulating solutions.
- *Give lots of options.* Big decisions are almost never made by just a few people. Broad consultation and ultimately consensus are needed to gain acceptance of ways to solve problems that have eluded the very best professionals in any field of endeavor. It is far better to offer half a dozen ideas than to insist on just a couple. In fact, the evaluator might well want to label the solutions as *options for improvement* instead of *recommendations*. Everyone wants the former; sometimes, people resent the latter.

Methodology

Evaluation reports need to describe the methods used to obtain findings. The goal here is to explain just the right amount—not too much, not too little. The advice is

- Don't get carried away.
- Still, describe the whole approach.
- Briefly discuss its shortcomings.

Evaluators are naturally keenly interested in their methodologies and need no encouragement to talk about them. However, clients and stakeholders are mostly interested in findings and recommendations. They will start by assuming that the evaluator has done a professional job and are not interested in plowing through page after page of methodology.

At the same time, advocates or defensive managers who do not like the findings and recommendations will immediately attack the methodology. A full description of the methodology will uphold the findings in the report, the integrity of the evaluator, and even the evaluation profession itself. Hence, to have impact, the evaluator faces a significant challenge: keeping the description of methodology succinct yet complete and compelling. Here are some hints on how to achieve this balance:

- Keep the description of methodology very brief in the executive summary—no more than one paragraph.
- Put a page or two in the body of the report.
- Provide a full description in an appendix.
- Offer ways for the reader to contact the author for more information about the methods.

Evaluators sometimes take too narrow a view of their own methodologies. They focus on their surveys, correlation analyses, focus groups, and other such techniques. They sometimes regard their literature reviews, stakeholder consultations, and analyses of laws and regulations as background work that precedes the formulation of their methodology. However, their clients think that these chores are important, too, and the simple recitation that these tasks have been performed adds much credibility to the report.

No methodology is perfect. There are always shortcomings, and if the evaluator does not acknowledge them, others certainly will highlight them in the public comments that will inevitably follow. But if the evaluator discusses them briefly, the report comes across as quite professional. It is ironic that pointing out the flaws of one's own methodology gives the report greater credibility, but that is the case. At the same time, the shortcomings section does not have to be lengthy or exhaustive. There is no point in going on and on, telling readers why they should not believe anything they read in the report.

The Audience

A report's audience is the set of people the evaluator wants to read the evaluation and be influenced by it. From the perspective of obtaining impact, the audience can be more precisely defined as the set of people who are or should be involved in deciding matters covered in the report. They consist of two groups: thought leaders and other interested persons.

Thought Leaders

In every field of endeavor is a group of people recognized as the movers and shakers. They are the thought leaders. An understanding of the existence and functioning of thought leaders is extremely important:

- An evaluation report will have no impact unless it impresses the thought leaders.
- Thought leaders will not be impressed unless they read the report.

For an evaluation report to have impact, it must persuade the movers and shakers of the merits of its findings and recommendations. No significant action will occur until they all agree, or at least agree to disagree. But action will occur if they do.

The set of thought leaders for a particular evaluation is concrete. Their names can be listed. In a large corporation they include board members, the chief executive officer, the chief financial officer, key stockholders, and heads of large operating departments or services sectors. In an accounting or law firm, they are the partners and administrators. In the federal government, they consist of key members of Congress and their staffs, executives of affected federal agencies, representatives of industry and beneficiary groups or activists, and the Office of Management and Budget. In states and local governments, they include the governor, mayor, legislators, council members, chief executive officer, budget officials, department or agency heads, program directors, and local stakeholder groups. In nonprofit foundations, they are the board members and top staff. On a smaller scale, the thought leaders are the owners and managers of a small business.

In order for a report to have impact, the evaluator must make sure that the evaluation results are known by the thought leaders. The following actions are therefore essential in persuading the thought leaders to read the report:

- Make a list of the thought leaders who have influence on the matters discussed in the evaluation report.
- E-mail them each a copy of the report.
- Make the report very easy for them to read.

Other Interested Persons

In addition to the thought leaders, numerous individuals who are not influential now might very well become so—such as students and researchers. Many others will not care about the topic of the report—until they read it. Through reports, evaluators can inspire others to become movers and shakers. Think back on your own development and recall the things that influenced you to become an evaluator or a leader in a subject that you are now evaluating. Chances are these things included reports, articles, and books.

The problem for evaluators is that they cannot make a list of these people, yet need to get the report to them. The way to do this is to have reports published and disseminated through professional journals, newsletters, and books. Better yet, use the Internet. Electronic outlets are now ubiquitous. In recent years some important reports were never published in hard-copy form.

The Medium

Reports and other publications convey a message using several different carriers simultaneously, each one interacting with the other and all of them important. I am using the word *medium* to refer not simply to the general, classic type of publication—television, newspapers, radio—but to cover anything necessary to deliver the message: the color of the ink, the grammar of the sentence, the size of the paper, the method of binding the reports, the writing style, the U.S. mail, the Internet, the type size, the fonts, the overheads, television sets, newspapers, newsletters, panel discussions, and much more. All of these are important.

The Six Basic Formats

If I were writing this chapter fifteen or twenty years ago, I would have started by describing a convenient standard report format—something to follow and deviate from. Today, however, electronic information technology has completely changed the way we communicate. Almost anyone can produce, and virtually everyone consumes—and expects to find material in the form of—videos, overhead projector slides, PowerPoint presentations, audio recordings, CDs, web pages, and electronic newsletters, among many other choices. Newsletters abound, all hungry for material to fill in the white spaces before deadline. Cottage advocates open websites, publish newsletters using Internet list servs, post blogs, publish on YouTube, and send messages to worldwide audiences. How can an evaluator efficiently put the message of a report out to the world through all the different media that are available?

The answer is to concentrate on the message and to become facile at using electronic processors to adjust it to the publication format and medium at hand. To do so requires mastering communication at approximately six levels of detail and format styles:

- The Mom Test summary
- The killer paragraph
- The outline
- The two-page executive summary
- The ten-page report
- The technical report

We will look at these six basic formats. As an aid to the discussion, I have created examples of the formats using material from an evaluation published by the U.S. Department of Health and Human Services, Office of Inspector General (OIG) on recruiting foster parents (2002). I will illustrate the first four of the six basic formats as I explain each one. The last two formats—the ten-page report and the technical report—are too long for this book. However, the principles for writing them will, I hope, be clear enough when we discuss those topics.

Box 28.1 displays some key background information about problems in recruitment of foster parents at the time the Office of Inspector General conducted its study and about the evaluation approach that the OIG used.

Keep this background in mind, as the next sections of this chapter illustrate how the results of the study could be portrayed at several levels of detail.

The Mom Test Summary.   If you skipped the section describing the Mom Test, go back and read it now. Box 28.2 provides a summary for the foster care recruitment report that passes the Mom Test.

The Killer Paragraph.   The one or two sentences written to pass the Mom Test are needed mostly for oral presentation of the study results—the quick statement at the beginning of the meeting and the explanation in the hallway on the way to the meeting, for example. The equivalent written version is the *killer paragraph.*

A compelling paragraph can be useful on many occasions. For example, delivery of the report to the client is typically done by letter or memo. The place for the killer paragraph is after the "Dear So-and-So" and the line that says, "I am happy to send you the report." At this point, a good, concise paragraph

Box 28.1. Background on Recruitment of Foster Care Parents

Most children in foster care are cared for in foster family homes; some are in institutions, group homes, or other group settings. Most foster parents are nonrelatives. In early 2000, there were approximately 581,000 children in foster care. Forty-seven percent were cared for in private homes by nonrelative foster parents. At that time many states were experiencing a shortage of families willing and able to provide foster care, especially families to care for children with special needs, such as adolescents with psychological or mental disabilities or even adolescents in general. Other children who are difficult to place include sibling groups and children with mental, behavioral, and emotional challenges and children with special physical needs (such as HIV-positive children, babies addicted to drugs, and babies with shaken baby syndrome).

States were using a variety of methods to recruit foster families, including a combination of media, that is, television public service announcements, radio campaigns, newspaper advertisements, magazine advertisements, brochures, and even billboards. They were also using such recruitment tools as magnets, bookmarks, coffee mugs, T-shirts, pins, rubber balls, grocery bags, calendars, and lapel pins. Other methods included making presentations to local civic and religious organizations and running booths at state and county fairs, malls, school events, and health fairs. Still, state efforts were falling short.

In order to gain a better understanding of this problem, the Office of Inspector General surveyed, by mail, the foster care program managers for the fifty states, the District of Columbia, Puerto Rico, and the Virgin Islands, gathering information about state policies, practices, and processes for recruitment, and the barriers states were encountering in their recruitment efforts. The OIG then selected five states that accounted for 53 percent of the nation's foster children, were geographically diverse, and reflected a mix of county- and state-administered foster care systems. In these states the OIG interviewed state foster care program managers and conducted focus group discussions with foster parents and child welfare staff. Through these methods, survey staff heard firsthand from foster families, caseworkers, caseworker supervisors, foster care recruitment specialists, and staff from private foster care agencies with whom the state foster care agency contracts. These discussions and interviews occurred in both urban and rural areas.

Box 28.2. Mom Test Summary for Foster Parent Recruitment Report

Current methods to recruit foster parents are falling short because they are focused on the wrong audience. Instead of using broad-based media such as TV, radio, and magazines to recruit foster parents from the general public, recruiters should use networks of current foster parents to reach families willing and able to care for the most challenging children.

is far more compelling than one or two pages of text. A strong paragraph, because of its short, stand-alone format, cries out: "Bottom line, here's what we found." Once that point is made, don't dilute it with more words. Anyone who wants more can read the report.

The killer paragraph is a lot more, too. It is the abstract that appears first in the version of the report that is published in a professional journal. It is the first paragraph in the news article that someone else writes about the findings. It is the brief summary that appears on the first page of a trade group's or professional organization's newsletter that talks about the report on the inside pages. It is the description that appears in a compilation of multiple study findings being sent to some important person. It is what shows up in a literature review. It is what makes it onto the computer screen when someone does a word search and the report makes the list.

The killer paragraph may be the only thing that most people will ever know about all that work the team accomplished. It had better be good. Box 28.3 contains some tips on how to write this paragraph, and Box 28.4 provides an example.

The Outline.   Few other instruments achieve emphasis and clarity of thought as effectively as outlines do. Outlining helps the writer decide what is important and helps the listeners or readers to focus. A topic outline provides a visual reinforcement of an oral presentation. It makes it easier for clients to organize their own thoughts, and it helps them remember what has been said or written. These features make a one-page outline highly useful to pass around the table at the start of the presentation on the report's findings and recommendations.

Box 28.3. Tips on Writing the Killer Paragraph

- *Focus on findings and recommendations.* These are the most important parts of the report. Devote most of the words in this paragraph to them.
- *Limit methodology.* The least important part of the paragraph is the methodology. Try to make only a passing reference to it.
- *Be concrete.* Do not just serve up sweeping generalities. Include concrete facts—numbers and examples.
- *Prioritize.* There is no need to mention every finding and recommendation, just the major ones.
- *Avoid abbreviations.* Do not use any abbreviations or technical language.
- *Be brief.* Aim for about twelve lines or a quarter of a page of text. Never exceed one-third of a page.

A sentence outline, in which the first thought (at least) of each major section is expressed in a single sentence, is a very handy briefing document that can stand on its own. Forcing yourself to render the main thoughts in sentences is a good discipline to promote clarity, precision, and emphasis. More important, the result will become the backbone of the executive summary and the report itself, and a powerful tool for communicating findings and recommendations.

Box 28.4. Killer Paragraph for the Foster Parent Recruitment Report

Increasingly, state foster care programs are having difficulty recruiting foster parents for difficult to place children. In response, they have ramped up their efforts by investing in television public service announcements, radio campaigns, newspaper advertisements, and magazine advertisements, as well as making presentations to local civic and religious organizations and running booths at state and county fairs, malls, school events, and health fairs. Still, their efforts are falling short. After interviewing foster parents, caseworkers, and other experienced frontline staff, the Office of Inspector General has concluded that current efforts are focused on the wrong audience. Instead of using broad-based media such as TV, radio, and magazines to recruit foster parents from the general public, recruiters should use networks of current foster parents to reach families willing and able to care for the most challenging children. The report also recommends promoting positive public perceptions of foster care, better information sharing, and more technical assistance for foster care program managers.

A topic outline, which uses phrases instead of sentences for key ideas, is useful as the table of contents for the report and as a briefing document or visual aid when giving an oral briefing. It is less tedious to read than a sentence outline, and sometimes makes it easier for an audience to follow major threads of thought. The trick is to strike a balance between brevity and completeness and between summary concepts and key facts.

For all these reasons, it is worthwhile to take the trouble to prepare an outline. The topic outline for the foster care recruitment report in Box 28.5 illustrates how integral the outline is to the report itself and to other documents derived from it.

The Two-Page Executive Summary.   For serious readers, the two-page executive summary is the most important part of the study. The principles for writing it are generally the same as for the paragraph-length version but there is more room to elaborate. Box 28.6 contains some additional tips. For the entire executive summary for the foster parent recruitment report, see Exhibit 28.1.

The Ten-Page Report.   Dollar for dollar, minute for minute, the best investment any of us will ever make in reaching our goal to make a difference in this world is in writing a compelling ten-page report. It will reach more thought leaders than anything else you do. It will outlast every speech you ever make. It may reach people not yet born. It can easily be mounted on the Internet, and people may read it without even printing it out. Except for the following section on technical reports, almost everything else discussed in this chapter relates to how to produce this document.

Box 28.5. Topic Outline for the Foster Parent Recruitment Report

Purpose: To assess states' efforts to recruit foster parents

Background—Foster Children
- 581,000 children in foster care in 2000
- 47 percent cared for by nonrelative foster parents
- 26 percent cared for by relatives
- Many children have special emotional or physical needs, such as
  Adolescents
  Sibling groups
  Children with mental, behavioral, and emotional challenges
  HIV-positive children
  Babies addicted to drugs
  Babies with shaken baby syndrome

Recruitment of Foster Parents
- State agencies are ramping up recruitment efforts, including
  Public service announcements on TV, radio campaigns, billboards
  Presentations to civic and religious groups and at fairs, malls, school events
- Still, shortages continue

Methodology
- Mail survey to fifty states, D.C., Puerto Rico, Virgin Islands
  Information requested on state policies, practices, recruitment processes, barriers
  Forty-one responses received, representing 81 percent of children in nonrelative care

- In-depth information from five states, purposefully selected
  Geographically diverse
  Contain 53 percent of nation's foster children
  Include mix of county- and state-administered systems
- In the five states, interviews and focus group discussions involving
  Fifteen foster parents
  Seven child welfare staff
  Both urban and rural areas

Findings
- Recruitment efforts not focused on families willing and able to care for most challenging children
- States underusing most effective tool—foster parents
- Poor public perceptions of foster care and cumbersome requirements have negative impact
- States unable to measure success of recruitment efforts

Recommendations
- Target recruitment on parents for children who are most difficult to place
- Use current foster families in recruitment efforts
- Promote positive public perception of foster care
- Improve information sharing about effective practices and increase technical assistance to program managers

Box 28.6. Tips on Writing the Executive Summary

- Prioritize. Concentrate on the findings and recommendations.
- Start the findings on the first page, a third of the way up from the bottom or higher.
- Flesh out the recommendations, starting them about the middle of the second page.
- Limit discussion of the methodology. Use no more than a short paragraph to describe the methodology. Use plain language.
- Do not squeeze material in by using small type sizes or narrow margins. The idea is to make the report easy to read, not hard to read.
- Do not use footnotes. Save those for the body of the report (if you need them at all).
- Use headlines, and put the main point of each paragraph in the first sentence.

The ten-page report can be thought of as an extended version of the executive summary. Just flesh out the summary with key facts, explanations, and context.

The Technical Report.   For some audiences, a ten-page report is not enough. This is particularly true of researchers, academics, policy analysts, program staff, and specialists; these individuals are likely to need context and details about methodology. They won't believe anything in the report unless it contains these additional layers of information and discussion of that information. However, there is considerable variation in how finely honed and polished this material needs to be, which depends on the subject matter and the field of inquiry. Depending on whom you are trying to reach, you may need none, one, or more than one technical report, each tailored to a specific client or audience. Box 28.7 contains tips about how hard to work on this report and how to package these deeper layers of knowledge.

Writing Style and Layout

Because evaluators write for impact, they have to capture the reader's attention, hold it, and focus it. However, important people who read a lot also read fast, so evaluators have to write for the way they read, that is, by skimming. To really understand how busy people read reports, evaluators first have to understand how they see these documents.

Layout and Typography.   The executive reader skimming a report initially reads everything but the plain text. Therefore the report writer needs to make sure that the important material in the report is announced by the layout, the typography (font styles and sizes and formats such as boldface and underlining), and the graphics. The general principles for employing such enhancements are as follows.

- Use layout and typographical enhancements to highlight your main points.
- Don't use such enhancements for anything else.

Box 28.8 provides tips on the kinds of enhancements to use and the kinds to avoid.

Box 28.7. Tips on Producing a Technical Report

- For executives and senior program managers, skip the appendixes.
- Program and policy staff typically want detailed tables, frequency distributions of responses to survey questions, the list of survey recipients, and published guides gathered over the course of the evaluation. Give this information to them, but skip the step of writing a high-quality tome. Send them copies of file tables, e-mail them the database versions of this material, or send all this material to them on a CD.
- For technical experts and some researchers, it is probably worthwhile to prepare formal technical reports that look professional and are easy to use.
- For the research community at large, the world of academics, and serious policy researchers, take the time to prepare solid, comprehensive reports. Then take the ten-page report and rename it "Executive Report." Now everyone will be pleased. The executives have a report especially written for them and the deep thinkers have what they want—thoughtful context and careful methodology.

Box 28.8. Tips on Text Enhancements

Enhancements to Use
- *Outline.* The message is in the outline, so make it jump off the page by using the topic outline phrases as the headlines in the text.
- *Bold text.* Put the three to five key findings and recommendations in boldface type.
- *Type size.* Increase the type size a couple of points for the major findings and key recommendations.
- *Lists.* Put the subfindings and subsidiary recommendations or options into lists.

Enhancements to Avoid
- *Excess.* Using layout and text enhancements is like shouting. If you shout everything, you shout nothing. Only three to five thoughts should jump off each page.
- *Footnotes.* Do not put footnotes in the executive summary. One of these side remarks may shift the attention of executive readers away from the main ideas.
- *All caps.* Do not use all caps for more than one or two short words. This style is hard to read.
- *Abbreviations.* Abbreviations, usually written in all caps, look like enhanced text. They are not what the writer wants skim-reading executives to pay attention to.
- *Italics.* Do not use italics in subheads. Italics are ambiguous enhancements: to some people they appear emphatic; to others they seem parenthetical. Thus, they may deemphasize things for some people instead of emphasizing them. Use italics only within the body of the text to distinguish or emphasize words or phrases.

EXHIBIT 28.1. EXECUTIVE SUMMARY FOR THE FOSTER PARENT RECRUITMENT REPORT.

Department of Health and Human Services
Office of Inspector General
MAY 2002
Recruiting Foster Parents
Purpose

To assess states' efforts to recruit foster parents.

Background

State child welfare agencies are tasked with the responsibility of protecting children from abuse and neglect, which sometimes requires that children be removed from their homes and placed in foster care. Based on information reported to the Administration for Children and Families (ACF) via the Adoption and Foster Care Analysis and Reporting System (AFCARS), as of March 31, 2000, there were 581,000 children in foster care. Forty-seven percent of those children were cared for in non-relative foster family homes.

The ACF has regulatory oversight of the Title IV-E foster care program. The Title IV-E foster care program is designed to assist states in covering the costs for children in foster care by providing states with unlimited matching funds for children who meet income eligibility and other program requirements. Federal expenditures for the Title IV-E foster care program totaled $4 billion in fiscal year (FY) 1999 and $4.3 billion in FY 2000. Federal funding for the Title IV-E foster care program totaled $4.4 billion in FY 2001. Estimated federal funding for the program is $5.1 billion in FY 2002.

This report focuses on states' efforts to recruit foster care families. A separate report, "Retaining Foster Parents" (OEI-07-00-00601), addresses the issues associated with the retention of these families. We used two mechanisms to conduct this inspection. We used a mail survey to obtain information from the foster care program managers in the fifty states, the District of Columbia, Puerto Rico, and the Virgin Islands to determine their efforts to recruit foster care families. We also conducted focus group discussions with child welfare staff and foster parents in five states.

Findings

Recruitment Efforts Do Not Focus on Families Willing and Able to Care for the Most Challenging Children

The foster care agencies use recruiting methods designed to cast a wide net and recruit a large volume of prospective foster parents. However, many families recruited in this manner are unwilling to care for school-age children, teenagers, and children with special needs. These children constitute the largest portion of children in foster care, thus creating an urgent need to recruit families who are willing and able to provide them with care.

States Are Underutilizing Their Most Effective Recruitment Tool—Foster Parents

Only seven states are using foster parents regularly in their recruitment efforts, even though survey respondents in twenty states said they find foster parents to be one of the most successful recruitment tools. Foster parents are effective recruiters because they share information about the need for foster parents through word-of-mouth contact and can promote the idea of fostering just by their presence in the community.

Poor Public Perceptions of Foster Care and Cumbersome Requirements Have a Negative Impact on Recruitment

Poor public perceptions of foster care discourage prospective foster parents. Unfavorable media portrayals depicting tragedies and abuses endured by foster children perpetuate negative perceptions about the current foster care system. Delayed responses to inquiries about becoming a foster parent, stringent requirements, and the length of time involved in becoming a foster parent also adversely affect states' recruitment efforts and reinforce existing reservations about fostering.

States Are Unable to Measure the Success of Their Recruitment Efforts

The lack of performance indicators and information about recruitment expenditures renders many states unable to measure the success of their recruitment efforts. States lack the tools necessary to identify which methods of recruitment are most beneficial and cost effective.

Recommendations

Our review allowed us to take a retrospective look at the effectiveness of foster care recruitment efforts. This review indicates that it may be time to rethink some aspects of the recruitment process. Clearly, substantial progress can be made towards improving recruitment efforts through the combined efforts of states, ACF, and national organizations, with particular emphasis on:

- Targeting recruitment efforts on parents for children who are the most difficult to place;
- Promoting positive public perceptions of foster care; and
- Improving information sharing about effective practices among key stakeholders and increasing technical assistance for program managers.

Source: Executive Summary of *Recruiting Foster Parents*, May 2002, U.S. Department of Health and Human Services, Office of Inspector General.

Graphs, Tables, and Other Large Graphics.   Graphs, tables, formulas, and pictures, collectively referred to as graphics, are often used in evaluation reports.

Readers like them because they highlight and explain complex and important subjects. Readers also like to analyze and interpret them themselves. These graphics can also be visually interesting, artful, and attractive. Evaluators like them because they are helpful in analyzing data, are effective tools of presentation, and are an expression of their profession. Evaluators also like pictures because they provide an entertaining backdrop for what might be professional-sounding but otherwise dull prose.

Unfortunately, with one exception, these are all reasons why evaluators should not put these particular types of graphics in their reports. Here is why not.

Large graphics are far more noticeable than any of the other enhancements already discussed: type size, bold and italic type, lists, and so on. Imagine that you are skimming a report. What you notice are the large graphics—the graphs, pictures, cartoons, tables, and formulas. Now apply the fundamental principal of enhancements to large graphics: "Use graphics to highlight and clarify your message. Don't use them for anything else." Is the graph you notice while skimming the report about the main message? Is it about the major finding? Is it about the most important recommendation? If so, it should be there. If not, it should not be used.

Graphs and tables are also tools for analyzing. They can reveal relationships, distinctions, trends, significant differences, and inconsistencies. They can also be useful for describing and emphasizing. But graphs that are good for analyzing may not be best for describing or emphasizing. For example, a key correlation might have been revealed with the help of a graph with one independent and four dependent variables, dozens of data points, and four different families of curves. But the best graph for emphasizing and explaining the correlation might be a simple straight line that illustrates the general nature and magnitude of the relationship between two variables. Clearly, the second one should go in the report, even if the evaluator is prouder of the first one. Box 28.9 gives more advice about graphics.

It is worthwhile elaborating on the fourth tip in Box 28.9. Recall that a major reason for using a large graphic is to illustrate critical background information or emphasize major findings. For this reason, you can really exploit graphs by making your message explicit in the title. Consider, for example, Figure 28.1, a graph that could be used to set the focus of the foster parent recruitment report. Then look at Figure 28.2, which is the same graph but with a title in the form of a short sentence that tells the story.

Box 28.9. Tips on Using Large Graphics in Reports

- If you use graphics at all, include one for the most critical piece of background information or one or two for the most important findings. Otherwise do not use any, because any idea associated with a graphic automatically becomes a major topic or finding in the reader's mind, even if it is not one.
- Use one or two graphics in the ten-page report. Put lots more in technical reports, where they are more useful analytically.
- Keep graphics simple. For graphs, use standard types with few bars, lines, and slices. Limit their detail and style to the default versions commonly available in grant-producing software. They are easy to produce and read.
- Instead of noun phrases, use abbreviated versions of the major findings as titles of graphs and tables, in order to drive the point across. See the examples on the next page.
- In a short report, limit the number of rows and columns in tables to two or three each. This creates emphasis. Omit interior lines for demarking rows and columns. They are not needed for short tables and are visually distracting.
- Long, complicated tables can be useful in long technical reports, although even there they can be boring and exhausting to the reader.
- Make graphs and tables large enough to read. Watch out for and avoid tiny text or numbers in the keys, source notes, and axis data points.

FIGURE 28.1. GRAPH WITH A TYPICAL TITLE FOR THE FOSTER PARENT RECRUITMENT REPORT.

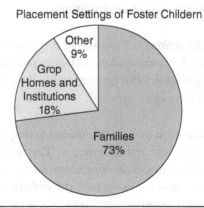

Placement Settings of Foster Childern

Source: Adapted from information in U.S. Department of Health and Human Services, Office of Inspector General, 2002.

FIGURE 28.2. GRAPH WITH A MESSAGE IN THE TITLE FOR THE FOSTER PARENT RECRUITMENT REPORT.

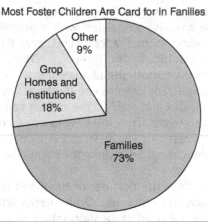

Most Foster Children Are Card for In Fanilles

Other 9%

Grop Homes and Institutions 18%

Families 73%

Source: Adapted from information in U.S. Department of Health and Human Services, Office of Inspector General, 2002.

Power Writing. Power writing is a writing style intended to be very easy to understand and emphatic. It is defined by this purpose and by the techniques that it uses to achieve them. It lends itself very well to use in evaluation reports because it forces the writer to get to the point and enables the reader to grasp the main message and the thread of logic underlying the findings and recommendations. It provides simple explanations but without superficiality. Box 28.10 explains how to do power writing.

Physical Considerations. Even the best report that serves up insightful findings and practical recommendations using cogent and unforgettable prose and mind-grabbing graphics can be forgettable if some simple but crucial physical considerations have been ignored.

Color. Even the most ordinary household computer can easily produce sharp color images and text enhancements. This is especially useful for graphs, because the colors allow distinctions beyond those that can be illustrated using black, white, and gray tones. In fact, the default versions of the simple graphs produced by most popular word processing programs use color. The bright colors also give reports an attractive, appealing professional appearance. By all means, take advantage of these color features to enhance your reports, especially if your main reporting outlet will be the Internet or an e-mailed PDF or if your report will be printed out on paper by a professional print shop or publisher.

Box 28.10. Tips on Power Writing—How to Do It

- The most important sentence of any paragraph is usually the first; sometimes it is the last.
- Try to express the principal thought of each paragraph in the first sentence, which makes skim reading easy.
- Use the last sentence as the power sentence if you need the paragraph itself to introduce the power thought, lead the readers up to it, or surprise them with it.
- Use the body of the paragraph to elaborate on or introduce the power sentence. Elaboration includes evidence, explanation, effects, and pros and cons.
- Readers are put off by long sections of unrelieved type. Try to keep paragraphs down to a quarter of a page and never more than a third of a page.
- Break sentences into small chunks. Try to avoid sentences of more than two lines each. Long sentences are a real put-off for skim readers and can be confusing.
- Avoid technical jargon. Executives are able to express complex thoughts in common language and appreciate others who can do the same thing.
- The passive voice leads to ambiguity and complex sentence structure. It obfuscates. Use it when that is what you want to do (as you may sometimes deliberately and legitimately choose to do). Otherwise, use the active voice.
- Do not use abbreviations. Spell the name or phrase out fully on the first use. After that you may be able to use a shorter version of the name or a pronoun (such as "it," if it is clear within the context).

Be careful though. Most professional offices also have color printers, but because of their expense, they use them only for important briefings or for special copies of reports that will be handed out to important, senior-level officials. Copies of your e-mailed color report rendered in black and white (*grayscale*) by the ubiquitous black and white printers used in most professional work offices may actually look awful. Colored graphs may look muddy in grayscale, and the distinctions between the sectors in pie charts or adjoining sections of other colored graphs may disappear.

To solve this problem, you have to experiment a bit to develop a version of the graph that will look professionally sharp, with the necessary distinctions showing clearly in either color or black and white formats.

Paper Copies.   More and more, professionals, including thought leaders and key staff, read electronic versions of reports on computer screens. However, some still prefer paper copies, especially if they read while traveling or bring home things to read at night. So it is still worthwhile investing in a good paper copy. However, the paper copy they read will most likely be a copy that someone other than you has given them, a fact that leads to two fundamental principles:

- Make it easy for others to print or copy your report.
- Make it hard for them to ruin it in the process.

As obvious as these principles seem, they are frequently violated, and with disastrous results. Box 28.11 has tips for these principles.

Box 28.11. Tips on Helping Others to Make Great Copies of Your Reports

- Others are far more likely to copy the shorter version (such as an executive summary or short executive report) than the longer technical version.
- Make it easy to remove the cover. Staple it on, or put the report in a folder or three-ring binder. That will make it easier to copy the report.
- Print on only one side of the paper. Although newer copy machines can easily print both sides of a document page, more than half the time it does not happen. If your report pages are printed on both sides, odds are high that many readers will receive a copy with every other page missing.
- If you want a nice colored version to hand out, also produce a sharp black and white version, with appropriate reformatting, to use for making black and white copies.
- Let the first inside page be a black and white version of the cover. The recipient will instinctively use it for making copies, and subsequent readers will not be introduced to a murky version of the report with an illegible title, the inevitable result of copying the colored cover.
- Use standard business-size paper so no one has to fuss with different paper trays in copying the report.

Electronic Reports. It is now easy to e-mail the report to others or to put it on the Internet. But the electronic version will also get mangled when opened unless precautions are taken. Remember that the message has to be carried by the layout, the typography (font characteristics like styles, sizes, bold, and underlining), and the graphics. Yet, that is the part that is least likely to come out as it originally looked.

Even if recipients have the same word processor, even the same version, the report will not necessarily come out on the recipient's end looking like the original. That is because the font may be slightly different on different computer screens and printers. Even a slight difference can cause a word to slip down to the next line or up to the previous line. That one word can shorten or lengthen a paragraph or page by a line; the latter event can leave the reader at the other end with orphan text (the last line of a paragraph at the top of the next page) and widow headers (a header at the bottom of the page whose associated text starts on the next page). Far worse, it can cause an entire graph or table to slip to the next page, leaving a huge white space on one page and totally destroying the pagination and layout of the entire rest of the report. Other things can go wrong, too. In lists, for example, the tabbing distance may not be the same, and the wraparound programming will be foiled, turning carefully crafted lists into unreadable jumbles of words and spaces.

Box 28.12. Tips on Producing Reliable Electronic Reports

- *PDF.* Produce a PDF version if possible. It preserves text almost exactly as you see it. Almost all computers include at least a read-only version of this program. One way to create PDFs if one does not have the dedicated software is to use a printer that will scan a document and send the scan to one's computer as a PDF file, which can then be e-mailed.
- *Web version.* Many word processors give you the option of saving your report in web format (HTML). Although it will look different from the written report, you can edit the web version to make it clear and attractive.
- *Web posting.* If you can, post the report on the web and send recipients the web address. You can also e-mail a click-on web link quite easily, which is universally readable and transmits quickly, or copy the link into an e-mail, relieving recipients of the chore of pulling down an attachment. Be careful with the spacing in your report, though. Do not use the computer's tab, insert, or centering features. Instead, type spaces one at a time to achieve these effects.

Evaluators may have to do some extra work to avoid all these problems, but given the pervasive use of e-mail and the Internet, it may be well worth the effort. See Box 28.12 for some tips on how to do this.

Presentations.   A speech or presentation can make a powerful impression on others. If they are stakeholders or other important people, this is an unparalleled opportunity to persuade them of the wisdom of the report.

Speech is also ephemeral. Word of mouth about how good a speech or presentation was can extend its effects, but only to a few people and only so far as the person relating what was said can also speak or write effectively and can represent the presentation accurately. All the ideas in the presentation will go through the sieve of others' minds and will be bent and colored by their interests, biases, and how their minds work. Make it easy for them to get the story right. Give them a piece of writing that they can copy and attach to meeting minutes or use as an outline and reminder of the concepts when they write articles based on it.

Box 28.13. Tips on Preparing Overheads and Handouts

- *Six-slide limit for overheads.* If you need to use more slides, put the additional information in a handout. This is not a hard-and-fast rule, though. Much depends on the pace and style of presentation.
- *Five-line limit per slide.* With more lines, the type is too small to be read. Nevertheless, there is much room for exceptions. The size of the room and the screen make a big difference.
- *Topic phrases only.* Do not use complete sentences.
- *Color slides.* Use the color in the overhead slide projections to advantage, but be careful that the text is readable. Dark backgrounds make this difficult.
- *Black and white handouts.* Create handouts in black and white.
- *Pictures.* Add a cartoon or picture to each slide to set the mood and make the slide more interesting. However, make sure the pictures are related to the message. Otherwise, the audience will enjoy the slide show and forget your message.

Evaluators can greatly enhance their speech with information projected on a screen through slides. And they can put their point across effectively at a briefing if they give everyone a handout that emphasizes the important points. Box 28.13 has suggestions for doing both. An example of a slide presentation for the foster parent recruitment report can be found in Exhibit 28.2.

Conclusion

Be sure to break any of these rules and ignore any hints that do not make sense for your situation. There are many cases in which what has been suggested in this chapter does not apply. However, to put things in perspective, Boxes 28.14 and 28.15 set out a simple formula and a golden rule for writing for impact.

EXHIBIT 28.2. SLIDE PRESENTATION FOR THE FOSTER PARENT RECRUITMENT REPORT.

Recruiting Foster Parents

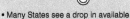

Purpose: To Assess States' Efforts to Recruit Foster Parents

Foster Children

- 581,000 foster children in 2000
- 73% are cared for in families
- Many have special needs
  - o Adolescents
  - o Sibing groups
  - o Mental, behavioral, emotinal challenges
  - o HIV positive
  - o Drug addicted
  - o "Shakan baby" syndrome

Recruitment

- Many States see a drop in available foster parents
- They are ramping up recruitment efforts
  - o Public service announcements
  - o Newspapers
  - o Presentations to civic and religious groups
  - o Presentations at fairs, malls, schools
- Still, shortages continue

Evaluation Methodology

- 50 State mail survey
  - o State policies
  - o Recruitment methods
  - o Recruitment barriers
- 41 responses received
  - o Repersent 81% of children in non-relative care
- 5 Stae in depth review
  - o Geographically diverse
  - o Contains 53% of foster children
  - o Mix of State and county run systems
- Interviews and focus groups with
  - o 115 forster parents
  - o 107 chid welfare staff

Findings

- Current methods focus on wrong audience
  - o Most families with unwilling or unable to care for children with severe prolems
  - o Best source would be netwoks of current foster parents
- Barriers
  - o Unfavorable public perception of foster care
  - o Cumbersome requirements
- States unable to measure success of specific recruitment techniques

Recommendations

- Use netwoks of foster parents to reach parents willing to care for hard-to-place children
- Promote positive puplic perception of foster care
- Share effective practices
- Provide technical support to child welfare office

Box 28.14. Formula for Success

- *The Mom Test.* Summarize the report in one or two simple, compelling sentences.
- *Findings.* Provide two to five findings that bring new facts or insights to the subject matter.
- *Options and recommendations.* Offer numerous practical options for solving the problems raised by the findings.
- *Power writing.* Get to the point, and use simple, clear sentences.
- *Layout, typography, and graphics.* Use these tools to highlight the message.
- *Thought leaders.* Put the report into the hands of all the key stakeholders.

Box 28.15. Golden Rule

- Make the message jump off the page.
- Make sure nothing else does.

Reference

U.S. Department of Health and Human Services, Office of Inspector General. *Recruiting Foster Parents.* OEI-07–00600. Washington, DC: U.S. Department of Health and Human Services, May 2002. http://oig.hhs.gov/oei/reports/oei-07–00–00600.pdf.

CHAPTER TWENTY-NINE

CONTRACTING FOR EVALUATION PRODUCTS AND SERVICES

James B. Bell

The goal of evaluation contracting is to procure needed evaluation services and products from an appropriately qualified evaluation contractor. The procurement process usually involves a competition among prospective contractors, or *offerors*, which results in a contract award. The contract specifies the expected services and products and financial and administrative terms and conditions under which the evaluation will be conducted. Evaluations might also be *contracted for* under grants, cooperative agreements, or other types of formal agreement with similar provisions.

Types of contractors include large and small for-profit firms, academic institutions, nonprofit agencies, and solo consultants. Despite the existence of a formal agreement, *sponsors*—the organizations that procure evaluations—are highly dependent on how well contractors understand and respond to their intent. Is the contractor—with the sponsor's support and oversight—able to execute the series of day-to-day activities that will yield high-quality products and services that fulfill the intent of the contract?

The practical advice in this chapter focuses on five areas:

- Creating a feasible, agreed-on concept plan
- Developing a well-defined request for proposal (RFP)
- Selecting a well-qualified evaluator that fulfills the intent of the RFP
- Constructively monitoring interim progress
- Ensuring product quality

The guiding principles in each area encourage sponsors to shepherd their investment throughout the course of an evaluation (see Box 29.1). The sponsor should then be able to use the evaluation products to enhance performance or communicate the value of the program evaluated and also build internal evaluation capacity. These principles respond to formidable challenges that can affect the timeliness, cost, and quality of evaluation products. For instance, a usual practice is to divide procurement responsibilities among several sponsor staff members. With multiple involved parties from both the sponsor and contractor organizations, keeping everyone's efforts productively aligned throughout the evaluation is an overriding concern. The contractor staff members answer to a leadership authority whose priorities for use of staff at a particular time may or may not align with the sponsor's expectations. The challenges are heightened because evaluations differ with regard to purpose, scope, size, method, work plan complexity, and cost. Evaluation projects also differ with regard to the nature of the program or organization being evaluated and the characteristics of the sponsor—as well as in the qualifications and working style of the contractor staff.

These types of challenges affect the likelihood that evaluation products will meet high technical standards. For example, contractor staff members may possess strong methodological capabilities, but their efforts might be hindered by a weak working knowledge of the subject program. Moreover, staff members may be unaware of the organizational dynamics within and around the program.

Box 29.1. Five Principles for Successful Evaluation Contracting

Principle 1. Establish a solid foundation by creating a feasible, approved concept plan that outlines key elements of the procurement.

Principle 2. Ensure that offerors will understand the key elements of the purchase by developing a well-defined, appropriately prescriptive request for proposal (RFP).

Principle 3. Select a well-qualified evaluator that fulfills the intent of the RFP and adapts to changing circumstances as needed.

Principle 4. Constructively monitor interim progress to shepherd high performance by the contractor, without unnecessarily interfering or hindering progress.

Principle 5. Ensure the quality and usefulness of major products by promoting early review and discussion of emerging findings, using internal briefings to conserve resources.

The number of active evaluation contracts is not known, but it is reasonable to surmise that thousands are currently underway throughout the world involving hundreds of millions of dollars. Despite this large investment, little practical advice has been written on contracting for evaluation services and products. Stufflebeam's *CIPP Evaluation Model Checklists* (2007) offers ten checklists of activities to consider for a variety of evaluation types such as context evaluation and impact evaluation. The first checklist addresses contractual agreements. (Other relevant publications are listed in the Further Reading section at the end of the chapter.)

The remainder of this chapter is organized by five principle focus areas. The discussion of each area begins with a description of the sponsor-created document(s) within that area. This is followed by a description of the opportunities and challenges and practical suggestions for navigating the procurement process within each area. For each area, a chart identifies the most frequently occurring *pitfalls* and practical suggestions, or *tips*, for avoiding those situations. The practical suggestions are intended to aid sponsor staff responsible for accomplishing the goal of evaluation contracting. Contractor staff should also benefit because successful evaluations reflect a productive collaboration between sponsor and contractor staffs. In addition, even though tasking in-house staff to conduct an evaluation does not technically constitute *contracting*, the same principles and practical suggestions given in this chapter should apply in that situation as well.

Besides funding level, large- and small-scale evaluations are distinguished by variations in features, such as availability of sponsor labor to manage and oversee the procurement and sponsor organization size and standard procurement processes. The practical advice herein concentrates on how to apply key principles for large evaluations that generally involve more rigorous procedures. But small evaluations benefit from at least minimal attention to each key consideration for each procurement step. Advice is offered below on scaling down sponsor activities and documentation for small evaluations. While small evaluations benefit from considering key points for large evaluations, the sponsor effort expended should be commensurate with the funding level of the evaluation.

Creating a Feasible, Approved Concept Plan

Most evaluation procurements require prior approval from a high-level sponsor official with the authority to commit resources. Those who are directly involved in the procurement gain this approval by submitting a short *concept plan* (or *purchase plan*). This document also serves as a vehicle for gaining internal agreement on the plan's key elements among such sponsor staff members as those who are responsible for the program that will be evaluated and those who will be responsible for overseeing the evaluation. The first step in successful evaluation contracting is the creation of a feasible, approved concept plan. Feasibility is judged by the match between the expected technical products and delivery schedule on the one hand and the estimated cost and period of performance on the other. An unfeasible concept plan results when those involved in shaping the plan are not sufficiently knowledgeable about the amounts of labor and calendar time needed to develop the intended evaluation products.

The evaluation marketplace presents an array of types of services that might contribute to fulfilling the mandate of an evaluation. It is important to distinguish between evaluation studies and applied research and to recognize the overlap of information technology (IT) services with either evaluation studies or applied research. For example, if an organization obtains applied research or IT services in support of strengthening its program evaluation capacity, these purchases should be guided by an overarching plan—one that guides the ways in which the IT or applied research supports program evaluation. An organization might hire an IT service provider to create an automated records system that yields evaluation data as a by-product of administrative record keeping. In turn, those records might be tabulated and analyzed to generate valued statistical reports, such as month-to-month changes in the number of clients served and trends in client characteristics—two, valued process evaluation measures for most client-serving programs and organizations. A brief summary of practical suggestions for overcoming a major pitfall in concept planning is shown in Box 29.2.

Box 29.2. Tips on Creating a Feasible, Approved Concept Plan

Pitfall
The evaluation starts with unreasonable expectations, ambiguous aims, or internal disagreements that continue throughout the procurement, undercutting product quality and usefulness.

Tips
- Decide on key elements—subject, scope and purpose, main products, delivery schedule, total cost estimate, period of performance, and procurement approach.

- Verify that prominent internal and external stakeholders agree on key elements (if agreement is uncertain, use evaluability assessment techniques before the purchase or as the contractor's first step).
- Ensure that products and services are deliverable within the delivery schedule and budget.
- Ensure that the evaluation contributes to building sponsor capacity to purchase evaluation in addition to fulfilling the immediate contract intent.

Key Elements of a Concept Plan

The following are key elements of a concept plan that must be *decided on*, but not exhaustively documented:

- The subject and purpose
- The intended audience for the findings
- The major product(s) that will be forthcoming
- The product delivery schedule
- The period of performance
- The expected total cost
- The procurement approach

The discussion at this stage might also touch on related matters, such as the preferred data collection and statistical analysis methodologies. In essence the concept plan is the foundation for the ensuing evaluation and sets the stage for developing a detailed request for proposal (RFP). Mistakes, such as a concept plan that contains an unrealistic match between desired products or types of activities and expected costs and schedule, will hinder later phases of evaluation—ultimately undercutting the quality and usefulness of the products.

The level of detail in the concept plan might vary depending on factors such as contract approval requirements and practices of the sponsor and scale and complexity of the evaluation. When an evaluation is a high priority for the organization or represents a relatively large investment, a greater amount of discussion and deliberation is likely to occur before approval is gained. Regardless, the upcoming procurement is described with the detail needed for the approval process, rather than at the more detailed level needed for the ensuing RFP.

For small evaluations, it is advisable to consider each key element of a concept plan in an organized manner, such as a meeting of key staff members. However, concept plan documentation might be one page. If necessary because of limited available staff time, a small evaluation sponsor should place the greatest attention on the evaluation subject and purpose, intended completion date, and expected cost. Initial decisions on these elements will enable procurement of a small evaluation to move forward.

Shaping a Feasible Concept Plan

Sponsor staff shoulders the burden of creating a concept plan. Primary responsibility usually rests with the *project officer*. This role might be filled by the person who must gain approval to obligate organization funds for the evaluation. Regardless, several sponsor staff members are likely to be involved in decisions that affect specific aspects of the evaluation and also in the multiple stages involved in administering the procurement.

Subject and Intent. The creation of a concept plan usually begins with thoughtful consideration of the mandate or impetus for the evaluation: Who is requesting it? Which program or organization will be the subject? What is the purpose of the evaluation? What is the scope of measurement? How much flexibility do sponsor staff members have in interpreting how to respond to the impetus or mandate?

The impetus for most evaluations is an external mandate, such as a requirement in authorizing legislation, a charge from a foundation's board of directors, or a government accountability requirement like that in the Government Performance and Results Act (GPRA). Conversely, some evaluations are driven by an internal interest, which allows greater flexibility with regard to the purpose, design, and cost. When an external mandate calls for a certain type of evaluation, the sponsor's discretion is constrained in such areas as how the evaluation is designed. These constraints can be troublesome when the external mandate is unrealistic with respect to considerations such as the maturity of the subject program or the state of available measurement technology. For example, it is not uncommon for an external mandate to require intermediate or long-term outcome measures before the subject program is fully implemented.

The mandate is considered first so that ensuing decisions about key elements are consistent with the driving reason for the evaluation purchase. The mandate may be from external or internal sources and have a single or multiple dimensions. For example, a mandate might call for measuring program outcomes for accountability purposes *and* for examining organizational processes to identify inefficiencies.

Ideally, each evaluation should be part of a larger strategy to enhance program and organizational performance, communicate the value of the program evaluated, or enhance transparency and accountability and also to build the sponsor's internal evaluation capacity. This suggests that a new evaluation should be considered and shaped from multiple perspectives in order to respond to both the immediate mandate and contribute to a larger strategy of program or organization performance enhancement.

Intended Audience(s).   The identity of the intended audience should be clarified early because it affects the content and style of evaluation products. Intended audiences can range across numerous subgroups or be narrowly defined. Typically, the types of audiences include some mix of the following groups: funding and oversight officials; local, state, and federal program staff and officials; clients and advocacy groups; frontline staff in a particular field, such as child welfare or HIV prevention; clients and advocacy groups; elected officials and policy staff in the legislative and executive branches of government; boards of directors of foundations and other nonprofit officials; and evaluators and researchers.

Careful audience identification is important because a technically proficient evaluation might not meet the expectations of oversight officials, interested stakeholders, and other internal and external audiences. An unfavorable opinion of the evaluation products can damage the sponsor's general reputation—especially with oversight officials and external stakeholders. When doubt exists, stakeholders' and other audiences' expectations for evaluation information should be examined and confirmed, either as part of the sponsor's procurement planning or during an evaluation-planning activity built into the start of the contract.

Products and Schedule.   The concept plans become more concrete when the focus shifts to the intended main products and delivery schedule. If the evaluation is responding to an external mandate, for example, it is likely that specific questions on program performance must be addressed in a report that is due on a certain date. Thus the main product—usually a final evaluation report—must contain certain measurements in a form that yields credible answers for the intended audiences.

Period of Performance.   Although closely related to the delivery schedule that denotes due dates for major products, the period of performance refers to the start and end dates of the contract. Sometimes there is not enough time between the start and end dates to allow for creation of the intended products. For example, the concept plan might envision a survey that requires time-consuming approvals, as is the case for surveys conducted under federal contracts. The federal Office of Management and Budget must approve these surveys, and the review process can take many months or even a couple of years.

Total Cost.   The amount of money available to fund the evaluation sets boundaries on all other key elements of the concept plan. A well-defined RFP is untenable unless the funding level is established (whether or not the total cost is to be communicated to prospective contractors in the RFP). Moreover, it is not possible to consider the feasibility of the plan without a total cost estimate.

Evaluation budget estimation is plagued by uncertainties. The following are four examples that seem prevalent and influence evaluation cost: (a) the extent to which new data collection instruments and protocols must be developed; (b) the extent to which the collection of data is dependent on the cooperation of parties outside the control of the evaluator or sponsor; (c) the extent to which contractor staff has a proven record of undertaking similar tasks successfully; and (d) the extent to which the client is likely to be heavily involved in all phases of the evaluation.

Procurement Approach.   The choice of procurement approach is a pivotal decision because it affects both the amount of effort sponsor staff members expend during the solicitation as well as the potential offerors involved in the competition. Typically, the sponsor staff member responsible for overseeing the administrative and financial terms of the contract or contract officer is heavily involved in this decision.

The most basic and commonly used approach is a *full and open* competition with only a few eligibility restrictions on potential offerors. For example, the procurement might be limited to legal entities in the United States or to entities based in a specific U.S. state or region. However, depending on the rules governing the sponsor, there may be myriad other restrictions and limitations, including so-called set-asides for small, minority-owned or woman-owned businesses. There are numerous set-aside categories defined by characteristics of the candidate business owners or legal status of these businesses (for-profit versus nonprofit). A staff who is creating a concept plan needs to be aware of the set-aside options, if they exist, and then must determine whether the organization prefers certain procurement approaches that restrict eligibility or limit competition.

Some organizations, especially when purchasing small evaluations, employ an incremental approach to streamline the pre-solicitation phase, which extends up to the finalization of a contract. The first step is to solicit brief concept proposals. Then, based on the sponsor's review of these proposals, a small number of offerors are chosen to submit full-scale proposals. This tactic has the advantage of limiting the investment at the beginning of the solicitation process for both the sponsor and the offerors. The sponsor does not have to create a fully developed RFP, and the interested offerors do not have to write full-scale proposals until their concept proposals are accepted.

One of the most pronounced changes in the evaluation marketplace is the growing use of so-called umbrella contracts or other forms of pre-qualification, which often go by more technical names, such as *ID/IQ Task Order Contracts*. Several state agencies also have adopted this practice. These contracts enable purchasers to prequalify numerous evaluation service providers in anticipation of the issuance of *request for task order projects* or (RFTOPs) for specific evaluations. The establishment of a pool of prequalified contractors increases the likelihood that at least some evaluators will submit proposals when an RFTOP is issued.

In some instances when an umbrella contract or pre-qualified group does not exist, sponsors preselect a small number of competitors and send the RFP to them directly. This practice, *limited competition*, is useful when a sponsor knows a small group of well-qualified evaluators and is reasonably confident a sufficient number will respond to a given RFP. Otherwise, a limited competition can backfire, leaving the purchaser without an appropriately qualified offeror. The use of limited competition can be more resource intensive for the sponsor than the previously described umbrella contracts or prequalified groups of evaluators.

A sponsor occasionally desires to retain a specific contractor to conduct an evaluation, based on prior experience with that contractor or the contractor's reputation. This practice, known as *sole source procurement*, greatly simplifies the purchase. The contractor enters the process earlier than would be acceptable in an open competition. In turn, the contractor can help to shape the evaluation. The success of this practice rests on the integrity of the contractor. There are no competitors to ensure for the sponsor that the proposed technical approach and cost equate to what might be achieved in either a full and open or a limited competition. That said, the sponsor's job is eased considerably because much of the effort involved in the pre-solicitation and contractor selection phases of the procurement is avoided.

Developing a Well-Defined Request for Proposal

The existence of a feasible approved concept plan (or purchase plan) positions the sponsor staff to develop a well-defined RFP (sometimes referred to as a *request for application* or RFA). An RFP documents the sponsor specifications for what will become the technical and business provisions of the evaluation contract. The technical specifications in the RFP are analogous to the blueprints for a brick-and-mortar construction project. The RFP should be unambiguous and offer an appropriate level of prescription—a level that accurately conveys the technical and cost expectations without being overly directive in areas better addressed by offerors based on their relevant experience and expertise. Potential offerors should be able to demonstrate how the intent of the evaluation will be realized through their proposed technical approaches. In the worst case, an overly prescriptive RFP might actually dissuade offerors' creative responses by requiring unrealistic activities, products, or data collection and analysis procedures.

A program's history of evaluation is significant with regard to developing an RFP. Must new measures be developed and tested, or will the evaluators use existing, well-accepted measurement tools? How did intended audiences view prior evaluations? Conducting the first evaluation of a program or an organizational component presents more challenges than carrying out an evaluation that replicates a well-established and accepted technical approach. In the latter, high-quality execution is expected; in first-time evaluations, methodology and data collection instrument development usually is a major activity. The design of the evaluation and the amount of professional staff effort needed can greatly affect the complexity of contracting for evaluation.

A brief summary of practical suggestions for overcoming a major pitfall in RFP development is shown in Box 29.3.

Determining RFP Content

An RFP contains two interrelated parts that guide the technical and business aspects of the evaluation purchase. In many cases, these parts are separately submitted and reviewed. Usually, a cover letter conveys the name of the project, offeror eligibility criteria, proposal due date, and sponsor contact information, including the electronic or physical address where proposals are to be submitted. There might also be a requirement for a notice of intent to submit a proposal—an advised technique for gauging how many and which offerors are likely to respond to the RFP. When the competition is restricted to certain types of organizations, such as nonprofits, small, or minority-owned businesses, it should be noted in the cover letter. The cover letter should also offer to respond to questions from potential bidders by a certain date and state that all questions and responses will be shared with all potential bidders.

Box 29.3. Tips on Developing a Well-Defined RFP

Pitfall

An incomplete, ambiguous, or overly prescriptive RFP interferes with an offeror's ability to demonstrate optimal ways to fulfill the evaluation intent.

Tips

- Include sufficient detail on key technical elements—unambiguous and no missing key elements.
- Be appropriately prescriptive—allow offerors to demonstrate creativity to fulfill the intent of the evaluation.
- Present a few overarching evaluation questions to help clarify the purpose (not a great number of narrow, disconnected questions that do not correspond to the scope and purpose).
- Emphasize the main products and major tasks.
- Emphasize the needed substantive and methodological staff qualifications.
- Require a task-level staff-loading chart (described later) for at least the first year of a multiyear contract (allocations of labor in out years can be less precise, but a task-level staff-loading chart should be created before the start of each year).
- Include a total cost estimate expressed as dollars or gross amount of labor (total hours or person-years).

The RFP guides the ensuing steps in the procurement by presenting in greater detail key elements of the concept plan and adding elements that are needed for the competition, such as proposal instruction and proposal review criteria. The RFP should include the anticipated cost of the evaluation (that consideration is sometimes, mistakenly, not disclosed until competing evaluators have had a chance to propose a cost).

Instead of offering comprehensive detail, sponsors of a small evaluation should create a minimal RFP that contains brief statements on essential key points in each proposal section. Sponsors of small evaluations also should encourage questions from, and dialogue with, prospective offerors; shifting some of the burden of clarification to offerors who must interpret guidance in the RFP. Providing key information in each section should allow offerors to respond to an RFP. Another tactic for small evaluation RFPs is to limit the number of proposal pages to ten or fewer and be directive about including specific items, such as a list of deliverable products and delivery dates, a staff loading chart, or a staff qualifications matrix.

Period of Performance.   A potential offeror's first concern is likely to be the dates on which the evaluation will start and end; this information is conveyed in both the main text of the RFP and the cover letter. Without these dates, it is impossible for an offeror to begin gauging whether there is sufficient calendar time to accomplish all the tasks in the statement of work (as described later) with available resources.

Subject and Background.   Evaluations focus on a specific program, program component, or organizational component that defines the subject and scope of evaluation measurement. Evaluation subjects operate in a real-world environment that includes, for instance, program history, evolution, and current policy issues and decision-making agenda. The board of directors of a foundation might desire an evaluation to inform a future decision on whether to expand a program that receives favorable support from stakeholders but lacks independent evaluation. In order to respond astutely to the RFP, prospective evaluators need this information—including the description of subject program and background on why it was formed, how it has evolved, and the board's questions on performance. It is not necessary for the sponsor to present an exhaustive description of the evaluation subject and background. However, the amount of information should be sufficient to enable an offeror to do his own investigation and development of the background section of the technical proposal. If they exist, descriptions of prior evaluations with citations or reference materials should be noted.

Statement of Work.   As the core technical section of an RFP, the *statement of work* (SOW) addresses the evaluation purpose, the main products and delivery schedule, and the expected major tasks and activities or workplan. The SOW should focus on the desired contents and style of deliverable products—the tangible results of an evaluation. These products generally are written reports, but they might also be databases, focus group meeting transcripts, analytical programming (software code statements), audio or visual recordings, or other items generated or collected during the evaluation.

Products to be submitted to the sponsor are considered *deliverable products.* Products developed for internal purposes that are not submitted to the client, such as notes from field interviews, are considered *interim products* and are used to develop deliverable products. The SOW must identify expected deliverable products in sufficient detail to guide an offeror's response. For example, if the sponsor desires a glossy final report suitable for widespread dissemination to the public, this requirement should be expressed because it has direct implications for both needed labor—graphic design expertise—and other direct costs, such as color layout and printing.

The SOW might address aspects of the research design, such as whether to employ a random assignment or quasi-experimental research design or whether, in the case of a qualitative evaluation, to use focus groups, field observations, or semi-structured in-person interviews.

Tasks, subtasks, and activities are the mutually exclusive units of effort (labor), or *building blocks*, into which an evaluation project is subdivided to enable creation of a workplan. *Activities* are the smallest discrete unit here, so multiple activities make up a *subtask*. In turn, multiple subtasks make up a *task*. All project effort should be accounted for in these interrelated units of effort when an offeror creates a technical proposal.

A common error is to present a large number of tasks—more than six to eight—or an overly detailed subtask structure for one or more tasks. Although it is important to identify major tasks, sponsors can over-specify the structure of a technical work plan. As a rule, the sponsor should limit specification to generic units of effort (tasks), such as "develop an evaluation plan" or "collect data from each grantee." A SOW should identify nonnegotiable task or subtasks, such as "submit a draft final report four months before the end date," "conduct a start-up meeting within two weeks of the EDOC [effective date of the contract]," or "conduct two site visits to each grantee over the five-year period of performance." The RFP should state the expected dates for delivering products and finishing tasks.

Estimated Budget. An RFP should include an estimated total budget, expressed as a monetary value or a level of effort (such as person-hours or person-years of labor). The estimate typically offers the annual or multiyear total cost of the project—not the budget for individual project tasks or products. That said, one of the most controversial issues in RFP development is whether to include an estimated budget. Unless the RFP is very specific and detailed about how the evaluation is to be conducted, contractors can scale the evaluation in substantially different ways, depending on the amount of resources assumed to be available for the contract. Without information on available resources, bidders must guess. This guessing game benefits only bidders that somehow gain privileged information on the available amount or are able to deduce the amount from past experience.

Regardless, some sponsors continue to believe it is imprudent to include the funding available for the project, whether in the form of a monetary value or an estimated amount of labor. This position is based on the suspicion that the offerors will simply build up costs to the estimated amount, even if there are less expensive ways to accomplish the same deliverable products. Even though that pricing behavior is possible, the more likely result is that competing contractors will propose the most robust affordable methods. In other words, because a competition is under way, the offerors' incentive is to propose the highest quality technical approach that is achievable with the estimated budget.

Technical Proposal Instructions.   The sponsor can decrease the burden on its own reviewers and encourage precision in offerors' technical proposals by supplying a recommended outline and section-level instructions for those proposals. The proposal outline and section instructions should align with the proposal review criteria (and vice versa). In other words, if one criterion is "the extent to which the offeror demonstrates an understanding of the subject program and emergent policy issues and trends that affect the program," then the outline and instructions should elicit that information from offerors. For instance, requesting a proposal front section entitled "understanding of the problem" or "background" will usually elicit this information.

It is advisable to set strict page limits for the technical proposal (meaning reviewers stop reading and scoring when the page limit is exceeded). The preferred mode is to set an overall limit for the main body of the technical proposal, which allows offerors the freedom to allocate pages to their competitive advantage. Offerors will align page distribution with the points assigned to proposal review criteria (see the following section). A page limit of thirty to forty pages is typical for a technical proposal for a full-scale evaluation sponsored by a federal agency. This limit does not include résumés and descriptions of past evaluation projects, which can be supplied in an appendix. It is also advisable to provide guidance on font size and page margins.

Technical Proposal Review Criteria.   Not surprisingly, the proposal review criteria should parallel the recommended technical proposal outline, which should align with the types and relative importance of information needed to score competing proposals. As a group, the criteria should be comprehensive and reasonably precise, but not too detailed.

With regard to comprehensiveness, the criteria should separately address each of the following domains in the proposal:

- Understanding of the subject and background
- Appropriateness of the proposed technical approach, focusing on data collection and analysis methods

- Feasibility of the workplan, focusing on the description and explanation of deliverable and interim products, tasks, subtasks, and schedule
- Substantive and methodological qualifications of the staff, focusing on the presence of needed qualifications and demonstrated success in conducting similar evaluations
- Qualifications of the offeror (so-called corporate qualifications)
- Quality of the management plan, focusing on project organization, allocation of labor or staff loading, and mechanisms for internal progress monitoring and quality assurance

The scoring weights allocated among these criteria during the review vary somewhat across procurements. The two most important criteria relate to staff qualifications and technical approach. An evaluation is most likely to succeed if the right people are applying the right approach. In a 100-point scoring scheme, these two criteria combined should receive a majority of the points, perhaps 35 and 25 points, respectively. The understanding of the subject would then receive half (20) of the remaining points. With 10 points each, the scoring of corporate qualifications and the management plan will not affect the outcome of the competition, unless these domains are scored very low.

Business Proposal Instructions.   The instructions for the business proposal are often a standardized boilerplate that is used by a sponsor for all procurements, which may limit sponsor latitude to tailor business proposal instructions for a given RFP. When flexibility exists, the sponsor should require submission of a proposed budget that breaks out costs by person, task, and year. Because some competitions are restricted to certain eligible organizations, such as nonprofits, small businesses, or minority-owned entities, the instructions must cite the applicable organization eligibility criteria. For example, different annual revenue thresholds are used to define a small business.

Writing an RFP

A well-defined RFP clearly describes what is expected from the evaluation contractor without being overly prescriptive about aspects that should be left to the experts who will conduct the evaluation. There are areas in which sponsors sometimes become overly prescriptive. For example, a well-meaning sponsor staff member might argue persuasively to colleagues that an evaluation should require annual field visits to multiple community grantees over a five-year period of performance. He or she might not recognize the trade-off in cost between these yearly visits and other data collection activities that could strengthen evidence on outcome achievement. Many experienced evaluators would contend that the added value of information gained by five visits per grantee is not commensurate with the cost and that three or two field visits supplemented with telephone conference calls would achieve similar measurement information at a substantially lower cost. In turn, the saved resources could be redirected to other complementary data collection and analysis activities, such as a client survey or analysis of secondary data from grantee records. Thus, an overly prescriptive mandate on field visits might actually undercut the potential value of products gained from the evaluation.

The burden of writing an RFP can be eased by relying on an example, an RFP used for a past similar evaluation. When available and truly comparable, such an example provides an established template or outline, and sponsor staff members can modify this existing text rather than spend time creating all new text. Over-reliance on the language in an existing RFP might have negative consequences. For example, a new RFP might thoughtlessly borrow from an earlier RFP the requirement for a telephone survey. This might be done without recognizing the high per-respondent cost of a telephone survey and the comparatively smaller total budget for the new evaluation. A more reasonable requirement for the new evaluation might be a mail or web survey with a lower per-respondent cost or a request that the offeror recommends and justifies a survey methodology.

It is also possible to lessen the burden of RFP development on internal staff by engaging contractors, consultants, or other outside parties. Typically, outsider parties who assist at this stage of the procurement are precluded from competing for the evaluation contract.

Selecting a Well-Qualified Evaluation Contractor

After completing a well-defined (appropriately prescriptive) RFP, the focus shifts to the most important activity in the procurement process—selecting a well-qualified evaluator who will fulfill the sponsor's intent. This means ensuring that candidate contractors receive and respond to the RFP, reviewing and scoring their proposals, and negotiating the final contract. Thus, the release of the RFP into the evaluation marketplace initiates the competition.

This section presents detailed suggestions for reviewing proposals and selecting an evaluator that apply to large and small evaluations. However, strict adherence to the guidance might be too resource intensive for a small evaluation. With regard to this seminal step in the procurement process, those in charge of a small evaluation should concentrate their efforts on selecting proposal reviewers, focusing review on contractor staff qualifications. In small evaluations, weak proposals should be quickly eliminated and dialogue initiated with not more than a couple leading competitors. Oral discussions then can address many topics that for a large evaluation would require more extensive documentation.

A brief summary of practical suggestions for avoiding the pitfall resulting from failing to select a well-qualified evaluator is shown in Box 29.4.

Reviewing Proposals

A contractor's response to an RFP consists of a technical proposal and a cost or business proposal. In most competitions, assessment of the quality of the technical proposal should receive the greatest attention and be completed before an accompanying business or cost proposal receives in-depth attention. Only the business proposals of the technical proposals that score in the competitive range should receive careful scrutiny. This cutoff should be a predetermined score that is high enough to warrant a contract award—usually at least 80 out of 100 points, which might float higher when there are multiple high-scoring technical proposals, but it should rarely drop below 75.

Box 29.4. Tips on Selecting a Well-Qualified Evaluation Contractor

Pitfall
The chosen evaluator fails to perform as expected.

Tips
- Provide advance notification of forthcoming evaluations to promote and increase availability of prospective offerors.
- When pressed for sponsor labor to manage the procurement, establish umbrella contracts or a pool of pre-qualified offerors or adopt a phased solicitation process.
- Request notices of intent to submit a proposal.
- Ensure that proposal reviewers have both independence and an appropriate range of expertise.
- Ensure that the proposed contractor staff has demonstrated through performance on similar past assignments the substantive (topical) knowledge and methodological qualifications needed to conduct the evaluation.
- Ensure that the selected offeror's understanding of the problem accurately describes the current state of the subject program or organization.
- Ensure that the technical approach addresses the key evaluation questions with appropriate methods.

Technical proposal review processes vary across sponsors. The review process may involve only one or two reviewers' reactions to submitted proposals, or a multi-tier process may be used to ensure objectivity and transparency. The procedures tend to be simpler for small evaluations launched by smaller organizations. Government agencies and large foundations tend to have elaborate review processes and detailed procedures. For example, a large organization's technical proposal review is likely to involve two levels of initial scoring in which a panel of reviewers applies the *proposal evaluation criteria* stated in the RFP. The first level is scoring by individual reviewers, and the second is collective or panel scoring in which all the individual scores are combined (or averaged).

When all reviewers score all proposals using their own interpretation of scoring standards, variability among reviewers is less problematic. But when the review process involves assigning primary and secondary reviewers to avoid requiring each reviewer to score all proposals, the difference in scoring stringency among individual reviewers impacts overall review panel scores. A proposal that is reviewed only by a stringent scorer(s) would receive a lower score than a proposal of similar quality reviewed only by a more lenient scorer(s). To lessen this scoring dilemma, it is advisable to allow for group discussion and revision of reviewers' original scoring. Without extensive reviewer training and practice, reviewers are unlikely to uniformly apply the evaluation criteria. Group discussion allows the panel score to be a more meaningful reflection of how the reviewers collectively rate proposals in relation to one another.

In addition to generating a numerical score, the technical review should identify questions about and weaknesses in each proposal. These are compiled into a single consolidated written list for use in a later stage of the competition (as described later in the "Best and Final Negotiations" section) and also might be used for a debriefing of unsuccessful bidders.

Selecting the Evaluation Contractor

The selection process culminates with a signed evaluation contract. One of the challenges is to ensure that well-qualified evaluators learn about the RFP and decide to submit a proposal. Another is deciding how to gauge the relative weight of past performance of key staff members on similar evaluations on the one hand and the quality of the proposed technical approach on the other. The demonstrated ability to achieve high performance should trump the ability to conceptualize and articulate a technical approach. After all, a proposed technical approach is a written plan, which is not equivalent to successful performance throughout all phases of an evaluation. However, there should be opportunities, especially on smaller projects, for less established evaluators who demonstrate promise through their training, limited experience, and technical proposal writing skills. In fact, the sponsor of a small project should be concerned with whether a highly qualified individual evaluator has enough available time. However, there are good reasons why a highly qualified evaluator might make a time commitment to a small evaluation, such as topical or methodological interest.

Identify Candidate Evaluators.   An evaluation purchase will fail unless at least one well-qualified evaluator submits a proposal. Perhaps the process should be postponed until there is reasonable assurance that qualified offerors will submit a proposal. There are several ways to reach out to candidate evaluators. Most sponsors have a history of prior evaluations. Prospective evaluators track upcoming evaluations through contacts with sponsor staff members and searches of relevant websites or documents. From a sponsor's perspective, the objective is to draw interest from as many well-qualified evaluators as possible to ensure strong competition.

Evaluators have established methods of tracking upcoming projects, and there are numerous websites that post RFPs, such as the federal government's Fed Biz Ops site (which replaced the earlier hard-copy *Commerce Business Daily*) or postings on state agency or foundation websites. A concern is that by the time an RFP is released—usually with a thirty-day or shorter response time—it is difficult for prospective bidders to assemble a competitive team and write a strong proposal. Some sponsors disseminate a forecast of upcoming evaluations, which is helpful to ensure that evaluators will be ready to respond when the RFP is released. Unfortunately, this practice is not widespread, so there are many instances when well-qualified evaluators are unable to respond to an RFP with a short submission deadline.

Disseminate the RFP.   Over the past several years, tracking services have emerged that scour the websites of government agencies, national and international foundations, and other large organizations for evaluation RFPs. On a fee-for-service basis, these firms use keyword searches to identify evaluations that are posted on websites that carry a voluminous number of RFP announcements for all types of goods and services—not just evaluations. Increasingly, the websites of professional associations such as the American Evaluation Association are used by smaller foundations to post evaluation RFPs. Government agencies, however, are bound by procurement regulations on how, where, and when evaluation RFPs are posted. Evaluations are handled the same way as all other government procurements, which further complicates identifying upcoming evaluations among the many upcoming agency-sponsored purchases.

Form a Review Panel. The sponsor's review follows different pathways for a technical proposal and a business (or cost) proposal. The technical proposal usually has the highest priority and therefore receives the most intensive scrutiny. Most evaluation RFPs state that technical quality supersedes price considerations in the selection of a contractor. Also, the cost proposals accompanying technical proposals that have scored in the competitive range are sometimes the only ones that receive a thorough financial and administrative review. This review is carried out by sponsor *contract officers* and *contract specialists,* staff members who manage the financial and administrative requirements of the procurement.

Depending on sponsor organization policy and practice, an "independent" review panel might be convened to score proposals according to the RFP proposal evaluation criteria. In some nongovernment organizations, the review is conducted solely by those who wrote the RFP. When an independent panel conducts the review, there is an effort to minimize real and apparent conflicts of interest among those who are chosen to serve on the panel. For instance, the official in charge of the subject program is not likely to serve as the chair of the review panel, although it is not uncommon for that person, or other program representative(s), to be on the panel. The person who will serve as the sponsor's *technical project officer* for the evaluation often chairs the review panel. Other members of the panel should reflect the types of substantive and methodological expertise needed to conduct the evaluation. It is advisable to achieve both independence and balance in perspectives and expertise among reviewers, lest the scoring focuses myopically on one or a few areas. The contract officer might also be on the panel (or be a consultant to the panel) to focus on the financial and contract administrative aspects of the purchase.

Typically, a panel has a small number of members (four to six), so there are inevitable gaps in expertise that should be acknowledged. When an important matter for which the panel lacks expertise is at issue such as in-depth knowledge on a proposed statistical analysis technique, a bona fide expert should be asked to assist but only if the issue is a major factor in the competition.

An array of more or less elaborate processes is employed by review panels. One option is that all members review and score each proposal. Alternatively, a *primary* and one or more *secondary* reviewers might be assigned to each proposal. The latter process is used when there are a large number of proposals to consider or a short period in which to complete the review.

The following sections discuss considerations related to each section or topic that is normally addressed in a technical proposal review. The order of this discussion and level of detail are meant to signal their relative importance in selecting an evaluator. Because the qualifications of the proposed staff—especially the proposed project director's record of positive performance in conducting similar evaluations—are the most likely determinant of a successful purchase, the discussion begins with that topic.

Review Staff Qualifications. The proposed staff should possess the qualifications needed to conduct the planned evaluation activities on schedule in a high-quality and effective manner. This is best demonstrated through performance on similar past evaluations. The RFP should request a staffing matrix and accompanying text on qualifications to ease reviewers' scoring of proposed staff qualifications. The substantive (subject matter) knowledge and methodological qualifications needed to conduct the evaluation are arrayed on the rows, and the identities of proposed staff are the column headings. The cells in the matrix are then marked to indicate the individuals whose qualifications demonstrated in past similar or related evaluations match those needed for the current evaluation. An offeror's staff qualifications matrix should be scrutinized with regard to comprehensiveness and balance across needed areas of experience and expertise.

The marked cells are not sufficient evidence of a desired qualification. Therefore, the reviewers should carefully review the accompanying text and résumés of key staff members, especially if they are not known to the reviewers through past performance. If necessary, reviewers should craft follow-up questions about the qualifications of key staff members for possible use during best and final negotiations.

Substantive qualifications are the knowledge, skills, and experience that demonstrate familiarity with the program and subject area: Is enough basic understanding of the program and environment present in proposed staff members to provide a foundation for executing the evaluation? Without staff members who have training and experience in the applicable data collection and analysis methods, the evaluation will founder. Reviewers' assessments of the methodological qualifications of proposed staff should reflect the requirements of each stage of the evaluation: research design and instrument development, data collection, data analysis and interpretation, and report writing. It is useful also to consider distinctions among social science research methods—such as survey research, statistical modeling, and various qualitative approaches.

In scoring the qualifications of proposed staff, reviewers should make allowances for the transfer of knowledge and skills across evaluations. For example, with regard to transferable substantive qualifications, a currently popular initiative in many social programs is *services integration* or the coordination of services across multiple provider organizations. Knowledge gained about services integration in one program arena should apply in evaluations of other social program arenas with services integration objectives. Similarly, common functions and processes are present in most social programs. Administration and management, financing, frontline service delivery, case management, and manual and automated record keeping are functions found in most social programs. Knowledge and experience in these functional areas are transferable across programs. Moreover, evaluations can be successfully conducted by staff with a low level of substantive knowledge if the project allows for a learning period.

In scoring the proposed staffing, attention should be paid to the mix of senior, midlevel, and junior staff members, including the amount of labor proposed for each individual. The mix of staff levels and labor hours should be appropriate to the creative and problem-solving challenges of the evaluation. For example, a program that has not been previously evaluated requires a greater share of effort by senior staff. In contrast, in a project that is a replication of an earlier evaluation, midlevel and junior and support staff may play a larger role. The senior staff members will retain technical leadership and other overarching responsibilities, but their share of total project labor should decline in an evaluation where the detailed technical approach is being replicated. The reviewers should pay close attention to the total amount of time to be devoted to the evaluation by key senior staff, particularly the project director. These staff members must devote sufficient effort to ensure high-quality products. It is not uncommon for offers to propose highly regarded senior staff with a proposed level of effort that is not sufficient to allow them to make a contribution to the evaluation.

Finally, individual staff members should have interpersonal skills and experiences appropriate to their roles in the project. Because such attributes are less likely than others to be formally documented, it is advantageous to check references or, if feasible, meet with proposed staff members during best and final negotiations.

Review the Technical Approach. This review should focus on whether the proposed approach is responsive to the expressed aims of the evaluation with regard to information collection and analysis. If the RFP lists key questions, an introductory overview should describe how the questions will be answered, including the research design, the methods and instruments for data collection and analysis, and the content of main products. There should be a discussion of the rationale for these decisions and the strengths and potential limitations of the proposed technical approach. The sponsor should encourage offerors to discuss alternatives, if there are viable options within a general technical approach. For example, the RFP might call for data available from multiple sources. An offeror would then be expected to discuss the methodological and cost trade-offs between the data sources.

After these key elements have been assessed, the reviewers should assess the proposed sequence of tasks, subtasks, activities, and interim products that will be completed. The reviewers should be able to understand how the evaluation will be conducted and assess whether the work plan seems reasonable given the technical challenges and the proposed staffing and schedule. An offeror's work plan should incorporate sponsor guidance and provide the necessary structure for contractor management and sponsor oversight if the proposal is successful. Tables and charts that depict these items—such a product delivery schedule, a Gantt chart showing task start and end dates, and a task-level staff loading chart—establish conventions that will be used to communicate about progress if a contract is awarded.

Review the Understanding of the Problem.　Ideally, the offeror's discussion of background should accurately describe the subject program's current state, evolution, and existing data systems, as well as other pertinent aspects of its operating environment and context. It should convey knowledge of salient aspects of the subject area within and around the scope of the evaluation. For example, in a national evaluation of a family court improvement fund, this discussion should address federal program guidelines for court improvement and the operations of local family court and child welfare systems. There should be an understanding of the philosophical and historical underpinnings of child welfare case adjudication and the variations in family court and child welfare systems across state and local jurisdictions.

For some evaluations, deep understanding of the subject program is less important, allowing for less emphasis on this qualification. For example, an evaluation that narrowly examines secondary data on client characteristics might not need staff with in-depth knowledge, although even such narrow focused efforts can benefit from program knowledge.

Review Corporate Qualifications.　The evaluation contract is between the sponsor and the organization that employs the staff members who will conduct the evaluation. This arrangement introduces another level of complexity into the procurement. Hence there is a need to review offeror qualifications to confirm a record of positive performance on similar evaluations with regard to maintaining staffing and completing tasks and products both within the estimated budget and on time.

Review the Management Plan.

An RFP should include an estimate of total cost expressed as a gross monetary value (dollars) or gross labor amount (level of effort expressed in person-hours or person-years). The RFP instructions should require the offerors to turn the estimated total budget into a much more detailed allocation of labor hours for each task and staff member. A *staff-loading chart* is a spreadsheet that shows the allocation of labor, usually person-hours, across tasks or products.

The need for offerors to have the flexibility to fit labor allocations to technical requirements stems from a typical evaluation activity that will consume different amounts of labor depending on how it is conducted. For example, if a "start-up meeting" is required in the RFP, one could estimate fewer than ten hours of labor for a telephone meeting or as much as fifty or more hours for an in-person meeting. The difference in needed labor is accounted for by variation in factors, such as (a) the number of evaluation team members who will attend, (b) the extent of new document preparation required for the meeting, (c) the number of cycles of sponsor review and comment on materials that will be presented or discussed in the meeting, (d) whether long-distance travel is involved, (e) the number of sponsor staff members who will attend and whether it is the evaluation team's responsibility to organize their participation, (f) whether the evaluation team will host the meeting at the contractor's facility, and (g) other special considerations that may be present.

If the proposed staffing includes more than a few people, they should be organized into teams with well-defined roles that facilitate full use of their capabilities. The use of teams, and especially the exchange of information among teams, suggests a collegial structure that still allows the structure and focus needed to accomplish project tasks and responsibilities. The number of teams, team size, and scope of team responsibility should be consistent with the number of project staff members, the evaluation purpose, and the expected products and general workplan of the evaluation.

If there are technical teams, the team leaders should also be on a management team to shepherd their collective efforts. Working closely with the project director, the team leaders have a key role in project management. The management team is involved in most aspects of planning evaluation assignments, monitoring technical progress, and interpreting and integrating products and results from completed evaluation activities. The management team ensures that the evaluation parts are brought together and shaped through internal peer review into the products that present the evaluation results.

For many evaluations, a sponsor workgroup and an external advisory group are also advantageous add-ons to the organization structure. A workgroup helps to promote an exchange of information among the project staff members and individuals representing the sponsor organization or subject program. Program managers and policymakers should be involved if they are expected to use evaluation findings to improve program performance. An external advisory group is composed of independent experts on the evaluation subject or methodology. The group effort usually is applied to quality assurance at critical stages of the evaluation.

Conducting Best and Final Negotiations.   There are two types of best and final negotiations. The most common is a final round of competition among a small number of offerors with the highest technical scores. The other involves only the offeror with the highest technical score. In either case, this final stage of the selection process is the sponsor's last opportunity to resolve major issues before a contract is finalized and before the sponsor's leverage to exact changes is reduced. The best and final negotiations process usually involves the sponsor forwarding to the offeror questions about both the technical and business proposals with a short deadline for a response. Oftentimes the questions focus on the total cost, the distribution of labor among proposed staff, or the schedule. For example, the sponsor might ask about the roles that proposed consultants are expected to play in the project. There might be questions to elicit more details about a particularly important task or product. The sponsor might ask for more explanation about how the offeror will simultaneously conduct complex, multiple data collection activities or how it will synthesize findings from quantitative and qualitative analyses. It is advisable to arrange an in-person or telephone meeting involving key representatives of the sponsor and offeror as part of the negotiations.

Constructively Monitoring Interim Progress

After a contract is awarded, the responsibility of monitoring the contractor's technical progress falls to the project officer or the sponsor employee assigned to project officer–style duties. To guide monitoring expectations, the project officer relies on the delivery schedule, the workplan, staff-loading chart, and the detailed budget determined during best and final negotiations.

The project officer exercises leverage on contractor performance through her or his authority to approve the contractor's monthly invoices and progress reports. It is unlikely that a monitoring plan can be effective without continuous adaptation throughout the life of the project. It is advisable to hold a kick-off meeting to revisit the project plan and discuss the monitoring procedures. The relevant senior staff members of the sponsor and contractor should attend. A key discussion topic should be the sponsor's responsibility with regard to facilitating contractor access to information resources under sponsor control. This might include access to documents and databases as well as people who may be reluctant to cooperate with the contractor without encouragement from the sponsor. A summary of practical suggestions for avoiding pitfalls in progress monitoring is shown in Box 29.5.

Interim progress monitoring absorbs evaluation resources. Monitoring that is too demanding can use unwarranted amounts of project resources, but too little may permit the squandering of project resources on unproductive efforts. The intensity of monitoring is appropriate when the forward momentum of the evaluation is maintained or enhanced. Effort should not be distracted from productive project activity for monitoring purposes, nor should evaluation resources be wasted on unproductive efforts because monitoring did not detect a contractor performance problem. There are many other ways in which interim progress monitoring can derail. A common mistake, for example, is acceptance that a data collection task is completed while data cleaning and quality assurance are still underway. Depending on the number and types of errors detected, a substantial effort might be needed to resolve the errors.

Sponsor monitoring effort is reduced by selection of an appropriately qualified evaluator—a contractor that has a demonstrated record of effectively managing the inevitable unanticipated issues and problems that occur in evaluations. Regardless, the more monitoring information required from the evaluator, the greater the sponsor effort is required to review and act on findings. For small evaluations, monitoring might focus on contractor progress on main tasks involved in producing the main deliverable product: typically a final report. For example, if the evaluator identifies a few major interim tasks and target dates, periodic updates on completion should be sufficient to allow sponsors to track progress on the main deliverable in relation to expenditures. A simple table that displays total costs incurred to date and task status can be provided by the evaluator. These updates—usually monthly—will allow sponsor staff members to identify problems that require action, such as a revised work plan to address an emergent issue.

Box 29.5. Tips on Constructive Interim Progress Monitoring

Pitfalls

The evaluation proceeds more slowly and expensively than expected or misses chances to avoid problems and capitalize on opportunities.

Tips

- Maintain a constructive collaborative relationship between the sponsor's project officer and the contractor's project director.
- Support the contractor, especially on issues where the sponsor exercises greater control, such as gaining access to documents, databases, and people.
- Create a minimally burdensome progress report format, but require more detail if progress flags.
- Defend against unrecognized shifts in the evaluation mandate by periodically revisiting and discussing that mandate throughout the project period.

Reviewing Progress Reports and Invoices

To establish the progress report template, start with the intended completion dates for major tasks and products—such as completion of a literature review or a data collection and analysis plan—and then move backward. Monitoring milestones for each major product should be defined by considering the main steps in product development. Sometimes a task involves a relatively small amount of labor and substantial calendar time. An example of a calendar-intensive activity is acquisition of data from a government agency, which might involve multiple levels of review and approval. However, any activity requiring support and effort outside the span of control of the contractor should be carefully thought through when setting a monitoring schedule. Avoid a progress-monitoring report format based solely on expended resources and elapsed time, for example, monthly progress markers unrelated to product completion. Such a format disregards the natural development cycle for evaluation products.

It is advisable to create a standard table format to reduce the amount of text required in progress reports. One tactic is to focus on exceptions to planned progress. The contractor reports only an impending delay or labor overrun that will affect the planned schedule for delivering products or expending labor. For this approach to be effective, the contractor must be able to detect trends away from the plan in advance, rather than after a deviation has occurred.

Although there is increasing use of project-tracking software, such as Microsoft Project, these tools are not always well suited to relatively small projects and have drawbacks that should be noted. For example, the use of these tools can absorb inordinate amounts of resources and require monitoring information to fit a standard format that might not align with evaluation task structures. These tools can encourage overly detailed tracking that draws resources away from more productive evaluation activities. That said, some sponsors have already instituted such tracking and management software and made its use mandatory.

Monitoring Process

Interim progress monitoring should be a constructive endeavor, one that encourages recognition of and creative response to opportunities and problems. The monitoring process should enable the project officer to shepherd an evaluation to completion on schedule with the budgeted resources. Progress monitoring also should help contractors to identify opportunities to enhance the value of the evaluation product(s). Common monitoring problems can be avoided by focusing on a well-specified product delivery schedule, well-timed monitoring reports, and effective use of monitoring information.

The monitoring process should be flexible enough to allow contractor staff to complete evaluation products. For example, evaluations are fraught with delays that cannot be predicted or controlled by the contractor because they are caused by such things as an inability to schedule planned stakeholder interviews as quickly as planned or the unexpected absence of a contractor staff member due to illness. The project officer has to be accommodating without ignoring major milestone completion dates. In the example of slower than expected completion of stakeholder interviews, the project officer can encourage the contractor to advance the schedule for one or more other activities to compensate for lost time on the interviews.

Throughout an evaluation, multiple lines of effort are proceeding simultaneously, and that allows this flexibility. Continuing the example of the delayed stakeholder interviews, the contractor could expedite the work on a literature review task or an assessment of the utility of readily available secondary data sources—two lines of effort that will be needed when the stakeholder interviews are completed. In the worst case, the number of stakeholder interviews might be reduced so the evaluation can proceed. Some of the interviews could be conducted later when stakeholders are available.

Well-defined interim project milestones borrowed from the workplan and delivery schedule in the finalized technical proposal and well-timed monitoring do not alone guarantee effective use of progress-monitoring information. The project officer who monitors must be able to interpret information on progress and respond appropriately. She or he must be able to engage in constructive discussions with the contractor's project director. In turn, the project director should know how to adjust contractor staff assignments in response to monitoring findings.

It is not enough for the project officer and the project director to establish a workable monitoring process. In an evaluation with more than a small number of staff members, it is especially important that the mid-level management staff is able to establish internal monitoring processes overseen by the project director. These mid- and lower-level contractor supervisory staff members must be able to interpret monitoring data and to adjust the assignments of their supervisees accordingly. Although it is not part of a project officer's duties to be involved in internal management, it is within her or his purview to inquire of the project director how these processes are working—especially if a consistent pattern of inadequate progress is detected.

Checking the Mandate During the Evaluation

In rare instances, either the project director or the project officer may change the contractor's or the sponsor's interpretation of the mandate during the course of the evaluation. This change must be immediately disclosed to the other party, and agreement should be reached on any shift in the evaluation mandate. Representing the sponsor's interests, the project officer may respond to a changed agenda for decision making during the course of the evaluation. For example, a new legislative proposal or executive initiative may cause the sponsor to shift its views of the preferred measurements taken and analyses performed during the evaluation. Sometimes, the project officer is slow to communicate to the project director that the sponsor expectations for the evaluation have changed.

To defend against unknown shifts in the evaluation mandate, the project director and the project officer should periodically revisit and discuss the evaluation mandate throughout the project period. They can integrate checks on the mandate into routine evaluation activities, such as sponsor review of the data collection and analysis plan. By describing to the sponsor the data that will be collected and analyses that will be performed, the contractor staff creates an opportunity for discussion of possible shifts in expectations for the evaluation. Whether or not changes are identified, the project record should note that the sponsor has rechecked the mandate.

Finally, sometimes a shift in the evaluation mandate is so great that a separate and distinct effort to renegotiate the project purpose, budget, and schedule is required. A change in program leadership, for example, might precipitate such major renegotiations. When this happens, it will probably be necessary to modify the contract.

Assuring Product Quality and Usefulness

The tangible evidence of a successful evaluation is a well-received final report that contains high-quality evaluation information. This and other deliverable reports should communicate the essence of the evaluation in language suitable for the general public, minimizing the use of jargon and insider language. What practical steps can a project officer take in concert with the project director to ensure that reports meet this requirement? Although it is not the responsibility of the project officer and other sponsor staff members to micromanage major products, they should have a strong understanding of how to shepherd products toward crucial milestones in product development. They should facilitate communications between those who initiated the evaluation and the evaluation contractor. Overall, the project officer should devote considerable attention to the specifications for and development of major products. A summary of practical suggestions for avoiding pitfalls through ensuring product quality is shown in Box 29.6.

Box 29.6. Tips on Ensuring Product Quality and Usefulness

Pitfalls
Reports do not accurately convey key evaluation findings in concise, clear language, or rewriting consumes too much of the available resources.

Tips
- Devote considerable attention to the development of major products.
- Encourage, and if necessary require, the use of a stepwise report development process to enable sponsor involvement and conserve project resources.
- Have the contractor start early on analysis, interpretation, and shaping the language of findings using partial data.

The sponsor is advised to require through the RFP that the contractor develop written reports in four steps, with involvement in each step by the project officer and, if warranted, other sponsor staff members and outside experts. This approach is predicated on establishing early agreement about the content of a report through outlines and briefings before extensive labor is expended writing the full text of the report.

The first step is to agree on the outline of each major report. This outline explains the report's purpose, the titles and intended contents of the chapters and sections, and the planned length and style of the document. Agreement on the outline for the final report and other important products should be accomplished in the first technical meeting between the project officer and project director. One way to codify the project's technical mandate—such as the evaluation purpose, subject, and methods—is to develop a detailed outline of the planned evaluation report(s). The final report outline should be referenced as a source of guidance, often in the early preparation phase of the evaluation and throughout the data analysis phase. The possible need to modify the report outline should be part of a continuing dialogue involving contractor staff, the project officer, and representatives of the subject program.

At the earliest point in the evaluation when preliminary data analyses are completed, the sponsor should request development of a briefing package following the outline. The briefing, which is the second step in the report development process, should cover the key points in each chapter and section of the report. The objective is to summarize the essence of the report before actual writing begins. In a briefing format using charts, tables, graphs, other exhibits, and other short forms of written communication such as bulleted lists, the content of the forthcoming report(s) can be discussed without expending the labor required to develop high-quality narrative text. These first two steps of report development are comparatively inexpensive, designed to convey report contents without incurring the cost of writing fully developed documents.

Typically, creation of the briefing can start well before data collection is finalized by using partial data and preliminary analysis results. A common mistake is to wait too long before beginning to analyze, interpret, and craft key messages for the final report. In most evaluations, the main findings are revealed with partial data. Waiting for finalized, cleaned data limits the amount of calendar time and labor available for carefully considering the results, refining the analysis, and honing the written language needed to communicate findings and implications. It is crucial to establish adequate controls on the distribution of a preliminary briefing. The project officer should limit access to those sponsor staff members intimately involved in the evaluation. The contractor staff must exercise similar protections on unauthorized distribution.

The third step should yield a full-scale draft report, which is normally one of the most expensive evaluation activities. Although the report should be complete and readable, the emphasis should be on technical content. Final editing and polishing of the document should be postponed until the technical contents of the final report are reviewed and commented on by the sponsor. The draft final report should be reviewed by the project officer, subject program staff members, and any outside experts engaged as advisers. Distribution of a draft report should be carefully controlled; the project officer should limit reviewers to those who are familiar with the project and understand that the draft report is not a final product.

The final step in report development is polishing the written document to ensure effective communication of the evaluation results to the intended audience(s). If the contractor is new to the sponsor, the project officer should assist in this step by providing examples of reports that demonstrate the sponsor's preferred writing style and presentation format. The project officer should be aware that some reports, such as those intended for very limited internal audiences, do not require the same level of editing and production sophistication as a high-profile document intended for distribution to the general public. A project officer's demand for over-polishing absorbs resources that might have been more usefully spent on more important evaluation activities.

For small evaluations, the quality assurance process can be streamlined by limiting the number of pages in the main body of a report. Much of the technical information on the evaluation subject, purpose, and the methods and data that support main findings can be contained in appendices. Limiting the number of sponsor-affiliated reviewers or requiring a confidential independent review as part of the contract are other ways to assure product quality, while containing burden on sponsor staff members.

Conclusion

This chapter has offered practical suggestions for avoiding pitfalls in the evaluation contracting process that could impede procuring needed evaluation products and services from an appropriately qualified evaluation contractor. The advice covers the steps in contracting from creating a feasible, approved concept plan to ensuring the quality and usefulness of major evaluation products. Much attention was devoted to sponsor-created documents, such as a well-defined, appropriately prescriptive request for proposal (RFP), and key sponsor activities, such as constructively monitoring interim progress. Nevertheless, successful evaluation contracting ultimately depends on the collective technical competencies and communication skills of both contractor and sponsor staffs. Every evaluation presents unique technical and logistical challenges that require resourcefulness by contractor and sponsor staff members who are mutually committed to achieving success.

While the aforementioned advice applies to all evaluation purchases, allowances and adjustments that reduce sponsor effort are needed for small evaluations to ensure a proper balance of sponsor effort in relation to size and complexity of the evaluation.

Reference

Stufflebeam, D. L. *CIPP Evaluation Model Checklists* (2nd ed.). Kalamazoo, MI: Western Michigan Evaluation Center. www.wmich.edu/evalctr/checklists. 2007.

Further Reading

Della-Piana, G., and Della Piana, C. K. "Evaluation in the Context of the Government Market Place: Implications for the Evaluation of Research." *Journal of Multidisciplinary Evaluation*, 2007, *4*(8), 79–91.

Mattessich, P. W. *Planning, Contracting, and Managing for Useful Results*. St. Paul, MN: Amherst H. Wilder Foundation Publishing Center, 2003.

Nathan, R. P. "Point/Counterpoint: Can Government-Sponsored Evaluations Be Independent?" *Journal of Policy Analysis and Management*, 2008, *27*(4), 926–944.

National Cancer Institute Assessments Branch. *Evaluation Contracting Guide: Evaluation Contracting Process*. Bethesda, MD: National Cancer Institute, Office of Science Planning and Assessment, 2007.

Smith, S. R., and Smyth, J. "Contracting for Services in a Decentralized System." *Journal of Public Administration Research and Theory*, 1996, 2, 277–296.

Stufflebeam, D. L. "Lessons in Contracting for Evaluations." *American Journal of Evaluation*, 2007, *21*(3), 293–314.

Western Michigan University, Evaluation Center. *Evaluation Checklist Project*. www.wmich.edu/evalctr/checklists, 1999.

Wisconsin Department of Health and Family Services, Office of Strategic Finance Evaluation Section. *DHFS Evaluation Resource Guide*. http://dhs.wisconsin.gov/aboutdhs/OPIB/policyresearch/EvaluationResourceGuide06–06.pdf, 2006.

CHAPTER THIRTY

USE OF EVALUATION IN GOVERNMENT

The Politics of Evaluation

Joseph S. Wholey

Today those in government face demanding constituencies, interest groups and advocacy groups with legitimate but conflicting interests, and aggressive media scrutiny. Global, national, and local forces demand higher levels of transparency, performance, and accountability, and public trust in government remains low. The meanings of *transparency, accountability*, and *performance* have changed to include outcomes—results that typically lie beyond the control of any one agency or program.

To promote transparency and accountability, legislators, foundations, and other funders are requiring agencies and grantees to measure policy and program outcomes. To meet demands for higher levels of performance, those in government and in nonprofit organizations must find ways to focus reasonable fractions of their resources on specific results and garner the political and bureaucratic support needed for progress toward those results.

Other chapters in this volume discuss challenges in deciding whether and when to evaluate, what to focus on, and how to evaluate—and provide suggestions for overcoming those challenges. In other literature Wilson, Radin, and others have noted that programs vary greatly in terms of the feasibility of performance measurement (see Radin, 2006; Wilson, 1989).

Harry Hatry (personal communications, December 2009, January 2010) has identified political and bureaucratic challenges that manifest themselves when public officials decide what will be evaluated, the evaluation's scope and timing, who will be invited to submit evaluation proposals, the criteria for evaluating proposals, and the persons who will rate the proposals—any and all of which could affect the evaluation. These issues are worthy subjects for another volume and another day, although James Bell (in Chapter Twenty-Nine in this volume) touches on some of them.

After a brief review of some of the developments in use of evaluation in government over the last forty years, this chapter focuses on (1) political and bureaucratic challenges that affect the use of evaluation findings, and especially those that affect the use of evaluation findings to improve program performance; and (2) approaches that evaluators can use to help overcome those challenges. Although the discussion focuses on use of evaluation in government, where political and bureaucratic challenges are especially abundant, much of the discussion applies to the nonprofit sector as well.

Use of Evaluation in Government

Evaluation is used in government to *increase transparency, strengthen accountability*, and *improve performance*—all terms in good political currency. Evaluation is used to inform and assist policy and management decision making, and is at times used to improve the performance and value of public programs—although many political and bureaucratic challenges stand in the way. A *program* is a set of resources and activities directed toward one or more common goals. Programs may include entire agencies, categorical programs, block grant programs in which funds can be used more flexibly, intergovernmental and public-private programs, and *horizontal*, or *cross-cutting*, programs in which multiple agencies share common goals. In many cases program implementation involves managers in a network of agencies.

Program improvement is an especially important use of evaluation because public programs tend to live on once they are created and develop constituencies. Although many examples can be found in which evaluation has been used to improve public programs, all too often evaluations are completed, disseminated, and then remain on the shelf.

Use of evaluation has grown in the U.S. government in response to legislative and executive initiatives, many of which carry political overtones. Use of evaluation grew exponentially in the 1960s. Many evaluation studies were conducted in response to the Economic Opportunity Act of 1964, which was proposed by President John Kennedy and passed by the Congress partly as a tribute to the fallen president. Thousands of local evaluation studies were conducted under the Elementary and Secondary Education Act of 1965 in response to a provision, inserted by Senator Robert Kennedy, requiring that every local Title I project be evaluated every year—although lack of comparability of those studies made it impossible to learn much from them at state or federal levels.

Evaluation grew in the U.S. Department of Health, Education, and Welfare (now the Department of Health and Human Services) after President Johnson's Child Health Act of 1967 amended Title V of the Social Security Act to allow the department to "set aside" (use) *up to* 0.5 percent of maternal and child health program funds for program evaluation and grew even more when the Public Health Service Act was amended to allow the department to set aside *up to* 1 percent of public health program funds for evaluation. In the Department of Labor, evaluation of job training programs grew when funds were made available under the Economic Opportunity Act and under the Social Security Amendments of 1967.

In the 1970s, many local governments began to use performance measurement systems. Dayton, Ohio, and Sunnyvale, California, were among the leaders: Dayton monitored department performance in terms of annual performance targets and allocated salary increases to department heads based in part on department performance; Sunnyvale monitored the quality and results of local services as well as citizen satisfaction, used performance information to achieve progress toward local goals and objectives, and reported to citizens on needs and results.

At the federal level, many agencies and programs were using performance measurement systems as early as the 1970s. The U.S. Employment Service, for example, measured the performance of each state employment security agency and allocated funds for the staffing of state agencies, based in part on their performance in terms of national objectives such as placement of job applicants; placement of veterans, unemployment insurance recipients, and minorities; and the wage levels, expected duration of employment, and skill levels of jobs filled. The Bureau of Community Health Services set performance targets such as immunizing at least 90 percent of young children and allocated additional staff and grant funds to high-performing regions; regional offices allocated additional grant funds to high-performing projects. The U.S. Office of Education set targets for the student loan program—to lower the default rate, move loans from default to repayment status, and collect money due the government—and established incentive systems under which regional office staff could compete for cash incentives and other awards. And use of evaluation studies continued to grow. The Department of Labor, for example, funded a multiyear evaluation of the Job Corps, a high-cost residential program designed to improve the job prospects of unemployed high school dropouts.

Since the 1970s, governments and agencies at all levels have established *performance management systems* in which agencies establish outcome-oriented goals and performance targets, monitor progress, stimulate performance improvements, and communicate results to higher policy levels and the public. Since the mid-1990s, "New York City and, subsequently, the City of Los Angeles saw crime rates plummet after each adopted CompStat" (Office of Management and Budget, 2010, p. 73). Partly because individual evaluation studies are typically time-consuming and are often ignored and because measurement and reporting of the extent of progress toward program goals fits comfortably under the definition of program evaluation, a growing number of evaluators have become involved in these management reform efforts (see National Academy of Public Administration, 2008; Wholey, 1983).

Since the 1990s, use of performance measurement systems has grown in the federal government in response to the requirements of the Chief Financial Officers Act of 1990 (which requires federal agencies to measure program performance, report annually on the results of agency operations, and provide a list of their evaluation studies), and use of performance measurement systems has grown even more in response to the Government Performance and Results Act of 1993 (GPRA). The GPRA requires federal agencies to: develop and update multiyear strategic plans that include outcome-related goals, prepare annual performance plans that include numerical performance targets (in some instances, qualitative targets) for their programs, report annually on program performance in terms of the annual targets, and annually report the findings and recommendations of completed evaluation studies. The legislation that became the GPRA was proposed by a conservative Republican Senator, William Roth, and was based partly on the experience of Sunnyvale, California, after Sunnyvale's former mayor, John Mercer, joined Senator Roth's staff. Roth's bill, which at one time was known as the "Bang for the Buck Act," was amended based on input from the Office of Management and Budget when Senate committee chairman John Glenn signed on as a co-sponsor; GPRA then passed the Senate. GPRA was finally enacted in the next Congress, passing the House partly as a courtesy to the newly elected president, Bill Clinton, who saw GPRA as a quality management initiative that would help in "reinventing government."

GPRA's passage benefited from the political support of the National Academy of Public Administration and the American Society for Public Administration; both organizations passed resolutions and testified that GPRA was supported by public managers. Most federal managers have not been happy with the implementation of GPRA, however: GPRA implementation typically has not involved program managers in defining the goals and targets used to measure "performance"; has imposed increased burdens on managers, staff, and grantees; and has not provided the promised increase in management flexibility in return for those increased burdens.

Use of performance measurement systems also grew in many state governments in the 1990s in response to gubernatorial and legislative initiatives, though some of these efforts faltered in response to fiscal and other challenges (see Aristigueta, 1999). In Florida and Texas, for example, the leadership of governors and subsequent legislation spurred such efforts; in Oregon and Virginia, the state legislatures took the lead. Performance measurement has also grown in state and local government to provide data on the results of federal grant programs.

In the 2000s, high-stakes performance measurement spread to every state and every school district under the provisions of President George W. Bush's No Child Left Behind Act. President Bush's Office of Management and Budget stimulated performance measurement in terms of *multi-year* performance targets and strongly encouraged "rigorous" evaluation studies using experimental designs by requiring federal agencies to respond to its Program Assessment Rating Tool (PART), which was developed when future governor Mitch Daniels directed OMB. Both the No Child Left Behind Act and the PART process remained controversial as President Bush completed his term, partly because their benefits did not appear to match their costs.

During the Obama Administration, OMB repeatedly reinforced its emphasis on rigorous evaluation studies, but indicated that randomized experiments were not the only path to rigor (Office of Management and Budget, 2009). OMB encouraged both the *production* and *use* of information from performance measurement systems and evaluation studies. In 2009, agency heads were asked to develop, commit to, and manage toward a limited number of high-priority performance goals that reflected key agency missions and demonstrated programs' direct public value. The goals and short-term targets were set to be achieved by 2012. With the passage of the GPRA Modernization Act of 2010 (GPRA Modernization), priority goals between and across agencies became a statutorily mandated activity for the twenty-four largest federal agencies along with periodic reviews and public reporting requirements. The law requires that agency priority goals be updated every two years, with quarterly reviews by the agencies' chief operating officers (COO), and cross-agency or agency strategic goals are updated once every four years. GPRA Modernization also better aligned numerous other performance and strategic planning timeframes with election cycles to accommodate priorities when a new president is elected.

As required by GPRA Modernization, OMB created a federal *performance portal*, Performance.gov, to communicate priority goals and results to the public and to congressional leaders (Office of Management and Budget, 2010). The Performance.gov website, launched in 2011, featured the full suite of government priority goals listed by agency and program. Each goal included a designated leader to improve transparency and to encourage accountability for goal attainment.

OMB initiated a series of evaluation initiatives in the first two years of the Obama Administration focused on increasing evaluation funding, strengthening agency capacity to produce and use evaluation, and improving access to data. The Administration proposed new funding for a suite of specific program evaluations and for enhanced federal agency evaluation capacity in targeted agencies. While only a portion of the requested evaluation funds were ultimately appropriated by Congress, additional resources were made available for evaluation during the Obama Administration through the increased use of evaluation set-asides, where a percentage of program funding was directly allocated to performance and evaluation activities. The administration also modified grant criteria for certain programs to increasingly emphasize evidence-based practices in areas such as teen pregnancy prevention and home visiting for parents. In addition, OMB coordinated a series of interagency workshops around common evaluation themes such as creating independent evaluation offices, procurement strategies, and integrating performance and evaluation systems (Office of Management and Budget, 2013). Some of the Obama Administration's planned efforts to improve access to federal data have been fully implemented, such as the launch of data.gov, but other proposed policies have yet to be enacted (Office of Management and Budget, 2014a,b).

While OMB encourages agencies to integrate performance systems and evaluation activities, the coordinating guidance for the two systems tends to not be integrated within OMB or in federal agencies. In addition to the existing performance office at OMB, the Obama Administration created an additional Evidence and Innovation Team to coordinate the government-wide evaluation initiatives. However, many federal agencies still maintain performance operations within budget offices and situate evaluation staff in other program or support offices.

GPRA Modernization effectively modified how federal agencies develop and report on key agency goals, yet whether this information is utilized by the public and congressional leaders is to be seen. Similarly, efforts to improve the production of evaluation in federal agencies have seen mixed results government-wide, although additional efforts to generate more evaluations and to provide searchable websites to disseminate evaluation results are underway in criminal justice, education, health, and labor programs.

Political and Bureaucratic Challenges Affecting Use of Evaluation

Many political and bureaucratic challenges affect the use of evaluation to improve results. At times, the term *politics* refers not only to partisan politics but also to bureaucratic politics: political challenges abound in many arenas in which people are more concerned with their own or their organization's interests than with evaluation findings or the public good. Political challenges affecting the use of evaluation include the nature of the federal system, in which both the federal government and the states are sovereign; the everchanging balance of power between the legislative and executive branches of government and between the two major political parties; intraparty rivalries; and individual legislators' pride of authorship of specific policies and programs. Political challenges abound within the bureaucracy as well.

Exhibit 30.1 identifies a host of political and bureaucratic challenges affecting the use of evaluation in government—in particular, challenges affecting the use of evaluation findings to improve public policies and programs. Use of evaluation may be hampered, for example, by fragmentation of power, interest group pressures, competing goals, organizational systems and cultures, changes in organizational leadership, lack of coordination among agencies, or lack of willingness to use evaluation information when it is available.

Eleanor Chelimsky (2009) has identified three levels of political pressure in the environment in which evaluations are conducted: "the overall 'checks and balances' architecture of government," "the *bureaucratic climate* within the agency," and the "*dominant professional culture* of the agency" (p. 52; emphasis in original). Her first level of political pressure may be found in the first category of challenges in Exhibit 30.1; her second level in the other eight categories; and her third level of political pressure may be found in challenges relating to agency cultures and to lack of cooperation within and among agencies. She notes that political pressures affecting evaluators are complex, always present, and always changing.

Although evaluators may see themselves as here to improve program performance, elected officials, political appointees, and career executives and managers all tend to place greater weight on political and bureaucratic factors, including their needs to respond to the crisis of the moment, to develop

EXHIBIT 30.1. POLITICAL AND BUREAUCRATIC CHALLENGES AFFECTING USE OF EVALUATION

1. Institutional challenges: fragmentation of power among the Congress, the executive branch, and the courts; among congressional committees; and among federal, state, and local governments; legal and regulatory requirements; legislative and budget processes
2. Political challenges (narrowly defined): constituency, interest group, and advocacy group pressures; partisan politics; intraparty rivalries; individual legislators' pride of authorship of specific policies or programs
3. Competing ideologies, values, and goals
4. Organizational cultures, structures, policies, systems, and procedures
5. Changes in the organizational environment
6. Changes in organizational leadership
7. Lack of coordination and cooperation within agencies; overlapping accountability frameworks
8. Lack of interagency coordination and collaboration; overlapping accountability frameworks
9. Lack of willingness to use evaluation findings

and maintain policies that reflect the interest of their various constituencies, and to protect "their" programs from the harm that even well-intentioned evaluations might cause. Many of these challenges also affect the use of evaluation in nonprofit organizations, where boards of directors and program managers may have little interest in use of evaluation.

Overcoming Political and Bureaucratic Challenges

Although these challenges to use of evaluation may seem overwhelming (and such challenges cannot always be overcome), four approaches can be helpful:

1. Redesigning management systems to focus on results
2. Creating incentives for higher program performance
3. Developing agreement on key national, state, or community indicators
4. Developing performance partnerships

Although these approaches lie beyond evaluators' usual focus, appropriate involvement of evaluators in all four—at least when offering recommendations or options for program improvement—could greatly improve evaluators' effectiveness and help improve the performance and value of public programs.

TABLE 30.1. OVERCOMING POLITICAL AND BUREAUCRATIC CHALLENGES.

Challenges	Approaches for Overcoming Challenges			
	Redesigning Management Systems to Focus on Results	Creating Incentives for Higher Program Performance	Developing Agreement on Key Indicators	Developing Performance Partnerships
1. Institutional	X	X	X	X
2. Political (narrowly defined)	X	X	X	X
3. Competing goals	X	X		X
4. Organizational cultures and systems	X	X		X
5. Changes in the environment	X	X	X	
6. Changes in leadership	X	X		
7. Lack of coordination in agencies	X	X		
8. Lack of interagency coordination	X	X	X	X
9. Lack of will to use evaluation findings	X	X	X	X

Note: Row and column headings are abbreviated; "X" indicates that a specific approach can help overcome specific challenges.

Table 30.1 identifies approaches that may be helpful in overcoming each of the political and bureaucratic challenges listed previously. The following pages discuss the four approaches.

Redesigning Agency Management Systems to Focus on Results

Agency cultures are often dominated by standard operating procedures that are controlled by Congress, the White House, or central management agencies. Agency management systems typically focus on process and give little attention to the results of the agency's programs. Evaluators should, when appropriate, recommend or provide options for redesigning agency management systems (planning, budgeting, financial management, personnel management, information resource management, program management, procurement, grants management, audit, accounting, evaluation, and data systems) to focus on program goals. In some cases, evaluators can assist in redesigning agency management systems to focus on results.

In the 1970s, at least three federal agencies refocused agency management and evaluation systems on results. First, with the participation of regional offices and grantees, the Bureau of Community Health Services managed the Community Health Centers program using program objectives, performance indicators, and performance targets that had been developed with the participation of regional offices and grantees over a four-year period. The bureau allocated additional staff and grant funds to high-performing regions; regional offices allocated additional grant funds to high-performing projects.

Second, the Department of Labor funded a multiyear evaluation of the Job Corps that included a sophisticated analysis comparing the program's costs with the dollar value of the program's benefits.

And third, in response to inputs from both program advocates and skeptics, in 1978 Congress authorized the Department of Agriculture to "set aside" (use) *up to* 0.5 percent of program funds for the Special Supplemental Nutrition Program for Women, Infants, and Children (WIC) (*up to* $3 million per year) for evaluating program performance, evaluating WIC's health benefits, and administering pilot projects. The department funded a number of evaluations, including a more definitive evaluation of the WIC program, and completed an evaluation synthesis that compared program costs with the program's benefits.

In the early 1980s, these three agencies used evaluation to help protect effective programs from elimination or deep budget cuts. In the face of the Reagan Administration's successful efforts to reduce spending in domestic programs and consolidate categorical programs into block grants, Congress maintained a number of effective programs.

Although the Reagan Administration targeted the Community Health Centers program for conversion to a primary care block grant to the states, for example, Congress arranged for the program to continue. The Community Health Centers program was generally regarded as well managed and effective in providing primary health care to those in medically underserved areas. Though Congress reduced funding for the Community Health Centers program in fiscal year 1982, Congress increased funding for the program in subsequent years.

Although Congress agreed to a 60 percent reduction in federally funded employment and training programs between 1981 and mid-1983, Congress maintained and then increased funding for the Job Corps—partly on the basis of a longitudinal evaluation that included a cost-benefit analysis showing that the Job Corps' economic benefits to society exceeded the program's costs.

And although Congress agreed to substantial cuts in other nutrition programs between 1981 and 1983, arguments of program effectiveness and "cost-effectiveness" were used in congressional decisions to maintain the WIC nutrition program, which the Reagan Administration had proposed, including in the maternal and child health block grant to the states; to minimize WIC program cuts in fiscal year 1982; and to expand the WIC program substantially in subsequent years. There was evidence from evaluation studies and an evaluation synthesis that WIC improves nutrition, increases infants' birthweight, produces healthier babies, improves children's growth and development, and produces significant medical savings by reducing the need for expensive neonatal intensive care.

Since 1995, the Veterans Health Administration (VHA) has redesigned agency management systems to focus on results, created incentive systems focused on results, created performance partnerships with public and private sector organizations, and used performance measurement systems and evaluation studies to improve the quality of VHA services. VHA is the nation's largest health care network, with more than 150 medical centers, 800 outpatient primary care clinics, 100 nursing homes, forty rehabilitation treatment programs, and 200 readjustment counseling centers. VHA provides some of the nation's highest quality health care, though twenty years ago the quality of its services left much to be desired (see Longman, 2007; National Academy of Public Administration, 2008; Oliver, 2007). Though more will always need to be done and two wars have strained VHA capacity, VHA has significantly improved the quality of the health care that it delivers (Jha, Perlin, Kizer, and Dudley, 2003).

Beginning in 1995, VHA transitioned from an inpatient-focused organization to a system focused on high-quality outpatient care. VHA is now organized into twenty-one Veterans Integrated Service Networks (VISNs), each of which includes many medical centers, outpatient clinics, and nursing homes. VHA regularly measures patient satisfaction, waiting times, and the quality of the health care that it provides. The agency uses such performance information to motivate managers and staff, allocate and reallocate resources, and redirect program activities (Hatry, Morley, Rossman, and Wholey, 2003). To stimulate high organizational performance, VHA negotiates performance agreements with network directors, giving heavy weight to quality, cost, and outcome objectives, including patient access, patient safety, appropriate health care, and cost of care; network directors then negotiate performance agreements with their medical center directors, clinical managers, and others reporting to them. Network directors are given quarterly feedback on performance in terms of their network performance plan. In performance review meetings, network directors share best practices, identify problems, and discuss steps that VHA and individual networks are taking to solve problems.

Creating Incentives for Higher Program Performance

If evaluators seek to have their work used in government, they should look for ways to alter the individual and organizational incentives systems that drive behavior. Evaluators should be alert to opportunities for agencies to create intangible and financial incentives for improved agency and program performance—or to create penalties for poor program performance. Where appropriate, evaluators can recommend or offer options for changes in incentive systems that would focus on program results. In some cases, evaluators can help design such systems. Incentives can be directed to agency or program managers, to individual staff members, to groups of staff members, or to entire organizations (Table 30.2).

To be effective, incentives must be tailored to the individuals or groups to be motivated. (Although I tend to emphasize positive incentives, penalties such as unfavorable publicity or financial penalties are more effective in many situations.) In public and nonprofit organizations, intangible incentives are particularly important. Policymakers, executives, and managers can stimulate better organizational performance by giving visibility, increased responsibility, or more interesting assignments to those whose organizations perform well or improve their performance, for example. "Perks" such as more flexible working hours or additional leave can also be used to stimulate improved performance; agencies can reward managers and staff members whose organizations perform well.

Frequent feedback on performance and performance-focused meetings can stimulate higher program performance, as can public recognition, organizational report cards, and support for budget proposals. Among the most powerful incentives in public and nonprofit organizations is the time and attention of senior officials. In VHA, for example, executives can develop performance agreements with senior managers focusing on organizational performance, provide frequent feedback on organizational performance, and meet regularly with managers and staff to build commitment to high(er) organizational

TABLE 30.2. INCENTIVES FOR HIGHER PROGRAM PERFORMANCE.

	Incentives for Managers and Staff	Organizational Incentives
Intangible Incentives	Performance-focused meetings with senior managers	Performance-focused meetings
	Honor awards	Honor awards
	Public recognition	Public recognition Organizational report cards
	Favorable publicity Increased responsibility	Favorable publicity
	More interesting work	Challenging new projects Support for budget proposals
	Removal of constraints	Removal of constraints
	Delegation of authority	Delegation of authority
	Better office space or better parking More flexible hours Additional leave	
	Performance agreements	Performance agreements
Financial Incentives	Cash awards	Allocation of overhead resources
	Pay raises	Allocation of discretionary funds Discretionary use of savings
	Promotions	Staff increments Renewal of discretionary grants Extension of contracts

performance. VHA executives' annual evaluations and bonuses depend to some extent, for example, on organizational performance; and executives whose organizations are not doing well may be reassigned or encouraged to retire.

Agencies can also use organizational report cards to stimulate higher program performance. Gormley (2004) presents a number of examples in which organizational report cards have been effective in stimulating higher performance in the health care, job training, elementary and secondary education, higher education, child care, and environmental protection arenas. Some of these report cards use *risk-adjusted* performance measures to control for the influence of client characteristics on program outcomes.

Because the use of financial incentives is typically constrained, two types of intangible incentives are particularly important: removal of constraints and delegation of authority. It may be possible to get relief from higher-level requirements, and it may turn out that some "requirements" on agencies and programs are self-imposed.

Financial incentives can, of course, be powerful motivators. Promotions, bonuses, and pay raises can be used to stimulate and reward high (er) program performance; group awards can be given to all those on a team or in an organization that has moved to higher performance levels. Modest staff increments or awards of discretionary funds can be used to stimulate and reward effective organizational performance. Resource distribution to VHA's health-care networks depends primarily on the number of veterans served; network directors then allocate and reallocate resources to meet performance goals, including quality, cost, and outcome goals.

Discretionary use of (say) 50 percent of budget savings can be used to stimulate more efficient performance. And renewal of discretionary grants or contracts can be conditioned on high or improved performance by grantees or contractors.

Developing Agreement on Key National, State, or Community Indicators

Key indicator systems, such as Oregon Benchmarks, Virginia Performs, and the Casey Foundation's Kids Count, inform members of the public, advocacy groups, legislators, public and nonprofit agencies, and other constituencies about trends in health, education, social, economic, and environmental conditions, for example, trends in teenage pregnancy rates, crime rates, high school graduation rates, unemployment rates, and water quality. United Way of America notes that community indicators "can present a compelling snapshot of a community's status [and] may serve as powerful catalysts to . . . fostering collaboration and mobilizing resources" (United Way of America, 1999, p. 1). Kamensky and Burlin (2004) and their colleagues discuss networks and partnerships through which two or more agencies may work to achieve national-, state-, or community-level results that citizens value and that no single agency could have produced alone.

The use of key indicators increases the demand for reliable performance measurement systems and evaluation studies and can stimulate the use of evaluation findings among many actors who may wish to learn about approaches that have been effective in improving conditions and who can influence legislation, regulations, and budget allocations. When appropriate, evaluators can assist policymakers by identifying options for development of key national, state, or local indicators and, in some cases, by assisting in creation and maintenance of such indicator systems.

Many states have developed agreement on systems of key statewide indicators. As noted above, for example, state legislatures took the lead in development of key state indicators in Oregon and Virginia (see Aristigueta, 1999; Council on Virginia's Future, 2010).

Efforts were undertaken in the mid-2000s to develop a set of key national indicators—economic, health, education, social, environmental, and security indicators—that could inform public officials and members of the public about problems and progress across the United States and no doubt stimulate political responses to perceived needs. By 2008, with the help of the Institute of Medicine, the nonprofit organization State of the USA had developed a set of twenty health and health care *yardsticks*, including indicators of health outcomes, indicators of health-related behaviors, and indicators related to the state of the health system: for example, self-reported health status, injury-related mortality, physical activity, health care expenditures, and insurance coverage (Institute of Medicine, 2009; State of the USA, 2010).

Developing Performance Partnerships

Contextual factors affect any organization's ability to produce intended outcomes, and it typically takes the efforts of more than one agency or program to produce intended outcomes. When intended program outcomes are changes in conditions (rather than outcomes for clients in a program), *performance partnerships* may be a natural follow-on to development of key indicators at the national, state, or community levels. In performance partnerships, two or more organizations agree to take joint accountability for achieving specific outcomes, agree to allocate some of their resources to partnership efforts, and take responsibility for producing specific outputs to help achieve the intended outcomes. Performance partnerships use information from performance measurement systems and evaluation studies to track the extent of progress; identify where inputs, outputs, or outcomes fall short of intended levels; and learn how to improve performance and results. Evaluators can assist policymakers and managers by identifying factors that affect achievement of intended outcomes, by recommending or identifying options for development of performance partnerships, and in some cases by assisting in creation and maintenance of performance partnerships.

Bardach (1998) describes a number of performance partnerships among state and local agencies, each of which he calls an *interagency collaborative capacity* (ICC). Each ICC is a virtual organization to which two or more agencies allocate personnel, budget, authority, or other resources to the ICC and work together to increase public value (economy, efficiency, effectiveness, or fairness). Some of the ICCs Bardach describes are efforts to redesign and integrate social services in a community or region. He notes that Healthy Start,

California's school-linked health and social services program, increased access to health care and reduced student mobility in many communities and that Maryland's Systems Reform Initiative was associated with reductions in out-of-home placements of at-risk children. Bardach concludes that ICCs must be designed to "give line staff teams and the implementing network an unusual degree of flexibility" (p. 161). He also states that "[u]p to a point interagency financial relations can be structured to provide incentives for desired performance. But after that point, constructive dialogue, on a foundation of trust, is required" (p. 162).

The Healthy People program is a Department of Health and Human Services performance partnership that was developed to influence public health trends in favorable directions. The goals of the program are to (1) help people of all ages to increase life expectancy and improve their quality of life and (2) eliminate health disparities in the population, such as disparities by gender, race or ethnicity, education, or income. Under the Healthy People program, research and evaluation studies and performance measurement systems have supported establishment of and progress toward the nation's Health Objectives for 1990, for 2000, and for 2010. Although specific appropriations have not been required, Congress has supported the program and has incorporated relevant Healthy People objectives into a number of federal programs.

Performance targets set in the Healthy People program have stimulated performance partnership efforts among many federal agencies, state agencies, communities, and nonprofit organizations. Healthy People 2010 includes 467 objectives (performance targets) in twenty-eight focus areas. Among these focus areas are quality health services, environmental health, injury and violence prevention, mental health and mental disorders, physical activity and fitness, and public health infrastructure. Work is now under way on Healthy People 2020 (www.healthypeople.gov).

Conclusion

Use of evaluation in public and nonprofit organizations has grown in the United States over the last forty years. Performance measurement systems and evaluation studies are used to increase transparency, strengthen accountability, and support policy and management decision making. Sometimes evaluation is used to improve the performance of public and nonprofit organizations.

Political and bureaucratic challenges will always affect the use of evaluation in public and nonprofit organizations, and no approach will work 100 percent of the time. Four approaches can be used to help overcome political and bureaucratic challenges affecting the use of evaluation: (1) redesigning agency management systems to focus on results; (2) creating incentives for higher program performance; (3) developing key national, state, or community indicators; and (4) creating performance partnerships. Each of the four approaches creates new forces that can help in overcoming challenges to use of evaluation and thus help to improve the performance of public and nonprofit agencies and programs.

When appropriate, evaluators should identify opportunities for the use of these approaches, separately or in combination. In some cases, evaluators can move beyond typical evaluation roles and assist in agency efforts to redesign agency management systems or create new incentives; to develop agreement on key national, state, or community indicators; or to develop performance partnerships. In these ways, evaluators can help public and nonprofit organizations to improve the performance and value of their programs and services.

References

Aristigueta, M. P. *Managing for Results in State Government.* Westport, CT: Quorum Books, 1999.

Bardach, E. *Getting Agencies to Work Together.* Washington, DC: Brookings Institution Press, 1998.

Chelimsky, E. "Integrating Evaluation Units into the Political Environment of Government: The Role of Evaluation Policy." In W.M.K. Trochim, M. M. Mark, and L. J. Cooksy (eds.), *Evaluation Policy and Evaluation Practice.* New Directions for Evaluation, no. 123. San Francisco, CA: Jossey-Bass, 2009.

Council on Virginia's Future. *Virginia Performs.* http://vaperforms.virginia.gov/index.php, 2010.

Gormley, W. T., Jr. "Using Organizational Report Cards." In J. S. Wholey, H. P. Hatry, and K. E. Newcomer (eds.), *Handbook of Practical Program Evaluation* (2nd ed.). San Francisco, CA: Jossey-Bass, 2004.

Hatry, H. P., Morley, E., Rossman, S. B., and Wholey, J. S. *How Federal Managers Use Outcome Information: Opportunities for Federal Managers.* Washington, DC: IBM Center for The Business of Government, 2003.

Institute of Medicine. *State of the USA Health Indicators: Letter Report.* Washington, DC: National Academies Press, 2009.

Jha, A. K., Perlin, J. B., Kizer, K. W., and Dudley, R. A. "Effect of Transformation of the Veterans Health Care System on Quality of Care." *New England Journal of Medicine,* 2003, *348*(22), 2218–2227.

Kamensky, J. M., and Burlin, T. J. (eds.). *Collaboration: Using Networks and Partnerships.* Washington, DC: IBM Center for The Business of Government, 2004.

Longman, P. *Best Care Anywhere: Why VA Health Care Is Better Than Yours.* Sausalito, CA: PoliPoint Press, 2007.

National Academy of Public Administration. *After Yellow Ribbons: Providing Veteran-Centered Services.* Washington, DC: National Academy of Public Administration, 2008.

Office of Management and Budget. *Increased Emphasis on Program Evaluations.* Memorandum M-10–01. Washington, DC: Office of Management and Budget, 2009.

Office of Management and Budget. *FY 2011 Budget of the United States Government, Analytical Perspectives.* Washington, DC: Office of Management and Budget, 2010.

Office of Management and Budget. *Next Steps in the Evidence and Innovation Agenda.* Memorandum M-13–17. Washington, DC: Office of Management and Budget, 2013.

Office of Management and Budget. *FY 2015 Budget of the United States Government, Analytical Perspectives.* Washington, DC: Office of Management and Budget, 2014a.

Office of Management and Budget. *Guidance for Providing and Using Administrative Data for Statistical Purposes.* Memorandum M-14–06. Washington, DC: Office of Management and Budget, 2014b.

Oliver, A. "The Veterans Health Administration: An American Success Story?" *Milbank Quarterly,* 2007, *85*(1).

Radin, B. A. *Challenging the Performance Movement.* Washington, DC: Georgetown University Press, 2006.

State of the USA. *Our Work.* www.stateoftheusa.org/ourwork/index.asp, 2010.

United Way of America. *Community Status Reports and Targeted Community Interventions: Drawing a Distinction.* Alexandria, VA: United Way of America, 1999.

Wholey, J. S. *Evaluation and Effective Public Management.* Boston, MA: Little, Brown, 1983.

Wilson, J. G. *Bureaucracy: What Government Agencies Do and Why They Do It.* New York: Basic Books, 1989.

CHAPTER THIRTY-ONE

EVALUATION CHALLENGES, ISSUES, AND TRENDS

Harry P. Hatry, Kathryn E. Newcomer, Joseph S. Wholey

Many opportunities exist for evaluators to help public and nonprofit organizations to improve program design and program performance. This handbook presents a variety of approaches for evaluating program performance and getting evaluation results used. In this final chapter we discuss important topics not directly addressed in the preceding chapters. First we address four challenges: (1) quality control of the evaluation process; (2) selection and training of evaluators; (3) standards and ethics in evaluation work; and (4) getting others to use evaluation findings to improve programs. Then we examine the relationship between performance monitoring systems and evaluation studies, discuss trends in program evaluation, and present some concluding observations.

Challenge 1: Controlling the Quality of the Evaluation Process

Those responsible for evaluations, whether in government agencies, nonprofit organizations, or academic institutions, can take steps to ensure the quality of their evaluation work, whether evaluation studies or ongoing performance monitoring. Earlier chapters suggest a number of quality control steps to take in managing *individual* evaluations—for example, checking for missing data and checking for consistency in the definitions of data items when data are collected from different offices or different years.

Here we are concerned with quality control of the entire evaluation process. Here are suggestions for steps that evaluators can take:

- Provide for peer review of evaluation designs and draft evaluation reports. The peer review might be undertaken by evaluators in the agency, evaluators in another part of government, or experts from universities or consulting firms.
- Give staff in the agencies and programs that have been evaluated the opportunity to respond to draft evaluation findings. This step is valuable both politically and for quality control. The feedback can identify important problems in the evaluation itself. In an evaluation of drug programs in Dade County, Florida, for example, the agencies whose programs were evaluated noted after reviewing the draft report that an important group of client records had been overlooked by the evaluators. This required the evaluation team to reopen its data collection and analysis activities and rework its findings.
- Provide for periodic, independent, external reviews of the agency's evaluation activities, as the U.S. Government Accountability Office (2007) has suggested. Such reviews should identify any patterns of weakness in evaluation designs, data collection procedures, or report presentations and suggest steps to increase the technical quality and usefulness of the evaluation findings. Reviewers might also identify alternative approaches not currently being used by the evaluators.
- Regularly review the work of evaluation contractors and provide oversight of evaluation contractors' work, including reviews of evaluation designs and draft evaluation reports (see Chapter Twenty-Nine). After the final report has been submitted, the quality and timeliness of the contractor's performance should be assessed, taking into consideration the time and other resources that were available.
- Place primary responsibility for data quality on the program managers and staff who oversee data collection. This is the first line of defense against bad procedures and data.

Challenge 2: Selecting and Training Evaluators

Finding skilled, trained evaluators is an important prerequisite for quality evaluations. An evaluation usually requires a team rather than a single individual.

Collectively, the team members are likely to need an understanding of organizational contexts; legislative mandates; evaluation designs; and data collection, data processing, and data analysis methods. They should also be able to listen well and to communicate evaluation findings and recommendations clearly, both orally and in writing. All the needed knowledge and skills do not usually reside in a single individual, however. An evaluation team can also add outside members for services such as survey research, data processing, and editing.

Educational background is informative but by no means likely to be conclusive in selecting evaluation personnel. Good grades in evaluation-related courses will likely increase the probability that candidates know what they are doing, at least with regard to the technical aspects of evaluation work. But some individuals with such training do not adapt well to environments in which resource constraints preclude elaborate designs such as controlled experiments. We have worked with many fine evaluators whose backgrounds may seem quite surprising, such as history majors and lawyers. Program evaluators need logical, systematic approaches to their work as well as cultural humility: the ability to apply such approaches can be found in people with many different backgrounds.

Although on-the-job training will improve evaluators' skills, agencies should provide additional training opportunities for both experienced and newer evaluation staff. Training should cover such topics as the latest thinking on evaluation designs, statistical techniques (such as those used for selecting samples and analyzing data), questionnaire design, working with program personnel, and effective presentation of evaluation results. The rapid introduction of new technology (as is occurring in data collection, data processing, mapping, and report presentation) makes it imperative to keep up with what can be done most efficiently and with maximum quality.

Challenge 3: Maintaining Standards and Ethics

Certain norms should guide all evaluators' work. In planning their work, for example, evaluators should ensure that evaluation criteria are relevant and that evaluation findings will be available in time for important policy and management decisions. Within constraints on available resources, evaluators should ensure that that their data and conclusions are valid. They should ensure adequate training for data collectors, pretests of data collection schemes, ongoing quality control testing of data collection, and security of the resulting data so as to protect the confidentiality of those from whom information was collected.

Ethical challenges are common in evaluation work due to the applied and political nature of the work, along with the existence of diverse sources of guidance that do not suggest a single "correct" response to a given ethical dilemma. Indeed, evaluators encounter competing ethical frameworks—including teleological and deontological theories, universalist and relativist perspectives, and descriptive and prescriptive approaches to valuing—that offer conflicting guidance for resolving ethical challenges and assessing the merit and worth of programs. While professional codes of conduct provide a useful starting point for ethical practice, such general principles are open to interpretation and do not indicate one course of action for a particular scenario. There has been and continues to be widespread recognition that evaluators need ethical training (see Morris, 2008).

Of most concern is that information obtained in evaluations should not violate the anonymity, confidentiality, or privacy rights of program participants or anyone on whom or from whom information was obtained—whether from records, surveys, or interviews. If the evaluators want to quote or refer to particular individuals, they will usually need to obtain the written permission of the people to be cited. For some evaluations, the evaluators will be required to obtain informed consent prior to obtaining records on or conducting interviews with individuals; for example, they need to obtain permission from parents before surveying schoolchildren. The Education Commission of the States (1991) defines *informed consent* as follows: "A person must voluntarily give his or her consent before information about that person can be released to someone else, and consent must be based on a full understanding of what information will be exchanged, with whom it will be shared, and how it will be used" (p. 2). The commission's report on information sharing is a good source for a comprehensive discussion of the meaning of confidentiality. Sieber (1992) offers useful guidance on working with internal reviewers to ensure that research is done ethically.

Obtaining informed consent forms can become quite cumbersome and time consuming. Evaluators should determine in advance what requirements apply to a particular evaluation. Evaluators may have to consider alternatives such as requesting data without any personal identifiers or requesting group data only. Both options, however, preclude linking data on the same individuals from different sources.

Virtually all evaluations will be subject to formal requirements to protect the rights and welfare of human subjects, such as the requirements of the Health Insurance Portability and Accountability Act (HIPAA) and of an institutional review board (IRB). Most research organizations, such as universities doing research or evaluation studies involving human subjects, have an institutional review board. IRBs review evaluation plans prior to implementation to ensure that evaluations protect any private information obtained. (Chapter Nine offers suggestions for working with IRBs during the evaluation planning process.)

Standards exist for many subgroups of evaluation professionals (Davis, 1990). The so-called Yellow Book standards of the U.S. Government Accountability Office (2007) guide the work of GAO auditors and evaluators as well as those in agency offices of inspector general and state and local auditors. The Joint Committee on Standards for Educational Evaluation (2010) has published a set of standards for evaluation of education programs; these standards focus on propriety, utility, feasibility, and accuracy. The American Evaluation Association (2004) has developed a detailed set of principles titled *Guiding Principles for Evaluators* and has endorsed the Joint Committee's evaluation standards.

If evaluation findings are likely to influence public support for the program or to have substantial political or program repercussions, evaluators may face pressures to slant their findings in one direction or another. They may receive more or less subtle cues from evaluation sponsors indicating that such slanting is desired. These situations are always difficult. Evaluators who face such pressures and are unable to resolve them appropriately may find that their reputations suffer. One possible solution is for the evaluator to indicate the assumptions that would lead to a particular conclusion and then show in a sensitivity analysis how different assumptions would lead to different conclusions. Another option the evaluator can take in extreme circumstances is whistle-blowing; for example, reporting to the appropriate authorities that such pressures have been exerted. If the pressures are subtle, however, whistle-blowers may find themselves in untenable situations later. It is import to consider ways in which findings may be misrepresented ahead of time in order to take adequate precautions.

Challenge 4: Using Evaluation Findings to Improve Programs

For evaluation to be worth the effort, evaluation findings and recommendations must be used by executives, managers, legislators, or other funders. Evaluation is often threatening to those whose programs are being evaluated. Evaluations may provide ammunition for those who want to eliminate the program, reduce program expenditures, or dramatically change the program's direction. We believe, however, that a major purpose of most program evaluations should be to provide information that helps to improve programs and services, not solely to save money. For example, at the U.S. federal level the GPRA Modernization Act of 2010 placed greater emphasis on this purpose than the Congress had given it in the Government Performance and Results Act of 1993. Effective use of evaluation findings and performance data requires capacity-building within any organization to support learning and using information to improve program performance. Here are suggestions for increasing the use of evaluation findings to improve programs:

- Encourage high-level agency officials to establish an annual evaluation agenda and support inclusive participation in selecting the foci of evaluation work. (This will likely engender more interest in the findings, both among those officials and among their staff members.)
- With the evaluation sponsors, seek to emphasize that improving the program is a major purpose of the evaluation. This can blunt at least some program concern about being threatened by the evaluation. Then include specific program improvement suggestions and recommendations in the final report (or in an attachment). Make sure that all suggestions and recommendations flow from the findings. (See Chapter Twenty-Seven for advice on making effective recommendations.)
- Make sure that the evaluation findings become available in a timely way. Avoid extending deadlines beyond a time when the findings' usefulness will likely diminish.
- As suggested in a number of the previous chapters, involve potential users in developing the evaluation questions.
- Ask major stakeholders such as program officials to review an early version of the evaluation report with its preliminary findings (without giving up control of the final wording).
- For major evaluations, arrange for a prestigious advisory committee that reviews both the evaluation design and the preliminary findings.
- Make sure the report is well written, is clear, and contains some form of executive summary/highlights. (See Chapter Twenty-Eight for suggestions on writing for impact.)
- Offer briefings on the evaluation findings—both to program managers and staff members and to other agency officials.
- Suggest to the program managers that they hold "How Are We Doing?" sessions with their staffs to discuss evaluation findings and recommendations.
- When appropriate, offer recommendations or options for redesigning agency management systems or incentive systems, developing agreement on key indicator systems, or creating performance partnerships.

- If it does not violate contractual or other obligations, develop a dissemination plan for use after the report has been released. Such a plan might include publicizing the findings in journal articles, webinars, op-ed pieces, blogs, and the like.

The Relationship Between Performance Monitoring and Evaluation

Considerable differences of opinion exist among evaluators as to how performance measurement, or monitoring, and evaluation studies are related, in particular the extent to which they are at odds with or complement each other. We suggest that viewing ongoing performance measurement, or monitoring, as well as targeted analysis of programmatic and administrative data (frequently called data analytics), as subfields of evaluation practice holds promise for public and nonprofit organizations to take better advantage of evaluators' skills, and to forge a more strategic, and likely more effective, approach to using evaluation to inform and improve program management.

Evaluation embraces a broad confederation of methods and disciplinary approaches to assess the value and worth of programs and policies that can be integrated in day-to-day practice. In the same way that logic modeling, impact evaluations, and case studies may be pursued in complementary fashion, so can performance measurement be viewed as another significant sub-field of evaluation practice that is complementary with many other evaluation approaches. Furthermore, as with performance measurement, many evaluation methods may be undertaken on a quick-turn-around and periodic or continuous basis, especially by evaluators located inside an organization. Characterizing performance measurement as something distinct from evaluation has led to a persistent and pervasive separation among groups of people, which has been costly in terms of both resources and organizational learning. Hence, we see little theoretical or practical basis for viewing performance measurement as separate from evaluation practice.

We believe that the presence of performance measurement tends to encourage the use of other forms of evaluation. First, the information on programs obtained through regular performance measurement often raises questions as to why program operations or outcomes are as good or bad as they are. This is likely to occur, particularly in situations when outcomes failed to meet targets or were much better than targets. In these cases, the performance data inevitably lead to asking why the deviations have occurred and thus to greater support for evaluation studies. Usually, because of a lack of time or other resources, public organizations may seek less expensive ways to obtain such information. When the stakes are high, however, public organizations and foundations are likely to press for in-depth evaluation studies.

Second, if an organization regularly collects performance data, this can enhance the ability of evaluators to undertake evaluation studies by providing ready-made data. For example, if an outcome-monitoring system has been obtaining feedback from clients of health or social service programs at regular intervals, subsequent evaluations can use such information and not rely solely on after-the-fact data collection, saving time and funds and perhaps providing better evaluation information.

It is not widely recognized that the availability of regularly collected performance information also has the potential for encouraging small-scale randomized controlled experiments. For example, if a program is regularly collecting outcome information and program officials want to test a new intervention without immediately applying it across the board, evaluators would need only to develop the process for random assignment of future clients to the new or to the old intervention (as described in Chapter Seven) and add to the database the information on which clients received which intervention. This possibility applies primarily to relatively small-scale interventions and interventions that are limited to one organization. (However, various matched-pair designs might be used involving multiple locations in the country.) This random assignment option has very rarely been used to date, but we believe it has a considerable and untapped potential. Such randomized experiments might even be undertaken by organizational staff with little outside assistance. (Note that the outcome information from performance measurement systems is not likely to exactly match the needs of a particular evaluation study. However, if the program's performance monitoring process includes client outcome data identified by demographic and service characteristics, the evaluators are likely to be able to obtain a great deal of the information that they need.)

If performance measurement and data analytics are viewed as parts of evaluation practice—parts that can benefit from insights from other evaluation practitioners—public and nonprofit organizations will be better positioned to build intellectual and organizational capacities to learn, improve, and be accountable. Public agency managers and executives could be better served if they receive a unified message and appropriate training on how to interpret and use performance data, data analytics, and other forms of evaluation work to inform their learning and decisions. Evaluation capacity could also be better positioned and distributed within an organization to provide this training to enhance the evaluation competencies needed from all—from front-line staff to line managers to top leaders.

Trends in Program Evaluation

Here we provide our thoughts about six trends in program evaluation likely to continue into the next decade. The coming decade is likely to be a period of unsurpassed advances in technology and transparency and an increasing focus on the use of evaluation to support evidence-based policy. The term *evidence-based policy* is a vague one, but it generally means that rigorous evidence is used to inform decision-making. How that evidence should be generated has been and continues to be contested, as we discuss further below.

Information Technology

New technology, some of which we can only guess at, is likely to add to the richness of the data available and the increasing ability to process large amounts of data in a practical way. For example, as indicated by Berman and her colleagues (in Chapter Sixteen), the use of mobile devices, bolstered by the use of photography and videotaping (and perhaps even holographic devices), is likely to be used increasingly to track the physical condition of a variety of service elements, such as roads, parks, buildings, housing, and neighborhoods. These devices can be used to obtain the more accurate and timely data and the more comprehensive information that are useful to evaluation users. It may be that, in the future, trained observers will be able to make their ratings based on information collected by orbiting space satellites.

Data entry and analysis are almost certain to become much faster and less expensive for evaluators (balanced by the cost of the new technical equipment). Technology is already available that permits direct real-time entry of field-collected data into computers; for example, observations of problems in the field can be translated directly into work orders for repair and maintenance crews. Direct translation of voice to electronic forms will become common, enabling evaluators to use that quicker and easier form of data entry with, for example, information obtained through field interviews.

Evaluators' use of the Internet for literature reviews, online surveys, and dissemination of evaluation findings will increase (as discussed in Chapter Eighteen). Use of online libraries and good search engines will help evaluators to quickly identify relevant research and evaluation studies. In the right circumstances, web-based surveys can reduce data collection costs and speed data analysis.

Surveys will increasingly be administered through wireless communications devices as well as over the Internet until some better technology comes along. However, obtaining good response rates will likely be a growing problem, with survey experts trying to determine how to overcome the obstacles from people's use of multiple media and how to motivate people to respond.

Continued breakthroughs in technology, including those mentioned in the previous paragraphs, are likely to mean that data, processed and analyzed, should become available much more quickly than before, providing much shorter turnaround times, even for the findings from large-scale surveys. Technology is also changing the way that reports are disseminated. When evaluation reports are not confidential, evaluators are posting PDF files of their reports on their organizations' websites, for example.

Big Data

Information technology is making it considerably easier to link information on individual clients' demographic characteristics, the type and amount of service provided to each client, and client health outcomes and financial data – providing what some refer to as "*big data*." While the private sector has been quick to mine large linked data sets on consumer choices and habits, the ability to link and then mine government generated data has raised both opportunities and challenges for evaluators as well. Information on client characteristics and receipt of services can be linked to the considerably better outcome data that are becoming available (for example, see van Staa, Goldacre, Gulliford, Cassell, Pirmohamed, Taweel, Delaney, et al., 2012). Similarly, much more attention is being given to tracking clients and events across programs, both within an agency and across agencies. However, privacy issues and the need to protect the privacy of individuals will continue to be a major concern in such applications. Evaluators will still need to make sure findings cannot be attributed to specific persons without their permission.

We are likely to see considerably more comparative data covering programs and agencies having similar missions, not only in the United States but across the globe. Globalization will assuredly affect the evaluation community, if for no other reason than the fact that evaluation information will be coming from all over. Improved translation capability will likely increasingly break down the current barriers to the use of such information. Many countries, and countries on most continents, are beginning to generate sizeable amounts of evaluation information—and pretty soon the penguins of Antarctica may be providing evaluation information.

Agency record data are likely to continue be the major data source for much outcome data. Evaluation studies will be able to make considerably more use of the data coming from ongoing performance monitoring systems, assuming that these systems continue to improve their quality and coverage of key outcomes.

Data Visualization

The use of geographic information systems, "GIS," to analyze data with spatial attributes in program evaluation is still relatively new, but it shows promise for enhancing data collection, and improving the communication, use, and accuracy of program evaluation results (Azzam and Robinson, 2013; Booza, Bridge, Neale, and Schenk, 2010; Koschinsky, 2012). The use of GIS is helpful in collecting and analyzing data from geographically dispersed programs, as it can facilitate the investigation of variation in both program implementation and key elements of the environment that tend to vary nonrandomly across space (such as population density, access to resources, community norms, infrastructure, population composition, convenience of location, and weather).

One of GIS' greatest strengths is the ability to quickly and clearly visualize geographic data. Most GIS platforms were designed for both cartography and spatial analysis, and can easily produce attractive, highly-customizable maps and graphics derived from the underlying data. This capability is important because graphics communicate information more clearly than text or chart-based alternatives for audiences of evaluation.

In fact, "*data visualization*" has recently become a popular objective for evaluators who wish to communicate effectively findings of their work. Reporting of evaluation findings can certainly be enhanced by the greater use of color and graphics. Advances in computer and copying technology are increasingly allowing easier production of attractive, multicolored reports. Presentations in 3-D seem just around the corner.

These technological developments in both GIS and the use of other data visualization techniques seem likely to increase the quality and richness of evaluation reporting. A danger here, however, is that overdone visuals may confuse readers or deflect questions about the accuracy and validity of the evaluation findings. Evaluators will need to avoid complicating their reports unnecessarily and thereby missing the forest for the trees of technology.

Complex Adaptive Systems

Interest in how to apply principles from systems theory and complexity theory to better analyze complex programs has been increasing and is likely to continue to increase into the near future. Most programs exhibit the characteristics of complex adaptive systems according to the Williams and Hummelbrunner (2011), as they are composed of interacting, semi-autonomous agents (either individuals or subordinate organizations, or both) whose actions are difficult to predict, and that often self-organize new patterns of behavior over time. Michel Quinn Patton has drawn attention to the complexity involved in program implementation, and he defines complex systems as "characterized by a large number of interacting and interdependent elements in which there is no central control" (Patton 2011: 1), and complex adaptive systems as "a dynamic network of many interacting parts, continuously acting and reacting. The results of these interactions are dynamic, emergent, uncertain, and unpredictable" (Patton 2008: 369). Jonathan Morell has also embraced the application of complexity theory in evaluation practice as he calls for evaluators to diagnose, anticipate, accommodate, and address "surprises" that inevitably occur in evaluation practice (2010).

The increasing call to evaluate programs that seek to improve well-being in delineated geographical areas (such as communities or neighborhoods) that use multiple services and multiple agencies, as discussed in Chapter Eleven, clearly adds considerable evaluation complexity. Funders and other decision-makers often oversee multiple programs, and programs almost always exist within a web of overlapping and interlocking interests that extend well beyond the program itself. A key promise of complexity theory is to be able to account for these factors in a useful way in an evaluation.

Ray Pawson (2013) provides a useful framework for designing evaluations that is sensitive to them any sources of complexity. He argues that to account for complexity and complex adaptive systems, a longer-term view is needed to build—over time, and after many evaluations—general knowledge about how similar programs work. "The basic antidote to complexity," he says, "is for inquiry to be iterative" (Pawson 2013, 84).

Evaluation Mandates

Many foundations and even national governments are increasingly issuing requirements that programs be evaluated—for example, every five years in Canada and Japan. Relatedly, a major recent development has been the emergence across the United States and the world of "Pay for Success" (PFS) programs. This approach has achieved wide interest very quickly—even though as of this writing it has not yet been proven to be successful. A major element of these PFS arrangements is the requirement for some form of evaluation to determine whether the provided service has met targets so that funders can be fully paid for the service costs and for success payments.

Mandatory evaluation via cost-effectiveness studies and benefit-cost analyses has recently become popular among some foundations, for example, Pew, and politicians who are asking for evidence to compare the costs of achieving desired outcomes through different programs. The Washington Institute for Public Policy has drawn much national attention, including from the Obama Administration and the U.S. Congress, for its path-breaking work in using benefit-cost and cost-effectiveness analyses to compare social programs (see www.wsipp.wa.gov/).

However, many close observers of evaluation practice have been quick to acknowledge challenges to across-the-board evaluation requirements (see Dahler-Larsen, 2012). John Mayne posits that evaluation use results when the supply of credible and timely evaluative information matches decision-makers' demand, but that the "supply-push" assumption of providing more and better evaluation has not been effective without a concurrent "demand-pull" framework to balance it (2010). Ray Rist is similarly skeptical, and argues that organizations are over-supplied with information already (2006).

Demand for Rigorous Evidence

The assumptions underlying the promotion of evidence-based decision making in government and in the nonprofit sector are that, first, the more rigorous the social science research design, the more credible are the evaluation findings; second, systematic reviews of rigorous evaluation studies of the same intervention can produce especially credible findings; and third, rigorous evaluations can produce models of "demonstrated evidence-based interventions" (DEBIs) for replication.

Widely recognized criteria by which the rigor of evaluation studies can be rated are accepted, but not all criteria are viewed as equal by evaluation professionals. Most advocates of systematic reviews tend to believe that true experiments are far better than any other design. The term for experimental designs that has become fashionable in the twenty-first century is random control trials (RCTs), since that is the term used in medical research for tests of the efficacy of new drugs. Many of those supporting evidence-based policy view RCTs as the "gold standard" for designing any research or evaluation study (for example, the Coalition for Evidence-Based Policy, see Coalition for Evidence-Based

Policy, 2012). While there is disagreement within the evaluation profession regarding the sanctity of RCTs, and the relative weight to be given to different evaluation designs, the acceptance of the value of the "evidence-based" label is widespread and here to stay.

Significant implications of the prevalence of the acceptance of the goal of rigorous evidence for evaluation practice include: higher demands being placed on those reporting outcomes or evaluation findings to demonstrate the quality of the evidence they produce; a lack of a clear, shared understanding about when evidence is good enough; and, given the homage paid to RCTs, more uncertainty among both evaluators and audiences about how to produce high-level evidence in fieldwork where random assignment is simply not an option or is highly difficult to sustain. It is challenging—and expensive—to produce compelling "evidence" about the impact of public and nonprofit programs.

At the same time, ever-tighter public agency budgets are likely to continue. The environment in which managers and evaluators work is becoming even more challenging. However, the increasing need to justify expenditures with results and the push for evidence-based policy provide opportunities for expanding evaluation efforts. Taxpayers and legislators will likely be even more insistent on economy, efficiency, and identifying what they are receiving for their money. This will continue to encourage public officials at federal, state, and local levels, and others providing funding or using public funds, to justify their funding with some form of evaluation information. However, a frugal outlook can also, paradoxically, lead to curtailing the funds needed for evaluation studies and performance monitoring systems.

It is inevitable that controversy will continue over performance monitoring and evaluation requirements. Many service organizations believe that evaluation activities reduce funding for their direct services to clients and thus are harmful. In addition, questions about the capacity of service organizations to undertake such efforts are, and will continue to be, a major concern. These concerns are legitimate. If funders and the service organizations themselves are to make evaluation efforts worthwhile, they need to use the evaluation information to help improve their programs.

Both service organizations and funders need help in developing their capacity to support evaluation efforts. We hope that more will be done in future years to alleviate both of these concerns.

It seems likely that university training in such subjects as public policy, public administration, business administration, public health, education, criminal justice, and social work will increase the attention curricula give to evaluation because of the increased interest in evidence-based practice. (Similarly, more in-service training in evaluation is likely to occur in government and in nonprofit organizations.) In the long run, this should build the demand for evaluation. Students' understanding of evaluation will likely make them less fearful of it and make them better future users of evaluation information.

Final Thoughts

At the beginning of this handbook, we noted two primary reasons for evaluation activities: to achieve greater accountability in the use of public or donated funds and to help agency officials improve the effectiveness of their programs. We believe that the second purpose should usually be the primary one. In the long run, improving services and program outcomes should be the main rationale for allocating resources to evaluation, whether for evaluation studies or for ongoing monitoring of program results. This is the most important cost-effectiveness test for program evaluation—whether benefits to citizens from improved programs are worth the costs of evaluations.

Given the trend toward increased monitoring and evaluation of the performance of programs operated by public and nonprofit organizations, the challenge for evaluators will be to respond to these new opportunities and help ensure that evaluation leads to more effective programs. Because most government and nonprofit agencies operate under severe financial constraints, evaluation funds will always be vulnerable. Thus, it is vital that evaluators produce usable and useful information from their work. Evaluators should document the effects that their evaluations have and develop case studies of evaluations that have been used to add value to government programs.

Evaluators should devise evaluation practices that are as low cost as possible, both to reduce their vulnerability to budget cuts and to get the most product from limited resources.

Program evaluation, whether produced at low cost or high cost, is by no means a panacea. It does not substitute for *quality implementation* of programs. It will not always provide definitive information as to program impacts. What evaluation can do is provide reasonably reliable, reasonably valid information about the merits and results of particular programs operating in particular circumstances. Necessary compromises will inevitably mean that the users of the information will be less than fully certain of the validity of the evaluation findings. In a world full of uncertainties and hazards, however, it is better to be roughly right than to remain fully ignorant.

References

American Evaluation Association. "Guiding Principles for Evaluators." www.eval.org/p/cm/ld/fid=51. 2004.

Azzam, Tarek, and Robinson, David. "GIS in Evaluation: Utilizing the Power of Geographic Information Systems to Represent Evaluation Data." *American Journal of Evaluation*, 2013, *34*(2), 207–224.

Booza, Jason C., Bridge, Patrick D., Neale, Anne Victoria, and Schenk, Maryjean. "Incorporating Geographic Information Systems (GIS) into Program Evaluation: Lessons from a Rural Medicine Initiative." *Journal of the American Board of Family Medicine*, 2010, *23*(1), 59–66.

Coalition for Evidence-Based Policy. "How Low-Cost Randomized Controlled Trials are Possible in Many Areas of Social Policy." http://coalition4evidence.org/wp-content/uploads/uploads-dupes-safety/Rigorous-Program-Evaluations-on-a-Budget-March-2012.pdf. 2012.

Dahler-Larsen, Peter. *The Evaluation Society*. Stanford, CA: Stanford University Press, 2012.

Davis, Dwight. "Do You Want a Performance Audit or an Evaluation?" *Public Administration Review*, 1990, *50*(1), 35–41.

Education Commission of the States. *Confidentiality and Collaboration: Information Sharing in Interagency Efforts*. Washington, DC: Education Commission of the States, 1991.

Joint Committee on Standards for Educational Evaluation. *The Program Evaluation Standards* (3rd ed.) Thousand Oaks, CA: Sage, 2010.

Koschinsky, Julia. "The Case for Spatial Analysis in Evaluation to Reduce Health Inequities." *Evaluation and Program Planning*, 2012, *36*(1), 172–176.

Mayne, John. "Building an Evaluative Culture: The Key to Effective Evaluation and Results Management." *Canadian Journal of Program Evaluation*, 2010, *24*, 1–30.

Morell, Jonathan. *Evaluation in the Face of Uncertainty: Anticipating Surprise and Responding to the Inevitable*. New York: The Guilford Press, 2010.

Morris, Michael (Ed.) *Evaluation Ethics for Best Practice: Cases and Commentaries*. New York: The Guilford Press, 2008.

Patton, Michael Quinn. *Utilization-Focused Evaluation* (4th ed.). Thousand Oaks, CA: Sage, 2008.

Patton, Michael Quinn. *Developmental Evaluation: Applying Complexity Concepts to Enhance Innovation and Use*. New York: Guilford Press, 2011.

Pawson, Ray. *The Science of Evaluation: A Realist Manifesto*. Thousand Oaks, CA: Sage, 2013.

Rist, Ray C. "Conclusion: A Brief Critique." In Ray C. Rist and Nicoletta Stame (eds.), *From Studies to Streams: Managing Evaluative Systems* (283–286). New Brunswick, NJ: Transaction Publishers, 2006.

Sieber, Joan. *Planning Ethically Responsible Research*. Thousand Oaks, CA: Sage, 1992.

U.S. Government Accountability Office. *Government Auditing Standards: 2007 Revision*. Washington, DC: U.S. Government Accountability Office, 2007.

U.S. Government Accountability Office. *Program Evaluation: A Variety of Rigorous Methods Can Help Identify Effective Interventions*. Washington, DC: U.S. Government Accountability Office, 2009.

van Staa, Tjeerd-Pieter, Goldacre, Ben, Gulliford, Martin, Cassell, Jackie, Pirmohamed, Munir, Taweel, Adel, Delaney, Brendan, et al. "Pragmatic Randomised Trials Using Routine Electronic Health Records: Putting Them to the Test." *BMJ*, 2012, *344*. www.bmj.com/content/344/bmj.e55.

Williams, Bob, and Hummelbrunner, Richard. *Systems Concepts in Action: A Practitioner's Toolkit*. Stanford, CA: Stanford University Press, 2011.

NAME INDEX

Page references followed by *e* indicate an exhibit; followed by *t* indicate a table; followed by *b* indicate a box.

A

Abadie, Alberto, 276
Abbott, A., 453
Abdullah, R. B., 390, 396
Abma, T. A., 286, 580
Abravanel, Martin, 271
Achilles, C. M., 692
Ackermann, F., 45, 46, 48, 50, 51, 52
Adams, William C., 321, 474, 492
Agle, B. R., 37
Alberti, P. M., 390, 396
Allison, Graham, 185
Allison, P. D., 330
Altman, D. G., 161
Ammons, D. N., 129
Andrew, Bahati, 392, 406
Aranda, Claudia L., 320, 383, 384, 386, 391, 407
Arisigueta, M. P., 802
Armbrecht, Eric S., 405
Armor, D. J., 714
Askew, K., 289*t*, 296, 311
Atkins, David, 670*b*

A (continued)

Auspos, Patricia, 260, 261, 263, 264, 274
Azzam, Tarek, 248, 253, 826

B

Bank, Roy J., 386
Banks, S., 252
Bardach, E., 812, 813
Barnett, Steve, 669*b*
Barnow, B., 181
Barron, M., 209
Barton-Villagrana, H., 229, 255
Beard, J., 294
Beaty, T., 233
Beck, S., 233
Bedell, J. F., 396
Beelman, A., 687
Befani, B., 582
Begdell, J. F., 390
Belfield, Clive R., 669*b*
Bell, James B., 700, 765
Bellotti, J., 450
Benjamin, L., 293
Berger, V. W., 161

B (continued)

Berk, M. L., 215
Berk, R. A., 688
Berliner, D. C., 118
Berman, Barbara J. Cohn, 321, 412, 708
Bernanke, Ben, 260, 263
Berner, M., 702
Bernstein, D., 109
Beverly, M. G., 289*t*, 296, 311
Bickman, L., 64
Bifulco, Robert, 139
Birks, Y. E., 169, 173
Bisgaier, Joanna, 389, 405
Blair, J., 367*e*
Bloom, G. A., 39
Blumberg, S. J., 352
Boardman, A. A., 638
Boback, N., 255
Bog, Debra, 4
Bone, Sterling A., 386
Boodoo, G. M., 302
Booza, Jaon C., 826
Boruch, Robert F., 105, 230, 474, 559, 673, 676, 681, 692, 702, 710, 719

Page references followed by *fig* indicate an illustrated figure; followed by *e* indicate an exhibit; followed by *t* indicate a table; followed by *b* indicate a box.